C̶u̶l̶t̶u̶r̶a̶l̶ populism

This book provides a novel understanding of current thought and enquiry in the study of popular culture and communications media. The populist sentiments and impulses underlying cultural studies and its postmodernist variants are explored and criticized sympathetically. An exclusively consumptionist trend of analysis is identified and shown to be an unsatisfactory means of accounting for the complex material conditions and mediations that shape ordinary people's pleasures and opportunities for personal and political expression.

Through detailed consideration of the work of Raymond Williams, Stuart Hall and 'the Birmingham School', John Fiske, youth subcultural analysis, popular television study, and issues generally concerned with public communication (including advertising, arts and broadcasting policies, children's television, tabloid journalism, feminism and pornography, the Rushdie affair, and the collapse of communism), Jim McGuigan sets out a distinctive case for recovering critical analysis of popular culture in a rapidly changing, conflict-ridden world.

The book is an accessible introduction to past and present debates for undergraduate students, and it poses some challenging theses for postgraduate students, researchers and lecturers.

Jim McGuigan lectures in Communication Studies at Coventry University.

Cultural populism

Jim McGuigan

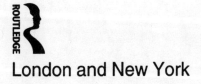

London and New York

First published in 1992
by Routledge
11 New Fetter Lane, London EC4P 4EE

Simultaneously published in the USA and Canada
by Routledge
29 West 35th Street, New York, NY 10001

Reprinted 1993

© 1992, Jim McGuigan

Typeset in Baskerville by LaserScript, Mitcham, Surrey
Printed and bound in Great Britain by Mackays of Chatham PLC,
Chatham, Kent

British Library Cataloguing in Publication Data
A catalogue record for this book is available from the British Library.

Library of Congress Cataloging in Publication Data

McGuigan, Jim
Cultural populism by Jim McGuigan.
   p. cm.
   Includes bibliographical references and index.
   1. Culture. 2. Popular culture. 3. Populism. 4. Subculture.
   5. Mass media and youth. I. Title.
HM101.M357 1992   92–248
306–dc20   CIP

ISBN 0–415–06294–2
ISBN 0–415–06295–0 (pbk)

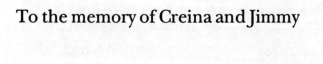
To the memory of Creina and Jimmy

It's an occupational hazard for intellectuals, regardless of their politics, to lose touch with the stuff and flow of everyday life.

(Marshall Berman 1984)

Contents

Acknowledgements

I should like to acknowledge the help of numerous people who contributed either directly or indirectly to the writing of this book, only a select few of whom are named here. Mike Peters' criticisms were invaluable and I am indebted to him for improving the linguistic precision of the manuscript. Rob Burkitt and Ann Gray also provided penetrating albeit differential readings, for which I am extremely grateful. Lesley Watson, Christopher and Jenny survived the experience of living with a project not of their own choosing but which called upon extraordinary powers of endurance, at least from Lesley, in conditions that they made possible. Many students in Leeds served as guinea pigs, whether they knew it or not, and I remember them with fondness. And, finally, I must thank Chris Rojek at Routledge for his encouragement and quite awesome efficiency.

Leeds,
December 1991

Introduction

This book is intended as a sympathetic critique of cultural populism. Since it may, contrary to my wishes, be read as an unsympathetic critique, the reasons for questioning cultural populism at all need to be signalled clearly from the outset. There is, however, a problem of definition, which must be dealt with first. The term 'cultural populism' is frequently used in passing but, to my knowledge, has never really been given a precise definition. A number of writers, whom I regard as cultural populists, use the term loosely to attack other writers with whom they disagree. That is why I choose to define 'cultural populism' fairly precisely here and with a comparative neutrality that distinguishes my usage sharply from the main alternative, largely commonsensical and exclusively pejorative usages.

For the purposes of conceptual precision, it is necessary to consider the term 'populism' separately from 'culture', at least initially, in order to reflect upon the varied meanings of their actual and potential combination. 'Populism' is much more commonly used in political discourse than in cultural discourse – however, not with any great precision, but nearly always with negative connotations, usually meaning something like 'the mobilisation of political majorities around a set of simple and probably disingenuous slogans', perhaps appealing to 'the lowest common denominator'. For instance, Margaret Thatcher was called a populist by her opponents and so is Boris Yeltsin. Such politicians are not called populist by their own supporters. The accusation of 'populism' implies reckless and unscrupulous demagogy. Direct popular appeal, over the heads of other politicians, is often commented upon as disreputable: making promises that cannot be kept, offering solutions that are unrealistic. Politicians, as practical intellectuals in the power game, it might therefore be assumed, should know better: they know what is possible; ordinary people do not.

An elementary deconstruction of the uses of 'populism' would identify its binary opposite, which is, of course, 'elitism'. Nobody, well hardly anyone nowadays, is a self-confessed 'elitist'. Being thought an 'elitist' is just as bad as being a 'populist', if not worse. Both 'populist' and 'elitist' are, in effect, terms of abuse, used by intellectuals, whether formally engaged in politics or not, who may be deliberately vague about where they themselves stand. In this book the term 'elitist' is used occasionally as convenient shorthand for ideological positions that are disrespectful of ordinary people's tastes, whilst also recognising, however, that 'elitist' itself erases important differences and nuances of intellectual standpoint when applied too casually.

Populism has been defined with conceptual neutrality and studied extensively in political science, which is how I appropriate it with reference to the study of 'culture' in the broadly anthropological sense normally deployed in communication, cultural and media studies. Conceptual clarity matters, although 'cultural populism' is not a strictly analytical category and it resists semantic fixity. In the academic context, discussed here, 'cultural populism' refers to diffuse political sentiments associated routinely with certain analytical protocols rather than the kind of dispassionate scientificity claimed by a 'paradigm'.

Similar to non-academic political discourse, the term 'populist' generally carries negative connotations in both theoretical and everyday discourses on culture. For example, the punk-style classical violinist, Nigel Kennedy, has been labelled a 'populist', meaning, in a journalistic context, someone who has sold out his 'serious' cultural status for popular approval and commercial success. Again, and echoing judgemental political commentary, implicit in such a labelling is an unspoken elitist assumption, that if Kennedy were to re-don his tie and tails, and cease to be attractive to people who know nothing about classical music, he would be less objectionable to the *cognoscenti*.

Any form of culture that appeals to ordinary people could reasonably, in my view, be called 'populist culture' with no necessarily evaluative judgement implied, although this is rarely so in prevailing cultural discourses. The popularisation of classical music, moreover, is a very particular case since, by and large, the most popular forms of culture are not generally disseminated from 'high' to 'low' in such a way. In the main, chart music and television programming, for instance, are much more firmly grounded, for good commercial reasons, in the tastes and preferences of ordinary people. They may be appropriated by serious, 'elite' culture (for example, Lennon and McCartney reminding 1960s intellectuals of Schubert) but that is not the meaning of 'cultural populism' recommended here. Yet, my recommendation does have something to do with the link between intellectuals and the culture of ordinary people.

'Cultural populism', in my usage, is further distinguishable from two closely connected practices: one, a practice of primary cultural production, and the other, a secondary, academic and educational practice of studying popular cultural texts as an extension of, say, literary criticism. The first of these two practices, which some authors have called 'aesthetic populism', typically refers to how popular cultural elements are inscribed in 'serious' works of art or how serious work is adapted to popular contexts. Self-consciously 'postmodernist' cultural production is thus sometimes defined as 'aesthetic populism', to which I shall return. For the moment, I would merely observe that this is not new. 'Serious' culture, the kind of culture which becomes canonised as 'art', has always refreshed itself from the springs of popular culture, as the Russian formalists pointed out many years ago with their idea of 'the canonisation of the junior branch'. I do not consider this to be 'cultural populist'. Nor do I consider the study of popular cultural texts to be, by definition, populist. Popular culture has indeed become widely academicised in recent years. No longer is it thought illegitimate to study, say, Hollywood films or romance fiction. A much greater range of texts are now studied: and frequently they are found, with the aid of sophisticated reading techniques, to be much more complex and interesting than academic conservatives had ever imagined. This, again, is not new and there is nothing inherently populist about it. When nineteenth-century cultural critics began studying the English novel as seriously as the poetry of ancient Greece and Rome, it was believed at first to be a dangerously standard-lowering activity.

Intellectual retrieval and study of popular culture are not, then, sufficient conditions for the definition of 'cultural populism' proposed in this book. In my foregoing remarks, I have registered less circumscribed uses of the term that cannot, and should not, be legislated against simply to reduce ambiguity. The usage, which best serves the purpose of my argument, however, is closer to the would-be neutrality of political science than any of the cultural or political discourses that are, I would argue, more often than not silently elitist. The following definition is the one that I propose. *Cultural populism is the intellectual assumption, made by some students of popular culture, that the symbolic experiences and practices of ordinary people are more important analytically and politically than Culture with a capital C.* It may be that the use of upper-case for words like 'Culture' and 'Art' is the immediate typographic signifier of cultural elitism in English (though not of course in German). That cultural analysts of a populist persuasion are mainly concerned with types of product and the sociality of their reception rather than the selective naming of works and authors is also in itself significant. A Derridean would, no doubt, have much to say about this. The definition offered here, however, is deliberately minimalist (and not, as must be obvious, entirely neutral) but one which suffices for the task of tracing and questioning the main trajectory of the British school of thought known as 'cultural studies', which has growing influence internationally and especially in the English-speaking world; and which variously interrelates and overlaps with the fields of communication studies and media studies.

One or two further qualifications are required. The term 'ordinary people' is, admittedly, problematic. For me, it is an open category constructed in opposition to 'intellectuals', who serve as the agents of 'exceptional' culture, the senior branch from the point of view of academic conservatism. These terms can be endlessly unpacked or deconstructed, a practice which, in my opinion, defers rather than advances understanding. The vital point is to do with the *positive relationship* between intellectuals and popular culture. Apart from those comparatively few pioneers who 'discovered' and became fascinated by 'folk' culture in the past, cultural critics generally evinced a contemptuous attitude to popular culture, either explicitly or implicitly. An appreciative, non-judgemental attitude to ordinary tastes and pleasures, which has now become increasingly common amongst intellectuals, is a great advance, at least in the academy. In that sense, I am perfectly happy to declare myself a 'cultural populist'. It is necessary to make such a declaration because this book criticises some aspects of 'cultural populism'. Two current developments prompted me to write on these matters. First, an *uncritical* populist drift in the study of popular culture, a discernible narrowing of vision and fixation on a self-limiting set of issues. Second, historical changes in the experiential conditions of ordinary people that are not, I believe, grasped adequately by an exclusively interpretative approach to popular culture, the direction in which a great deal of theorising and research has gone. This book is dedicated to exploring the prospects for critical renewal in the field and to the possibility of a *critical populism*, which can account for *both* ordinary people's everyday culture *and* its material construction by powerful forces beyond the immediate comprehension and control of ordinary people. That can only be achieved if certain artificial barriers between schools of thought are broken down.

The book is divided into three parts. The first part looks at the emergence of popular cultural study and its relation to populist politics. The exchange between intellectuals and ordinary people's culture is treated as inherently paradoxical. And the formation of what has become known as a distinctly British cultural studies approach is shown to be rooted in populist sentiments, specifically with reference to the work of Raymond Williams, Stuart Hall and the Birmingham University Centre for Contemporary Cultural Studies. Furthermore, it is suggested that cultural populism is not a unitary phenomenon. Two very different responses to the perceived elitism of 'the mass culture critique' are traced: the first moving towards a 'productionist' opposition to mass culture, and the second drifting into a 'consumptionist' elimination of the older distinction between 'popular' and 'mass' culture. The latter trajectory has entered the mainstream, and arguably become *the* mainstream position, for Anglophone studies of popular culture. This consumptionist position, dubbed 'the new revisionism' by leading critics of cultural populism, is called into question from the perspective of the political economy of culture, which insists upon a determinate relation between the production and consumption of symbolic forms. A paradigm crisis in contemporary cultural studies, of which the uncritical populist drift is a symptom, is identified and related to the internal contradictions of neo-Gramscian hegemony theory, which once cohered the field of study in opposition to the political economy perspective. Critical questions of politics, judgement and explanation are posed with the aim of reopening dialogue between hegemony theory and political economy.

The second part concretises these developments in, first, the study of youth culture and, second, of popular television. It is argued that neo-Gramscian hegemony theory's approach to subcultural analysis was deconstructed and reorientated towards what became an uncritical understanding of youth cultural consumption. A similar trajectory is traced in the construction of 'popular television' as an object of study, exemplified by the turn towards 'the active audience', which in spite of its evident advantages neglects the economic, technological and political determinations of televisual culture. The uncritical endorsement of popular taste and pleasure, from an entirely hermeneutic perspective, is curiously consistent with economic liberalism's concept of 'consumer sovereignty', the weaknesses of which are particularly manifest in the debate concerning broadcasting policy conducted in Britain since the early 1980s. These developments are related to the recomposition of hegemony during the 1980s and its implications for the study of popular culture and the politics of democratic reform.

The third part examines some disconfirming instances for cultural populism around popular consumption, class, gender and sexuality, race and ethnicity. British tabloid journalism, American-originated feminist campaigns against pornography and the Rushdie affair are selected as case studies that call into question an exclusively populist approach to cultural study. An adequate account of contemporary popular culture, it is suggested, demands analysis of public communication, institutional power and, in a materialist perspective, socio-economic relations. This argument is taken further in the final chapter, where issues of postmodernism and cultural populism are addressed. Aiming to broaden the purview of populist-inspired analysis, the case of collapsing communism is examined to illustrate the pincer movement of capitalist economic and cultural power under postmodern conditions of increasing globalisation. The various meanings and still uncertain consequences of this rupture with a past configuration, which once divided the world in now suddenly unfamiliar ways, are integrally related to the general argument of the book. In conclusion, some urgent considerations for cultural critique are mooted.

Part I

Theoretical politics

Chapter 1

Populism and ordinary culture

The question as to who 'the people' are, where they/we will be
made to stand, line up and be counted, the political direction
in which they/we will be made to point: these are questions
which cannot be resolved abstractly; they can only be answered
politically.

(Bennett 1986a: 20)

To throw some light on discussions about the 'people' and the
'popular', one need only bear in mind that the 'people' or the
'popular' ('popular art', 'popular religion', 'popular medicine',
etc.) is first of all one of those things at stake in the struggle
between intellectuals.

(Bourdieu 1990: 150)

Tony Bennett's statement above comes from an article which
summarises a once-compelling approach to popular cultural
analysis, that of neo-Gramscian hegemony theory. The statement
is unintentionally ironic because the Right in Britain had recently
accomplished what Bennett and similar critics believed the Left
should be doing. At its height, 'Thatcherism' effectively mobilised
'the people' for authoritarian government by speaking the
language of 'setting the people free' (Gamble 1988). From the
perspective which constructed Bennett's battle-cry, Stuart Hall
drew the conclusion that the opposition had better start 'learning
from Thatcherism' (March 1988). Later in this chapter I shall be
considering what that meant for students of popular culture.

Pierre Bourdieu's statement, quoted from a paper originally
delivered at Lausanne in 1982, problematises the study of popular
culture and it differs somewhat from the cultural politics of
Bennett and Hall. Bourdieu's statement is a sardonic and wicked

contribution. To suggest that discoursing on 'the popular' is some kind of intellectual game in which participants in the cultural field, education and so on, struggle to make themselves heard and to win symbolic power in the clash of contending ideologies is not only sardonic and wicked: it is also an historical truism. After all, the whole idea of 'popular culture' is *intellectual*: 'popular culture was not identified by the people but by others' (Williams 1983a: 237). Who were these others? Intellectuals, of course. Who else? Johann Gottfried Herder, the German philosopher, is to blame. Towards the end of the eighteenth century, Herder and his followers made the distinction between 'learned culture' and 'popular culture'. Then they set about studying the latter, no doubt to the astonishment of many of the self-consciously 'learned'. This 'discovery of popular culture' (Burke 1978) in Germany around the time that industrial capitalism was being forged in Britain and modern democracy was emerging bloodied from the turmoil of the American and French Revolutions had both aesthetic and political dimensions.

In terms of aesthetics, the discovery of popular culture is related to the Romantic reaction to Classicism, the attempt to break with excessively formalistic, dry and unemotional art. To recover something of the vital impulses of ordinary people, their apparent spontaneity and disregard for propriety, their 'naturalness', are amongst the themes which cut both ways: back to a myth of an 'organic' past in contrast to a 'mechanical' present, or forward to a Utopian future of popular emancipation. It is no accident that the great Welsh cultural theorist Raymond Williams should most famously have opened his account of 'culture' with a book on English Romanticism and its conservative and radical strands: *Culture and Society*, published in 1958.

The discovery of popular culture was also an expressly political move, related to ideas of nationhood; thereby linked to a third constitutive feature of modernity, the formation of national identity, in addition to industrialisation and democratisation. An interest in the original 'folk' inflection of popular culture had greater resonance in peripheral nations, in Brittany rather than Paris and in Scotland, Wales and Ireland rather than England. The study of 'folklore', coined by William Thoms in 1846, has an affinity to subordinate localities, regions and aspiring nations, collecting and cataloguing fragments from a lost world of folk-song, oral story-telling, festive ritual and the rest. Such

practices can function as a retreat from contemporary
identity, pleasure and expression, in view of which Pet.
(1981) has named the cults of a certain apolitical conservatism
with a small 'c': the cults of 'primitivism', 'purism' and 'commu-
nalism'. The sentimental attachment to some pure, unsullied,
primitive and originally peasant, or peasant-like, community has
recurred intermittently with reference to urban as well as rural
contexts: from nostalgic studies of traditional working-class
neighbourhoods, best exemplified by Richard Hoggart's founding
classic of cultural studies, *The Uses of Literacy* (1957); to the
consumption 'tactics' and meaningful 'poaching' of ordinary
people generally in contemporary city locales, documented by
Michel De Certeau (1984).

Now, let us return to Bourdieu's sardonic observation
concerning the symbolic 'strategies' deployed by students of
popular culture. It offers a reflexive means of putting the
relationship between populism and ordinary culture in
perspective.

BOURDIEU'S PARADOX

Bourdieu draws attention to the problem of speaking about
popular culture and the relation of such intellectual discourse
both to the internal machinations of the academy and to the
outside world. Bourdieu (1984) has written at great length on
'distinction' strategies whereby symbolically powerful groups,
intellectuals of one kind or another, mark out their positions in
society. The symbolically powerful draw the borderlines between
what Mikhail Bakhtin (1984) called 'official' and 'unofficial'
cultures – broadly speaking, the demarcation of Culture with a
capital 'C', on one side, and the pastimes and pleasures of ordinary
people, the non-intellectuals, on the other. These processes are
complicated immensely when intellectuals, usually on the lower
rungs of distinction, become interested in popular culture.

In his Lausanne paper, Bourdieu prefers to talk specifically
about popular language rather than popular culture in general.
The paradox of cultural populism is neatly summed up by his
following questions:

> When the dominated quest for distinction leads the dominated
> to affirm what distinguishes them, that is, that in the name of

which they are dominated and constituted as vulgar, do we have to talk of resistance? In other words, if, in order to resist, I have no other resources than to lay claim to that in the name of which I am dominated, is this resistance? Second question: when, on the other hand, the dominated work at destroying what marks them out as 'vulgar' and at appropriating that in relation to which they appear as vulgar (for instance, in France, the Parisian language), is this submission? I think this is an insoluble contradiction: this contradiction, which is inscribed in the very logic of symbolic domination, is something those who talk about 'popular culture' won't admit.

(1990: 155)

Bourdieu's paradox is not only about ordinary language – the tension between 'vulgar' and 'official' discourses – but also about socially constructed actors engaged in a practice: in this case, theorising and studying popular culture. There is a sociology to be written about those who wish to speak of 'the popular' within the academy, a Bourdieuan, infinitely regressing project if ever there was one. This book is not such a sociology, though it has it in mind. Cultural studies, as practised in Britain, is a peculiarly congenial site of work for intellectuals of working-class origin, for women, for people of colour, in general for those from positions of social subordination and marginality, but not exclusively so. Academic cultural studies may not be a popular discourse, yet it is not strictly an official discourse either. It is, rather, a semi-official discourse mainly due to a politically impelled engagement with popular culture. Cultural studies has been perceived from above as excessively political and excessively popular in its orientations, which at least in ambition is not a misperception. The symbolic power of such a perception has kept it comparatively marginal in the academy, even now, related perhaps to its growing journalistic influence beyond the usual confines of academe. In effect, cultural studies is caught in something of a trap, caught between the power points of official academic discourse and what I would call its populist political sentiments.

As far as I can gather, Bourdieu is not unduly bothered by the 'insoluble contradiction', the dilemmas and traps, of his paradox, because he believes 'resistance' to oppressive power 'occurs on terrains altogether different from that of culture in the strict sense of the word' (1990: 155). He means in the fields of economic and political practice, which is why his views are rather different from those of Bennett and Hall. Bourdieu's own paradox, incidentally, has not prevented him from discoursing on the popular, with his theory of 'the popular aesthetic', which affirms the 'continuity between art and life' (1984: 32) in contradistinction to the refinements of conservative high culture and also *avant-garde* 'distanciation'.

POPULIST SENTIMENT

I want to argue that at the heart of British cultural studies – and also impinging upon the cognate fields of communication and media studies – there is populist sentiment, but hardly any 'sentimentality'[1] is discernible: present-day students of popular culture are too street-wise for that. Although the cultural studies approach considered here is not wholly encompassed by populism, a non-populist cultural studies is very nearly a contradiction in terms: it is an academic game which might do better calling itself something else.

To use the noun 'sentiment' is risky because it instantly invokes the adjective 'sentimental', as it does in *The Oxford English Dictionary*:

> **Sentiment** . . . n. **1.** a mental attitude produced by one's feeling about something; a verbal expression of this; an opinion. **2.** emotion as opposed to reason; sentimentality.

The next entry is '**Sentimental** . . . romantic or nostalgic feeling . . . showing or affected by emotion rather than reason'. In his invaluable *Keywords* Raymond Williams notes that such a delimitation of meaning is traceable back to late Romanticism, enunciated by Robert Southey during his conservative old age: 'the sentimental classes, persons of ardent or morbid sensibility' (quoted by Williams 1983a: 283). In Williams's judgement 'this confusion permanently damaged *sentimental*'. Who knows? Perhaps 'sentiment(al)' can be re-articulated and used neutrally alongside the less discredited term 'sensibility', which has an interesting connection with 'sense', *pace* Jane Austen (1811/1989). 'Sentimentality', 'sense and sensibility' apart, using the term 'sentiment' enables me to avoid using Williams's concept 'structure of feeling' to characterise 'populism' as Ken Hirschkop does, a little too loosely in my view, to characterise Williams's own complex populism (Hirschkop 1989). To suggest that a theory or a field of intellectual enquiry is grounded in certain sentiments is hardly in itself contentious except in the most rigorously positivistic discourses of social and cultural science. That cultural studies has values and that practitioners are passionate about what they do should not alarm anyone: it would be much more alarming if cultural studies lacked such qualities.

What, then, do I mean by 'populist sentiment'? Roughly, it is a sense of commitment to 'the people' and their struggles, reminiscent of Bertolt Brecht's concept of the 'popular':

> Our concept of what is popular refers to a people who not only play a full part in historical development but actively usurp it, force its pace, determine its direction. We have a people in mind who make history, change the world and themselves. We have in mind a fighting people and therefore an aggressive concept of what is *popular*.

> (1938: 81)

This is the fighting talk of an eccentric partisan of 1930s Popular Front communism, bellicose in a manner that 1990s radical sensibility, informed by feminism and knowledgeable about the fate of 'actually existing socialism', would typically find problematic. Brecht's revolutionary populism reads poignantly in the 1990s so soon after the events when the people of the now defunct German Democratic Republic rejected a nominally Marxist regime in favour of capitalism, a regime with which Brecht had evinced solidarity when he returned from the United States to make his home in the East of Germany after the Second World War.[2] The recent fate of Brecht's chosen homeland also illustrates the fact that populism is not necessarily socialist.

How are we to make sense of the meaning of this slippery phenomenon, populism, which I am suggesting lies at the heart of cultural studies? As Ernesto Laclau (1977) has observed, it is 'a concept both elusive and recurrent' (p. 143). 'Elusive', difficult to define; 'recurrent', a label readily applied by political commentators and also, increasingly, by cultural critics. However, it is a concept more commonly used and understood in discussions of politics than of culture. For political science, the *Narodnivestvo* movement, emerging in the 1870s when intellectuals went to the peasantry to find a solution to the ills of czarist Russia, and the short-lived American Populist Party of the 1890s, representing farmers against monopoly capital and New York finance (Webster, D. 1988), are the paradigm cases. Other historical cases frequently mentioned include Central European peasant movements, African liberation movements, Perónism, movements with a radical rhetoric eschewing 'class', plus communist variants such as Maoism.[3] In searching out examples, one can range back through British history to the fourteenth-century Peasant Revolt and up to the recent Anti-Poll Tax Campaign when 'carnival turned to carnage' in Trafalgar Square on 31 March, 1990. That conjunction, 'carnival'/'carnage' (from *New Statesman and Society*, 6 April 1990) is an interesting one for our purposes here. That's the problem. There are so many potential examples to be winkled out: for instance, one must not fail to mention the Paris *événements* of 1968 in a book on cultural studies. Nowadays, 'populism' is often used with reference to resurgent nationalist and ethnic movements, especially in the former Eastern bloc. Can we generalise from so many discrete cases? Is populism a movement or an ideology, or a combination of the two? Are we forever reduced to producing descriptive inventories, or can some structural principle of action and circumstance be divined? Structural functionalists have argued that 'populism arises as a response to the problems posed by modernity and its consequences' to do with the tension between advanced and backward regions (Stewart 1969: 180). This would square, I suppose, with 'the discovery of popular culture' at that transitional moment between 'tradition' and 'modernity'.

Laclau (1977) is not satisfied with the structural functionalist account and its formalist typology of tradition and modernity, the eruptions occurring in the interregnum telling us no more than we already know. Instead, Laclau recommends the analysis of specifiable historical conjunctures rather than a priori manipulations of ideal types. For him, populism is not inherent in the movement, nor in the ideology, but in the articulation of 'non-class contradictions' into political discourses originating in class contradictions. In Laclau's subsequent theorising, with Chantal Mouffe, 'class' looms much less large, if at all, as a fundamental and generative grounding (Laclau and Mouffe 1985). That does not, however, substantially affect this explication. Two points are crucial here. First, 'the people' do not exist in any finite sense: they are an articulation of political discourse. Political discourse interpellates a subject, a subjectivity and a subjecthood

(Althusser 1970/1984). This is, in a sense, a 'culturalist' argument: politics as the production of identity. The Weberian Donald MacRae (1969) said virtually as much, in rather different terms, in remarking that populism is 'about personality' (p. 160). Second, according to Laclau, politics is, furthermore, about 'the "people"/ power bloc contradiction' (1977: 166). It never presents itself as an unmediated struggle between classes. The problem of populism, then, is both dissolved *and* expanded to subsume the whole terrain of politics. Whoever gets to speak on behalf of 'the people' against the current construction of 'the power bloc' is winning the game, albeit only for the time being, according to the radical democratic theorisation – see O'Shea (1984), on Thatcherite rhetoric from this perspective. That politics is thus culturally implicated in 'the interpellation of subjects', is what enabled Stuart Hall to say:

> Popular culture is one of the sites where this struggle for and against a culture of the powerful is engaged: it is also the stake to be won or lost *in* that struggle. It is the arena of consent and resistance. It is partly where hegemony arises, and where it is secured.
>
> (1981: 239)

Hall did, however, wish to quibble with Laclau's formulation because he thought it depended too much on the Latin American experience of subordinate classes being articulated against the dominant classes through populist discourse. It neglected their articulation to the dominant classes in other contexts: for instance, Thatcherism in Britain. Thus, Hall wished to qualify the political range of 'populism' and contrast it with 'popular-democratic', which, by definition for him, is not available to the political Right (1988a: 140). Such a view could, none the less, reasonably be considered a populism of the democratic Left, still appreciating Hall's vital distinction between something like genuine democracy and what inadequately passes for it in the British parliamentary system. Incidentally, Hall's complaint concerning Laclau's Latin American particularity is somewhat peculiar when one considers the right-wing populist mobilisation of women against the socialist Allende regime in Chile during the early 1970s, which contributed to the 1973 military coup, analysed brilliantly by Michele Mattelart (1986).[4] Moreover, there is a danger in Hall's position of reducing culture entirely to politics and, more seriously, of collapsing politics into cultural politics *tout court*.

How does all this relate to popular cultural analysis? Throughout the course of this book I shall be exploring exactly that question, amongst others. For the moment, two examples can be sketched in before moving on to a more detailed treatment of the matters in hand: the interpretation of popular literature and the politics of carnival, both of which constitute problems in the study of popular culture in early modern Europe *and* the study of contemporary culture in the concluding years of the twentieth century.

When we analyse popular literature, popular television and so on, what inferences can we make about their meaning in relation to the conditions of 'the people'? Peter Burke has posed this question with reference to the *Bibliothèque Bleue*, seventeenth-century French chap-books. Folklorists have studied them as sources of popular culture without properly asking who produced them and for whom? Burke demonstrates that they were written by members of the clergy and the aristocracy, not by the French peasantry, which does not imply they were imposed simply as a deliberate policy of church and state. Their readership, in conditions of comparatively low levels of literacy, most likely consisted of 'prosperous peasant families within a given community, the "brokers" between that community and the outside world' (1981: 220). That these texts inscribed ideologies congenial to ecclesiastical and aristocratic power should come as no surprise, nor should we infer that they necessarily represented peasant attitudes and values:

> To treat the *Bibliothèque Bleue* as direct evidence of the attitudes of the French craftsmen and peasants of the seventeenth and eighteenth centuries is like treating TV shows and tabloid newspapers as direct evidence of the British working class today.
> (Burke 1981: 221)

However, in his detailed study of the subject, *Popular Culture in Early Modern Europe* (1978), Burke argues that texts like that of the *Bibliothèque Bleue* can tell us something if read 'obliquely', mainly because the clergy and aristocracy in early modern Europe were not so separated from 'the people' as the producers of comparable popular cultural forms are today; that is why the chap-books were such powerful tools of 'hegemony'. What Burke is drawing attention to is the situation pertaining prior to the rigid separation between intellectuals and ordinary people with the advent of fully fledged modernity: the sharp division between high and popular culture.

This first example raises questions about imposition: how popular culture is produced for 'the people' and what that means to them. The second example looks at the relationship the other way round: what culture produced by 'the people' means to intellectuals and 'the power bloc', the case of carnival.

Contemporary theoretical interest in 'carnival' and the 'carnivalesque' is largely inspired by the writings of the Russian critic Mikhail Bakhtin, suppressed under Stalinism but resuscitated from the 1960s when his major work of cultural analysis, *Rabelais and His World*, was eventually published in the Soviet Union and soon after translated into English.[5] In *Rabelais and His World* (1984) Bakhtin sought to explain the production of François Rabelais's *Histories of Gargantua and Pantagruel*, one of the precursors of the novel, in relation to the popular culture of sixteenth-century France, especially the tradition of carnival. For Bakhtin, carnival in this period is characterised by ritual spectacle, verbal comedy and marketplace speech. Carnival represented a moment of participatory celebration, inversion of hierarchies and vulgar expression, an unofficial 'second life' of the people, which is appropriated and re-presented in Rabelais's grotesquely funny, parodic and satirical writing. This intimate relationship between literature and popular culture, in spite of the well-known connotations of the term 'Rabelaisian', had been underestimated by other scholars, such as Rabelais's distinguished English translator J.M. Cohen (1955).

According to Bakhtin, with the advent of modernity, the literary and the popular separated: grotesque realism became a subordinate, comparatively disreputable strand in the history of the novel; and, '[t]he carnival spirit with its freedom, its utopian character oriented toward the future, was gradually transformed into a mere holiday mood' (1984: 33). Although historically, in Bakhtin's estimation, carnival became degraded, it has proved of immense interest to contemporary cultural analysis, seeking out traces of the carnivalesque in the modern media and their possible meanings under postmodern conditions (Stam 1988). Carnival is also a politically contentious phenomenon, seen by some as 'counter-hegemonic subversion' and by others as merely '*licensed* . . . popular blow-off' (Eagleton 1981). In this respect, it has been illuminated by Tony Bennett (1986b) with reference to the 'traditional' English working-class seaside resort of Blackpool.

However, carnival is not just of academic interest: it is also a palpable presence in contemporary Britain, thanks to the Afro-Caribbean community. In the past, carnival was not so prominent in Britain as in Southern Europe; some have said, because of the weather! However, it has certainly become a prominent form since the inception of the Notting Hill Carnival in 1965, which has grown into the largest street festival in Europe. Kwesi Owusu (1986) traces the carnival's history and relates it to the participatory, media-mixing tradition of 'orature'. In the late 1970s the Metropolitan Police sought to close off the streets to carnival and there were bloody clashes in Notting Hill. Since then it has become a much more legitimate event, in which black people and others join in a multi-media expression of shared popular identity – licensing the blow-off instead of repressing it?

One of the largest carnivals in Britain outside London takes place in the Chapeltown district of Leeds: its success and struggle illustrate some of the enduring issues around carnival. Vi Hendrickson, recalling fond childhood memories of carnival on the Caribbean island of Nevis, served on the Chapeltown Carnival organising committee in the early 1980s. Ten years later she felt the carnival had become 'a closed shop' whereby some leading members of the community were substituting themselves for the community, making it difficult to participate. She also complained of the ways in which the police and the Labour council treated the carnival. I think it is instructive to quote all her remarks concerning the carnival from the report in *Leeds Other Paper* (17 August 1990):

[When the Chapeltown Carnival began in a small way a few years ago] We weren't very confident of ourselves as black people then and were always looking to see how white people in Chapeltown would take it . . . . I do remember carnival being an exciting time and something to look forward to. It was a landmark in terms of black people coming into their own and organising their own festival . . . now, no one is sure of how to get involved in the preparations, it seems to be a closed shop. The only way to get in is if you happen to know who's on the committee. Those who see the carnival as a tourist attraction and not a political event are being extremely naive. The fact that we gather *en masse* on the street is political, the fact we have policemen overseeing what we do is political, the fact that we've allowed the route to be curtailed over the years is political. The Leeds route is getting shorter each year and that has a lot to do with who controls the city. In the old days we used to be able to take the parade down to the Town Hall. Now the police and the council decide how black people should express them-selves . . . . The carnival organisers need to recognise the power and contribution of women within the carnival movement. And recognise that without their enormous skills there would be no carnival . . . . They are spending public money and we have a right to know where it goes and how it's spent . . . . We should also be told of the negotiations that take place between the carnival committee and the police . . . . There's a whole generation of young people out there who don't express their culture through steel bands and costumes but also have something to say. Their contribution is absent from the carnival . . . . The organisers seem to be concerned solely with the actual event and not so much with the community. To me they are interlinked, you can't have one without the other.

This is only one voice and a slightly bitter and no doubt contestable one at that. Yet Vi Hendrickson does raise issues which have tested the ingenuity of the most sophisticated cultural analysts: the relationship between popular politics and culture under present conditions; the micro and macro processes of hegemony; mechanisms of inclusion and exclusion; relations between 'old' and 'new' popular culture and so on. Her words speak volumes. However, it is to the theorists of popular culture that we must now turn. Raymond Williams and Richard Hoggart, Stuart Hall and Edward Thompson are generally acknowledged to be the major figures in the formation of the British cultural studies approach, all of them associated with the 'New Left' from its inception in the 1950s. Here I shall concentrate on Williams and Hall, the two of this quartet most inclined to formal theorising. Hoggart is considered more fully in Chapter 2, but Thompson's inestimable work is not treated in any detail since it focuses mainly upon the history of the past rather than the present.

'CULTURE IS ORDINARY'

As Stuart Hall (1980a) has observed, there are no 'absolute beginnings' in the formation of cultural studies, a field characterised by the confluence and pursuit of diverse lines of enquiry. None the less, Raymond Williams's resonant phrase from 1958, 'culture is ordinary', and his insistence that this is 'where we must start' is as good a place as any to begin ('Culture is ordinary', reprinted in Williams 1989a). It is a clear and concise rebuttal of what, for purposes of brevity, can be labelled 'elitist' conceptions of culture. In British intellectual life, this is inscribed most celebratedly by Matthew Arnold's wish, expressed during the political upheavals of the 1860s (Williams 1970), to make 'the best that has been thought or known in the world current everywhere'. Arnold feared the potentially dire consequences for his 'philistine' class of enfranchising the anarchic 'populace' and so, where possible, he recommended the dissemination of 'sweetness and light', especially a secular religion of 'English Literature', through education and cultural policy to 'these masses', with the aim of tempering their vulgar and dangerous propensities (Arnold 1970).

Williams's resonant phrase is, outside the context of English cultural criticism, an anthropological banality, not a fresh sociological insight, curiously inspired by the arch-conservative T.S. Eliot's *Notes Towards the Definition of Culture*, where he says:

> it is the culture of a society that is fundamental . . . . It includes all the characteristic activities and interests of a people: Derby Day, Henley Regatta, Cowes, the Twelfth of August, a cup final, the dog races, the pin table, the dart board, Wensleydale cheese, boiled cabbage cut into sections, beetroot in vinegar, nineteenth-century gothic churches and the music of Elgar.
>
> (1948: 21, 31)

Eliot's patronisingly hierarchical conception of culture descended from the apex of individual cultivation, through national symbols and down to folksy working-class customs and habits. Enunciated within the English tradition, however, Eliot's sociological turn helped Williams (1979) to breach F.R. Leavis's (1930) critical dam, which assigned to the exceptionally cultured a task of protecting authentic 'minority culture' from the breakers of inauthentic and popular culture in a modern, 'mass civilization'. Williams inserted the anthropological notion of 'ordinary culture', treating lived experiences and everyday practices as more socially meaningful than the refined judgements of all-too-readily discriminating critics, into this perennial and principally literary debate (P. Anderson 1969; Mulhern 1979; Baldick 1983). The battle lines that were drawn up by Leavis and others in Britain and elsewhere have periodically been retraced ever since; for example, after the Second World War with the advent of universal secondary education and the rapid expansion of commercial media, which seemingly exacerbated the dangers of John Stuart Mill's (1974) 'levelling down' and 'Americanisation' (Hebdige 1982a). That cultural critics in the United States during the 1950s, also feared what guardians of English culture were complaining about only confirmed the diagnosis (Carey 1989; Ross 1989).

Anthropologists had established a respectable academic discipline for studying the lived cultures of 'others' in colonised territories (Beattie 1966). To anthropologise one's own culture, however, is another matter. Even when the anthropological gaze returned to the imperial shores it focused upon others – for example, in the practice of Mass Observation, perhaps the most important precursor of cultural studies. From the late 1930s until the late 1940s, Mass Observation mobilised middle-class explorers to investigate the habits and customs of, at first exclusively, the industrial working class 'up North', more systematically than the earlier journalistic forays of Mayhew and Orwell; yet it was still hopelessly empiricist in its method, piling up fascinating information with no satisfactory means of making sense of it, although bequeathing a rich archive to historians (Calder 1969; Jeffrey 1978). The year before Williams declared culture to be ordinary, Richard Hoggart had turned the anthropological gaze inwards by publishing the report of his own recovery of Northern working-class roots, *The Uses of Literacy* (1957), the book which actually introduced something like a cultural studies mode of thought to a wider public. Nevertheless, it was Williams (1958 and 1961) who spelt out the issues most sharply, in a way which enabled him to remind practitioners of the 'real project' of cultural studies towards the end of his life in the late 1980s ('The future of cultural studies', in Williams 1989b).

Williams criticised both commercial, mass-communicated culture, as presently constituted, and the received, downright snobbish culture that he encountered as a Welsh working-class scholarship boy at Cambridge University in the 1940s. He wanted to cut through this distinction by rethinking questions of culture and politics:

> A culture has two aspects: the known meanings and directions, which its members are trained to; the new observations and meanings, which are offered and tested. These are the ordinary processes of human societies and human minds, and we see through them the nature of a culture: that it is always both traditional and creative; that it is both the most ordinary common meanings and the finest individual meanings. We use the word culture in these two senses: to mean a whole way of life – the common meanings; to mean the arts and learning – the special processes of discovery and creative effort. Some writers reserve the word for one or other of these senses; I insist on both, and on the significance of their conjunction. The questions I ask about our culture are questions about our general and common purposes, yet also questions about deep personal meanings. Culture is ordinary, in every society and in every mind.
>
> (1989a: 4)

For Williams, it was the 'conjunction' of 'the most ordinary common meanings' and 'the finest individual meanings' that mattered. The refusal to give up on the project of creative 'discovery' detaches him from an uncritical populist endorsement of mass consumption and taste. But, at Cambridge, during the post-Second World War period, Williams equally resisted the then communist as well as mainstream Leavisite assumption that 'the masses' were benighted by the denial of capital 'C' Culture. It did not square with his own experience of working-class community and culture in Wales. Yet, in spite of his refusal simply to invert the terms of the prevailing cultural debate, Williams would be called a 'populist', in the pejorative sense used by orthodox Marxists, for giving insufficient weight to class struggle in his interactionist theory of culture as 'the study of relationships in a whole way of life' (1961). He did, however, respond eventually to Edward Thompson's (1961) criticisms of the elision of power and the connection to that which is '*not* culture', specifically the class system of socio-economic relations, from his early theoretical formulation (Williams 1973).

Throughout the course of his work,[6] Williams theorised an approach which he later, in the 1970s, came to call '[c]ultural materialism . . . the analysis of all forms of signification . . . within the actual means and conditions of their production' (1981: 64–5), constructed in an unorthodox relationship to Marxism and retaining the initially populist impulse of his earlier writings. Quite consistently, Williams rejected the 'base–superstructure' model of socio-economic and cultural arrangements, which in its cruder versions claimed that dominant ideas and institutions (the superstructure) simply reflect ruling-class interests in an exploitative economy (the base). Williams, like Thompson, preferred the alternative and much more open-ended claim that 'social being determines consciousness', a fundamentally materialist proposition reconcilable with the appreciation of popular creativity, demonstrated by Thompson's *Making of the English Working Class* (1963). For Williams, the base–superstructure model was 'not materialist enough' (1977a: 97) because it tended to consign culture to a purely ideational superstructure, whereas cultural production is, in reality, a material phenomenon in two main senses: first, as a meaningful transformation of materials in social interaction (language and so on); and, second, constituted within determinate economic relations (such as circulation of capital). In reality, culture is part of 'the base', and increasingly so in advanced capitalist societies, where communication technologies and cultural industries are of immense economic importance (1978).

In his 'base–superstructure' article (1973), Williams argued that Antonio Gramsci's conception of hegemony is superior to the dominant ideology thesis of the base–superstructure model, since it facilitates an understanding of the complex interplay of cultural forces within a social totality. When ideology is conceptualised as only the distorted 'reflection' of power relations and contradictions in 'the base' its livedness is thereby denied. That which is lived cannot be entirely illusory: it is represented in common sense, the practical reasoning of everyday life and, because hegemonic leadership is never all-pervasive, the nexus of culture and ideology is one of perpetual negotiation between contending forces. To explore the complexity of hegemony, Williams categorised cultural practice in terms of *dominant, residual* and *emergent* formations, with both residual and emergent subdivided into *alternative* and *oppositional.*

During the 1980s, Williams noted that hegemonic dominance was becoming progressively transnational, motivated by the globalisation of capitalism and the terror of a renewed Cold War, stated most sharply in his last great work of cultural and political analysis, *Towards 2000* (1983b).[7] Cultural power, *en route* to the millennium, was not only represented by the cardinal principle of possessive individualism: in addition, Williams identified what he called 'Plan X' – a nihilistic politics of 'strategic advantage' on a global scale (1983b: 244), of which Thatcherism was a local manifestation. However, Willams was no pessimist: he also discerned 'resources of hope' rising from below, subordinate cultural forces that can be clarified with reference to his model of hegemony. The dominant culture never commands the field entirely: it must struggle continually with residual and emergent cultures. Residual culture, by definition, derives from the past, usually rooted, under predominantly secular and urban conditions, in religious and rural practices, presenting resistance and challenge to the current hegemonic system: a major example would be the rise of Islamic fundamentalism. Williams himself, however, was more interested in emergent and oppositional formations, carrying potential for a new, previously unimaginable, social order. Because emergent culture is different from anything that went before, it is tempting to mistake apparent novelty, so characteristic of capitalist cycles of renewal, for forms and practices that really do make a difference. It is more reliable, perhaps, to study emergent cultures historically. From this perspective, the working-class and women's movements are justifiably seen as historical forms of emergence, signifying collective and liberating possibilities, the oppositional power of which has frequently been neutralised by incorporation into dominant hegemonic arrangements whilst also, however, winning genuine concessions.

Williams made a vital distinction between alternative and oppositional practices. Alternative culture seeks a place to coexist within the existing hegemony, whereas oppositional culture aims to replace it. For instance, there is a world of difference between a minority 'back-to-nature' cult and the ecology movement's global reach. In his later work, Williams managed to combine an enduring commitment to class politics, put into such disarray and discredit by the recomposition of capitalist hegemony, with hope in the 'new social movements', especially 'peace, ecology and feminism'. He was also sensitive to the dialectic of alternative and oppositional in more narrowly defined practices of cultural production, in film, television and so on, and the risks associated with, on the one hand, self-excluding purity and, on the other, compromised incorporation. The central problem, for Williams, turned on the articulation of popular movements and emerging forms of cultural production into a counter-hegemony, totalising opposition to 'Plan X'. Separated and divided, they are inherently vulnerable to neutralising and marginalising mechanisms, institutionally, societally and globally.

I have concentrated here on Williams's comparatively later ideas since they still speak directly to our present condition. However, it is also important to appreciate the continuity in Williams's thought from the time when he announced, polemically, that 'culture is ordinary'. Williams's populism persistently brought into the foreground the question of democracy, placing him on the incorruptible side of Hall's binary opposition between popular-democratic and merely populist politics. Writing in 1959 he said:

> Nothing has done more to sour the democratic idea, among its natural supporters, and to drive them back into angry self-exile, than the plain, overwhelming cultural issues: the apparent division of our culture into, on the one hand, a remote and self-gracious sophistication, on the other hand, a doped mass.
>
> (reprinted in 1989a: 17)

Williams not only strove to democratise cultural theory, he intervened politically by making very specific policy suggestions. The first two policies proposed in 'Culture is ordinary' were tame indeed: comprehensive education and increased expenditure on arts and adult education. The third proposal, however, would seem, according to 1990s conventional wisdom, even more dangerously radical and unrealistic than it did at the end of the 1950s: finding ways of replacing advertising revenue for newspapers with public funds.

In a subsequent piece, 'Communications and community' (1961, also reprinted in 1989a), Williams distinguished between four different systems of communications: authoritarian, paternal, commercial and democratic. The tension between paternal and commercial systems had more or less superseded the authoritarian legacy in Britain since the nineteenth century, or so it appeared in the late 1950s and early 1960s. Both had strengths and weaknesses but, instead of either, Williams favoured a democratic system, a possibility rather than an actuality anywhere: in the main, publicly owned facilities leased out to cultural producers representing real constituencies of variable social identity, as the institutional alternative to state control and untrammelled market forces, a prospect more remote and unfashionable now than it was then. Politically, it can be argued, Williams overstated the cultural question with an almost touching faith in modernity: 'the central problem of our society, in the coming half-century, is the use of our new resources to make a good common culture; the means to a good, abundant economy we already understand' (1989a: 10). He was later to revise that judgement in the light of resurgent class conflict from the late 1960s and, subsequently, ecological politics (1983b).

If I have positioned Williams like a Colossus at the entrance to cultural studies it is not because he said it all but because his vision of a 'common culture' founded in participatory democracy remained on the agenda, at least sentimentally, through the various theoretical twists and turns over the following years, which at times virtually displaced it. By the late 1980s, Williams looked back with horror at some of those twists and turns because, in his opinion, they had led cultural studies away from its popular educational project. From the 1970s onwards, cultural studies was carried along on successive waves of what Williams considered to be idealist theorising, mainly derived from Saussurian linguistics, resulting in specialised academicism and loss of historical imagination. Williams claimed that such 'theory' was elitist even when applied to the study of popular culture. Whether this claim was just or not, his meaning is clear when one thinks of the title of a book on popular culture edited by Colin MacCabe, a notable proponent of what Williams dubbed 'the new conformism', a legacy of heady 1970s theoreticism: *High Theory/Low Culture* (1986).[8] Williams's argument that cultural studies is peculiarly obliged to account for the formation of its own project was well put and a chastening reminder: 'the real problem of the project as a whole, which is that people's questions are not answered by the existing distribution of the educational curriculum, can be forgotten' (1989b: 159). Speaking at the 1986 conference of the Association for Cultural Studies, Williams urged upon his audience the paramount task of contesting the new educational utilitarianism, 'work experience' and so forth, 'a definition of industrial training which would have sounded crude in the 1860s' (1989b: 160).

Although he does not name him, Williams's criticisms were also aimed unmistakably at his old New Left comrade Stuart Hall, who did more than anyone to establish cultural studies as a nearly respectable subject during his directorship of the Birmingham University postgraduate Centre for Contemporary Cultural Studies in the 1970s. Williams questioned Hall's dating of the inception of cultural studies from the publication of certain texts: Richard Hoggart's *The Uses of Literacy* (1957), Edward Thompson's *The Making of the English Working Class* (1963), Williams's own *Culture and Society* (1958) and *The Long Revolution* (1961), 'the original "curriculum" of the field' (Hall 1980b: 16). Such a text-based history, according to Williams, obscured the practices that went into making those books and the educational context in which they were made: adult education, a curriculum negotiated with working-class students from the late 1940s and throughout the 1950s. These were students who had questions to ask that could not be answered by the established disciplines of Literature and History, thus, calling forth an exploratory approach, in effect an interdisciplinary cultural studies approach. Drawing on that memory, Williams criticised the Open University's Popular Culture course of the 1980s for producing a non-negotiated curriculum in which students were positioned as passive consumers of a newly reified branch of academic knowledge as though the subject matter had little to do with their own lives.

What, then, are we to make of the subsequent development of cultural studies, since, say, the founding of the Birmingham Centre in 1964 by Richard Hoggart? There is a voluminous and growing literature on this, which I do not intend to survey in depth.[9] Here I shall confine myself to reflections on cultural studies from within the Centre which was so important in establishing the field of study and, in the next chapter, return specifically to Hoggart's contribution. Michael Green has traced the emergence of contemporary cultural studies out of the discipline of English (1982), and Richard Johnson has written a number of illuminating pieces, ranging across various aspects of the Centre's work in the 1970s and 1980s (1979a, 1979b, 1980, 1986). Feminist (CCCS Women's Studies Group 1978) and black political (Gilroy 1987) perspectives have made internal criticisms of great consequence. And, nearing the end of his directorship at the Centre, Stuart Hall mapped the development of cultural studies up to 1980. Hall's (1980a and b) accounts are the best known: they point up many of the difficulties with making sense of such a complex, forever shifting field of interdisciplinary study.

Before considering Hall's maps I want to suggest that there are, broadly, three levels at which the development of cultural studies can be addressed. First, in terms of the movement of ideas within the field, the succession, incommensurability and interaction between different paradigms and problematics. This is the most conventional means of accounting for an academic project. Second, cultural studies may be considered in terms of its formation, as Williams insisted it should. This involves addressing institutional and historical contexts of emergence and transformation. Third, one can explore its politics of representation, the mechanisms of inclusion and exclusion which regulate agency within the field: basically, who gets to define the issues and with what purposes. To account for cultural studies on all of these three levels would require another book, a quite different book from this one. Comprehensive histories of British cultural studies or, specifically, of the so-called 'Birmingham School', not to be confused or conflated with Williams's own quite individual project, which never really established a 'school' as such, are for others better placed experientially than myself to write. My purpose in opening up the problem of accounting for cultural studies here is much more limited: to draw attention to its populist impulses. This can to some extent be clarified by Hall's maps. In effect, Hall has addressed all three levels, with a stress, however, on the first and second.

In his 'Two paradigms' essay (1980a), Stuart Hall very nearly abstracts cultural studies from its institutional and historical contexts: talking of cultural studies as though it were more than the work of the Birmingham Centre while, none the less, being mainly grounded in the ideational movements of that Centre. He names two paradigms, 'culturalism' and 'structuralism': the first, an indigenous British tradition emerging from the New Left of the late 1950s (the inaugural 'texts' of Hoggart, Williams and Thompson); the second, a French tradition imported into Britain from the 1960s and especially post-1968 (Lévi-Strauss, Barthes, Althusser). At one time it seemed as though structuralism had superseded culturalism, but Hall insists (in 1980) that there are strengths and weaknesses in both, seen from the perspective of hegemony theory. Culturalism can be aligned with Karl Marx's 'men [sic] make their own history', and structuralism with 'not in conditions of their own making'. This is the basis for Hall's particular neo-Gramscian synthesis, subsuming the respective strengths of culturalism and structuralism. Culturalism's 'experiential pull' enables it to stress human agency and expression in concrete historical circumstances without, however, adequately specifying the conditions of action. On the other hand, structuralism's linguistic model, which posits that language speaks us, draws attention to structured conditions (not only language but ideology and class relations) within which action is generated. The influence of Louis Althusser's anti-humanism is crucial here in advancing structuralism's case. The key term for culturalism is 'culture': for structuralism, it is 'ideology', conceived as the subject's imaginary relation to its conditions of existence.

Culturalism and structuralism are not the only paradigms identified by Hall in his 'Two paradigms' essay. In addition to these 'names of the game', he offers his own synthesis and goes on to mention three other contenders, each of which he treats with scepticism. Two of these contenders are 'poststructuralist': the reintroduction of the subject, a decentred not a humanist subject, in Lacanian psychoanalysis, which evacuates the analysis of social formation for the analysis of subjectivity; Foucauldian discursive formation analysis, which traces the specificities of power/knowledge operations but at the expense of analysing the articulation of determinate instances in a social formation; that is, it departs from the effort to theorise a non-reductive alternative to the base–superstructure model of orthodox Marxism, a project which characterised both culturalism and structuralism in their different ways. The final paradigm mentioned by Hall is the political economy of culture, which he rejects because it does not resolve Marxism's problem of economic reductionism, his own special demon.

Read in isolation, Hall's 'Two paradigms' essay would give the impression that cultural studies was perhaps a philosophical subdiscipline. And a reader unfamiliar with this theoretical terrain may not be much enlightened by the foregoing and very condensed summary of Hall's influential survey. Complicating matters even further, it is now out of date, preceding as it does the extraordinary efflorescence of poststructuralist and postmodernist theorising in the 1980s. But if you read Hall's other mapping piece, 'Cultural studies and the Centre' (1980b), it all makes much more practical sense because the theoretical acrobatics are there situated within a particular research institute, the Birmingham Centre for Contemporary Cultural Studies itself. The second essay presents a much messier picture, identifying other important strands of thought (for instance, interpretative sociology and Sartrean existentialism), false starts, dead ends, the difference between actually doing concrete research and theorising it, in a collective endeavour, sometimes harmoniously, sometimes antagonistically, built around workshops rather than academic individualism. Also, as well as registering the dizzying 'impact of the structuralisms', Hall registers the 'impact of the feminisms' – that is, a political rather than principally intellectual movement, in the 1970s. This leads us back to considering the relationship between cultural studies, institution and history and, in particular, the political radicalism of the post-'68 research student generation before the Thatcherite backlash was to transform the rules of the game so dramatically in the 1980s.

It also connects up with the main point I want to make here concerning the representational politics of cultural studies. This can be introduced by a quotation from *Women Take Issue*, produced by the Centre's Women's Studies Group:

> When we decided to do this book we thought we were deciding to produce the eleventh issue of *Working Papers in Cultural Studies*. Ten issues, with only four articles concerning women – it seemed about time. Women's continued 'invisibility' in the journal, and within much of the intellectual work done within CCCS (although things are changing), is the result of a complex of factors, which although in this particular combination are specific to our own relatively privileged situation are not unique to it.
>
> (CCCS Women's Studies Group 1978: 7)

The authors proceed to tell a familiar story of women's silence in a male-dominated discourse, the problem of whether to adopt a separatist stance or try to de-masculinise the whole process from top to bottom.[10] They also remark, 'Women's studies, like black studies, as a subject or discipline, has political not academic roots' (p. 9). Several years later, another graduate of the Centre, Paul Gilroy, had this to say in *There Ain't No Black in the Union Jack*:

> This book has a second more parochial aim [in addition to tracing the history of British racism] related to its origins in the

field of cultural studies. It seeks to provide, more implicitly than explicitly, a corrective to the more ethnocentric dimensions of that discipline . . . . The marginalisation of 'race' and racism has persisted even where cultural studies have identified themselves with socialist and feminist aspirations.

(1987: 12)[11]

These criticisms, made from female and black experiences within cultural studies, and specifically from within the Birmingham Centre, are not by any means peculiar to cultural studies. Similar criticisms have been made and acted upon in the wider society, most markedly in public-sector institutions. Cultural studies, then, like any other socially responsible intellectual practice, is affected by broad-based issues around discrimination and representation. But, and much more to the point, it is these issues, especially in their subjective and discursive aspects, that are integral to cultural studies, not only for the political sympathies of agents in the field but in deciding upon what to study and how to study it: this constitutes a democratic imperative, stimulated by 'underdog' sentiments. Although similar sentiments operate in the adjacent fields of media and communication studies, sociology and contemporary literary theory, it is in cultural studies where they have been most intensely felt and pronounced. However much we trace and map the movement of ideas in cultural studies, its institutionalisation in research centres, proliferating under-graduate and postgraduate degree courses, its presence in further and secondary education, the journals, associations and conferences where debates are conducted and fresh directions explored, the field of study is not intelligible without recognition of its populist impulses, and what I aim to show are some of their attendant dilemmas. Analytical objects are not only the product of academic theories. The energising sentiments may be populist but that does not mean, however, that cultural studies could in any way be reduced to a simplistic, atheoretical populism, merely telling it from the point of view of one socially subordinate constituency or another. The theories and methods are sophisticated and various, with a will to eclecticism, the sense of which is captured in Richard Johnson's (1986) 'realist hypothesis', seeking to reconcile probably irreconcilable epistemological positions: 'What if the existing theories, their methods and their results actually correspond to different sides of the same process?' (p. 283).

'BETWEEN THE GRAND OLD CAUSE AND THE BRAND NEW TIMES'

Contemporary cultural studies developed rapidly at Birmingham in the 1970s. Newly imbibed theories and proliferating socio-cultural differences spawned lines of enquiry and issues to engage, giving an impressive dynamism to the nascent field of study. The core problematic of ideological reproduction through popular culture was continually modified in response to a steady flow of mainly French ideas concerning language, power and subjectivity. And, empirical research projects were triggered off by a succession of constituencies to re-present: class, generational, gender/sexual and ethnic/racial. During that most fecund period of the Birmingham Centre, specificity was linked to complexity in a totalising framework. This was later to be called into question, usually from elsewhere, by the modish deconstructionist currents of the 1980s, frequently claiming that totalisation, making holistic connections between ostensibly discrete phenomena, is somehow inherently *totalitarian.*

In the mid-1970s, however, theoretical effort was devoted to producing a revised model of the social whole against 'expressive' and 'essentialist' conceptions of totality. Stuart Hall, drawing on both Louis Althusser and Antonio Gramsci, stressed that project in his mapping essays. Society was conceived of as inherently complex: the various 'instances' of the 'superstructure' irreducible to a single 'basic' contradiction, that of the forces and relations of production. Ideological formations were separated out rigorously and their articulation to the state and (possibly) the mode of production traced rather than presumed. The approach was interactive: specific social and signifying practices related dialectically through a complex totality, with the economic only determinate in 'the last instance', if at all.

'Articulation' is probably Stuart Hall's most important conceptual addendum to Gramscian thought, inspired originally by Ernesto Laclau (1977). Hall explained his usage of the term in an interview with Lawrence Grossberg, the leading North American interpreter of British cultural studies, in 1986:

> I always use the word 'articulation', though I don't know whether the meaning I attribute to it is perfectly understood. In England, the term has a nice double meaning because 'articulate' means to utter, to speak forth, to be articulate. It

carries that sense of language-ing, of expressing, etc. But we also speak of an 'articulated' lorry (truck): a lorry where the front (cab) and back (trailer) can, but need not necessarily, be connected to one another . . . . So the so-called 'unity' of a discourse is really the articulation of different, distinct elements which can be rearticulated in different ways because they have no necessary 'belongingness'.

(Grossberg and Hall 1986: 53)

One might observe, facetiously no doubt, that a 'back (trailer)' without a 'front (cab)' to pull it along would be stationary. Although Hall was elaborating on discourse/subjectivity in the interview with Grossberg, 'articulation' also illuminates how contemporary cultural studies theorised the relation of 'the cultural' to 'the economic', which is where it parts company with the political economy of culture. Political economists, in this field, generally insist on some necessary articulation between economic dynamics and cultural processes, whether systemically (capital accumulation and social reproduction) or institutionally (advertising, media ownership and control), though not automatically submitting the latter simply to a function of the former in either case (Garnham 1979; Golding and Murdock 1979; Jhally 1989), nor denying the importance of subjectivity, as cultural autonomists usually claim they do. Hall (1983) has conceded some ground to political economy, remarking that perhaps it is wiser to see the economic as determinate in 'the first instance' rather than in 'the last instance' (Murdock 1989a). Yet, 'the lonely hour' has scarcely ever arrived for contemporary cultural studies, early or late. Hall's concession did not substantially affect the predominantly interpretative style of research associated with Birmingham, which scrupulously avoided economic reductionism by normally steering clear of economic determinations.

Contemporary cultural studies increasingly autonomised itself as a distinct 'school of thought' with a growing reputation at home and abroad. Having summarily dismissed the political economy of culture (Hall 1980a), the Centre aimed to out-distance the pioneering work of Raymond Williams as well. For instance, Hall (1980c) criticised Williams's emphasis on 'the indissoluble elements of a continuous social-material process' by arguing that '[a]nalysis must deconstruct the "lived wholeness" in order to think its determinate conditions' (p. 101).[12] This methodological protocol, in epistemological and practical terms, is not contentious. No analysis could grasp the whole of life in one totalising movement. And, the breaking down and parcelling out of analytical tasks within a shared problematic, which happened at the Birmingham Centre, is fundamental to the intellectual division of labour in anything but the most individualised and imperious research. However, the pursuit of one question, or what is typically a cluster of questions, is likely to result in criticisms of partiality, of leaving something out, of neglecting important determinations, of not taking *absolutely everything* into account. For example, 'Why did Thatcherism become so popular?' is one such question open to the critique of partiality. It is, of course, the question which made Stuart Hall so famous in the 1980s.

Hall wanted to account for how Thatcherism, as an ideology, had won the battle for hearts and minds in the 1970s and then why it sustained hegemonic leadership through the following decade. He introduced his concept of 'authoritarian populism', to characterise Thatcherism, in the pages of *Marxism Today* (January 1979), five months before Margaret Thatcher's first of three successive general election victories:

> What we have to explain is a move toward 'authoritarian populism' – an exceptional form of the capitalist state which, unlike classical fascism, has retained most (though not all) of the formal representative institutions in place, and which at the same time been able to construct around itself an active popular consent.
>
> (in Hall and Jacques 1983: 22)

In a series of influential articles, throughout the 1980s, Hall went on to analyse how Thatcherism exploited the crisis of social democracy and mobilised mass support for harsh economic and disciplinary measures in ways that ran deeper than election-campaigning techniques, concentrating particularly on the ideological struggle to transform common sense from collectivist dependency on 'the nanny state' to the virtues of 'possessive individualism' and competition, a veritable cultural revolution.[13]

Jessop *et al.* attacked the authoritarian populism thesis in *New Left Review* in 1984, to which Hall replied (reprinted in 1988a). This exchange is worthy of consideration still since it clarifies the focus and the limits of Hall's particular thesis on Thatcherism and, to some extent, his general *modus operandi*. Bob Jessop and his co-authors charged Hall with 'ideologism' and neglect of the economic both in terms of structural explanation (for example, monetarism's function in class struggle) and the 'rewards' of Thatcherism (for instance, income-tax cuts). Furthermore, Jessop *et al.* argued that the concept of authoritarian populism was fraught with 'significant inconsistencies and ambiguities' because it sometimes stressed the 'authoritarian, disciplinary, coercive pole' and at other times the 'popular, populist and consensual pole' (1984: 35). They made a wide range of subsidiary points in this their first attack on Hall and the tendency he represented.[14] But, in sum, their critique rested on the claim that Hall had exaggerated the unity and strength of Thatcherism whilst undervaluing its weaknesses and sources of resistance to it. Hall replied by arguing that, first, Jessop *et al.* had treated his thesis at a level of generalised abstraction that he had never intended, hence enabling themselves to challenge the interpretation of ideology as a totalising analysis. He claimed that his intention was much narrower and more specific. And, with Gramsci, he would never deny 'the decisive nucleus of economic activity' (1988a: 156). Second, Hall contended, it was wrong to question the concept of authoritarian populism for referring to inconsistencies in the Thatcherite project. That was, in a sense, the whole point of it: Thatcherism had combined authoritarian *and* populist elements. Third, Hall repudiated any suggestion that his position conceded total hegemony to Thatcherism. He always saw it as an unstable project, in spite of its evident success at the time.

Hall's defence can be substantiated further if one refers back to the remarkably prescient *Policing the Crisis* (1978), perhaps the most impressive achievement of the Birmingham Centre during its heyday. In the early 1970s, Hall and his co-researchers became interested in the moral panic around 'mugging' and its connotations of an alien, black threat to law and order on the city streets of Britain. This developed into a conjunctural analysis of the British crisis and the 'exceptional state' solution:

> We identify, here, four principal aspects: the political crisis; the economic crisis; the 'theatre' of ideological struggle; the direct interpellation of the race issue into the crisis of British civil and political life. All four themes must be understood as unrolling within an organic conjuncture whose parameters are

overdetermined by two factors: the rapid deterioration of Britain's economic position; and the maintenance of a political form of 'that exceptional state' which gradually emerged between 1968 and 1972 and which now appears, for 'the duration' at least, to be permanently installed.

(Hall *et al.* 1978: 306)

All this before the election of the first Thatcher government! The conditions of Thatcherism's emergence are dated way back to a decade before, the failures of Wilsonian social democracy and Heath's Selsdon man strategy, underpinned by the long-term decline of the British *economy:* no mere 'ideologism' this. Although the economic was not neglected, this mode of political analysis was, nevertheless, distinguished by its stress on the complex relations between struggle for hegemonic leadership of the state *and* the ideological work in civil society required to bring it about: including right-wing 'think tanks' like the Centre for Policy Studies, the Institute of Economic Affairs and the Adam Smith Institute; dominant ideological news of industrial conflict and race relations; and authoritarian populist campaigns against 'permissiveness' (Hall 1980d). It emphasised the state and ideology: and, one obvious lesson of Thatcherism flowing from such a problematic was that ideological work at both of the Gramscian levels of 'philosophy' and 'common sense' is a necessary precondition for political power in a liberal parliamentary system. How, then, could a popular-democratic opposition have been mobilised effectively against Thatcherism's populist exploitation of discontent and anxiety? What answer was there to Thatcherism's promise to put the 'Great' back into Britain by acting belligerently abroad and by creating a 'popular capitalism' at home? Hall's authoritarian populism thesis was not only an account, however partial, of Thatcherism; it was also a provocative challenge to the Left, which he reckoned lacked cultural nous. This latter point can be illustrated with a quotation from his 1984 article, 'The culture gap', where he discusses the changes in everyday life brought about by postwar consumerism:

Consumer capitalism works by working the markets; but it cannot entirely determine what alternative uses people make of the diversity of choices and the real advances in mass production which it also always brings. If 'people's capitalism' did not liberate the people, it nevertheless 'loosed' many individuals into a life somewhat less constrained, less puritanically regulated, less strictly imposed than it had been three or four decades before. Of course the market has not remained buoyant and expansive in this manner. But the contradictory capacity, for a time, of the system to pioneer expansion, to drive and develop new products and maximize new choices, while at the same time creaming off its profit margins, was seriously underestimated. Thus the left has never understood the capacity of the market to become identified in the minds of the mass of ordinary people, not as fair and decent and socially responsible (that it never was), but as an expansive popular system.

(Hall 1988a: 215)

The insistence on the need to understand how Thatcherism addressed popular aspirations displayed a compelling sense of where 'ordinary people' were in their everyday lives, something which could not be ignored by, in Hall's words, 'the grand old cause' of socialism. A sense of 'the brand new times', also in his words from 1985, was needed to grasp contemporary forms of subjectivity and the actual conditions under which people live (Hall 1988a: 243). Present here, however, is also that ambiguously populist embrace of consumer capitalism which resulted in some polemical and frequently quite blinkered criticism of Hall alleging that he had learnt too much from Thatcherism.

Hall's observations on popular consumption invert the pessimistic mass culture critique (to be discussed in the next chapter), which assumes that ordinary people are somehow enslaved by consumerism and manipulated by the capitalist media. In contrast, cultural populism, of which I take Hall's work to be an inspiration, conceives of ordinary people as active pleasure-seekers and trusts in the good sense of their judgement. Such a left-democratic attitude, however, is not held consistently without costs. For example, writing with Martin Jacques on Band Aid and Live Aid, Hall applauded their anti-Thatcherite sentiments ('People Aid – a new politics sweeping the land', *Marxism Today*, July 1986; reprinted in Hall 1988a). The Live Aid concert, beamed around the world by satellite, and similar events of the 1980s, were perhaps signs of a changing sensibility, and it was indeed encouraging to see a popular concern for others, especially the starving of Ethiopia, when Thatcherism promoted selfishness and insularity. Hall and Jacques argued that only popular music could have mobilised such generosity, yet, surprisingly, they found the meaning of Band Aid's *Don't They Know It's Christmas?* and the virtual absence of black performers unworthy of comment. Less optimistic commentators took a contrary view, that ethnocentric and conscience-salving charity, albeit brashly hedonistic, was consonant with Margaret Thatcher's return to 'Victorian values'. Later and comparable events, such as Nelson Mandela's seventieth birthday concert, were less questionable on these grounds. The key issue, for the purposes of this discussion, is not strictly whether Hall and Jacques or the grumbling party-poopers were right, but how unqualified enthusiasm for anything remotely 'popular' slides into uncritical populism, about which I shall have much more to say in the rest of this book. To take another brief example, which has a rather different provenance: Hall and Jacques approved keenly of the 1981–86 Greater London Council's innovative cultural policies (also in Hall 1988a), more instantly recognisable as 'popular-democratic' than mass-mediated charitable entertainment. Unfortunately, for exactly that same kind of reason, the second Thatcher government abolished the Labour-controlled GLC, thus demonstrating how *realpolitik* can obliterate popular power at a stroke.

In concentrating on some of Stuart Hall's political writings here, my aim has been to indicate the connection between contemporary cultural studies and left-democratic populism rather than to interrogate the full subtleties of his theoretical position. Hall is not, by any means, the sole representative of this intellectual mix: he was, however, the most eloquent and credible exponent of cultural populism during the 1980s.

Towards the end of the 1980s, and before the fall of Margaret Thatcher herself, the state/ideology problematic circulating around Thatcherism began to be displaced in the pages of *Marxism Today* and also, somewhat hesitantly, in cultural studies by a very different problematic, one addressing longer-run and global forces, the key terms of which are 'culture' and 'economics':

The 'New Times' argument is that the world has changed, not just incrementally but qualitatively, that Britain and other advanced capitalist societies are increasingly characterised by diversity, differentiation and fragmentation, rather than homogeneity, standardisation and the economies and organisations of scale which characterised modern mass society. This is the essence of the so-called transition from 'Fordism', which defined the experience of modernity in the first two-thirds of the 20th century to 'Post-Fordism'. In economic terms, the central feature of the transition is the rise of 'flexible specialisation' in place of the old assembly-line world of mass production. It is this, above all, which is orchestrating and driving on the evolution of this new world. However, this must not be seen as exclusively an economic development, in the narrow sense. Just as Fordism represented, not simply a form of economic organisation but a whole culture – what Gramsci in 'Americanism and Fordism' called a new epoch of civilisation within advanced capitalism – so post-Fordism is also shorthand for a much wider and deeper social and cultural development.

(Hall and Jacques 1989: 11–12)

Crucially, this declaration of 'New Times' called for a further shift of attention away from the capitalist mode of production to its modes of reproduction and consumption, thus bringing to the foreground 'the cultural' to an even greater extent than before. According to the thesis, as discussed by Hall in his 'Brave new world' essay in the October 1988 edition of *Marxism Today* (reprinted with revisions as 'The meaning of new times' in Hall and Jacques 1989), the cultural phenomena associated with 'postmodernism' ('difference', 'subjectivity', 'identity') and the economic phenomena associated with 'post-Fordism' (information technology, robotics, disorganisation and reorganisation of systems of production/consumption) have some sort of relation to each other, the implication being that economic causation had returned to the agenda. This is an interesting turnabout if one remembers that it was Hall who consigned the political economy of culture perspective to the dustbin of base–superstructure Marxism when he surveyed the contending paradigms of cultural studies several years ago. The New Times thesis did not, however, constitute a reversion to economic reductionism, but it did open up a space for dialogue between two hitherto counterposed positions. In my view, the separation of contemporary cultural studies from the political economy of culture has been one of the most disabling features of the field of study. The core problematic was virtually premised on a terror of economic reductionism. In consequence, the economic aspects of media institutions and the broader economic dynamics of consumer culture were rarely investigated, simply bracketed off, thereby severely undermining the explanatory and, in effect, critical capacities of cultural studies. Some believe that the New Times thesis retains those weaknesses: 'New Times was born in the throes of political pragmatism under the sign of cultural theory bereft of economic reasoning' (Sivanandan 1990: 4). Commenting on the *Manifesto for New Times*, Judith Williamson (1989) expressed a similar view, suggesting that 'New Times' displays the same excessively ideological reading of culture and politics as the earlier Thatcherism thesis, and is peculiarly complicit with the *populist* delusions fostered by the political Right since the 1970s. Nicholas Costello and his co-authors (1989) have challenged the economic analysis battened on to the New Times thesis and the inferences that are drawn from it for working-class politics and culture. It undercuts arguments for socialism and, at best, brings into the foreground 'identity' and 'new social movement' politics (Rutherford 1990). The curious thing, however, is that the New Times thesis actually brought economic reasoning back into the cultural debate, switching from a state/ideology problematic, in the analysis of Thatcherism and authoritarian populism, to a culture/economic problematic, as Thatcherism went into decline and appeared less momentous in retrospect. The post-Fordism thesis of the regulation school of economists was seized upon for some rough-and-ready economic equivalent to the manifest cultural changes associated with postmodernity.

Recently, Angela McRobbie (1991a) has tried to make sense of the paradigm crisis in contemporary cultural studies. The old Althusserian/Gramscian synthesis of the Birmingham Centre no longer holds sway. Searching questions concerning modernity/postmodernity have superseded it. McRobbie identifies two particular strands in this respect: the radical critique of postmodernism and the New Times cultural politics of consumerism and playful identity. She attacks both unreservedly. According to her, the work of Fredric Jameson (1991) and David Harvey (1989), whom she regards as entirely hostile critics of postmodernism, merely reruns a discredited economic reductionism. And, even worse, New Times writers have lost all sense of the determinate relations between production and consumption, for instance, treating shopping as unproblematically pleasurable. That consumption is part of the material and unequal drudgery of social reproduction is missed by this 'cultural populism' (p. 14), a term used entirely pejoratively by McRobbie. She recommends a return to neo-Gramscian hegemony theory, which once mapped out the field, a kind of middle-ground position between the extremities of economic reductionism and insouciant hedonism. There are two main faults in McRobbie's argument: a slippage and a misrepresentation. The first is to do with her own position, which I believe, and aim to show in Chapter 3, is itself rooted in cultural populism – not in my vocabulary a term of abuse. Her critique of an undialectical consumptionist perspective is incisive. Like Sinbad, however, McRobbie wants to lure the genie back into the bottle but, unlike Sinbad, she can't do it. There is no retreat into some primordial haven in a rapidly changing world. This relates to the second fault in McRobbie's argument, her misrepresentation of the work of such writers as Jameson and Harvey, who do indeed re-articulate economics and culture but not in the crudely reductionist, or 'reflectionist', manner which she suggests. I shall explain why when considering their work and its implications for cultural studies in Chapter 6.

NOTES

1   Michael Schudson (1987) has also discussed populist 'sentiment' in communication and cultural studies but much more pejoratively than I do here.
2   Brecht famously wrote a short poem which comments ironically on the communist regime's brutal suppression of the East Berlin workers' revolt in 1953:

The solution

After the uprising of the 17th of June
The Secretary of the Writers' Union
Had leaflets distributed in the Stalinallee
Stating that the people
Had forfeited the confidence of the government
And could win it back only
By redoubled efforts. Would it not be easier
In that case for the government
To dissolve the people
And elect another?

(Brecht 1976: 440)

3 See the collection of papers from a 1967 London School of Economics symposium on populism, edited by Ghita Ionescu and Ernest Gellner (1969).

4 Michele Mattelart's analysis of right-wing populism and women in Chile could usefully be compared with Beatrix Campbell's (1987) study of women and Conservative Party politics in Britain, influenced by Stuart Hall's authoritarian populism thesis on Thatcherism.

5 Ken Hirschkop has contributed a valuable bibliographical essay on Bakhtin to the wide-ranging set of essays for which he is joint editor (Hirschkop and Shepherd 1989).

6 Alan O'Connor (1989) has written a book-length appreciation of Raymond Williams. Similarly to the book of essays edited by Terry Eagleton (1989), O'Connor concentrates mainly on the literary-political aspects of Williams's work. The discussion here draws on my own article which deals more specifically and at greater length with Williams's contribution to communication and cultural studies (McGuigan forthcoming).

7 Williams's posthumously published *The Politics of Modernism* (1989b) is an incomplete collection of disparate pieces and, for this reason, cannot be considered his last major study of culture and politics, which, therefore, remains *Towards 2000* from 1983.

8 Raymond Williams's characteristically oblique criticisms of structuralist and poststructuralist theoreticism were no doubt unfair and too sweeping, but he was not particularly inclined to sectarian squabbling. In fact, he displayed impressive solidarity with Colin MacCabe himself when he was denied tenureship at Cambridge in the early 1980s (see Williams 1981).

9 Of the literature on cultural studies, here are some of the more important texts: Rosalind Coward's (1977) '*Screen* theory' critique of class reductionism in 1970s Birmingham CCCS work; Terry Lovell's (1980 and 1981) Marxian realist critique of the Althusserian impact on cultural studies; Steve Baron's (1985) discussion of its significance for sociology; Lawrence Grossberg's (1983 and 1988) Left-postmodernist appraisals; John Fiske's (1987a) summary of British cultural studies approaches to television; Patrick Brantlinger's (1990) survey and discussion of the relationship between cultural studies and American studies; and Graeme Turner's (1990) introduction to British cultural studies.

10 For an up-to-date discussion of the relations between feminism and cultural studies, see Sarah Franklin *et al.* (1991).

11 On the question of race, the most important publication emanating from Birmingham was *The Empire Strikes Back* (CCCS 1982a), with which Gilroy was heavily involved.

12 Hall's argument concerning the separation of analytical elements was closely modelled on Karl Marx's (1973) methodological Introduction to the *Grundrisse* (Hall 1974a). His work, during the 1970s, was very much influenced by Louis Althusser (1966 and 1968). However, Hall's mature theoretical positions are most adequately described as neo-Gramscian. His best-known work draws on Antonio Gramsci's

Prison Notebooks (Hoare and Nowell-Smith, 1971) in a novel and fertile manner.

13 The authoritarian populism thesis derived from Gramsci's theory of hegemony, Poulantzas's analysis of authoritarian statism and Laclau's account of populism and popular-democratic struggle. See Hall's 'Popular-democratic vs authoritarian populism', originally published in 1980 and reprinted in Hall (1988a), and his elegant discussion of how to explain Thatcherism (1988b).

14 See Bob Jessop *et al.* (1990) for further elaboration on their critique of the authoritarian populism thesis, and Colin Leys (1990) for a commentary, defending the neo-Gramscian account.

Chapter 2

Trajectories of cultural populism

Although populist sentiment in contemporary cultural thought ranges across otherwise divergent positions, these positions share a commonly negative response to the elitist critique of mass culture, which has ideological origins that stretch back to the ancient Greek patrician's fear of the plebeian 'crowd' (Giner 1976). In the modern era, the mass culture critique was theorised and spread widely as educated common sense. The most conservative versions, dating from the nineteenth century, stressed an absolute division between inferior majorities and refined minorities. For example, the German philosopher Friedrich Nietzsche had this to say:

> In every healthy society there are three types which condition each other and gravitate differently physiologically; each has its own hygiene, its own field of work, its own sense of perfection and mastery. Nature, not Manu, distinguishes the pre-eminently spiritual ones, those who are pre-eminently strong in muscle and temperament, and those, the third type, who excel neither in one respect nor the other, the mediocre ones – the last as the great majority, the first as the elite.
>
> (1888: 645)

Nietzsche believed that 'the mediocre' of his day would have been happy in their mediocrity if it were not for 'the socialist rabble' stirring up false ideas of equality in their inherently feeble minds. In these circumstances, 'the pre-eminently strong in muscle and temperament' had a job to do on behalf of 'the pre-eminently spiritual ones'. Shorn of Nietzsche's belligerence, social and cultural thought rooted in such neo-aristocratic sensibility has provided a set of springs for a very strange assortment of bedfellows during the twentieth century, not only conservatives (like Ortega, Gasset and T.S. Eliot) but also liberals and socialists (see Swingewood 1977; Bennett 1982; Brantlinger 1983; Ross 1989), and, latterly, the ex-leftist 'new philosophers' of Paris (Hughes 1990). To explicate cultural populism's 'difference', however, it is the liberal and radical versions that require the closest examination.

In Victorian Britain, both Matthew Arnold (1970) and John Stuart Mill (1974) were worried that democratic emancipation, which as good liberals they supported in principle, would lower standards of culture and of political discourse. As a solution, Arnold recommended the aesthetic education of 'the masses', a recommendation put into practice with great fervour, especially from the 1920s onwards, by English literary criticism's petit bourgeois 'discrimination' strategy. The Leavisites, in particular, complained about the morally debilitating effects of mass communication, the threat posed not only by newly burgeoning commercial media but even the early BBC! To stem the tide, F.R. Leavis and Denys Thompson published a seminal guidebook for teachers of English and History, *Culture and Environment*:

> Those who in school are offered (perhaps) the beginnings of education in taste are exposed out of school to the competing exploitation of the cheapest emotional responses; films, newspapers, publicity in all its forms, commercially catered fiction – all offering satisfaction at its lowest level, and inculcate the choosing of the most immediate pleasures, got with the least effort . . . . We cannot, as we might in a healthy state of culture, leave the citizen to be formed unconsciously by his [sic] environment; if anything like a worthy idea of satisfactory living is to be saved, he must be trained to discriminate and resist.
>
> (1933: 3, 5)

These words, 'discriminate and resist', ring out across the decades in the study of mass-popular culture. In spite of its extremely limiting consequences for cultural education, the strategy advocated by the Leavisites did have the distinct virtue of at least putting the products of the modern media on the curriculum, albeit once there only to be derided by the all-knowing teacher. The discrimination strategy framed the cultural debate into which Raymond Williams intervened during the 1950s and was still setting the agenda when the National Union of Teachers held its conference on 'Popular Culture and Personal Responsibility' in 1960 (Lusted 1985). Both Williams's book, *Communications* (1962), and the book edited by Denys Thompson, *Discrimination and Popular Culture* (1964), also much-read, emanated from that conference.

The most theoretically sophisticated version of cultural elitism came, however, from the Left, specifically the neo-Hegelian Frankfurt School of Social Research, which was exiled in the United States during the Hitler period. It was, in fact, these radical scholars who coined the term 'mass culture', originally suggested to Max Horkheimer and Theodor Adorno by the Nazi propaganda machine but encountered again, in a rather different form, when they arrived, as suspicious European intellectuals, in the 'New World'. They believed that under liberal democratic conditions the capitalist media were being used to manipulate 'the masses' and consumer culture to buy them off, thereby suppressing critical reason and eliminating the possibilities of revolutionary social change: 'In democratic countries, the final decision no longer rests with the educated but with the amusement industry. Popularity consists of the unrestricted accommodation of the people to what the amusement industry thinks they like' (Horkheimer 1941: 303). The Frankfurt School's ideological critique rested upon a conception of mass-mediated knowledge and, more insidiously, mass-popular pleasure as somehow essentially alienating. For instance, Adorno (1941) notoriously attacked the vogue for jazz bands and jitterbugging from this rarified standpoint. He completely failed, as is well known, to appreciate the radical roots of black music. By the 1950s, Adorno (1954) was also denouncing what he considered to be the psychological damage caused by television's anti-aesthetic.

In the late 1940s, Adorno and Horkheimer (1947) had replaced the concept of 'mass culture' in their theoretical discourse with 'the culture industry' (Jhally 1989). The latter concept was supposed to be more damning since it combined two incompatible terms – 'culture' and 'industry' – whereas 'mass culture' might be misconstrued as authentically proletarian (by suggesting the Leninist sense of 'the masses'). Curiously, the now banal insight that popular culture is produced industrially, distributed and consumed according to commercial imperatives in a capitalist economy, is probably critical theory's most incisive and enduring contribution (Garnham 1987; Bronner and Kellner 1989; Jameson

1990). On the other hand, the persistently negative connotations of 'mass culture' render it much less usable, most certainly for cultural populism.

One of the earliest theoretical responses to a taken-for-grantedly demeaning view of ordinary people's tastes and pleasures was the American structural functionalist (Shils 1971; Gans 1974) challenge to the literary intellectuals' Frankfurt School-influenced (MacDonald 1953) critique of mass culture (Ross 1989).[1] This mainstream American sociological position of the 1950s, with its uncritical account of the system-stabilising 'functions' of popular culture, has been unwittingly echoed by British cultural populism, as we shall see. But, before considering that, let us return to the classic populist critique of 'mass communication', a term closely connected to the idea of 'mass culture':

> There are in fact no masses; there are only ways of seeing people as masses . . . . What we see, neutrally, is other people, many others, people unknown to us. In practice, we mass them, and interpret them, according to some convenient formula. Within its terms, the formula will hold. Yet it is the formula, not the mass, which is our real business to examine . . . . [It is founded in] a concept of society which relegates the majority of its members to mob status. The idea of the masses is an expression of this conception, and the idea of mass communication a comment on its functioning.
>
> (Williams 1958: 289, 293)

Raymond Williams himself never altered his judgement that the 'mass' formula should be scrupulously avoided because of its irredeemable association with contemptuous elitism and 'mob' psychology (Heath and Skirrow 1986). Although sympathetic to Williams's argument, John Corner (1979) has proposed that such terminology can still be used neutrally to refer to large-scale distribution of messages in complex societies without necessarily carrying unwarranted assumptions concerning audience homogeneity and passivity; and indeed it is frequently used thus, quite unobjectionably, in the literature.

Having outlined some of the key themes of 'cultural elitism', I want now to trace the two main trajectories of its opposite, 'cultural populism', in Britain since the late 1950s. The first trajectory is on the cusp of the mass-culture critique and cultural populism proper, represented by the work of Richard Hoggart and Jeremy Seabrook but given a more radically populist meaning by the movement for 'cultural democracy' from the 1970s, illustrated here by the ideas of Su Braden and John McGrath. Ultimately, the first trajectory arrives at a position which opposes popular cultural production almost entirely to mass cultural consumption. The second trajectory, exemplified by hegemony theory in the 1980s, retained a critical tension between 'popular culture' and 'mass culture', forging a dialectical perspective on symbolic exchange until, however, under the strain of its own internal contradictions, the synthesis imploded and ultimately dissolved in the work of some authors, most notably John Fiske, into an uncritical celebration of mass-popular cultural consumption, a position which James Curran (1990) and Philip Schlesinger (1991) have labelled 'the new revisionism'. At the end of the chapter, I shall review the principal objections to this terminally uncritical populism.

'UNBENDING THE SPRINGS OF ACTION'

Richard Hoggart's celebrated and widely read book, *The Uses of Literacy* (1957), more than any other publication, shifted the cultural debate in Britain from a stark opposition between elitist minority culture and lowly mass culture towards a serious engagement with the value and the values of majority cultural experience. Hoggart made influential discriminations *within* the field of ordinary people's culture (see his 'Culture: dead and alive', reprinted in Hoggart 1970a), discriminations that were then inscribed into the work of the Centre for Contemporary Cultural Studies, founded by him on assuming the professorship of English at Birmingham University in 1963 (Corner 1991). Peter Wiles (1969) has called Hoggart an 'urban populist'. Hoggart's 'populism', however, was extremely qualified: first, by his distinctly 'English' contempt for commercially imposed 'mass culture', the critical implications of which he never pursued with the vigour of Jeremy Seabrook; and, second, by his antipathy to the radical populism of the 'cultural democracy' movement in publicly subsidised community arts.

Read now, *The Uses of Literacy* seems less daring than Roland Barthes's *Mythologies*, published that same year in France. Barthes's semiological method allied to a critique of ideology yielded a series of scintillating essays on the codes of wrestling, press photography, cinema and so on. They demythologise the naturalising ruses of mass-distributed popular culture and manage to circumvent the pedestrian Anglo-American mass culture debate (Barthes 1972). Hoggart's tone, in comparison, is one of a secular priest legitimated by his own humble origins, his scholarship-boy background and the judgemental idiom of Leavisite criticism. He read the English working class as fleeting figures in a landscape (that the Penguin paperback edition had a Lowry on the cover from the 1960s is not irrelevant), and he railed against the pernicious impact of specifically 'American' mass culture, which was, in his judgement, 'unbending the springs of action'.

The Uses of Literacy is divided into two parts. Part One, entitled 'An "old" order', is an impressionistic reflection on community life in the industrial North of England: Hoggart himself came from Leeds and grew up in Chapeltown and Hunslet, providing his book with a strong sense of locality. Part Two, entitled 'Yielding place to the new', is a critical reading of mass publications and includes some sideways swipes at milk bars, frequented by the young, and their blaring juke boxes. The basic theme of the book is the erosion of the old culture by the new:

> My argument is not that there was, in England one generation ago, an urban culture still very much 'of the people' and that now there is only a mass culture. It is rather that appeals made by the mass publicists are for a great number of reasons made more insistently, effectively, and in a more comprehensive and centralised form today than they were earlier; that we are moving towards the creation of a mass culture; that the remnants of what was at least in parts an urban culture 'of the people' are being destroyed; and that the new mass culture is in important ways less healthy than the often crude culture it is replacing.
>
> (1957: 24)

Hoggart's nostalgic recollections of his own childhood and his account of the residual customs, habits and irreverent 'them' and 'us' attitudes of the white working class living in terraced cottages and meeting out on the street evoked the world still conjured up many years later by the long-running television serial, *Coronation Street* (1960–), a neighbourly and vibrant existence, ordinary people making the best of their situation without too much emphasis on squalor, cultural difference and social conflict (Critcher 1979; Dyer *et al.* 1981). Like *Coronation Street*, the appearance of Hoggart's book was timely, coinciding with the moment when urban planners, fired by the promise of modernity, were in fact transforming the communal space of that intimate way of life with slum clearances, the building of green-belt estates and inner-city tower blocks. In the second part of the book that he had originally wanted to call *The Abuses of Literacy*, Hoggart's literary readings of the newer genre fiction and magazines are very critical indeed of their, to him, degraded sentiments, yet as he eventually confessed in his autobiography, the examples quoted were, in fact, invented by himself at the request of his publisher, who was anxious about libel (Hoggart 1990). The methodological validity of the exercise notwithstanding, Hoggart's work did anticipate both the ethnographic and textual analysis strands of subsequent cultural studies.

The success of Hoggart's book with 'the general reader' turned him into a pivotal figure *institutionally* and very nearly a household name.[2] And, at Birmingham University, he was able to introduce popular cultural study as an addition to the main business of academic English. His inaugural lecture, 'Schools of English and contemporary society' (reprinted in Hoggart 1970b), set out the programme for the new research centre, of which there were to be three kinds of enquiry: historical and philosophical; sociological; literary critical. The point was to 'evaluate' the forms of popular culture, determine their place in society and clear up the 'muddle' of the cultural debate. In 1964 the Birmingham Centre's first report listed the initial seven projects to be undertaken:

1 Orwell and the Climate of the Thirties
2 The Growth and Change in the Local Press
3 Folk Song and Folk Idioms in Popular Music
4 Levels of Fiction and Changes in Contemporary Society
5 Domestic Art and Iconography in the Home
6 Pop Music and Adolescent Culture
7 The Meaning of Sport and its Presentation.

(CCCS 1964: 6–7)

This was an ambitious and wide-ranging programme of research, especially considering that the Centre had very little money except for a small grant from Penguin Books, which funded a research fellowship.

Hoggart's distinction between the 'processed' and the 'lived' in 'popular culture', against an undifferentiated and prejudicial notion of 'mass culture' as a basis for discriminating judgement (Hoggart 1970a: 130), was applied by the Centre's research fellow, Stuart Hall (in an earlier incarnation from the one discussed in the last chapter). Hall wrote *The Popular Arts*, yet another guidebook for teachers of English, with Paddy Whannel, education officer at the British Film Institute:

> In terms of actual quality (and it is with this, rather than with 'effects', that we are principally concerned) the struggle between what is good and worthwhile and what is shoddy and debased is not a struggle *against* the modern forms of communication, but a conflict *within* these media . . . . If we believe that one of the central purposes of education is to train the ability to discriminate, then we can see that the introduction of the study of the popular arts into the curriculum is less the imposition of a new subject than an extension of this basic aim to cover new and highly relevant areas of experience.
>
> (Hall and Whannel 1964: 15, 388–9)

The Leavisite terminology and solemn moral purpose hardly require comment. However, Hall and Whannel were at pains to distance their approach from that of F.R. Leavis and Denys Thompson, informed as they were by Williams's stress on 'ordinary culture' and Hoggart's discriminations. Hall and Whannel, in contrast to the unreconstructed Leavisites of the 1960s, were not so perturbed that most young people watched television, listened to pop music and went to the cinema, instead of reading 'good literature', visiting art galleries and attending classical music concerts. They advocated a 'widening' of the English curriculum to help students develop a discriminating attitude to their preferred forms and media. Teachers should introduce them, for instance, to the classics of European cinema and draw their attention to the *auteurs* of Hollywood in order to broaden their experience. Len Masterman (1980) later produced a devastating critique of this modified 'discrimination' strategy, its still confidence-sapping judgementalism and imposition of teacherly taste. But, in the early 1960s, Hall and Whannel's *The Popular Arts* was at the forefront of progressive education. The turn to 'the popular arts' and the cinema in particular had already been given an official nod of approval by the 1963 Newsom Report, *Half Our*

Future, concerned with working-class underachievement: and it was in this space that subsequent developments in film, television and media education occurred. These academic and educational trajectories should not, however, be taken as the only strands of thought on the cusp of the mass culture critique and cultural populism.

Although Hoggart opened up the study of popular texts and contexts, his own position was always embattled and became increasingly unfashionable, from the late 1960s, in the intellectual circles that he had once inspired, mainly due to his gloomy prognosis that mass culture was overwhelming the authentically popular. Such populist pessimism, however, was taken much further than Hoggart by the passionate jeremiads of Jeremy Seabrook. Seabrook and his occasional co-author, Trevor Blackwell, are strangely marginal to academic cultural studies (in spite of the fact that Blackwell himself studied at the Birmingham Centre in the 1970s). If mentioned at all, they are usually dismissed peremptorily. For instance, Alan Tomlinson (1990a) has observed acidly that Seabrook and Hoggart both represent 'a sad, dislocated, elitist, and perhaps menopausal, critique' (p. 17). In my opinion, Seabrook is not so conveniently sectioned off, since he enunciates a sensibility that has considerable social and political resonance.

Seabrook writes in a documentary mode which validates general argument with the words of ordinary people. His early books, such as *City Close-up* (1971), are composed mainly of lengthy passages of quoted speech from interviews, not tape-recorded but reconstructed afterwards. Presumably, this dubious method is used in order to facilitate 'natural' conversation. The effect on the reader, however, can be quite the opposite to Seabrook's intention. This is particularly noticeable in the later books, such as *The Leisure Society* (1988), where Seabrook's linking passages of commentary are fuller. Sometimes his interlocutors come across like ventriloquist dummies. None the less, these ordinary voices also frequently suggest striking insights.

There is running right through Seabrook's work a 'tragic vision', as Huw Beynon (1982) puts it: the fall from a pre-welfare-state dignity of labour to the compulsive and illusorily egalitarian mass consumption fostered by late capitalism. The title of one of Seabrook's best-known books is the tormenting question, *What Went Wrong?* (1978). The political hopes of a socially emancipated working class were, in his estimation, dashed on the rocks of a merely ostensible economic emancipation. And, when mass unemployment returned with a vengeance in the early 1980s, shattering the normative expectations cultivated by post-Second World War social democracy, the casualties were abandoned with no resources of resistance, hoist on the petard of short-lived affluence:

> Because the draining away of much of the strength of the working class has taken place under a huckster's cry of gifts, rewards, offers and prizes, it is harder to perceive than that other, older poverty. Its very intangibility makes it difficult to reduce to words. But it is no less real; it is a feeling, gnawing, corrosive, inescapable. It is not by chance that everything in Western culture is so readily turned into the visible, the palpable, image and commodity, what Guy Debord describes as the 'society of the spectacle'. Everything that exists becomes pictures, objects that can be seen and handled and which give an impression of multifarious richness and diversity. This is perhaps a metaphor for the way in which all the plundered attributes of working-class collectivism have been transformed. The anguish, the pain and loneliness which have been inflicted in exchange for all those positive intangibles are, like them, not acknowledged; and they remain buried beneath the torrent of visual stimuli, the manufactured excitement of buying and selling.
>
> (Seabrook 1982: 38)

Seabrook's writings are replete with such synoptic statements concerning the moral corruption of the working class and the worthlessness of mass culture:

> It is not so much that capitalism has delivered the goods to the people, as that the people have been increasingly delivered to the goods.
>
> (1988: 183)

> One of the great paradoxes is that the exaltation of the individual must seek its fulfilment through what are essentially mass markets: people whose individuality is actually impaired by the fact that they read the same newspapers, see the same television programmes, eat the same foods, dress in the same fashions, worship the same shadowy creatures promoted by

show business . . . . We should not be afraid to speak of the decay of a culture which is dominated by an ideology that teaches that life is something out of which it is the individual's highest duty to get as much money, sex and fun as he or she may; the dehumanizing of people in what is mistakenly called 'popular culture' (for it belongs to capitalism) in its 'entertainment' industry, with its cult of violence and pornography and degradation of human relationships.

(1990: 38, 166)

The recurrent themes of the mass culture critique are evident enough in Seabrook's despairing words. My main reason for quoting him at length is to illustrate the combination of radical pessimism with the search for a popular agency to reverse the process. Zygmunt Bauman (1987) argues that modern intellectuals in their now apparently *passé* wish to legislate rather than merely interpret have typically sought, at least until very recently, an agent for their project. For much of the twentieth century the leading candidate was the proletariat: but, with 'the emancipation of capital from labour' (the technological replacement of labour and the formation of a dual labour market divided into a minority of privileged workers and a disposable majority of peripheral and service workers), that particular agent of guaranteed historical transformation has disappeared (Gorz 1982 and 1985). Not even Seabrook and Blackwell, who have consistently spoken out on behalf of the poor, believe that an immiserated underclass can realise the socialist project. Now they argue that 'the myth of socialism', which promised so much and failed in its own terms, is subordinate to 'the green myth'. Capitalism and its erstwhile mimic, communism, despoils the Earth in its endless drive for productive growth and expanded consumption. The ecological *and* cultural costs are too great for us all:

The green myth has the undoubted advantage of appearing to be true . . . . [It is] deeply radicalizing, vibrant with emancipatory promise . . . . At the individual level, what myths and religions primarily offer is a vision of unity, a sense of wholeness, a feeling of reconciliation between the individual and the universe, between the one and the many.

(Blackwell and Seabrook 1988: 97, 98, 101)

All our differences (individual, class, gender, sexual, racial, ethnic and so on) can thus be subsumed, according to this quasi-mystical inflection of the mass-culture critique. Our shared natural and survival interests make us 'one people', which must be the ultimate populist promise. That such a conception of 'the people' seems of necessity to be displaced temporally from the present either into a lost past or into a Utopian future undermines its contemporary appeal, except as a persistently critical reminder that life could be better.

A more narrowly cultural but equally radical strand of this populism against mass-culture trajectory is the movement for 'cultural democracy'. During the 1960s, educational and cultural policy spending expanded in order to open up social 'access'. However, the idea of 'access' was a two-edged sword. What did 'access' mean in the cultural field? Access to established forms of art and knowledge or the means of production to redefine art and knowledge in the interests of hitherto excluded groups? The Arts Council meant the first, but it could hardly ignore the second meaning, articulated most energetically by community artists and political dramatists in the 1970s. They entered the margins of state funding while simultaneously denouncing the state and all its works, a somewhat contradictory position (Kelly 1984). John McGrath of the 7.84 Theatre Company, for instance, wanted a popular working-class theatre not only to oppose the theatrical culture of the National Theatre but to support counter-hegemonic struggles against the dominant institutions of capitalist society as a whole (McGrath: 1981). As money tightened in the late 1970s, the social democrats presiding over the Arts Council were seeking a way out. Su Braden's book of 1978, *Artists and People*, presented them with a heaven-sent opportunity:

> Before we can talk about 'community arts' or 'artists in residence', it must be understood that the so-called *cultural heritage* which made Europe great . . . is no longer communicating anything to the vast majority of Europe's population . . . . It is not that these cultural forms are 'above people's heads' but that it is a *bourgeois* culture and therefore only immediately meaningful to that group. The great artistic deception of the twentieth century has been to insist to *all* people that this was *their* culture. The Arts Council of Great Britain was established on this premise.
>
> (1978: 153)

The Secretary General of the Arts Council, Roy Shaw, attacked Braden's 'vulgar Marxism' in a *Guardian* review (20 September 1978); and the Vice-chairman of the Council, none other than Richard Hoggart, weighed into the debate as well. Hoggart (1979) defended the Arts Council's prioritising of expenditure on 'the main performing arts in particular (drama, music, opera, ballet)', in order to keep seat prices down at venues such as the Royal Opera House in Covent Garden, instead of wasting limited revenue upon what he dubbed disparagingly as 'participant, grass-roots, democratic and popular arts' (p. 238). At the 1980 symposium on 'Excellence and Standards in the Arts', Hoggart (1980) criticised cultural relativists, citing Braden in particular, and also the 'cultural slumming' of some academics (I wonder whom he was thinking of?). He went on to say, 'in both educational and arts writing over the last ten years, left-wing writers have got away with murder' (p. 30).

Hoggart's apparent inconsistencies distanced him from the cultural democratic movement with its various inflections of class, gender and race, a much more whole-hearted populism than he ever evinced. Braden's arguments for community photography can be taken as exemplary of oppositional cultural democracy and its uncompromising case against 'the dominant culture' of both 'art' and 'mass media':

> as a purveyor of dominant cultural bias, photography is capable of forming the vanguard of any invasion: an invasion where the incursionists take with them the ideologies, conventions and often the context from their own world as they launch themselves on the world of others. Alongside popular music and television, photography is the modern tool through which the dominant culture transmits its philosophies.
>
> (1983: 1)

Here Braden is referring to documentary photography's depiction of the oppressed from the viewpoint of the oppressor culture, an often-cited example of which is the sentimentally liberal work of Donald McCullen. As Barthes (1961) pointed out, photography is particularly seductive since it functions as 'a message without a code' (p. 17), by which he means that photography's iconic significations look like unmediated transcriptions of reality. This 'reality effect' of the photograph (and other textual forms) is routinely 'deconstructed' in communication, cultural and media studies. It is one thing, however, to reveal the absent codes of photography but quite another to produce 'different' photographic images. Braden proceeds:

> The alternative to cultural invasion is the altogether more conscious, more painstaking one, described by the educationalist Paulo Freire as 'cultural synthesis', in which the incursionists become collaborators, integrated with the people and acting with them in collective authorship.
>
> (1983: 1)

According to Braden, oppositional cultural workers should find ways of collaborating with the oppressed in their *self* representation.

This relates, by a circuitous route, to Williams's concern about the loss of a popular educational project in cultural studies, discussed in the last chapter. For instance, Andrew Dewdney and Martin Lister sought, with limited success, to apply contemporary cultural studies to photographic education at the Inner London Education Authority's Cockpit Arts Workshop during the 1980s:

> the underlying creative project of our generation was set by this felt need for a clearer understanding and more relevant forms of cultural practice. What we see now is that over fifteen years the first part of that generational project has been expressed by the development of courses and centres which do pay critical attention to how historical changes and shifts inform the framework of expression and communication. The courses we have in mind are those where social, economic and historical forces are made central to the perceptions and analysis of cultural forms. It is a pity, although to be expected, that these developments have been almost wholly confined to degree courses in higher education, rather than in the formation of newer kinds of popular cultural and educational institutions.
>
> (Dewdney and Lister 1986: 6)

Dewdney and Lister stress the empowerment of practical photography for young people, not only as a technical practice but as a critical sense-making activity. The schism between such developments in media education, more widespread in fact than Dewdney and Lister imply in the quoted passage, and the mainstream trajectory of cultural studies raises complex and difficult questions. Time and again it has been found that cultural production interests school students and community groups more than the study of consumption, the direction in which theoretical cultural studies has gone. Community arts, in contrast, have explored the possibilities of alternative and oppositional production. The radical populist intent of such practices came under attack from the Right during the 1980s, not surprisingly. It also, not so predictably, came under attack from the Left. Geoff Mulgan and Ken Worpole (1986), arguing the late-GLC case 'for a shift away from the traditional, patronage-based models of funding towards new forms of investment and regulation' (p. 10), challenged the 'indifference to possible audiences' (p. 87) of many community arts projects. Just 'doing it' very often seemed to be enough: little attention was paid to audience-formation and marketing (Lewis *et al.* 1986). A new spirit was in the air which insisted that the 'enterprise culture' could no longer be simply opposed in circumstances where state funding was being reduced or withdrawn. A good illustration of what was at stake for populist cultural politics is the fate of the 7.84 Theatre Companies in England and Scotland.

The story of how 7.84 (England) lost its Arts Council grant and its subsequent failure to benefit from GLC and Labour Movement patronage is told in John McGrath's 1990 book, *The Bone Won't Break*. McGrath also tells of how he left 7.84 (Scotland) because he could not agree with the new commercial 'realism' of publicly subsidised art. Clearly, these experiences were personally painful since McGrath had turned away from the lucrative terrains of television and film writing in the early 1970s to found 7.84 as a popular-democratic alternative at a moment of radical optimism. My purpose here in discussing some of McGrath's ideas is not to explain what happened to the political theatre movement and 7.84 in particular during the changing conditions of the 1980s: rather, it is to register what was at one time a compelling instance of populism against mass culture.

McGrath defines popular culture, first, in opposition to official 'serious' culture, 'the culture of working people in their areas' contrasted with the allegedly national 'dominant high culture which the middle and upper classes are mainly qualified to consume' (1990: 57). On the politics of public arts funding, this is close to the nub of the matter. However, McGrath's notion of 'the popular' is on a broader basis defined as the source and practice of resistance to 'mass culture'. He talks of mass production and standardisation in industrial societies in a manner not markedly different from the Leavisites and mass-culture critics in general: '[t]he real problem . . . involves the character of modern industrial society, and the nature and control of the mass media' (p. 60). Leisure-time privatisation, the role of television, the motor car and package holidays are all treated negatively by McGrath and he complains about the reduction of 'occasions for social exchange' taking place in the contexts of face-to-face interaction. This relates to the value of 'presence' in theatre compared with the technological impersonality of mass media. McGrath himself would probably argue that there is nothing inherently alienating about television as such, that the problem lies in who owns, controls and dictates the programming in capitalist society. None the less, he does view 'the effects of mass-production on the standardisation of popular culture' (p. 61) with a grim negativity. McGrath goes on to say:

> So the implication is that live, communally-generated and experienced popular culture rooted in the traditions of long-established communities is on the decline, and being replaced by the consumption in small groups of a standardised, non-local, non-specific culture created by those very groups of people who wish to exploit the backward elements in popular culture for their own commercial or political ends, the people who oppose any struggle for popular culture as interfering with nature.
>
> (1990: 62)

Speaking as a cultural producer, McGrath recognises opportunities for exploiting contradictions in the dominant system (for example, radical television programmes), but he believes these opportunities have become fewer and further between due to the increasingly market-regulated environment of transnational cultural production and distribution. And, as McGrath insists, the social democratic dissemination of high culture to the masses is no alternative. Thus, he kept faith with the original project of 7.84, to collaborate with local popular cultures, the best example of which was the Scottish ceilidh play, *The Cheviot, the Stag and the Black, Black Oil*, performed both in community centres and on television in the early 1970s (see McArthur 1978). It is significant, however, that such a practice should have been most successful in relatively unindustrialised rural settings –

settings like the Highlands of Scotland, internationally emblematic in terms of the relationship to the oil industry. It is on the
peripheries of the industrial world where this variant of populist
cultural politics makes the most obvious sense, reminding us of
'the discovery of popular culture' historically during the transition
from 'tradition' to 'modernity'. Similar to that of Seabrook and
Blackwell, McGrath tends to envisage the future in the imagery
and poetry of the past,[3] but the main weakness is not wherefrom
the poetry is drawn but its limited grasp on the dynamics of
contemporary cultural consumption. Populism against mass
culture is framed by a production-end model of consumption, not
unlike the distinctly anti-populist critical theory of Adorno and
Horkheimer. To assume that production determines consumption
may be a classically Marxist assumption, yet even Karl Marx (1973)
emphasised the dialectic of production and consumption:
'Without production, no consumption; but also, without
consumption, no production; since production would then be
purposeless' (p. 91).

Mike Featherstone (1990a) identifies two main alternatives to a
productionist perspective on consumption in the sociology of
culture, both of which were considered briefly in the last chapter:
the mode of consumption perspective, exemplified by Pierre
Bourdieu's work on distinction and taste; and the study of
pleasure, of which Mikhail Bakhtin's work on carnival is one
source (incidentally, also an influence on McGrath's recent
thinking). These perspectives frame but do not exhaust the
analytical positions taken on cultural consumption. The next
section traces the emergence of an exclusively consumptionist
approach to popular culture out of a once dominant hegemony
theory, which is ironic when one considers Tony Bennett's (1986a)
mandarin dismissal of populism against mass culture in the
context of extolling the virtues of hegemony theory: 'left-wing
populism, in its unqualified forms is, fortunately, no longer a
flourishing species' (p. 17).

FROM HEGEMONY THEORY TO THE NEW REVISIONISM

'Booms' in academic stocks and shares come and go (Morris
1988). The market for popular cultural critique slumped badly
during the 1980s after an initial high. At the beginning of the
decade, hegemony theory soared; but, by the end of the decade,

everybody seemed to be buying into the new revisionism. This rise and fall in values represents the second major trajectory of cultural populism considered here.

Hegemony theory framed the Open University's hugely influential distance-learning course 'U203 Popular Culture', which ran from 1982 to 1987. The OU is renowned for curriculum innovation in higher education due to the wide dissemination of its teaching materials, and this course was no exception. Following the lead set at Birmingham by Stuart Hall, who had recently become Professor of Sociology at the OU, Tony Bennett and some of his colleagues on the Popular Culture course team wanted to weld together the disparate strands of cultural studies with 'the turn to Gramsci' (Introduction to Bennett *et al.* 1986); and, to draw lessons for cultural politics from it.[4] In order to reconstitute the study of popular culture, Hall's division between culturalist voluntarism and structuralist determinism had to be overcome. In the 1970s, this paradigmatic divide had been marked out broadly by the tension between the Centre for Contemporary Cultural Studies (CCCS) and the Society for Education in Film and Television (SEFT).

SEFT and its internationally acclaimed journal, *Screen*, was the most important alternative site to Birmingham's CCCS for theorising popular culture. If CCCS tended to veer towards 'culturalism', SEFT was unremittingly 'structuralist', or rather, combining structural linguistics with Althusserian Marxism and Lacanian psychoanalysis, 'poststructuralist' (Coward and Ellis 1977). This French-inspired school differed sharply from the principal orientations of indigenous cultural studies, which had opened up to continental theory but not with the same exclusivity. The heady theoretical brew concerning 'textuality' and 'subject positioning', published by *Screen*, gave it a distinctly elite caste compared with the plebeian sympathies of CCCS. *Screen* theory took for granted that bourgeois and patriarchal ideologies thoroughly infused mainstream media, disturbed occasionally by 'trouble' in Hollywood texts and subverted by *avant-garde* film practices, but leaving virtually no conceptual space for the audience as a social rather than textual construct. Louis Althusser's theory of ideology supplied philosophical weight to this textual determinism. According to Althusser (1970), 'ideology in general' reconciled subjects to their conditions of existence and 'ideological state apparatuses', including communications and

cultural institutions, pumped them full of 'nationalism, chau-
vinism, liberalism, moralism, etc.' (p. 28), thereby securing the
reproduction of capitalist social relations. The ideological model
was extended to cover the systematic reproduction of patriarchal
relations as well, signalling an eventual shift from structuralist
Marxism to feminist psychoanalysis. Textual discourses of
cinematic realism, identification and scopophilia were endlessly
unravelled in the early work of *Screen* theorists such as Colin
MacCabe (1974) and Laura Mulvey (1975), somehow protected by
'theory' from the effects of dominant ideologies. Although
complex, subtle and revisable, their original message was also
functionalist, predictable and insistently unpopular.[5]

In cultural studies, around the inception of the OU's Popular
Culture course, we find the distinctly anti-realist chronology
whereby the ideas of a contemporary theorist, Louis Althusser, still
writing in the 1970s, are superseded by those of an Italian
politician, Antonio Gramsci, who died in 1937. Gramsci's legacy,
for cultural studies, was a set of enigmatic notes from his final
eleven years of life spent languishing in Mussolini's prisons (Hoare
and Nowell-Smith 1971). These notes, written in code to evade the
fascist prison censors, are open to multiple interpretation. None
the less, they offered a way of theorising culture and power in
advanced capitalist societies more nuanced than the dominant
ideology thesis, whether in the demotic version of cultural
democracy, echoing the mass culture critique, or in the theoretical
machinery of Althusserianism and its progeny.

The editors of the extracts from Gramsci's prison notebooks in
the Open University reader, *Culture, Ideology and Social Process*
(Bennett *et al.* 1981a) focus on the centrality of 'hegemony' in the
Italian revolutionary's writings. The concept of hegemony refers to
how the dominant class bloc in society constructs and sustains its
leadership over subordinate groupings. The crucial point is that
hegemony does not rely most effectively on coercion (although
that is always a possibility) but instead on a complex process of
winning *consent* to the prevailing order. As Raymond Williams
(1973) put it, hegemony 'saturates society', legitimated by
intellectual strata but flowing through ordinary practices and
meanings in common sense reasoning and everyday
representations, working as a kind of social 'cement'. However, it
never sets solid: hegemonic leadership is never accomplished once
and for all. There is a constant battle in which the ruling bloc has

to struggle for leadership against various resistances and oppositions. Sometimes the ruling bloc makes concessions to subordinate forces and, at other times, hard-won rights and opportunities are withdrawn. The particular hegemonic configuration at any one time depends on economic conditions and the current balance of power between contending forces. Hegemony is, then, endless struggle.

Gramsci himself actually made what amounted to a programmatic statement for cultural studies: 'It would be interesting to study concretely the forms of cultural organisation which keep the ideological world in movement within a given country, and to examine how they function in practice' (quoted by Bennett *et al.* 1981a: 195–6). And he goes on to say: 'The methodological criteria on which our own study must be based is the following: that the supremacy of a social group manifests itself in two ways, as 'domination' and as 'intellectual and moral leadership' (Bennett *et al.* 1981a: 197). So, according to Gramsci, cultural analysis should be situated within the problematic of hegemony, a piece of advice taken to heart and circulated with great aplomb by Stuart Hall (1980a).

Gramsci's purpose in recommending such study was not academic. His thinking was forged out of the specific historical circumstances in which Italian fascism had defeated socialism and communism. He wanted to understand what had happened and to rebuild an oppositional politics. The concept of 'the national-popular' is of paramount importance in this respect. Gramsci complained bitterly that in Italy, '[t]he lay forces have failed in their historical task as educators and elaborators of the intellectual and moral awareness of the people-nation' (in Forgacs and Nowell-Smith 1985: 211). The Roman Catholic church, the split between northern industrialism and southern agrarianism needed to be taken into account by a progressive and modernising political project. Gramsci believed the failure to organise a broad oppositional alliance had enabled the fascists to seize power. Parallels with the era of Thatcherism in Britain seemed, to some, clear and unmistakable. The 'universal class' was anything but standing in line ready for a frontal assault on the state, yet the women's movement, blacks, gays, CND and a multitude of community and single issue campaigns suggested that all was not lost. According to David Forgacs (1984), '[i]t is these two things arrayed against one another – the new state formation and the heterogeneous oppositional forces – which produce the need for a concept like the national-popular' (p. 84).

In a more strictly academic context, while the OU course was under preparation, Tony Bennett (1980) declared, 'the concept of popular culture is virtually useless, a melting pot of confused and contradictory meanings capable of misdirecting enquiry up any number of theoretical blind alleys' (p. 18). He then set about reviewing the extant usages of the concept, four in all: first, 'well-liked by many people'; second, 'a residual category consisting of those forms that are "left over" once the sphere of high culture has been defined'; third, 'a synonym for "mass culture"'; fourth, 'forms of cultural practice that are firmly rooted in the creative impulses of "the people" or particular sections of the people'. The first two usages are easily enough discarded. 'Well-liked by many people' is merely a quantitative observation, not a concept; and, besides, forms which would not usually be considered popular have large numbers of admirers, such as grand opera. Where do you draw the line? The second usage is more promising in this respect: that which remains once the line has been drawn for 'high culture'. However, such a solution is static and unhistorical since the most elementary knowledge of cultural history indicates that forms cross the line: for example, Shakespearian theatre started out as 'popular'. Historically shifting definitions and distinctions are woven into Bennett's eventual synthesis of the third and fourth usages. The third usage, 'popular culture' as a synonym for 'mass culture', is represented by the political variations of the mass culture critique, running from conservative and liberal elitism to the Frankfurt School. The trouble is it only sees popular culture as imposed by commercial interests on a gullible and dopey mass: that won't do for the populist sentiments of neo-Gramscian hegemony theory. The fourth usage is the romantic popular culture perspective from below,[6] of which radical populism against mass culture is an instance. Bennett recognised it as the main contender hitherto for a serious political engagement on the terrain of popular culture. The problem with this position, however, is that it conceives of commercial 'mass culture' as wholly meretricious and, most erroneously, it has an essentialist conception of 'the people' as a fixed entity forever waiting in the wings for their call on to the stage of history, already fully formed and authentic.

Bennett's solution was to keep 'popular culture' definitionally open, not as an inventory of forms or essential meanings but as a field of continually changing relations between the 'imposed from above' and the 'emerging from below': in effect, to historicise the concept as a site of perpetual struggle, negotiation and transaction, inspired by Gramsci, mediated by Hall. As he says:

> To rethink the concept of popular culture in and through the concept of hegemony is thus to define it as a system of relations – between classes – which constitutes one of the primary sites upon which the ideological struggle for the production of class alliances or the production of consent, active or passive, is conducted.
>
> (Bennett 1980: 26)

This rethinking of popular culture spawned a proliferation of research and pedagogy in either direct or indirect relation to the OU course, situating text/context analyses within critical and historical frameworks. Yet, although it offered a means of cohering the hitherto boundless field of cultural studies, the dialectical synthesis of neo-Gramscian hegemony theory was, nevertheless, an unstable project for several reasons. It demanded at least some residual attachment to historical materialism, underpinned by a theory of class relations, however non-reductionist. Radical feminists and some socialist feminists would not accept such an implicit privileging of capitalism over patriarchy as the determinate structure of social relations (see Segal 1987). Furthermore, the national-popular concept, appropriated by Hall and others in relation to Britain, is in danger of suppressing the specific dynamics of black and ethnic struggles, as Paul Gilroy (1987) argued forcefully (in fact, the Popular Culture course paid hardly any attention to race). Moreover, hegemony theory's break with the dominant ideology thesis may be considered less than complete:

> the truth conditions for this version of the theory of hegemony are very similar to Adorno's theory of mass popular culture. For Adorno, popular culture is ideological and furthermore articulates a dominant ideology. For the Gramscians, popular culture typically takes a hegemonic form to which other cultures are subordinated, while being a site of struggle. For both positions, popular culture has ideological force and both have to submit to similar tests of that force. The disagreement is only about *how* that force is achieved.
>
> (Abercrombie 1990: 202)

For neo-Gramscian hegemony theory, this methodological cut may not be quite so fatal as it first appears since there is perhaps a certain incommensurability between the sociological critique of 'the dominant ideology thesis' and interdisciplinary study of popular culture.

Nicholas Abercrombie and his co-authors (1980) made out a compelling case and modified their position in response to popular cultural studies (1990), but their wish to show that capitalism is sustained by 'the dull compulsion of economic relations' (Marx quoted by Hill 1990: 3), not by ideological domination, set itself a larger problem than did the OU course. Bennett and his closest collaborators were less concerned with explaining how capitalism is sustained than with tracking particular forms of hegemony through British history:

> we would argue that it is misleading to construe hegemony solely as a *condition* and, correspondingly, to view the task of historical interpretation as being to ascertain its presence or absence in any period. The concept refers rather to an always active and continuing *process*, the struggle between contending social forces for cultural and political leadership. Instead of asking whether hegemony exists or not, we would try to identify the *particular forms* this struggle took at a particular moment, the conditions bearing upon that struggle, and so on.
>
> (Bennett and Donald 1981: 79–80)

This is a protocol for historical research, inspired by the Birmingham Centre's distinction between 'expansive hegemony' and 'hegemonic crisis' (Hall *et al.* 1978). At moments of expansive hegemony there is a powerful ideological principle of articulation ('affluence', 'law 'n'order', 'popular capitalism', 'classless society' and so on), whereas moments of crisis occur when a new articulation is required, which may result in a fundamental transformation of the structure or not, as the case may be.

If there are problems with distinguishing hegemony theory from the dominant ideology thesis, the problems of reconciling it with a theory of pleasure are potentially insurmountable. Taking popular culture seriously involves, as Colin Mercer (1986) observed, taking pleasure seriously. However, Marxism has never been too strong on the question of pleasure, with the notable exceptions of Brecht and Bakhtin. Mercer made a strenuous attempt to address the question of pleasure from a neo-Gramscian standpoint: accounting for 'active consent'. Pleasure, albeit ideologically implicated, however, exceeds the problematic of hegemony. Of necessity, Mercer had to consider other problematics, most notably Lacanian psychoanalysis (see Turkle 1979) and Michel Foucault's attention to the body as the site of power, body politics instead of the body politic (see Foucault 1977 and 1979). Fantasy, the unconscious, the split subject (Lacan), disciplinary discourses of the body (Foucault) and hedonism (the later Barthes of *plaisir* and *jouissance* 1975) are all relevant to opening up the question of pleasure but none of them quite resolves the question of hegemony. Mercer opted for a Foucauldian emphasis on the micro-politics of the body:

> Photography, film, detective fiction can be taken as key instances in the contemporary cartography of pleasure. They, amongst others, constitute a plurality of powers and potentials, a technology of the body and of the social which makes up – elaborates – a dense texture of complicities, of subjectivities, which are formed not just 'in the head' but across the space of the body too.
>
> (1986: 66)

The synthesis of Gramscian state politics and Foucauldian body politics is a promising one. Already, Edward Said had combined Gramsci, Foucault and Williams convincingly in his study *Orientalism* (1978). More difficult to reconcile are psychoanalytic and sociological explanations of pleasure, as Terry Lovell argued from a perspective close to hegemony theory:

> Any Marxist theory of consumption would have as its central category 'use-value', and would focus on 'the pleasure of the text'. It is true that Althusserian and Lacanian currents in cultural studies have turned to this important question of pleasure, but its meaning has been restricted to the narrow Freudian sense. Cultural products are articulated structures of feeling and sensibility which derive from collective, shared experience as well as from individual desires and pleasures. The pleasure of the text stems at least in part from collective utopias, social wish fulfilment and social aspirations, and these are not simply the sublimated expression of more basic sexual desires.
>
> (1980: 61)

Although psychoanalysis has much to say about the specifically psychic and erotic mechanisms of pleasure, this social conception increasingly guided cultural populist thinking in the 1980s. It not only went beyond the psychologistic limitations of Freudian theory; it also called into question Marxist theories of commodity fetishism, the subsumption of use value by exchange value, and the alienation of 'real needs' by 'false' ones. The capitalist mode of production and market forces, according to Lovell, do not legislate for the social use or meaning of cultural commodities, whether primarily functional (such as clothes) or primarily symbolic (for example, television programmes). There is space, then, for active consumption and production of meaning: a space which has since been explored in terms of both the modes and pleasures of consumerism.

That is the kind of position given a Foucauldian gloss in the following passage from Mica Nava's article, 'Consumerism and its contradictions':

> consumerism can be argued to exercise control through the incitement and proliferation of increasingly detailed and comprehensive discourses. Yet because of the diffuse nature of this control, because it operates from such a multiplicity of points and is not unitary, it is also vulnerable. If this is the case, then contemporary preoccupations with imagery and the buying of things can be understood not only as part of this new technology of power, but as, variably (sometimes simultaneously), both as a form of subjection to it and a form of resistance. They are not inherently one thing or the other, since, if consuming objects and images is potentially subversive, this potential is countered always by its potential reappropriation and transformation into yet another mode of regulation.
>
> (1987: 207)

Nava's slippery rubric, reminiscent of Bennett's definitionally open popular culture, is proposed as a 'more nuanced understanding of subjectivity' and is orientated to women's power in consumption. She deliberately counterposes this sphere to the boys' sphere of economics and production. Always to return questions of consumption to production is both conceptually impoverished and also, from Nava's feminist variant of cultural populism, patriarchal theorising. However, the consumerist departure from hegemony theory's dialectical balancing act is not peculiarly feminist since, as Nava observes, such a rubric is 'a form of permission entitling members of today's left intelligentsia to enjoy consuming images and commodities' (p. 209). In that remark one can detect an enormous sigh of relief at being let off the hook of 'puritanical' critique *per se*: the cultural analyst now allowed to enjoy herself (and himself) instead of constantly having to expose the dire workings of 'the system' and its dreadful ideologies. Here we begin to see the drift into an uncritical populism, of which I shall take John Fiske's work on television and popular culture as a revealing instance.[7]

Fiske's agenda, it should be noted, borrows some items from feminist cultural studies, including rejection of the simplistic binary of positive/negative imagery and the exploration of feminine empowerment in media and consumer culture, but it carries the revisionist logic of those emphases to an outer limit that, I believe, few feminists would wholly agree with. The much-debated case of Madonna is indicative. When she burst upon the scene in 1985, several British feminists sought to make sense of Madonna. Diana Simmonds disputed the authenticity of her earthy image (*Marxism Today*, October 1985), whereas Judith Williamson stressed the irony of Madonna's self-presentation and her sly complicity with ordinary women's feelings: 'It is this flaunting of her fame that ties Madonna so firmly to other women and girls' (*New Socialist*, October 1985). And Cheryl Garratt observed, 'men are terrified of Madonna, which is part of the reason why other women love her so' (*Women's Review*, March 1986).[8] It is interesting, then, that Fiske chose Madonna's videos and her youthful female fans to demonstrate the respective merits of '*Screen* theory' and 'cultural ethnography' in his summary of British cultural studies approaches to television (1987a). '*Screen* theory' here stands for structuralist, linguistically based textual analysis of how texts position subjects; and 'cultural ethnography' stands for the interpretation of ordinary people's experiential accounts and pleasures. Fiske analysed the punning strategies of Madonna's early videos like *Material Girl*, and he interviewed young girls about what they thought of Madonna, her actual meaning for them. He says: 'Cultural analysis reaches a satisfactory conclusion when the ethnographic studies of the historically and socially located meanings that *are* made are related to the semiotic analysis of the text' (1987a: 272). A pleasing symmetry indeed: meaning is conceived of as a transaction between semiotic structures and interpretative subjects, but, in spite of Fiske's reference to 'historically and socially located meanings', comparatively decontextualised, at least in terms of the dialectic of cultural production and consumption, and isolated from time–space co-ordinates. Fiske's often quite acute analyses are largely confined to the hermetic encounter between the consumer and the commodity, the reader and the text, qualified only by a broad definition of 'text' and a free-floating 'intertextuality' borrowed from poststructuralism.

Significantly, in a book-length study of television (1987b), Fiske says next to nothing about institutional change in television during the 1980s: vital issues to do with de-regulation/ re-regulation and technology, for instance, are simply banished since, for Fiske, they are not pertinent to questions of interpretation. That there is no discussion of the policy clash between public service and free market principles over the organisation of broadcasting, especially in the British context from which Fiske and his approach originally hail, is a sad omission in the work of a theorist claiming to provide a critical understanding of television.

Thus, following Bourdieu, Fiske separates 'the cultural economy' (symbolic exchange between texts and audiences) from 'the financial economy' (where the television industry is located). Fiske believes it is completely unnecessary to interpret the meaning of the former in relation to the commercial operations of the latter: 'In this book I have argued against the common belief that the capitalist cultural industries produce only an apparent variety of products whose variety is finally illusory for they all promote the same capitalist ideology' (1987b: 309). This is a routine objection to the mass culture critique and the alleged cultural homogenisation and ideological closure said, by some radical critics, to result automatically from capitalist media production and distribution. Fiske, alternatively, stresses the variety and openness of mainstream television texts, enhanced rather than diminished by commercially populist imperatives (for instance, he makes a great deal of *Dallas*'s appropriation by people of widely divergent cultures during the 1980s).

A satisfactory theory of television, I would suggest, needs to account for the multi-dimensional interaction of production and consumption at both economic and symbolic levels, giving due weight to textual diversity and audience differences, as Fiske rightly recommends. Yet, in practice, Fiske merely produces a simple inversion of the mass culture critique at its worst, thereby reducing television study to a kind of subjective idealism, focused more or less exclusively on 'popular readings', which are applauded with no evident reservations at all, never countenancing the possibility that a popular reading could be anything other than 'progressive'. Fiske's television viewers, unlike Madonna, do not live in the material world or, for that matter, in a world where sexism, racism and xenophobia circulate amongst ordinary people.

Fiske's two-volume book on popular culture (1989a and 1989b), makes the rationale for bracketing off history, macro-politics and economics even more explicit. He recruits several not entirely compatible theoretical authorities to support his views (Bakhtin, Barthes, Bourdieu, De Certeau, Foucault, Gramsci, Hall, to mention a few). They are raided and sanitised in order to help him beat the drum against those whom he argues cannot see the micro-politics of popular culture in consuming practices and reading pleasures because they are so hopelessly fixated on macro-politics and the machinations of the cultural industries. Which is not to say that Fiske himself has any illusions about where the products actually come from. In various selections and combinations throughout *Understanding Popular Culture* (1989a) and *Reading the Popular* (1989b) the ultimate provider is named: 'white patriarchal bourgeois capitalism'. This empty rhetorical hybrid, however, has no real analytical function to perform because, in Fiske's scheme of things, 'the people' are not at all ground down or denied by the reified monster that supplies the goods. In effect, there is a striking homology between Fiske's 'semiotic democracy' and the ideal of 'consumer sovereignty' in free market economics, in spite of his extreme aversion to economistic reasoning. Repressed materials will always return, if only in symptoms open to differential decoding.

Under modern conditions, according to Fiske, there is no way in which the material artefacts of popular culture can be made by 'the people': that folkish practice is a thing of the past. But, contemporary popular culture is indeed 'produced' by 'the people', metaphorically speaking, in the transaction between the dominant culture's products and their consumption by subordinate groups: working-class, female, black and so on. Apparently, 'popular readings' of commodity texts are by virtue of social subordination never complicit with any kind of domination: '[t]here can be no popular dominant culture, for popular culture is formed always in reaction to, and never as part of, the forces of domination' (1989a: 43). Ordinary people persistently 'evade' and 'resist' the oppressive and make their own personally liberating meanings through consumption. Hence, shopping malls, video arcades, the beach, TV game shows, jeans and many other products of 'white patriarchal bourgeois capitalism' become sites and artefacts for pleasures that are 'progressive' though not of course 'radical'. Mass culture critics of Right and Left were wrong to assume that such forms are in any way pacifying. Fiske insists that the opposite view is mistaken too, in effect undermining his own position: unqualified celebration of popular culture is blind to the power relations, the dialectic of domination and subordination. That insight is what distinguishes the radical theorist like Fiske from the mere populist, according to him. There are plenty of examples in Fiske's work, however, to suggest the contrary. Drawing especially on Michel De Certeau's *The Practice of Everyday Life* (1984), Fiske's ordinary human being is a tricky customer, negotiating and manoeuvring the best out of any conceivable situation. For example, Fiske tells us admiringly that '[t]he young are shopping mall guerrillas par excellence' (1989a: 37). Unemployed youth's 'trickery' (changing price tags on clothing, and so forth) and 'tactics' (such as trying on a jacket and walking off in it) are compared with the survival tactics used by the Vietcong against the US Army in the 1960s, a comparison of astonishing insouciance that does justice neither to the perils of guerrilla warfare in a swamp nor to petty theft in a shop.

Fiske's conception of popular culture, with its ostensibly critical pedigree, represents a drastic narrowing of vision: the gap between 'popular' and 'mass' culture is finally closed with no residual tension; the relation between interpretative cultural studies and the political economy of culture is obliterated from the surface of the argument. The critical purview of cultural analysis is effectively reduced to a pinpoint seen through the wrong end of a telescope. Fiske's outer limit position represents a kind of neo-Benthamite radicalism, combining utilitarian pleasure-seeking implicitly, and in fact quite consistently, with *laissez-faire* economics, but does not, curiously enough, include Foucault's (1977) paranoid obsession with the panopticon, the political technology of surveillance actually invented by Jeremy Bentham in the early nineteenth century. Fiske backs popular cultural study into a narrow corner of the field, breaking with any effort to explore the complex circuits of culture, including production as distinct from productive consumption, and the temporal and spatial contexts of culture in a conflictful world.

One can overestimate the importance of Fiske in the study of popular culture. He is essentially a good populariser of difficult ideas and a bowdleriser of their subversive implications, not by any means an original thinker. His work, however, is symptomatic of a general trend: that of 'the new revisionism'. Philip Schlesinger (1991) characterises this as 'a collapse into subjectivism . . . a hermeneutic model of media consumption' that 'forces a breach between politico-economic arguments about the production of culture and the ways in which it is consumed and interpreted' (pp. 148–9). The provenance of the new revisionism, observes Schlesinger, is contemporary cultural studies, which as we have seen was at one time cohered by neo-Gramscian hegemony theory.

James Curran (1990), concentrating on 'mass communication research' rather than 'popular culture' in the broadest sense, has traced in detail the emergence of the new revisionism and suggested that it is not as new as it seems. Reacting against the critical paradigms of both political economy and hegemony theory, several leading students of the media turned towards a much more diffuse concept of power, sometimes inspired by an optimistic reading of Foucault (1977 and 1979), but actually reminiscent of many themes associated with the liberal pluralist paradigm of American mass communication research from the 1940s onwards and promoted in Britain, since the 1960s, by the 'uses and gratifications' school. For Curran, the new revisionism is concerned specifically with *audience* and *cultural value*. In audience research, 'the focus of attention shifted from whether media representations advanced or retarded political and cultural struggle to the question of why the mass media were so popular' (Curran 1990: 146). And '[t]he other notable contribution of revisionist thinking has been to reject the elitist pessimism about mass culture that was a significant strand within the radical tradition, represented by the Frankfurt School' (p. 154).

This is entirely consistent with the view expressed here that the new revisionism is the latest trajectory of British cultural populism: themes of audience empowerment, pleasure and 'popular discrimination', a term used quite constructively by Fiske, are fundamental to it. My own attitude to this research trajectory is ambivalent. It is genuinely illuminating in the better work of writers like Angela McRobbie and David Morley, but it also involves a retreat from more critical positions. In many ways such a trajectory is understandable, considering how difficult it has become to challenge present conditions with theoretical and political conviction. None the less, there are questions of critique, quality and explanation to be revisited and developed further if we want to avoid abjectly uncritical complicity with prevailing 'free market' ideology and its hidden powers. The exemplary figure in this respect, John Fiske, is frankly self-conscious about overstating the case in his fashionable disdain for anything which is not immediately 'popular'. Concluding a recent essay, Fiske remarks:

> The challenge offered by popular culture . . . comes from outside this social, cultural, and academic terrain [of 'high or bourgeois art']: the structure of this essay around the antagonism between dominant and popular culture is intended to emphasize this challenge and to help resist its incorporation. If, as a result, I am charged with oversimplifying the dominant, then this is a price which my academic politics lead me to think is worth paying.
>
> (1991: 115)

It is a curious conception of 'the dominant' in the cultural field that confines it to the official terrain of 'high or bourgeois art' and has no sense of a much more dominant set of market-based arrangements that were not, in the past, treated so favourably by academics. 'High or bourgeois art' has arguably become too easy a target, and perhaps something of a straw man, for a new generation of intellectual populists to attack. Fiske's politics is actually quite a pervasive 'academic politics' and, for this reason, his work should not be simply ignored as a peculiar aberration or considered in isolation from more substantial work, such as that of Paul Willis's (1990a and b) 'common culture' research, which is discussed in the next chapter.

QUESTIONING POPULISM

In this chapter I have traced two trajectories of cultural populism: the first, leading to a *productionist* view of popular culture; the second, leading to a *consumptionist* view. On the cusp of the mass culture critique, the cultural democracy movement tried and failed to establish a kind of dual power in the cultural field based on a popular system of production opposed to the dominant system. This project fell foul of the rightward turn in Britain from the late 1970s, which reconstructed the conditions of political and cultural hegemony, undermining the public sector and applying free market ideology across the institutional practices of British society. Radical populism had a contradictory love/hate relationship to social democracy but, more seriously, it underestimated popular powers of cultural consumption. The second trajectory, by contrast, was eventually to reach a position which vastly overestimated consumer power, falling into an uncritical populism not entirely different from right-wing political economy.

Between these two extremes, neo-Gramscian hegemony theory aimed to account dialectically for the interplay of the 'imposed from above' and the 'emerging from below'. Within contemporary cultural studies this continues to be a residual position and perhaps, if Angela McRobbie (1991a) is right, the preferred one. However, as I argued at the end of the last chapter, the field of study has fragmented, with leading positions restructuring around the opposition and interactions between postmodernist theory and new revisionist thought and practice (Morris 1988). To some extent, McRobbie is right to argue that hegemony theory offers a means of cohering the field, but it has never done so adequately due to the original schism with the political economy of culture. Although it is possible, and desirable, to have a situation of methodological pluralism, the uncritical drift of popular cultural study is encouraged by the failure to articulate consumption to production. Hegemony theory bracketed off the economics of cultural production in such a way that an exclusively consumptionist perspective could emerge from its internal contradictions: that is one of the reasons why it ceased to be the organising framework it once was.

My doubts concerning this trajectory are not unique. Several other commentators have also questioned the drift into uncritical populism from a number of different perspectives. To conclude this chapter, I shall briefly survey the extant arguments around three themes: *political critique, qualitative judgement* and *social scientific explanation.*

In 1987, Paul Willemen, the film theorist, noted

the abdication of critical responsibility in favour of the celebration of existing patterns of consumption based on a principled refusal to countenance the possibility that vast sections of the population have come to derive pleasure from conservative oriented media discourses.

(1990: 105)

He suggested that formerly radical critics were now conniving, in effect, with the intensified commodification of culture by affecting disingenuous solidarity with ordinary people and their preferences. Willemen's tone is harsh and moralistic, but perhaps justifiably so when one considers the knowledge and choices open to the highly educated in comparison with most people (Bourdieu 1984). Approaching the issue from a rather different angle than Willemen, Jostein Gripsrud (1989) argues that an unquestioning endorsement of 'the popular' is downright hypocritical on the part of critics who are themselves well endowed with cultural capital and possess privileged access to both 'high' and 'popular' culture. Their specialised competences are undeniable and should, therefore, be used in the service of an 'emancipatory knowledge interest' (Habermas 1972), not abrogated.

This general line of argument was initiated on the British Left by Judith Williamson's much-debated polemic in the February 1985 issue of *New Socialist*, where she said:

The original context of any product is that of its production. The one feature shared by Hoggart, whose argument is limited to the sphere of leisure and domestic culture, and the post-punk stylists within cultural studies, whose concern is with the meaning of consumerism alone, is an absence of any sense of a relationship between the spheres of production and consumption.

(1985: 19)

Williamson did not deny the power and meaning of 'consuming passion' but she did stress that consumption is unequal; not everyone has the same material access to commodities or an equivalent range of choices: 'The idea that ideologies including consumer fads are increasingly "cut loose" from the economic "base" has become more and more fashionable on the left at a time when these levels have rarely been more obviously connected' (1985: 20). Pre-empting Mica Nava, Williamson pointed out that sections of the radical intelligentsia were bored with the puritanical zeal of revolutionary politics, and wanted to enjoy themselves and become relevant again. Eighteen months later, Williamson resumed her attack, prompted by recent tributes to Mills and Boon romances, the joys of TV game shows and the subversiveness of (Princess) Sarah Ferguson's public image. She saw all this as symptomatic of a postmodern populism:

> One of the big tenets of 'post-modernism' is subjectivity. People are 'allowed' to be subjective 'again', to enjoy, to say what they feel. But the new yuppie-left pop culture craze is peculiarly phoney and non-subjective, for while it centres on *other* people's subjectivity (all those TV watchers who love *The Price is Right* or *Dynasty*) it allows the apparently left-wing practitioners of it to conceal theirs. How about a radical left critique of *The Price is Right?* With all our education, have we nothing more to say than 'people like it'?
>
> (1986a: 19)

Polemical and vulnerable to counter-attack, Williamson none the less posed some of the key questions, mainly concerning the politics of cultural analysis, and she reminded radical intellectuals of a certain critical responsibility. In some quarters she was misconstrued as having reverted to an early Frankfurt School position, most notably by Cora Kaplan (1986a), who replied in the pages of *New Socialist*. Kaplan put the elementary semiological argument that textual meanings change according to reception contexts. For instance, outside its American context of production, *Dallas* was likely to be read ironically, particularly by British viewers, amused by the excessive display of opulence, whereas the meaning of *Dallas* in the United States would be more conservative. Kaplan had a point (audience studies of *Dallas* are discussed in Chapter 4), but as a challenge to Williamson's argument concerning the institutional structures of production/consumption, cultural and material inequality, it rather missed the point. Kaplan's chosen example is significant for another reason: her belief that Williamson was merely re-running the old elitist attack on 'American' popular culture, a favourite theme of the mass culture critique. Kaplan's main example, against Williamson's presumed anti-Americanism, was Steven Spielberg's film version of Alice Walker's novel, *The Color Purple.* In an unguardedly literary moment of textual essentialism, Kaplan said the film de-radicalised the novel's meaning (namely it was not so 'good'). Despite its faults, however, the film succeeded in communicating a black feminist sensibility hitherto unfamiliar to British audiences (Kaplan 1986b). It is very odd that Kaplan should select a comparatively unusual 'serious' film version of a 'serious' novel to make her case concerning the progressiveness of Hollywood cinema abroad.

Commenting on the Williamson–Kaplan debate, Duncan Webster (1988) opined that Williamson, like many British Leftists, allowed opposition to US foreign policies to cloud her appreciation of American popular culture. Both Kaplan's and Webster's arguments are perplexing since Williamson did not criticise *American* popular culture specifically in the first place: she questioned the uncritical endorsement of mass popular culture, full stop. And, as Webster himself registered, Williamson (1986b) has made sophisticated and appreciative analyses of popular culture, including American-produced: witness her enthusiasm for Madonna quoted earlier in this chapter. So, what was the counter-attack about? One of the most pervasive dogmas of cultural populism: the remotest hint of anti-Americanism instantly brands the critic a European elitist and, therefore, out of order. Like all easily taken-for-granted domain assumptions, this populist reflex suppresses important questions. For example, does questioning the United States' 'global culture' and raising issues of, say, identity and self-determination in subordinate nations really constitute grounds for being judged a snob? And, furthermore, why should such considerations be construed as necessarily contemptuous of ordinary people's tastes? Incidentally, Williamson never ventured on to such treacherous terrain, though she might have done.

Another issue, and partially separable from political critique, is the crisis of qualitative judgement, not exclusively in communication, cultural and media studies but throughout the humanities. Cultural populism, in one way or another, disputes absolutist criteria of 'quality'. Who is to say whether a text is good or bad, or whether a reading practice is adequate to the text or deficient? By and large, mass culture critics had no doubts on these matters: they were confident in their capacity, usually legitimated by academic position and participation in the networks of 'serious' culture. They felt able to pass judgement on mass cultural consumption, to denounce it comprehensively or to make evaluative discriminations between the authentically popular and the usual rubbish foisted upon most people. Undiluted cultural elitism no longer washes. Cultural populism dealt it a fatal blow: opening up the range of 'texts' worthy of study (from grand opera to soap opera, from lyric poetry to disco dancing), evincing humility towards popular tastes and installing the active audience at the centre of the picture. None of this is *unpolitical.* It challenges the traditional academic politics of the humanities, as Michael Schudson (1987) quite rightly notes with some dismay, surveying recent developments in the US university system. The drift into relativising populism could put professional critics like himself out of work. Schudson's response is not, however, that of a conservative academic only worried about his job. For him, the present situation poses genuine dilemmas. Schudson welcomes the sociologising of cultural analysis from both the production and consumption ends of the circuit, yet he regrets the decline of the university's moral authority:

> I end up caught between a belief that the university should be a moral educator, holding up for emulation some values and some texts (and not others), and a reluctant admission that the basis for defining moral education is an unfinished, often unrecognised task . . . . [I]f we learn to be self-conscious about the implicit hierarchies of taste and value we live and teach by, will we locate adequate grounds for our moral claims? What ground can we stand on, especially when the trends that favour relativism are so much more powerful and cogent (to my own mind) than the rather arbitrary and ill-defined hierarchies of value they so pointedly confront?
>
> (1987: 66–7)

The dilemmas are real enough. Although Schudson does not resolve his own dilemmas, he is courageous to have mentioned them at all, since the pitfalls are so enormous that silence on these matters is undoubtedly the safest and most common option. Like Gripsrud (1989), Schudson slides back into a position where he is obliged to defend the superior judgement of professional criticism on more or less traditionalist grounds. They are both admirably circumspect about doing so. Some others are not, however, like the English critic Tony Dunn. In a notoriously provocative and perhaps tongue-in-cheek *Guardian* article, Dunn (1987) recommended a recovery of uncompromising Wildean elitism as the best alternative to taking 'the path of populism' which meets 'not the people but video promoters, fashion editors and Arts Council bureaucrats'.

Introducing a collection of essays on 'quality' in television which try to unblock the judgemental *impasse*, Geoff Mulgan (1990) argues that 'an alternative to the stale debate between a crude populism . . . and an equally crude elitism' (p. 6) must be sought. I agree with him, but it is easier said than done. One of the most promising signs, however, is that some latter-day cultural populists have begun to voice self-doubt: for example, Charlotte Brunsdon. Addressing an American audience, she asked: ' *What is good television?* This has not been a very fashionable question for television scholars in the UK' (1990a: 59). In that paper, Brunsdon roamed around why the question had been neglected, reviewing literary reception studies, ethnographic and subcultural approaches, and the 'redemptive reading' of popular texts. Wisely perhaps, from her position, she avoided answering the question. In a second stab at the problem, Brunsdon (1990b) mentioned a 'marked populism' (p. 71) in British television studies, a refusal to judge which eventually winds up in political quietism, especially when faced with urgent policy debates over 'quality television'. So, in order to clarify what might be at stake, she ran through various discourses on 'quality', discarding each in its turn, and reaching no satisfactory solution.

Brunsdon's discursive survey covered traditional aesthetics, professional codes, realist paradigms, entertainment and leisure codes and moral paradigms. Concluding that cultural populists should reveal their own surreptitious judgements and 'talk about them' (p. 90), Brunsdon (1990b) effectively proposed greater academic self-consciousness and scholarly reflexivity so that students of popular culture might again be able to speak, at least subjectively, about the unavoidable problem of judgement. Going somewhat further than Brunsdon was prepared to do, John Mepham (1990) has suggested boldly that 'quality television' is indeed identifiable, if not objectively then intersubjectively. Whatever the programme category, 'serious' or 'popular', quality programming is socially recognisable as *diverse, usable* and *truthful* – ethical rather than purely aesthetic criteria (Mepham's ideas are considered more fully in Chapter 4).

Circulating around the 'quality' problem for cultural populism is the residual issue of 'progressiveness'. At one time, judgemental practice in the field of study concentrated heavily on either identifying textual forms that were thought to be intrinsically 'progressive' or, in a more complex version, institutional and historical contexts that were conducive to the reception and activation of potentially 'progressive' meanings (Caughie 1980). This fitted with hegemony theory's emphasis on perpetual 'struggle', not to mention radical populism's contestatory cultural politics. However, in the 1980s, some were to argue that 'progressivism' was far too politically earnest and of doubtful popularity (Ang 1987). It had been assumed that opportunities for alternative and oppositional representations were more favourable in the area of 'serious' rather than 'popular' television, for institutional and ideological reasons (Murdock 1980). This assumption was also widely rejected in cultural populist circles during the 1980s.

In my view, the excessively audience-orientated and one-dimensional consumptionist perspectives have led to a lamentable foreclosure on questions concerning both 'quality', in the broadest sense, and the narrower sense of 'progressiveness', resulting in confused and hopeless silence. Production and textual determinations were too readily dissolved into uncritical constructions of 'popular reading'. However, one also has to remember that earlier positions were excessively political and sometimes tended towards restrictive judgementalism.

Finally, there are explanatory issues that are, in part, separable from political critique and qualitative judgement. This is obvious in a social scientific framework yet not always so evidently the concern of cultural criticism. For example, in his incisive critique of the British monarchy and its role in maintaining an archaic and comparatively undemocratic state, *The Enchanted Glass*, Tom Nairn remarks:

> People enjoy the Monarchical twaddle, and show very little sign of being robotized or 'brain-washed'. They relish the weird mixture of cheap fun, exalted moments and great spectacles, and come back for more. Whatever it all means, that meaning is sustained and apparently continually refreshed by a genuine, positive will more significant than any amount of peevish grousing about cost.
>
> (1988: 53)

Nairn is a republican abolitionist, but he believes the monarchy's popularity has to be understood, not only critiqued or judged. An interpretative, non-judgemental approach, such as that of cultural populism at its best, is indispensable but not, however, sufficiently explanatory.

In a similar vein, Geoffrey Nowell-Smith says with a crystal clarity often lacking in discussions of popular culture: 'the term popular culture retains its value when one is talking about the people who make it popular – that is, when one is talking about the people who keep a particular cultural form going by being the public for it or by being its producers' (1987: 87). That observation summarises the territory traversed in this chapter. Nowell-Smith went on to argue, however, that an exclusive attention to 'the popular' may distract critical analysis from focusing upon how the cultural field works in general. Accordingly, when 'the popular' is suspended, two major realities come sharply into focus:

1 Modern culture is capitalist culture . . .
2 Modern culture also takes the form of a single intertextual field, whose signifying elements are perpetually being recombined and played off against each other.

(1987: 87)

Contemporary cultural objects are mainly commodities produced and circulated for financial valorisation through exchange and consumption. That is not confined to 'popular' culture. 'High' cultural objects are also caught up in the process of capital accumulation, however much traditionalists may wish to ignore the fact. Of special interest is the postmodern interaction of forms and meanings across once heavily policed borders of cultural value and politics; and the complex relations between symbolic and material configurations at national, global and local levels. The old socio-cultural distinctions and hierarchies have not disappeared but they are becoming less important. Under these conditions, the rediscovery of popular culture is not so daring after all. Nobody is going to be shocked in the Senior Common Room or in the Student Union Bar if you talk about the textual playfulness and popular appeal of the latest Madonna film: it's probably already on the curriculum.

In the world syncretic culture of postmodernity nothing is sacrosanct; no boundary, either hierarchical or spatial, is forever fixed. There are, none the less, persistent tensions between centrifugal and centripetal forces, most importantly between globalisation and experientially situated cultures. Culture in general is of heightened significance in a world of international information flows and shared forms of popular entertainment, all of which is greatly enhanced by the newer technologies, especially satellite communications (Robins 1989). A crucial analytical task now is to reconnect interpretation and understanding, of one's own culture and of others, with explanation of the structures and processes that are recomposing these cultures. As Graham Murdock (1989a), for instance, has rightly observed, the 'interplay between the symbolic and the economic' (p. 45) has never been more pronounced and demanding of critical attention. Murdock (1989b) also calls for a renewal of interdisciplinarity, a breaking down of intellectual barriers between theoretical disciplines and methodologies, to address changing material conditions and cultural locations, broadening out rather than narrowing in.

Over the next two chapters, in order to concretise the arguments made so far, I shall discuss past and present work on youth culture and television, the two principal foci of British cultural populism, and in the final chapters discuss issues which transcend its self-imposed limitations.

NOTES

1   Andrew Ross (1989) has shown how the Frankfurt School critique appealed to Dwight MacDonald's (1953) erstwhile Trotskyism, initially opposed to the American Communist Party's populist cultural politics, launched in the 1930s and still evident around the Rosenberg spy trial of the early 1950s (see Ross's fascinating study of this in his first chapter). The American version of the mass culture critique fused with liberal Cold Warism, bringing Leftists like MacDonald himself, Irving Howe, Norman Mailer and C. Wright Mills into an implicit alliance with real Cold Warriors such as Leslie Fiedler and the *Encounter* writers. It is interesting to note, in light of Ross's historical excavation, that *Marxism Today*'s populism, which became so controversial on the Left at its height during the 1980s before the magazine's closure in the wake of Soviet communism's collapse in 1991, was actually quite consistent with a long tradition of Western communist strategy.

2   Richard Hoggart gave impassioned witness to the literary merit of *Lady Chatterley's Lover* at the obscenity trial of Penguin Books in 1960 (see Sutherland 1982). He also served on the Pilkington Broadcasting Committee, which criticised ITV's commercialism and recommended the setting up of BBC2. Hoggart is reputed to have written the Pilkington Report, though he denies this himself (Corner 1991). He

left Birmingham to become Deputy Director of UNESCO at the end of the 1960s and, in the 1970s, his major public role was as Vice-Chairman of the Arts Council of Great Britain.

3   John McGrath's ideas can be seen within a radical tradition stretching back at least to William Morris, the late-nineteenth-century Romantic Marxist. Morris's Utopian novel, *News from Nowhere* (1890/1970), projected a post-revolutionary and *post-industrial* 'golden age' into the future. He believed that human happiness depended on the bringing together of art and work, so that everyone would become a *cultural producer*. See E P.Thompson (1977) on the educative value of such revolutionary romanticism.

4   Andrew Tolson (1986) has made a Foucauldian critique of the OU Popular Culture course's political pretensions.

5   See Simon Clarke *et al.* (1980) for criticisms of Althusserian-influenced film studies and E.P. Thompson's (1979) much-debated critique of Louis Althusser and his British followers. Both Colin MacCabe (1976) and Laura Mulvey (1981) produced important auto-critiques of their earlier positions. Also, see Willemen (1978) and Williams (1977b) for criticisms of '*Screen* theory'. A more sympathetic treatment, which also gives a psychoanalytic and poststructuralist gloss to the OU Popular Culture course, is Antony Easthope's (1988) book, *British Post-structuralism.*

6   Tony Bennett (1980) includes 'history from below', associated with E.P. Thompson (1963) and Sheila Rowbotham (1973), in his fourth category of popular culture. Also, see Schwarz (1982) in the Birmingham CCCS's (1982b) major publication on cultural history.

7   John Fiske's position is not only indicative of the critical decline of British cultural studies, for which he is considered a leading representative in Australia and the United States, though not so much in Britain. Fiske's own brand of uncritical populism goes back much further, at least to his association with John Hartley at the Polytechnic of Wales. Their 1978 book, *Reading Television,* for instance, extolled television's 'bardic function' in contrast to the then more influential critiques of broadcasting's function as an apparatus of dominant ideology.

8   Madonna is a rather problematic case for exclusively consumptionist analysis since she is not just any old pop star but a generally recognised 'author' and controller of her own commodified image. She is, moreover, prepared to take creative and calculatedly commercial risks with her popularity. The 1990 'Blond Ambition' Tour which was subsequently exploited by her film, *In Bed with Madonna* (1991), broke the bounds of respectability and brought the censure of the Vatican down on Madonna's deliberately subversive head. See Skeggs (1991) for a defence of Madonna's erotic politics against feminist criticisms.

Part II

Analytical objects

Chapter 3

Youth culture and consumption

This chapter examines and concretises the mainstream trajectory of contemporary cultural studies around the substantive theme of youth culture and consumption, concentrating mostly on 'the Birmingham School'. That designation – 'Birmingham School' – derives from the international reception of British cultural studies in the Anglophone world, especially the United States, during the 1980s (see Brantlinger 1990). It homogenises and abstracts a body of work from its real conditions of production: the real conditions were heterogeneous and interactive with research outside the Birmingham Centre for Contemporary Cultural Studies. Hence, a number of caveats must be entered into the account.

First, participants in the Birmingham School of the 1970s did not always see eye to eye with one another on all aspects of youth cultural analysis: the comparative exclusion of girls from the earlier research is the best-known case in point (McRobbie 1980). Second, their subsequent work, as we shall see, diversified to a certain extent. Third, the Birmingham research on youth culture and consumption from the heyday of the 1970s is significant for its synthesis of disparate theoretical traditions, underpinned by a certain populist sentiment, owing much to various strands of American sociology of deviance, including the anomie paradigm, labelling theory and naturalistic methodology (see Taylor *et al.* 1973, and Young 1974), which had already informed the British National Deviancy Symposium from the late 1960s (see Cohen, S. 1971, and Taylor and Taylor 1973). Fourth, the Birmingham Centre's reputation for innovative youth cultural study, however, is well justified because of its distinctive combination of sociological deviancy theory with neo-Gramscian hegemony theory and Barthesian semiology. Working-class subcultures of 'resistance' – teds, mods, rockers, skins, punks and so on – were read *politically* as symbolic challenges to the dominant culture, not as signs of social pathology. It is this committedly oppositional account of subcultural creativity 'from below' that I consider to be populist and which some other commentators have called 'romantic' (for example, Woods 1977).

My survey traces a circular route taken by British youth cultural study, broadly within the Birmingham ambit, from the 1970s to the 1990s. In the 1970s, the Birmingham Centre sought to link youth culture to the social relations of production, leisure to work and class structure, subsuming yet also criticising the young consumer and juvenile delinquency concerns of functionalist sociology. During the 1980s, youth was returned once more to consumption exclusively in the writings of latter-day cultural populists, illustrated here by Paul Willis's theoretical reflections on the Gulbenkian study of youth, art and culture, *Common Culture*, published in 1990.

Before proceeding with the main substance of my argument, a couple of points need to be made by way of setting the scene: first, with regard to 'youth' as a modern discursive object; and, second, with regard to the convergence of academic and journalistic discourses on 'youth'. Dick Hebdige (1982b) has argued, in an extremely influential article on photography and youth, 'Hiding in the light', that 'youth' tends to be constructed across two separate yet sometimes intermingling discourses: of 'trouble' and of 'fun'. News and documentary discourses have typically brought into the foreground working-class juvenile delinquency. In contrast, youthful hedonism in a harmless, classless mode is highlighted by advertising and entertainment discourses. The youthful consumer is a semiological construct of consumer capitalism in the second half of the twentieth century, coming to prominence with the American-originated 'teenager' of the 1950s.

The figure of the troublesome youth, however, is older. For example, in the late 1890s, the 'hooligan' was the 'folk devil' and focus of 'moral panic', using Stanley Cohen's (1973) famous terms coined in his classic study of the 1960s mods and rockers, where he analysed the amplification of their misdemeanours by 'the control culture'. Geoffrey Pearson (1983) has shown that the hooligan panic of the 1890s displayed many of the features which became familiar many years later, after the Second World War, so familiar, in fact, that they were thought mistakenly by some to be entirely

novel: media sensationalising of popular pastimes like street celebrations turning into violent clashes with the police, outrageous
styles of dress and deportment, the sense of an alien presence (the
Irishness of 'hooligan'), public debate over punishment and
rehabilitation. According to Pearson, it was the knife-carrying
hooligans, with their donkey fringes and flared trousers, who
inspired Baden-Powell to found the Boy Scout movement.
Baden-Powell feared that if these young tearaways were not taught
the virtues of military imperialism then they might succumb to the
subversive influence of socialism. The hooligan panic is a
little-remembered instance of bourgeois anxiety concerning 'the
dangerous classes'. It is also an early instance of the processes of
surveillance, punishment and education of the working-class
young which were much sophisticated, though hardly successfully,
in twentieth-century social science, social work and penology.
Radical conceptions of youth culture, including the recovery and
sympathetic 'reading' of delinquescent expression, are sometimes
tempted into romanticising the 'resistance' of disadvantaged,
exploited and oppressed groups, in a kind of reaction formation:
a potentially irresponsible viewpoint when one considers, say, the
connection between the naturalised label 'hooligan' and football
spectatorship, a phenomenon which has little romance about it.

Similarly there is a tendency to overstate the cultural power of
youth in the sphere of consumption, which I shall be considering
later in this chapter. Youth-orientated journalism has a vested
interest in doing so, to flatter the youthful consumer's powers of
musical and fashion discrimination or perhaps, in the more
'serious' forms, to arbitrate on taste, to signify where the action is,
in magazines emerging in the 1980s such as *The Face* and its
successors, even occasionally mobilising the authority of youth
cultural theorists like Hebdige and McRobbie themselves. Angela
McRobbie (1989a) has, in fact, pointed to a convergence between
the theorising discussed in this chapter and cultural journalism,
particularly of the youth-orientated variety. The convergence,
however, is not only confined to youth cultural commentary. For
instance, *Marxism Today* and *The New Statesman and Society* caught
on to contemporary cultural studies in the 1980s, as did BBC
television's *The Late Show*, to mention some of the prominent
examples. Paul Willis (1990a) talks of 'the rise of common
culture'. This might more accurately be described as 'the rise of
cultural populism', which is by no means only an academic

phenomenon. In addition to the general media impact of populist cultural analysis, McRobbie (1989a) noted the shift within the Birmingham tradition of contemporary cultural studies towards more journalistic modes of writing under material conditions of cutbacks in higher education and lack of research funding. In the 'enterprise culture' of the 1980s, then, critical academia became much more market-led, submitting itself to the regulations of the market in several notable ways.

ANALYSING SUBCULTURE

Subcultural analysis in the 1970s challenged a conventional wisdom of the 1960s, promoted by both journalistic and socio-logical commentary on the implications of expanding popular consumption: the claim that the postwar 'affluent society' had emancipated the working class and especially the working-class young. Graham Murdock, of Leicester University's Centre for Mass Communication Research, mapped out the issues very clearly around the time when the Birmingham Centre was making a name for itself in subcultural analysis. Murdock (1975) disputed 'the myth of classlessness', founded on three propositions: first, that people born after the Second World War had no memory or fear of the economic depression and social deprivation which marked the 1930s since they had not lived through it themselves; second, and this follows directly from the first proposition, the working-class young, unlike their parents, had developed a generational consciousness instead of a class consciousness due to diminishing material inequality between the classes; third, the new generational consciousness had been shaped by the symbols, styles and meanings of youth-orientated consumer culture and popular music. 'The generation gap' was held to have replaced social class as the main source of conflict in Britain.

Sociologists like Murdock and the Birmingham researchers of the 1970s were keen to prise open that ideological framework by returning youth to class and, therefore, to the social relations of production without, however, denying the increasing importance of commercial leisure in the formation of identity. To quote Murdock:

the involvement of particular groups of adolescents in patterns and styles of leisure can be explained in terms of their continuing attempt to negotiate and resolve the contradictions in their class situation as mediated firstly through their work situation (which for adolescents under sixteen is their school situation), and secondly through their non-work situation in the family and local neighbourhood.

(1975: 119–20)

Murdock and Guy Phelps (1973) demonstrated a class motivation for popular musical taste amongst the young. Working-class skinheads, they found, preferred reggae for dancing: it resonated with their collectivism. On the other hand, middle-class youth preferred the contemplative individualism of 'underground' rock. And, despite the fact that many middle-class kids adopted a hippy, counter-cultural style, they were educational successes, but working-class skins were not.

Mike Brake's definition of 'subculture' is similar to Murdock's formulation although it does not translate class experience so directly into popular taste:

> subcultures arise as attempts to resolve collectively experienced problems resulting from contradictions in the social structure . . . they generate a form of collective identity from which an individual identity can be achieved outside that ascribed by class, education and occupation.

(1985: ix)

Such formulations and definitions were close to the Birmingham CCCS position spelt out in *Resistance through Rituals* (Jefferson 1975). There is a difference, however, to do with the politics of 'resistance', the assumption that subcultures not only arise as expressive, problem-solving responses to socially structured experiences but also constitute oppositional messages. *Resistance through Rituals* presented a conceptual model and a set of case studies elaborating on that basic proposition. It was not, however, the first major statement of the Centre on youth culture. 'Subcultural conflict and working class community' by Phil Cohen, published in the second issue of *Working Papers in Cultural Studies*, laid the groundwork for the more totalising approach of *Resistance through Rituals*.

Phil Cohen's (1972) seminal article is reminiscent of the early Chicago School's ecological perspective (see Madge 1963) in so far as it is concerned with spatial organisation as well as social structure and historical change. He was interested in how working-class communities in the East End of London, with their extended kinship networks, ecology of closely related work and residence, and local economic diversity linked to the docks, had changed during the 1950s and 1960s. Population was redistributed to green-belt estates and high-rise blocks of flats, familial ties severed and the economy restructured with the decline of the Port of London. In this socio-ecological context and its attendant planning blight, Commonwealth immigrants were scapegoated, becoming the object of racist resentment for a disorganised white working class.[1] The 'respectable' working class were, argued Cohen, 'caught in the middle of the two dominant, but contradictory ideologies of the day: the ideology of spectacular consumption, promoted by the mass media, and the traditional ideology of production, the so-called work ethic' (p. 21). Tension was felt most acutely by working-class men who had been taught that their effort in production was the proof of their masculinity. It is also with reference to this tension between production and consumption that Cohen sought to explain the formation of working-class subcultures of the young in which boys predominate. The subcultural response was formed in the interaction between the parent culture, rooted in the relations of production, and the consumer, mass-mediated culture, offering rather different identity-building resources:

> the latent function of subculture is this – to express and resolve, albeit 'magically', the contradictions which remain hidden or unresolved in the parent culture. The succession of subcultures which this parent culture generated can all be seen as so many variations on a central theme – the contradiction, at an ideological level, between traditional working-class puritanism and the new hedonism of consumption.
>
> (1972: 23)

The subcultural response took different forms – for instance, mod mobility or skinhead lumpenness – but each seeking to retrieve symbolic cohesion from the wreckage of commonly disorganised working-class backgrounds. Cohen's theorisation of class and youth intersecting with production and consumption inspired important work to follow.

The long conceptual essay, 'Subcultures, cultures and class', introducing *Resistance through Rituals*, was written by John Clarke,

Stuart Hall, Tony Jefferson and Brian Roberts. It provided an abstract framework to the Birmingham School's work on subcultural analysis in the mid-1970s, which is represented more concretely by the writings of Paul Willis, Dick Hebdige and Angela McRobbie, the authors to be considered most fully in this chapter. 'Subcultures, cultures and class' gives what is usually considered a 'culturalist' definition of 'culture', influenced by Raymond Williams and E.P. Thompson: 'Culture is the way, the forms, in which groups "handle" the raw material of their social and material existence' (Clarke *et al.* 1975: 10). The emphasis on 'experience' is grounded first and foremost, for these authors, in class experience, because class is the principal structuring division of capitalist society. In consequence, the notion of a single, undifferentiated culture is untenable. Class-cultural differences are further complicated by generational differences, associated with which are distinct subcultures. The descriptive category, 'youth culture', is displaced and replaced by generationally specific subcultures, a socio-structural conceptualisation:

> In modern societies, the most fundamental groups are the social classes, and the major cultural configurations will be, in a fundamental though often mediated way, 'class cultures'. Relative to these cultural-class configurations, *sub*-cultures are sub-sets – smaller, more localised and differentiated structures, within one or other of the larger cultural networks. We must, first, see sub-cultures in terms of their relation to the wider class-cultural networks of which they form a distinctive part. When we examine the relationship between a sub-culture and the 'culture' of which it is a part, we call the latter the 'parent' culture.
>
> (Clarke *et al.* 1975: 13)

This codified the ideas of Murdock, Brake and Phil Cohen, and British researchers' general indebtedness to American anomie theory, initiated by Robert Merton and developed in the sociology of deviance by Albert K. Cohen, Richard Cloward and Lloyd Ohlin (see Traub and Little 1980). The Birmingham authors cited these sources and proceeded to define their contribution in pushing subcultural analysis forward. They questioned the definition of subculture as 'problem-solving' and suggested that it did not satisfactorily plumb the internal complexity and dynamic of particular subcultural forms. Phil Cohen's notion of a 'magical solution' was an advance but the historical conditions and semiological differences between subcultural responses were insufficiently specified by it: for instance, the alternative styles of mod 'classlessness' and parodic accentuation of working-classness by the skinheads.

The theoretical sources for reconstructing subcultural analysis *à la* Birmingham were neo-Gramscian hegemony theory and Barthesian semiology. Hegemony theory was written into the Birmingham account of postwar British social history, elaborated in detail by the later *Policing the Crisis* (Hall *et al.* 1978). In the 'Subcultures' essay this produced a reinterpretation of the distinguishing features of postwar Britain: comparatively widespread affluence, growth of mass-communicated culture, the hiatus between pre- and postwar generations, extended secondary education and the emergence of youth-orientated cultural forms, the features which gave rise to the myth of classless youth or, as the Birmingham authors put it, 'youth as a metaphor for social change'. Like Murdock, they disputed the erosion of class inequality and conflict, drawing on the work of John Westergaard and Henrietta Resler (1975), and they reinterpreted the significance of postwar 'affluence', 'consensus' and 'embour-geoisement', a hegemonic articulation bursting asunder with renewed industrial conflict and cultural politics from the late 1960s under the pressure of Britain's longer-term economic decline relative to comparable countries. As the Birmingham authors observed, '[a] hegemonic cultural order tries to *frame* all competing definitions of the world within its range' (p. 39). The importance of spectacular subcultures here is not that they represent the whole of 'youth' in some homogeneous 'youth culture' but, in their practices of 'winning space' within and against the hegemonic order, they constitute fragile, transient and minority forms, issuing symbolic challenges to the dominant culture and its definitions. They do not have political strategies for structural change: their solutions are magical and imaginary, which is not to say they do not matter. And, moreover, it is asserted baldly that there is 'something privileged about the specifically *generational experience* of the young' (p. 49).

The fusion of Gramscian Marxism with Barthesian semiology, only dealt with briefly in the 'Subcultures' essay, is the central hinge of the Birmingham position on subcultural analysis. It recognised and valued rather than denounced youth cultural consumption: subcultures and their 'focal concerns' were thus seen as formed by the creative appropriation of commodities, specifically those of youth-orientated fashion and music industries. The Birmingham authors noted, 'commodities are also cultural *signs*' (p. 55). The stylistic ensembles which distinguish subcultures from one another and from 'straight' styles involve a reordering of the meaning of commodified objects in use. The sign has no fixed and immutable meaning: it is made to mean. Key concepts here are those of *homology* and *bricolage*, concepts with a structuralist pedigree.[2] At Birmingham, Paul Willis was the first to use the concept of homology: 'Essentially it is concerned with how far, in their structure and content, particular items parallel and reflect the structure, style, typical concerns, attitudes and feelings of the social group' (1978: 191). Willis (1972) had already analysed the meaning of the motorcycle in bike-boy culture. In a separate essay in *Resistance through Rituals*, John Clarke defined 'Lévi-Strauss's concept of *bricolage* – the re-ordering and re-contextualisation of objects to communicate fresh meanings, within a total system of significances, which already include prior and sedimented meanings attached to the objects used' (1975: 177). And, he gave an early example from the 1950s: 'the "Edwardian look" (an upper class and student revival), borrowed by the Teddy Boys, re-combined with extraneous items, the bootlace tie and the brothel-creepers, emerged with a new and previously uncharacteristic meaning' (p. 178).

To conclude this exposition of 'Subcultures, cultures and class', the distinction between working-class subculture and middle-class counter-culture should also be mentioned. According to Clarke *et al.*, working-class subcultures are distinguished by their collectivist, gang-like qualities from the more diffuse and individualistic forms of the middle-class counter-cultures associated with hippies and students. Both were thought to manifest a serious crisis of authority in Western capitalism generally, not only in Britain.

STUDYING RESISTANCE

The broadly 'culturalist' and 'structuralist' strands in Birmingham subcultural analysis are best exemplified by the work of Paul Willis and Dick Hebdige respectively. There was considerable interaction and overlap between these strands. However, the alternative methodological strategies of ethnographic field work, on the one hand, and the reading of subculture as 'text', on the other, call into question accounts which oversimplify the unity of the Birmingham School's perspective.

Paul Willis was the chief exponent of ethnographic practice at Birmingham during the 1970s. His work flowed from what he himself has called 'the "naturalist" revolt' in sociology (Willis 1980), originated by the Chicago School and developed in the new deviancy research of the 1960s, associated with figures like Howard Becker (1963/1973) in the United States and David Downes (1966) in Britain. Willis was not uncritical of this tradition: he questioned its anti-theoreticism and the inverted complicity with positivism of formalistic 'qualitative methodology', favouring himself a more 'reflexive', politically self-aware approach. Yet he stressed 'a profoundly important methodological possibility' of practices such as participant observation: 'that of *being "surprised"*, of reaching knowledge not prefigured in one's starting paradigm' (1980: 90). With unusual passion, Willis opened the book version of his doctoral thesis, *Profane Culture*, with a statement which encapsulates his enduring commitment to ethnographic fieldwork:

> The sheer surprise of a living culture is a slap to reverie. Real, bustling, startling cultures move. They exist. They are something in the world. They suddenly leave behind – empty, exposed, ugly – *ideas* of poverty, deprivation, existence and culture. Real events can save us as much as philosophy.
>
> (1978: 1)

Combined in Willis's work is this sense of the irreducibility of lived culture, its very *livedness*, and complex theorisation, nicely illustrated by the division of his classic, *Learning to Labour – How Working-Class Kids Get Working-Class Jobs* (1977), into two parts: the first, an ethnographic voicing of the group of working-class 'lads' he had studied, and the second, an abstract discussion of questions of social reproduction, 'the cultural level', agency and structure. Throughout his work Willis runs an ongoing dialogue between his own culturalist leanings and structuralist arguments which, in Jean-Paul Sartre's (1963) words, do not grasp 'the profundity of the lived': or, to paraphrase Sartre in words that Willis might have used, 'the profanity of the lived'.

In *Profane Culture* (1978) Willis compared hippy and bike-boy cultures of the late 1960s and early 1970s, acknowledging their class differences but insisting on the contradictory creativity of both. The emphasis on 'contradiction' in lived culture is central to Willis's earlier position, whether in the post-revolutionary strategies for a pre-revolutionary situation of his preferred youth cultures or the self-ensnaring of working-class boys in accomplishing their transition from failure at school to the lower echelons of manual work. A characteristic argument of Willis's pre-empted the critics of the dominant ideology thesis: 'the dominant class is most victim to the illusions and false promises of its own ideology' (1978: 5); 'the working class does not have to believe the dominant ideology' (1977: 123). Neither middle-class counter-culturalists nor working-class trouble-makers were victims of dominant ideology. They saw through it in one way or another: 'hippy culture makes a penetrating criticism of the philistinism and inner contradictions of capitalist society' (1978: 172); 'the one distinctive and often unrecognised potential that working-class cultural creativity and insight really does have. It is embedded in the only class in the capitalist social formation which does not have a structurally based vested interest in mystifying itself' (1978: 122–3).

Willis's *Learning to Labour* (1977) set itself the following problem: 'The difficult thing to explain about how working-class kids get working-class jobs is why they let themselves' (p. 1). The book reported on Willis's ethnographic study of a group of working-class boys in Wolverhampton during their final years at school before winding up on the shop floor of local factories. This group, known as 'the lads', constantly resisted the process of schooling, refusing to play the game, unlike the 'ear'oles' who hoped to improve their prospects by acquiring educational certification. In spite of their 'self-damnation', however, the members of the 'male school counter-culture' were probably not mistaken, in Willis's judgement, to absorb themselves in the pleasures of profane leisure and precocious sexuality instead of their lessons. Their cultural practice was, however, a contradictory amalgam of 'penetrations' and 'limitations': penetrating insights into the real conditions of their existence as future labourers for capital, and ideological limitations which 'confuse and impede' them. They penetrated the 'teaching paradigm' which promises knowledge and personal advancement in return for obedience and docility, thereby exposing the inherent contradiction of meritocracy in which, by definition, only a very few can actually rise. But their rejection of mental work and casual acceptance of manual work certainly narrowed their horizons: and, furthermore, their aggressive masculinity and racism divided them oppressively from girls and ethnic minority groups with whom, in reality, they had much in common.

I shall return to these 'limitations', particularly that of masculinity, in the next section. For now, I want to consider what separates Willis's wish to be surprised by ethnographic findings from Hebdige's alternative semiological approach to youth cultural analysis. Willis himself summed up the common Birmingham School stress on the creative appropriation of commodities and their use in strategies of resistance, for example, when 'leisure is brought into the work-a-day world *as a contesting and resisting agent*' (1982: 94). However, there was a theoretical difference over whether 'the cultural level' should be considered homologous with collective experience in such practices or autonomous in the more semiological sense of 'signifying practice'. Willis's disagreement with semiology, however, was not so sharp as his dispute with functionalist and economistic views of the social reproduction of labour power as somehow automatic: he wanted to insist on a certain autonomy of cultural agency, as in the case of the lads' 'self-damnation'. The question was: how autonomous?

The work of Dick Hebdige not only represented an alternative methodological strategy from Willis's but it also marked a watershed in subcultural analysis, shifting from a class-based sociology to a more complex understanding of social difference, particularly with regard to race, and an ostensible liberation of the sign from social structuration. His widely read *Subculture – the Meaning of Style*, published significantly in the final year of the 1970s, is a text disordered by the difficulties of holding together sociology and semiology in a much harder-to-read temporal context than that of *Resistance through Rituals*, published just four years earlier.

Before discussing Hebdige's book, a brief digression to put it in local context is required. This was the post-punk moment when the heroic succession of postwar subcultures came suddenly to a halt. Already, Ian Taylor and David Wall (1976), commenting on the glamrock cult of the early 1970s, had argued that intensified commercialisation of youthful leisure had brought about the manufacture of subcultural styles 'from above'. They suggested that glamrock and glitter were devices for selling new fashions, dreamt up by designers and the music industry, thereby short-circuiting the processes of subcultural emergence 'from below', an observation which anticipated the dynamics of a new 'postmodern', post-punk sensibility arising in the next decade. Beginning with the mod revival at the end of the 1970s, youth culture in the 1980s was characterised by the recycling and multiplication of older styles, constructing a kind of subcultural free market for young people. Punk itself, the most recent, was endlessly recycled and there were revivals of rocker in heavy metal, of hippy, of skin and so forth. During the 1980s, then, youth culture turned increasingly in on itself and nostalgia became all the rage. Few original and different subcultures emerged, with some minor exceptions such as the new romantics and the gothics, until the acid house phenomenon of the late 1980s. It is an irony of youth culture that acid house, premised on 'fun', signified by primary colours and ecstatic dancing, should have become a major focus of 'trouble', in Hebdige's (1982b) own terms. It had striking similarities to pre-1980s subcultures, at first mysterious and strange, an object of myth and speculation, to some extent deliberately cultivated. Combining lightly hedonist and mildly puritanical elements, acid house seemed to issue little threat, except for the illegality of warehouse parties and noise in the shires, yet it met with a social control response comparable to the fate of spectacular subcultures back in the 1960s. In the autumn of 1988, the tabloid press whipped up a panic concerning the use of psychedelic drugs and, in the summers of 1989 and 1990, police took action against parties on the outskirts of London and elsewhere (see Redhead 1990).

The acid house phenomenon and Hebdige's own work indicate why the class-structural model of *Resistance through Rituals* was too cumbersome and unworkable for analysing the complexities of youth cultural meanings. In *Subculture* (1979), Hebdige's tenuous linkage of sociology and semiology broke towards a poststructuralist fascination with the play of signifiers and away from 'experience'. Hebdige has consistently produced insightful readings of 'style' (for example, his early essay on the mods, 1975a) and cultural syncretism ('Reggae, rastas and rudies', 1975b, also published in *Resistance through Rituals*). The title of his later book, *Cut 'n' Mix* (1987), captures the sense of cultures combining and recombining, of bits and pieces plucked from various sources and then put together in novel combinations, such a typical feature of black music from the time of slavery to rap and hip-hop, and which is emblematic of the postmodern supersession of cultural 'purity', the blurring of boundaries between different forms and styles.

Diverging from the other Birmingham School authors of the 1970s already mentioned in this chapter, Hebdige was preoccupied by race rather than class, out of which his central thesis on subculture flowed: 'the history of post-war British youth culture must be reinterpreted as a succession of differential responses to the black immigrant presence in Britain from the 1950s onwards' (1979: 29). Phil Cohen had, in passing, addressed skinhead racism. The original skins were ska and reggae fans but similarly to the teds, fans of blues-influenced rock and roll; some of them attacked black people. In addition to this contradictory response by sections of white youth to 'the black immigrant presence', Hebdige analysed the situation of young blacks of Afro-Caribbean origin born in Britain: 'Somewhere between Trenchtown and Ladbroke Grove, the cult of Rastafari became a "style": an expressive combination of "locks", of khaki camouflage and "weed" which proclaimed unequivocally the alienation felt by young black Britons' (p. 36). For the rastas, Jamaican music and the mythic return to Africa were subcultural resources of resistance, and, as it turned out, a model for some young whites to imitate. Simon Jones's (1988) ethnographic study, *Black Culture, White Youth*, pursued Hebdige's insights in a manner closer to Willis's approach. That Jones found a few young whites who actually wished to be black culturally is a particular variation on Hebdige's theme of widespread borrowing from black culture by white youth: for instance, mods appropriated the style of the American ghetto hipster. Hebdige went so far as to argue: 'We can watch, played out on the loaded surfaces of British working-class youth cultures, a phantom history of race relations since the war' (p. 45).

The argument concerning race blended into Hebdige's analysis of style, illustrated by his reading of punk in the somewhat strained claim concerning its 'white "ethnicity"' and dadaistic play with national symbols such as the Union Jack and the Queen, signifying a tortured alienation (p. 65). Punk was, in fact, Hebdige's major example in the book of the 'semiological guerrilla warfare' (Eco 1967) conducted by youth subcultures against the dominant culture, sporadic code-breaking raids, 'oblique challenges'. The peculiarity of punk, brought out so well by Hebdige, is that its *bricoleur* function went beyond all earlier forms of subcultural *bricolage* by quoting from *them*, thus producing a reflexive statement on spectacular subculture:

> Punk reproduced the entire sartorial history of post-war working-class youth cultures in 'cut up' form, combining elements which had originally belonged to completely different epochs. There was a chaos of quiffs and leather jackets, brothel creepers and winkle pickers, plimsolls and plastic macs, moddy crops and skinhead strides, drainpipes and vivid socks, bum freezers and bovver boots – all kept 'in place' and 'out of time' by the spectacular adhesives: the safety pins and plastic clothes pegs, the bondage straps and bits of string which attracted so much horrified and fascinated attention. Punk is therefore a singularly appropriate point of departure for a study of this kind because punk style contained distorted reflections of all the major post-war subcultures.
>
> (Hebdige 1979: 26)

Indeed, it is youth cultural consumption itself which became at this juncture self-referentially generated, given a Kristevan gloss later in the book by Hebdige: a semiotic disruption of the symbolic (see Moi 1986). However, in *Subculture*, Hebdige still retained a link with the sociological roots of subcultural analysis, especially by identifying an homology of structures between punk and the state of the nation:

> In the gloomy apocalyptic ambience of the late 1970s – with massive unemployment, with the ominous violence of the Notting Hill Carnival, Grunwick, Lewisham and Ladywood – it was fitting that the punks should present themselves as 'degenerates'; as signs of the highly publicized decay which perfectly represented the atrophied condition of Great Britain . . . . And if a style is to catch on, if it is to become genuinely popular, it must say the right thing at the right time. It must anticipate or encapsulate a mood, a moment. It must embody a sensibility, and the sensibility which punk style embodied was essentially dislocated, ironic and self-aware.
>
> (1979: 87, 122–3)

Hebdige's book certainly anticipated or captured a mood, the mood of a growing pessimism in contemporary cultural studies attendant upon Britain's turn to the Right, at the end of the 1970s, and a growing hesitancy about the rationalist pretensions of radical critique: that is probably why, of all the 'classics' of the Birmingham School, *Subculture* was most read and did not date so quickly as its subject matter.

Soon, even in the highly qualified version propounded by Hebdige, subcultural analysis came under attack from critics wishing to drop the Marxist ballast once and for all in favour of a poststructuralist linguistic model. Dave Laing passed sentence on Birmingham subcultural theory in his alternative reading of punk:

> Dick Hebdige's *Subculture* provides a valuable summary of the basic themes of the subculture idea, but a few further comments are necessary here. First, it is worth recalling the functions served by the theory when it was developed by a group of *marxist* sociologists in the early 1970s. It both tied the activities of youth to a specific social class (thus attacking the 'myth' of a classless youth life-style) and also validated the apparently aimless activities of the mods, skinheads and others in terms of class struggle: even when they seemed to be mere consumers or delinquents, these kids were acting out a proletarian destiny, reacting against capitalism.
>
> (1985: 123)

Laing's barb about '*marxist* sociologists' pierced *sociologism* as much as Marxism. In *One Chord Wonders*, Laing argued that punk rock was a musical genre, first and foremost, and that Hebdige's subcultural reading of punk missed this point fatally. Laing, in effect, questioned the reduction of a significatory phenomenon to a social movement for some dubiously political purpose. Even on the subcultural front, Laing disputed Hebdige's reading of punk signification: for instance, by questioning its disarticulation/re-articulation of the swastika's fascist meaning. Following Barthes and Kristeva more consistently than Hebdige, Laing emphasised the semiological subversiveness of punk music, with its 'geno-song' disrupting the comforting referentialism of 'pheno-song', on the side of *jouissance* rather than *plaisir*, however, without shaking the citadels of the state. For Laing, punk rock was polysemic, mobilising different kinds of discontent and musicologically at odds with normative politics, except in its duller forms. Moreover, Laing argued that its social base was not in some unmediated relation to jobless working-class youth ('Dole queue rock') but situated specifically in relation to educational institutions, the crisis of comprehensive schools and the longstanding musical milieu of art school bohemia. Also, punk musicians were exactly that – musicians, professionally and, therefore, economically positioned differently from the industrial proletariat; still, however, resistant to big capital by producing and distributing their music independently, 'the indies', seizing a certain measure of control but, when successful, vulnerable to the blandishments and cash of the major record companies.

GENDERING YOUTH

If Dave Laing's critique of subcultural analysis in the case of punk was epistemological, from a poststructuralist position hostile to materialist cultural theory, then perhaps Angela McRobbie's feminist critique was less fundamental theoretically. Her criticisms came from inside the Birmingham Centre and constituted only a piecemeal departure, taken a little further by consumerist and postmodernist ideas as the 1980s wore on (McRobbie 1986 and 1991b). McRobbie's much-repeated claim that 1970s subcultural analysis was characterised by masculine bias, male researchers writing endlessly about putatively radical youth groups, publicly visible styles and forms dominated by boys, is undoubtedly right: and, in discussing that work so far the gender question has been reserved in order to address it more thoroughly in this section.

Yet, as McRobbie (1980) herself argued in 'Settling accounts with subcultures', although girls were marginalised, it did not necessarily follow that the whole perspective was worthless: she never denied the importance of class or the subversiveness of spectacular subculture: 'For as long as I can remember, collective expressions of disaffiliation from Authority and the hegemony of the dominant classes (by either sex) have sent shivers of excitement down my spine' (1980: 48). McRobbie explored two feminist options with regard to subcultural analysis: first, discard the existing literature and begin again by studying the ideological construction of girls' culture; second, reconcile commitment to girls' culture with a critical revaluation of subcultural theory. She proposed the latter option because, amongst other things, it opened up the issue of masculinity as well as femininity in youth culture. With this purpose in mind, she re-read the subcultural 'classics': Willis's *Learning to Labour* and Hebdige's *Subculture*. The issue of masculinity, McRobbie noted, was there in the classics as a kind of trouble in the text. For instance: 'One striking feature of Willis's study is how unambiguously degrading to women is the language of aggressive masculinity through which the lads kick against the oppressive structures they inhabit' (pp. 40–1). Failing to investigate working-class families and patriarchal structures, Willis preferred instead to consider aggressive masculinity's role in dignifying manual work for men against 'pen-pushing'. However, Willis (1982) did eventually concede some ground to McRobbie.

During the 1980s, study of masculinity came to the fore across a range of disciplines (for example, Metcalf and Humphries 1985; Easthope 1986; Segal 1990). Andrew Tolson, of the Birmingham School, published his *The Limits of Masculinity* as early as 1977, but this was comparatively isolated work at the time, not only at Birmingham. *Vis-à-vis* youth culture, the study of football hooliganism might have illuminated masculinity more in connection to, say, 'the magical recovery of community', territorial behaviour at football grounds (Jefferson 1975; Clarke 1978; Critcher 1982). All of this remained comparatively undeveloped, however, especially in gender terms. David Robins and Phil Cohen (1978) studied the obnoxious behaviour of Arsenal fans in their book *Knuckle Sandwich*, and, in a later book, Robins (1984) remarked, '[d]ecent, law-abiding citizens, who still believe that England is a basically tolerant country, are definitely in for a shock if they ever meet Barry Watts' (p. 116). Nowhere in the Birmingham-related literature is such aggressive masculinity 'romanticised': the aim was to understand, interpret and make sense of practices that could hardly be held up for approval. In comparison with figurational sociology's account of football hooliganism a decade later, subcultural analysis was non-judgemental when perhaps, in hindsight, it should have judged. Eric Dunning and his co-researchers remark:

> football hooligans and comparable groups are severely restrained in the formation of their personalities, their values and their actions by their restricted life experiences, their lack of comparative knowledge, and by constraints which lead to this interest and involvement in publicly aggressive forms of masculinity and 'street style'.

> (1988: 220)

These figurational sociologists argue that gendered power relations in working-class culture generate the aggressive masculinity associated with some young football fans. For them, this is connected to a long historical process of 'de-civilizing' the 'underclass', brought about by Britain's rigid and un-accommodating social structure (see Walvin 1986). Outlined only briefly here, the argument of Dunning and his colleagues is distinctly anti-populist and it exposes the issue of selectivity in contemporary cultural studies. Typically, subcultural analysis and its successors searched out signs of creativity and negotiated self-expression, veering away judiciously from disconfirming instances. And this is true of McRobbie's work as well as the masculine-biased work that preceded it.

I want now to reconstruct the feminist revision of subcultural analysis to the point where it turned from a dialectical model of production/consumption to an exclusive concern with consumption. In McRobbie's first attack on masculine bias, with Jenny Garber, published in *Resistance through Rituals*, the distinguishing features of Birmingham subcultural analysis were listed: centrality of class: spheres of school, work, leisure and family; social context of subcultural emergence; structural change in postwar Britain. Then, they said, '[w]e must, however, *add* [my emphasis] the crucial dimension of sex and gender structuring' (1975: 210). Their argument was consistent with 1970s Marxist feminism: girls' marginality in youth culture related to the 'secondariness' of women's place in the home and family, the sphere of social reproduction, as opposed to the men's sphere of production. In effect, women and girls are engaged in much less publicly visible activities than men and boys. This was partly qualified in some subcultures. They cited mod, in which girls' participation was more prominent than in the more masculine subcultures such as rocker and skinhead, though girls were not absent from them either. Garber and McRobbie were, of course, writing before punk broke in 1976, the least masculine-dominated of the major subcultures and a subculture in which girls appeared shocking in the garb of 'degraded femininity' (Hebdige 1982b).

In their original article, Garber and McRobbie fixed upon teeny bopper culture as the site of girls' subcultural formation, not so much a street form but enacted in girls' bedrooms with, in the 1970s, pictures of Donny Osmond, for instance, on the walls. Although they underplayed it, teeny bopper culture and fantasies projected on to pop stars always had an expressively public dimension, very public indeed at concert performances by favoured idols, at least since the Beatles, but first manifested by older girls in the enthusiastic reception of Johnny Ray in Britain *before* rock and roll, and reputedly worrying to parents, incidentally, along with anxieties and recurrent panics over under-age sex. Garber and McRobbie hesitated to define the teeny bopper phenomenon as 'resistance' since, in their view, 'it is one of the most highly manufactured forms of available youth culture – it is almost totally packaged' (p. 220). They concluded that the best route for feminist analysis might be 'to move away from the subcultural group phenomenon' because it 'may not be the most likely place where those equivalent rituals, responses and negotiations will be located' (p. 221).

McRobbie (1978) did that in her ethnographic study, 'Working-class girls and the culture of femininity', a feminist companion to Willis's *Learning to Labour*. Like Willis, after *Profane Culture*, McRobbie was less concerned with distinctive subcultural styles than with more mundane processes of 'resistance', especially to schooling, by the working-class young. The fourteen- and fifteen-year-old working-class girls whom McRobbie met at the Mill Lane youth club in Birmingham were well aware of their class and gender subordination. But, she found 'two saving factors' linked to 'the contradictions and apparently unresolvable conflicts which the girls' culture had to deal with and somehow accommodate': 'best friend relationships' and 'immersion in the ideology of romance' (pp. 97–8). The girls had a fatalistic attitude to their futures, taking for granted an inevitable marriage with its potentially negative entailments. Nevertheless, in the meantime, solidarity with their best friends and harbouring fantasies of a glamorous life enabled them to cope. Like Willis's lads they rejected education and were contemptuous of middle-class 'swots', their lack of style and their sexual inhibitions. McRobbie's girls would introduce expressive 'femaleness' into the classroom, flaunting their precocious womanhood to the chagrin of teachers. Sensitive to the paradox of these tactics, McRobbie echoed Willis's 'self-damnation':

> Marriage, family life, fashion and beauty all contribute massively to this feminine anti-school culture and, in doing so, nicely illustrate the contradictions inherent in so-called oppositional

activities. Are the girls in the end not simply doing exactly what is required of them – and if this *is* the case, then could it not be convincingly argued that it is their own culture which itself is the most effective agent of social control for girls pushing them into compliance with that role which a whole range of institutions in capitalist society also, but less effectively, directs them towards?

(1978: 104)

McRobbie (1982) explored the 'ideology of adolescent femininity' in her seminal study of the girls' magazine *Jackie*. There she stressed the ideological elimination of difference, particularly class and ethnic differences, between girls, in the way the various textual elements of the magazine produced a subject positioning around 'the personal' and 'romantic individualism'. The *Jackie* article is methodologically more akin to semiology than the ethnographic study of working-class girls, and is comparable with work in feminist film theory on textuality and subjectivity (Kuhn 1982): it also had similarities to Judith Williamson's (1978) *Decoding Advertisements*. However, McRobbie's *Jackie* article was framed by a general position on the study of popular cultural texts which is directly apposite to cultural populism. McRobbie dismissed 'the traditional thesis' of Leavisite discrimination and orthodox Marxist (and, by implication, feminist) 'conspiracy' theory on the manipulative function of 'mass culture'. The third possible approach to studying *Jackie* 'reverses both of the first two arguments . . . pop music and pop culture as meaningful activities' (p. 267). She attributed this 'populist' position to Willis: it is the argument concerning the popular 'reappropriation' of commodities. In the case of *Jackie*, it would suggest that girls are not just 'dopes' of the text but actively involved in using the magazine for their own self-activated purposes. According to McRobbie, this is a great improvement on 'traditional' and 'conspiracy' thinking. However, in her estimation at that time, it is 'of limited usefulness when applied to teenage girls and their magazines'. Girls 'play little, if any, role in shaping their popular culture and their choice in consumption is extremely narrow' (p. 267). McRobbie's position, stated in the *Jackie* article, was neo-Gramscian, drawing attention to how 'hegemony is sought uncoercively on this terrain', the terrain of civil society which works, under capitalism, through ideologies of 'freedom' and 'choice'. In studying a text like *Jackie*, then, it is necessary to grasp a certain dialectic of pleasure and oppression, how that which is freely chosen by the subject also serves to subjugate. McRobbie insisted that '*Jackie* is a force to be reckoned with by feminists' (p. 282). She recommended a two-pronged strategy. First, for teachers and youth workers to help girls 'deconstruct' the naturalising ideology of such magazines and similar cultural forms. The volume, *Feminism for Girls* (McRobbie and McCabe 1981), was an important contribution to such work. Second, and more ambitiously, to produce a feminist magazine for girls, which was implemented, marginally, in a one-off television programme made by the Birmingham Film and Video Workshop, *Girl Zone*, transmitted on Channel Four in a late-night ghetto slot in 1986, and by the alternative publication, *Shocking Pink*. However, McRobbie soon withdrew her own commitment from such explicitly contestatory cultural politics, indicated by her autocritique of the *Jackie* article in 1984:

> I wanted images and stories that were more down to earth, more real, and I commented sourly on how the picture stories ended with a kiss as though there was nothing else beyond. I consciously played down or ignored the role of fantasy in popular fiction and implicitly argued for more representations of *real* girls confronting *real* issues . . . this is a distinction which I no longer hold to be so useful. Daydreaming during work, as an added and therefore positive input, or else just as a distraction, is still nevertheless as much an *experience*, a piece of reality, as is babysitting or staying in to do the washing. What is more, to ignore these more private aspects of everyday experience is to avoid considering their function and how they make sense in terms of politics and social change.
>
> (1984: 160)

In addition to revaluing fantasy, McRobbie (1991b) also concurred with the critique of textual determinism in her original *Jackie* article (Barker 1989), its non-dialogic assumption being that the text necessarily positioned the reading subject within patriarchal ideology. Such an alternation of perspective, however, was not only to do with recognising a faulty application of semiology but is related to changes in the object of analysis. Since the late 1970s, mainstream girls' magazines have indeed changed, to what extent is perhaps a moot point. For example, *Just Seventeen* played down romance and began dislocating fixed notions of femininity in a manner consistent with 1980s 'popular feminism' (Stuart 1990). The conservative *Jackie* declined in popularity, and then had to adapt to the shifting mores of adolescent girls in order to survive commercially. In the light of these developments, McRobbie no longer believed that radical alternatives to the mainstream were necessary or, for popular pleasure, strictly desirable. She recommended that female students of communications media should consider seeking employment on publications like *Just Seventeen* because of 'the space these magazines offer for contestation and change' (1991b: 186).

By arguing for a politics of style at the beginning of the 1980s, in response to Hebdige's prevarications on the matter, McRobbie had begun to push the logic of her position onwards from the Marxist-feminist discourse of radical engagement with youth culture: 'it will be necessary to supplement the established political triad of class, sex and race with three more concepts – *populism, leisure* and *pleasure*' (1980: 48). McRobbie is reluctant to drop older commitments as she discovers new ones. However, her subsequent work has been distinguished by an ever more open-minded populist appreciation of mainstream youth culture: disco-dancing as feminine empowerment and dance generally as disruptive of fixed gender identities (1984); retro-style in fashion as produced from below by the poor and unemployed buying second-hand clothes; shopping as a creative, self-validating act (1989b); and, the as yet unrealised potential of teenage pregnancy and single parenthood for avoiding economic dependency in working-class marriage (1991b).

In the 1980s, many of the suddenly old shibboleths of New Left cultural politics tumbled down like dominoes, evident in McRobbie's work but stated most boldly by Erica Carter. To quote McRobbie once more:

> Contemporary feminism has been slow to challenge the early 1970s orthodoxy which saw women as slaves to consumerism. Only Erica Carter's work has gone some way to dislodging the view that to enjoy shopping is to be passively feminine and incorporated into a system of false needs.
>
> (1989b: 24–5)

Carter's (1984) scathing view of masculine-biased research on youth culture, in fact, exceeded the terms of McRobbie's revision.

Subcultural theory was, according to Carter, founded on a set of 'unspoken oppositions': conformity/resistance, harmony/ rupture, passivity/activity, consumption/appropriation, femininity/ masculinity. Following the deconstructionist procedure of Jacques Derrida (Norris 1987), she revalued the hitherto negative, 'conformist' terms in these binary oppositions, particularly the category of consumption, worked out with reference to consumerism in the Federal Republic of Germany in the 1950s. She suggested that market research categories, with their fine distinctions of lifestyle and gender, are superior to the blunt instrument of neo-Gramscian class analysis upon which the Birmingham School model of subculture was based, because they actually address youthful desires and the felt needs of young girls. This is strictly relevant to the matters in hand: 'If subcultural theory has traditionally remained standing somewhat suspiciously on the sidelines of commercial youth culture, the same has not always been true of research into girls' culture' (p. 188). Rejecting subcultural theory, Carter extolled the market as 'a vast machine for the regulation of interconnecting circulatory flows . . . capital and labour . . . money, commodities, visual and textual signifiers through the circuits of consumption unlocked by capital' (p. 189). It is an interactive information system with obvious advantages over and above financial valorisation and capital accumulation. Carter's enthusiasm for the market was not unqualified, yet she insisted that its revaluation in the study of youth culture is long overdue:

> If anything is to be learned about the lived realities of consumption, then we must shift the terms of the youth culture debate, looking first at the dominant forms of a supposedly conformist culture of consumerism (as well as its everyday subversions). One route into this project is the examination of teenage lifestyles: of their assemblage on the production line of commodities for the teenage market, and their deconstruction, appropriation, subversion and reassemblage by teenage girls themselves.
>
> (1984: 198)

There is a decisive switch here from the critique of what were once considered monolithic structures – capitalism and patriarchy – to a more accommodating attitude. Carter's quotation from a West German girl underlines the exclusively consumptionist turn: 'I can't change things, I can't think plastic out of my world, and so I try to turn the tables on it and see what's actually good about it' (p. 214).[3]

CONSUMING PASSIONS

During the 1970s, contemporary cultural studies named the enemy confidently from theoretical positions informed at first by Marxism and then subsequently by feminism (to a lesser extent, black politics). The grounds of such critical thought were increasingly called into question in the 1980s for internal and external reasons. As we have seen, the tension between masculine-biased subcultural theory and feminism was resolved for some by the revaluation of consumption practices, inspired by a populist reading of Michel Foucault on 'micro-politics' (Gordon 1980; Nava 1987).

However, struggles over knowledge and power in academic cultural studies were small beer compared with the recomposition of hegemony in the wider society. In Britain acutely, but not only there, doubt was cast upon older radical wisdoms concerning the mechanisms and possibilities of social emancipation. The New Right's success had much to do with how it worked upon real conditions and desires, addressing ordinary people's material aspirations and stressing the sense of personal freedom and choice engendered by the market (Hall 1988a). The promise of public solutions to private problems was increasingly delegitimated and the welfare state undermined. Thatcherism rewrote the rules of the game by trying to create an 'enterprise culture' founded upon competitive individualism and consuming passions (Keat and Abercrombie 1991). There is no direct translation of this hegemonic project into contemporary cultural studies. Criticism, however, became boring for some, and the moment arrived to revise radical wisdom. For instance, Kathy Myers (1986) challenged anti-consumerism and called for the reappraisal of advertising and marketing, citing their deployment by the GLC's failed campaign to save itself in the mid-1980s. The new thinking was not confined to learning from the enemy but also involved dumping many once cherished assumptions, for example, those of classical Marxism. Following the latest French guru, Jean Baudrillard, Myers (1986) rejected the old distinction between 'use value' and 'exchange value', and between 'real needs' and 'false needs'.

In his earlier synthesis of semiology with political economy, Baudrillard (1988) adapted Marxism to the conditions of modern consumer society. That required serious attention to signifying practice (Kellner 1989a). By emphasising the sign value of the commodity in addition to exchange value, Baudrillard had wanted to extend the theory of commodity fetishism to account for an historical situation in which the reification of human labour and the ideology of consumption had, seemingly to him, become overwhelming: use value was thus entirely subsumed under exchange value and given a semiological form. This sense of total ideological entrapment, similar to Adorno's pessimistic critique of mass popular culture, is not so different from the postmodern nihilism Baudrillard later espoused: the claim that reality is no longer separable from signification, that we live in a hyperreal world of simulacra.

Neo-idealist theory (Dews 1987), however, is quite different from latter-day British cultural populism, for which it is rather convenient actually to retain a distinction between use value and exchange, thus facilitating the argument that there is use in excess of exchange value: that, for instance, young people are able to use commodities in creative ways which have nothing meaningfully to do with their role in the circulation of capital. This is the kind of limit position now reached by contemporary cultural studies.

Paul Willis's reports on the Calouste Gulbenkian Enquiry into Arts and Cultural Provision for Young People, *Common Culture* (1990a) and *Moving Culture* (1990b), exemplify the strengths and weaknesses of latter-day cultural populism. *Moving Culture* summarises for a non-specialist readership the findings of an ethnographic research project conducted by Joyce Canaan in Wolverhampton, and fifteen other commissioned studies from around the country on various aspects of youth culture and consumption. *Common Culture*, the text discussed here, expands upon the research findings and situates them within a developed theoretical framework. The Gulbenkian Enquiry is a collective project, bringing together the contributions of several researchers well-known and respected in the field of cultural studies, including Angela McRobbie, and for this reason it may be taken as representative of a whole strain of thought, broadly that of 'the new revisionism'. However, Willis's own personal predilections are evident in the texts, repeating many of his arguments from *Profane Culture* and *Learning to Labour*, plus refinements from the collectively gathered research findings. In this discussion, then, 'Willis' is the authorial marker but keeping in mind that he speaks from a position not entirely reducible to himself.

Introducing its case, *Common Culture* polemicises against certain orientations of public arts policy: the dominant tradition of 'high art' enacted by the postwar attempt to disseminate it to the masses through agencies like the Arts Council, and the 'community arts' movement which at one time seemed to be the main alternative to that tradition. Neither has successfully addressed young people in general. The dominant arts tradition is simply irrelevant, appealing to a tiny minority of any age group, but especially the young. This is an argument long canvassed by the community arts movement in its mission to break down barriers between 'art' and 'people' with participatory projects. Although ostensibly in contest with the dominant tradition, in truth, Willis contends, community arts share the very same assumption: the belief that only by being introduced to 'the arts' do ordinary people become creative. Willis insists they are already creative, already symbolically active, producing meanings of aesthetic value. He uses the authority of Raymond Williams to back up this claim. The title of the book, *Common Culture*, invokes Williams's reworking of Tawney's concept. R.H. Tawney saw 'common culture' as the universal dissemination of established art and culture. Williams (1958) disagreed with Tawney and, instead, argued for analysis of culture as anthropologically grounded and, politically, for popular access to the means of defining culture and its production. In spite of what Willis says, Williams's actual position was opposed to endorsement of market-based cultural consumption as presently constituted: to accomplish 'common culture', whether rightly or wrongly, Williams believed production had to be democratised. Willis's assertion that 'common culture' already exists fully formed in the everyday *consuming* practices of young people would make the old man spin in his grave. According to Willis, the contemporary achievement of 'common culture' has not yet been properly recognised. His avowed intention is to bring it to recognition.

Willis (1990a) also attacks what he calls 'academic semiology', accusing it of 'cultural populism', the discovery of '"art equivalents" in popular texts' (p. 5). His usage of 'cultural populism' is very nearly the opposite of mine. Willis means the appropriation of popular cultural artefacts as 'art', of which there are many versions, including '*Screen* theory'. Such a procedure is not strictly 'populist' since, for it, discourses of 'the people' and 'popular creativity' are unnecessary or, at most, optional extras. 'Unofficial' culture is quite routinely made 'official' when selected and canonised according to traditional *non-populist* criteria of judgement (see Williams 1961). On the other hand, Willis's own approach is indeed 'cultural populist', in the sense used in this book.

Against the aesthetic canonisation of the once profane, Willis prefers a sociological understanding of culture as lived practice, not static artefact. In order to get by day-to-day, everyone has to do 'necessary symbolic work'. Sociality is communication, the use of language and the body in everyday interaction. As Erving Goffman (1969) argued, there is a dramaturgy of ordinary life: people produce themselves as social actors, observing rules of symbolic exchange and role-playing scripts. From this flows identity and solidarity, affirming 'our active sense of our own vital capacities', says Willis (p. 12). Under contemporary conditions, personal affirmation has less to do with paid labour than with leisure, facilitated by the active use of commodities: 'Oddly and ironically, it is from capitalism's own order of priorities, roles, rules and instrumentalities *in production* (ironically, of leisure goods and services too) that informal culture seeks escape and alternatives in capitalist *leisure consumption*' (1990a: 19). Although sensitive to the 'irony', Willis's argument lacks ambiguity: capitalism both constrains *and* enables, defining the dominant and permitting the subordinate, thereby traversing the whole field of possibility. This argument is fleshed out by Willis's concept of 'grounded aesthetics . . . the yeast of common culture' (p. 21). For Willis, aesthetic qualities do not reside in the artefact but in its use. 'Official arts' reify artefacts as though they carry with them essential meanings that only need to be understood correctly by the consumer. Thus, the active role of consumption, reading as rewriting, for instance, is downgraded or simply ignored. 'Grounded aesthetics', in contrast, privileges the act of consumption, the construction of meaning in use, drawing attention to a complex, mediated process whereby the consumer brings knowledgeability to the artefact and does not just submit to its inherent charms. Specifically, products of the market relation, therefore, do not automatically legislate for their own use. People have to do something with them. And, as Willis remarks, '[c]ommercial cultural commodities are all most people have' (p. 26). Against the Baudrillardian thesis that postmodern culture is characterised by an implosion of meaning, surfaces with no depth, Willis asserts the meaningfulness that most people get out of what is on offer. 'The style and media theorists . . . are hoist by their own semiotic petards', incapable of grasping 'the movement of the real world' (p. 27).

These abstract arguments, not in themselves original, are concretised in *Common Culture* with evidence from Joyce Canaan's research and the fifteen area studies, covering young people's involvement with television and video, popular musical forms and technologies, fashion, hairstyle, sport, magazines, drinking, fighting and advertising. For instance, young people are found to be knowledgeable and discriminating television viewers, preferring soap opera of all the programme genres for its 'realism' yet not in a naïve 'reflectionist' sense. Their use of popular music is complex and varied, not only in terms of taste but also with regard to technologies of reception, playback and production, selecting and recombining meanings actively.

Willis pays particular attention to the ways in which consuming practices become production practices through home-taping, re-recording and mixing. He is keen to avoid making absolute distinctions of gender and ethnicity amongst the mainly working-class young people in the study. But Willis does give due consideration to practices associated particularly with black youth: the use of sound systems, DJ-ing, rapping and so forth. Also, following Kobena Mercer, he remarks upon hairstyle as 'a key site of semantic struggle' (p. 92), especially for young blacks. However, in youth cultural consumption there is constant interaction and borrowing, complicating ethnic differences and to some extent gender differences as well.

The substantive material reported on in both *Moving Culture* and *Common Culture* is richly detailed and closely attuned to particularities which are not easily or desirably overgeneralised. None the less, the substantive material is meant to demonstrate the general arguments concerning 'symbolic creativity' and 'grounded aesthetics'. In some areas this is more convincing than in others: television, popular music and fashion being credible examples. Other instances are less conveniently incorporated.

Willis admits so himself on the question of drinking and fighting by young working-class men. In the section on such behaviour he strives to be non-judgemental, mainly concerned with questioning 'tabloid headlines' to do with aggressive masculinity, suggesting that drinking and fighting are nothing like as mindless or widespread as is typically made out. They constitute a kind of Brechtian everyday theatre, especially in bellicose gesturing. At this juncture the relation of general argument to particular examples, both present and absent, becomes overstretched and unconvincing. There is, remarkably, no discussion of young people's symbolically creative use of tabloid newspapers like the *Sun*, which sells between three and four million copies daily and is read by three times that number of people, many of them young. As Ken Worpole (1990) commented in a review of *Common Culture* and *Moving Culture*, 'however creative and re-productive young people are with many cultural forms, the case of the brutalism of the popular press needs particular consideration' (p. 44). The silence here is very loud.

It is important to register that Willis is only too well aware of some criticisms that may be levelled at his and his collaborators' work. In an afterword to *Common Culture*, he defends its central thesis against a criticism already made by Simon Frith, who raised the question of 'quality', venturing that not all culture has equal worth. Willis's answer to this is that the meanings and values of a cultural artefact depend on activation in use: they can never be decided in abstraction from real sociality. However 'good' an artefact might be judged by academic critics, that does not count for much unless it resonates with ordinary people's judgement in their everyday lives. On that point, Willis simply repeats the argument from *Profane Culture* on 'homology'. Thus, the validity of Frith's question is, in effect, denied.

Willis also notes a potential criticism of his work to be made from 'the now orthodox Gramscian perspective' on popular culture as a site of struggle between 'the people' and 'the power-bloc'. The trouble with this perspective, for Willis, is its excessively macro-level of reasoning, whereas his own interests are more microscopic. He is concerned with very specific practices and meanings, not with whole social processes dealt with at such a level of generality and malleability of analysis that nothing much in particular can be learnt. Willis aligns himself on the side of 'agency' as opposed to 'structure' in social and cultural theory, somewhat disingenuously when one considers his faith in market capitalism's capacity to deliver the goods for everyone's creative use. Willis, significantly, closes the book by referring to the gulf between Left intellectuals and ordinary people and, moreover, the manifest failure of socialism in the late twentieth century (p. 158). The aim, therefore, is clearly to challenge worn-out radical assumptions rather than worn-out conservative ones. In consequence, Willis really has nowhere else to look than to the unqualified pleasures of consumer sovereignty in the marketplace. At best this is a libertarian humanism of uncertain political provenance, at worst it signals a loss of conviction in any grounds for criticising what exists in a world where human happiness does not seem wholly ubiquitous and where, apparently, there is no compelling vision of a better future.

In *Common Culture,* Willis summarises the material provided by Mica and Orson Nava on advertising art and youthful tele-literacy. Although advertising may be manipulative, Willis reports, its scope for creative appropriation by the young is great. It is worth paying closer attention to the case of advertising and young people, filled out by the Navas in their article in the first issue of the *Magazine of Cultural Studies* (March 1990). The Navas are extremely impressed by the respect shown by the advertising industry to young people, viewing them as 'discriminating and hard to reach', which invalidates the 'received wisdom' concerning

> images of undereducated undiscriminating and undisciplined young people who are addicted to TV and who mindlessly imbibe the advertisers' message along with the materialist values of the consumer society. Characteristic of this view is the notion that there exists a simple cause and effect relationship between advertising and the purchasing of commodities.
>
> (1990: 15–16)

Young people, it seems, are not sold on commodities by television advertisements but they do enjoy watching them from an aesthetic point of view:

> Our argument therefore is twofold: an analysis of the mode in which the commercial is consumed not only gives us insight into the cultural skills of young people, it also radically interrogates conventional divisions between art and advertising.
>
> (1990: 16)

The Navas rail against the denial of artistic status to advertising and they seek to establish its aesthetic worth, combining Willis's sense of 'cultural populism' with mine, on a number of counts: the technical, formal and ideational interaction with the visual arts (ads with cinematic models, and so on) and the overlap of directorial personnel (ads made by illustrious film directors). Some advertisements are acclaimed by industry awards even when not effectively increasing sales: for example, Ken Loach's celebrated *Guardian* ad of the mid-1980s in which a skinhead, apparently attacking a bourgeois gentleman, is in the end shown to be rushing to his aid, rather like latter-day cultural populists themselves. The Navas are also impressed by postmodern referentiality in TV commercials, not only when they quote from 'art' forms but in their occasionally witty citing of each other. The Navas' clinching and quite staggeringly absurd assertion is that advertisements are 'no more inherently implicated in the economic organisation of life than any other cultural form'! (my exclamation mark) (p. 21).

This claim made by the Navas for advertising aesthetics is in one sense merely banal. Thirty years previously Raymond Williams, observed that advertising is 'the official art of modern capitalist society' (1960/1980: 184). That displeased Williams, since he regarded advertising as distorted communication and hugely wasteful, no doubt a quaintly old-fashioned view. There is nothing much at stake, however, in admitting advertising to the canon of 'art'. It is well known that television advertisements are aesthetically sophisticated and enjoyed by many people, including the young: after all, they are the most expensive category of television programming, costing a great deal of money to make and slot into schedules, especially in Britain, far outstripping the production costs of even filmed drama. The famous Levi ads, shot to the standards of multi-million-dollar Hollywood movies, are indeed visually stunning. And, of course, for commercial television, the basic economic function of advertising revenue has priority, anyway, over programming quality (Smythe 1981). That the ads are sometimes better to watch than the programmes is a very old audience cliché.

To suggest that the aesthetic purpose of expensive television advertising exceeds its commercial purpose *for the industry* is frankly risible, yet one can see where it comes from: professional advertising ideology. Consider Jules Goddard's (1985) 'marketing

view of advertising', the argument that ads are themselves
commodities manufactured by advertising agencies for sale to
other manufacturers, not principally vehicles for persuading
consumers to spend *their* money. Such thinking on the part of the
advertising profession is a significant phenomenon in its own
right. It is a pseudo-scientific kidology, whereby organisations (in
business, politics and so on) are persuaded, up to a point, that they
cannot do without lavish advertising and marketing campaigns
even when such practices might fail in their ostensible aims of
selling commodities or winning votes. None the less, over time,
advertising as simulated commerce meets certain material limits.
Although the advertising industry awards itself prizes for artistry,
the bottom line standard of judgement, for the agency and its
client, is pecuniary. When a campaign does not increase or
maintain sales then, prosaically, the client may go elsewhere
regardless of the kudos bestowed upon it by the agency and the
advertisements' poetic bravura.[4]

From a critical perspective, it is constructive to invert the Nava
thesis by examining how advertising discourses shape other texts.
This has been done with particular reference to the commodity
form of Music Television, where art and advertising discourses are
deliberately blurred by advertising (Kaplan 1987; Jhally 1989).
Everybody knows, of course, that pop videos are advertising
vehicles. Other examples are less blatant, for instance: designer
imagery and positioning of products in mainstream films; and
toy-marketing in children's television programmes.

However, the Navas are absolutely right to reject Vance
Packard's (1957) purely manipulative theory of advertising and
Herbert Marcuse's (1964) philosophically sophisticated
'one-dimensional man' thesis. Both were indeed 'demeaning' to
ordinary people in their time. And perhaps some intellectuals still
hold a similarly pessimistic view of advertising and consumerism.
But, for popular cultural analysis, in the early 1990s, these are straw
men from a dim and distant past. Contemporary critics of
advertising, such as Wolfgang Haug (1986), Sut Jhally (1987),
Stuart Ewen (1988), William Leiss and his co-researchers (1990),
are all extremely conscious of the active, symbolic aspects of
consumption, yet they are ignored by the Navas. What
distinguishes the work of these critics from the brand of cultural
populism discussed here is that they seek to analyse the circulation
of commodities, their sensuous aspects and historical contexts,

mediated by advertising and marketing, rather than confining themselves one-dimensionally to the point of consumption.[5]

The stark contrast between critical analysis and the new revisionism can be illuminated further by Judith Williamson's (1978) concluding remarks in her widely acknowledged classic, *Decoding Advertisements*, which the Navas mention all too briefly. At length and with numerous examples, Williamson demonstrated how advertising modes of address work in relation to ideology and subjectivity. Having torn them apart, she then concluded on a tragic but embattled note: 'ideologies cannot be known and undone, so much as engaged with – in a sort of running battle, almost a race since the rate at which their forms, especially advertising, reabsorb all critical material, is alarmingly fast' (p. 178). For some cultural analysts, the race became too fast, the absorbing powers of advertising too great, to do anything but simply regurgitate the industry's own astute professional ideologies as though this were a mould-breaking discovery, thereby retreating into a Nava-Nava-land where all critical passion is consumed.

NOTES

1   Questions of class, race and youth are developed with impressive sophistication in Phil Cohen's later work (e.g. 1988).
2   Lucien Goldmann's (1975) use of 'homology' in the sociology of literature as well as Claude Lévi-Strauss's (1969) use of *'bricolage'* in anthropology. The application of structuralist concepts to popular culture was pioneered by Roland Barthes (1957/1972). An article of his was published in the first issue of *Working Papers in Cultural Studies* in 1971, and Barthes's study of 'the fashion system' is cited in the 'Subcultures' essay.
3   Male writers on youth culture began saying similar things in the 1980s. Simon Frith (1983): 'The issue, finally, is not how to live outside capitalism . . . but how to live within it' (p. 272). Iain Chambers (1986): 'If you live in a black-and-white world, and prefer the security of an abstract utopia to the potential of the present, then contemporary popular culture merely seems to be the predictable product of capitalism and consumerism' (p. 190).
4   The rigours of the market should not be underestimated. For instance, there are plenty of examples from US commercial television where series are withdrawn after only a few episodes if audiences are too low and advertising revenue suffers, a fate which nearly befell both *Hill Street Blues* (Gitlin 1984) and *Cagney and Lacey* (D'Acci 1987).

5   In a subsequent article, Mica Nava (1991) addresses this critical strand
    of thought without, however, distinguishing it to any significant
    degree from earlier 'manipulation' theory. There, the potential for
    political activity around consumerism, associated with Green politics,
    is emphasised, but she does not revise her celebratory judgement
    concerning advertising's popular appeal for young people
    irrespective of what is being advertised.

Chapter 4

Popular television

During the 1980s, 'popular television' became a key object of analysis for what Richard Collins has called 'the Siamese twins of media and cultural studies' (1990: 31). The study of popular television has multiple institutional sites and draws upon various research traditions in Britain. However, the British Film Institute, in particular, had a pivotal role in promoting popular television study[1] and, closely connected, the International Television Studies Conferences at London University's Institute of Education attracted scholars from around the world to address television from a number of different perspectives (Drummond and Paterson 1986 and 1988). Television analysis, nationally and internationally, is extremely diverse: it is not my aim to survey it generally. The specific focus here is on the valorisation of popular modes of television-viewing in mainly British media and cultural studies. Studying television at all, never mind in its mainstream forms and in relation to audience preferences, was tantamount to a populist move for the traditional humanities, which happily left this *merely popular* medium, characterised by formal hybridity and social mundanity, to 'numbers-crunching' sociology until recently. Film studies was about as far as academic cultural critics would go, and then only on the margins. In this intellectual context, Raymond Williams's *Television, Technology and Cultural Form* (1974), like so much of his work, was ground-breaking, yet not wholly isolated even in the mid-1970s.

Williams (1974) tried to define the cultural and historical distinctiveness of broadcast television. First, people normally 'watch television' rather than discrete programmes. Television discourse takes the form of a 'flow' of diverse programming elements in temporal sequence. To some extent, television schedules *us* in a reciprocal relation to domestic routines. When we enter the 'flow', in effect we enter a complex montage of interacting significations. Second, Williams identified television's contribution to 'mobile privatisation': the public world is made available in new and extensive ways within the private space of the home, accentuating the typical condition of daily life in advanced industrial societies. We travel, imaginatively at least, and stay put simultaneously (Williams 1983b). 'Flow' and 'mobile privatisation' were not the only potential socio-cultural dimensions of televisual technology. Broadcast television had, for quite specific historical reasons, become institutionalised in these particular uses.

John Ellis (1982) questioned Williams's concept of 'flow' and his critical concern about the blurring of separate programming categories (for example, advertising and drama). For Ellis, the peculiarity of broadcast television discourse included the 'segment', a short bit of information, exemplified by the spot advertisement, and also manifestly evident in news and entertainment programmes made up of brief items. Segmental structuring, however, is ubiquitous in television: for instance, very noticeably so in soap operas, where usually a cut from one scene to another coincides with a transition between two of the several storylines. These segments of 'clinches' fit with the distracted mode of attention in the domestic viewing context, distracted in comparison, that is, with the more overwhelming experience of cinema-spectating.

The turn towards popular television as a privileged object of analysis in the 1980s is not only related to these pioneering theorisations but also, and perhaps more importantly, to the paradigm crisis in British media and cultural studies. Speaking at the 1989 BFI conference on 'Film and Media Studies in Higher Education', Richard Collins suggested that the dominant ideology thesis, which had organised the field since the 1970s, was no longer dominant ('Paradigm lost?', reprinted in Collins, R. 1990). Nicholas Abercrombie and his co-authors (1980) found scant evidence of dominant ideological influence over widespread social beliefs and practices. And Conrad Lodziak (1986) challenged media-centred versions of the dominant ideology thesis with regard to television, distinguishing between 'the power to produce programmes' and 'the power-effectiveness of the programmes on the audience' (p. 3). There was plenty of evidence that powerful social groups had enormous though not exclusive influence over programming ideologies, but it did not follow that these ideologies were decisive in the reproduction of social relations. The 'ideological effect' (Hall 1977), in the strong sense, remained unproved.

Collins concluded that although postmodernist aesthetics and the new revisionist populism, exemplified by John Fiske (1987b), had destabilised the dominant ideology thesis, there was as yet no satisfactory new paradigm which could explain the complex relations between mediated culture and social structure. Reviewing *The Media Reader* (Alvarado and Thompson 1990) the following year, Brian Winston (1990) seemingly answered Collins's question, 'Paradigm lost?' with 'Paradigm found'. Lumping together the dominant ideology thesis with behaviourist media effects research, Winston remarked: 'Till now the dominant paradigm has been that we who consume mass messages are essentially passive receivers upon whom the products of such media act' (p. 16). The 'new paradigm', variously germinated by Raymond Williams, psychoanalysis, feminism and black politics, 'has been slowly aborning'. It is founded in 'the idea that audiences might rework media messages'. Winston oversimplified matters greatly. None the less, the shift towards the *active audience* in television and media study generally, a radical *rapprochement* with the functionalist tradition of uses and gratifications research (Blumler *et al.* 1972), has indeed been a leading trend in recent years. Some strands of this trend manifest 'uncritical populism'. However, it has also been a hugely valuable move forward from the excesses of both behaviourism and Marxism in the study of television. It does not in itself constitute a satisfactory alternative paradigm for reasons that will become clearer as the chapter unfolds.

'Taking popular television seriously' (Dyer 1985) was stated with polemical verve and impressive conviction by the BFI's Channel Four television series in 1986, *Open the Box*, and in Jane Root's (1986) accompanying book of the same title. That intervention went well beyond the earlier attempt to translate film theory into television genre analysis (for example, the material collected in Bennett *et al.* 1981b) by emphasising the domestic conditions of reception and audience activity, providing a more adequate account of the social psychology of television than purely textual analysis of programmes could ever produce. However, in attacking the 'viewer as zombie' myth propounded by writers like

Marie Winn (1977), it tended to tip the balance towards uncritical populism. Root equated Winn's behaviourist evidence of the allegedly harmful effects of television on children and her self-righteous familial ideology with critiques of racism and sexism in popular programming (Ferguson, B. 1984 and 1985). Throughout her book, Root celebrates *ad nauseam* the pleasures of television-viewing and audience empowerment, reminding the reader eventually, as an afterthought, that the producers of television have more power over the medium than the consumers (p. 120). A number of authors went overboard, in the mid-1980s, to celebrate popular television from an active audience viewpoint (examples are Taylor and Mullan 1986 and Fiske 1987b). Michael O'Shaughnessy (1990) has summarised the terms of what had become a new orthodoxy and, commenting on the use of *vox pop* in the BBC consumer show, *That's Life*, he displays a common hesitancy between hegemony theory and latter-day cultural populism: 'Is this the challenge or incorporation of alternative voices?' (p. 101).

Doubts concerning populism in popular television study had already been lodged by John Caughie in the early 1980s: 'the danger has to be noted that the popular can become the guarantee of politics, and the attention to programmes and programme categories with high ratings can become a politically self-justifying imperative' (1984: 117). He went on to argue that the historical transition in the meaning of 'the popular' from 'the property *of* the people, through packaging *for* the people, to consumption *by* the people' poses problems of critical judgement in cultural analysis. The first sense of 'the popular' is at best historically residual and not where the action is under advanced capitalist arrangements: however, Caughie warned, 'in settling for consumerist notions of popular culture there should be some of the uneasiness of an historical compromise, and a hesitation about a meaning naturalised by capitalism' (p. 118).

This sense of unease was enunciated by Andrew Goodwin, also in the early 1980s, when he questioned the editorial line of the short-lived *teleaste* magazine, *Primetime*. The editors of *Primetime*, in seeking to sustain a memory for the transient products of television and even to construct a canon of 'classics' (*The Prisoner* and so on), had attacked 'the literary mafia' representing 'the cultural-class system' and its contempt for popular television (vol. 1, no. 3, March–April 1982). Goodwin was permitted to reply in the next issue, expressing his 'fear . . . that we will merely replace elitism with populism' (1982: 2). He pointed out that 'the dominant class' was not univocal in relation to television by distinguishing between its cultural and economic 'wings'. The 'cultural wing' was indeed 'elitist' but it was responsible for public service broadcasting whereas the 'economic wing' had no such sense of responsibility in pushing the *laissez-faire* myth of 'giving the public what it wants'. Moreover, according to Goodwin in 1982, it was wrong to speak of 'popular television' since the system was thoroughly 'unpopular', from a certain perspective – in effect, the perspective of radical populism against mass culture. The system does not 'belong' to the people, argued Goodwin: they may enjoy consuming the programmes but they have precious little control over production decisions or access to programme-making. In the 1990s, such an argument for cultural democracy reads as naïve now that empowerment is so much defined by the capacity to consume rather than to produce. Nevertheless, Goodwin's prognosis was not far off the mark:

> if we look towards the next decade of British television it would seem that the 'economic' wing of 'the cultural-class system' is about to go on the rampage. In the face of this onslaught (increasing commercialisation of television through home video sales, the internationalisation of the market-place, the abandonment of public service ideals in the satellite and cable markets) the 'cultural' wing looks positively progressive. Now this wing is not the same as 'the literary mafia', but it does share a hostility to a second group of gangsters – the national and multinational corporations without whom no modern 'cultural-class system' would be complete.
>
> (1982: 3)

Goodwin's argument assumes that the politics of television can only be partially understood as the clash of contending cultural forces since television is also an institution of enormous economic significance. In the study of popular television, however, the relationship between the cultural and the economic has been comparatively neglected. Active audience research and the meaning of television in everyday life took a certain priority during the 1980s. Such research was rarely linked to the complex economic determinations, technological and policy changes occurring around television nationally and internationally.

To clarify what is at stake, then, in studying popular television, this chapter traces the switch from the Birmingham encoding/decoding model, associated uneasily with the dominant ideology thesis, to the ethnography of viewing contexts; the development of feminist work on continuous serials and the international circulation of the most widely viewed television of the 1980s, *Dallas*; the increasingly vexed question of children's television-viewing with the decline of public service principles of broadcasting; and, concluding with a discussion of the gulf between political economy and cultural analysis of television.

WATCHING TELLY

If the Judaic God had created the world as an advanced industrial civilization from scratch (s)he would probably have spent the seventh day in front of the television set. However, it is unlikely that even the Supreme Being could have watched attentively for the full twenty-four hours: the most resolute couch potatoes find it hard staying awake for such an unbroken stretch. Normally, we spread that average length of viewing time over the whole week, which no doubt raises our level of attention but not necessarily to any great heights. Much of the time we are doing something else as well (Collett 1986), though occasionally we may be permitted, depending on the particular balance of power in the home, to concentrate on our favourite programme (Morley 1986).

Across the various paradigms, scholarly disputes, denunciations and celebrations, it is now generally agreed that, in Neil Postman's words, 'the single most important fact about television is that people watch it' (1986: 94). Postman himself regards this as an unfortunate fact: we are 'amusing ourselves to death', according to him. Although Postman is one of the more interestingly hostile critics of 'the medium', his views meet with little sympathy in present-day popular cultural study. Postman's neo-McLuhanite position is essentialist and arrogant, yet consistent with what some authors claim 'ordinary people' have said to them, troubled by their 'addiction' to 'the plug-in drug' (Winn 1977) or the 'hypnotic effect' of 'the evil eye' (Playfair 1990).

That most people devote a great deal of their leisure time to watching telly, whether distractedly, guiltily or pleasurably, was not traditionally the main consideration for media researchers. The study of attitudinal, cognitive and behavioural 'effects' of television rather than the experience of watching it seemed more pertinent for all sorts of commercial, ethical and political reasons, the reasons that brought major research funding. However, since the early days of mass communications research, there have been counter-traditions sceptical of extravagant stories about the alleged effects of media messages on audiences. In James Halloran's (1970) much quoted statement, 'We must get away from the habit of thinking in terms of what the media do to people and substitute for it the idea of what people do with the media'. This liberal pluralist view, which conceptualises the media–audience relation as a negotiated transaction, contrasted sharply with claims made by mass culture critics and experimental psychologists that audiences were vulnerable to manipulation. There is, however, a problem concerning active media use, against effects research, to do with whether the audience member is to be conceived of as a free-wheeling individualist or as a social individual, roughly, between psychologism (the usual criticism of 'uses and gratifications' research) and sociologism (a tendency, in spite of disclaimers to the contrary, of the 'encoding/decoding' model – see Lewis 1983). Both are in danger of collapsing the discursive specificity of the media message into already constituted dispositions or meaning frames. In the case of television, that may lead to its complex systems of visual and aural signifiers being treated as entirely indeterminate.

Does the text have any determinate status? The influential work promoted by the Society for Education in Film and Television's journal *Screen* (see Brewster *et al.* 1981), in the 1970s, refused both empirical psychology and sociology, relying instead on self-sufficient textual study, consciously informed by Lacanian psychoanalysis and unconsciously by sociological assumptions (Morley 1989). Films were said to position spectating subjects through linguistic and psychic mechanisms inscribed in the cinematic text: so audience research was not required. *Screen* theory's textual determinism was thus open to the critique that it represented yet another version of manipulative media theory, typically negligent of the socio-cultural resources that actual audience members bring to decoding texts (Morley 1980a).

Running alongside the development of '*Screen* theory' was the formulation of the encoding/decoding research model at the

Birmingham Centre for Contemporary Cultural Studies under the aegis of Stuart Hall (1974b), which defined audiences in much more active terms. It is significant, however, that these two contrasting approaches took different forms and media as objects of study: SEFT concentrating on feature films in cinema; CCCS concentrating on television news and current affairs programmes (Hall *et al.* 1976). Perhaps it is the case that cinema has a more determinate effect on its spectator than television does on its viewer. Sitting in a darkened auditorium amongst strangers in front of a large, brightly lit screen is very different from glancing at the telly amid the hustle and bustle of domestic life, except for the solitary, particularly old people (Tulloch 1989). Whatever the differences, any general theory of text–audience relations should be able to account for such differences (Kuhn 1984). Hitherto, there has been remarkably little research on cinema audiences, and this is unlikely to change considering the long-term decline of the cinematic institution (Docherty *et al.* 1987). Nowadays, most people watch their films on the box, perhaps simulating the conditions of cinema by turning the living-room lights down or off. With film-dedicated satellite channels and the introduction of wide-screen, high-definition television, the approximation to cinematic spectatorship will become increasingly available to those who can afford it.

The Birmingham encoding/decoding model was not only concerned with the activity of audiences but also with the effectivity of texts in the attempt to go beyond the consumer sovereignty of uses and gratifications research. In that sense, it was linked to hegemony theory's refinement of the dominant ideology thesis. Instead of treating television as merely a purveyor of ruling-class 'bias', it was supposed to reconcile the active audience concept with the ideological process of winning consent to the prevailing order, for instance, the ostensibly open yet, in fact, narrowly circumscribed terms of British parliamentary democracy (Hall 1972 and 1977). Stuart Hall (1982) persistently argued that television was implicated in the 'production of consent' and not simply the 'reflection of consensus', as defined by dominant interests and powers in society. As a model of communication, in practice, the 'encoding/decoding' formulation proved flexible almost to the point of incoherence due to the double-edged implication of ideological effectivity *and* audience activity.

Hall (1974b and 1980b) was impressed by Umberto Eco's

(1965) argument that because the modern 'mass' media address heterogeneous audiences, audiences with diverse cultural backgrounds, aberrant decoding of the message is, therefore, normal and only to be expected. Volosinov's (1929) theory of the *multi-accentuality* of signs, motivated by 'the class struggle in language', and Barthes' (1964) work on visual connotations and ideology, also enabled Hall to conceptualise the television message as *polysemic*, as always open to differential decoding. However, Hall insisted that television messages are not wide open to any decoding: they are encoded in such a way as to *prefer* a reading and to restrict the potential range of other readings. The preferred reading is structured by dominant ideological discourses in the wider society, the closure enacted and given specific inflections through the professional codes of television production. There are, then, two distinct and separable moments in the circulation of the message between production and consumption: encoding and decoding.

In order to explore how *preferred* readings and other readings might operate, Hall appropriated Frank Parkin's (1973) class-based value systems: dominant, negotiated and radical. Parkin wanted to explain how working-class people resisted and/or were incorporated into the unequal system of rewards in Western capitalist societies. According to him, resistance derived from the radical political values of socialist parties, whereas dominant values, the values adopted by working-class conservatives, derived from establishment institutions that represent the covert interests of the ruling class. Normally, Parkin suggested, working-class people negotiated a set of beliefs somewhere between the dominant and radical value systems, motivated by their own existential circumstances. Parkin's ideas were inserted into the encoding/decoding model, intended originally to analyse the ideological effectivity of 'factual' television.

Concentrating on news and current affairs, where ideology was assumed to be most evident, Hall distinguished between *dominant, negotiated* and *oppositional* decodings. Dominant decoding occurs when the preferred meaning is taken more or less straight; oppositional decoding questions the legitimacy of the message; negotiated decoding, the most common, involves various possibilities of reading dependent on the experiential circumstances and preoccupations of viewers. The model suggested that differential decodings were socially motivated by class and situation. For example, it was assumed that trade unionists viewing industrial conflict stories would make either negotiated or oppositional readings depending on their distance from or involvement in disputes.[2] It was necessary to 'test' such empirical 'hypotheses' if the model was to produce more than theoretical speculation. The task of doing so fell to David Morley, who had been engaged in constructing protocols for ethnographic audience research since the early 1970s (Morley 1974).

With Charlotte Brunsdon, Morley published a short monograph on the semiological paradigms and syntagmatic chains of the early evening news and magazine programme *Nationwide*, in 1978. He went on to conduct a celebrated audience study of the programme's mode of address and ideological problematic using the encoding/decoding model (1980b and 1981a). Morley showed episodes of *Nationwide* to several groups divided into two social classes as conventionally defined: managers and full-time students (middle class), apprentices and trade unionists (working class). They were all attending courses of one kind or another: with his 'captive' audiences in the classroom, then, Morley could discuss their interpretations of *Nationwide*. Morley's analysis of transcripts from tape-recorded discussions broadly confirmed the model's distinctions between dominant, negotiated and oppositional codes. However, many data were also thrown up which exceeded the limits of a simplistic and reductionist class analysis of television decoding. There were significant cross-cutting differences to do with age, gender and race/ethnicity. This worried Morley and he concluded *The 'Nationwide' Audience* with a chapter on the anomalies and theoretical issues arising. He argued particularly that the model needed to be complexified by *interdiscourse*, a concept borrowed from the discourse theorist Michel Pecheux. It refers to the way *social subjects* are interpellated and constructed across a range of discourses, not just textual discourses (as in *Screen* theory) or by class discourses (as in the primitive version of the encoding/decoding model).

Morley's application of the encoding/decoding model in his *Nationwide* audience study was criticised systematically, not least of all by Morley himself.[3] Justin Wren-Lewis (Lewis 1983) complained that Morley's *Nationwide* analysis was insufficiently semiological, in effect, reducing television to a conveyor belt of dominant ideological meanings produced elsewhere, by 'primary definers', thus denying television's autonomy as signifying practice. The problem turned for Wren-Lewis on how the preferred reading was identified in the first place. He argued that it could not logically be elicited prior to audience research. Martin Jordin and Rosalind Brunt (1988) challenged Wren-Lewis's 'empiricist illusion' (p. 236). They argued that the real problem with Morley's research ran much deeper because his qualitative ethnography was compromised by the positivistic protocols of quantitative audience research method (a criticism that could equally well be made of Morley's later *Family Television* study). Unlike Wren-Lewis, Jordin and Brunt remained in touch with the dominant ideological aspect of hegemony theory by insisting that preferred readings could indeed be isolated *textually* prior to audience research, the investigative task then becoming to study all decodings as a potentially infinite range of negotiations with the preferred reading. Although these two sets of criticisms are different, they wind up making a similar proposal for a more thoroughgoing ethnography of audiences, unweighed-down by the pre-suppositional baggage of the original encoding/decoding model, which is more or less the position Morley arrived at himself through his autocritique.

Morley (1981b and 1986) became dissatisfied with the artificiality of watching and discussing television programmes with specially selected groups in educational institutions. He wanted to interview people in their homes, the 'natural setting' where they actually watch television. Morley had also become dissatisfied with Frank Parkin's Weberian scheme of class value systems. It was a superficial theory of class but, more seriously, it obscured social differences of age, gender, race and ethnicity. One way out of the impasse was to dispense completely with such global value systems and to consider instead the relations between textual genres as frameworks of meaning and audience sub-groups in the interdiscursive contexts of everyday life. *Screen* theory was already concerned with genre and gender from a feminist perspective but only at the level of textual processes. Instead, Morley drew on Pierre Bourdieu's and Jean-Claude Passeron's (1977) concept of *cultural competence*. The theory of differentially acquired competences, hierarchically ordered as *cultural capital* and distributed unequally, provided a means of rethinking the diverse experiences and knowledges socially situated groups bring to their use of television and the shaping of their programme preferences.

Concurrently, at the CCCS, work along these lines was conducted by Charlotte Brunsdon and Dorothy Hobson, who were interested in soap opera and women. They took the Birmingham-based soap, *Crossroads*, as their exemplar. *Crossroads* was one of the most despised programmes on British television, despised by professional broadcasters themselves for its poor production values as well as by cultural elitists and by men in general. It was the acme of junk television and its audience was predominantly female. Brunsdon (1981) insisted, in the face of such prejudice, that pleasurable viewing of *Crossroads* depended on viewers being competent in various kinds of knowledge: of the genre, of the specific serial, and in terms of 'the socially accepted codes and conventions for the conduct of personal life'. In a patriarchal society, it is mainly women who are competent in this respect because of the domestic roles assigned them. Most men did not like *Crossroads* because they were not competent enough to appreciate its popular appeal. Hobson wrote a book on *Crossroads* (1982), which drew on her informal viewing and conversation about the programme with women in their own homes; a precursor of the spate of ethnographic audience research in British television study later in the 1980s.

In his *Family Television – Cultural Power and Domestic Leisure* (1986), Morley sought to synthesise audience interpretations of television with its social use, to reconcile encoding and decoding with uses and gratifications: and, in so doing he staked out a comparatively new terrain for British research, though one already explored extensively in the United States by James Lull (1990). Morley summed up his shift of position clearly:

> having previously argued that the critical formula was that of a programme's ideological problematic plus its mode of address (in relation to audience 'tastes', cultural capital and political views), I now want to extend the formula to include a third term, which is that of audience 'availability' (both in terms of physical presence and freedom from competing demands on attention).
>
> (1986: 48)

The great weakness of the encoding/decoding model was that it paid too little attention to viewing contexts and, in consequence, failed to account for patriarchal power relations in the home. Such relations are frequently at the heart of the social practice of watching telly: for instance, who chooses which programmes and/or channels to watch, who is permitted to watch attentively, who controls the remote control.[4] The power of the father is implicit in these considerations. Morley found that women's opportunities for viewing and their genre preferences were substantially different from those of their male partners. For many women the home is a place of work, whereas men usually experience it rather more as a place of leisure. Men are allowed to watch more attentively and their choices of viewing are related to this: for example, their preference, in comparison with women, for 'serious' documentaries. Women are rarely permitted to watch with undivided attention: that is one of the reasons why the fragmented and repetitive structures of soap opera are so popular with the female audience.

Thus, Morley (1986) commented upon gendered power relations with reference to the social use of television and programme preferences. He also stressed the importance of contradictory decodings and how they complicate our understanding of subjectivity, citing Ernesto Laclau and Chantal Mouffe's (1985) argument that the subject is split *socially*, not just psychologically as in the abstract universalism of Jacques Lacan's (1968 and 1970) model of consciousness/unconsciousness: 'the same man may be simultaneously a productive worker, a trade union member, a supporter of the Social Democratic Party, a consumer, a racist, a home owner, a wife beater and a Christian' (Morley 1986: 42). Following Laclau and Mouffe, Morley pointed to the lack of necessary class-belongingness of subjective interpellations. But there is a rank ordering of discursive resources in the constitution of the subject, he contended, whereby some are more prominent than others, especially gender and class discourses.

Morley visited only eighteen lower-middle-class and working-class nuclear families in south London, all of them white. This was a narrow selection in terms of household, class, race and region. The fact that the research was, as Morley insisted, a modestly resourced *pilot* project, to be followed perhaps by more extensive enquiry, did not prevent the provisional sketch of *Family Television* from becoming a touchstone 'classic'.

Other researchers went further in refining Morley's basic insights from both the *Nationwide* study and *Family Television*. Since the mid-1980s there has been an extraordinary proliferation of small-scale ethnographic audience research in Britain and elsewhere (for example, Seiter *et al.* 1989). Two notable British examples are the studies by Ann Gray (drawn upon by Morley 1986) and Marie Gillespie. Both Gray and Gillespie concentrate on the use of the video cassette recorder, the most successful new domestic television technology during the 1980s, much more important than the piecemeal development of cable and satellite services in that decade.

Ann Gray (1987a)[5] studied television-viewing practices and VCR use in West Yorkshire, mainly in the town of Dewsbury. She interviewed an ethnically homogeneous selection of thirty women from across the official classification of socio-economic groups. Her research is thus revealing about cultures of gender and class. Interviewees were asked to colour-code the use of domestic technology: pink for feminine, blue for masculine and lilac for feminine/masculine. Washing machines, apart from the motor, came out as pink; VCRs as mainly lilac, except for the deep indigo of the timer function. The conventional gendering of domestic technology, according to Gray, is further accentuated by industrial design: sleek black, high-tech VCRs (masculine); white, chunky-dialled washing machines (feminine). The timer function on VCRs is off-putting for women yet they routinely operate time settings on washing machines. In addition to the gendering of domestic technologies, Gray also developed a typology of viewing contexts and film genre preferences (p. 47), which confirmed the rigidities of male (such as war) and female (melodrama, for example) tastes. Gray found that gender differences and power imbalances were most pronounced in working-class households. Although her sample was small and quite self-consciously incommensurate with positivistic surveys, Gray's open-ended interviews indicated some important features of cultural power in northern English family life.

Marie Gillespie (1989) studied the viewing of Hindi ('Bombay') films on video amongst families of Indian origin in Southall, west London. This family viewing situation, she found, functioned differently for grandparents, parents and children, but for them all it is a crucial site for negotiating Asian British identity. Gillespie observes:

The exclusion and marginalisation of many people in Southall from mainstream British society, coupled with the failure to provide adequate leisure/culture facilities, has (like among the *Gastarbeiter* (guest worker) Turkish community in West Germany) contributed to an important home video culture.

(1989: 228)

For older viewers the films offer nostalgia and opportunity to socialise the young into the language and images of their culture of origin. However, the young, according to Gillespie, have mixed feelings about such films. Girls tend to be less critical than boys and they become engaged by the narrative and spectacle of the films. The boys, typically, are more concerned with questions of representation and evince embarrassment at India's 'backwardness'. There is thus a familial tension between traditional and modern values manifested in shared viewing of the films. As Gillespie comments, 'it would appear that Hindi films can serve to legitimate a particular view of the world and at the same time to open up contradictions within it' (p. 237).

These studies by Gray and Gillespie combine residual aspects of encoding/decoding with the shift towards the study of viewing contexts, but they also raise larger issues to do with the complex cultural circuits of gender and ethnicity, power and identity, that go beyond exclusively television analysis. The sense that this strand of audience ethnography poses more questions than it alone can answer has been discussed usefully by Janice Radway (1988). Radway's (1987) research on women's reading of romantic fiction in the United States has manifest affinities with British approaches to the study of television-viewing, on which she herself has commented.[6] But Radway subsequently became dissatisfied with the fragmentation of lived experience produced by only superficially ethnographic and media-specific interview studies, including her own earlier work. She says:

the ethnographic method has been applied until now in an extremely limited fashion both to reception studies and media analysis. In anthropology, of course, an ethnography is a written account of a lengthy social interaction between a scholar and a distant culture. Although its focus is often narrowed in the process of writing so as to highlight kinship practices, social institutions or cultural rituals, that written account is rooted in an effort to observe and to comprehend the entire tapestry of social life.

(1988: 367)

Radway concluded that audience ethnography was far too modest. She proposed, instead, collaborative research projects to study 'leisure worlds' in specific localities and communities, to obtain a better understanding 'of the culture of leisure and consumption at the present historical moment' (p. 372). The ambitiousness of such a proposal situates television-viewing within the interacting series of leisure uses in mundane temporal and spatial contexts. Whether it will be implemented adequately and succeed in producing new knowledge is yet to be seen.

Radway's proposal moves a long way from the originating question of television audience ethnography: what do television programmes mean to actual audiences? It is a question which took the semiology of popular culture seriously by rejecting textual determinism, assuming that a message is made to mean in the process of decoding. As we have seen, such a question leads into another set of questions concerning how people watch television within the highly differentiated routines and power structures of everyday life, which ultimately exceed the terms of small-scale and easily managed media-centred studies. However, the following passage from Roger Silverstone's 'Television and everyday life' encapsulates the potential of a still developing field of enquiry:

Television as 'text' and television as technology are united by their construction, their recontextualization, within the practices of our daily lives – behind and beyond the closed doors of our houses – in our displays of goods and cultural competences, both in private and in public. If we are to make sense of the significance of these activities, which after all, are the primary ones for any understanding of the dynamics of the pervasiveness and power of the mass media in contemporary culture, then we have to take seriously the varied and detailed ways in which they are undertaken. This is the basis for the case for an ethnography of the television audience, and for a commitment to ethnography as an empirical method.

(1990: 186)

Although this remains a favoured direction for communication, cultural and media studies in the 1990s, more modest questions and questions of a rather different kind should not be precluded by it. Audience ethnography can illuminate the social dynamics of viewing practices and audience tastes, but these must also be related to how programmes represent the world and the pleasures they offer, as we shall see in the next section on soap opera. Moreover, issues to do with production in the narrow sense, what is actually provided, cannot simply be inferred from an exclusive attention to consumption, since the conditions for television and other media are not only determined by audience feedback. As Ien Ang (1991) has shown, 'critical' researchers were discovering, in the 1980s, what television companies had known all along about active and recalcitrant audiences, and the consequential difficulties of commodifying them for sale to advertisers. This recognition of a mutuality of knowledge and power does not necessarily reconnect hermeneutic understanding, however, with analysis of economic, political and technological forces over which ordinary people have little control or even comprehension.

SOAPING FEMINISM

The main trajectory of popular television studies in the 1980s was away from cultural criticism, effectively implying that audience research and textual analysis were mutually exclusive options. Christine Geraghty (1991) protests in her book *Women and Soap Opera* that 'in the urge to speak to "real viewers" the pendulum should not swing so much the other way that textual work which is sensitive to the positions offered to the audience is no longer feasible' (p. 7). She has little to fear, since ethnography is much harder and more expensive to do than textual analysis. Besides, the reduction of texts to their contexts of reception, at the logical extreme, reaches the absurdity of Berkeleyan subjective idealism, which totally denies the materiality of the object.

Another and related trajectory, already under way at the beginning of the 1980s, was the shift from the study of exceptional television forms, such as 'serious' authored drama (Brandt 1981), to the study of unexceptional, mainstream forms, popular series and serials, especially soap opera. This partly reflected institutional changes: the decline of the single play and its replacement with cinematic hybrids, made-for-TV feature films and mini-series/serials. It also reflected the popular audience-orientated trend associated with ethnographic studies. That is not all-consuming, however, since many one-off productions have gone to the 'cutting edge' of permissible representation, in the judgement of some critics (Tulloch 1990) – to name but a few: *Boys from the Blackstuff* (1982), *Edge of Darkness* (1985) and *Oranges are not the Only Fruit* (1990). Each of these examples, all originally televised on BBC2, attracted large audiences (in the region of 5 to 10 million). Such programmes pose questions about 'progressive' innovation and 'quality' that have been neglected by cultural populism, questions considered in the next section, specifically with reference to children's programming.

Of all the staple television drama genres (including, for instance, police series and situation comedies), most scholarly attention was lavished upon soap opera in the 1980s, mainly because it is the perfect test case for popular television analysis. In Britain, the home-made soaps consistently occupy the top rating positions but watching them is no longer habitually derided as the lowliest form of cultural distinction. Their seriality, repetitiveness and domesticity exemplify general features of broadcast television. Moreover, their feminine mode of address drew support from those feminists who had tired of 1970s ultra-radicalism. Thus, in the late 1970s and early 1980s, soap opera was raised to the quintessence of popular television.

This was not the first time that soap opera had been the object of serious scholarship. Back in the 1940s, American mass communications research, at its inception, dispelled alarm concerning the effects on house-bound women of listening to day-time radio serials, the prototype of the genre, sponsored by soap powder manufacturers. The psychiatrist Louis Berg had claimed they caused 'acute anxiety state, tachycardia, arrythmias, increase in blood pressure, profuse perspiration, tremors, vasomotor instability, nocturnal frights, vertigo, and gastrointestinal disturbances' (quoted by Allen 1985: 21), a claim based ludicrously on subjecting himself to an intensive listening period. This was the familiar pseudo-scientific stuff of moral panic over popular culture. Herta Herzog (1942) produced a classic response when she argued, in the light of empirical audience research, that listening to soaps fulfilled already constituted psychological and social needs for women. And, in 1948, Lloyd Warner and William Henry defended soaps opera's function in confirming women's domestic roles as wives and mothers (Allen 1985: 28). It is not surprising, then, that post-1968 feminism had originally evinced hostility to a cultural form apparently designed expressly to keep women in their place.

Charlotte Brunsdon (1987) suggests that 'the contradictory feminist response to soap opera' (p. 147) is related to a tension between principles of realism and pleasure. In the 1970s many feminists complained about stereotypes and called for more realistic depictions of women, thereby seeking, observes Brunsdon, an ideal reality beyond the actual feminine experiences and problems dealt with pleasurably in soap operas. Her observation epitomises a mellowing of feminist cultural politics, renouncing opposition to the mainstream and also rejecting *avant-garde* alternatives to it. For instance, Laura Mulvey's (1975) psychoanalytic critique of classic Hollywood pleasures and her own resolutely anti-populist film-making practice (for example, *Riddles of the Sphinx*, 1978 – see Kuhn 1982) became suddenly unfashionable. Such radical feminist strategies 'suffer from an element of pessimism', according to Lorraine Gamman and Margaret Marshment (1988: 2), and were ineffectually maximalist. Alternatively, engagement with the mainstream offers the best prospect for women, which is the view that came to predominate in the 1980s.

As in other areas of popular cultural study, there is a discernible hovering here between the dialectical populism of hegemony theory and the uncritical populism of new revisionism. This may be illustrated by referring to two talks on soap opera given by academics at Edinburgh International Television Festivals, the first in 1977 and the second in 1985. The Television Festival is mostly attended by broadcasting professionals to discuss developments within the industry. In 1977, when Richard Dyer, Terry Lovell and Jean McCrindle delivered a paper on 'Soap opera and women', it was met with uncomprehending disbelief (I know because I was there). Dyer *et al.* challenged the masculinity of the festival, pointing to the paucity of women participants and absence of women's issues apart from this one session on soap opera. At that festival both Raymond Williams and Dennis Potter had spoken of 'Realism and non-naturalism', prompted by John McGrath's (1977) famous denunciation of television naturalism at the previous year's festival. None of them addressed the representation of women in their arguments concerning the politics of television drama.

By contrast, Dyer *et al.* explained their interest in the mundane form of soap opera: its traditional association with women, both in terms of representation and of viewing preference. The genre had 'limits' but it also offered 'possibilities' for 'critical feminism'. *Coronation Street* showed 'strong, independent women from whom much of the action is generated'. Nevertheless, Dyer *et al.* still found soap opera 'largely contemptible', and said it should be 'uncompromisingly attacked' because the power structures which oppress women were not adequately represented in the programmes. So they were not only drawing attention to the contradictory potential of soaps: their own position could also be construed as internally contradictory and inconsistent, displaying the problem of holding together a notion of ideological effect with an appreciation of popular pleasure, typical of the field of study. As well as bearding the broadcasters in their den, on more academic terrain, Dyer *et al.* attacked the Althusserian/Lacanian critique of realism:

> This anti-realism too easily slides over into hostility to all or most popular forms and conventions. We wanted to study soap opera precisely because it *is* popular, it is for and about women, it is not prestigious and we wanted to discover why it gives pleasure to millions of people and to relate that to its ideological effects.
>
> (1977: 26)

In addition to finding it 'contemptible', then, Dyer *et al.* were prepared to say boldly positive things about soap opera: 'the pleasure it takes in the close details of life', 'entertainment as validation' and 'open-endedness'. They also referred to the British soaps' evocation of Utopian feelings of 'intensity', 'transparency' and 'community', especially in the fictionalised working-class world of *Coronation Street*. Christine Geraghty (1991) later took this up in her comparison of British and American prime-time soaps, also using the two other categories of Utopian feeling, defined elsewhere by Richard Dyer (1977), 'abundance' and 'energy', more characteristic of the American programmes.

Dyer, Lovell and McCrindle's 1977 intervention was seminal: it presaged a classic study of *Coronation Street* (Dyer *et al.* 1981), and it put soap opera firmly on the agenda of feminist cultural politics in Britain. They were calling for a radicalisation of the potential inherent in the genre, something which the Channel Four programme, *Brookside*, launched in 1982, manifested in a highly qualified way (Geraghty 1983). *Brookside*, with its comparatively larger range of masculine identificatory characters and treatment of public issues like unemployment, made soap opera more appealing to men as well as women. Yet, by doing so, it may have contributed to a dilution of the genre's feminine appeal, a strategy which *Crossroads* eventually aped, fatally, as it happened (Geraghty 1991).

At the 1985 Edinburgh Television Festival, Dorothy Hobson also bearded the broadcasting professionals in their den, but in a much less conflictual manner than Dyer, Lovell and McCrindle had done in 1977. She objected to the way soaps were still held in contempt by broadcasters themselves. Her argument was that soap opera was good for both television companies and for viewers: everyone should be pleased. And she sought to eliminate residual feminist doubts concerning the genre:

> Questions about soap opera being a closed form of drama which is ultimately conservative because the resolutions are never progressive, do not take into account the work the audience contributes to the understanding of the drama. Ultimately, I would argue, the soap opera is one of the most progressive forms on television because it is a form where the audience is always in control. The production can include whatever solution it wishes, the viewer *always knows best*. They will always re-interpret the ending and make allowances for the dramatic needs of the programme, or the ignorance of reality on the part of the producers . . . . Soap opera is not pulling drama down a slippery slope – it is a major form of television art.
>
> (1985: 60)

The openness of the genre (its continuousness and sense of an unresolved future), alluded to by Hobson, is one of the principal arguments for the femininity and feminist potential of soap opera. However, Hobson adds to this an extreme version of the active audience concept (it does not matter how storylines are resolved since audiences will make their own judgements) and the bid for artistic status, similar to the Navas' thesis on advertising. Furthermore, like John Fiske's position, the audience is said to be so satisfied with what is currently on offer that there is no imaginable reason for demanding anything better. It is a Panglossian view of popular culture: all is well in the best of all possible worlds.

Although soap opera theorists generally fulfil Roland Barthes' injunction that it is necessary to be a fan in order to be a critic, few are as unreflexive about the genre as Dorothy Hobson. Christine Geraghty (1991), the leading British writer on soap opera, admits to a certain ambivalence about it. She believes the genre offers a space for women which exercises their skills and validates their sense of reality, but that does not mean these potentials are always activated by the audience. Geraghty is sceptical of sweeping claims to do with audience empowerment, though she resists the tendency more common in American writing simply to infer audience positioning from the text itself. The classic instance of such textual determinism is Tania Modleski's (1984) argument that soaps, by offering multiple and shifting identifications across the ensemble of characters, produce the audience position of 'a sort of ideal mother: a person who possesses greater wisdom than all her children' (p. 92). Reporting on an ethnographic study of American soap-viewing, Ellen Seiter and Gabriele Kreutzner have commented on the unsatisfactoriness of Modleski's thesis, while also indicating a more dialectical view than uncritical writers, thereby refusing Hobson's choice: 'Modleski offers no possibility for *conscious* resistance to the soap opera text: the spectator position is conceived of in terms of a perfectly 'successful' gender socialization entirely in keeping with a middle-class (and white) feminine ideal' (Seiter *et al.* 1989: 237).

In the literature there has been an ongoing debate about what actually constitutes the soap opera genre. For instance, Muriel Cantor and Suzanne Pingree (1983) tried to confine it to the 'classic' form of American day-time serials, the form upon which latter-day Australian soaps like *Neighbours* are modelled: daily episodes and production techniques scarcely updated from those of 1950s live television. They insisted, with good reason, that these serials are very different from prime-time shows like *Dallas* and *Dynasty*, made expensively on film and aimed at the international market. And, there is a problem about whether or not, for example, Brazilian tele-novellas (Mattelart, M. 1986), which are usually concluded after six months, count. The British early evening form is yet another variation, not running every weekday but still continuous and evocative of real time passing (Geraghty 1981). Across the various programmes labelled 'soap opera' there are differences to do with the number of interweaving storylines, continuousness, organisation of time and space, *mise-en-scène* and ideological thematics. More important than purity of definition, however, is what Geraghty (1991) describes as the 'blurring of boundaries between soap opera and other genres' (p. 4): for example, the multiple narrative structure of *Hill Street Blues* was similar to programmes which would more readily be identified as 'soap opera'. The 'postmodernist' *Twin Peaks* drew on elements of American prime-time soap, combining them with 'whodunnit' police investigation and surrealist 'arty' cinema (Boyd-Bowman 1990). *Twin Peaks* also brought the masculinisation of soap opera to a new and troubling frontier, actually crossing the border into pornographic-style violence against women.

The main concern here is not with definitional problems or the misappropriation of soap opera, however, but rather with, firstly, its feminist appreciation and, secondly, the globalisation of an American form. Thus, research on *Dallas*, assuming it to be in some sense a soap opera, is especially pertinent. For instance: Ien Ang's (1985) study of Dutch women's reading of *Dallas*; Elihu Katz and Tamar Liebes's (1986) cross-cultural study of audience decodings in Israel and the United States; and the European comparative study of serial fiction by Alessandro Silj *et al.* (1988), *East of Dallas*. During the 1980s, *Dallas* was the most widely viewed television programme in the world. It ran from the late 1970s into the 1990s and, as the selection of research mentioned indicates, it became the object of intense academic inquiry, coinciding with an increased globalisation of the television market. Anxiety about institutional change was famously enunciated, in the mid-1980s, by the then BBC Director General Alistair Milne's disingenuous prediction that it might all lead to 'wall-to-wall-*Dallas*' (Dunkerley 1987) – disingenuous, because he oversaw the successful campaign to win *Dallas* back for BBC transmission when Thames Television outbid the £30,000 fee per episode, paid by the BBC until then, by offering the American production company, Lorimar, £50,000 (which was still only approximately 15 per cent of the production cost for each episode). This was cheap popular television indeed for British public service broadcasting, much cheaper to rent than the costs of making the more modest home-based soaps such as the BBC's own *EastEnders*.

In her *Watching Dallas* (1985), Ien Ang synthesised textual analysis from film studies with the move towards television audience research. She put an advertisement in the Dutch women's magazine, *Viva*, requesting letters from viewers to comment on *Dallas*'s pleasures and its lowly cultural standing. Her forty-two replies came overwhelmingly from women (three men replied). Ang read these letters 'symptomatically', in the Althusserian term, relating their commonsensical individualism to extant ideologies of 'mass culture' and 'populism'. This apparently scanty empirical evidence was used cleverly by Ang to refine and substantiate her theoretical arguments concerning realism and melodrama, cultural value, feminism and pleasure with regard to *Dallas*.

Ang distinguished between 'empiricist realism', 'classical realism' and her own idea of 'emotional realism'. *Dallas* fans, Ang found, considered it 'realistic', thus calling into question the usual criticism of the programme's 'unrealistic' representation of opulent family life and personalised motivation around the Texas oil business. 'Empiricist realism', based on a reflectionist assumption, could not possibly explain this; nor could Colin MacCabe's (1974) critique of realist illusionism explain it without treating the viewers as mere dupes of the text, which is why his 'classic realism' thesis is thoroughly unacceptable to cultural populism. Both perspectives, according to Ang, are caught up in a cognitive-rationalism which fails to grasp the affective impulses of pleasurable meaning in fiction and fantasy. Ang insisted that for many women *Dallas* was *emotionally realistic*, for example, because of the identification some of her respondents made with Sue Ellen's desperate efforts to cope with her villainous husband, J.R., and to establish her own space (see Ang 1990a). It did not matter that Sue Ellen's lifestyle was so much richer than that of her female fans. In fact, it was an added attraction. For Ang, Sue Ellen's plight exemplified the programme's 'tragic structure of feeling', derived from 'the combination of melodramatic elements and the narrative structure of soap opera' (1985: 78).

Although Ang failed to make the connection explicit, this notional 'tragic structure of feeling' is remarkably similar to the Lacanian tension between imaginary unity and symbolic difference (Lacan 1968 and 1970), a major preoccupation of *Screen* theory (Mulvey 1975; MacCabe 1976). Considered from that perspective, the human condition is universally tragic due to perpetual disruption and splitting by the unconscious of conscious desires for a sense of personal wholeness and self-realisation, originally initiated by the infant mirror phase and played upon persistently by larger-than-life identificatory figures in films and advertising. Quite differently from those idealisations, in *Dallas*, just as the characters seemed to be getting on top of their problems everything fell apart on them again: their projects were repeatedly thwarted by forces beyond their control. Ang argued that these repetitive frustrations invoked women's position within patriarchy: masochistic but emotionally realistic and, hence, mistakenly denounced by feminists for not being 'right on'.

In addition to the 'tragic' structure of the *Dallas* text, Ang interpreted different readings of the programme in relation to ideologies of mass culture and populism. Some viewers were ambivalent about enjoying *Dallas* because they knew that it was 'bad' culture. To solve this problem, they adopted an 'ironic viewing attitude', whereby a sense of intellectual superiority and discursive control could be sustained by running commentary on the ridiculous behaviour and events depicted in *Dallas* (Ang cited Foucault 1981, to support her argument here). Other viewers, however, had no such problem to negotiate: they knew what they liked and that was it; their own autonomous judgement was all that mattered. Ang remarked astutely:

> There exists a cynical dialectic between the intellectual dominance of the ideology of mass culture and the 'spontaneous', practical attraction of the populist ideology. The stricter the standards of the ideology of mass culture are, the more they will be felt as oppressive and the more attractive the populist position will become. This position offers the possibility, contrary to the morals of the ideology of mass culture, of following one's own preferences and enjoying one's own tastes.
>
> (1985: 115)

This dialectic is ruthlessly exploited by commercial media's propagation of the idea that 'indeed there's no accounting for taste'. However, it also resonates with Bourdieu's (1984) concept of the 'popular "aesthetic" . . . the exact opposite of the bourgeois aesthetic' (Ang 1985: 116), a direct and uninhibited immersion in preferred cultural experiences rather than the obligatory self-distancing of the educated.

Audience responses to *Dallas* illustrate *both* differences of cultural disposition *and* a certain universality constructed historically by American-based entertainment industries. It is important to stress this *double* aspect, since in the populist literature (including Ang 1985 and 1990b, and Morley 1989) a great deal has been made of the former at the expense of the latter in the habitual *anti*-anti-American mode. Katz and Liebes (1986), from a uses and gratifications perspective, have shown how the programme was differentially decoded by people of diverse cultural origins in Israel and how *Dallas* was read as a realist representation of affluent US society the further viewers were away from it culturally and geographically. The international role of such programmes was also explored in the comparative study of serial fiction in several European countries, *East of Dallas*. Alessandro Silj *et al.* (1988) argue that notions of American cultural imperialism associated with programmes like *Dallas* are far too simplistic. Crucially, they are never the *most popular* programmes of their kind in European countries, yet they are more popular than, say, similar French programmes in Britain or British programmes in Germany:

> *Dallas*, and American serial fiction in general, is always the loser when competing with fiction produced by European countries; but, to continue the sports metaphor, it wins the indirect challenges. If, in each country, national programmes occupy the top positions in the audience ratings, the public's second choice *never* falls on programmes produced by other European countries. American is the *lingua franca* of the European market of television fiction.
>
> (Silj *et al.* 1988; 199)

This finding undermines the European Commission's official encouragement of 'pan-Europeanism' in television associated particularly with satellite broadcasting and the interests of European-based media conglomerates. However, the issue of the second-rung popularity of programmes like *Dallas* needs to be delved into further. It raises the question of globalising culture (Featherstone 1990b): is 'global culture' American culture writ large or something else? Silj *et al.* say:

> Contrary to European fiction many American programmes are free from references to real situations (social and political) and often even to time, thereby favouring a symbolisation of characters and situations and this, in turn, increases the audience potentially able to identify with the stories told.
>
> (1988: 207–8)

Thus, the 'universal' appeal of *Dallas* and such texts generally is to do with a lack of specific cultural reference: that is what makes them so open. On the other hand, as Geraghty (1991) argues, the strength of British soaps and probably the reason for their much greater national popularity than American imports, judged by viewing figures, is exactly *their* cultural specificity, their capacity to engage in social dialogue, to touch upon the everyday lives of people domiciled in Britain. There is a two-way communicational process here, which is not wholly reducible to differential audience interpretations. Producers of national-based soaps are sensitive to the current preoccupations of their audiences – quite literally so in the case of viewers' letters (Hobson 1982) – in a way that impinges directly on their production decisions.

In the 1980s, British soaps went through a kind of modernisation process, particularly stimulated by new programmes, most important of which were *Brookside* (1982) and *EastEnders* (1985). From its launch, *EastEnders* represented the particular multicultural mix of British society and the reorganisation of local communities more intensively than its precursors, which is not to say the representation of black people went without justified criticism (Buckingham 1987a; Daniels and Gerson 1989). Like the American prime-time soaps, the British soaps started featuring gay characters and registering popular feminism explicitly but with more contextualised nuances than programmes with an international appeal. 'The nation' masks over internal differences and obscures transnational identities, as many critics have rightly argued. Yet its inscription in popular modes of address is also a localising and resistant force – to a degree seriously neglected by an exclusive focus on consumption. However limitedly, domestic forms of cultural production actually and potentially articulate the textures of daily experience more sensitively than global culture's universalising mode of address does or, from a commercial point of view, would wish to do. The greater popularity of home-grown soaps throughout Europe bears out this argument.

That the Australian import, *Neighbours*, reached levels of major British soap opera popularity (viewing figures above 15 million) in Britain itself by the late 1980s, however, complicates matters without, I would suggest, necessarily destroying the argument. *Neighbours* was a special case, not comparable with American export programmes. The peculiarly British appeal of *Neighbours* had much to do with its plethora of youthful identificatory characters and rescheduling between children's programmes and BBC1's *Six o'Clock News*. Until it was placed in this early evening slot, when adults join already 'captured' young viewers, the viewing figures for *Neighbours* had been quite modest.

CHILD-MINDING

Due to the programme's slipshod production values and astonishing youthful appeal, the sudden ascent of *Neighbours* to the top of the ratings at the end of the 1980s contributed to yet another cycle of the perennial debate over children's television-viewing. No discussion of popular television would be complete without considering the child's relation to it. Although anti-paternalism has made considerable headway, the tendency for latter-day cultural populism to coalesce with unrestrained commercialism becomes especially questionable with regard to children, owing to their comparative powerlessness, not only as audiences. The image of vulnerably innocent children may be out-dated, but it would be irresponsible to deny genuine concern about the programmes they watch.

The history of public debate and academic research on children and television is replete with unjustified alarmism, inconclusive findings and narrow-minded prejudice. Television has been blamed for all manner of 'effects' on impressionable young minds: causing children to act violently through the mechanism of 'imitation' (see McCron 1976, and Murdock and McCron 1979), retarding language acquisition, distracting from homework, confusing a fragile sense of reality (see Hodge and Tripp 1986), and umpteen other things, including the transmission of political ideologies under the cover of educational and ethical socialisation (Mattelart, A. 1979; Ferguson, B. 1984 and 1985). Many of the assumptions linked to such research were called into question by the media education movement, breaking with earlier 'discriminatory' approaches in the 1980s, but were then revived in the light of policy decisions to 'de-regulate' broadcasting at the end of the decade. Institutional change in broadcasting meant that the populist attack on behavioural and ideological 'effects' had to be qualified by critical discussion of the prospects for children's programming under less constrained market conditions than had prevailed hitherto. In this section I shall trace these developments briefly and outline the issues they have brought forth.

Reviewing the press response to the Department of Education and Science's 1983 report, *Popular TV and Schoolchildren* (reprinted in Lusted and Drummond 1985), the media educationalist David Lusted (1984) identified some of the recurrent ideological frameworks that have generated moral panics over children's television-viewing: the 'copycat', 'anaesthetic' and 'sex 'n' violence' theses. Each one functions differently. The 'copycat' thesis relates to long-held middle-class anxieties over working-class popular culture and the belief that certain messages and entertainment forms *activate* dangerous propensities: for instance, that television coverage of rioting causes youngsters to riot (see Tumber 1982) or that fictions of criminality cause juvenile delinquency (exemplified notoriously by William Belson's 1978 study). The 'anaesthetic' thesis, in contrast, reflects middle-class people's anxieties concerning their own children, the assumption being that watching television is *pacifying*. These behaviourist theses are mutually contradictory, of course: television is held to activate or pacify depending on the particular Pavlovian alarm bell being rung at the time. Both claims, in their contrasting ways, suppress complex questions of media representation and audience interpretation. The third ideological framework, the 'sex 'n' violence' thesis, propounded by Mary Whitehouse and her National Viewers and Listeners Association, now inscribed latently in a statutory body, the Broadcasting Standards Council, is founded more specifically on a puritanical view of representational morality *per se*. It is not entirely separable, however, from behaviourist theses which allege harmful effects of images on action.

All these ideological frameworks were variously invoked by sensational press stories about the findings of *Popular TV and Schoolchildren*. None of them was actually endorsed by the report itself, confused and internally contradictory though it was. The 'media education' movement, promoted by the British Film Institute in particular, seized upon the DES report and sought to articulate it against the dominant ideological frameworks. Lusted (1985) himself argued that the DES report was, in fact, consistent with recent media education's 'shift from a set of worries about television's effects to a set of questions about television's representation of the social world' (p. 11). And Richard Dyer

(1985), discussing the report as well, suggested that the key concept of 'representation' not only draws attention to textual politics: it 'should also make us think of the *audience*' (p. 45). Whatever popular television texts say, they speak to audience members who will make their own interpretations. In that sense, children are no less active viewers than adults.

Although television/audience research paradigms are not directly congruent with pedagogic questions, none the less there is a definite interaction between the active audience concept of media and cultural studies and the active learner of media education. There have been similar correspondences in earlier phases of media education: for instance, from a Leavisite perspective, teaching children to discriminate against homogenising and manipulative mass communications, or cultural critique from dominant ideology perspectives, both assuming that the modern media have negative effects that must be warded off. The turn away from these positions towards the active audience and popular pleasure has been pushed strenuously in the media educational writings of David Buckingham. Introducing a collection of observational studies on children and media in the classroom, Buckingham remarks:

> the 1980s have seen a renewed emphasis on the active role of media audiences. While in certain cases, this has been motivated by a form of populism – a desire to defend the preferences of 'ordinary viewers' at all costs – it has led to a widespread recognition of the diverse ways in which media texts may be used and understood.
>
> (1990: 10)

Searching out a 'new paradigm', Buckingham (1987b) has reviewed older ones: 'effects', 'uses and gratifications' and 'critical'. The third of these paradigms is of most significance for this discussion. It can be seen in the critique of the long-running magazine programme *Blue Peter*, by Buckingham's colleague at the London University Institute of Education, Bob Ferguson:

> The established universe of discourse of children's television may be characterised as Anglo-centric, often racist, sexist, royalist, pro-capitalist, ostensibly Christian and as generally arguing that the best way to deal with social problems is through benevolence . . . . [In programmes like *Blue Peter*] The

dominant discourse of children's television works to produce future citizens who are well socialised and the majority of child viewers ingest the discourse unquestioningly.

(1985: 48)

The polemical sweep with which the ideology of *Blue Peter* is summated here is one thing, but Ferguson's assertion, without any evidence of audience response, that it is *ingested unquestioningly* is highly problematic. Arguing against the implicit assumption of viewer passivity in Ferguson's position, Buckingham (1987b) contends that the active learner concept of cognitive psychology is better able to account for audience response. However, because it is confined to the micro-level (how individual children make sense), cognitive psychology is, therefore, less adequate than the semiological and sociological orientations of British media and cultural studies, according to Buckingham. A properly social conception of the learning and viewing subject is required.

Elsewhere, Buckingham (1989) argues a similar case against the American concept of 'television literacy'. This is an improvement on counterposing verbal literacy to television-viewing, but there are problems with applying linguistics to television, originally inspired by cine-semiotics. Although equally language-like, film and television are not languages, nor do they work in exactly the same significatory ways. Moreover, the conception of language deployed by US researchers is insufficiently dialogic. Quite apart from the Metzian delusion that a grammar of moving images can be theorised formally (see Monaco 1981), the fundamental fault with the analogy between verbal and film/televisual literacy is that children learn to speak and write as well as listen and read but they do not get to make television programmes. In spite of the widespread school-based practice of video production, children are normally placed in relation to television as consumers, though not as passive consumers. Buckingham (1989) observes, '[f]rom a "culturalist" perspective, the central paradox of mass communication is that in order to ensure its popularity it must allow for a wide diversity of different readings' (p. 19). He says we need a social theory of literacy, which draws upon reception aesthetics (see Holub 1985), dialogic linguistics (Bakhtin/Volosinov), and the social distribution of cultural powers and competences (Bourdieu).

The outstanding study, from broadly this kind of position, is that of the Australian researchers Bob Hodge and David Tripp, *Children and Television* (1986). They combined semiology, cognitive psychology and cultural ethnography with a precision and on a scale unmatched by any comparable research in Britain. Their three-year project, aided by four research assistants, involved 600 children and was funded by a Perth television station, apparently with no strings attached. Hodge and Tripp upset many deeply ingrained assumptions concerning children's television-viewing, most notably what they derive from watching cartoons. An episode of *Fangface* was analysed according to the techniques of structuralist narratology (Barthes 1966), but Hodge and Tripp avoid the 'semiotic trap' of inferring reading from purely textual analysis. The analysis was checked out and revised by what children from different age groups said about the programme. This overturned, for example, Hodge and Tripp's own presumption that the visual channel of meaning was always more important than the verbal channel. For children in the study, visual intelligibility was frequently triggered off verbally. Also, Hodge and Tripp demonstrate with considerable linguistic sophistication how cartoon-viewing helps young children develop from simple to complex grammatical structures, enhancing their verbal as well as audio-visual competence: for instance, by learning to understand cross-cutting parallel actions and the overall unfolding of the story. Hodge and Tripp comment:

> It is ironic that it is precisely the kind of programming that children have the greatest cognitive need for as they are approaching adolescence, that is most commonly subjected to criticism by lobbyists: cartoons and magazine programmes (studded with cartoons) for younger children and adult primetime series for older ones. The persistent popularity of such programme types with children, we would suggest, is a healthy sign, and not a danger signal, though that does not mean we believe that there could be no better programmes for children, or adults for that matter.
>
> (1986: 92)

Hodge and Tripp's work on 'modality' (reality/fantasy continua) indicates that most children at very young ages are capable of distinguishing fiction from non-fiction. Moreover, children's ability to grasp reality references in adult programming depends upon their stage of cognitive development: that which is unintelligible is edited out by the active mind of the child. So, according to Hodge and Tripp, it is mistaken to blame television for problems it does not create, such as schizophrenic conflation of fantasy with reality, or pathological retreats into the world of television, as in the famous case of the television-fixated boy, Garcia, which say more about the life circumstances of the child (isolation and neglect) than television's supposedly hypnotic influence.

Ironically perhaps, it is evidence of the positive attributes of children's television-viewing, running counter to wholesale denunciations of television as bad for kids, that puts the question of what kind of programming is provided for children so firmly on the agenda. The British Action for Children's Television (BAC TV) campaign begun in the late 1980s (Simpson 1989) and Maire Messenger Davies's book, *Television is Good for Your Kids* (1989), linked closely with BAC TV, take exactly this position. The campaign responded to two very important developments during the 1980s: toy-marketing through cartoon programmes, associated with the diminution of the American Federal Communication Commission's regulatory powers since 1984; and the British government's decision to de-regulate/re-regulate British commercial television in the late 1980s (leading to a legislative cycle completed at the end of 1990 with as yet uncertain consequences). These developments, plus the undermining of the BBC's finances, shifted issues dramatically. The polarisation of ideological demystification and popular television appreciation, exemplified by Buckingham's (1986) misleading assault on Len Masterman's 1985 book, *Teaching the Media* (see Masterman's reply 1986), obscured emerging issues of institutional change and 'quality'. To conclude this section, then, these matters are considered specifically with reference to the BBC's transmission of *Teenage Mutant Ninja/Hero Turtles* in 1990 and the urgency of re-engaging issues of qualitative judgement, issues not confined solely to children's television.

As BBC TV's own investigative documentary programme, *Public Eye*, put it in an edition entitled 'Toys and turtles' in December 1990, the flagship of British public service broadcasting had unwittingly plunged itself into an invidious position by screening the *Mutant Turtles* cartoon. The first five episodes of the cartoon were financed by the Los Angeles toy manufacturer, Playmates, in order to promote their products, the models and paraphanalia associated with what became a major children's cult, making huge profits for Playmates and its licensees. Although it did not show the first five episodes, the BBC was, nevertheless, complicit with covert advertising through entertainment, not for the first time (it had already televised *Thundercats*, also produced deliberately to sell toys, besides showing sponsored sporting events like the *Embassy World Snooker Championships*, which circumvents the prohibition against cigarette advertising on television). In the *Public Eye* programme, the BBC's defence, enunciated by the Head of Children's Programmes, Anna Home, and emphasised by the presenter, Peter Taylor, was that by renting the *Turtles* at £3,000 an episode it could thus make *The Chronicles of Narnia* at £400,000 per half-hour: actually in Taylor's *Guardian* article on the topic (10 December 1990) the figure quoted was £100,000, probably closer to the truth, yet still expensive children's programming. Peter Taylor's impassioned argument (BBC2, 14 December 1990) was twofold: first, drawing attention to the paradox that 'quality' television (*Narnia*) was made possible by the dubious cultural value of the *Turtles* cartoon and its commercial manipulation of children; second, to quote him:

> In the new world of multi-channeled de-regulated broadcasting programmes like these become even more attractive. What company in the business of maximising its profits would want to spend a fortune developing its own quality programmes when *Turtles* are cheap and ratings winners?

The connection between questions of 'quality' and 'de-regulation' is indeed important, though Taylor's argument is overstated and rooted in a seriously unexamined concept of quality. It is consistent with what John Mepham (1990) has identified as a traditional and no longer tenable public service notion, that some categories of programming are intrinsically of 'quality' whereas others are not, by definition.

British studies of popular television have tended to avoid evaluative judgement in reaction to these hierarchical assumptions whilst also implicitly judging, at the very least by virtue of the texts and audience contexts selected for analysis. For example, Rosalind Coward's (1990) discussion of *Turtles* stressed its 'postmodernist' and even 'subversive' qualities. According to Raymond Williams, there is no unitary standard of quality anyway: there are only standards, in the plural (1983a: 296). This would make possible the argument that the *Turtles* cartoon is good of its kind, but the criteria by which that can be said are complicated by the transience of audience approval (as a seven-year-old I know said in the summer of 1991, 'the *Turtles is passé*'). Where does such globalising American culture stand, for instance, in relation to the much-fêted yet distinctly untelevisual (in my opinion) English conservatism of *Narnia*, or in comparison with the underrated but boldly subversive *Maid Marion*, feminist and arguably dependent on a British viewing context to make sense? Are such questions, stated here very baldly, ruled out of court by the rejection of idealist aesthetics and paternalistic ideologies of quality?

Some commentators on broadcasting broke the silence concerning qualitative judgement that marked populist cultural thought during the 1980s (see Mulgan 1990). In particular, John Mepham (1990) has sketched out a set of judgemental principles which refuse both the terms of paternalist and free market ideologies. First, he insists on 'the Social Project' of cultural pluralism, '*a rule of diversity*' (p. 59). To shift the argument from 'quality' to 'diversity' is a characteristic move by critics of British government policies that rewrote the rules of the broadcasting game with little guarantee that different values and tastes would be respected. Mepham, however, goes further in proposing 'the Cultural Purpose' of providing '*usable stories*' and 'the Normative Framework . . . *an ethic of truth-telling*'. 'Excellence', according to these principles, should be demanded across the whole range of programming, not only in some minority sphere of 'quality'. Mepham suggests that people use television narrative fiction to make sense of themselves and their place in the world: for example, soap operas. He argues that sometimes such programmes tell the truth and sometimes they do not (the retrenchment of *EastEnders* in response to conservative criticism of its treatment of sexuality is cited as a case in point). Mepham's argument concerning 'truth' is not epistemologically naïve. There are many different kinds of truth, he says, and there are no certainties: 'The rule I am proposing is not that the quality of a story be assessed by whether or not it is true, but by whether or not it is governed by an ethic of truth-telling' (p. 69). According to Mepham, a 'quality' programme seeks to avoid 'the known forms and variety of mediocrity and falsehood' and increases the capacity for 'truth-telling in its audience' (pp. 70–1). These truth conditions would be difficult to decide upon, putting it mildly, but that is only to be expected in ethics and aesthetics. The reinsertion of aesthetic and ethical judgement into the debate is a vital rejoinder to the uncritical drift of cultural populism and its failure to dispute *laissez-faire* conceptions of consumer sovereignty and quality (Peacock *et al.* 1986), but it is not enough.

SWITCHING CHANNELS

To recapitulate, new revisionism emerged partly from the anomalies bequeathed by hegemony theory to cultural populism. By seeking to reconcile the dominant ideology thesis with the active audience a possible danger was always that the latter would eventually invert the former, which is to some extent what actually happened. The simple inversion of a binary logic – oppressive ideology/popular pleasure – can be traced back to the disabling schism between contemporary cultural studies and the political economy of culture (Hall 1980a; Jhally 1989).

As we have seen, John Fiske (1987b), outstripping Stuart Hall's qualified anti-economism, severed the 'cultural economy' entirely from the 'financial economy' in order to extol the achievement of really existing 'semiotic democracy', a position which suppresses questions of material inequality in the cultural field. Even the Peacock Committee (1986), appointed by the second Thatcher government to plot the 'de-regulation' of British broadcasting, quoted evidence to the effect that lower-income groups spend a greater proportion of their money on media goods but such expenditure rises *absolutely* with higher-income groups (see Golding 1990). And Graham Murdock (1990a) has pointed out that ownership of VCRs, for example, is correlated with income, rising with higher-income groups, contrary to the supposition that such technology is used more by lower-income groups. There is, then, a pronounced relation between material inequality and cultural inequality in the most basic sense of financial capacity to consume. New revisionists neglected this rather elementary relationship, being solely concerned with interpretation of textual and audience meanings during a period of dramatic institutional transformation in national and international broadcasting, conducted by politicians and business interests in ways that had potentially inegalitarian consequences.

Cultural populism meets up not only with *laissez-faire* economics but also, and probably just as unwittingly, with technological determinism around the study of media consumption and 'the new technologies' in isolation from economic analysis of communications and cultural industries. Studying the social use of VCRs, multi-channel cable and satellite television, music centres and recording decks, home computers and so on, without due consideration of the economic and political forces shaping product innovation, is unnecessarily one-dimensional. The consumption and production moments of cultural circulation and their interaction are thus fatally separated.

David Morley (1991), responding to criticisms of the new revisionism, which to some extent can be made of his own work, has suggested that the so-called 'micro' level of analysis (small-scale studies of cultural consumption) should be re-articulated with 'macro' analysis (large-scale studies of, say, globalising cultural production and circulation). But, similarly to Ien Ang (1990b), Morley insists on keeping the interpretation of cultural consumption always firmly at the centre of the analytical picture. Although Morley's position is defensible in many respects, it is difficult to see quite how an account of relevant economic dynamics can be built up satisfactorily from such an essentially hermeneutic perspective. The dynamics operating at the 'macro' level are not only subjectively 'meaningful' as and when they impinge upon cultural consumers: they are fundamentally about the disposition of material resources, corporate decision-making and capital investment. It is necessary, then, to take an historical and economically informed view of how television technologies become institutionalised in consumption processes if these complex and obscure dynamics are to be grasped at all.

Some of the new technologies are not, in fact, all that new: cable has been around since the 1930s and satellite since the 1960s. These delivery systems have been greatly refined since their inception, and their domestic usability adapted to facilitate a new cycle of commodity circulation and capital accumulation in the communications and cultural industries. In the early 1970s, Raymond Williams speculated that such technologies, integrated together, could produce 'locally based yet internationally extended television systems' (1974: 151), breaking with the nationalistic orientation of institutions like the BBC. Participatory democracy and mutual understanding might thus be improved, bringing about a further stage of 'the long revolution'. Yet, even then, Williams was pessimistic. He anticipated 'para-national corporations' controlling technological change, thereby over-riding democratic institutions and 'a short and successful counter-revolution . . . under the cover of talk about choice and competition' (p. 151).

Ten years later, Nicholas Garnham could observe Williams's gloomy prognosis coming closer to fruition. He was able, however, to give it a firmer grounding in political economy: 'This proliferation of potential channels is not a response to consumer demand but the result both of the search of multi-national hardware manufacturers for new markets, and of the industrial and financial strategies of various governments' (1984: 2). The goal of transnational media conglomerates to accumulate capital and governmental plans to switch from manufacturing-based to information-based economies both became centred to a significant degree on the television set. Other economic determinations include the need to open up fresh outlets for investment capital as the Third World debt crisis mounted and, specifically in Britain, the lobbying of advertising agencies for more plentiful means and lower rates to reach the consumer (O'Malley 1988).

Television viewers had been getting their pleasures on the cheap. They could be encouraged to pay a great deal more. The discrediting of the BBC licence fee as a 'poll tax', its mooted replacement by advertising (or more probably discretionary subscription), new pay-TV services, apparently free yet in reality consumer-funded advertising services, are all devices for extracting money from viewers, in addition to selling them the equipment. One likelihood is that, with the escalating price of watching television, the low-paid, the unemployed and many old-aged pensioners would be excluded from the choice of programming that better-off working-class people are generally most inclined to purchase. There are contradictions and paradoxes in such developments which are problematic for media capital too, as the early operators of cable and satellite television discovered in Britain.

Indifference to these matters in some areas of media study is far from novel: it also occurred when the dominant ideology thesis ruled the roost. Several years ago, Dallas Smythe (1977) put his finger on this 'blind spot' concerning political economy. He argued, against neo-Marxist ideologism, that the most important cultural commodity in advertising-funded media is not the message, the meaning of the soap opera or the news story, but the *audience*. Capitalist media organisations sell audiences to advertisers and, moreover, audiences themselves *work* to accomplish their own subjection to exploitative consumption and production relations (a very different inflection of the 'active audience' from that of new revisionism). They give up their leisure time *freely* for these purposes, but they have to be taught to do so. Smythe quotes the publisher's blurb for a book entitled *How Children Learn to Buy*:

> As the authors see it, consumption is a perfectly legitimate and unavoidable activity for children. Consequently they reject a strategy directed at protecting kids from marketing stimuli. What is necessary, then, is to acknowledge that children are going to watch television commercials and to prepare them to be selective consumers.
>
> (1977: 13)

Dallas Smythe's position is usually seen in Britain as crudely economistic.[7] His Canadian antipathy to US cultural imperialism (Smythe 1981) certainly pulls the argument towards reductionism. Yet such a no-nonsense viewpoint still breathes fresh air into the claustrophobic atmosphere of exclusively hermeneutic circles. It may, however, be considered incommensurate with the interpretive concerns of contemporary cultural studies: it is not about meaning, it is about political economy. That has something going for it, but not much if we are remotely interested in research that might contribute to democratic reform. The recourse to methodological pluralism can serve as a diversion here, especially when the connection between academic knowledge and pressing issues of public policy are at stake. The major problem with exclusively hermeneutic study of television is its incapacity to engage critically with such issues. This was particularly noticeable in the comparative failure of new revisionists to intervene constructively in British broadcasting debates of the 1980s.

As several policy-orientated theorists have argued, the cultural commodity is neither purely symbolic nor purely economic. In contrast to Smythe, the French sociologist Bernard Miège (1979) theorises the cultural commodity as complex and variable in form, not reducible to the commodification of audiences for sale to advertisers, however important that may be. And Pierre Bourdieu (1971) draws attention to the double value of cultural commodities as 'both merchandise and meaning' (p. 164). From the perspective on communications and culture of British political economy, Nicholas Garnham (1979 and 1987) has done most to unravel the cultural commodity's complexity, how it compares with and differs from other commodities that are not principally cultural but functional. Garnham is very careful not to reduce meaning to merchandise. He distinguishes between the use value of the cultural commodity and its exchange value in a manner similar to Terry Lovell's (1980) argument that the realisation of exchange value depends on supplying genuine use value. Cultural commodities are time-consuming bearers of meaning, particularly narrative forms, that are appropriated and used actively in ways capital must enable in order to ensure profitability. Furthermore, it is exceptionally difficult to predict the popular appeal of a cultural commodity. Hence, communications and cultural industries develop a repertoire of products to reduce risk, so that 'hits' pay for 'misses'. Novelty has to be constantly promoted because cultural commodities are not typically used up during consumption. You can eat a loaf of bread only once but you can watch a video or listen to a record several times. It is commercially imperative, therefore, to produce a steady flow of new attractions to distract from the lingering pleasures of older ones.

Significantly, political economists of communications and culture were much more critical of Conservative government broadcasting policies in the 1980s than were commentators associated with contemporary cultural studies. For example, Garnham (1983) was attacked for defending public service against free market manoeuvres by Ian Connell (1983), formerly of the Birmingham Centre. Before outlining their alternative positions, a brief résumé of the policy context is in order. During the 1980s, successive inquiries, reports, legislative proposals and enactments, initiated by New Right politics, sought to dispense with, or at least drastically reduce, public service regulation of the broadcasting system, to stimulate investment and to introduce market-based pricing mechanisms in the delivery of television (see Collins, R. *et al.* 1988, on the peculiarities of television economics that made this so difficult to accomplish). The first phase, in the early 1980s, associated with the Cabinet's Information Technology Advisory Panel (ITAP) and the Hunt Report on cable, envisaged the transition to an information-based economy on the back of entertainment-led cable services, financed entirely by private enterprise. That such policies and subsequent ones were poorly thought out and unsuccessful in their own terms due to consumer intransigence and delayed profitability need not detain us here. More to the point, for this discussion, are the issues raised concerning the fate of public service broadcasting in the much-hyped imminent cornucopia of multi-channel television, and whether or not diversity and accessibility would be enhanced or diminished.

Garnham (1983) proposed that the ideal of public service broadcasting should be defended, although there was much to criticise in its historical record, particularly paternalism and unaccountability. Connell (1983) countered by declaring this an idealist argument that missed the progressive potential of more open market arrangements for independent production companies and television viewers. Garnham, argued Connell, had forgotten the real history in which the advent of commercial television, during the 1950s, brought about a popularly responsive programming absent under the preceding BBC monopoly (see Crook 1986). Commenting on Connell's optimistic scenario, Carl Gardner (1984) observed that the British system had remained wholly public service in regulatory form after the introduction of commercial television alongside the BBC. It was erroneous simply to infer from the past performance of publicly regulated commercial services what de-regulated broadcasting might actually be like in the future. The difference between Garnham and Connell, however, is not only to do with problems of historical inference but to do with quite different conceptions of social empowerment in relation to television. Connell cited the work on soap-opera audiences of Dorothy Hobson to support his claim concerning the popular usability of commercial television, whereas Garnham emphasised broadcasting's role in the public sphere of information and democratic debate. They differed according to the relative weight to be placed on the social organisation of cultural production (Garnham) and the personal practice of cultural consumption (Connell). Garnham under-played the active audience and Connell overplayed it.

Although not fixed once and for all either conceptually or institutionally, public service broadcasting has rested hitherto upon two fundamental principles: guaranteed *diversity* and universal *accessibility* (Murdock 1990a and b). Programme diversity has several aspects, including range of genres (investigative documentaries to soap operas) and, increasingly, range of production sources (greatly expanded by Channel Four's transmission of independently made programmes in the 1980s). Diversity also refers to the expression of different points of view, especially political. Traditionally, this was confined to the parliamentary spectrum of politics, but in the 1980s, again with Channel Four leading the way, it was extended, albeit mainly on the margins, to include sexual politics, ethnic and racial identities. Accessibility is linked to universality, at least in terms of reception. Under public service arrangements, licence fee-payers have had the right to receive whatever was on offer. Hence, the BBC and the IBA would build transmission facilities to reach even very low-populated areas.

Free marketeers claim that diversity of provision can be improved but not as a public and universal right. Thus, viewers must choose whether or not they want to buy new reception devices, such as satellite dishes, and subscribe in order to descramble channels and to receive cable services. On the principle of accessibility there is no real dispute: free market operations are not, by definition, obliged to provide it universally (however, various obligations qualifying the market mechanism are written into publicly allocated franchises, otherwise de-regulation would come as too sudden a shock to the system). The dispute, from the perspective of privatisation, is over the actuality, not the principle, of diversity. From the perspective of public service, diversity is best secured by universal accessibility through tax-paying, either the old licence fee or, in future, from general taxation. As we actually move from one system to the other, from mainly public to private regulation, the television viewer is redefined from a *citizen* with guaranteed universal rights to a *consumer* capable (or not) of buying what might (or might not) be a more diverse range of programming.

Those who wish to retain public service on broadly universalistic grounds, although no longer exclusively, argue their case on this question of democratic citizenship and broadcasting. As Peter Golding (1990) insists, 'communicative competence and action, and the resources required to exercise them, are requisites for citizenship' (p. 99). The pro-public service case has been expressed most elegantly by Paddy Scannell (1989 and 1990). Scannell (1989) contends that 'communicative entitlement' is a necessary condition of democratic citizenship in a modern complex society. He also contrasts his own position explicitly with neo-Gramscian hegemony theory and its oscillation between the poles of the dominant ideology thesis and the new revisionism. According to Scannell, Stuart Hall's (1977) conception of the 'ideological effect' generated much too predictable accounts of how mainstream broadcasting reproduced dominant maps of meaning and social relations. On the other pole, Scannell also refuses populist complicity with Peacock's (1986) consistently *laissez-faire* redefinition of 'broadcasting as a private commodity rather than a public good' (Scannell 1989: 139), exemplified here by what some have considered to be Ian Connell's left-Thatcherite position.

By reconstructing the history of public service broadcasting, Scannell seeks to demonstrate its unfinished contribution to political and cultural democracy. Broadcasting produced a new kind of public in Britain, from the 1920s onwards, 'a general public', with routinely informed access to the issues of the day and regularly available entertainment forms which celebrate 'the pleasures of ordinariness' (p. 142). It is hard to imagine what life was like before broadcasting democratised 'the universe of discourse', intersecting with and restructuring the temporal rhythms of everyday life (Scannell 1988). This profound development occurred under public service arrangements in Britain, but it does not necessarily follow that they should persist for nostalgic reasons, or that in other countries the same was not accomplished by other arrangements. Scannell himself is not uncritical of British broadcasting's past record, especially its limited conception of democracy, deriving from the 1918 Representation of the People Act. In that sense, it is the product of a state system in which democratic rights are not entirely modern or sufficiently representative of socio-cultural plurality, a question that goes beyond broadcasting policies and structures as such. Public service broadcasting, according to Scannell, could never have achieved Jurgen Habermas's unattainable ideal of perfect 'communicative rationality'. More realistically, however, it has enhanced what Scannell calls 'reasonableness', and still remains a better prospect for deepening participatory conduct of public life than the dubious democracy of consumer sovereignty in the marketplace heralded by born-again free marketeers during the 1980s.

The defence of public service broadcasting, however well it is done on paper by Scannell and others, is arguably forced into a conservative position, in the sense of preserving existing structures against the winds of change. It may also seem futile to resist inexorable technological and economic forces bringing about transformations that are already, in fact, upon us. John Keane (1991), although an admirer of Scannell's defence, suggests that 'the contemporary case for public service media is trapped in a profound legitimation problem'. He identifies three weaknesses of the critique of de-regulation: first, 'neglect of the self-contradictory and self-paralysing tendencies of market-based communications'; second, 'insufficient attention . . . to the growth of state censorship'; third, 'unconvincing attempt to justify publicly the public service model against its enemies' (p. 116). Keane's solution is not to turn the clock back but to formulate a whole new model of democratic communications, inspired by Raymond Williams's (1962) wish to detach 'the idea of public service' from 'the idea of public monopoly'. Too easily, perhaps, defending public service becomes, in practice, defending the BBC instead of making bold proposals for 'new kinds of institution', as Williams recommended. Keane, a political scientist, is not first and foremost concerned with broadcasting, yet he accepts the argument that broadcasting is intimately bound up with politics and citizenship rights. Keane, following Williams, proposes a radical democratic rethink, a counter-factual modelling, which is unashamedly Utopian: 'What would a redefined, broadened and more àccessible public service model look like in practice?' (p. 124). It would depend on a completely new conception of citizenship, certainly as far as Britain is concerned, involving freedom of information, displacement of state sovereignty, essentially constitutional imperatives. That would render possible 'the development of a dense network or "heterarchy" of communications media which are controlled *neither by the state nor by commercial markets*' (p. 158). Keane's proposal is quite unrealistic, of course, and not entirely original. Many would find it utterly implausible. But, then again, who anticipated, fifteen or twenty years ago, that good old British public service broadcasting would suffer the hammering it has received in order to usher in Alan Peacock's (1986) equally implausible ideal of a perfectly competitive broadcasting market founded on the myth of sovereign consumption?

NOTES

1 Two consecutive BFI Summer schools were devoted to popular television in the early 1980s: 'TV fictions' (1981) and 'Who does television think you are?' (1982). From about this period the BFI archive placed greater stress on television acquisitions (Madden 1981); and its education department, through Easter schools, teaching materials etc., stepped up its commitment to the study of popular television. The BFI also organised 'One Day in the Life of Television' (1 Nov. 1st 1988), when all transmissions received in Britain were recorded for posterity and people were asked to fill in diary entries on their viewing that day, an event inspired by Mass Observation.

2 See Greg Philo (1990) for an up-date on television and industrial conflict, which takes a sceptical view of the ideological indeterminacy which characterises more fashionable strands of communication, cultural and media studies.

3 See David Morley (1989) for a summary of the criticisms, including the inapplicability of the 'preferred reading' to fiction programmes, and the reduction of cognitive understanding to ideological interpretation by the encoding/decoding model.

4 In the 1986 BFI/Channel Four series *Open the Box*, Morley described the television remote control as functioning for many male heads of household like 'a medieval symbol of authority' (ep. 1, 'Part of the furniture').

5 See Ann Gray's *Video Playtime – the Gendering of a Leisure Technology* (1992) for the details of her research and, also, Gray (1987b) on problems of populism and television audience research.

6 The study of women's reading of romance fiction has been one of the most fiercely debated and productive topics in feminist cultural studies. In addition to Modleski (1984) and Radway (1987), see Deborah Philips (1990).

7 Graham Murdock (1978) had a famous debate with Smythe on political economy and communications analysis, in which Murdock questioned the reduction of commercial media operations to what are, none the less, key economic dynamics. Smythe's weakness may, therefore, be that of having overstated a powerful insight. See Smythe's reply (1978) and Bill Livant's commentary (1979).

Part III

Contemporary issues

Chapter 5

Dilemmas of culture and politics

Before considering how to move beyond the self-imposed limitations of latter-day cultural populism, already signalled in the concluding section of the last chapter, I should like to summarise the main critical themes of this book. First, *an uncritical populist drift in contemporary cultural studies* has been identified. The case is stated polemically, accentuating discernible trends in order to highlight consequential dilemmas of culture and politics. That ordinary people use the symbolic resources available to them under present conditions for meaningful activity is both manifest and endlessly elaborated upon by the new revisionism. Thus, emancipatory projects to liberate people from their alleged entrapment, whether they know they are entrapped or not, are called into question by this fundamental insight. Economic exploitation, racism, gender and sexual oppression, to name but a few, exist, but the exploited, estranged and oppressed cope, and, furthermore, if such writers as John Fiske and Paul Willis are to be believed, they cope very well indeed, making valid sense of the world and obtaining grateful pleasure from what they receive. Apparently, there is so much action in the micro-politics of everyday life that the Utopian promises of a better future, which were once so enticing for critics of popular culture, have lost all credibility.

Second, *cultural populism's solidarity with ordinary people has become increasingly sentimental.* Retreating from contest with dominant powers in the cultural field, populists evince solidarity with ordinary people's capacity to win space from below. On several occasions in the course of this book, however, I have drawn attention to a disingenuous selectivity in populist cultural research, a characteristic veering away from disconfirming instances, instances when 'the people' do not quite measure up to sentimental expectations. In this chapter, I shall consider some disconfirming instances in order to pinpoint certain dilemmas thus produced and simultaneously evaded: the popularity of the British tabloid newspaper, the *Sun*; the issue of pornography and sexual violence; and the tension between British Muslims and the liberal intelligentsia around the Rushdie affair.

Third, *the taken-for-granted schism between micro-processes of meaning and macro-processes of political economy is one of the main reasons for cultural populism's limitations at the explanatory level.* The emphasis on text/context relations, mediated exclusively by audience activity and popular pleasure, fails to account adequately for the material conditions of culture and hence the complex dialectics of liberation and control. In spite of the acuity of much of this work in communication, cultural and media studies, none the less, it represents a drastic narrowing of vision. However active the reader, there still remains the question of what is read. To say so, in whatever manner one feels obliged, is not necessarily to retreat into textual objectivism. Yet, it must be said, the materiality of the text is not only to do with its activation in use but depends on its prior existence: it is materially produced, it is made available, it is offered for popular appropriation. Some texts get made and some do not; some stories are told and some are not. This is elementary and of necessity draws attention to the controlling institutions of cultural production and the conditions under which meaningful artefacts are circulated in the world.

Fourth, *grounds for criticism were deconstructed in response to 'the postmodern condition'* (or, slightly more colloquial but not much, 'New Times'). The connection between postmodernism and the new revisionism has only been made implicitly so far. In the next and concluding chapter, this connection is made explicit and its implications pursued in some detail. Jean-François Lyotard's (1984) announcement of the collapse of 'grand narratives', especially that of Marxism but associated with Enlightenment ideas of 'progress' generally, is echoed by recent cultural populism. It is unclear, however, to what extent this sudden loss of conviction in rational grounds for criticising and changing the world represents the experience of ordinary people. As I have already suggested, the uncritical drift in the field of study derives largely from an inversion of hyper-criticism, exemplified by the dominant ideology thesis in relation to the modern media and popular culture. Linked to this inversion is the fashionable procedure, sometimes given a Derridean imprimatur, of deconstructing cherished radical assumptions by, ostensibly, out-radicalising them. Such a mutating (mute? mutilating?) of intellectual practice probably says more about the competitive academy in the postmodern era than it does about the clash of contending forces in the world at large, which is another story.

In short, the study of culture is nothing if it is not about values. A disenchanted, anti-moralistic, anti-judgemental stance constructed in opposition to cultural and political zealotry only takes you so far. The posture may be cool, detached and irreverent but it is not value-free. New revisionism is rooted in populist sentiments of an increasingly slippery kind. And it is striking how a pact has been made, overtly or covertly, with economic liberalism, rediscovering the virtues of the market as a cultural provider and incitement to pleasure. Curiously, much less interest has been shown in political liberalism, by which I mean the discourse of rights, citizenship and democracy. Hyper-critics often argued, and some still do, that such values are illusory in practice, that they are only 'bourgeois freedoms'. And, indeed the gulf between formal and substantive rights is painfully obvious when the actual conditions of people at the subordinate echelons and on the margins of capitalist social relations are considered. However, the liberalisation of Marxism, which was one of the main planks of hyper-criticism, is relevant here:

> If liberalism's central failure is to see markets as 'powerless' mechanisms of coordination and, thus, to neglect the distorting nature of economic power in relation to democracy, Marxism's central failure is the reduction of political power to economic power and, thus, the neglect of the dangers of centralized political power and the problems of political accountability.
>
> (Held 1989: 166)

Adapting Jurgen Habermas's (1989) thirty-year-old thesis, *The Structural Transformation of the Public Sphere* (originally published in 1962), for present purposes: European bourgeois men secured liberties for themselves during the eighteenth and nineteenth centuries by constructing a 'public sphere' of information and debate.[1] To extend such liberties to others in terms of class, gender and race has been an enduring struggle and never with a fully egalitarian result anywhere for complex historical and structural reasons. To reconcile liberty and equality is, needless to say, a difficult matter. Some believe it is becoming harder, that the public sphere is shrinking rather than expanding, and this has much to do with the resurgence of economic liberalism. In the last chapter, with the intention of problematising our understanding of 'popular television', that was discussed with reference to the 'de-regulation' of broadcasting. When commercial imperatives gain the upper hand, as Nicholas Garnham (1990) observes, '[p]ublic communication is transformed into the politics of consumerism' (p. 111). We have seen how contemporary cultural studies, responding to 'New Times', became preoccupied with 'the politics of consumerism', illustrated particularly by the trajectory of youth subcultural analysis, charting what was once a neglected and hitherto downgraded terrain but one which has since become hugely over-occupied. The consequent evacuation by some of an older terrain, a terrain which requires re-occupying, that of critical analysis of 'public communication' (Ferguson, M. 1990), is the subject matter of this chapter. By means of three brief case studies of popular culture and politics, I aim to open up some urgent contemporary issues that exceed the limits of new revisionism.

SUN-SETTING

The problem: how does cultural populism account for the *Sun*? This is not a problem for anti-populism. The term 'populist' itself, in left-liberal discourses, frequently denotes the cultivation of popular ignorance and prejudice by the *Sun* and similar tabloids like the *Star*, the *Sport* and even the generally Labour-supporting *Mirror*. However, none of these rival papers has achieved quite such a successful combination of entertainment value and political suasion as the fun-loving, loony-left-bashing *Sun*. They are either insufficiently entertaining or less politically daring. The conventional wisdom of many liberals and leftists is that *Sun*-readers are 'indoctrinated' by the rabid reaction of Britain's largest circulation daily. Such intellectual common sense has difficulties responding to the routine defence of the *Sun*, that it gives readers what they want and, anyway, nobody forces them to buy the paper. The right-wing skewing of the British press, concentration of ownership and control, and market obstacles to a radical popular press are usually invoked but they do not in themselves account for the peculiar appeal of the *Sun*. From a populist perspective, the recourse to 'indoctrination' or, demotically, the 'stupidity' of *Sun*-readers is inadequate. The popular appropriation of the *Sun* has not, however, been celebrated by academic cultural analysts. With the partial exception of Mark Pursehouse's (1987) encoding/decoding analysis (considered later in this section), there is no fully fledged new revisionist appreciation of *Sun*-reading – as yet. The *Sun* remains a scandalous object and a problematic case for latter-day cultural populism. As Andy Medhurst (1989) observed on the twentieth anniversary of its acquisition by Rupert Murdoch, '[t]he *Sun* destroys the assumption that if something is popular it must be ideologically sound' (p. 41).

Some journalistic commentators have teased progressive sensibilities on this intractable problem of the *Sun*'s popularity, especially around the publication in 1990 of Peter Chippindale and Chris Horrie's book, *Stick It Up Your Punter! – the Rise and Fall of the Sun*, which traced the history of its production and demonised the editor, Kelvin MacKenzie, but did not try very hard to account for the *Sun*'s appeal from the point of view of the reader. Instead, Chippindale and Horrie were content to note signs of decline following Elton John's libel action, false allegations concerning Liverpool football fans crushed at Hillsborough, and governmental warnings of legislative control if the *Sun* and its ilk did not clean up their act. Reviewing *Stick It Up Your Punter!*, Julie Burchill defended the *Sun* against 'socialist puritanism', including Chippindale and Horrie's quite restrained criticisms: 'I probably wouldn't side with the *Sun* if I didn't find its detractors so morally duplicitous. Many of the attacks on it, as on Thatcherism, are veiled attacks on the English working class, which may be vulgar and crude but has a real lust for life' (1990: 36). In a *Guardian* review (12 November 1990), Roy Greenslade, ex-*Sun* journalist and then current editor of the *Daily Mirror*, also chided readers of 'the world's worst' (MacKenzie's nickname for the left-liberal *Guardian*). For communications analysis, such knock-about-stuff provides food for thought and raises the question of how a principled critique of the *Sun* might be mounted which is also sensitive to audience activity and popular pleasure, the basic themes of cultural populism. To explore this question, I want to consider how the *Sun* is so popular and why. My aim is not to produce a comprehensive explanation but rather to formulate the problem in such a way that the analytical tensions mapped out already become sharply focused.

From a political economy perspective, the *Sun* and its lucrative role in the 'Murdoch empire' of transnational press and television ownership is one of the quintessential instances of how the capitalist media operate. It is significant that James Curran's account of 'The press in the age of conglomerates' (Curran and Seaton, fourth edition 1991) pays special attention to the history of the *Sun* and News Corporation's other British national newspapers – *The Times* and *Sunday Times, News of the World* and *Today* – with a joint circulation approaching 12 million. The facts are well known but worth recalling. Concentration of ownership and control by three major proprietors increased to 75 per cent of national daily and 83 per cent of national Sunday circulation by the mid-1980s (Curran and Seaton, third edition 1988). These proportions dropped slightly to 73 per cent and 81 per cent respectively in 1988, which does not substantially alter the basic post-Second World War trend towards greater concentration. Nor did the introduction of computerised type-setting have the dispersal effect that some commentators predicted. The press baron had returned with a vengeance: the late Robert Maxwell (Maxwell Communications and the Mirror Group) vying with Murdoch for chief demon of the liberal-left intelligentsia in this respect, followed by the lower profile David Stevens (United Newspapers). The argument that such concentration restricts the diversity of the press is borne out by the overwhelming preponderance of right-wing newspapers, partly diluted by Maxwell's market-wise and residual right-wing Labourism. None of this, of course, was new in the 1980s. Press barons had used newspapers for their own personal aggrandisement and for political influence before. The point is, however, that extreme concentration plus proprietorial interference had worsened, reducing the modest editorial liberalisation of the 1960s. The case of the *Sun* exemplifies and accentuates it.

In 1964 the TUC sold its share in the *Daily Herald* to International Press Corporation. The *Herald* had been the labour movement's paper but, due to falling advertising revenue, as a result of its ageing working-class readership, it had ceased to be commercially viable, albeit still retaining a circulation of over a million. IPC made a short-lived attempt to turn it into a middle-market paper, aiming to combine a radical working-class readership with the progressive middle class, fatefully titling it the *Sun*. This did not work: it had already been tried to some extent by the *Herald* and was to be tried again, with terrible confusion and even more disastrous results, by the *News on Sunday* in 1987. IPC owned the market-leading tabloid, the *Daily Mirror*, so there seemed little point in competing directly with that: which is exactly what Murdoch decided to do so successfully when he bought the ailing *Sun* at a knock-down price in 1969. Its first editor under the new ownership, Larry Lamb, turned the *Sun* towards lewd entertainment and away from anti-Establishment news values by, for instance, introducing the topless Page Three Girl and muting its support for the Labour Party. In 1974, *Sun*-readers were advised to vote Conservative for the first time, though half of them still voted Labour. And, in 1978, the *Sun* surpassed the *Mirror*'s circulation shortly before Margaret Thatcher formed her first government. She had been attending *Sun* editorial meetings at this time. The fierce economics of the press, the rise of the New Right and the disorganisation and political realignment of sections of the working class, especially the 'C2s', fused together to produce the brash, Thatcherite daily which became a byword for the erosion of journalistic standards. Moreover, by the end of the 1980s, Murdoch had broken the resistance of the print unions with the dash to Wapping and the introduction of new printing technologies. Thus, the days of hot metal passed along with a tradition of radical popular journalism in Britain. There is little doubt that the *Sun* spearheaded the British press's contribution to the right-wing cultural and political revolution of the 1980s.

Discussing the role of the British press as a whole at the end of the Thatcher era, James Curran concluded in an austere fashion quite inimical to the pleasure politics of latter-day cultural populism:

> By contributing to the disorganization of oppositional forces in Britain the press helped to stabilise the social order . . . [endorsing] the principal tenets of capitalism – private enterprise, profit, the 'free market', and the rights of property ownership . . . . [It] promoted national identification at the expense of class solidarity. The press also reinforced political and social norms by mobilizing public indignation against a succession of public enemies . . . . The press also built support for the social system in less direct and obvious ways . . . . By

regularly reporting political and economic news as dis-
connected events, it encouraged acceptance of the economic
and social structure as natural – the way things are. Embedded
in its entertainment features also were values and assumptions
that were not as apolitical as they appeared to be at first sight.
Its expanding consumer sections concerned with television,
records, tapes, CDs, books, travel, motoring, fashion, health,
homes, bingo, and personal finance tacitly promoted the
seductive view that consumption is a way of expressing
individuality and of participating in a 'real world' that
transcends hierarchies of power.

(Curran and Seaton 1991: 125–6)

Implicit here is a view of cultural power linked not only to the
representation of politics but also to the relentless promotion of
popular consumerism, perhaps uncomfortably reminiscent of the
Frankfurt School's mass culture critique. Quite differently,
however, Curran's argument is substantiated by empirical study of
British media and society historically. It is not founded upon an a
priori and elitist assumption concerning the manipulation of 'the
masses'. In an article with Colin Sparks, Curran concedes a great
deal to the populist sentiments of the new revisionism.
Nevertheless, Curran and Sparks (1991) identify some of the key
limitations of its 'cultural relativism'. They insist that textual
polysemy is not limitless; that popular choice of reading is limited
by editorial exclusions of, for example, serious news from tabloid
papers; and that 'understanding' should not be confused with
'interpretation', as cultural populists tend to do. At the root of
these criticisms is the assumption that a notion of ideological
domination in some form, however qualified by recognition of
audience activity and popular pleasure, remains indispensable
and, at least at the textual level, discernible.

The concept of ideology as imbricated by the inegalitarian
power structures of capitalist society distinguishes a radical
critique from a liberal one. But, there is considerable room for
agreement on the typically liberal complaints concerning routine
inaccuracy, invasion of privacy (particularly of those not rich
enough or powerful enough to defend themselves), coarsening of
public sensibilities and proprietorial interference with editorial
decision-making, monopolisation and questionable business
practices. It is unnecessary to rehearse the usual catalogue of

charges that can be made against the *Sun* – and other papers – on such counts (see Chippindale and Horrie 1990, for chapter and verse). It is worth pausing, though, for a moment on these matters before addressing the ideological question: there are differences.

For instance, John Pauley (1988) has sought to puncture liberal myths held by American critics of Murdoch. He suggests that Murdoch's 'interference', his legendary 'hands-on' approach to management, his manifest deviation from the proprietorial norm, conveniently legitimates the otherwise paper-thin professional ideology that editorial freedoms are sacrosanct under liberal market conditions. Pauley also disputes the absolute separation of 'entertainment' from 'information' in official journalistic discourse. The Murdoch press's habitual transgression of the indistinct boundary between them reveals the fictionality of all news narrative, thereby subverting belief in factual truth, according to Pauley.

Liberal assumptions are also punctured by Murdoch's skilled circumvention of cross-media ownership prohibitions and his ability to delay the exercise of legal sanctions. In Britain, he has been given a comparatively free hand when it comes to anti-monopoly legislation: for instance, the acquisition of Times Newspapers in 1981 and Sky's takeover of British Satellite Broadcasting in 1990. For more radical critics than those only committed to all-too-frequently disappointed defence of the liberal principles of a 'free press', in News Corporation's financial problems, accumulating from debt-financed expansion insufficiently offset by alleged insider-trading and tax-avoidance,[2] there is some confirmation of an unfashionable assumption that even the boldest of entrepreneurs are not absolved from the auto-destructive tendencies of capitalism.

Returning specifically to the *Sun*: whatever the *Sun* does, it is done ideologically. The analysis of ideology, however, is not reducible to the study of ownership and control. The aim of capital is to make a profit: and the *Sun* has done that handsomely for News Corporation, partly subsidising Murdoch's loss-making satellite television. It is the only British national newspaper profitable on sales alone. Advertising revenue is more important for the 'quality' press than for 'popular' papers like the *Sun*, a significant index of inequalities of wealth in addition to those of power and knowledge. The capitalist organisation of the press permits the expression of critical views if they sell and attract advertisers: in that precise sense, it is ideologically 'neutral'. Press ideology, then, does not simply reflect the directly political interests of capitalism as a whole. Rather, the capitalist organisation of cultural production sets variable limits and enables possibilities that are articulated through a very complex set of mediations to power structures not solely reducible to the capital/labour relation on the grand scale. Although the *Sun* has a notable anti-union record, its racism and sexism have incensed critics probably most. A critique of *Sun* ideology would need to explore racist and sexist ingredients in, to use Stuart Hall's (1988a) term again, an 'authoritarian populist' mix. This stress on the systematic articulation of ideology to power in its multiplicity is quite different from the typical liberal usage of 'ideology' as always consciously held yet probably erroneous beliefs, as in 'Marxist ideology'.

The Althusserian conception of ideology as all-pervasive, as the unconscious mechanism of subjectivity, as 'universal' (Althusser 1970), and only intelligible to theoretical science, which at one time hypnotised radical critics, is no longer a convincing alternative to superficial liberal or economistic Marxist concepts. Althusserianism's once imperiously scientific logic is preserved residually, however, in post-Marxist theories of discursivity, which provide no basis for adjudicating truth claims at all. Conversely, from a realist position in epistemology, and in more classical usage, ideology retains utility as a critical concept (Lovell 1980), referring to systematically distorted ideas motivated by oppressive power. At the extreme, this includes lying. It is perfectly reasonable to criticise the *Sun* for telling lies, no doubt a banal point to make, but a point intended deliberately to offend against theoretical sophistry in contemporary cultural studies. If we cannot say the *Sun* has told lies on behalf of oppressive power then we are in trouble.

Ideology is not only about lying nor is ideological critique confined to demystification (see Eagleton 1991 for a survey of the many and varied uses to which 'ideology' has been put). There is also the routine exclusion and marginalisation of dissenting opinion. In the British press, as Mark Hollingsworth (1986) observes, 'radicals and dissenters . . . are stigmatised as irrational and unrepresentative . . . . Their alternative explanations of political and social realities are reported in terms of the personal quirks of a few individuals rather than a reasoned critique' (p. 4).

Hollingsworth is referring to the British press as a whole, and clearly there are plenty of exceptions to the rule. The *Sun*, however, is no exception. It has pursued campaigns of vilification, for example, on its own behalf, against Clare Short, MP, and her bill to outlaw the Page Three Girl, which mobilised many women's deeply felt objections (Benn 1988). To criticise the ideology of the popular press on grounds of lying and the suppression of dissent is worth doing in its own right, though only covering the tip of the ideological iceberg; and, such criticisms are not dependent on a dominant ideology thesis in the strong sense of the key determinant of social reproduction (Lodziak 1986).

Chris Searle's (1989) critique of the *Sun*'s racism is a good illustration of why certain issues should not be allowed to slip from view merely in order to refine the hermeneutic complexities of communication. Through a close reading of the *Sun* during the late 1980s, Searle elaborated on the interconnected themes of racism, xenophobia and populism. Concentrating on the *Sun*'s particular tropes around the representation of Africa, Arabs and Asians, Searle shows how the *Sun* constructs a belligerent Britishness, mobilising violent contempt for 'others' generally. It may well be that all news fictionalises, but the *Sun* takes it to such an extremity that Searle is impelled to ask, '[h]ow are the readers to know which of the stories are "made up" and which have any basis in truth?' (p. 13). As an educationist, Searle is concerned quite rightly with what 'the Murdoch curriculum', as he calls it, teaches readers. Unfortunately, his exclusively textual analysis and reasonable anger tempt him into a discourse of 'daily dose', 'brain shackles' and 'mind gangrene', which does less than justice to the communicative problem.

Mark Pursehouse's study of *Sun*-readers complicates the problem in a manner more congenial to the new revisionism yet he retains the critical edge of hegemony theory. His reading of the *Sun* text is consistent with Searle's. However, Pursehouse stresses a wider range of ideological elements and registers the paper's impressive rhetorical powers:

> The *Sun*'s text is complex. Populist interests in individuals, personalities, sex, scandal, violence, sport and amusement are presented in a lively, identifiable language and format which ideologically layers a heterosexual, male, white, conservative, capitalist, nationalist world view. Since the *Sun* appears to be

read by more people every day, than any other commercial reading material, we should pay attention to *how* it is read.

(1987: 2)

In the preliminary study of *Sun*-readers from which this quotation is taken, Pursehouse combined the encoding/decoding model with an interview method orientated towards audience context and readerly use: for instance, reading the *Sun* during tea breaks sometimes interactively with workmates. This enables him to bring out the nuances of reading very well, two aspects of which are of special interest: the similarities and differences between female and male readings. Both his female and male readers talk of the entertainment rather than news value of the *Sun*, though each reading is differentially negotiated. In a shame-faced manner, the men enjoy its sexism whereas the women do not complain, although sensing, however, that the paper is not really addressed to them. The crucial insight, confirmed by surveys and by intuition, is that *Sun*-readers do not expect reliable news or responsible interpretation of events: they read the *Sun*, in their own minds, more or less exclusively for light relief. An obvious implication is that something might be learnt from the *Sun*'s rhetorical techniques, its vernacular brilliance, by papers wishing to represent the world rather differently.

This point is probably consistent with John Fiske's (1989b) argument concerning 'popular news'. He concentrates, like a good cultural populist, on television rather than tabloid journalism, but the general argument is transferable or else it has no coherence whatsoever. In a characteristic new revisionist deconstruction, he inverts the usual critique around information/ entertainment:

> It would be better for TV news if it confidently asserted that its position in the repertoire of news media is one that makes its popularity its defining characteristic. It should, therefore, be evaluated less by informational criteria and more by those of popular appeal. We should demand of our television news that it makes the events of the world *popular*, that it subject them to popular taste and attempt to make them part of the popular consciousness of society.
>
> (1989b: 185)

This is exactly what the *Sun* has done so successfully. Yet, I am sure that Fiske would not endorse the *Sun*'s racism, sexism and the rest of it. Fiske wants popular news to address the diversity of subcultures, respecting cultural differences. Apparently, this is also what Rupert Murdoch himself favours, if we are to take seriously his remarks at the Edinburgh Television Festival in 1989. Extolling multi-channel commercial television against the stuffiness of British public service and 'Establishment' values, he said:

> Take the ethnic and racial minorities. How are they served? In Britain by one or two token programmes. But in the US 80 per cent of Hispanics have at least one Spanish only channel. There is a Black entertainment network and there is National Jewish TV. In New York alone, there are ten hours a week of Korean, Chinese and Japanese television.[3]

That, however, represents rather more the power of ethnic subcultural organisation and legitimation of domestic cultural differences in the United States, in comparison with Britain, than anything which Rupert Murdoch's television channels or chains of newspapers ever have or are ever likely to provide. The quoted passage and the rest of Murdoch's speech at Edinburgh evince a populism actually indistinguishable from Fiske's position: Murdoch also attacks patronising and elitist attitudes. To be fair, the strong argument for a cultural populism which does not support Murdoch's politics is that the form can be extricated from the content. That, however, is strictly a *formalist* argument and one which isolates an understanding of the *Sun* from political, economic and cultural contexts. Incidentally, this brings out a difficulty in Pursehouse's position too. His readers do not, he observes, interrogate the ideological framing of the *Sun* – quite understandably since their reading is not an analytical reading. But, that constitutes 'the ideological trap they find themselves in' (Pursehouse 1987: 32). None of his readers doubt they are the beneficiaries of a 'free press', which offers them genuine choice and diversity. Still, *they* choose to read the *Sun*. The possibility is thus raised that the *Sun*'s appeal is not only formal but that it is ideologically confirming, addressed to the taken-for-granted assumptions and expectations of readers, a discomfiture for the uncritical appreciation of popular preferences.

Reading the *Sun* may, therefore, combine what Ralph Miliband (1978) has called 'de-subordination', interlarded by resentment, with a deeply rooted and recently ascendant people's conservatism, a legacy, in part, of the British Empire and social democracy's cultural and political failure. In the year when the *Sun* became the most widely read national newspaper, Miliband said:

> there is at work in Britain a process which I will call *de-subordination* for want of a better term to convey what is involved. De-subordination means that people who find themselves in subordinate positions and notably the people who work in factories, mines, offices, shops, schools, hospitals and so on do what they can to mitigate, resist and transform the conditions of their subordination. The process occurs where subordination is most evident and felt, namely at 'the point of production' and at the workplace in general; but also wherever else a condition of subordination exists, for instance as it is experienced by women in the home, and outside.
>
> (1978: 402)

Sensitive to the politically indeterminate aspects of de-subordination, Miliband observes that it is a 'complex and diffuse phenomenon' which 'does not fit into familiar ideological slots' (p. 403). He also puts it in the context of the 'steady flow of reactionary ideas' (p. 405) during the 1970s:

> In a suitably charged social climate, and in conditions of considerable economic, social, political and cultural malaise and uncertainty, propaganda based on chauvinist, anti-black, anti-semitic, xenophobic, anti-left and other assorted slogans is likely to have some resonance, to put it no higher.
>
> (1978: 407)

What I am suggesting, then, is that the *Sun*'s success must be understood multi-dimensionally within a determinate historical conjuncture, the lineaments of which were identified early by both Stuart Hall and Ralph Miliband. To concentrate exclusively on the text–reader relation in isolation from historical sociology is inadequate and runs the risk of producing apologetics rather than reasoned critique. The *Sun* is, arguably, symptomatic of and contributory to a political culture in which popular pleasure is routinely articulated through oppressive ideologies that operate in fertile chauvinistic ground. It is populist in the worst sense. And, maybe, Julie Burchill (1990) is right. But this is not a 'veiled attack' on what she so interestingly calls 'the *English* working class'. It is not an 'attack' at all: it is rather a sober assessment of the unmaking of class politics and the conservative articulation of de-subordinate impulses. This is similar to Curran and Sparks's (1991) argument, but they qualify their argument by suggesting that the *Sun*'s popular appeal is contradictory: for example, by simultaneously legitimating royalty and exposing its foibles. To some extent, that must be so. As cultural populists have persistently argued, the amassing of large audiences and readerships depends on polysemy, by providing texts that can be read in different ways. This lends itself to a much more optimistic view of popular culture in Britain than other examples would indicate. To take a mundane yet poignant example, some of 'the people' turned the comedian Harry Enfield's intentionally despicable 'Loadsamoney' character into a hero of callous greed with the encouragement of the *Sun*. Such an example calls into question Fiske's bizarre claim that the popular appropriation of a cultural artefact is virtually by definition progressive but it is not alternative to Curran and Sparks's view, which is essentially critical of the *Sun* in spite of its contradictoriness. In effect, with all the qualifications taken into account, the *Sun*'s entertaining parody of a newspaper exemplifies how 'freedom of the press' defined exclusively in market terms can, under certain conditions, obstruct rather than enable informed citizenship. This is a peculiar paradox of liberal democracy.

CENSORING PORNOGRAPHY

Turning from an exclusive concern with cultural consumption towards the complexities of public communication returns us to the question of 'distortion'. Is it still credible to claim, in view of the discrediting of the dominant ideology thesis, that communicative distortions reproduce and aggravate distorted social relations? Such a question is premised on the feasibility of removing distortion from culture and politics, the potential for what Jurgen Habermas (1970) calls 'an ideal speech situation' (p. 144). According to Habermas, the aim of this abstract idealisation is to produce a genuinely open discourse of 'truth', 'freedom' and 'justice'. The Habermasian project is idealist in both the ethical and epistemological senses; and, perhaps, as sceptics observe, its lofty idealism distracts from what actually happens here and now, the unavoidable 'distortions' of 'real life'. Yet, without an ideal of what *ought* to be, how can we criticise what *is*? Imagining something better, however Utopian the fiction, is the cornerstone of criticism. This argument is directly relevant to feminist debates concerning pornography and censorship. Opposition to degrading representations of women assumes systematic distortion, specifically the power of men over women, and thereby implies hope that women can free themselves, obtain justice and define their own truths.

Fine ideals are all very well, but how are they to be realised? There is no feminist consensus on pornography and what should be done about it. Disputes between anti-porn feminists and anti-anti-porn feminists tend to be mutually destructive, manifesting deep schisms not only to do with the pornography issue. In the 1970s and 1980s, the women's movement split in several directions: 'liberal' feminists seeking advancement within 'the system'; 'radical' feminists wishing to overthrow 'the patriarchal system'; 'socialist' feminists refusing to separate gender relations entirely from multi-systemic forms of exploitation and oppression, including those of class and race. Some feminists are tempted to look back on the late 1960s and early 1970s as a mythical Golden Age of solidarity and common purpose. At that time, however, the women's movement shared in a purely libertarian opposition to censorship and puritanism. Even pornography was seen to be liberating, part of a sexual transformation which many feminists later came to regard with bitterness as largely defined by unreconstructed, albeit 'radical', men. As Andrew Ross (1989) points out, an 'unapologetically populist' pornographer like Al Goldstein, publisher of *Screw*, ostensibly spoke the language of 'sexual revolution' when he extolled the masturbatory pleasures of male truck drivers and conveniently ignored the exploitation of female pornography workers, the first and most obvious contradiction.

Recent apologists for the pornography business, the British journalists David Hebditch and Nick Anning evince a strictly capitalist logic shorn of any residual counter-cultural pretensions, celebrating the freedoms of both consumer and worker:

> If the world-wide porn business really does generate revenues in excess of $5 billion [probably a serious underestimate], it is only because consumers are ready, willing and able to pay over part of their hard-earned income. We found no evidence, nor was any presented to us, that pornography is in any way obligatory.

The industry thrives by popular consent. The question is, if so many people exercise that choice by voting with their money, who is to deny them the right? As one industry veteran observed: 'Nobody ever died from an overdose of pornography'.

(Hebditch and Anning 1988: 373–4)

Sickness unto death, however, is exactly what many anti-porn feminists allege to be the potential effect on the pornography-consumer's victim, usually a raped and battered woman. With astonishing flippancy, Hebditch and Anning sum up the generalised market conception of freedom underlying their defence of the pornography business: all those sovereign, mainly male, consumers 'voting with their money'. The cash nexus is also constitutive of the labourer's 'freedom' in production: it is hard to imagine women working in the pornography business for nothing. Alternatively, labour-power is not sold so much as coerced in child pornography. Some adult pornography workers have, unlike Hebditch and Anning's informants, been victims of coercion too: for example, Linda Lovelace-Marciano (see Everywoman 1988).

In this section, I shall concentrate on pornography and the struggle for women's liberation: first, because it calls into question any simple populist endorsement of popular taste and consumption (Ross 1989); and, second, because it came to occupy centre ground in feminist debates over culture and censorship in the 1980s (Chester and Dickey 1988). In a period of political reaction in the United States and Britain, radical feminists made the running around the issue of pornography, identifying it, controversially, as the essence of patriarchal oppression. Aside from the hyperbole, there are enormous problems with defining pornography and with charting its range and scope. Doubts abound concerning the opposition between pornography and erotica, the liberal distinction between 'hard' and 'soft' porn, and whether or not pornography as narrowly defined is distinguishable from, say, mainstream films representing violence against women, like *Fatal Attraction* in which the sexually active woman is repeatedly killed for disrupting the family. Although feminists, virtually by definition, would agree that sexist images and words are part of the semiological landscape of everyday life, disputes arise over the key sites of struggle and the wisdom of censorship strategies. Being for or against 'censorship' is the normal but misleading way of putting the question, though the word has a pejorative connotation even for those, in effect, advocating its general application to sexist representations. It is unlikely that any feminist would support 'freedom of expression' in child pornography or 'snuff movies' if they were indeed records of actual murder. Nor does any feminist, to my knowledge, advocate repeal of legislation against incitement to racial hatred.

The question is, then, what kind of censorship? And, moreover, to what extent and within what limits? These questions cannot be settled once and for all: cultural and political conditions change, definitions shift. Anti-anti-porn feminists have usually argued that the 1980s was a decade when calls for greater censorship played into the hands of moral reactionaries and habitually censorious governments. For instance, in the heightened homophobic climate of the AIDS panic (Watney 1987), Clause 28 of the British Local Government Act outlawed the 'promotion of homosexuality', including lesbianism, to be used against artists and educators. In the United States, exhibition of Robert Mapplethorpe's aesthetically approved homo-erotic photographs nearly fell foul of the 'three-pronged' obscenity test. On the representation of consensual S&M, some lesbians attacked pro-censorship feminists. The tensions and dilemmas are tortuous, to say the least.

Andrea Dworkin, author of a classic book on pornography (1981), and the lawyer Catherine MacKinnon, were invited to draft anti-pornography legislation for the City of Minneapolis in 1983, which was passed there and in Indianapolis but not implemented. In Minneapolis the Mayor vetoed the Council's ordinance and the Indianapolis ordinance was halted by an immediate Federal Court action. The legislation was held in both cases to contravene the First Amendment, the right to freedom of expression. Although various and normally incompatible political tendencies were temporarily allied together on both sides, the division amongst feminists is the most significant, between Women Against Pornography (WAP) and Feminist Anti-Censorship Task Force (FACT). A similar division was reproduced in Britain between the Campaign Against Pornography (CAP) and its breakaway group led by Catherine Itzin, Campaign Against Pornography and Censorship (CPC), on the one side, and various anti-anti-porn feminists on the other, such as Jean Seaton (1986) and Lynne Segal (1987 and 1990).

Itzin (1988) has spelt out the terms of the anti-porn campaign in Britain. In an article on the publication of the Minneapolis hearings (Everywoman 1988), Itzin identifies the novelty of Dworkin and MacKinnon's ordinance:

> What is radical about this US model for legislating against pornography is its understanding of pornography not only as a cause of violence to women (important as that is), but as a major contribution in creating negative attitudes of 'bigotry and contempt' and sexual inequality. Once and for all it is clear that pornography is a women's rights and civil liberties issue . . . defining pornography as sex discrimination ('the graphic sexually explicit subordination of women in words and pictures') and then stipulating that any single item of pornography will always include one or more of a number of presentations of women as sexual objects who are portrayed as enjoying pain or humiliation or as experiencing sexual pleasure in being raped, or penetrated by objects or animals, and so forth . . . . The legislative breakthrough is the combination of 'subordination' *plus* sex and violence, describing pornography descriptively and objectively for what it actually portrays and not subjectively as obscenity legislation does. At last there is an opportunity to include only that which is pornography (bearing in mind that the people who make it, sell it and buy it know exactly what it is) and to exclude everything that is not pornography.
>
> (1988: 22)

I have quoted Itzin at length because her position is frequently misrepresented. However, what she says requires further clarification. Fundamentally, Dworkin and MacKinnon claimed their ordinance was not censorship since it made possible civil action by women upon whom it would be encumbent to prove harm; that is, a posteriori action unlike, for instance, the a priori state censorship of the British Video Recordings Act (Barker 1984). In practice, this may be a fine distinction but it is important to bring out: it is the justification for claiming to be against *both* pornography *and* censorship. Such legislation is not directly transferable from the United States to Britain because British law does not include positive constitutional rights or provide for individual civil suits in redress of collective grievances, as does American legislation (Osman 1988). That is why Itzin proposed

British legislation on the model of the 1986 Public Order Act's provision against incitement to racial hatred. She wants to ban incitement to sexual hatred. There are two further points to make at this juncture. First, note the definition of pornography – 'graphic sexually explicit subordination of women in words and pictures' – quoted from MacKinnon (Everywoman 1988: 2), the difficulties with which are both elided and improved upon by Itzin's list of qualifying conditions. In the Minneapolis/Indianapolis ordinances the first and sufficient condition was 'women . . . dehumanized as sexual objects, things or commodities'. This would probably make a great deal of advertising illegal, which may have been the intention but it was not made explicit. Itzin wisely runs the wide-open first condition into the violence-stipulating second of the American ordinances' nine qualifying conditions, any one of which is sufficient. This matters because of the anti-porn campaigners' claim to textual objectivism, contrasted with obscenity law's subjectivist criteria of depravity and corruption. Second, there is the need to prove that pornography *causes* actual harm to women. The problems of proof and causality here are immense, especially in terms of the social scientific research cited by both the American and British campaigns (Henry 1988).

This brief discussion of Itzin's summary of the anti-porn position indicates that the question of censorship in feminist debates on pornography is 'riven with dilemmas and potential conflict' (Dickey and Chester 1988:1). What is pornography? What does it do? What should be done about it? What are the conditions of action and the potentially unintended consequences? Who should be opposed? Who should be allied with? Such questions, and many more besides, are addressed to cultural and political circumstances fraught with dissonance, quite apart from the fact that pornography is already comparatively restricted in Britain.

On these matters intellectual tunnel vision and ideological certainties will not do. In her book *The Pornography of Representation* (1986), Susanne Kappeler cites Deirdre English's argument that campaigning to censor pornography is a distraction from and an oversimplification of patriarchal oppression, the characteristically anti-anti-porn feminist position. Kappeler agrees, and wishes to 'shift the ground of the argument' (p. 2). I think her intention is admirable, but the way in which Kappeler puts it into practice creates further problems. She is less concerned with practical action than with understanding, which is undoubtedly what is needed. However, Kappeler undercuts the grounds of understanding, in effect, with her poststructuralist move of discursive violence, both in terms of her object and her own discourse.

This can be illuminated with reference to the story Kappeler adopts as a metaphor for her book: the murder of the young black farm worker, Thomas Kassire, by his boss in Namibia, Van Rooyen, a story told in the *Guardian Weekly* in 1984. What interests Kappeler in this story is the way the boy was tortured and *photographed* by and with the white farmer and his drunken mates. For Kappeler, this is a metaphor for pornography that condenses apparently every form of sadistic cruelty and domination known to her. There are two points to make, one positive and one negative, concerning Kappeler's appropriation of this terrible story. First, she uses it to undermine the behaviourism of the exclusively anti-porn position, which is founded on the proposition that pornography actually causes men to behave violently towards women. Kappeler quite rightly stresses the 'graphy' in 'pornography'. It is a representational practice, deploying words and images, and should be understood, according to Kappeler, as a form of symbolic violence which is real in itself, as real in a sense as rape and murder, the literal 'effects' claimed by anti-porn campaigners. Representation is indeed 'real' but, surely, we are talking about different orders of reality here? This leads on to my second point, the negative one. Kappeler conflates the symbolic violence of pornography, normally against women though in this case a man, with racial and class domination in which a white boss murders his black worker while simultaneously producing the evidence of his crime (the photographs), thus ensuring Van Rooyen's conviction. Throughout *The Pornography of Representation*, Kappeler reminds the reader of this primal scene, figuring 'the white man and his guests', as distilling the essence of Sadian pornography, the paradigm of the genre. In so doing she clouds understanding rather than clarifies, the worst aspect of which is the conflation of a general argument concerning sexist representation with a particular case of racist murder.

Black commentators on pornography, like Pratibha Parmar (1988) and Sona Osman (1988), have criticised such opportunistic conflation of difference. To quote Parmar's strictures against the 'false unity' of much feminist discourse:

this sisterhood of all women assumes that there are no significant differences between women, compared with the similarities of our experiences of pornography. I find such analysis Eurocentric and nationalist. It is also insulting in its simplicity. Feminism has a long history of divisions created out of an inability of the movement to deal with differences of race, class and sexuality.

(1988: 123)

Parmar goes on to highlight black women's (and men's) practical struggles against the racism of immigration controls, education, policing and so forth. And, in her contribution to the collection *Feminism and Censorship* (Chester and Dickey 1988), Osman questions the assumption held by Itzin and others that legislation against pornography modelled on incitement to racial hatred is the solution. Such legislation has not prevented violence against black people: why should one suppose it would prevent violence against women (1988: 153)?

In concluding this section, I want to make a modest contribution to the debate, like Kappeler, in order to shift the argument. In my opinion, her poststructuralist move does not help very much. The alternative, which I am proposing, derives from critical theory and is influenced by Jurgen Habermas's 'universal pragmatics'. It is concerned with the conditions of debate, not with adding to its substance. As Habermas says:

The goal of coming to an understanding is to bring about an agreement that terminates in the intersubjective mutuality of reciprocal understanding, shared knowledge, mutual trust, and accord with one another. Agreement is based on the corresponding validity claims of comprehensibility, truth, truthfulness, and rightness.

(1979: 3)

Habermas's ideal of 'undistorted communication' was originally inspired by the psychoanalytic situation in which the analysand learns to speak openly of his or her troubles. This 'ideal speech situation' is theorised by Habermas according to what he believes are the universal properties of linguistic communication. I have my doubts concerning the psychoanalytic analogy of social relations beyond the dyad, the abstract universalism of Habermas's model, and also the consensual as opposed to correspondence theory of truth upon which it is founded. None the less, as a practical means of unblocking distorted communications it has potential.

Drawing on Austin's speech-act theory, Habermas produces a tripartite distinction: *locutionary*, *illocutionary* and *expressive* (Pusey 1987). Locutionary speech-acts are assertions about an object. Illocutionary or cognitive speech-acts are intersubjective statements with propositional content. Expressive speech-acts are statements of authentic feeling. Thus, we have a tripartite classification of speech-act categories covering 'objective', 'intersubjective' and 'subjective'. For my purposes with regard to feminist pornography debates, these can be applied, at the risk of over-simplification, as follows: (1) *statements of fact*, or objective truth claims; (2) *statements of mutuality*, or dialogic closures and openings; (3) *statements of feeling*, or subjective truth claims.

One of the most tendentious aspects of anti-porn campaigning discourse is the blunt statement of fact concerning evidence of behavioural effects. This is complicated by the definitional problem of whether a narrow or a broad concept of pornography is being used and for what purposes. A precise and limited definition, distinct from sexist representation in general, is probably necessary for the issue of censorship to be posed at all. Although questionably objectivist, it is consistent with a view of pornography as symbolic violence, especially against women, and does not automatically entail a behaviourist reduction. Definitional precision cannot, however, solve the evidential problem of 'effects'. Laboratory experiments exposing male college students to violent pornography, using the Rape Myth Acceptance Scale, and statistical correlations between pornography and sexual violence, the kind of evidence reported by Ed Donnerstein at the Minneapolis hearings (Everyman 1988), have been treated with insufficient circumspection by pro-censorship campaigners. Apart from methodological objections to such research, the evidence thus produced is countered by similarly positivistic research which proves no direct correlation between consumption of pornography and acts of violence against women (see Henry 1988, and Segal 1987 and 1990). The criticisms of artificially constructed 'effects' research are well known and need no repetition (see McCron 1976). To be serious about the 'effects' of pornography, questions of fantasy, psychic intransigence and interpretation must come into the reckoning, subjective matters which do not lend themselves to isolation and dissection in a psychological laboratory. 'Soft' evidence, like text/context analyses and case studies of rapists and their victims, in addition to frequently used personal testimony by anti-porn campaigners, tell us much more, but they lack orthodox 'scientific' legitimacy.

In fact (a statement of fact!), we know very little indeed about the meaning, use and effect of pornography. There is, however, plenty of insightful speculation. For example, Lynne Segal (1987) has suggested that consuming pornography may be 'a compensatory expression of men's *declining* power . . . sexual anxiety and paranoia' rather than, as anti-porn feminists argue, their power over women (pp. 107–8). The growth of the pornography business, paradoxically, could be a sign of the comparative success of feminism, women's increasing independence and men's loss of 'emotional support and sexual servicing from women' (p. 107). Segal's argument, though unsubstantiated, is at least as credible as the claim that pornography is the root of all patriarchal evil.

Returning to Parmar's point about 'false unity': this is a major problem for feminism and especially for campaigning organisations that purport to speak on behalf of all women. Genuine grounds of mutuality depend on recognition and respect for differences. Perhaps the central issue, not only confined to feminism, is how people with divergent opinions and from different cultures might speak with one another on matters where agreement could be reached. One of the most striking features of the pornography debate is the way in which feminists hurl abuse at one another. This is usually associated with anti-porn feminists accusing anti-anti-porn feminists of being in league with pornographers. When, for example, Donnerstein detached himself from the American campaign it was said that he 'seems to have changed sides and now works for the pornography publishers and producers' (Everywoman 1988: 5). Such statements are very common indeed. However, similar statements are made from the other side too, especially against Andrea Dworkin. For example, Loretta Loach, reviewing Dworkin's *Letters from a War Zone* (1988), even when complaining about 'the language of conflict', described the book as 'rant and rhapsody' reminiscent of vulgar Leninism (*New Statesman and Society*, 20 May 1988). Lynne Segal (1990), normally a source of light on these issues, has even threatened to sue Dworkin for pornographic re-presentation in her own books were the catch-all legislation she advocates ever actually introduced. On a more constructive note, Segal advocates educative and agitational strategies against sexist representations and, in particular, what can reasonably be deemed 'pornographic'. That is a means of opening up dialogue instead of closing it down. An ongoing, never-ending dialogue, however, lacks the teleological purposefulness of a censorship campaign. None the less, legislation may not be the most *effective* means of countering pornography and sexism. The anti-porn position has been hugely educative, if not hitherto successful legislatively. At the very least, many people now think much more carefully about these issues, including men.

It ill behoves a man to say this, but the pornography debate has sometimes been conducted in ways inimical to feminism. Emotional solidarity, women supporting one another, in comparison to the way men more typically compete with one another and conceal their feelings, is attenuated by the divisiveness of the censorship question. Many feminists are simply unsure of what position to take. Considering how difficult it really is to decide, 'woolly-minded liberalism' deserves better treatment than fierce denunciation. Yet there is no doubt that many women find pornography, in particular, and sexist representations, in general, extremely distressing. With impressive honesty, voicing her personal doubts and reflecting on her own transition from an extreme pro-censorship to a more circumspect position, in an article entitled 'Snakes and ladders', Julienne Dickey concluded in a manner conducive to mutual understanding:

> The debate about solutions, legislative or otherwise, to media sexism and pornography will continue. Ideally we will see this as a strengthening process, refusing to allow it to divide us, but rather committing ourselves to listening respectfully to one another's arguments.
>
> (1988: 167)

AUTHOR-KILLING

When Roland Barthes (1968) declared 'the birth of the reader must be at the cost of the death of the Author' (p. 148), he did not mean what the Ayatollah Khomeini meant when he issued his *fatwa* against Salman Rushdie and Viking/Penguin, like a Chicago gangster, on St Valentine's Day 1989. Khomeini *really meant it*: the Islamic fundamentalist reading of *The Satanic Verses* (Rushdie 1988) called for the death of Rushdie, the blaspheming apostate. Barthes's iconoclasm was mild in comparison with that of the late Ayatollah. For Barthes, the meaning of a literary text has no authorial authority: it is produced by the reader's reading and not by the author's intention. This is true of all texts, though especially so, according to Barthes, of the modernist text's significatory indeterminacy, which inscribes multiple readings. In a similar vein, Umberto Eco (1981) theorised the 'open text' of serious modernism as opposed to the 'closed text' of popular realism. Cultural populism problematises such an elitist distinction, and so might the later Eco, author of *The Name of the Rose*.

On becoming a famous novelist himself, Eco (1985a) suggested that the *post*modernist text is characterised by 'double-coding'. It delivers both the realist pleasures of popular fiction and the modernist play with language: something there for both the people and the intellectuals to get their teeth into. Salman Rushdie's *Satanic Verses* are often called 'postmodernist', a label which he does not attribute to his own work. He usually calls himself a 'modernist'. That could be seen to indicate his implied readership: Western intellectuals, not ordinary Muslims and their mullahs. As a modernist, however, he would still have to assume the possibility of differential readings, which indeed Rushdie did until *The Satanic Verses* was 'misread' or simply not read at all, as he frequently complained, by those who found it offensive to their beliefs. On the first anniversary of the *fatwa*, Rushdie (1990) tried to authorise the meaning of his text, claiming that it did not actually mean what 'ordinary Muslims' thought it did. In effect, Rushdie's commitment to modernism and perhaps also modernity was qualified by seeking reconciliation thus. At the end of 1990, after nearly two years in seclusion, Rushdie announced, to everyone's surprise, his return to Islam, yet not the fundamentalist version which had imperilled him in the first place, as he stressed so bitterly a year later.

The rise of Islamic fundamentalism in recent decades constitutes a revolt against both capitalist and communist modernity (Hiro 1990), put into practice by the theocratic state of Iran, the pre-modern politics of which became infamously literary critical, legitimated by the leader as authoritative reader, just when populist fervour for the ten-year-old revolution had ebbed following a lengthy and stalemated war with Iraq.[4] Fundamentalism, of whatever kind, while being obsessed with the past, also tends to deny history as perpetual process. Maxime Rodinson (1979), taking an historical view, says that the cultural tradition of Islam must be understood at three levels: first, at that of the canonical texts, particularly the *Qur'an*; second, at that of the divergent sects and rival interpretations of holy law; and, third, at the level of the contextualised meanings and practices of Islam as it is lived. The lived experience of belief and moral regulation is a necessary level of properly materialist analysis. To 'know Islam' only in terms of the *Qur'an* and its various schools of thought (Sunni, Shia, Sufi and so on) would be idealist: so would knowledge derived exclusively from Western media 'coverage' (Said 1981). Meanings change depending on temporal and spatial circumstances, but fundamentalism seeks to fix them once and for all. There are, in Edward Said's formulation, borrowing Stanley Fish's concept, certain 'communities of interpretation' that conceal their respective interpretive procedures in a manner which facilitates mutual incomprehension and war. The Western media typically represent Islamic civilization in images of fanatical crowds and Hitlerian leaders: from the other side, the West is perceived by many Muslims as resolutely amoral and grossly materialistic. Wherever it takes hold of the popular imagination, fundamentalism ossifies meaning, setting it in ideational concrete: for instance, to set 'West' against 'East' or 'East' against 'West' indissolubly. In the case of the Occident, its superior economic, technological and military strength, taken for granted as somehow natural, is the advantage of power. In the case of Islamic fundamentalism, the mobilisation of the powerless is achieved by a scholarly and perhaps heretical priesthood interpreting canonical texts for contingent political purposes.

Knowledge of Islam is at the root of the problem in the Rushdie affair and also generally with regard to Occidental 'knowledge of the Orient'. Rushdie's offence was to do with excessive knowingness. Brought up as a Muslim, he knew only too well the legend of Satan's interference with the Archangel Gabriel's recitation of the words of Allah to Muhammad. This devilish intrusion, seized upon by medieval Christian ideologists and circulated as a rumour to discredit Islam's professed monotheism, indicated that Muhammad was apparently prepared to throw in three female gods temporarily in order to appease the polytheists of seventh-century Arabia. Rushdie added insult to crusading injury by calling his character Mahound, who founds a faith, 'the messenger-businessman'. 'Mahound' is one of those names for Muhammad, meaning 'devil', used by the Crusaders. Furthermore, Rushdie named the prostitutes at the Curtain brothel after Muhammad's wives. On page 376 of *The Satanic Verses* 'curtain' is translated as the Arabic 'hijab', the head-dress worn by Islamic women to conceal their hair. A connotation, immediately evident to the Muslim reader, is of false modesty covering up licentious carnality. This is related to an old Western depiction of Islamic women, excavated by Rana Kabbani (1986), and mythologised particularly by Richard Burton, the Victorian Orientalist. Burton's work effectively functioned as pornography for bourgeois gentlemen who denied their own wives expressive sexuality.

In Rushdie's novel, melding the offensive elements together, the Prophet Mahound (Muhammad) is represented as a hypocrite not only in theology but also in sexuality, subordinating women to male prerogatives: 'What finally finished Salman with Mahound: the question of the women; and of the Satanic verses' (Rushdie 1988: 366). As Shabbir Akhtar (1989) points out, the status of Muhammad in Islam is different from that of Moses in Judaism or Jesus in Christianity: he is held in even greater reverence. To insult the Prophet is to insult the faith. According to Rushdie (1990), none of the scurrilous fictions in his work should be taken literally since they are all 'dreamt' by his insane character Gibreel who, because similarly named, imagines himself to be the Archangel. Rushdie drew on crusading myths and nineteenth-century Orientalism (Said 1978; Sardar and Wynn Davies 1990) as a means of exploring his own 'God-shaped hole', he says. Unfortunately, Rushdie underestimated the historical forces at work in the contexts where his text might be interpreted: the right-wing Jamaat movement in Pakistan, the crisis of authority in Iran and, much nearer home, the smouldering disaffection of Muslim communities in Britain, especially Bradford. To underestimate the complex dialectics of text, sect and context in this way could yet prove fatal.

The Satanic Verses, a novel which itself wonderfully exemplifies Bakhtinian heteroglossia, proved to be an extraordinary incitement to discourse. So much has been written about the book and its author's plight that further comment may only add to a confusing babble of voices or simply be superfluous. Yet the cultural and political ramifications of the Rushdie affair are so enormous that they continue to intrigue. My own interest in the Rushdie affair is specifically to do with the gulf between the English literati and British Muslims, intellectuals and ordinary people. It opened up a set of ideological dilemmas for the chattering and scribbling classes, to some extent throwing their predominantly anti-racist and culturally relativist values into crisis.

Why did Muslims in Britain object so passionately to Rushdie's novel and how did the left-liberal intelligentsia respond? In general, Britain's million Muslims have sought to reproduce their cultures of origin in increasingly ghettoised neighbourhoods, surrounded by a social environment frequently experienced as hostile to them. The old Northern industrial city of Bradford came, during the Rushdie affair, to symbolise the embattled situation of many British Muslims. Mainly from Pakistan, Muslims originally settled in Bradford because the city's once-renowned but declining textile industry still offered employment, at low rates of pay, in the 1950s and 1960s. The present Islamic community of some 70,000 is comparatively poor yet dignified and, to an extent, self-sufficient, with a growing entrepreneurial middle class. When *The Satanic Verses* was ritually burnt outside Bradford's mock-Renaissance town hall in January 1989, the indigenous liberal conscience, if it can be reified as such, was instantly reminded of Nazi book-burnings. Why was this desperate action taken? Complaints had already been made for several months but they attracted little public attention. The Harley Street dentist Dr Hesham el-Essaway, chair of the Islamic Society for the Promotion of Religious Tolerance in the United Kingdom, wrote in protest to Rushdie's publishers about *The Satanic Verses* shortly following its publication in the early autumn of 1988 and received only a curt reply, although the book was banned in India and elsewhere around that time. In December, *The Satanic Verses* was burnt in Bolton, but it was the Bradford event which captured the media, thus achieving the first aim of any popular protest in a modern highly mediated society. Within weeks, six died in the Jamaat-inspired Islamabad riot, and Khomeini's *fatwa* was issued. The feelings of British Muslims could no longer be ignored or summarily dismissed.

In response, the British 'popular' press, as well as the 'quality' press, suddenly championed literary 'freedom of expression'. Newspapers like the *Sun*, however, had problems championing Rushdie himself, a black leftist from a privileged background. The opportunity once again to attack 'mad mullahs' and 'immigrants', including Rushdie, was irresistible for the *Sun* (Barker 1990), which confirmed what Muslim intellectuals and ordinary people alike suspected: they were living in a country that did not value them as citizens and had little to value in itself. When Muslim leaders took legal action against *The Satanic Verses*, they confronted the anomaly of the blasphemy law, which protects only Christianity, adhered to nominally by a majority of Britons, a state religion with very few devout believers yet a faith that the 1988 Education Act insisted should be foisted on all and sundry at school. From an Islamic perspective, this must have looked very peculiar indeed.

Serious debate on the Rushdie affair, as distinct from the cruder forms of popular media racism, was framed by 'the liberal conscience', the vicissitudes of which will be discussed in due course. Muslim voices had to be heard, if only to underwrite 'freedom of speech' or to isolate fundamentalist opinion in a television-studio discussion chaired by *The Late Show*'s Michael Ignatieff, the epitome of concerned yet intransigent liberalism. Of those who came into the public eye, Hesham el-Essaway, Kalim Siddiqui and Shabbir Akhtar were the most frequently called upon. The mild-mannered Essaway was treated with contempt by Rushdie on breakfast television while the writer was still free and arrogant. In spite of this, when a subsequently contrite Rushdie sought to build bridges with the Islamic community, Essaway acted as his mediator. In contrast, Siddiqui, of the pro-Iranian Muslim Institute, was always ready and willing to confirm the worst fears of the liberal consensus by flirting with incitement to murder. The most complex of these spokesmen was Shabbir Akhtar, whose book on the Rushdie affair, *Be Careful with Muhammad!* (1989), sheds considerable light for anyone, such as myself, who has only a passing acquaintance with Islam. Akhtar's defence of Islamic fundamentalism met with a reasoned response from no less a figure than ex-Labour Party leader, Michael Foot (see Apignanesi and Maitland 1989: 238-49).

Educated in Western philosophy at Cambridge and Calgary, Akhtar was not only able to joust with liberal intellectuals on their own ground, but also, as a Community Relations Officer in

Bradford, his arguments had an intimate relationship to ordinary Muslim feelings of a kind that Rushdie certainly could not claim. For example, in his book, Akhtar evokes the sense of hurt felt by the negative stereotyping of Muslims and Islamic ways of life in popular films and television programmes. To see one's cultural identity depicted routinely as barbaric must be galling, to say the least. In addition to describing the everyday experience of symbolic negation, to which Rushdie had unwittingly contributed, Akhtar produced a sophisticated philosophical and political critique of *The Satanic Verses*. First, he makes it quite clear that atheistic criticism of Islamic theology and social practice is wholly permissible and actually desirable:

> One has every right to be sceptical about the authenticity of the Koranic revelations vouchsafed to Muhammad. And there are valid doubts about the fairness of certain Islamic social norms, particularly those governing the lives of women. But slander or libel are not adequate substitutes for critique or reverent reservation.
>
> (1989: 28)

The main trouble with Rushdie's book, however, according to Akhtar, is the calculatedly offensive use of obscene language and abuse (Mahound, 'a smart bastard' with 'God's permission to fuck as many women as he pleases', to quote Rushdie). Akhtar remarks, 'Rushdie enters the mosque – but tactlessly refuses to take off his shoes' (p. 30). In fact, Akhtar himself shows Rushdie enormous respect by saying:

> *The Satanic Verses* fails to raise the truly central issues about a Muslim identity in the contemporary world of varied voices and irreligious confidences. It fails to set the agenda for the Islamic Enlightenment – a Muslim response to modernity.
>
> (1989: 31)

That is more than a back-handed compliment: to criticise Rushdie for failing 'to set the agenda for the Islamic Enlightenment'! How different it is from the observations of such secular minds as Fay Weldon – 'The Koran is food for no-thought' – and Conor Cruise O'Brien – 'Muslim society . . . repulsive . . . repulsive . . . repulsive' (both quoted by Kabbani 1989: 3–4).

It would be unfair to tar all Western liberal participants in the debate with the intemperate brush-strokes of Weldon and

O'Brien. The very words – 'Western', 'liberal', 'intellectual' – are far too general: they encompass many differences. The British meaning of 'liberal' is different from the principal North American one. In the United States it functions as a euphemism for 'left-wing', whereas in Britain it is often the butt of left-wing criticism. My own terminology, used in this chapter, of 'left-liberal' or 'liberal-left' fudges these differences. None the less, they refer, however loosely, to the prevailing universe of discourse in literary and socially critical circles on both sides of the Atlantic. Dissent from received opinion, hypocrisy and so forth, amongst literary intellectuals, is permitted and encouraged. Several notable inflections of left-liberalism were enunciated around the Rushdie affair, which can be clustered under three broad headings: *absolutist, autocritical* and *dialogic.*

Initial responses to the book-burning and the *fatwa,* especially by writers in defence of Rushdie, articulated an *absolutist* defence of 'freedom of expression' against the benighted values of Islamic fundamentalism, insisting on no back-sliding by publishers and booksellers. Akhtar (1989) calls this kind of position 'the Liberal Inquisition', and Richard Webster (1990) calls it 'authoritarian liberalism'. It asserts an absolute to which nobody really subscribes and, besides, one that is scarcely feasible. There are all sorts of restrictions on freedom of expression to protect individuals, groups and states. Censorship exists in both defensible and indefensible forms. The classic liberal case against censorship where harm cannot be proved (Mill 1974; Williams, B. 1981) is reasonable, yet inconsistencies and contradictions are rife in the real world. The British government protected Rushdie and his publishers while still trying to suppress Peter Wright's *Spycatcher,* which broke state 'confidentiality' but hardly gave away genuine 'secrets'. The liberal distinction between public and private is also a perpetual battleground, as in various issues concerning sexuality and its representation. And, with reference to the Rushdie affair, there is the issue of blasphemy law. Many liberals favour abolition because it discriminates in favour of Christianity, a view approaching common ground with Muslim critics. Some would like the blasphemy law replaced by provision against incitement to religious hatred, a position paralleling that of the anti-porn feminist notion of incitement to sexual hatred (Lee 1990).

Richard Webster's book *A Brief History of Blasphemy* (1990) presents a liberal *autocritique,* denouncing liberalism in broadly liberal terms. He challenges the Article 19 pamphlet, 'The Crime of Blasphemy', which advocated abolition 'without replacement' (Webster, R. 1990: 14). Webster takes this secularist case apart cleverly. He shows how the Western liberal concept of 'inner conscience' upon which it is founded is a secular transformation of Puritanism, the extreme Protestant revolt against Roman Catholicism. Most celebratedly, the Puritan poet John Milton argued the anti-censorship case from this position in the seventeenth century. According to Webster, the Rushdie affair 'is a clash not between religious authoritarianism and freedom but between two kinds of rigidity, two forms of fundamentalism' (p. 59). Paradoxically, absolute freedom of expression is 'a principle of intolerance', borne out by longstanding Occidental domination of the Orient, particularly the anti-Semitic tradition, documented excellently by Webster, in which Muslims have supplanted Jews as the main object of Christian contempt since the Holocaust. 'The problem with this position, if maintained consistently, is that it leads directly, by unstoppable logic into a completely amoral universe', contends Webster (p. 61). Few liberals, however, would go that far.

The problem with merely deconstructing Western values is that it does not address the *dialogic* task of mutual understanding, which involves recognition of sincerely held differences of opinion, including those of liberal-leftists, and willingness to explore grounds for agreement. A year after the *fatwa*, Akhtar argued that a decision not to publish a paperback version of *The Satanic Verses* would have enabled both sides to retreat with a limited victory (*Sunday Independent*, 4 February 1990). That did not happen when Rushdie subsequently concurred: warring positions were too entrenched. Bhikhu Parekh's suggestion that 'men and women of wisdom and goodwill' should 'get together and evolve a broadly acceptable consensus' (*Sunday Independent*, 11 April 1990) was also excessively optimistic. This kind of 'Habermasian answer . . . that we simply have to talk it over' (Eagleton 1990: 412) seems a remote possibility indeed in a world of *realpolitik*. There are very difficult issues of cultural identity at stake. In conclusion, I want to mention two such issues, both of which are central to the thematic structure of *The Satanic Verses*: Islamic womanhood and the migrant experience.

For liberal-leftists, the position of women within Islam is a major bone of contention. In his book on the Rushdie affair, Malise

Ruthven (1990) stresses the aspect of female subordination, quoting from the *Qur'an*: 'Men are managers of the affairs of women.' The weight of women's legal testimony as half that of men and 'the sexual double standard', whereby a woman's transgression is punished most severely, are not values that gell easily with Western feminism. Some women, however, have tried to reconcile feminism with Islamic culture. Rana Kabbani (1989), for instance, argues that Christianity, especially Roman Catholicism, and Judaism also deny women freedom. Much of what is commonly supposed about Islam in this respect is simply untrue. The brutal practice of clitoridectomy, contrary to common supposition, is a peculiarly African practice, in fact, and not legislated by Islam. And the actual institution of arranged marriage has a great deal to commend it in practical terms, according to Kabbani. Women are not necessarily forced to accept a partner they do not want. Kabbani goes still further: 'Muslim feminists no longer choose to model themselves on their western sisters . . . . Wearing the *hijab* can be a liberation, freeing women from being sexual objects, releasing them from the trap of Western dress and the dictates of Western fashion' (1989: 26, 27). Rushdie's feminism, as represented in *The Satanic Verses*, is closer to the politics of Women Against Fundamentalism (Sahgal and Yuval-Davis 1990) than to Kabbani's position. For an Indian with an Islamic background Rushdie's writings and his public pronouncements appeared curiously Eurocentric to Kabbani in a way which she questions, specifically around women's issues.

Rushdie's own formation, predominantly within Western elite culture, did indeed separate him rather sharply from the popular culture of Islamic communities in Britain and elsewhere. Bhikhu Parekh, a Hindu, made the point forcefully in an early commentary on the Rushdie affair:

As an immigrant, Rushdie sometimes seems to resent that everyone around him is not an immigrant; on other occasions, he is profoundly pleased that the natives have their roots intact and showers benediction. At a different level, he is both drawn towards and repelled by his fellow immigrants. He both fights them and fights for them; both resents them and delights in their world of certainties; cares for them but also tramples on their dearest memories and sentiments. He loves them as real human beings, yet he also turns them into an abstract cause;

and his holy anti-racism goes hand-in-hand with touches of contempt for them.

(1989: 31)

Yet more forcefully, Akhtar (1989) remarks, '[d]espite the prodigiously massive prestige that is attached to his name in anti-racist circles, I find it hard to believe that Rushdie has any real understanding of the daily headaches many ordinary blacks experience in this country' (p. 34). Akhtar attributes this to Rushdie's English public-school education and the self-insulating privileges of wealth.

The migrant experience, in its multiple and varied forms, precipitates a crisis of identity, catching people between at least two cultures. For many ordinary Muslims in Britain, the situation is one of doubt and uncertainty, a 'moral void', as Parekh (1989) puts it, alleviated by the certainties of 'the holy text' (p. 31). Rushdie's personal crisis of identity was compounded by the status of great writer in his own time, with a licence to speak freely, and his populist sympathies for the people he writes about for a Western readership. The fact of the matter is that *The Satanic Verses* was never addressed to ordinary British Muslims. Rushdie can hardly have expected them to wade through it. But the writer did himself come to recognise his own failure of communication. During the second year in hiding from indignant Muslims, he made a series of conciliatory moves. Rushdie objected to the British banning of *International Guerrillas*, the Pakistani film in which his fictionalised character is hunted down by assassins and at the end killed by a bolt from Heaven. And, on announcing his return to Islam, Rushdie went on local Southall radio, relayed to Bradford, to speak with ordinary Muslims, whose attitudes had hardened rather than softened over his offence and the intensified racism it had unleashed. Young Muslims, following the lead of their elders, were reluctant to forgive him (Flint 1990). Then, he was, however briefly (see Rushdie 1991), listening as well as speaking, engaging in dialogue, thus fulfilling what Edward Said (1981) says are 'the two necessary conditions for knowing another culture – 'uncoercive contact . . . through real exchange and self-consciousness about the interpretive project itself' (p. 142).

NOTES

1 See Nicholas Garnham (1990), ch. 7, 'The media and the public sphere'; James Curran's (1991) 'Rethinking the media as a public sphere'; and Michael Hofmann (1991a) on problems of applying Habermas's concept to contemporary television and politics.
2 These matters were explored rigorously and with considerable critical acumen by Christopher Hird's investigative television documentary, *Empire* (Channel Four, 20 December 1990).
3 This quotation is taken from the report of Rupert Murdoch's speech in the BBC's in-house journal, *Ariel* (29 August 1989).
4 Ervand Abrahamian (1991) argues that Khomeini was a 'populist' and not a 'fundamentalist' because he addressed the popular culture of Iranians in a charismatic manner rather than sticking rigidly to theocratic lore. Although this is a powerful argument, Abrahamian uses these terms in an unnecessarily essentialist way. Both 'fundamentalism' and 'populism' are historically variable constructions. It is inconceivable that a fundamentalism with popular appeal would not be populist in some sense: equally, a return to fundamentals is always a dubiously authentic claim necessarily adapted to the circumstances in which it is articulated.

Chapter 6

Anomie of the people

Constant revolutionizing of production, uninterrupted disturbance of all social conditions, everlasting uncertainty and agitation distinguish the bourgeois epoch from all earlier ones. All fixed, fast-frozen relations, with their train of ancient and venerable prejudices and opinions are swept away, all new formed ones become antiquated before they can ossify. All that is solid melts into air, all that is holy is profaned.

> (Marx and Engels 1967: 83 – originally published in 1848)

The era of simulation is . . . everywhere initiated by the interchangeability of previously contradictory and dialectical terms . . . the interchangeability of the beautiful and the ugly in fashion; of the right and the left in politics; of the true and false in every media message; of the useful and the useless at the level of objects; and of nature and culture at every level of meaning. All the great humanist criteria of value, all the values of a civilization of moral, civic and practical judgement, vanish in our system of images and signs. Everything becomes undecidable.

> (Baudrillard 1988: 128 – originally published in 1976)

So what's the difference: has anything really changed much since Karl Marx penned his brilliant description of modernity? Might he not have recognised the postmodern miasma of Jean Baudrillard? The difference could be that Marx thought that the condition he described was not permanent while Baudrillard, paradoxically, believes that his condition is. The historical formations described by both writers are similarly anomic, in the sense of conjuring up a socially experienced normlessness and meaninglessness.

Anomie is a *fin-de-siècle* concept of ancient origins. As Marco

Orru (1987) has shown, it can be traced back twenty-five centuries to fifth-century Greece and the Sophists. Its most famous usage, however, appeared towards the end of the nineteenth century in Emile Durkheim's *The Division of Labour in Society* (1964), originally published in 1893. This was not the first time that Durkheim had used the term. That was six years earlier, in his review of Jean-Marie Guyau's *L'Irreligion de l'avenir* (Orru 1987). Guyau argued that the religion of the future would be anomic, providing no universal precepts to guide the individual's actions. Anticipating Jean-Paul Sartre (1948), for Guyau, the individual was thus condemned to the freedom of inventing him- or herself. Unlike the ill-fated Guyau, Durkheim did not find this version of anomie one little bit liberating. He saw it as a recipe for anarchy and social disorder. The reason why I invoke anomie here is not because of any desire to resuscitate Durkheimian sociology but because it seems to capture the sense of Fredric Jameson's response to a novel form of spatial dislocation brought about by the globalisation of capitalism:

> this latest mutation in space – postmodern hyperspace – has finally succeeded in transcending the capacities of the individual human body to locate itself, to organise its immediate surroundings perceptually, and cognitively to map its position in a mappable external world.
>
> (1991: 44)

Nowadays, according to Jameson, people are not only confused socially; they are confused spatially; they don't know *where* they are. Jameson never uses the concept of anomie. Being a Marxist, he might have been expected to use the concept of alienation, rooted in a rather different set of assumptions from anomie (Horton 1964; Lukes 1967). The trouble with alienation, though, is that it refers to problems of identity derived from production, whereas postmodernity is best understood with regard to consumption and consuming identities in a global marketplace, which may or may not be a problem depending on where you stand with respect to postmodern discourse.

To what extent ordinary people in their enormous diversity suffer from anomie in a rapidly changing world is open to debate. Less debatable is the condition of radical intellectuals, denied the totalising guarantees of modernity, guarantees which, according to Jean-François Lyotard, hitherto impelled their projects. To quote him: 'I define *postmodern* as incredulity towards meta-narratives' (1984: xxiv). Following Ludwig Wittgenstein, Lyotard contends that knowledge has fragmented into a series of incommensurate 'language games', now conceived as postindustrial networks of information-processing. Knowledge, partial and imperfect, has superseded manufacture as the dynamic of such a society. Consequently, the grand narrative of labour and its emancipation, told by Marx, no longer makes sense:

> In contemporary society and culture – postindustrial society, postmodern culture – the question of the legitimation of knowledge is formulated in different terms. The grand narrative has lost its credibility, regardless of what mode of unification it uses, regardless of whether it is a speculative narrative or a narrative of emancipation.
>
> (Lyotard 1984: 37)

As many commentators have observed, Lyotard's claim is itself a grand narrative of sorts. Jurgen Habermas (1985) views this as the latest eruption of the counter-Enlightenment, an irrational rejection of the as-yet incomplete modern project. The postmodernists have switched their philosophical allegiance to the nihilism of Friedrich Nietzsche, the political implications of which are immediately evident to a German rationalist. With all its easily catalogued imperfections, overlooked by Habermas in his first foray against postmodern discourse, modernity still offers rational solutions to human problems, he insists.

On a less alarmist and more substantive level, the question turns on the scope and validity of postmodernist claims. Can, for example, postmodernism be bracketed off as a narrowly cultural matter, as an aesthetic convulsion, the latest avant-garde and yet another aestheticising trend in philosophy? To situate it thus is the characteristically late-modernist move taken by the sociologist Anthony Giddens. For him, the present socio-economic configuration is most accurately explained as *accentuated modernity*: 'Rather than entering a period of postmodernity, we are moving into one in which the consequences of modernity are becoming more radicalised and universalised than before' (1990: 3). This is indeed disconcerting and perplexing. Giddens points out that postmodernity used to be understood, in the Marxist scheme of things at least, as communism replacing capitalist modernity (p. 46). Giddens's own conception of modernity, in contrast, is multi-dimensional, covering the institutional matrix of capitalism, industrialism, surveillance and military power (p. 59). What has happened is that these defining features of modernity have become increasingly distanciated in time and space, the dynamics of which are no longer apprehendable at the level of the nation state but have to be grasped globally. Instead of Weber's 'iron cage' or Marx's 'monster', Giddens sees modernity as a 'juggernaut':

> a runaway engine of enormous power which, collectively as human beings, we can drive to some extent but which also threatens to rush out of our control and which could rend itself asunder. The juggernaut crushes those who resist it, and while it sometimes seems to have a steady path, there are times when it veers away erratically in directions we cannot foresee. The ride is by no means wholly unpleasant or unrewarding; it can often be exhilarating and charged with hopeful anticipation. But, so long as the institutions of modernity endure, we shall never be able to feel entirely secure, because the terrain across which it runs is fraught with risks of high consequence. Feelings of ontological security and existential anxiety will coexist in ambivalence.

(Giddens 1990: 139)

In my view, it is reasonable to treat the inflated claims of postmodern discourse with modernist scepticism, as does Giddens and also Marshall Berman in his celebrated study of modernity, *All that is Solid Melts into Air*, where he attacks 'a mystique of post-modernism, which strives to cultivate ignorance of modern history and culture, and speaks as if all human feeling, expressiveness, play, sexuality and community have only just been invented – by the post-modernists – and were unknown, even inconceivable, before last week' (1983: 33). However, Berman's own way of thinking about modernity provides an indispensable means of interrogating what David Harvey (1989) calls 'the condition of postmodernity'. Whether this is an accentuation of modernity or a sharp break into something else is the question I shall be going on to explore. Berman conceives of 'modernity' as the experiential mediation of 'modernisation' – the ever-expanding capitalist world market – and 'modernism' – the series of aesthetico-cultural responses to modernisation that, taken together, represent 'the modern movement' in art and philosophy

(Anderson, P. 1984). Modernity is, then, the dialectical meaning of modernisation/modernism for 'ordinary people and everyday life in the street' (Berman 1984: 123). This populist concern of Berman's, in spite of his avowed modernism, now has a distinctly *post*modern ring to it. In fact, several authors have already remarked upon the affinity between certain aspects of *post*modernism and *aesthetic* or, less frequently, *cultural populism.*

The most common summation of postmodern style and sensibility is 'the blurring of boundaries'. For instance, Mike Featherstone writes:

> If we examine definitions of postmodernism we find an emphasis on the effacement of the boundary between art and everyday life, the collapse of the distinction between high art and mass/popular culture, a general stylistic promiscuity and playful mixing of codes.
>
> (1991: 65)

Although a discourse on postmodernism along these lines can be traced back to American Pop Art of the 1960s, and no doubt further, it really came into its own with Charles Jencks's advocacy of postmodern architecture:

> To this day I would define postmodernism as I did in 1978 as *double coding: the combination of Modern techniques with something else (usually traditional building) in order for architecture to communicate with the public and a concerned minority, usually other architects.*
>
> (1986: 14)

The example of architecture is crucially important and perhaps the field in which 'postmodernism' definitely means something concrete (excuse the pun). Built space is instantly visible and routinely experienced in the quotidian by people indifferent to self-conscious architectural and philosophical discourses. For ordinary people, the reaction against the modern international style, from office blocks to public housing (Corbusier's 'machines for living'), is palpable and meaningful, albeit much exaggerated. It is a widely shared popular belief that urban planners made a terrible mistake in their reconstructions of the modern city, especially in the immediate post-Second World War period. Their buildings were alienating and often shoddy – instant slums. Postmodern architecture's orientation to the vernacular, older styles and contextual harmony, on the other hand, when done well, generally meets with approval even if it looks somewhat 'toytown'. And, yet, as Jencks observes, architects are also talking with one another in adopting these communicative principles.

Umberto Eco (1985a) appropriates Jencks's double-coding to characterise the kind of literary text which speaks simultaneously to the literati and a popular readership, spraying out erudite references whilst also providing the less culturally educated with a good story. Double-coding makes sense, too, of the kind of cinematic texts typically dubbed 'postmodernist', including the archetypal example, Ridley Scott's *Bladerunner*, and films with less immediately popular appeal, such as Wim Wender's *Wings of Desire* (Harvey 1989) and David Lynch's *Blue Velvet* (Denzin 1988). Television dramas like *Edge of Darkness* have been similarly identified (McGuigan 1986), but of more significance is the way in which the most popular medium can be thought of as institutionally postmodern, something implied by Eco's remarks concerning 'Neo-TV':

> The principal characteristic of Neo-TV is that it talks less and less about the external world. Whereas Paleo-TV talked about the external world, or pretended to, Neo-TV talks about itself and about the contact that it establishes with its own public . . . one can spend 48 hours a day in front of the TV, so there's no more need to come into contact with that remote fiction – the real world . . . . Now unreality is within everyone's grasp.
>
> (Eco 1985b: 19, 25)

In effect, the once *unpopular* elements of modern art have been reworked in popular contexts:

> 1 *Aesthetic Self-Consciousness or Self-Reflexiveness* . . .
> 2 *Simultaneity, Juxtaposition, or 'Montage'* . . .
> 3 *Paradox, Ambiguity, and Uncertainty* . . .
> 4 *'Dehumanization' and the Demise of the Integrated Individual Subject or Personality* . . .
>
> (Lunn 1985: 34-7)

These representational mechanisms, rendered commercially palatable, plus the recycling and mixing of older forms, mark out the contemporary postmodern popular, denounced by some as mere 'aesthetic populism' (Jameson 1991) and celebrated by

others as the newly democratised culture (Collins, J. 1990). Iain
Chambers, whose usage of the term is more or less consistent with
mine, makes the connection between 'cultural populism' and the
postmodern popular with unqualified enthusiasm:

> Inside this mobile collage a democracy of aesthetic and cultural
> populism becomes possible. The previous authority of culture,
> once respectfully designated with a capital C, no longer has an
> exclusive hold on meaning. 'High culture' becomes just one
> more subculture, one more option, in our midst. This forces a
> self-conscious reassessment in the recognition of what passes for
> contemporary knowledge; a posterior situation to the previous
> intellectual disdain for, and critical distance from, 'mass
> culture' and popular taste.

(1986: 194)

That Chambers is a graduate of the Birmingham Centre for
Contemporary Cultural Studies is no coincidence, for, as I have
argued in this book, populist sentiment was its energising impulse,
now given a postmodern twist. Steve Connor holds a similar view:

> Recent years have seen an explosion of interest in a whole range
> of cultural texts and practices which had previously been
> scorned by, or remained invisible to, academic criticism.
> Contemporary cultural critics, following the inspiring lead of
> Richard Hoggart, Raymond Williams, Roland Barthes and
> Stuart Hall, take as their subjects sport, fashion, hairstyles,
> shopping, games and social rituals, and unabashedly bring to
> bear on these areas the same degree of theoretical
> sophistication as they would to any high cultural artefact. In a
> sense, this is a postmodern phenomenon, for it is the mark of
> that levelling of hierarchies and blurring of boundaries which is
> an effect of the explosion of the field of culture described by
> Jameson in which the cultural and the social and the economic
> are no longer easily distinguishable one from another.

(1989: 184)

The cultural, the social and the economic cannot, however, be so
casually run into one another. They need to be separated out if the
articulations between them are to be understood and explained.
The present state of populist cultural analysis should not be
treated so complacently. Jim Collins (1990) has complained about
the excessively consumptionist emphasis in the field, which

dissolves the specificity of textual and production processes. And, on a more political note, Lawrence Grossberg (1988) questions 'The current roadblock in cultural studies – its inability to address the specificity of the relations between popular culture and systemic politics in the context of a hegemonic struggle' (p. 13). He blames this on the New Right's disorganisation of radical critique in the 1980s. The point is well taken, but I think it indicates a certain nostalgia for the moment of hegemony theory, which briefly gave coherence to critical analysis of popular culture in Britain. As I have argued in this book, the problem goes deeper than the uncritical drift out of hegemony theory: it derives from the original schism between the hermeneutic mainstream of British cultural studies and the political economy of culture. I wish, then, to develop my argument further by discussing theories which aim to account for postmodern culture in the context of socio-economic relations and changing identities, taking the case of collapsing communism to substantiate this materialist modification of cultural populism, and, in conclusion, to consider the prospects for critical renewal in the field.

LIVING IN THE (POST?)MODERN WORLD

Postmodern discourse must be contextualised historically and treated with scepticism if we are to extricate any enduring insights about popular culture from its iconoclastic declarations. Andreas Huyssen (1990) stresses 'the specifically American character of postmodernism' (pp. 362–3). For him, postmodernism's point of departure is the '"populist" trend of the 1960s with its celebration of rock'n'roll and folk music, of the imagery of everyday life and of the multiple forms of popular literature' which 'gained much of its energy in the context of the counter-culture and by a next to total abandonment of a critique of modern mass culture' (p. 366). In the following decade, it reappeared as a theme on the Parisian intellectual scene, particularly in the writings of Jean Baudrillard, the most important postmodern theorist for communication, cultural and media studies, who resituated postmodernism within the anti-populist mass culture critique.

Douglas Kellner has traced the development of Baudrillard's writings from a 1960s synthesis of historical materialism with semiology, in order to account for consumer manipulation, through a rejection of Marxism and towards an aristocratic nihilism in the 1970s and 1980s, when he eventually argued that highly technologised media, especially television, and 'the masses' had finally swallowed each other up:

> Baudrillard . . . suggests that the media intensify massification by producing mass audiences and homogenised ideas and experiences. On the other hand, he claims that the masses absorb all media content, neutralize, or even resist, meaning, and demand and obtain more spectacle and entertainment, thus further eroding the boundary between media and 'the real'.
>
> (Kellner 1989a: 69)

Baudrillard's provocative thematics of imploding reality – that representation is now 'hyperreal', that 'images', 'simulations' and 'simulacra' have become indistinguishable from social being itself – are overblown but not to be dismissed lightly. Perhaps they should be put to work as bold hypotheses for stimulating empirical enquiry, an approach inimical to Baudrillard's own casuistry.[1]

Baudrillard's 1985 essay, 'The masses – the implosion of the social in the media', summates his mature position and exemplifies how different it is from cultural populism. It is worth pausing for a moment to consider what he has to say. In this essay, Baudrillard revises his 'pessimistic' objection to both Marshall McLuhan's (1964) technological optimism, concerning the emergence of a 'global village',[2] and Hans Magnus Enzensberger's (1974) populist optimism, concerning the prospects for 'mass participation' in the modern media,[3] derived from Walter Benjamin and Bertolt Brecht. Baudrillard had stopped seeing 'the forced silence of the masses in the media' as 'a sign of passivity and alienation': instead, his revised perspective amounted to 'a vision of things which is no longer optimistic or pessimistic, but ironic and antagonistic' (1988: 208). He uses the example of opinion polls to illustrate this perspective, rejecting the naïve view that polling registers real opinions and also the critical view that it is used to manipulate the public. Opinion polls represent, rather, a simulacrum of public opinion, neither accurate nor manipulative, but efficacious for simulating politics in a depoliticised world. The fact of the matter is, according to Baudrillard, 'the masses' just don't care: 'the masses have no opinion and information does not inform' (p. 211), which is exactly the kind of effect of modern media on consciousness that Theodor Adorno and Max

Horkheimer feared back in the 1940s. The only difference between these critical theorists and the postmodern ironist Baudrillard is judgemental, not analytical. What modernist critics cannot understand, contends Baudrillard, is 'the evil genius of the masses' (p. 213). With cynical delight, Baudrillard declares, 'The mass knows that it knows nothing, and it does not want to know. The mass knows that it can do nothing, and it does not want to achieve anything' (p. 216). For ordinary people, then, politics is 'undecidable'. There is something chillingly perceptive about Baudrillard's observations on public opinion and politics . . . and yet.

In his book *Consumer Culture and Postmodernism* (1991), Mike Featherstone lodges sociological objections to the sweeping claims of postmodernist rhetoric. He calls for solidly grounded evidence of the impact of postmodernism on 'the lives of ordinary people' (p. 4). This is relevant to assertions both of popular powerlessness (postmodern elitism) and countervailing assertions of popular empowerment (postmodern populism). Specifically with reference to the populist celebration of consumer culture, Featherstone says: 'we need to ask the stark sociological questions about not only where the postmodern lifestyles take place; but how many people from which range of groups participate and for how long?' (p. 105). Featherstone argues convincingly that postmodernism is primarily to be understood, in Bourdieuan terms, as the product of the 'new cultural intermediaries' and perhaps only secondarily, or at second hand, as a truly popular phenomenon. These are not, however, mutually exclusive possibilities, though the latter is of more profound significance than the former, raising cultural and economic issues with regard to the everyday meanings and determinations of postmodern experience. Hermeneutic interpretations, the stock-in-trade of cultural populism, are necessary but insufficient. Materialist explanations of structural determination are also required, the kind of explanations that postmodernism itself, including its populist variants, would more often than not tend to rule out of order because of an alleged reductionism. In this sense, the writers whom I believe have produced the most compelling accounts of postmodernity are not themselves, strictly speaking, postmodernist: Alex Callinicos, Fredric Jameson, David Harvey, Scott Lash and John Urry. It is to their work that I shall now turn. To a lesser or greater degree, they all have something interesting to say about the production and consumption of postmodern culture in relation to capitalism, thereby linking cultural analysis with political economy.

Callinicos (1989 and 1990) is the only one of these writers wholly opposed to postmodern discourse. His book, *Against Postmodernism* (1989), is a sustained rationalist critique of its philosophical assumptions, following Habermas, and also of its political implications from a Trotskyist position. Callinicos's attack on the neo-Nietszchean strand of poststructuralist thought, underlying much of postmodern discourse, is in many respects quite devastating. That, however, is not the most distinctive part of his argument, which is to do with the connection between postmodernism and the thesis of postindustrial society, associated particularly with the work of the American sociologist Daniel Bell. Since the 1950s, Bell has argued that the epochal struggle between capital and labour has run its course. His original Cold War thesis, 'the end of ideology' (Bell 1960), has obvious resonance in the 1990s, with the recent collapse and continuing crises of regimes once officially committed to Marxism-Leninism. Bell's (1974) further and less overtly partisan claim that capitalism has ceased to function as an industrial system in the modern sense rests on a set of inferences concerning the discernible shift of labour from manufacturing to service sectors in advanced capitalist economies, the decline of Alvin Toffler's 'smokestack' industries and the rise of 'information' controlled by the technical-professionals (see Kumar 1978, and Boyne and Rattansi 1990). Like many other critics, Callinicos doubts that these trends have transformed capitalism beyond all recognition, unlike Lyotard (1984), who accepts the postindustrial thesis without question. Callinicos declares unreservedly: 'The idea of postindustrial society is, of course, nonsense' (1989: 121). Bell's argument is a kind of technologically determinist futurology, which does not square with the facts. As Callinicos points out, even in the United States, the service sector grew by only 0.8 per cent between 1970 and 1984. Labour in the manufacturing sector did indeed decline but productivity there increased, aided by robotic technology and computerised information.

Although such evidence calls into question the postindustrial thesis, Callinicos recognises that capitalism has not remained static. None the less, it persists as a globally exploitative system irrespective of local and mainly superficial changes. Callinicos gives some credence to theories of 'disorganized capitalism' and 'post-Fordism' but not much, due to their taintedness with 'New Times' revisionism. He does, however, give greater credence to the attendant thesis of a postmodern class, originating in Bell's (1976) later concern with 'the cultural contradictions of capitalism', though Callinicos refuses to see it as a class in itself. Rather, he prefers to regard postmodernists in 'the cultural mass' (Bell's term) as 'the children of Marx and Coca Cola'. Callinicos says: 'The political odyssey of the 1968 generation is, in my view, crucial to the widespread acceptance of the idea of a postmodern epoch in the 1980s' (p. 168). Disappointed by the failed prospects of revolutionary change, the radical middle-class youth of the 1960s, now middle-aged professionals, have settled for something less dangerous than storming the citadels of power:

> What could be more reassuring for a generation, drawn first towards and then away from Marxism by the political ups and downs of the past two decades, than to be told – in a style decked out with the apparent profundity and genuine obscurity of the sub-Modernist rhetoric cultivated by '68 thought – that there is nothing they can do to change the world? 'Resistance' is reduced to the knowing consumption of cultural products – perhaps the 'Postmodern' works of art whose authors have sought to embody in them this kind of thinking, but if not any old soap opera will do just as well.
>
> (Callinicos 1989: 170)

Scott Lash and John Urry's book *The End of Organized Capitalism* (1987), and Lash's *Sociology of Postmodernism* (1990) present a distinctive case concerning the relationship between capitalist transformation and postmodern culture. Their extensive treatment of the relationship constitutes a powerful critical response to the postindustrial thesis, but much less dismissively than Callinicos's critique. Adopting Claus Offe's (1985) concept of 'disorganized capitalism', Lash and Urry list its features as follows: growth of a world market, emergence of a service class, declining manual working class and national-level wage-bargaining, large monopolies overriding nation-state controls, diminution of class politics, increased cultural fragmentation and pluralism, decline of employment in extractive/manufacturing industries and of regionally specialised industry, decline in plant size and industrial cities. And, finally, 'appearance and mass distribution of a cultural-ideological configuration of "postmodernism'" affecting 'high culture, popular culture and the symbols and discourses of everyday life' (Lash and Urry 1987: 7). Their evidence is based on comparisons between Britain, the United States, France, West Germany and Sweden, which illuminates a great deal but tends to lose sight of the transnational dynamics of capitalism. Also, the discussion of postmodernism is only sketchily connected to these dynamics. For Lash and Urry, the disorganization of capitalism neither confirms postindustrialism nor does it represent a terminal crisis: rather, it is an updating of the system's still fundamentally intact social relations.

What has changed most notably is the cultural experience of living under capitalism. Lash and Urry believe that 'postmodernism' captures the texture of these lived relations, in both its commercially 'authoritarian populist' aspects, on the one side, and its youth culture and 'new social movement', unhierarchical aspects, on the other. It is neither inherently reactionary nor inevitably progressive but variable and contradictory in its effects. According to Lash and Urry, 'postmodernism' relates to the anti-auratic culture, spotted by Walter Benjamin (1936/1973) many years ago, and the return of the figural with the supersession of modernist abstraction (Lash 1990). The typical mode of attention is distracted and the attitude is irreverent. Lash and Urry identify three features of the postmodern social condition: '*semiotics of everyday life*' (cultural signs themselves become referents); '*new class fraction*' (the postmodernists); and, '*decentring of identity*' (multiple and overlapping subjectivities) (1987: 287–8).

Drawing on Pierre Bourdieu's (1984) ideas concerning 'the new petite bourgeoisie', 'habitus' and 'classificatory schemes', Lash and Urry thus provide a sociological account of postmodernist sociality, which is more substantial than Callinicos's narrowly political judgement. Bourdieu's dominant class is divided between 'the bourgeoisie' (high on economic capital but not always on cultural capital) and 'the intellectuals' (high on cultural capital but comparatively low on economic capital). Beneath these two groups are various *petit bourgeois* fractions competing with one another and with those above them. This is where Lash and Urry discern the social base for postmodern culture. The new petite bourgeoisie are engaged in occupational practices of 'presentation and representation' either in the public sector (for instance, youth workers) or private sector (for example, designers), usually without the prestigious credentials of the *haut bourgeois* intelligentsia with whom they may have a resentful relationship or, for the more acquisitive, the capitalist class whom they may seek to join. Lash and Urry remark:

> In promoting themselves, this new cultural petite bourgeoisie . . . encourages 'symbolic rehabilitation projects'; that is they give (often postmodern) cultural objects new status as part of rehabilitation strategies for their own careers. In their work in the media, in advertising, in design, as 'cultural intermediaries' they are taste creators.
>
> (1987: 295–6)

Moreover:

> this new petit bourgeois not only has a habitus which predisposes him or her to the reception of postmodern cultural objects, but . . . a pre-eminently *de*structured and decentred habitus . . . he or she is low on 'grid' (i.e. classificatory structures) and lives for the moment . . . . He or she is also low on 'group' (the strength of boundary between 'us' and 'them').
>
> (1987: 296)

Furthermore:

> A crucial effect . . . of the electronic media and spatio-temporal changes in our disorganizing capitalist societies has been the decentring of identities and the loosening or destructuring of group and grid.
>
> (1987: 299)

Lash and Urry's adaptation of Bourdieu to account for the postmodern class fraction is convincing, albeit schematic, and has influenced my own argument that the populist intervention in cultural knowledge can be understood, in the first instance, as a Bourdieuan struggle for symbolic power, representing fairly narrow interests yet similarly evincing a certain democratisation of culture: a postmodern populism.

Now, we must turn to the most renowned theorist of the articulation between postmodern culture and the global dynamics of capitalism, the American Marxist Fredric Jameson. During the 1980s, Jameson (1984, 1985 and 1988) put a much-debated set of arguments (see Kellner 1989b) on this articulation: the epochal significance of postmodernism, the eclipse of radical critique and politics, the rise of aesthetic populism and accentuated consumerism, the technological renewal of capital, the call for an aesthetic of cognitive mapping, and so forth. These arguments are resumed and extended in his monumental 1991 book, *Postmodernism or, The Cultural Logic of Late Capitalism*, the same title as his controversial 1984 article, which was published in *New Left Review*. To do justice to the complexity of Jameson's position would take too long: instead, my aim here is to outline his key arguments as briefly as possible without, I hope, distorting them.

In the introduction to his book, Jameson declares:

> It is safest to grasp the concept of the postmodern as an attempt to think the present historically in an age that has forgotten how to think historically in the first place . . . . Postmodernism is the consumption of sheer commodification as a process . . . the 'postmodern' is to be seen as the production of postmodern people capable of functioning in a very peculiar socioeconomic world indeed.
>
> (1991: ix, x, xv)

Whether it is 'safe' or not, this is a fairly bold sequence of observations. The tone might suggest that Jameson would be in the camp of modernist sceptics, but that is not quite so since his initial take on postmodernism is as the popular commercialisation of modernism in a way which diminishes its critical force. This really is a new formation, in which postmodernism represents the 'structure of feeling' (Williams's concept) of 'late capitalism'. Postmodern intellectuals are 'fascinated' by a 'whole degraded landscape of schlock and kitsch' (p. 2). Populism, however, is only part of the emergent 'hegemonic norm' or postmodern 'force field'. Jameson goes on to list its 'constitutive features':

> a new depthlessness, which finds its prolongation both in contemporary 'theory' and in a whole new culture of the image or the simulacrum; a consequent weakening of historicity, both in our relationship to public History and in the new forms of our private temporality . . . a whole new type of emotional ground tone . . . 'intensities' . . . the deep constitutive relationship of all of this to a whole new technology, which is itself a figure for a whole new economic world system . . . postmodernist mutations in the lived experience of built space

itself . . . the bewildering new world space of late or multinational capital.

(1991: 6)

In his subsequent writings, Jameson has become more circumspect about using Ernest Mandel's (1975) term, 'late capitalism', perhaps because there is nothing 'late' about this globalised capitalism at all, no longer confronted seriously by an alternative economic system. However, Mandel's scheme of capitalist 'stages' is essential to Jameson's own 'periodising hypothesis'. He offers an homology of the dominant aesthetico-cultural forms and transformations in the capitalist mode of production: realism corresponding to market capitalism and steam power; modernism to monopoly capitalism, electric and combustion power; and postmodernism to multi-national capitalism, electronic and nuclear power. This is extremely schematic and arguably reductionist, yet it does indicate a greater significance for postmodern culture than some perturbation of the *petit bourgeois* habitus. If Jameson is right, then everyone is caught up in an epochal transition and personally disorientating process. That is why he calls for an 'aesthetic of cognitive mapping – a pedagogical political culture which seeks to endow the individual subject with some new heightened sense of itself in the global system' (1991: 54). I shall be returning to the theme of cognitive mapping. Suffice it to say for the moment that Jameson's thesis has been widely disputed for being excessively totalising, for failing to account adequately for the precise mediations and experiential differences (see, for instance, Davis 1988) in this articulation of culture and economy on a global scale.

Responding to Jameson's 'daring thesis', David Harvey says, in *The Condition of Postmodernity*:

I think it important to accept the proposition that the cultural evolution which has taken place since the early 1960s, and which asserted itself as hegemonic in the early 1970s, has not occurred in a social, economic, or political vacuum.

(1989: 63)

He then sets about putting flesh on the bare bones of Jameson's skeletal articulation of postmodern culture to economics. Principally a literary theorist, Jameson's articulation proceeds from cultural critique, whereas Harvey, a geographer, derives his arguments with greater conviction from political economy: and, for this reason, Harvey is even more vulnerable than Jameson to the accusation that his approach is merely a last-ditch effort to breathe life into a properly dead and buried classical Marxism. This accusation, made for instance by Angela McRobbie (1991a), misses the distinctiveness of Harvey's approach, which returns a powerful sense of the dialectics of space and place to cultural studies.

Harvey agrees with Charles Jencks that the place where the symbolic break between modern and postmodern architecture occurred most precisely was St Louis, in the United States: the time, 3.32 p.m. on 15 July 1972; when the uninhabitable modern housing estate of Pruitt-Igoe was blown up. One can make too much of these events, not uncommon since, yet the dating does matter. From the mid-1960s capitalist societies faced a series of accumulating crises which came to a head in 1973 with the OPEC oil price hike and, during the Arab–Israeli War, the Arab embargo on oil exports to the West. Nothing would remain the same. According to Harvey, this was the conjunctural moment at which Fordism reached its nadir. It was probably also the moment when communism's mimicry of that system met its Waterloo, though nobody knew it at the time, and the history is yet to be written.

Following the French regulation school of economists, Harvey views 'recent events as a transition in the *regime of accumulation* and its associated *mode of social and political regulation*' (1989: 121). To sustain the accumulation process, capital must reproduce itself socially while simultaneously solving its two basic economic problems: price-fixing and labour-exploitation. During the post-Second World War period, these problems were solved by Fordism allied to Keynesian demand management economics, a system of mass-standardised production and consumption regulated by large-scale state intervention, ensuring a certain level and quality of existence for social majorities, especially in richer countries like the United States and Britain. Harvey observes:

> The break up of this system since 1973 has inaugurated a period of rapid change, flux and uncertainty. Whether or not the new systems of production and marketing, characterised by more flexible labour processes and markets, of geographical mobility and shifts in consumption practices, warrant the title of a new regime of accumulation, and whether the revival of

entrepreneurialism and of neo-conservatism, coupled with the cultural turn to postmodernism, warrants the title of a new mode of regulation is by no means clear.

(1989: 124)

Although very nearly agnostic on the accentuated modernity/ postmodernity debate, Harvey proceeds on the assumption that something of enormous significance has been happening, at least on the economic front. Fordism is a rigid system in terms of long-term investment, product design, labour markets and nation-state involvement, making it difficult to respond quickly to changing economic and cultural circumstances. Greater flexibility, in all these respects, is what distinguishes so-called 'post-Fordism'. It becomes easier to switch investment around, between businesses, regions and countries. Labour markets are restructured, creating a sharper division between 'core' well-paid, comparatively secure workers, and 'peripheral' low-paid, temporary and part-time workers. With labour power becoming a more flexible commodity, manufacturing processes also become more flexible, applying computerisation for rapid changes in product lines and aiding the feasibility of small-batch production, led increasingly by market research. Up-to-date knowledge is the key to commercial success at the level of the firm *and globally* as information technology enables capitalism to reorganise financial markets. The nation state plays a less pronounced role, legitimated by neo-classical economics. Under these conditions, Fordism is devolved to cheaper labour markets internationally, and, at the centre of the capitalist world economy, smaller-scale manufacture, subcontracting and networking, adapted to the tasteful and carefully cultivated whims of the 'lifestyle' consumer, become 'the leading edge', in Hall and Jacques's (1989) words, if not the exclusive mode.

The cultural aspects of these developments are in many respects new, yet, argues Harvey, the constitutive features of capitalism, which he analysed in *The Limits to Capital* (1982), are not fundamentally altered: capitalism is still growth-orientated, exploitative of labour, and technically and organisationally dynamic (1989: 180). In consequence, capitalism tends to *over*-accumulate, 'indicated by idle productive capacity, a glut of commodities and an excess of inventories, surplus money capital . . . and high unemployment' (p. 181). These are recurrent and unavoidable critical outcomes. Various techniques are used to ameliorate such outcomes: devaluation, macro-economic controls and, of particular interest to Harvey, absorption of over-accumulation 'through temporal and spatial displacement' (p. 182). Summarising a complexly technical argument, influenced by Henri Lefebvre's 'grid' of spatial practices (material, coded and representational), supplemented by considerations of accessibility/distanciation, appropriation, domination and production of space in time, Harvey says:

> Spatial and temporal practices are never neutral in social affairs. They always express some kind of class or other social content, and are more often than not the focus of intense social struggle. That this is so becomes doubly obvious when we consider the ways in which space and time connect with money, and the way that connection becomes even more tightly organized with the development of capitalism. Time and space both get defined through the organization of social practices fundamental to commodity production. But the dynamic force of capital accumulation (and overaccumulation) together with conditions of social struggle, render the relations unstable. As a consequence, nobody quite knows what 'the right time and place for everything' might be. Part of the insecurity that bedevils capitalism as a social formation arises out of this instability in the spatial and temporal principles around which social life might be organized (let alone ritualized in the manner of traditional societies). During phases of maximal change, the temporal and spatial bases for reproduction of the social order are subject to the severest disruption.
>
> (1989: 239)

The novelty of Harvey's analysis is not so much his account of the renewal of capitalism but, rather, the way he articulates the logic of capital to cultural change through the mediation of time–space relations. Historically, capitalism revolutionised time and space. For capitalism, time really is money. The exploitation of labour-time and the efficient use of time are, therefore, essential. Also, capitalism trades: it must, therefore, control space. Materially accurate mapping techniques arose with the expansion of world trade. The intensification of these practices characterises 'the condition of postmodernity', in Harvey's account, what he calls 'time-space compression'. The world speeds up and becomes smaller, which can be both exhilarating and disconcerting. To illustrate the point, Harvey refers to satellite communications: such 'systems deployed since the early 1970s have rendered the unit cost of communication invariant with respect to distance' (p. 293). Representations of distant events are received instantaneously throughout the world: we 'see', with astonishing immediacy, students protesting and getting massacred in Tiananmen Square, the Berlin Wall tumbling, dissident intellectuals mobilising the people in Prague, violent revolution in Romania, journalists falling about during air raids, military briefings and video games in the Gulf, and the operatic implosion of Soviet communism. Closer to home, the regime of flexible accumulation requires us to participate at high speed when the going is good, or the credit is available. The 'mobilisation of fashion' is a good example, whether it happens to be clothes or ideas.

There is no time for pause or reflection when you are living in the postmodern world; that is, if you go with the flow. To understand these experiences, some comprehension of the dynamics of postmodern capital is necessary but not, for Harvey, sufficient. Not all of us experience these processes in the same way: there are many differences in our time–space positioning: we cannot assume 'others' are similarly placed, socially, culturally, spatially or economically. But nobody's identity is fixed once and for all in the maelstrom of postmodernity: we move about, either imaginatively or physically. Identities are constantly dissolving and recomposing across many determinations, including those of a renewed, flexibly accumulating capital, which sweeps all before it but can never rest on its laurels, or else it is dead too.

CHANGING IDENTITIES

In a BBC2 *Late Show* interview at the end of 1989, the year of popular-democratic revolution in Eastern Europe, Stuart Hall remarked:

> When I ask somebody where they come from I expect nowadays to be told a very long story . . . . Everybody seems to come from about five different places and, in their heads, their sense of themselves, to be juggling a kind of set of world identities, as it

were, trying to find their place in a number of different possible senses of who they are.[4]

For Hall, evidently, this pluralisation of identity and decentring of subjectivity constitutes a creative *dis*placement in which the old fixities and certainties are shattered by what he calls 'a new dynamic culturally across the globe'. Such a sense of possibility was underscored, that winter of 1989, with the unfreezing of the Soviet bloc by extraordinarily peaceful uprisings in the German Democratic Republic and Czechoslovakia, followed by the more predictable violence of Ceauşescu's overthrow in Romania. Hall was less concerned with these unfolding events than with longer-term cultural exchanges brought about by post-imperial diasporas generally, manifested particularly by 'world music' in the widest sense, the globalised popular culture of the young. Not surprisingly, in the interview, Hall linked the physical and imaginary migrations of people to the broader dynamics of 'New Times', post-Fordism and postmodern culture.

*Dis*placement has contradictory aspects, simultaneously opening up new vistas and also uprooting people from where they want to be. Most migrations are painful, especially when they are not freely chosen but are enforced by considerations of economic necessity and political survival. The migrant, thus impelled to move, typically feels nostalgic for what has been left behind (Berger and Mohr 1975). Intellectuals may not suffer from this affliction so much as ordinary people. For that reason, they may regard a strong sense of place as reactionary and defensive (Massey 1991).

David Harvey (1990) attributes the 'tension between fixity and mobility' to destructive and constructive shifts of capital in the global economy. In Britain, we have seen the decimation of mining communities, once narrowly circumscribed and, hence, ultimately vulnerable places. Now, many Eastern Europeans hope to become beneficiaries of capitalist reconstruction in their places of work, so neglected and run-down under command economics. What is in doubt, however, is the extent to which over-accumulated capital deals with post-communist territories as outlets for investment in production and not only as expanded consumer markets. There is a temptation to treat these processes as thoroughly opaque and, therefore, entirely beyond popular control. In the everyday life-world, movements of capital are indeed obscure and experienced as uncontrollable. But, Harvey himself argues, there is a dialectic of space and place whereby ordinary people do find a measure of control, however limited: identities are forged out of this dialectic. Harvey (1990) gives the example of New York's Times Square, built by capital and turned into what Raymond Williams called a 'knowable community' by its ordinary users on the street.

A similarly knowable community is Doreen Massey's (1991) Kilburn High Road, an intersection of many cultures, most notably of English, Irish and Asian origin. Massey, refining Harvey's insights, calls for 'a global sense of place' which incorporates 'the power-geometry of time-space compression' (p. 25), to explore differential experiences of place, particularly between men and women. Some groups are 'in charge' of movement through space: 'the jet-setters, the ones sending and receiving the faxes and the e-mail, holding the international conference calls, the ones distributing the films, controlling the news, organising the investments and the international currency transactions' (p. 26). There are other groups, however, who get moved about, refugees seeking safe havens, like the Kurds in the wake of the Gulf War. And, there are yet others 'who are simply on the receiving end of time-space compression . . . eating British working-class style fish and chips from a Chinese take-away, watching a US film on a Japanese television; and not daring to go out after dark' (p. 26).

Identity is a collective phenomenon, never exclusively individual. It has most frequently been thought of in nationalistic terms, referring to what those within the boundaries of a nation-state are said to share. This conception masks over cultural differences: 'Great Britain' is a good example, made up of several nationalities, either through territorial division or migration. Against such 'imagined community' (Anderson, B. 1983), it is sometimes argued that 'real' identity is local, qualified perhaps by awareness of global dynamics, as Massey suggests. 'Real' identities are not, however, necessarily place-specific at all. There are 'communities of interest', in the old GLC term, which cut across geography. For instance, one might wish to refer to the 'Islamic nation' dispersed throughout Europe. 'Identities', 'communities' and 'nations' are always to some degree imaginary constructions of self; and they are now routinely negotiated in relation to globalising culture under postmodern conditions.

Philip Schlesinger (1991) has criticised Benedict Anderson's analysis of 'imagined communities' for not appreciating the role of the modern media in the reproduction and formation of identities, especially national ones. It is true that modern media, and broadcasting in particular, have played a major role in national identity-formation. The future likelihood, however, is that they may come increasingly to erode such identities, for better or for worse, as transnationalisation, economically and culturally, develops. This has already been very important in the collapse of communism, though conversely releasing hitherto suppressed ethnic and smaller national identities, usually with a *pre*-modern flavour. Schlesinger argues that the events of 1989 were 'an unprecedented challenge to long-standing patterns of cultural and political identity in Europe' (p. 176). More parochially, they present a challenge to students of communications media as well. He identifies

> [a] new and very practical task, that of tracking developments in the Eastern bloc . . . . [Specifically] one of the most interesting processes to observe in the coming years will be the political, economic and cultural responses to the invasion of East-Central Europe by capitalist multi-media enterprises. Will a durable 'public sphere' be established?
>
> (Schlesinger 1991: 176)

In formulating the question thus, Schlesinger quite wittingly opens up a can of analytical worms: the brand name on the can is 'cultural imperialism'. This has become a deeply unfashionable problematic, not least because of what John Tomlinson (1991) calls, 'the *hermeneutic naivety* of the discourses of cultural imperialism' (p. 34). In umpteen studies of the flow of cultural products from 'imperial' centres to their subordinate peripheries 'the crucial question of how ordinary readers read' (p. 43) has been neglected. This is a space where new revisionist perspectives on media consumption have made hay, demonstrating time and time again how audience activity and popular pleasure exceed symbolic imposition. The consumption of American cultural products across the globe, for instance, does not represent domination, according to latter-day cultural populism. Schlesinger spells out clearly the consequent analytical dilemma associated with such an aversion to economically informed communications analysis and cultural critique when he says: 'Between reliance on an outmoded and discredited model of media effects and a trendy subjectivism, current mediology has not much to offer in shedding light upon the constitution of collective identity in general and national identity in particular' (1991: 172).

At stake, then, is whether or not a theory of economic and cultural power depends upon a simplistic model of media 'effects'. Cultural populists are right to reject the latter but, in my view, they are mistaken in rejecting the former. It is indeed unsatisfactory to think of cultural imperialism as an attack on 'pure' subordinate cultures at the level of individual response. People, wherever they are, make syncretic use of the cultural products available to them. But this is not the only level at which the question can be posed. Tomlinson offers a means of circumventing Schlesinger's dilemma by recommending

> another way of formulating the domination involved in cultural imperialism. Instead of on the level of individual responses, it might be thought of in terms of the culture as a whole. The argument would run something like this: whatever the divergence in individual responses to cultural imports, domination is occurring where the 'autonomy' of a culture – roughly speaking, its right to develop along its own lines – is threatened by external forces.
>
> (1991: 95)

Subsequently, Tomlinson goes on to remark, '[w]hat is interesting about the changes in the planned socialist economies is that the desire for more consumer goods is linked with the desire for the political freedom of liberal democracies' (p. 131). The question of domination arises, however, concerning the extent to which the democratic revolutionaries in Eastern Europe were able to develop autonomous solutions or, contrary to their aims in many cases, were merely swapping one form of domination for another, the dictate of communism for the dictate of global capitalism, a cruel irony indeed. Put so baldly, the question answers itself, and an obvious critical reply to it would be: better the devil you don't know than the devil you know. Whatever the risks of massive economic and cultural upheaval, for the erstwhile subjects of communist autarky, they are preferable to acquiescing with a discredited and curiously archaic system.

The various sustained attempts to explain the deep causes and to chart the uncertain consequences of collapsing communism are beyond the scope of this discussion (see, for instance, Hobsbawm 1990; Callinicos 1991, and Miliband and Panitch 1991), but they cannot be wholly ignored should we wish to explore the cultural aspects of this momentous occurrence. The crisis of communist cultural and socio-economic arrangements, what Zygmunt Bauman (1990) has called 'the counter-culture of modernity', may represent one of the most important senses in which we can speak of 'postmodernity'. My own view is that the communist regimes were caught in a frozen state of modernity, having sought to complete the project initiated by capitalism, applying Fordist methods of production – and to a fatally lesser extent, consumption – with a vengeance, and despoiling nature to an even worse degree than capitalism itself in order to achieve that long-wished-for leap into the modern world. As we have seen, capitalism adapted its project ruthlessly from the early 1970s, leaving communism behind in the slipstream of history. 'The signs in the street' (Berman 1984) are relevant here: Eastern European cityscapes look for all the world like capitalist modernity *circa* 1960, which is fairly modern but not, as it turned out, modern enough. To quote Mary Kaldor, who summarises the key dynamic in 'the West' very well:

> Unlike in the East, economic restructuring took place in the West during the 1970s and 1980s. Fordist patterns of industrial development have been increasingly replaced by more flexible, decentralized resource-saving methods of production, applicable to both manufacturing and services and based on the revolution in what are known as information technologies. The pole of capitalist accumulation has shifted from the United States to Japan and, to a lesser extent, West Germany and the smaller West European countries.
>
> (1990: 31–2)

Robin Blackburn (1991) holds a similar view: that the failure of communism has to be explained with reference to the successful renewal of capitalism. He stresses the way in which '[t]he protracted Cold War imposed an increasingly strident technological blockade and contributed to incipient stagnation' (p. 30). And, worsening the situation, decision-making procedures in 'Soviet-type economies' led to backwardness, stifling innovation, especially by failing to exploit by-products. Domestic technological spin-offs from military and space industries were crucial to product-innovation in the West whereas, in the East, such opportunities were lost in a web of bureaucracy and prohibition. Defence spending drained resources, fatally denying Western levels of domestic consumption and product quality to ordinary people. External pressure and internally exacerbated economic stasis, moreover, were accompanied by cultural inertia:

> In the seventies and eighties, the cultural inertness of the Communist states made them vulnerable to the cultural vitality of the non-Communist world. The Communist authorities could not insulate their populations from the cultural products of the West, and on occasion actively promoted them . . . . Of course the vitality of popular culture in the West or South is not capitalist, drawing as it does on a variety of impulses, some of them utopian or resistant. But as the theorists of the 'society of the spectacle', or the postmodern, have pointed out, the cultural logic of late capitalism has been able to ally itself with the electronic media in ways that proved to be beyond the post-Stalinist command economies.
>
> (Blackburn 1991: 64–5)

In analytical terms, there is a substantial difference between whether one puts the weight of explanation on cultural-political determinations or on cultural-economic determinations of communist collapse. Stuart Hall and Fredric Jameson differed from one another on this point, with Hall emphasising democratic aspiration and the appeal of Western consumerism, while Jameson, consistent with his thesis on postmodernity, emphasised the incorporation of post-communist countries into global capitalism, something which even reform communists sought (Hall and Jameson 1990). On this issue, one cannot be strictly right or wrong. Yet, the difference does matter since it raises important questions of power and self-determination. Hall's position does not depart significantly from the liberal democratic view enunciated by Timothy Garton Ash in Britain and Francis Fukuyama in the United States. Garton Ash's (1990) brilliantly evocative journalistic writing on the 1989 events was framed by the assumption that liberal democracy and the benefits of market capitalism, very much in that order, were the inspirations of revolt. And, more hawkishly, Fukuyama (1990) saw the events as confirming his 'end of history' thesis, expounded in advance of autumn 1989 (Fukuyama 1989a and b).

It is easy enough to agree with Hall and Garton Ash, but Fukuyama's argument is much harder to swallow. However, the virtue of such a phenomenology of revolt is interpretive rather than explanatory. With the benefit of hindsight, in view of the disenchantment that set in soon after the heartening events of late 1989, the hard-boiled, depth materialism of Jameson's judgement is an indispensable corrective. The liberal democratic view did little more than endorse the delusion that a transition to Western European-style consumer capitalism, with Western Germany as the shining model to aim for, would actually happen more or less quickly once the magic of 'the market' was allowed to perform its tricks. Anything that is said, even now, remains very speculative. However, Bogdan Denitch's 'prognosis' of 'Mexicanization' seems closest to the mark for the time being:

> The post-communist politics of Eastern Europe will in many ways resemble Mexico, with all the present ambiguities of corporatism, corruption, a dynamic private sector, and a multitude of political parties, most of which have no effective access to power or broad support. One must not push the analogy too far, but it is richly suggestive. These will also be societies where the role of international financial institutions and banks will be important as well as a source of great internal hostility and controversy. These are part of the historical penalty being paid by these societies for the lost years under communist regimes.
>
> (1990: 39)

This may not be the fate of all the post-communist societies; exchanging 'Second World' status and the suppression of difference for a kind of 'Third World' status and widening disparities of wealth and opportunity. The case of East Germany is special (incidentally, Denitch, writing in 1989, did not anticipate its swift annexation by West Germany, which may undermine his predictive credibility). Some insouciant Western pundits forecast that Czechoslovakia and Hungary could reach Western European living standards quite soon, probably aided by membership of the EEC, though their export potential is doubted by wiser commentators in view of the eclipse of the protected Comecon market and such countries' own well-established competitive disadvantages in the global marketplace. Between even these two comparatively favoured ex-communist states there are important distinctions to be made. Neo-Stalinist for longer, since post-1968 'normalisation', Czechoslovakia avoided debt dependency whereas, superficially better prepared for coping with market forces, Hungary indebted itself heavily to Western financial institutions under Kadar's reform communist regime (Ray 1991). *Petit bourgeois* 'enterprise', 'anything-goes' culture and debtor status are a long way off from, say, the West German 'miracle'. The Hungarian situation may already exemplify the process of Mexicanisation (see Bihari 1991, for an incisive discussion of Hungary's problems). It is hard to generalise because of the peculiarities of each newly democratised or democratising country. Yet, taking two of the more critical examples, the effect of 'shock therapy' in Poland and, in the former Soviet Union, the persistent danger of authoritarian populist solutions to the chaos resulting from communism's self-immolation indicate anything but a smooth transition to Western-style consumer capitalism. Identities in the former Eastern bloc are indeed changing but in what ways are yet to be decided. Perhaps the postmodernists are right: undecidability is the present condition's mental set.

WRITING ON THE WALL

So far I have stressed the economic determinants of collapsing communism, especially those associated with Western capitalism's technological renewal. This does not, however, account sufficiently for the specific political and cultural processes of the 1989 revolutions and related developments across Eastern Europe. The romantic view is that people simply rose up in protest and toppled oppressive regimes in countries where the command economy was incapable of delivering the goods: end of story.

I would not deny the catalytic effect of these uprisings, prefigured by the Polish workers' movement of Solidarity in the early 1980s, and led with great courage by the dissident intellectuals of New Forum in East Germany and Civic Forum in Czechoslovakia at the close of the decade. Nor would I reduce these revolutions exclusively to the triggering effect of what Gennady Gerasimov has called 'the Sinatra doctrine' of Mikhail Gorbachev (Dawisha 1990). Democratic *revolutionary* populism did indeed precipitate systemic transformation in the Eastern bloc (Habermas 1990). But I am also struck by John Palmer's sombre observation:

The importance of revolution 'from below', of 'people power', in effecting these changes cannot be dismissed, and is rightly a source of great optimism for those in peace and opposition movements throughout Europe. But there is a grave danger that the gains of 1989 will fall prey to forces over which the citizen has little control.

(1991: 176)

These forces are economic, political and cultural: taken together they pose a question of hegemony in which popular forces play a part, but maybe a more limited part than radical democrats might wish. To understand the 'ideology of popular protest' (Rude 1980), one has to dig deeper than the philosophies of protest movements, into the grounds of unofficial culture and, in the case of the East, its articulation to Western values and practices.

Let us pause for a moment to consider 'the street culture of *glasnost*' on the Arbat pedestrian precinct, Moscow's Covent Garden, described by Leo Panitch and Sam Gindin:

The profusion of craft and artist stalls on the Arbat or at Ismaelovsky Park gives Moscow some of the vibrancy so notably absent in the past. Yet this directly blends with some of the most unsavoury aspects of the kind of market freedom we know in the West. There are, near the Arbat, many beggars pathetically attempting to scrounge a few kopeks by turning pity for their physical handicap or the visible impoverishment of their children into some sort of exchange value. Rather more pleasantly interspersed among the stalls are many buskers, such as a jazzband playing with gusto Dixieland renditions of Glenn Miller's hits . . . . Reflecting a far more traditional aspect of Russian culture, a much larger crowd gathers amidst the stalls to hear a poet declaim his verses in the richest of Russian tones. His poems are all political and splenetically anti-regime . . . . Thus does the politics of *glasnost* blend with the commercialism of *glasnost*. Indeed, among the crafts on the stalls themselves the hottest new commodity, produced by hundreds of political-artist entrepreneurs in an array of styles ranging from the most crudely painted to some of high artistic quality, is the 'Gorby' doll. Like the traditional Matrushka, it opens up to reveal a succession of dolls inside. Inside Gorbachev one invariably finds Brezhnev (usually bedecked in his military medals), then Krushchev (the one we bought is carrying a shoe), then Stalin (ours has a pipe in one hand and, held behind his back, a bloody dagger in the other), then finally, inside Stalin, there is always a tiny Lenin, looking sage or stunned, benevolent or evil, according to the whim, ideological orientation or sense of consumer demand of the dollmaker.

(1991: 29–30)

This is one of the most distinctively 'postmodern' scenes: the blurring of boundaries, the mixing of codes, the intermingling of high and popular culture, the playful seriousness of it all.[5] That is one thing it has in common with the official, deeply conservative Soviet-style culture: seriousness. Culture was very serious indeed: transgression could lead to death, incarceration or banishment. Soviet bloc countries have promoted and heavily subsidised classical music, opera and ballet for the masses. Popular culture was conceived of as 'folk culture', an authentic trace of the past. Books, films, television programmes all mattered in a terribly serious way. None of this, however, could possibly stand up to the commercialised popular culture of the West, with its irreverent, forever changing qualities (or, when not changing, recycling), so seductive, particularly for the young.

Boris Kagarlitsky (1988), coordinator of the Moscow Popular Front for *Perestroika*, recognised this when the prospects for autonomous reconstruction seemed more hopeful than Denitch's subsequently gloomier prognosis of Mexicanisation: 'The chief weakness of the new Left is the persistent gap between "high" culture and the "low" culture of the youth' (p. 338). What is this low culture of youth? Nothing less than the implantation of Western youth culture in its various permutations and combinations. It is well known that for many years in Eastern Europe, as elsewhere in the world, Anglo-American popular music and subcultural styles appealed to the young. You could see hippies and punks on the streets of East Berlin as well as Moscow throughout the 1980s; and, young East Berliners used to gather near the Wall to listen to the deliberately provocative open-air concerts just over the other side.[6] In one way or another, the writing was on the wall for a long time.

John Bushnell's study *Moscow Graffiti* (1990) beautifully captures the inroads of Western-related unofficial culture amongst the young since the 1970s. A regular visitor to Moscow, Bushnell notes that graffiti were seldom seen on the walls of the Soviet capital until the late 1970s when, suddenly, words and images connoting football support, rock music and counter-cultural politics began to appear. He says: 'Study of the graffiti opens up the history of the Soviet youth subculture because the graffiti have developed in tandem with the subculture' (1990: x). There are, however, particular national traditions which already made graffiti an important Russian form, specifically in the tradition of Kievan Rus, writing on church walls as a devotional act of Orthodox Christianity. Bushnell also considers the practice of childrens' graffiti, which because of the size of children tended to be low down on walls: it only rose up the walls in profusion towards the end of the 1970s, when teenagers took to it.

The earliest examples of this kind of graffiti were associated with the new soccer gangs, the *fanaty*, a neologism adopted by supporters of teams like Moscow Sparta. The word 'fan' appeared on walls, taken like many graffiti words from English, close to the Russian word 'fanat', but in the context of football hooliganism, which broke out around this time, connoting something very familiar in England and soon to become common in the Soviet Union. The next wave of graffiti was associated with Western rock music, against which the Soviet authorities gave up the battle during the 1970s. Performers from the West began to visit in the mid-1970s, most notably the German-based reggae band, Boney M, whose biggest hit was *Rah Rah Rasputin, Russia's Greatest Love Machine*. Heavy metal, the louder the better, has great appeal in Russia; and its keenest followers, the *metallisty*, are enthusiastic graffiti-writers as well, scrawling up the names of such bands as AC/DC and Kiss. Another strand, identified by Bushnell, relates to counter-cultural politics, the pacificism of the hippies and the nihilism of the punks. And there is also the cult of Mikhail Bulgakov, author of the much acclaimed novel *The Master and Margarita*. The stairwell of the apartment block where Bulgakov lived has been covered in graffiti referring to him and his famous book. Other graffiti writers include the *Afgansty*, veterans of the war in Afghanistan, some of whom were to adopt puritanical social attitudes in response to the Pandora's box of 'openness', and, yet more ominously, there are the *fashisty*, as the name suggests even further to the authoritarian right than the *Pamiat'* (Memory) movement.

Bushnell is reluctant to theorise the social and political significance of these 'writings on the wall', yet the implications are quite evident, both in terms of the 'resistance' model of subcultural theory and in terms of the popular imaginative practice which is crucial to understanding the decline of communist cultural hegemony: *interior migration*, symbolised by the language of the West, and in the narrow sense of language, English itself. In spite of his theoretical reluctance, Bushnell does make the basic empirical inference in this respect:

> Western popular culture and English, the principal language of that culture, have acquired prestige among Soviet young people, who live in a world saturated with Western symbols and artefacts . . . . We can read the defeat of the Soviet regime's efforts to control culture in the English the graffiti writers use, but even the language is Soviet rather than British or American.
>
> (1990: 197, 219)

Graffiti is, of course, a situated idiom, an argot, adapted to local circumstances whether it happens to be in New York, London, Moscow or Berlin. There was writing on the Berlin Wall too, but that was from the Western side rather than the Eastern, for obvious reasons. When the Wall fell and chunks of it became souvenir commodities, the more graffiti-decorated the chunk, the more valuable, fetching up to 40 Deutschmarks. As Lori Turner comments, 'The Wall, in fact, is turned into the trophy reserved for the winners of the cold war' (1990: 3).

Interior migration in the former German Democratic Republic was most profoundly represented by television-viewing rather than literally writing on the wall. Kurt Hesse (1990) sums up a view shared by many journalistic and academic commentators, based on his own research conducted with East German migrants to the West four years before 1989: 'In divided Germany in recent years an "electronic unification" took place in front of the TV sets day-by-day' (p. 355). Hesse interviewed 205 of the 25,000 East–West migrants during 1985, not an insignificant sample yet perhaps unrepresentative since these were people who actually left the GDR, always an exceptionally difficult thing to do whether illegally or legally under the Honecker regime. For these determined people, West German television had most importantly fulfilled the uses and gratifications function of *surveillance*. News and current affairs programmes, particularly *Kennzeichen D*, dedicated to reporting on life in the GDR, influenced their desire to leave. Interestingly, Hesse's interviewees were contemptuous of American entertainment programmes, particularly *Dallas* and

Denver (*Dynasty*), both of which were watched avidly by many East Germans in the 1980s. Complicating the picture further is the fact that GDR citizens in Dresden, where it was *not* possible to receive Western television signals, were disproportionately represented in the annual statistics of those applying for exit visas. As Hesse observes, 'they could not emigrate vicariously to the western world via the media' (p. 369), which may have contributed to their discontent, signified so vividly by media images of Dresdeners clambering aboard trains to the West in October 1989. Hesse concludes:

> Western TV in East Germany [had] a 'soma effect', as in Aldous Huxley's *Brave New World*: short-term satisfaction through relaxation provided by western TV. The long-term effects of western TV were not, however, system stabilising. Western TV regularly conveyed another world. This was not only a dream-world, which facilitated escape from everyday life, but was also a spur to compare realities and act on them. In October 1989 the people of the GDR decided that the time for action had come. This 'October Revolution' would not have happened at that time and in that way without the continual influence of western media, in particular western TV.
>
> (1990: 369)

The balance of Hesse's judgement seems to be about right: it differs from an extreme active audience perspective, which has no account of 'media influence', and also, at the other extreme, from the perspective which sees the media as all-powerfully 'manipulative'. What has to be appreciated is that television may work differently for different people under different circumstances: it can activate and it can pacify, depending upon audience predispositions and, nowadays, particular conditions of time–space compression. This opens up a number of questions concerning how television operated in the GDR and its political role during and after the popular uprising, which can be dealt with only briefly here.

Until 1973, the Socialist Unity Party dictatorship in the GDR sought to dissuade its subjects from watching West German television. Subsequently, the government actually promoted it by, for example, relaying signals to unfavourably located areas. Why? In a fascinating study of GDR culture and society, prior to the 1989 events, Duncan Smith (1988) offers three possible explanations for the communist regime's tolerance of Western television-viewing. The first explanation combines mass society reasoning with the orthodox Marxist-Leninist theory of ideological 'reflection'. Perhaps the regime believed the masses could thus be reconciled to staying put. Peter Hoff (1991) argues that this was indeed the regime's view of the role of television, pacification, both Western and Eastern (he also suggests that GDR television was not, in fact, as unpopular as it is usually made out to have been). Smith speculates, furthermore, that the regime's leaders may have believed that Western messages would be neutralised by the ideological effect of living under 'actually existing socialism', that the mundane medium of television, even when propagandising on behalf of the West, did not matter very much ideologically. Hoff confirms the likelihood of such a simplistic understanding of television by the Socialist Unity Party. However, Smith suggests a second explanation, that having so patently lost the ideological battle with their subjects, the leaders of the communist regime were prepared to accept a dependent status for the GDR in relation to its manifestly richer neighbour, the Federal Republic of Germany, leading nation in the EEC. There is a lot going for this explanation as well, since the GDR did have a kind of shadow membership of the EEC through its increasingly fraternal and economically advantageous relationship with the FRG during the 1980s. Perhaps the GDR authorities were trying to have it both ways. Third, Smith conjectures that the government might secretly have expected future unification on the terms of Western consumer capitalism; and, thus saw television as a means of stimulating consumerism for purposes of internal economic growth in the short to medium term and maybe eventual economic integration in the longer term. Smith himself believes there is some truth in all of these explanations, and I am inclined to agree with him.

Are these contradictory positions explicable or, yet again, must we remain undecided? I think the contradictions are explicable because of the enormous economic, political and cultural pressures on the GDR, a vulnerable outpost of Soviet communism, its comparative achievements in communist terms perpetually undermined by such close proximity to the glitteringly successful West Germany, representing the magical powers of capitalism's accentuated modernity so graphically with its high-tech gloss. The neo-Stalinist solution came to look less and less modern – or should we say postmodern? – as time passed.

It all came to a head, of course, in the late summer and early autumn of 1989 when East Germans ran away in huge numbers, first through the Austro-Hungarian border and then Czechoslovakia. The regime oscillated between battening down the hatches and permitting flight to the West in closed trains, fatal indecision culminating with the opening of the Berlin Wall at midnight on 9 November. Images of desperate people at border crossings, abandoned Trabants in Prague, and so on, had been relayed around the world and back to East Germans uncertain of their identity and, thus, prone to West German seduction. The sudden transition from interior migration to actual physical migration on such a dramatic scale finally destroyed communist hegemony in the East. The bravery of protesters, the church vigils, the demonstrations, especially in Leipzig, and the mass gathering in East Berlin's Alexanderplatz on 4 November, all contributed to the *coupure de courant*, but these forces were soon swept aside, their hopes of finding a 'third way', perhaps still inspired to some extent by Rudolf Bahro's *The Alternative in Eastern Europe* (1978), became a footnote to history. Paraphrasing a famous author, McKenzie Wark (1990) comments: 'When all that is solid melts into airwaves, people are forced to face, with delirious sense, their real relations, and bring them into line with "consciousness", or rather with unconscious desires' (pp. 37–8). Hitherto, the unconscious had not officially existed in East Germany. But what were these desires and how were they brought into line?

One particularly compelling account is that offered by the West German sociologist Michael Hofmann (1991b). He points out that East German television's brief flowering of critical commentary, once the dead hand of communism had been lifted, contributed to disillusionment with any autonomous reform solution: the decrepit state of the GDR and the corruption of its leaders were exposed. This reverberated intertextually with the glamorous iconography of consumer capitalism coming from the West, the reality of which was now available, so it seemed, to East Germans if they wanted it. The Christian Democrats exploited the situation swiftly while the Social Democrats issued their jeremiads about the costs of unification. Chancellor Kohl sealed the deal by offering one-to-one convertibility of the soft Ost Mark for the hard

Deutschmark in exchange for taking a ride with him, an offer which few East Germans, with otherwise unspendable money in the bank, could afford to refuse.

The key metaphor of this rapidly unfolding process, during the year between the original regime-breaking flight of ordinary people and the eventual unification of Germany, was the train. Already, the impatient were seen crossing the border to the West in ancient *Deutches Reich* trains. Then, the patient and circumspect became fearful of missing the train:

> The political symbolism of a unification train racing to its final destination had become the self-fulfilling prophecy of the year. It was entirely appropriate therefore that the West German government celebrated Unification Day by producing a video clip, which featured as its leitmotif an ultra-modern, high-speed train zooming through an Arcadian setting of complete harmony between East and West, man and nature, deep humanity and high technology. 'Vorsprung durch Technik': in the Autumn of 1990, the 'train to unity', having started out as a Chattanooga-Choo-Choo, became the Gold Coast Flyer, evoking Californian images of a new Gilded Age and of a new Barbary Shore.
>
> (Hofmann 1991b: 68)

The irony of all this is that East Germans, subjects of a police state, unable to travel freely, bewildered and seeking liberation, were, according to Hofmann's analysis, denied fully democratic rights in the deeper sense, which would have included sufficient time to decide their own futures. The public sphere became a tool of annexation rather than a forum of genuinely democratic debate and self-determination. This awkward squad attitude was expressed most famously in West Germany by the writer Gunter Grass, who for many years had argued against reunifying the state because the history of a unified Germany had been so appalling, instrumental in causing two World Wars. For expressing such views, Grass (1990a) was called, by some, 'a rootless cosmopolitan', the obverse of the worst kind of German national identity. When the popular slogan shifted from 'we are the people' to 'we are one people' during November 1989, the writing was apparently on the wall once more for anyone who did not fit into a very narrow conception of German national identity, particularly 'guest workers': the Turks in the West; the Vietnamese, Africans and

Poles in the East; 'the new wretched of the Earth' (Hughes 1990). East Germans themselves, their former homeland a *Schnappchen* ('real steal') for some Westerners, were now second-class citizens in the land of the almighty Deutschmark (Grass 1990b).

Frank Unger voices a much less pessimistic view of the unseemly haste with which German unification was conducted:

> From the politicians' viewpoint, German unification had to be managed at such breathtaking speed not because a growing nationalist sentiment in both parts of Germany propelled it, but precisely because nationalist sentiment in favour of unification was so feeble, especially in the larger part, the Federal Republic.
>
> (1991: 71)

It cannot be denied, however, that xenophobic nationalism has revived, predating German unification but fuelled by it, particularly in the economically devastated Eastern *Länder*. However, this is not a phenomenon confined only to Germany by any means. In addition to what Unger calls the 'patriotism of the international marketplace' (p. 75), marginalisation and hatred of subordinate peoples traverse the Continent and may well be enhanced rather than diminished by moves towards further integration of Europe: 1992 and all that. However benign some of the intentions, such as Gorbachev's 'common European homeland' and Jacques Delors's advocacy of social justice, generating as much if not more enthusiasm in Central and Eastern Europe than in Western Europe, peoples of non-European origin do not figure very prominently in the rhetoric. Jan Nederveen Pieterse (1991) echoes Denitch when he says that in the poorer parts of Europe, including the western and southern fringes, there is developing 'a European Mexico syndrome – a border-zone where economic, political, cultural, religious and demographic differences accumulate to create a gap between worlds, a zone of confrontation' (p. 5).

To clarify the issues at stake, Philip Schlesinger (1991) stresses 'the question of inclusion and exclusion, or, putting it differently, where Europe stops' (p. 188). David Morley and Kevin Robins (1989 and 1990) propose a structuralist variation on this theme by arguing that identity is formed according to constructions of 'difference' between 'self' and 'others'. In an article which begins by discussing the issue of the troubling aspects of German *Heimat*, these authors say that the problem of Europe is its self-definition in opposition to the other of 'America', a view consistent with one of the key domain assumptions of new revisionism, that all 'European' criticisms of the United States' cultural power and resistance to it are rendered somehow illegitimate by implicit 'elitism'. More constructively, they proceed to consider the equation of Europeanness and Christendom, which seems closer to the heart of the matter: 'Islam . . . is now the primary form in which the Third World presents itself to Europe' (1990: 16). One might add that this is also the principal signifier of 'otherness' for the United States and its 'New World Order', though Morley and Robins are predictably silent there. The crucial point is that for both 'Europe' and 'America' assertions of unified identity are assertions of superiority, born of economic and cultural power: they should, therefore, be questioned and analysed critically.

CONCLUSION – CRITICAL RENEWAL?

These concluding remarks do not summarise the book as a whole but instead are intended to develop the arguments of this chapter, which in themselves aim to extend and deepen an essentially sympathetic critique of cultural populism. For purposes of clarification, though, I shall remind the reader of my two main reasons for writing this book. First, I became concerned about a discernible narrowing of vision in cultural studies, exemplified by the drift into an uncritical populist mode of interpretation. I support the wish to understand and value everyday meanings, but, alone, such a wish produces inadequate explanation of the material life situations and power relations that shape the mediated experiences of ordinary people. This leads directly to my second reason for opening up the question of cultural populism: the sense that the world is changing in ways that exceed the analytical capacity of a narrowly interpretive approach, illustrated here by the collapse of communism and its ideological implications for popular-democratic politics. Although such changes are of global significance (Wallerstein 1990), they cannot be left exclusively to systemic theories which override mundane issues of lived experience (Boyne 1990). To a certain extent, then, I see this book as presenting a case for greater dialogue between mainstream cultural studies, as practised in Britain, and the political economy of culture. I am quite definitely not advocating an economically reductionist cultural analysis. Economic determinations, however, have been mistakenly bracketed off because of some earlier traumatic encounter with the long redundant base–superstructure model of 'orthodox' Marxism, a trauma represented symptomatically by a debilitating avoidance syndrome. Moreover, an exclusively interpretive approach not only manifests explanatory inadequacies; it also diminishes the critical powers of cultural analysis. Real grounds for criticising socio-economic conditions and cultural arrangements are thereby deconstructed, severing any link between what *is* and what *ought* to be, a thoroughly conservative severance, in spite of the radical rhetoric, and ultimately complicit with the oppressive powers it claims to oppose.

One of the recurrent clichés of social and cultural analysis today is the idea of 'criticism without guarantees'. If this means that rational critique and the ruse of history are not one and the same, it is hardly disputable. Many past critics did, from our vantage point, mistakenly believe that historical logic was on their side, justifying their self-appointed task of bringing the truth to conscious realisation irrespective of the human costs, thus hastening the inevitable outcome. How wrong they were, it is easy to say. No guarantees ever really existed: unintended consequences are the rule, not the exception. The difference between us and them is that we know we don't know anything for sure, which may give us a fragile sense of superiority. We can only wonder at their intellectual hubris and blithe certainty, which must have been comforting. They had maps; we have not. Yet, today, there are some who are sure and they do have maps or, rather, 'game plans' (Williams 1983b): they, however, are not the critics. For us critics, ours is an age of 'disorientation' resulting 'from the sense many of us have of being caught up in a universe of events we do not fully understand, and which seem in large part outside our control', in Anthony Giddens's words (1990: 2). Giddens is one of the proponents of 'criticism without guarantees' but not, I fancy, without grounds. Social criticism emerges from a perception of present wrongs – the real grounds. Furthermore, it is inspired by the conviction that human relationships could be better in the future – a Utopian desire.

It is interesting that critical theorists such as Anthony Giddens, in sociology, and Fredric Jameson, in cultural analysis, should resort to Utopianism. Is it because communism, the degraded realisation of Utopia in the twentieth century, has failed? Zygmunt

Bauman (1976) argued several years before the Berlin Wall was breached that the accomplishment of 'actually existing socialism' had dealt a damaging blow to Utopian hopes. Neither Giddens nor Jameson, however, resemble nostalgists for neo-Stalinism, of whom there are few. No, their Utopianism responds to a shared perception of contemporary social and spatial disorientation, but they do differ: Jameson sees the current condition as one of postmodernity, whereas Giddens sees it as accentuated modernity. For Jameson, the problem is first and foremost cultural: it turns on 'how to imagine Utopia' (1988: 355) in a critical context that has been disabused of such imaginings. Jameson proposes an 'aesthetic of cognitive mapping' to enable personal and political reorientation, although he is vague enough about the idea to avoid the obvious dangers of preaching. Nancy Fraser has asked him why he recommends 'cognitive mapping' as an aesthetic and not a social scientific strategy (Jameson 1988: 358). Jameson replied by arguing that social science cannot address the subject's imaginary relationship to its conditions of existence, in Althusser's famous phrase: compared with the emotional appeal of art, he seems to be saying, social science is *too cognitive.*

Giddens's (1990) position, though more prosaic, is in some ways bolder since he is prepared to connect an ostensibly scientific practice, sociology, to Utopian desire. His concept of 'Utopian realism' gathers up critical insight, political anticipation and institutional possibility. For example, Giddens believes there are finite limits to capital accumulation, making endless growth an impossible means of eliminating scarcity. The wasteful dynamics of global capitalism must, therefore, be checked, and wealth redistributed equitably in order to move beyond a condition of persistent ecological and military risk. Various movements for peace, democracy, ecology, for collective and self emancipation, old and new, are mutually implicated in the Utopian project since they all offer visions, 'counter-factual models', for a better world. Giddens contends that until the oppressed of one kind or another are liberated and technology is properly humanised, we cannot speak of *post*modernity. In the meantime, a critical social science has much to criticise and plenty of territory to chart.

What is the purpose of Utopian thought? To answer this question, Ruth Levitas (1990) has reviewed definitions of Utopia according to *content, form* and *function.* There is not the space here to discuss the Utopian imaginary in terms of generic form and 'good society' content (see Kumar 1991). Of greater immediate relevance is Utopianism's *function*, which has generally been oppositional, a means of criticising prevailing conditions by measuring them against an idealised future (Utopia) or a refraction of the present (dystopia). There is a danger in taking Utopia, however sketchy, too seriously. When treated as a blueprint, history tells us, Utopia has a habit of turning into dystopia. Where does that leave us? Following Miguel Abensour and Edward Thompson (Anderson, P. 1980), Levitas suggests that the purpose of Utopia is not so much to serve as a *catalyst* of change, to specify what should be done, but as a *critical tool*, analytically useful, in 'the education of desire'. For her, '[t]he essence of Utopia seems to be desire – the desire for a different, better way of being' (p. 181), of an historically variable kind, never fixed in the mind once and for all.

Utopian desire is not confined to the crazed imaginings of intellectuals. Richard Dyer (1977) finds it represented in commercial entertainment forms and, therefore, resonant with the wishes of ordinary people. Drawing on Hans Magnus Enzensberger's (1974) argument that '[c]onsumption as spectacle is – in parody form – the anticipation of a Utopian situation', Dyer sketched five categories of 'Utopian sensibility': *abundance, energy, intensity, transparency* and *community*. Each of them is structured in opposition to actual conditions: *scarcity, exhaustion, dreariness, manipulation* and *fragmentation*. The Utopian sensibilities parodied in popular entertainment are, then, imaginative compensations for living in less than satisfactory conditions. That is why popular culture matters so much. Everybody wants a 'better way of being': the question is, however, on what terms? This is at the heart of the critical problem to do with cultural populism: whether or not we believe that's all there is. At the beginning of this book I outlined why Raymond Williams is probably the single most important founding figure of populist cultural studies. Williams's understanding of contemporary sources of pleasure was less optimistic than many of those who have followed the tracks he marked out. In 1980, for instance, he observed 'a potentially lethal combination of abstract desire and practical cynicism' on the brink of a renewed Cold War (1980: 268). Now that the Cold War has been won, partly because of quite concrete desires, have we seen an end to 'practical cynicism'? I think not.

The enormous revival of Utopian thought in recent years is

heartening for anyone who does not blink at the contemporary world through rose-tinted spectacles. It is vitally important, however, to distinguish between *critical Utopia* and *achieved Utopia* (Baudrillard's term with reference to 'America'). The most pronounced versions of Utopia today are not those of the critics. *Achieved Utopia* is, of course, oxymoronic, as Jean Baudrillard (1989) would readily acknowledge with his cheek-bursting tongue. Krishan Kumar (1991) reminds us: 'Utopia is nowhere (*outopia*) and it is also somewhere good (*eutopia*)' (p. 1). One really has to be very suspicious of any claim that Utopia is an actual place that exists here and now, even if the claim is made in jest. Francis Fukuyama (1990), however, makes exactly this claim in deadly earnest. According to him, countries like the United States and Britain are 'post-historical', among the cluster of nations, which must include Japan, Germany and a few others, that are shining examples of the 'liberal democratic revolution and the capitalist revolution'. All other countries aspire to the same condition. Fukuyama, writing out of the US State Department, is unabashedly neo-Hegelian, which is a much more complex position to hold than the usual critical understanding of his 'end of history' thesis credits. It does not mean that world stasis has occurred but it does mean that the universal spirit is real and you could find it in George Bush's United States, John Major's Britain and Helmut Kohl's Germany. There is nothing better to be expected: put your critical Utopias away and enjoy the taste of 'the real thing' – that is, if your place in the world is a favoured one. This Western triumphalism is ideology neat and simple: questions of wealth and poverty, technological and ecological imbalances, exclusion and otherness, are not denied: they are merely consigned to their subsidiary places in the conservative imaginary of achieved Utopia.

Take, for example, 'America', at Baudrillard's instigation. It is interesting that European critics have tended to read Baudrillard on 'the microcosm of the West' – United States, California, Disneyland – as an apologia, albeit ironic, whereas American critics have seen it rather more as a putdown by an old-world intellectual (Denzin 1991). Baudrillard's discontinuous aphorisms and self-contradictions, however witty and thought-provoking, amount to little more than the end-game of a cynical mind. We may do well to forget Baudrillard and read Mike Davis's *City of Quartz* (1990) on Los Angeles instead. From this point of view, Disneyland is anything but 'the "real" America' (Baudrillard 1988:

172). The reality is hyperreal enough. A city of the insurgent Pacific Rim economy, with Japanese capital holding the whip hand over US business, staggering disparities of wealth and power, racist imbrications of class and ethnicity, built-spaces such as the Ronald Reagan Office Building in downtown designed for surveillance, and ruthless policing of boundaries, keeping people firmly in their places, 'Fortress LA', reminiscent of 'Fortress Europe'. This city of dreams, Hollywood and untold exploitative riches is the embodiment of both Utopia and dystopia, depending on the perspective from which you see it: 'Somewhere between . . . Gramscian optimism and . . . Frankfurt School pessimism lies the real possibility of oppositional culture' (Davis 1990: 87). In reality, Los Angeles is divided between an 'emerging, poly-ethnic and *poly-lingual* society', soon to constitute a majority on the excluded margins, and the shrinking Anglo-American 'corporate celebration of "postmodern" Los Angeles' (p. 24), a veritable powder keg. Future prospects for popular resistance and cultural expression, as ever, remain open to speculation. But it is not much help for falsely modest intellectuals merely to record how well ordinary people are doing against the overwhelming odds. There are urgent critical tasks, especially the task of calling into question the myth of achieved Utopia, which rests so complacently at present on the claim that 'the market'[7] with its proven dynamism can solve all our problems.

NOTES

1   Baudrillard's (1991) inability to distinguish between simulacra and real events enabled him to suggest, a few days before fighting began, that the Gulf War was 'impossible' since it had already been fought on television. This was indeed a 'media war', 'modelled' preceding and during hostilities, effacing lived reality with high-tech specularity, overloading viewers with information while simultaneously withholding strategic knowledge and images of death. Although Baudrillard's deliberately ironic conceit illuminates such processes, the soon-to-be casualties of 'incontinent ordnances' and 'carpet-bombing' may not have appreciated his wit.

2   Marjorie Ferguson (1991) has demonstrated Baudrillard's indebtedness to McLuhan, particularly the concept of 'implosion', taken from *Understanding Media*.

3   There is a persistent affinity between certain themes in Enzensberger's writings and British cultural populism, from the 1970s through to the 1990s.

4   Stuart Hall's brilliant 1991 television documentary series, *Redemption Song* (BBC2), explored questions of cultural syncretism and multiplication of identities in the Caribbean, while in a sense recovering his own Jamaican roots.

5   Panitch and Gindin's account of 'the street culture of *glasnost* ' is actually rather dignified. From the late 1980s, beggary became extremely widespread on the city centre streets of Moscow, as did hard currency transactions, not to mention the obligatory queues that have a culture all of their own since many Muscovites spend a couple of hours per day in them.

6   The spectacular performance of Pink Floyd's *The Wall* at what was left of *the* Wall in July 1990 must have been a poignant and heavy-handed reminder for many young ex-GDR citizens.

7   Jameson (1991) has remarked, in view of the actual processes of monopolisation and consumer manipulation, that 'the "market" turns out finally to be as Utopian as socialism has recently been held to be' (p. 278).

Bibliography

Abercrombie, N. (1990) 'Popular culture and ideological effects', in Abercrombie, N. *et al.* (1990).

Abercrombie, N., Hill, S., and Turner, B. (1980) *The Dominant Ideology Thesis*, Hemel Hempstead: Allen & Unwin.

Abercrombie, N., Hill, S., and Turner, B. (1990) *Dominant Ideologies*, London: Unwin Hyman.

Abrahamian, E. (1991) 'Khomeini – fundamentalist or populist?' *New Left Review* 186, March–April.

Adorno, T. (1941) 'On popular music', in *Studies in Philosophy and Social Science* IX (1).

Adorno, T. (1954) 'Television and the pattern of mass culture', *Quarterly of Film, Radio and Television* 8; reprinted in B. Rosenberg, and D. Manning White (eds) (1957) *Mass Culture*, Glencoe, Ill.: Free Press.

Adorno, T. and Horkheimer, M. (1947) 'The culture industry – enlightenment as mass deception', extracted from their *Dialectic of the Enlightenment* in J. Curran *et al.* (1977).

Akhtar, S. (1989) *Be Careful with Muhammad! – the Salman Rushdie Affair*, London: Bellew.

Allen, R. (1985) *Speaking of Soap Operas*, Chapel Hill, NC: University of North Carolina Press.

Althusser, L. (1966 – original French publication, 1969) *For Marx*, London: Penguin.

Althusser, L. (1968 – original French publication, with Etienne Balibar, 1970) *Reading Capital*, London: New Left Books.

Althusser, L. (1970 – original French publication) 'Ideology and ideological state apparatuses', in *Essays on Ideology* (1984), London: New Left Books/Verso.

Alvarado, M. and Thompson, J. (eds) (1990) *The Media Reader*, London: British Film Institute.

Anderson, B. (1983) *Imagined Communities*, London: Verso.

Anderson, P. (1969) 'Components of the national culture', in A. Cockburn, and R. Blackburn (eds) *Student Power*, London: Penguin.

Anderson, P. (1980) *Arguments within English Marxism*, London: Verso.

Anderson, P. (1984) 'Modernity and revolution', *New Left Review* 144, March–April, London.

Ang, I. (1985) *Watching Dallas – Soap Opera and the Melodramatic Imagination*, London: Methuen.

Ang, I. (1987) 'The Vicissitudes of "Progressive Television"', in *New Formations* 2, London: Methuen.

Ang, I. (1990a) 'Melodramatic identifications – television fictions and women's fantasies', in M. E. Brown (ed.) *Television and Women's Culture – The Politics of the Popular*, London: Sage.

Ang, I. (1990b) 'Culture and communication – towards an ethnographic critique of media consumption in the transnational media system', *European Journal of Communication* 5 (2–3) (June), London: Sage.

Ang, I. (1991) *Desperately Seeking the Audience*, London: Routledge.

Angus, I. and Jhally, S. (eds) (1989) *Cultural Politics in Contemporary America*, London: Routledge.

Apignanesi, L. (ed.) (1986) *ICA Documents 4 and 5 – Postmodernism*, London: Institute for Contemporary Arts.

Apignanesi, L. and Maitland, S. (1989) *The Rushdie File*, London: Fourth Estate.

Arnold, M. (1970) *Selected Prose*, London: Penguin.

Austen, J. (1811/1989, with Tony Tanner's Introduction) *Sense and Sensibility*, London: Penguin.

Baehr, H. and Dyer, G. (eds) (1987) *Boxed In – Women and Television*, London: Pandora.

Bahro, R. (1978) *The Alternative in Eastern Europe*, London: New Left Books/Verso.

Bakhtin, M. (1984) *Rabelais and His World*, Indiana University Press.

Baldick, C. (1983) *The Social Mission of English Criticism 1848–1932*, London: Clarendon Press.

Barker, M. (ed.) (1984) *The Video Nasties – Freedom and Censorship in the Media*, London: Pluto Press.

Barker, M. (1989) *Comics – Ideology, Power and the Critics*, Manchester: Manchester University Press.

Barker, M. (1990) '*Sunlight on Salman*', *Magazine of Cultural Studies* 1.

Baron, S. (1985) 'The study of culture – cultural studies and British sociology compared' in *Acta Sociologica* 28 (2).

Barrett, M., Corrigan, P., Kuhn, A., and Wolff, J. (eds) (1979) *Ideology and Cultural Production*, London: Croom Helm.

Barthes, R. (1961) 'The photographic message', in S. Heath (1977).

Barthes, R. (1964) 'The rhetoric of the image' in S. Heath (1977).

Barthes, R. (1966) 'Introduction to the structural analysis of narratives', in S. Heath (1977).

Barthes, R. (1968) 'The Death of the author', in S. Heath (1977).

Barthes, R. (1972/1957 – original French publication) *Mythologies*, London: Jonathan Cape.

Barthes, R. (1975) *The Pleasure of the Text*, London: Jonathan Cape.

Baudrillard, J. (1988) *Selected Writings*, Cambridge: Polity Press.

Baudrillard, J. (1989) *America*, London: Verso.

Baudrillard, J. (1991) 'The reality Gulf', *Guardian* (11 Jan; reprinted from *Liberation*.

Bauman, Z. (1976) *Socialism – the Active Utopia*, London: George Allen and Unwin.

Bauman, Z. (1987) *Legislators and Interpreters – On Modernity, Post-Modernity and Intellectuals*, Cambridge: Polity Press.

Bauman, Z. (1990) 'From pillars to post', *Marxism Today* (Feb.), London.

Beattie, J. (1966) *Other Cultures – Aims, Methods and Achievements in Social Anthropology*, London: Routledge.

Becker, H. (1963/1973) *Outsiders*, New York: Free Press.

Bell, D. (1960) *The End of Ideology*, New York: Free Press.

Bell, D. (1974) *The Coming of Post-industrial Society*, London: Heinemann.

Bell, D. (1976) *The Cultural Contradictions of Capitalism*, London: Heinemann.

Belson, W. (1978) *Television Violence and the Adolescent Boy*, Farnborough: Saxon House.

Benjamin, W. (1936) 'The work of art in the age of mechanical reproduction', in *Illuminations*, W. Benjamin (1973), London: Fontana.

Benn, M. (1988) 'Page 3 – and the campaign against it', in G. Chester and J. Dickey (1988).

Bennett, T. (1980) 'Popular culture – a "teaching object"', in *Screen Education* 34 (spring).

Bennett, T. (1982) 'Theories of the media, theories of society', in M. Gurevitch *et al.* (1982).

Bennett, T. (1986a) 'The politics of the "popular" and popular culture', in T. Bennett *et al.* (1986).

Bennett, T. (1986b) 'Hegemony, ideology, pleasure – Blackpool', in T. Bennett, *et al.* (1986).

Bennett, T. and Donald, J. (1981) 'Postscript to Block 2', in *U203 Popular Culture*, Milton Keynes: Open University Press.

Bennett, T., Martin, G., Mercer, C., and Woollacott, J. (eds) (1981a) *Culture, Ideology and Social Process*, London: Batsford.

Bennett, T. Boyd-Bowman, S., Mercer, C., and Woollacott, J. (eds) (1981b) *Popular Television and Film*, London: British Film Institute.

Bennett, T., Mercer, C., and Woollacott, J. (eds) (1986) *Popular Culture and Social Relations*, Milton Keynes: Open University Press.

Berger, J. and Mohr, J. (1975) *A Seventh Man*, London: Penguin.

Berman, M. (1983) *All that is Solid Melts into Air*, London: Verso.

Berman, M. (1984) 'The signs in the street – a response to Perry Anderson', *New Left Review* 144 (March–April).

Beynon, H. (1982) 'Jeremy Seabrook and the British working class', in M. Eve, and D. Musson (eds) *The Socialist Register* 1982, London: Merlin Press.

Bihari, P. (1991) 'From where to where? – reflections on Hungary's social revolution', in R. Miliband and L. Panitch (1991).

Blackburn, R. (1991) 'Fin de siècle – socialism after the crash', *New Left Review* 185 (Jan.–Feb.).

Blackwell, T. and Seabrook, J. (1988) *The Politics of Hope*, London: Faber & Faber.

Bloch, E., Lukacs, G., Brecht, B., Benjamin, W., and Adorno, T. (1977) *Aesthetics and Politics*, London: New Left Books/Verso.

Blumler, J., Brown, R., and McQuail, D. (1972) 'The television audience – a revised perspective', in D. McQuail (ed.) *Sociology of Mass Communications*, London: Penguin.

Bourdieu, P. (1971) 'Intellectual field and creative project', in M. Young (ed.) *Knowledge and Control – New Directions for the Sociology of Education*, London: Collier Macmillan.

Bourdieu, P. (1984) *Distinction*, London: Routledge.

Bourdieu, P. (1990) 'The uses of the "people"', in *In Other Words*, P. Bourdieu, Cambridge: Polity Press.

Bourdieu, P. and Passeron, J-C. (1977) *Reproduction in Education, Society and Culture*, London: Sage.

Boyd-Bowman, S. (1990) 'Peak time television', *Magazine of Cultural Studies* 2.

Boyne, R. (1990) 'Culture and the world system', in M. Featherstone (1990b).

Boyne, R. and Rattansi, A. (eds) (1990) *Postmodernism and Society*, London: Macmillan.

Braden, S. (1978) *Artists and People*, London: Routledge.

Braden, S. (1983) *Committing Photography*, London: Pluto Press.

Brake, M. (1985) *Comparative Youth Culture*, London: Routledge.

Brandt, G. (ed.) (1981) *British Television Drama*, Cambridge: Cambridge University Press.

Brantlinger, P. (1983) *Bread and Circuses – Theories of Mass Culture as Social Decay*, Ithaca, NY. and London: Cornell University Press.

Brantlinger, P. (1990) *Crusoe's Footprints – Cultural Studies in Britain and America*, London: Routledge.

Brecht, B. (1938) 'Against Georg Lukacs', in E. Bloch, *et al.* (1977).

Brecht, B. (1976) *Poems, Part Three 1938–1956*, London: Eyre Methuen.

Brewster, B., Buscombe, E., Hanet, K., Heath, S., Kristeva, J., Kunkzel, T., Metz, C., and Willemen, P. (1981) *Screen Reader 2 – Cinema and Semiotics*, London: Society for Education in Film and Television.

Bronner, S. and Kellner, D. (eds) (1989) *Critical Theory and Society – a Reader*, London: Routledge.

Brunsdon, C. (1981) '"Crossroads" – notes on soap opera', *Screen* 22 (4), London.

Brunsdon, C. (1987) 'Feminism and soap opera', in K. Davies *et al.* (1987).

Brunsdon, C. (1990a) 'Television – aesthetics and audiences', in P. Mellencamp (1990).

Brunsdon, C. (1990b) 'Problems with quality', *Screen* 31 (1).

Brunsdon, C. and Morley, D. (1978) *Everyday Television – 'Nationwide'*, London: British Film Institute.

Buckingham, D. (1986) 'Against demystification – "Teaching the media"', *Screen* 27 (5).

Buckingham, D. (1987a) *Public Secrets – EastEnders and Its Audience*, London: British Film Institute.

Buckingham, D. (1987b) *Children and Television – an Overview of the Research*, London: British Film Institute.

Buckingham, D. (1989) 'Television literacy – a critique', Radical Philosophy 51.

Buckingham, D. (1990) 'Media education – from pedagogy to practice', in D. Buckingham (ed.) Watching Media Learning, London: Falmer Press.

Burchill, J. (1990) 'Gotcha!', New Statesman and Society (16 Nov.).

Burke, P. (1978) Popular Culture in Early Modern Europe, London: Temple Smith.

Burke, P. (1981) 'The "discovery" of popular culture', in R. Samuel (1981).

Bushnell, J. (1990) Moscow Graffiti – Language and Subculture, London: Unwin Hyman.

Calder, A. (1969) The People's War, London: Jonathan Cape.

Callinicos, A. (1989) Against Postmodernism – a Marxist Critique, Cambridge: Polity Press.

Callinicos, A. (1990) 'Reactionary postmodernism?', in R. Boyne and A. Rattansi (1990).

Callinicos, A. (1991) The Revenge of History – Marxism and the East European Revolutions, Cambridge: Polity Press.

Campbell, B. (1987) The Iron Ladies – Why do Women Vote Tory? London: Virago.

Cantor, M. and Pingree, S. (1983) The Soap Opera, Beverly Hills: Sage.

Carey, J. (1989) Communication as Culture, London: Unwin Hyman.

Carter, E. (1984) 'Alice in the consumer Wonderland' in A. McRobbie and M. Nava (1984).

Caughie, J. (1980) 'Progressive television and documentary drama', Screen 21 (3); reprinted in T. Bennett et al. (1981b).

Caughie, J. (1984) 'Television criticism – "A discourse in search of an object"', Screen 25 (4–5).

CCCS (1964) First Report, Birmingham: University of Birmingham.

CCCS Women's Studies Group (1978) Women Take Issue, London: Hutchinson.

CCCS (1982a) The Empire Strikes Back – Race and Racism in 70s Britain, London: Hutchinson.

CCCS (1982b) Making Histories – Studies in History-writing and Politics, London: Hutchinson.

Chambers, I. (1986) Popular Culture – the Metropolitan Experience, London: Methuen.

Chester, G. and Dickey, J. (eds) (1988) Feminism and Censorship – the Current Debate, Bridport: Prism Press/Campaign for Press and Broadcasting Freedom.

Chippindale, P. and Horrie, C. (1990) Stick it Up Your Punter! – the Rise and Fall of the Sun, London: Heinemann.

Clarke, J. (1975) 'Style', in T. Jefferson (1975).

Clarke, J. (1978) 'Football and working class fans', in R. Ingham, (ed.) Football Hooliganism – the Wider Context, London: Inter-Action.

Clarke, J. Critcher, C., and Johnson, R. (eds) (1979) Working Class Culture – Studies in History and Theory, London: Hutchinson.

Clarke, J., Hall, S., Jefferson, T., and Roberts, B. (1975) 'Subcultures, cultures and class', in T. Jefferson (1975).

Clarke, S., Lovell, T., McDonnell, K., Robins, K., and Seidler, V. (1980) *One-Dimensional Marxism – Althusser and the Politics of Culture*, London: Alison and Busby.

Cohen, J. (1955) 'Introduction' to *Gargantua and Pantagruel*, François Rabelais, London: Penguin.

Cohen, P. (1972) 'Subcultural conflict and working-class community', in *Working Papers in Cultural Studies* 2, Birmingham CCCS.

Cohen, P. (1988) 'The perversions of inheritance – studies in the making of multi-racist Britain', in P. Cohen, and H. Bains (eds) *Multi-Racist Britain*, London: Macmillan.

Cohen, S. (ed.) (1971) *Images of Deviance*, London: Penguin.

Cohen, S. (1973) *Folk Devils and Moral Panics*, London: Paladin.

Collett, P. (1986) 'Watching the TV audience', International Television Studies Conference, London University Institute of Education.

Collins, J. (1990) *Uncommon Cultures – Popular Culture and Post-Modernism*, London: Routledge.

Collins, R. (1990) *Television – Culture and Policy*, London: Unwin Hyman.

Collins, R., Curran, J., Garnham, N., Scannell, P., Schlesinger, P., and Sparks, C. (eds) (1986) *Media, Culture and Society – a Critical Reader*, London: Sage.

Collins, R., Garnham, N., and Locksley, E. (1988) *The Economics of Television*, London: Sage.

Connell, I. (1983) 'Commercial broadcasting and the British Left', *Screen* 24 (6).

Connor, S. (1989) *Postmodernist Culture – an Introduction to Theories of the Contemporary*, Oxford: Basil Blackwell.

Corner, J. (1979) '"Mass" in communication research', *Journal of Communication* (winter).

Corner, J. (1991) 'Studying culture – reflections and assessments. An interview with Richard Hoggart', *Media, Culture and Society* 13 (2), London: Sage.

Costello, N., Michie, J., and Milne, S. (1989) *Beyond the Casino Economy*, London: Verso.

Coward, R. (1977) 'Class, "culture" and the social formation', in *Screen* 18 (1).

Coward, R. (1990) 'Invasion of the Turtles', *New Statesman and Society* (24 Aug.).

Coward, R. and Ellis, J. (1977) *Language and Materialism – Developments in Semiology and the Theory of the Subject*, London: Routledge.

Critcher, C. (1979) 'Sociology, cultural studies and the post-war working class' in J. Clarke *et al.* (1979).

Critcher, C. (1982) 'Football since the war', in B. Waites, *et al.* (1982).

Crook, G. (1986) 'Public service or serving the public – the roots of popularism in British television', International Television Studies Conference, London University Institute of Education.

Curran, J. (1990) 'The New Revisionism in mass communication research

– a reappraisal', *European Journal of Communication* 5 (2–3) (June), London: Sage.

Curran, J. (1991) 'Rethinking the media as a public sphere' in P. Dahlgrin, and C. Sparks (eds) (1991) *Communication and Citizenship – Journalism and the Public Sphere*, London: Routledge.

Curran, J., Gurevitch, M., and Woollacott, J. (eds) (1977) *Mass Communication and Society*, London: Edward Arnold.

Curran, J. and Seaton, J. (1988, third edn; 1991, fourth edn) *Power Without Responsibility – the Press and Broadcasting in Britain*, London: Methuen/Routledge.

Curran, J. and Sparks, C. (1991) 'Press and popular culture', *Media, Culture and Society* 13 (2) (April), London: Sage.

D'Acci, J. (1987) 'The case of Cagney and Lacey', in H. Baehr, and G. Dyer (1987).

Daniels, T. and Gerson, J. (eds) (1989) *The Colour Black – Black Images in British Television*, London: British Film Institute.

Davies, K., Dickey, J., and Stratford, J. (eds) (1987) *Out of Focus – Writings on Women and the Media*, London: Women's Press.

Davis, M. (1988) 'Urban renaissance and the spirit of postmodernism', in E. Kaplan (1988).

Davis, M. (1990) *City of Quartz – Excavating the Future in Los Angeles*, London: Verso.

Dawisha, K. (1990) *Eastern Europe, Gorbachev and Reform*, Cambridge: Cambridge University Press.

De Certeau, M. (1984) *The Practice of Everyday Life*, Berkeley: University of California Press.

Denitch, B. (1990) *The End of the Cold War*, London: Verso.

Denzin, N. (1988) '"Blue velvet" – postmodern contradictions', *Theory, Culture and Society* 5 (2–3) (June), London: Sage.

Denzin, N. (1991) '"Paris, Texas" and Baudrillard on America', *Theory, Culture and Society* 8 (2) (May), London: Sage.

Dewdney, A. and Lister, M. (1986) 'Youth and photography', in *Ten: 8* 2, Birmingham.

Dews, P. (1987) *Logics of Disintegration – Post-Structuralist Thought and the Claims of Critical Theory*, London: Verso.

Dickey, J. (1988) 'Snakes and ladders', in G. Chester, and J. Dickey (1988).

Dickey, J. and Chester, G. (1988) 'Introduction' to G. Chester, and J. Dickey (1988).

Docherty, D., Morrison, D., and Tracey, M. (1987) *The Last Picture Show? – Britain's Changing Film Audiences*, London: British Film Institute.

Downes, D. (1966) *The Delinquent Solution*, London: Routledge.

Drummond, P. and Paterson, R. (eds) (1986) *Television in Transition*, London: British Film Institute.

Drummond, P. and Paterson, R. (eds) (1988) *Television and its Audience*, London: British Film Institute.

Dunkerley, C. (1987) *Television Today and Tomorrow – Wall-to-Wall-Dallas*, London: Penguin.

Dunn, T. (1987) 'Take a walk on the Wilde side', *Guardian* (10 Feb.)

Dunning, E., Murphy, P., and Williams, J. (1988) *The Roots of Football Hooliganism*, London: Routledge.

Durkheim, E. (1964) *The Division of Labour in Society*, New York: Free Press/Collier Macmillan.

Dworkin, A. (1981) *Pornography – Men Possessing Women*, London: Women's Press.

Dworkin, A. (1988) *Letters from a War Zone*, London: Secker & Warburg.

Dyer, R. (1977) 'Entertainment and Utopia', *Movie* 24 (Spring); Reprinted in R. Altman (ed.) (1981) *Genre – the Musical*, London: Routledge.

Dyer, R. (1985) 'Taking popular television seriously', in D. Lusted, and P. Drummond, (1985).

Dyer, R., Geraghty, C., Jordan, M., Lovell, T., Paterson, R., and Stewart, J. (1981) *Coronation Street*, London: British Film Institute.

Dyer, R., Lovell, T. and McCrindle, J. (1977) 'Soap opera and women', *Edinburgh International Television Festival 1977 Programme*, London: Broadcast.

Eagleton, T. (1981) *Walter Benjamin – or Towards a Revolutionary Criticism*, London: New Left Books/Verso.

Eagleton, T. (ed.) (1989) *Raymond Williams – Critical Perspectives*, Cambridge: Polity Press.

Eagleton, T. (1990) *The Ideology of the Aesthetic*, Oxford: Basil Blackwell.

Eagleton, T. (1991) *Ideology – an Introduction*, London: Verso.

Easthope, A. (1986) *What a Man's Gotta Do – the Masculine Myth in Popular Culture*, London: Paladin.

Easthope, A. (1988) *British Post-structuralism*, London: Routledge.

Eco, U. (1965) 'Towards a semiotic inquiry into the television message', in *Working Papers in Cultural Studies* 3 (1972), Birmingham CCCS.

Eco, U. (1967) 'Towards a semiological guerrilla warfare', in U. Eco, (1987).

Eco, U. (1981) *The Role of the Reader*, London: Hutchinson.

Eco, U. (1985a) *Reflections on The Name of the Rose*, London: Secker & Warburg.

Eco, U. (1985b) 'A guide to the neo-television of the 1980s', *Framework* 25.

Eco, U. (1987) *Travels in Hyperreality*, London: Picador.

Eliot, T.S. (1948) *Notes towards the Definition of Culture*, London: Faber & Faber.

Ellis, J. (1982) *Visible Fictions*, London: Routledge.

Enzensberger, H. (1974) *The Consciousness Industry*, New York: Seabury Press.

Everywoman (1988) *Pornography and Sexual Violence – Evidence of the Links*, London: Everywoman.

Ewen, S. (1988) *All Consuming Images – the Politics of Style in Contemporary Culture*, New York: Basic Books.

Featherstone, M. (1990a) 'Perspectives on consumer culture', in *Sociology* 24 (1).

Featherstone, M. (ed.) (1990b) *Global Culture – Nationalism, Globalism and Modernity*, London: Sage.

Featherstone, M. (1991) *Consumer Culture and Postmodernism*, London: Sage.

Ferguson, B. (1984) 'Black Blue Peter' in L. Masterman (1984).

Ferguson, B. (1985) 'Children's television – the germination of ideology', in D. Lusted, and P. Drummond (1985).

Ferguson, M. (ed.) (1990) *Public Communication – the New Imperatives*, London: Sage.

Ferguson, M. (1991) 'Marshall McLuhan revisited – 1960s Zeitgeist victim or pioneer postmodernist?' *Media, Culture and Society* 13 (1) (Jan.), London: Sage.

Fiske, J. (1987a) 'British cultural studies and television', in R. Allen (ed.) *Channels of Discourse*, London: Methuen.

Fiske, J. (1987b): *Television Culture*, London: Methuen.

Fiske, J. (1989a) *Understanding Popular Culture*, London: Unwin Hyman.

Fiske, J. (1989b) *Reading the Popular*, London: Unwin Hyman.

Fiske, J. (1991) 'Popular discrimination', in J. Naremore, and P. Brantlinger (eds) *Modernity and Mass Culture*, Indiana University Press.

Fiske, J. and Hartley, J. (1978) *Reading Television*, London: Methuen.

Flint, J. (1990) 'Tragedy in the name of Allah', *Observer* (11 Feb.).

Forgacs, D. (1984) 'National-popular – genealogy of a concept', *Formations of Nation and People*, London: Routledge.

Forgacs, D. and Nowell-Smith, G. (eds) (1985) *Antonio Gramsci – Selections from Cultural Writings*, London: Lawrence & Wishart.

Foster, H. (ed.) (1985) *Postmodern Culture*, London: Pluto Press.

Foucault, M. (1977) *Discipline and Punish – the Birth of the Prison*, London: Allen Lane.

Foucault, M. (1979) *The History of Sexuality*, Vol. 1, London: Penguin.

Foucault, M. (1981) 'The order of discourse', in R. Young (ed.) *Untying the Text*, London: Routledge.

Franklin, S., Lury, C., and Stacey, J. (1991) 'Feminism and cultural studies – pasts, presents, futures', *Media, Culture and Society* 13 (2) (April), London: Sage.

Frith, S. (1983) *Sound Effects – Youth, Leisure and the Politics of Rock'n'Roll*, London: Constable.

Fukuyama, F. (1989a) 'The end of history?', *National Interest* 16 (summer), Washington, DC.

Fukuyama, F. (1989b) 'The end of hysteria?' *Guardian* (15 Dec.).

Fukuyama, F. (1990) 'Forget Iraq – history is dead', *Guardian* (7 Sept.).

Gamble, A. (1988) *The Free Economy and the Strong State – the Politics of Thatcherism*, London: Macmillan.

Gamman, L. and Marshment, M. (eds) (1988) *The Female Gaze*, London: Women's Press.

Gans, H. (1974) *Popular Culture and High Culture*, New York: Basic Books.

Garber, J. and McRobbie, A. (1975) 'Girls and subcultures', in T. Jefferson (1975).

Gardner, C. (1984) 'Populism, relativism and left strategy', *Screen* 25 (1).

Garnham, N. (1979) 'Contribution to a political economy of mass communication', *Media, Culture and Society* 1 (2) (April), London: Academic Press; reprinted in Garnham (1990).

Garnham, N. (1983) 'Public service versus the market', *Screen*, 24 (1), London; reprinted in Garnham (1990).

Garnham, N. (1984) 'Introduction' to A. Mattelart *et al.*, *International Image Markets*, London: Comedia.

Garnham, N. (1987) 'Concepts of culture – public policy and the cultural industries', *Cultural Studies* 1 (1), London: Methuen; reprinted in Garnham (1990).

Garnham, N. (1990) *Capitalism and Communication – Global Culture and the Economics of Information*, London: Sage.

Garton Ash, T. (1990) *We the People – the Revolution of '89*, London: Penguin/Granta Books.

Geraghty, C. (1981) 'The continuous serial – a definition', in R. Dyer *et al.* (1981).

Geraghty, C. (1983) '"Brookside" – no common ground', *Screen*, 24 (4–5).

Geraghty, C. (1991) *Women and Soap Opera*, Cambridge: Polity Press.

Giddens, A. (1990) *The Consequences of Modernity*, Cambridge: Polity Press.

Gillespie, M. (1989) 'Technology and tradition – audio-visual culture among South Asian families in West London', *Cultural Studies* 3 (2), London: Methuen.

Gilroy, P. (1987) *There Ain't No Black in the Union Jack*, London: Hutchinson.

Giner, S. (1976) *Mass Society*, London: Martin Robertson.

Gitlin, T. (1984) *Inside Primetime*, New York: Pantheon.

Goddard, J. (1985) 'Editorial' from *International Journal of Advertising* 4 (4); reprinted in M. Alvarado, and J. Thompson, (1990).

Goffman, E. (1969) *The Presentation of Self in Everyday Life*, London: Penguin.

Golding, P. (1990) 'Political communication and citizenship – the media and democracy in an inegalitarian social order', in M. Ferguson (1990).

Golding, P. and Murdock, G. (1979) 'Ideology and the mass media – the question of determination', in M. Barrett *et al.* (1979).

Goldmann, L. (1975) *Towards a Sociology of the Novel*, London: Tavistock.

Goodwin, A. (1982) 'Unpopular television', *Primetime* 1 (4).

Goodwin, A. and Whannel, G. (eds) (1990) *Understanding Television*, London: Routledge.

Gordon, C. (ed.) (1980) *Michel Foucault – Power/Knowledge*, Brighton: Harvester.

Gorz, A. (1982) *Farewell to the Working Class – an Essay on Post-industrial Socialism*, London: Pluto Press.

Gorz, A. (1985) *Paths to Paradise – on the Liberation from Work*, London: Pluto Press.

Grass, G. (1990a) *Two States – One Nation? – The Case Against German Reunification*, London: Secker & Warburg.

Grass, G. (1990b) 'The business blitzkrieg', *Weekend Guardian* (20 Oct.).

Gray, A. (1987a) 'Behind closed doors – video recorders in the home', in H. Baehr, and G. Dyer (1987).

Gray, A. (1987b) 'Reading the audience', *Screen* 28 (3).

Gray, A. (1992) *Video Playtime – the Gendering of a Leisure Technology*, London: Comedia/Routledge.

Green, M. (1982) 'The Centre for Contemporary Cultural Studies', in P. Widdowson, (ed.) (1982) *Re-reading English*, London: Methuen.

Gripsrud, J. (1989) '"High culture" revisited', in *Cultural Studies* 3 (2), London: Methuen.

Grossberg, L. (1983) 'Cultural studies revisited and revised', in M. Mander (ed.) *Communications in Transition*, New York: Praeger.

Grossberg, L. (1988) *It's a Sin*, Sydney: Power Publications.

Grossberg, L. and Hall, S. (1986) 'On postmodernism and articulation – an interview with Stuart Hall', in *Journal of Communication Enquiry* 10 (2), (summer), Iowa Centre for Communication Study.

Gurevitch, M., Bennett, T., Curran, J., and Woolacott, J. (eds) (1982) *Culture, Society and the Media*, London: Macmillan.

Habermas, J. (1970) 'Toward a theory of communicative competence', in H. Dreitzel, (ed.) *Recent Sociology no. 2 – Patterns of Communicative Behaviour*, New York: Macmillan.

Habermas, J. (1972) *Knowledge and Human Interests*, London: Heinemann.

Habermas, J. (1979) *Communication and the Evolution of Society*, London: Heinemann.

Habermas, J. (1985) 'Modernity – an incomplete project', in H. Foster (1985).

Habermas, J. (1989 – original German publication 1962) *The Structural Transformation of the Public Sphere – an Enquiry into a Category of Bourgeois Society*, Cambridge: Polity Press.

Habermas, J. (1990) 'What does socialism mean today? – The rectifying revolution and the need for new thinking on the left', *New Left Review* 183 (Sept.–Oct.).

Hall, S. (1972) 'External/internal dialectic in broadcasting', in Fourth Symposium on Broadcasting, University of Manchester.

Hall, S. (1974a) 'Marx's notes on method: a reading of the "1857 Introduction"', in *Working Papers in Cultural Studies* 6, Birmingham CCCS.

Hall, S. (1974b) 'The television discourse – encoding and decoding', *Education and Culture* 25, UnESCO.

Hall, S. (1977) 'Culture, the media and the "ideological effect"', in J. Curran *et al.* (1977).

Hall, S. (1980a) 'Cultural studies – two paradigms', *Media, Culture and Society* 2 (2); reprinted in R. Collins *et al.* (1986).

Hall, S. (1980b) 'Cultural studies and the centre – some problematics and problems', in S. Hall *et al.* (1980).

Hall, S. (1980c) 'The Williams interviews', *Screen Education* 34; reprinted in T. Eagleton (1989).

Hall, S. (1980d) 'Reformism and the legislation of consent', in J. Clarke *et al.* (eds) *Permissiveness and Control – the Fate of the Sixties Legislation*, London: Macmillan.

Hall, S. (1980e) 'Encoding/decoding', in S. Hall *et al.* (1980).

Hall, S. (1981) 'Notes on deconstructing "the popular"', in R. Samuel (1981).

Hall, S. (1982) 'The rediscovery of "ideology" – return of the repressed in media studies', in M. Gurevitch *et al.* (1982).

Hall, S. (1983) 'The problem of ideology – Marxism without guarantees', in B. Matthews (ed.) *Marx 100 Years On*, London: Lawrence & Wishart.

Hall, S. (1988) 'Thatcher's lessons', in *Marxism Today* (March); reprinted in S. Hall (1988a).

Hall, S. (1988a) *The Hard Road to Renewal*, London: Verso.

Hall, S. (1988b) 'The toad in the garden – Thatcherism among the theorists', in C. Nelson and L. Grossberg (1988).

Hall, S., Connell, I., and Curti, L. (1976) 'The "unity" of current affairs television', *Working Papers in Cultural Studies* 9, Birmingham CCCS.

Hall, S., Critcher, C., Jefferson, T., Clarke, J., and Roberts, B. (1978) *Policing the Crisis*, London: Macmillan.

Hall, S. and Jacques, M. (eds) (1983) *The Politics of Thatcherism*, London: Lawrence & Wishart.

Hall, S. and Jacques, M. (eds) (1989) *New Times*, London: Lawrence & Wishart.

Hall, S. and Jameson, F. (1990) 'Clinging to the wreckage', *Marxism Today* (Sept.).

Hall, S., Hobson, D., Lowe, A., and Willis, P. (eds) (1980) *Culture, Media, Language*, London: Hutchinson.

Hall, S. and Whannel, P. (1964) *The Popular Arts*, London: Hutchinson.

Halloran, J. (1970) *The Effects of Television*, London: Panther.

Harvey, D. (1982) *The Limits to Capital*, Oxford: Basil Blackwell.

Harvey, D. (1989) *The Condition of Postmodernity*, Oxford: Basil Blackwell.

Harvey, D. (1990) 'From space to place and back again: reflections on "the condition of postmodernity"', paper delivered at the 'Futures' conference, Tate Gallery, London (23 Nov.).

Haug, W. (1986) *Critique of Commodity Aesthetics – Appearance, Sexuality and Advertising in Capitalist Society*, London: Macmillan.

Heath, S. (ed.) (1977) *Roland Barthes – Image-Music-Text*, London: Fontana.

Heath, S. and Skirrow, G. (1986) 'An interview with Raymond Williams', in T. Modleski (1986).

Hebdige, D. (1975a) 'The meaning of mod', in T. Jefferson (1975).

Hebdige, D. (1975b) 'Reggae, rasta and Rudies', in T. Jefferson (1975).

Hebdige, D. (1979) *Subculture – the Meaning of Style*, London: Methuen.

Hebdige, D. (1982a) 'Towards a cartography of taste 1935–1962', in B. Waites *et al.* (1982).

Hebdige, D. (1982b) 'Hiding in the light', in *Ten: 8* 9, Birmingham; reprinted in Hebdige (1988).

Hebdige, D. (1987) *Cut 'n' Mix*, London: Comedia.

Hebdige, D. (1988) *Hiding in the Light*, London: Comedia.

Hebditch, D. and Anning, N. (1988) *Porn Gold – Inside the Pornography Business*, London: Faber & Faber.

Held, D. (1989) *Political Theory and the Modern State*, Cambridge: Polity Press.

Henry, A. (1988) 'Does viewing porn lead men to rape?' in G. Chester, and J. Dickey (1988).

Herzog, H. (1942) 'What do we really know about daytime serial listeners?' in P. Lazarsfeld, and F. Stanton (eds) *Radio Research 1942–43*, New York: Duel, Sloan and Pearce.

Hesse, K. (1990) 'Cross-border mass communication from west to east', *European Journal of Communication* 5, London: Sage.

Hill, S. (1990) 'Britain – the dominant ideology thesis after a decade', in N. Abercrombie *et al* (1990).

Hiro, D. (1990) *Islamic Fundamentalism*, London: Paladin.

Hirschkop, K. (1989) 'A complex populism – the political thought of Raymond Williams', *News from Nowhere no. 6, Raymond Williams – Third Generation*, Oxford English Ltd.

Hirschkop, K. and Shepherd, D. (eds) (1989) *Bakhtin and Cultural Theory*, Manchester: Manchester University Press.

Hoare, Q. and Nowell-Smith, G. (eds) (1971) *Selections from the Prison Notebooks of Antonio Gramsci*, London: Lawrence and Wishart.

Hobsbawm, E. (1990) 'Goodbye to all that', *Marxism Today* (Oct.).

Hobson, D. (1982) *Crossroads – the Drama of a Soap Opera*, London: Methuen.

Hobson, D. (1985) 'Slippery soaps', *Edinburgh International Television Festival 1985 Programme*, London: *Broadcast*.

Hodge, B. and Tripp, D. (1986) *Children and Television*, Cambridge: Polity Press.

Hoff, P. (1991) 'Continuity and change – television in the GDR from autumn 1989 to summer 1990', in G. Nowell-Smith, and T. Wollen (1991).

Hofmann, M. (1991a) 'Exploding a few myths on television and politics – Habermas's "The structural transformation of the public sphere" Revisited', International Television Studies Conference, London University Institute of Education.

Hofmann, M. (1991b) 'The unity train', in G. Nowell-Smith, and T. Wollen (1991).

Hoggart, R. (1957) *The Uses of Literacy*, London: Chatto and Windus.

Hoggart, R. (1970a) *Speaking to Each Other Volume One – About Society*, London: Chatto and Windus.

Hoggart, R. (1970b) *Speaking to Each Other Volume Two – About Literature*, London: Chatto and Windus.

Hoggart, R. (1979) 'How should we pay for the arts?' *New Society* (2 Aug.).

Hoggart, R. (1980) 'The crisis of relativism', *New Universities Quarterly* 35 (1), Oxford: Basil Blackwell.

Hoggart, R. (1990) *A Sort of Clowning*, London: Chatto and Windus.

Hollingsworth, M. (1986) *The Press and Political Dissent – a Question of Censorship*, London: Pluto Press.

Holub, R. (1985) *Reception Theory*, London: Methuen.

Horkheimer, M. (1941) 'Art and mass culture', in *Studies in Philosophy and Social Science* IX (2).

Horton, J. (1964) 'The dehumanization of anomie and alienation – a problem in the ideology of sociology', *British Journal of Sociology* 15 (Dec.).

Hughes, H.S. (1990) *Sophisticated Rebels – the Political Culture of European Dissent 1968–1987,* Cambridge, Mass.: Harvard University Press.

Huyssen, A. (1990 – originally published 1984) 'Mapping the postmodern', in J. Alexander, and S. Seidman, (eds) *Culture and Society – Contemporary Debates,* Camrbdige: Cambridge University Press.

Ionescu, G. and Gellner, E. (eds) (1969) *Populism – its Meaning and National Characteristics,* London: Weidenfeld and Nicolson.

Itzin, C. (1988) 'The campaign trail starts here', *Guardian* (2 Feb.).

Jameson, F. (1984) 'Postmodernism, or the cultural logic of late capitalism', *New Left Review* 146 (July–Aug.).

Jameson, F. (1985) 'Postmodernism and consumer society' in H. Foster (1985).

Jameson, F. (1988) 'Cognitive mapping', in C. Nelson and L. Grossberg (1988).

Jameson, F. (1990) *Late Marxism – Adorno, or, The Persistence of the Dialectic,* London: Verso.

Jameson, F. (1991) *Postmodernism or, The Cultural Logic of Late Capitalism,* London: Verso.

Jefferson, T. (ed.) (1975) *Resistance through Rituals,* Birmingham CCCS; republished by Hutchinson, London, 1976.

Jeffrey, T. (1978) *Mass Observation – a Short History,* Birmingham CCCS Occasional Paper.

Jencks, C. (1986) *What is Post-Modernism?* London: Academy Editions.

Jessop, B., Bonnett, K., Bromley, S., and Ling, T. (1984) 'Authoritarian populism, two nations and Thatcherism', *New Left Review* 147.

Jessop, B., Bonnett, K. and Bromley, S. (1990) 'Farewell to Thatcherism? Neo-liberalism and "New Times"', *New Left Review* 179.

Jhally, S. (1987) *The Codes of Advertising – Fetishism and the Political Economy of Meaning in the Consumer Society,* London: Francis Pinter; republished by Routledge, London, 1991.

Jhally, S. (1989) 'The political economy of culture', in I. Angus, and S. Jhally (1989).

Johnson, R. (1979a) 'Histories of culture/theories of ideology – notes on an impasse', in M. Barrett *et al.* (1979).

Johnson, R. (1979b) 'Three problematics – elements of a theory of working-class culture' in J. Clarke *et al.* (1979).

Johnson, R. (1980) 'Cultural studies and educational practice', *Screen Education* 34.

Johnson, R. (1986) 'The story so far – and further transformations?' in D. Punter (ed.) *Introduction to Contemporary Cultural Studies,* London: Longman.

Jones, S. (1988) *Black Culture, White Youth,* London: Macmillan.

Jordin, M. and Brunt, R. (1988) 'Constituting the television audience – a problem of method', in P. Drummond, and R. Paterson (1988).

Kabbani, R. (1986) *Europe's Myths of Orient,* London: Pandora.

Kabbani, R. (1989) *A Letter to Christendom,* London: Virago.

Kagarlitsky, B. (1988) *The Thinking Reed – Intellectuals and the Soviet State from 1917 to the Present,* London: Verso.

Kaldor, M. (1990) 'After the Cold War', *New Left Review* 180 (March–April).

Kaldor, M. (ed.) (1991) *Europe from Below – an East–West Dialogue*, London: Verso.

Kaplan, C. (1986a) 'The culture crossover' in *New Socialist* (Nov.).

Kaplan, C. (1986b) *Sea Changes – Culture and Feminism*, London: Verso.

Kaplan, E. (1987) *Rocking Around the Clock – Music Television, Postmodernism and Consumer Culture*, London: Methuen.

Kaplan, E. (ed.) (1988) *Postmodernism and its Discontents*, London: Verso.

Kappeler, S. (1986) *The Pornography of Representation*, Cambridge: Polity Press.

Katz, E. and Liebes, T. (1986) 'Mutual aid in the decoding of *Dallas* – preliminary notes from a cross-cultural study', in P. Drummond and R. Paterson (1986).

Keane, J. (1991) *The Media and Democracy*, Cambridge: Polity Press.

Keat, R. and Abercrombie, N. (eds) (1991) *Enterprise Culture*, London: Routledge.

Kellner, D. (1989a) *Jean Baudrillard – from Marxism to Postmodernism and Beyond*, Cambridge: Polity.

Kellner, D. (ed.) (1989b) *Postmodernism, Jameson, Critique*, Washington, DC: Maisonneuve Press.

Kelly, O. (1984) *Community, Art and the State – Storming the Citadels*, London: Comedia.

Kuhn, A. (1982) *Women's Pictures – Feminism and Cinema*, London: Routledge.

Kuhn, A. (1984) 'Women's genres', *Screen* 25 (1).

Kumar, K. (1978) *Prophecy and Progress – the Sociology of Industrial and Post-industrial Society*, London: Penguin.

Kumar, K. (1991) *Utopianism*, Milton Keynes: Open University Press.

Lacan, J. (1968) 'The mirror-phase as formative of the I', *New Left Review* 51.

Lacan, J. (1970) 'The insistence of the letter in the unconscious', in J. Ehrmann (ed.) *Structuralism*, New York: Anchor Books..

Laclau, E. (1977) *Politics and Ideology in Marxist Theory*, London: New Left Books/Verso.

Laclau, E. and Mouffe, C. (1985) *Hegemony and Socialist Strategy*, London: New Left Books/Verso.

Laing, D. (1985) *One Chord Wonders – Power and Meaning in Punk Rock*, Milton Keynes: Open University Press.

Lash, S. (1990) *Sociology of Postmodernism*, London: Routledge.

Lash, S. and Urry, J. (1987) *The End of Organized Capitalism*, Cambridge: Polity Press.

Leavis, F.R. (1930) *Mass Civilization and Minority Culture*, reprinted in his *Education and the University* (1979), Cambridge: Cambridge University Press.

Leavis, F.R. and Thompson, D. (1933) *Culture and Environment*, London: Chatto and Windus.

Lee, S. (1990) *The Cost of Free Speech*, London: Faber & Faber.

Leiss, W., Kline, S. and Jhally, S. (1990) *Social Communication in Advertising*, London: Routledge.

Lévi-Strauss, C. (1969) *Totemism*, London: Penguin.

Levitas, R. (1990) *The Concept of Utopia*, Hemel Hempstead: Philip Allen.

Lewis, J. Wren- (1983) 'The encoding/decoding model – criticisms and redevelopments of research on decoding', *Media, Culture and Society* 5.

Lewis, J., Morley, D., and Southwood, A. (1986) *Art Who Needs It? – The Audience For Community Arts*, London: Comedia.

Leys, C. (1990) 'Still a question of hegemony', in *New Left Review* 181.

Livant, B. (1979) 'The audience commodity – on the "blindspot" debate', *Canadian Journal of Political and Social Theory* 3 (1).

Lodziak, C. (1986) *The Power of Television*, London: Francis Pinter.

Lovell, T. (1980) *Pictures of Reality*, London: British Film Institute.

Lovell, T. (1981) 'Marxism and cultural studies' in C. Gledhill (ed.) *Film and Media Studies in Higher Education*, London: British Film Institute.

Lukes, S. (1967) 'Alienation and anomie', in P. Laslett and W. Runciman (eds) *Philosophy, Politics and Society* Series III, Oxford.

Lull, J. (1990) *Inside Family Viewing – Ethnographic Research on Television's Audiences*, London: Routledge.

Lunn, E. (1985) *Marxism and Modernism*, London: Verso.

Lusted, D. (1984) 'Feeding the panic and breaking the cycle – "Popular television and schoolchildren"', *Screen* 24 (6).

Lusted, D. (1985) 'A history of suspicion – educational attitudes to television' in D. Lusted and P. Drummond, (1985).

Lusted, D. and Drummond, P. (eds) (1985) *TV and Schooling*, London: British Film Institute.

Lyotard, J. (1984) *The Postmodern Condition – a Report on Knowledge*, Manchester: Manchester University Press.

McArthur, C. (1978) *Television and History*, London: British Film Institute.

MacCabe, C. (1974) 'Realism and the cinema – notes on some Brechtian theses', *Screen* 15 (2); reprinted in T. Bennett *et al.* (1981b).

MacCabe, C. (1976) 'Theory and film – principles of realism and pleasure', *Screen* 17 (3).

MacCabe, C. (ed.) (1986) *High Theory/Low Culture*, Manchester: Manchester University Press.

McCron, R. (1976) 'Changing perspectives in the study of mass media and socialization' in J. Halloran (ed.) *Mass Media and Socialization*, Leeds: International Association for Mass Communication Research.

MacDonald, D. (1953) 'A theory of mass culture' in B. Rosenberg and D. White, (eds) (1957) *Mass Culture – the Popular Arts in America*, Glencoe, Ill.: The Free Press.

McGrath, J. (1977) 'TV drama – the case against naturalism', *Sight and Sound* 46 (2), London: British Film Institute.

McGrath, J. (1981) *A Good Night Out – Popular Theatre: Audience, Class and Form*, London: Methuen.

McGrath, J. (1990) *The Bone Won't Break – On Theatre and Hope in Hard Times*, London: Methuen.

McGuigan, J. (1986) 'The cognitive dimension – "Edge of Darkness"',

International Television Studies Conference, London University Institute of Education.

McGuigan, J. (1992) 'Reaching for control – Raymond Williams on mass communication and popular culture', in W. Morgan and P. Preston (eds) *Raymond Williams – Education, Politics and Letters*, London: Macmillan.

McLuhan, M. (1964) *Understanding Media*, London: Routledge.

MacRae, D. (1969) 'Populism as an ideology', in G. Ionescu and E. Gellner (1969).

McRobbie, A. (1978) 'Working class girls and the culture of femininity', in CCCS (1978).

McRobbie, A. (1980) 'Settling accounts with subcultures' in *Screen Education* 34; reprinted in Bennett *et al.* (1981a).

McRobbie, A. (1982) '*Jackie* – an ideology of adolescent femininity', in B. Waites *et al.* (1982).

McRobbie, A. (1984) 'Dance and social fantasy' in A. McRobbie and M. Nava (1984).

McRobbie, A. (1986) 'Postmodernism and popular culture', in L. Apignanesi (1986).

McRobbie, A. (1989a) 'Introduction' to A. McRobbie (1989c).

McRobbie, A. (1989b) 'Second-hand dresses and the role of the rag market', in A. McRobbie (1989c).

McRobbie, A. (ed.) (1989c) *Zoot Suits and Second-Hand Dresses*, London: Macmillan.

McRobbie, A. (1991a) 'New times in cultural studies', *New Formations* 13 (Spring), London: Routledge.

McRobbie, A. (1991b) *Feminism and Youth Culture*, London: Macmillan.

McRobbie, A. and McCabe, T. (eds) (1981) *Feminism for Girls – an Adventure Story*, London: Routledge.

McRobbie, A. and Nava, M. (eds) (1984) *Gender and Generation*, London: Macmillan.

Madden, P. (1981) *Keeping Television Alive*, London: British Film Institute.

Madge, J. (1963) *The Origins of Scientific Sociology*, London: Tavistock.

Mandel, E. (1975) *Late Capitalism*, London: New Left Books/Verso.

Marcuse, H. (1964) *One Dimensional Man*, London: Routledge.

Marx, K. (1973) *Grundrisse*, London: Penguin.

Marx, K. and Engels, F. (1967) *The Communist Manifesto*, London: Penguin.

Massey, D. (1991) 'A global sense of place', *Marxism Today* (June).

Masterman, L. (1980) *Teaching about Television*, London: Macmillan.

Masterman, L. (1984) *Television Mythologies – Stars, Shows and Signs*, London: Comedia.

Masterman, L. (1985) *Teaching the Media*, London: Comedia.

Masterman, L. (1986) 'Reply to David Buckingham', *Screen* 27 (5).

Mattelart, A. (1979) *Multinational Corporations and the Control of Culture – the Ideological Apparatuses of Imperialism*, Brighton: Harvester Press.

Mattelart, M. (1986) *Women, Media, Crisis*, London: Comedia.

Medhurst, A. (1989) 'Sunsational', *Marxism Today* (Nov).

Mellencamp, P. (ed.) (1990) *Logics of Television*, London: British Film Institute.

Mepham, J. (1990) 'The ethics of quality in television', in G. Mulgan (1990); reprinted in *Radical Philosophy* 57 (spring 1991).

Mercer, C. (1986) 'Complicit pleasures', in T. Bennett *et al.* (1986).

Messenger Davies, M. (1989) *Television is Good for Your Kids*, London: Hilary Shipman.

Metcalf, A. and Humphries, M. (eds) (1985) *The Sexuality of Men*, London: Pluto Press.

Miège, B (1979) 'The cultural commodity', *Media, Culture and Society* 1 (3), reprinted in B. Miege (1989) *The Capitalization of Cultural Production*, New York: International General.

Miliband, R. (1978) 'A state of de-subordination', *British Journal of Sociology* 29 (4).

Miliband, R. and Panitch, L. (1991) *Socialist Register 1991*, London: Merlin Press.

Mill, J.S. (1974 – originally published in 1859) *On Liberty*, London: Penguin.

Modleski, T. (1984) *Loving with a Vengeance – Mass-produced Fantasies for Women*, London: Methuen.

Modleski, T. (ed.) (1986) *Studies in Entertainment – Critical Approaches to Mass Culture*, Indiana University Press.

Moi, T. (ed.) (1986) *The Kristeva Reader*, Oxford: Basil Blackwell.

Monaco, J. (1981) *How to Read a Film*, New York: Oxford University Press.

Morley, D. (1974) 'Reconceptualising the media audience – towards an ethnography of audiences', Birmingham CCCS Occasional Paper.

Morley, D. (1980a) 'Texts, readers, subjects', in S. Hall *et al.* (1980).

Morley, D. (1980b) *The 'Nationwide' Audience*, London: British Film Institute.

Morley, D. (1981a) 'Interpreting television – a case study', *U203 Popular Culture*, Milton Keynes: Open University Press.

Morley, D. (1981b) 'The Nationwide audience – a critical postscript', *Screen Education* 39.

Morley, D. (1986) *Family Television – Cultural Power and Domestic Leisure*, London: Comedia.

Morley, D. (1989) 'Changing paradigms in audience studies', in E. Seiter *et al.* (1989).

Morley, D. (1991) 'Where the global meets the local – notes from the sitting room', *Screen* 32 (1) (spring).

Morley, D. and Robins, K. (1989) 'Spaces of identity: communications technologies and the reconfiguration of Europe', *Screen* 30 (4).

Morley, D. and Robins, K. (1990) 'No place like *Heimat* – images of home(land) in European culture', *New Formations* 12 (Winter), London: Routledge.

Morris, M. (1988) 'Banality in cultural studies', in *Block* 14, reprinted in P. Mellencamp (1990).

Morris, W. (1970 – originally published in 1890) *News from Nowhere*, London: Routledge.

Mulgan, G. (ed.) (1990) *The Question of Quality*, London: British Film

Institute.

Mulgan, G. and Worpole, K. (1986) *Saturday Night or Sunday Morning?* – *From Arts to Industry, New Forms of Cultural Policy*, London: Comedia.

Mulhern, F. (1979) *The Moment of 'Scrutiny'*, London: New Left Books.

Mulvey, L. (1975) 'Visual pleasure and narrative cinema', *Screen* 16 (3); reprinted in T. Bennett *et al.* (1981b).

Mulvey, L. (1981) 'Afterthoughts on "Visual pleasure and narrative cinema"', *Framework* 15–17.

Mungham, G. and Pearson, G. (eds) (1976) *Working Class Youth Culture*, London: Routledge.

Murdock, G. (1975) 'Education, culture and the myth of classlessness', in J. Howarth and M. Smith (eds) *Work and Leisure*, London: Lepus Books.

Murdock, G. (1978) 'Blindspots about Western Marxism – a reply to Dallas Smythe', *Canadian Journal of Political and Social Theory* 2 (2).

Murdock, G. (1980) 'Authorship and organisation', *Screen Education* 35.

Murdock, G. (1989a) 'Cultural studies at the crossroads', in *Australian Journal of Communication* 16.

Murdock, G. (1989b) 'Critical inquiry and audience activity', in B. Dervin, *et al.* (eds) *Rethinking Communications* vol. 2 *Paradigm Exemplars*, London: Sage.

Murdock, G. (1990a) 'Television and citizenship – in defence of public broadcasting', in A. Tomlinson (1990b).

Murdock, G. (1990b) 'Redrawing the map of the communications industries – concentration and ownership in the era of privatization', in M. Ferguson (1990).

Murdock, G. and McCron, R.(1979) 'The television and delinquency debate', *Screen Education* 30.

Murdock, G. and Phelps, G. (1973) *Mass Media and the Secondary School*, London: Macmillan.

Myers, K. (1986) *Understains – the Sense and Seduction of Advertising*, London: Comedia.

Nairn, T. (1988) *The Enchanted Glass*, London: Radius Books.

Nava, M. (1987) 'Consumerism and its contradictions', *Cultural Studies* 1 (2), London: Methuen.

Nava, M. (1991) 'Consumerism reconsidered – buying and power', *Cultural Studies* 5 (2, London: Methuen.

Nava, M. and Nava, O. (1990) 'Discriminating or duped? – Young people as consumers of advertising/art', in *Magazine of Cultural Studies* 1 (March).

Nelson, C. and Grossberg, L. (eds) (1988) *Marxism and the Interpretation of Culture*, London: Macmillan.

Nietzsche, F. (1888) 'The Antichrist', in W. Kaufmann (ed.) (1968) *The Portable Nietzsche*, New York: Viking.

Norris, C. (1987) *Derrida*, London: Fontana.

Nowell-Smith, G. (1987) 'Popular culture', *New Formations* 2, London: Methuen.

Nowell-Smith, G. and Wollen, T. (eds) (1991) *After the Wall*, London: British Film Institute.

O'Connor, A. (1989) *Raymond Williams – Writing, Culture and Politics*, Oxford: Basil Blackwell.

Offe, C. (1985) *Disorganized Capitalism*, Cambridge: Polity Press.

O'Malley, T. (1988) *Switching Channels – the Debate over the Future of Broadcasting*, London: Campaign for Press and Broadcasting Freedom.

Orru, M. (1987) *Anomie – History and Meanings*, London: Allen and Unwin.

O'Shaughnessy, M. (1990) 'Box pop – popular television and hegemony', in A. Goodwin and G. Whannel (1990).

O'Shea, A. (1984) 'Trusting the people – how does Thatcherism work?' in *Formations of Nation and People*, London: Routledge.

Osman, S. (1988) 'Should it be unlawful to incite sexual violence?' in G. Chester and J. Dickey, (1988).

Owusu, K. (1986) *The Struggle for Black Arts in Britain*, London: Comedia.

Packard, V. (1957) *The Hidden Persuaders*, London: Longman.

Palmer, J. (1991) 'Europe after the Revolutions', in M. Kaldor (1991).

Panitch, L. and Gindin, S. (1991) 'Perestroika and the proletariat' in R. Miliband and L. Panitch (1991).

Parekh. B. (1989) 'Between holy text and moral void', *New Statesman and Society* (24 March).

Parkin, F. (1973) *Class Inequality and Political Order*, London: Paladin.

Parmar, P. (1988) 'Rage and desire – confronting pornography', in G. Chester and J. Dickey (1988).

Pauly, J. (1988) 'Rupert Murdoch and the demonology of professional journalism', in J. Carey, (ed.) *Media, Myths and Narratives*, Newbury Park: Sage Annual Review of Communication Research, vol. 15.

Peacock, A. *et al.* (1986) *Report of the Committee on Financing the BBC*, London: HMSO Cmnd 9824.

Pearson, G. (1983) *Hooligan – a History of Respectable Fears*, London: Macmillan.

Philips, D. (1990) 'Mills and Boon – the marketing of moonshine', in A. Tomlinson (1990b).

Philo, G. (1990) *Seeing and Believing – the Influence of Television*, London: Routledge.

Pieterse, J.N. (1991) 'Fictions of Europe', *Race and Class* 32 (3) (Jan.-March), London: Institute of Race Relations.

Playfair, G. Lyon (1990) *The Evil Eye – the Unacceptable Face of Television*, London: Jonathan Cape.

Postman, N. (1986) *Amusing Ourselves to Death*, London: Methuen.

Pursehouse, M. (1987) *'Life's More Fun with Your Number One Sun' – Interviews with some Sun-Readers*, Birmingham CCCS Occasional Paper.

Pusey, M. (1987) *Jurgen Habermas*, London: Tavistock.

Radway, J. (1987) *Reading the Romance*, London: Verso.

Radway, J. (1988) 'Reception study – ethnography and the problem of dispersed audiences and nomadic subjects', *Cultural Studies* 2 (3), London: Methuen.

Ray, L. (1991) 'A Thatcher export phenomenon? The enterprise culture in Eastern Europe', in R. Keat and N. Abercrombie (1991).

Redhead, S. (1990) *The End of the Century Party – Youth and Pop Towards 2000*, Manchester: Manchester University Press.

Robins, D. (1984) *We Hate Humans*, London: Penguin.

Robins, D. and Cohen, P. (1978) *Knuckle Sandwich – Growing Up in the Working-class City*, London: Penguin.

Robins, K. (1989) 'Reimagined communities? European image spaces, beyond Fordism', *Cultural Studies* 3 (2), London: Methuen.

Rodinson, M. (1979) *Marxism and the Muslim World*, London: Zed Press.

Root, J. (1986) *Open the Box*, London: Comedia.

Ross, A. (1989) *No Respect – Intellectuals and Popular Culture*, New York/London: Routledge.

Rowbotham, S. (1973) *Hidden from History*, London: Pluto Press.

Rude, G. (1980) *Ideology and Popular Protest*, London: Lawrence & Wishart.

Rushdie, S. (1988) *The Satanic Verses*, London: Viking.

Rushdie, S. (1990) 'In good faith', *Sunday Independent* (4 Feb.).

Rushdie, S. (1991) 'One man in a doomed balloon', *Guardian* (13 Dec.).

Rutherford, J. (ed.) (1990) *Identity – Community, Culture, Difference*, London: Lawrence & Wishart.

Ruthven, M. (1990) *A Satanic Affair – Salman Rushdie and the Wrath of Islam*, London: Hogarth Press.

Sahgal, G. and Yuval-Davis, N. (1990) 'Refusing Holy Orders', *Marxism Today* (March).

Said, E. (1978) *Orientalism*, London: Routledge.

Said, E. (1981) *Covering Islam – How the Media and the Experts Determine How We See the Rest of the World*, London: Routledge.

Samuel, R. (ed.) (1981) *People's History and Socialist Theory*, London: Routledge.

Sardar, Z. and Wynn Davies, M. (1990) *Distorted Imagination – Lessons from the Rushdie Affair*, London: Grey Seal Books.

Sartre, J. (1948) *Existentialism and Humanism*, London: Methuen.

Sartre, J. (1963) *Search for a Method*, New York: Knopf.

Scannell, P. (1988) 'Radio times – the temporal arrangements of broadcasting in the modern world', in P. Drummond and R. Paterson (1988).

Scannell, P. (1989) 'Public service broadcasting and modern public life', *Media, Culture and Society* 11 (2).

Scannell, P. (1990) 'Public service broadcasting – the history of a concept' in A. Goodwin and G. Whannel (1990).

Schlesinger, P. (1991) *Media, State and Nation – Political Violence and Collective Identities*, London: Sage.

Schudson, M. (1987) 'The new validation of popular culture: sense and sentimentality in academia', *Critical Studies in Mass Communication* 4 (March).

Schwarz, B. (1982) 'The "people" in history – the Communist Party Historians Group 1946-56', in CCCS (1982b).

Seabrook, J. (1971) *City Close-up*, London: Penguin.

Seabrook, J. (1978) *What Went Wrong?*, London: Gollancz.

Seabrook, J. (1982) *Unemployment*, London: Paladin.

Seabrook, J. (1988) *The Leisure Society*, Oxford: Basil Blackwell.

Seabrook, J. (1990) *The Myth of the Market*, Bideford: Green Books.

Searle, C. (1989) *Your Daily Dose – Racism and the Sun*, London: Campaign for Press and Broadcasting Freedom.

Seaton, J. (1986) 'Pornography annoys', in J. Curran *et al.* (eds) *Bending Reality – the State of the Media*, London: Pluto Press.

Segal, L. (1987) *Is the Future Female? – Troubled Thoughts on Contemporary Feminism*, London: Virago.

Segal, L. (1990) *Slow Motion – Changing Masculinities, Changing Men*, London: Virago.

Seiter, E., Borchers, H., Kreutzner, G. and Warth, E-M. (1989) *Remote Control – Television, Audiences and Cultural Power*, London: Routledge.

Shils, E. (1971) 'Mass society and its culture', in B. Rosenberg and D. White (eds) *Mass Culture Revisited*, New York: Van Nostrand Reinhold.

Silj, A., Alvarado, M., Chaniac, R., Torchi, A., O'Connor, B., Bianchi, J., Hofmann, M. (1988) *East of Dallas – the European Challenge to American Television*, London: British Film Institute.

Silverstone, R. (1990) 'Television and everyday life – towards an ethnography of the television audience' in M. Ferguson (1990).

Simpson, P. (1989) *Children in the Market Place*, London: British Action for Children's Television.

Sivanandan, A. (1990) 'All that melts into air is solid – the hokum of new times', in *Race and Class* 31 (3), London: Institute of Race Relations.

Skeggs, B. (1991) 'A spanking good time', *Magazine of Cultural Studies* 3 (spring).

Smith, D. (1988) *Walls and Mirrors – Western Representations of Really Existing Socialism in the German Democratic Republic*, New York: University Press of America.

Smythe, D. (1977) 'Communications – blindspot of Western Marxism', *Canadian Journal of Political and Social Theory* 1 (3).

Smythe, D. (1978) 'Rejoinder to Graham Murdock', *Canadian Journal of Political and Social Theory* 2 (2).

Smythe, D. (1981) *Dependency Road – Communications, Capitalism, Consciousness and Canada*, New Jersey: Ablex.

Stam, R. (1988) 'Mikhail Bakhtin and Left cultural critique', in E. Kaplan (1988).

Stewart, A. (1969) 'The social roots', in G. Ionescu and E. Gellner (1969).

Stuart, A. (1990) 'Feminism – dead or alive?' in J. Rutherford (1990).

Sutherland, J. (1982) *Offensive Literature – Decensorship in Britain 1960–1982*, London: Junction Books.

Swingewood, A. (1977) *The Myth of Mass Culture*, London: Macmillan.

Taylor, I. and Taylor, L. (eds) (1973) *Politics and Deviance*, London: Penguin.

Taylor, I. and Wall, D. (1976) 'Beyond the skinheads – comments on the emergence and significance of the glamrock cult', in G. Mungham and G. Pearson (1976).

Taylor, I., Young, J., and Walton, P. (1973) *The New Criminology*, London: Routledge.

Taylor, L. and Mullan, B. (1986) *Uninvited Guests – the Intimate Secrets of Television and Radio*, London: Chatto and Windus.

Thompson, D. (ed.) (1964) *Discrimination and Popular Culture*, London: Penguin.

Thompson, E.P. (1961) '"The Long Revolution" Part 1', *New Left Review*, 9–10.

Thompson, E.P. (1963) *The Making of the English Working Class*, London: Gollancz.

Thompson, E.P. (1977) *William Morris – Romantic to Revolutionary*, London: Merlin Press.

Thompson, E.P. (1979) *The Poverty of Theory and Other Essays*, London: Merlin.

Tolson, A. (1986) 'Popular culture – practice and institution', in C. MacCabe (1986).

Tomlinson, A. (1990a) 'Introduction – consumer culture and the aura of the commodity', in A. Tomlinson (1990b).

Tomlinson, A. (ed.) (1990b) *Consumption, Identity and Style*, London: Routledge.

Tomlinson, J. (1991) *Cultural Imperialism*, London: Pinter.

Traub, S. and Little, C. (eds) (1980) *Theories of Deviance*, Illinois: Peacock.

Tulloch, J. (1989) 'Approaching the audience – the elderly', in E. Seiter *et al.* (1989).

Tulloch, J. (1990) *Television Drama – Agency, Audience and Myth*, London: Routledge.

Tumber, H. (1982) *Television and the Riots*, London: British Film Institute.

Turkle, S. (1979) *Psychoanalytic Politics – Jacques Lacan and Freud's French Revolution*, London: Burnett Books/André Deutsch.

Turner, G. (1990) *British Cultural Studies – an Introduction*, London: Unwin Hyman.

Turner, L. (1990) 'The Berlin Wall – fragment as commodity', in *Border/Lines* (Fall), Toronto.

Unger, F. (1991) 'Speaking of unity', in G. Nowell-Smith and T. Wollen (1991).

Volosinov, V. (1929 – original Russian publication 1986) *Marxism and the Philosophy of Language*, Cambridge, Mass.: Harvard University Press.

Waites, B., Bennett, T., and Martin, G. (eds) (1982) *Popular Culture – Past and Present*, London: Croom Helm.

Wallerstein, E. (1990) 'Culture as the ideological battleground of the modern world-system', in M. Featherstone (1990b).

Walvin, J. (1986) *Football and the Decline of Britain*, London: Macmillan.

Wark, M. (1990) 'Europe's masked ball – East meets West at the Wall', *New Formations* 12 (winter).

Watney, S. (1987) *Policing Desire*, London: Comedia.

Webster, D. (1988) *Looka Yonder! – the Imaginary America of Populist Culture*, London: Routledge.

Webster, R. (1990) *A Brief History of Blasphemy – Liberalism, Censorship and 'The Satanic Verses'*, Southwold: Orwell Press.

Westergaard, J. and Resler, H. (1975) *Class in a Capitalist Society*, London: Heinemann.

Wiles, P. (1969) 'A syndrome, not a doctrine – some elementary theses on populism', in G. Ionescu and E. Gellner (1969).

Willemen, P. (1978) 'Notes on subjectivity', *Screen* 19 (1) (spring).

Willemen, P. (1990) 'Review of John Hill's "Sex, class and realism – British Cinema 1956-1963"', in M. Alvarado and J. Thompson (1990); originally published in *Framework* 35 (1987).

Williams, B. (ed.) (1981) *Obscenity and Film Censorship*, Cambridge: Cambridge University Press.

Williams, R. (1958) *Culture and Society*, London: Chatto and Windus.

Williams, R. (1960) 'Advertising – the magic system', *New Left Review* 4; reprinted in R. Williams (1980).

Williams, R. (1961) *The Long Revolution*, London: Chatto and Windus.

Williams, R. (1962) *Communications*, London: Penguin.

Williams, R. (1970) 'A hundred years of culture and anarchy', in R. Williams (1980).

Williams, R. (1973) 'Base and superstructure in Marxist cultural theory', *New Left Review* 82; reprinted in R. Williams (1980).

Williams, R. (1974) *Television, Technology and Cultural Form*, London: Fontana.

Williams, R. (1977a) *Marxism and Literature*, Oxford University Press.

Williams, R. (1977b) 'A lecture on realism', *Screen* 18 (1) (spring).

Williams, R. (1978) 'Means of communication as means of production', in R. Williams (1980).

Williams, R. (1979) *Politics and Letters*, London: New Left Books.

Williams, R. (1980) *Problems in Materialism and Culture*, London: New Left Books/Verso.

Williams, R. (1981) 'Marxism, structuralism and literary analysis', *New Left Review* 129; reprinted as 'Crisis in English studies', in R. Williams (1983c).

Williams, R. (1983a) *Keywords*, London: Fontana.

Williams, R. (1983b) *Towards 2000*, London: Chatto and Windus.

Williams, R. (1983c) *Writing in Society*, London: New Left Books/Verso.

Williams, R. (1989a) *Resources of Hope*, London: Verso.

Williams, R. (1989b) *The Politics of Modernism*, London: Verso.

Williamson, J. (1978) *Decoding Advertisements*, London: Marion Boyars.

Williamson, J. (1985) 'Consuming passion', in *New Socialist* (Feb.); reprinted in J. Williamson (1986b).

Williamson, J. (1986a) 'The problems of being popular', in *New Socialist* (Sept.).

Williamson, J. (1986b) *Consuming Passions*, London: Marion Boyars.

Williamson, J. (1989) 'Even new times change', in *New Statesman and Society* (7 July).

Willis, P. (1972) 'The motorbike within a subcultural group', in *Working Papers in Cultural Studies* 2, Birmingham CCCS.

Willis, P. (1977) *Learning to Labour – How Working-Class Kids Get Working-Class Jobs*, Farnborough: Saxon House.

Willis, P. (1978) *Profane Culture*, London: Routledge.

Willis, P. (1980) 'Notes on method', in S. Hall *et al.* (1980).

Willis, P. (1982) 'Male school counterculture', Unit 30 of U203 *Popular Culture*, Milton Keynes: Open University.

Willis, P. (1990a) *Common Culture*, Milton Keynes: Open University Press.
Willis, P. (1990b) *Moving Culture*, London: Calouste Gulbenkian.
Winn, M. (1977) *The Plug-in Drug*, New York/London: Viking/Penguin.
Winston, B. (1990) 'Paradigm found', *Listener* (21 June).
Woods, P. (1977) 'Youth, generations and social class', units 27–28 of E202 *Schooling and Society*, Milton Keynes: Open University.
Worpole, K. (1990) 'Total culture', *Marxism Today* (Sept.).
Young, J. (1974) 'New directions in subcultural theory', in J. Rex (ed.) *Approaches to Sociology*, London: Routledge.

Name index

Subject index

would show that *no* housewives go out to
 wife who keeps house, then the question
y-wed in a one-room flat with her husband
arly all the time is really a "housewife."
e the wife who has a maid to do most of the
t interpretations will lead to different
.

sometimes associated with the population
nt may not be known; for example, the
in England with unsuspected diabetes.
asy to collect figures for such a population.
ould be clear that, before any figures are
eful consideration should be given to the
roposed survey.

y often it is impracticable to obtain in-
item in the population and we have to be
tion of all such items.   Such a fraction is

 a group of items taken from the population

METHODS OF COLLECTION

ned.   We have seen that figures relating
tion can be obtained either from the whole
 a sample.   Whichever approach is decided
bination of the following methods can be

ation.—For example, counting for oneself
of cars in a car park.
.—Asking personally for the required in-

rom published statistics.
ionnaire.—Sending a questionnaire by post
ng completion.

ation.   This is the best method, as it reduces
rrect data being recorded.   Unfortunately
be used, generally on account of the cost.
nomical, for instance, to follow a housewife

PART TWO

THE COMPILATION AND PRESENTATION
OF STATISTICS

keeping, the survey
work! If it means a
arises whether a new
away on business ne
And should we includ
housework? Differe
results in the analysi

Another problem
is that its full exte
number of people
Obviously it is not e
To sum up, it sh
collected at all, car
population of any

3. Samples. Ve
formation on every
satisfied with a fra
known as a sample
A *sample*, then, is
for examination.

SECTION 7

1. Methods outl
to a chosen popula
population or from
on, one or a com
adopted:

(a) *Direct obser*
    the number
(b) *Interviewing*
    formation.
(c) *Abstraction*
(d) *Postal quest*
    and request

2. Direct obser
the chance of inc
it cannot always
It would be unec

Before
be collecte
aspect of
arise in col
based on s

Always
than the o
original fig
will be, at
since it may

SECTI

1. Altern
data. The

(a) the en
(b) a sam

First, thougl

2. Populat
the specific
we want to
know what pi
then our "po
we wish to kn
population is
not the same
may be forei
should be care

For instance
wives who go
If it is taken to

B

around for a month in order to find out how many times she vacuumed the lounge, quite apart from the practical difficulties. At other times this method cannot be used because the information cannot be directly observed, *e.g.* where people would spend their holidays if they had unlimited money.

3. Interviewing. A disadvantage of interviewing is that inaccurate or false data may be given to the interviewer. The reason may be (*a*) forgetfulness, (*b*) misunderstanding the question, or (*c*) a deliberate intent to mislead.

For example, a housewife who is asked how much milk she bought the previous week (*a*) may have forgotten, (*b*) may include —or fail to include—any milk bought by her husband, or (*c*) may overstate the amount because she has a number of children and feels she ought to have bought more than she did.

Another disadvantage of interviewing is that if a number of interviewers are employed they may not record the answers in the same way as the investigator himself would.

For example, to the question "Did you watch the XYZ TV programme last night—yes or no?" the interviewer may get the answer, "Well, part of it, then someone came and we switched off." He may well record this as a "no" answer, while the investigator may be taking it that such answers are recorded as "yes."

Different standards like this can easily result in the wrong conclusions being drawn from the survey. One way of overcoming this disadvantage is to train the interviewers very carefully so that they record data in *exactly* the same form as the investigator himself would record it.

4. Abstraction from published statistics. Any data that an investigator collects himself are termed *primary data* and, because he knows the conditions under which they were collected, he is aware of any limitations they may contain.

Data taken from other people's figures, on the other hand, are termed *secondary data*. Users of secondary data cannot have as thorough an understanding of the background as the original investigator, and so may be unaware of such limitations.

Statistics compiled from secondary data are termed *secondary statistics*. Obviously the compilation of such statistics needs care, in view of the possibility of there being special features concerning the earlier statistics, or the population concerned, which are not known to the compiler. For example, a table relating to unemployment may cover only *registered* unemployment; if this fact were not indicated, a subsequent investigation using the figures in conjunction with *unregistered* unemployment figures could result in quite false conclusions.

For this reason anyone wishing to use published statistics should consider the purpose for which they were originally compiled. In many Government publications, the statistics *are* compiled in the knowledge that they will be used in the production of secondary statistics. Such statistics are carefully annotated and explained so that users will not be misled, and secondary statistics may be prepared from them with reasonable confidence. However, many others are published in connection with a specific inquiry and it may be very dangerous to use them as a base for the compilation of secondary statistics.

5. Postal questionnaire. This is the least satisfactory method, for the simple reason that only relatively few such questionnaires are ever returned. A return of 15% is often considered good response for certain types of survey, although reminder notices can usually improve the percentage. Moreover, the questionnaires which are returned are often of little value as a sample, since they are frequently biased in one direction or another.

For example, a questionnaire relating to washing-machine performance will be returned mainly by people with complaints, who are only too pleased at the chance to air them. Satisfied users will probably not bother to reply. A conclusion, based on the returned questionnaires, that washing machine performance was on the whole bad would therefore be a false conclusion.

Bias of this sort is rarely as obvious as in the above example, and so cannot be allowed for in any analysis of returned questionnaires. Postal questionnaires therefore are not recommended unless one of the following conditions applies:

(a) Completion is a legal obligation (*e.g.* Government surveys).

(b) The non-responders are subsequently interviewed in order to obtain the required information.

(c) An appropriate sample of the non-responders is interviewed and the results indicate that failure to reply *is in no way connected with any bias*.

6. Design of a questionnaire. If a questionnaire is to be used—either as a postal questionnaire or as a basis for interviewing—the following points should be observed in its design:

(a) Questions should be *simple*.

(b) Questions should be *unambiguous*.

(c) The best kinds of question are those which allow a *pre-printed answer* to be ticked.

(d) The questionnaire should be as *short* as possible.

(e) Questions should be *neither irrelevant nor too personal*.

(f) *Leading questions should not be asked*. A "leading question" is one that suggests the answer, *e.g.* the question "Don't you agree that all sensible people use XYZ soap?" suggests the answer "yes."

(g) The questionnaire should be designed so that the *questions fall into a logical sequence*. This will enable the respondent to understand its purpose, and as a result the quality of his answers may be improved.

SECTION 8.   RANDOM SAMPLES

1. The problem of bias. Taking a sample is not simply a matter of taking the nearest items. If worthwhile conclusions relating to the whole population are to be made from the sample it is essential to ensure that the sample is free from *bias*, *i.e.* allowing a particular influence to have more importance than it really warrants.

Assume, for example, that we wish to know what proportion of Europeans are fair-haired. If we took a sample wholly from Stockholm, our conclusion based on it would be wrong, because Swedes are a fair-haired nation. Our sample would thus allow "fair-hairedness" to have an importance greater than is warranted, *i.e.* it would be biased towards "fair-hairedness."

Unfortunately it is not sufficient merely to ensure there is no *known* bias in our sample. *Unsuspected* bias can equally invalidate our conclusions. So the question arises as to how one can select a sample that is free even from unknown bias.

2. What is a random sample? The problem of unsuspected bias can be solved by taking a *random sample*. A random sample is a sample selected in such a way that every item in the population has an equal chance of being included. This is the only type of sample which we can be confident is free from bias.

There are various methods of obtaining a random sample but they all depend on the selection being wholly determined by chance.

One may imagine such a selection being made by writing the name (or number) of each item in the population on a slip of paper and then drawing from a hat, as in a lottery, the required number of slips to make up the sample. Although this gives the idea behind "random selection," in practice great care has to be taken that no bias can possibly arise—for instance, in this method adjacent slips could conceivably stick together. Probably the best method of selection is to number all the items and then allow a computer to throw out a series of random numbers which will identify the items to be used in the sample.

3. Random samples are not perfect samples. Finally, students should appreciate that a random sample is not necessarily a good cross-section of the population.

Drawing the names of Europeans out of a hat *could* result in a sample containing all Swedes—though it is highly unlikely. Thus a random sample too can be one-sided, and does not *guarantee* a sample free from bias. It simply guarantees that the *method of selection* is free from bias. This is a rather subtle difference, but an important one.

SECTION 9. NON-RANDOM SAMPLING

1. Bars to using random samples. Occasions often arise when the selection of a pure random sample is not feasible. These obstacles arise:

    (a) when such a sample would entail much expensive travelling for the interviewers;

    (b) when "hunting out" the people selected would be a long and uneconomic task.

(c) when all the items in the population are not known. It would be impossible to select a random sample of fair-haired mothers, for example, since there is no list of such mothers from which the names can be copied on to slips of paper!

These bars are overcome by using *multi-stage*, *quota* and *cluster* sampling respectively.

2. Multi-stage sampling. In this technique the country is divided into a number of areas, and three or four areas are selected by random means. Each area selected is again sub-divided and another small sample of areas selected at random. This process may be repeated until ultimately a number of quite small areas in different parts of the country have been selected. A random sample of the relevant people within each of these areas is then interviewed.

Although the technique does involve sending interviewers to different parts of the country, once an interviewer is in an appropriate area he can carry out all his interviews with virtually no further travelling. This brings the cost of the survey within reasonable bounds.

3. Quota sampling. To avoid the expense of having to "hunt out" specific people chosen by a random sample, interviewers are told to interview all the people they meet, up to a given number, which is called their *quota*. Such a quota is nearly always divided up into different types of people (*e.g.* working class, upper class, etc.) with sub-quotas for each type. The object is to gain the benefits of stratification (*see s.* **10.** 2).

4. Cluster sampling. In this technique the country is divided into small areas, much as with the multi-stage method. The interviewers are sent to the areas with instructions to interview every person they can find who fits the definition given (*e.g.* fair-haired mothers).

This sort of sampling could be applied where surveys of (say) home workshops, or oak trees, were required. It should be carefully distinguished from multi-stage sampling, where the object is to cut down costs. Generally, cluster sampling is used when it is the *only* way a sample can be found.

SECTION 10. SYSTEMATIC AND STRATIFIED SAMPLING

1. Systematic sampling. This is simply a short-cut method for obtaining a virtually random sample. If all the items in the population are listed and a 10% sample (say) is required, then the sample can be selected by taking every tenth item on the list, providing there is no regularity within the list such that items ten spaces apart have some special quality. If by mischance there happened to be some pattern in the list that coincided with the sampling interval, the sample would be biased: for instance, every tenth house in a street might have a bay window and therefore be slightly more expensive. Such bias is not common, however, and systematic sampling can often be safely used.

2. Stratified sampling. It is important to note that none of the techniques so far mentioned is better than a pure random sample. Stratified sampling is *better* than purely random methods and must therefore be distinguished from the others. In order to use it, one has to know what groups comprise the total population, and in what proportions.

For instance, in a survey relating to lung cancer among smokers there will be pipe smokers and cigarette smokers. As the proportion of each can easily be found, stratified sampling can be employed. The technique involves the following steps (assuming in this case that the relevant proportions are 3 : 7):

(a) Decide on the total sample size (say 1,000).
(b) Divide this into sub-samples *with the same proportions as the groups in the population* (300 and 700).
(c) Select at random from each strata the appropriate sub-sample (300 pipe and 700 cigarette smokers).
(d) Add the sub-sample results together to obtain the figures for the overall sample.

The reason why stratified sampling is an improvement over a pure random sample is that it lessens the possibility of one-sidedness. As we have seen, a random sample of Europeans *could* be composed wholly of Swedes. But if it were arranged that the sample should contain different proportions of each nationality according to the size of the country's population, a one-sided sample would be impossible.

PROGRESS TEST 3

1. List (a) the advantages and (b) the disadvantages of a postal questionnaire as opposed to a personal interview.*

2. What comments have you to make on the following statement made in *Mack's Mag*?*

"We thought we would like to learn something of the physical characteristics of our readers, so ten newsagents were selected and an observer stationed at each.   This observer noted down physical facts about every person who bought a copy of *Mack's Mag* and the results of this random sample will be published in next week's issue."

3. What sampling methods would you use to obtain the following information?*

(a) Ages of Australian-born persons resident in the U.K.
(b) Health details relating to U.K. borough councillors.
(c) Heights of employees (male, female and juvenile) employed in a large factory.
(d) The views of the public on Sunday trading.

CHAPTER IV

TABLES

It is a psychological fact that data presented higgledy-piggledy are far harder to understand than data presented in a clear and orderly manner. Consequently, the next step after the figures have been collected is to lay them out in an orderly way so that they are more readily comprehended. A very good form of layout is one of columns and rows. Such a layout is known as a *table*.

EXAMPLE
The following data are the result of an imaginary survey into the cinema-going and television-watching habits of adult males in Great Watchet. The same information is presented in two ways: first in narrative form, *i.e.* written sentences, and then in tabular form. It is obvious which is the clearer and more concise.

(1) *Narrative form*

A survey of adult males in Great Watchet, taken in September 19—, by personal interview, showed that 122 of the 2,049 single men under 30 attended the cinema less than once a month; 1,046 attended one to four times a month, and 881 more than four times a month. Of the single men over 30 the respective figures were 374, 202 and 23, a total of 599. As regards television viewing, 830 of the single men under 30 viewed less than 15 hours a week, the other 1,219 viewing 15 hours or more. For single men over 30 these figures were 358 and 241 respectively. As regards the married men, 1,404 of the under-30's attended the cinema less than once a month, 289 attended one to four times a month and 112 more than four times a month. For those of 30 and over the figures were 1,880, 115 and 10 respectively. TV viewing figures showed that 1,162 married men under 30 viewed less than 15 hours a week and the remaining 643, 15 hours or more. Of the "30 and over" group, 484 viewed less than 15 hours and 1,521 viewed 15 or more hours a week.

2) *Tabular form*

TABLE 1.   SURVEY OF CINEMA ATTENDANCE AND TELEVISION VIEWING AMONG ADULT MALES IN GREAT WATCHET, SEPTEMBER 19—

	Single		Married	
	Under 30	30 and over	Under 30	30 and over
Cinema attendance:				
Less than once a month	122	374	1,404	1,880
1–4 times a month	1,046	202	289	115
More than four times a month	881	23	112	10
Total	2,049	599	1,805	2,005
Television viewing:				
Less than 15 hours a week	830	358	1,162	484
15 hours or more a week	1,219	241	643	1,521
Total	2,049	599	1,805	2,005

Source: *personal interview*

SECTION 11.   PRINCIPLES OF TABLE CONSTRUCTION

1. Imagination and common sense are needed. The construction of a table is in many ways a work of art. It is not enough just to have columns and rows: a badly constructed table can be as confusing as a mass of data presented in narrative form. Yet, as with a work of art, it is difficult to lay down precise rules that will apply to all cases. For this reason the student should construct his tables as common sense guides him—and the sounder his common sense, the better will his tables be.

On the other hand, there are certain principles which must be observed in the construction of *all* tables. A trace of imagination can often improve a table, but to ignore any of these principles will only result in a loss of clarity and impact which might be compared with mumbling instead of speaking out clearly.

2. The basic principle. Of all the principles of table construction, there is one which is basic: *construct it so that the table achieves its object in the best manner possible.* This means the student must ask himself at the very beginning, "What is the purpose of this table?" Some of the possible reasons for which a table may be constructed are:

(*a*) To present the original figures in an orderly manner.

(*b*) To show a distinct pattern in the figures.

(*c*) To summarise the figures.

(*d*) To publish salient figures which other people may use in future statistical studies. (Many Government statistics are produced for this purpose, and the student is warned against using such tables as models if his own table is produced for a different purpose.)

Frequently table construction involves deciding which columns of figures should be adjacent to each other. For example, would Table 1 be improved if "Under 30" and "30 and over" had been the main column headings, with each broken down into "Single" and "Married" sub-headings? The answer depends, as always, on the purpose of the table. If the activities of *age-groups* are to be compared, it is best as it stands. But if a comparison between men of different *marital status* were required, the change would be an improvement.

Other kinds of decision must also be made. For instance, what totals should be shown? Should percentages be added? Should some figures be combined, or even eliminated? Invariably, the basis of all these decisions is the purpose to which the table will be put.

3. Other principles of table construction. The following additional principles should also be observed:

(a) *Aim at simplicity.* This is vitally important. A table with too much detail or which is too complex is much harder to understand, and so defeats its own object. *Remember:* it is better to show only a little and have that little understood than to show all and have nothing understood.

b) *The table must have a comprehensive, explanatory title.*
If such a title would be too long, then a shorter one
may be used together with a sub-title.

(c) *The source must be stated.*   All figures come from somewhere and a statement of the source must be given,
usually as a footnote.

(d) *Units must be clearly stated.*   It is possible to reduce the
number of figures by indicating in the title or in the
headings the number of thousands, or other multiples of
ten, each figure represents (*e.g.* writing "£000" in the
title indicates that all figures in the table are in thousands of pounds).

(e) *The headings to columns and rows should be unambiguous.*
It is very important there should be no doubt about the
meaning of a heading.   If a lengthy heading would be
necessary to remove ambiguity, then a short heading
may be used with a symbol referring the reader to a
footnote containing a more detailed explanation.

(f) *Double-counting should be avoided.*   If a table shows
"People in X: 100", and also "People in X and Y: 500"
then the 100 people in X appear twice in the table.
This is "double-counting" and, as it is apt to mislead,
should normally be avoided.   Cumulative figures may,
of course, be shown but should be identified as such.

(g) *Totals should be shown where appropriate.*   They are
used in a table for one of the following purposes:

   (i) To give the overall total of a main class.
  (ii) To indicate that preceding figures are sub-divisions of
     the total.
 (iii) To indicate that all items have been accounted for
     (*e.g.* if a survey of 3,215 people is presented in a table,
     "Total 3,215" indicates that all the people surveyed
     appear in the table, *i.e.* there are no gaps).

(h) *Percentages and ratios should be computed and shown if
appropriate.*   Frequently figures in tables become more
meaningful if they are expressed as percentages, or
(less often) as ratios.   In constructing a table, therefore,
it is important to decide whether or not it can be improved in this way.   If it can, additional columns
should be inserted in the table and the percentages (or
ratios) computed and entered.   Such percentages and
ratios are sometimes called *derived statistics.*

4. Advantages of tabular layout. Comparison of narrative and tabular form as in the Example at the beginning of this chapter shows that tabular presentation has several distinct advantages, quite apart from being more readily intelligible:

(a) It enables required figures to be located more quickly.

(b) It enables comparisons between different classes to be made more easily.

(c) It reveals patterns within the figures which cannot be seen in the narrative form (*e.g.* in Table 1 cinema attendance is mainly confined to the younger men).

(d) It takes up less room.

PROGRESS TEST 4
(*Answers on pages* 249–51)

1. In 1958, 1,090 million passenger journeys were made on British Railways, yielding £137·6 million in receipts. Of the journeys, 351 million were at full fares, 426 million at reduced fares and an estimated 313 million by season ticket holders. By 1961, journeys at full fares had fallen by 78 million, reduced fare journeys were up by 9 million and season ticket journeys up by 4 million.

During the same period, receipts from full fares went up from £74·0 million to £79·7 million, reduced fares went up from £46·1 million to £54·1 million and season ticket receipts increased by £5·9 million.

Draw up tables which will summarise the above information and will bring out the principal changes between the two years, and compute derived statistics where appropriate. (I.O.T.).

2. Boys in Xville can be classified as regards age, height (T, tall; S, short), intelligence (G, good; P, poor), and complexion (F, fair; D, dark). A survey of 13 and 14 year olds has shown the number of boys of each combination to be as follows:

13-year olds		*14-year olds*	
T, G and F —	8	T, G and F —	7
T, G and D —	7	T, G and D —	6
T, P and F —	9	T, P and F —	8
T, P and D —	6	T, P and D —	6
S, G and F —	10	S, G and F —	9
S, G and D —	5	S, G and D —	7
S, P and F —	5	S, P and F —	9
S, P and D —	7	S, P and D —	5

Tabulate these data for use by a headmaster about to start a school in the town.*

3 Criticise the following table:

Castings	Weight of metal	Foundry hours
Up to 4 cwts	60	210
Up to 10 cwts	100	640
All higher weights	110	800
Others	20	65
	290	2,000

CHAPTER V

GRAPHS

Tables, as we have seen, make data easier to understand. A further improvement in this respect can often be obtained by representing the data *visually*. Such an improvement stems from another psychological fact—that people, not being computers, are able to see spacial relationships much better than numerical relationships.

For example, in comparing sales of A with sales of B in the following table, what conclusions can you draw?

	1958	1959	1960	1961	1962	1963
Sales of A (units)	1,121	1,230	1,339	1,452	1,568	1,681
Sales of B (units)	492	541	602	644	691	738

It takes a certain amount of study to see that sales of A increase each year by more units than sales of B. But it is obvious at once when the same data are shown visually: *see* Fig. 1.

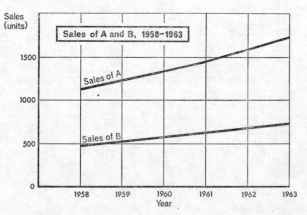

Fig. 1.—*Graph as a means of comparing sales*

Such visual presentation can take many forms, but they can all be divided into two main groups, *graphs* and *diagrams*. The difference between them is not very important; basically a graph is a representation of data by a continuous curve on squared paper, whilst a diagram is any other two-dimensional form of visual representation. Note that a line on a graph is always referred to as a *curve*—even though it may be straight. Diagrams are discussed in Chapter VIII.

SECTION 12.   PRINCIPLES OF GRAPH CONSTRUCTION

Graph construction, like table construction, is in many ways an art. However, like tables again, there are a number of basic principles to be observed if the graph is to be a good one. They are as follows.

1. The correct impression must be given. Since graphs depend upon visual interpretation, they are open to every trick in the field of optical illusion. Note, for example, the difference between the impressions gained from the two graphs in Fig. 2 (*a*) and (*b*). They are one and the same graph; but in the second one the horizontal scale is only one-third the size of the first. Thus scale manipulation can considerably alter the dramatic impact of a graph. Needless to say, *good* (*i.e.* accurate, undistorted) presentation ensures that the correct impression is given.

2. The graph must have a clear and comprehensive title.

3. The independent variable should always be placed on the horizontal axis. When starting a graph the question always arises as to which variable should be placed on the horizontal axis and which on the vertical. Careful examination will generally show that the figures relating to one variable would be quite unaffected by changes in the other variable. The variable that will not be affected is called the *independent* variable and should be placed on the horizontal axis (*s.* **46.** 4). Time, for example, is *always* the independent variable and so is always on the horizontal axis.

4. The vertical scale should always start at zero. Again this is done to avoid giving wrong impressions: *see* Fig. 2 (*a*) and (*c*). If it is not practical to have the whole of the vertical scale running from zero to the highest required figure, then the scale may be such that it covers only the relevant figures *providing* that zero is shown at the bottom of the scale and *a definite break in the scale is shown* (*see* Fig. 3).

5. A double vertical scale should be used where appropriate. If it is desired to show two curves which normally would

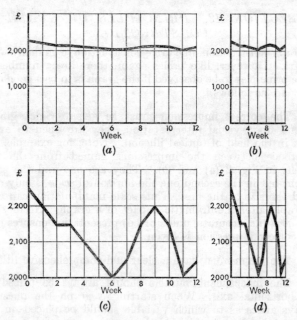

FIG. 2.—*Effect of using different scales for the same graph*

(*a*) Correctly scaled graph. (*b*) Graph with horizontal scale one-third of correct scale. (*c*) Zero omitted on the vertical scale. (*d*) Zero omitted and horizontal scale one-third of correct.

The student may find it difficult to realise that these four graphs involve identical figures. They should serve as a warning of the distortion that can result from badly chosen scales

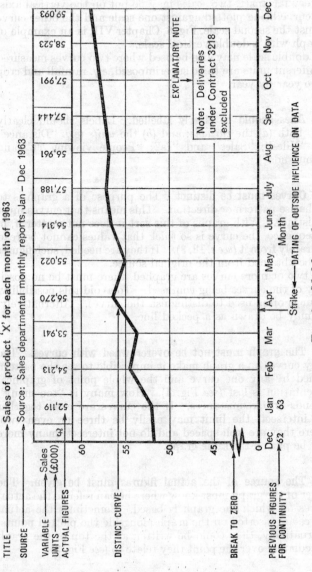

Fig. 3.—*Model graph*

lie very far apart, two scales may be put on the vertical axis, one curve being plotted against one scale and the other curve against the second scale. Fig. 8, Chapter VII, is an example of a graph with a double vertical scale.

A double scale may also be used where two curves measured in different units are to be superimposed, *e.g.* rainfall and crop value year by year.

6. Axes should be clearly labelled. Labels should clearly state both (*a*) the *variable*; and (*b*) the *units* (*e.g.* "Distance" and "Miles"; "Sales" and "£s"; "People viewing TV" and "Thousands").

7. Curves must be distinct. The purpose of a graph is to emphasise pattern or direction. This means that curves must be distinct. With graphs of this sort it does not matter if, in consequence, the curve is so thick that values cannot be read accurately from it (*see s.* **13.** 3). If they are needed, such figures can be obtained from the original source.

If two or more curves are graphed, there must be no possibility of the curves being confused. To avoid this possibility, colour is often used to distinguish the curves. Alternatively, one may be drawn as a pecked line.

8. The graph must not be overcrowded with curves. Too many curves on a graph make it impossible to see the pattern formed by any one curve and the whole point of graphical presentation is lost (*see* Fig. 4). How many is "too many" depends on circumstances. If the curves are close together and intersect, the limit may easily be three or even two. Where they are well spaced and do not intersect, many more may be put on the same graph.

9. The source of the actual figures must be given. The reader of the graph must know where he can refer to the actual figures on which the graph is based. Sometimes the actual figures are inserted on the graph alongside the plotted points. Alternatively, they could be written at the top of the graph immediately over the point they relate to (*see* Fig. 3).

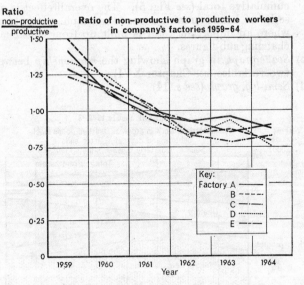

FIG. 4.—*Graph with too many curves*

NOTE, incidentally, that ratios are plotted at mid-points of years. This indicates that each ratio is an average for the year (*see s.* **16**.2). Note too that, when mid-points are to be plotted, the ambiguity is lessened if periods are shown as lying between points (as here) rather than at single points as in Fig. 3

SECTION 13.   TYPES OF GRAPH

1. Types of graph.

(a) *Time series:* a graph showing changes in value of one or more items from one period of time to the next. This is the commonest form of graph, and it is called a *historigram* (*i.e.* like "history-gram") or *time series graph*. Do not confuse historigram with *histogram* (*s.* 28).

(b) *Band chart:* a graph involving a number of curves. Each curve represents one stage in the build-up of a cumulative total (*see* Fig. 5). The overall effect is of a series of bands running across the graph. It is of use where an important total is built up from continually changing sub-figures.

(c) *Scattergraph:* a graph showing the *relationship* between two variables (*see* Chapter XVI).

(d) *Semi-log. graph* (*see s.* 14).

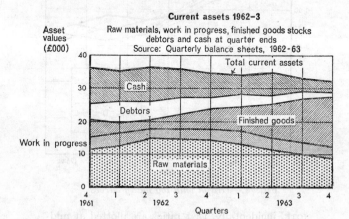

Current assets 1962–3

Asset values (£000)

Raw materials, work in progress, finished goods stocks debtors and cash at quarter ends
Source: Quarterly balance sheets, 1962-63

FIG. 5.—*Band chart*

2. Plotting points on a time series graph. A certain amount of care is needed when plotting points on a time series graph. There is some confusion on this topic, as many statisticians maintain that values should be plotted at the *mid-point* of the period to which they relate. However, a businessman who saw his total sales figure for the whole of 1964 plotted at 30th June would have difficulty in reading the graph. In view of this, two working rules are suggested:

(a) Plot *totals* at the *end* of the period to which they apply.

(b) Plot *averages* at the *mid-point* of the period to which they apply.

Rule (a) must be applied with discretion. For instance, in the Z chart (*s.* 17) the rule must be followed; but, when plotting yearly figures in relation to a trend line (*ss.* 71 and 72), totals must be plotted at the mid-points of periods.

3. Statistical graphs are not mathematical-type graphs. It is important to appreciate that the graphs considered here are designed only *to present information*. They must be distinguished from graphs of the mathematical type, which are used to determine otherwise unknown values. In the latter case, a very thin line must be drawn so that values can be read off accurately. Graphs which only present information should not be used to determine figures, except approximately; the main consideration is that they should be *distinct* even though it results in a very thick curve (*see s.* **12.** 7).

SECTION 14. SEMI-LOG. GRAPHS

1. When to use semi-log. graphs. So far we have only considered the ordinary kind of graph, called the *normal scale graph*. It has one limitation in that it gives the wrong impression of rates of change. From the graph in Fig. 1, based on the figures given at the beginning of this chapter, it can be seen that sales of A have increased more than sales of B. But *the percentage increase for the six years is the same*, namely 50%—sales of A in 1963 were 50% greater than in 1958 and so were sales of B.

If then we want a graph that shows which product is increasing its sales faster, in terms of percentage increase per annum, we cannot use a normal scale graph. To get the right impression we need a *semi-log. graph* (or *chart*). (*See* Fig. 6.) This type has a *logarithmic scale on the vertical axis* (*see* Fig. 7; note that the normal scale is retained on the horizontal axis —hence *semi*-log. chart).

2. Features of a semi-log. graph.
(*a*) If a single curve is plotted on a semi-log. graph (*see* Fig. 7):
    (i) The slope of the curve indicates the *rate* at which the figures are increasing.

        NOTE: For convenience it is assumed that the figures are increasing, although of course everything said here applies equally to decreasing figures.

    (ii) If the curve is a straight line, *the rate of increase remains constant*. Thus is the rate is 20% per annum then the increase will always be 20% of the *previous* year's total (*see* curve C in Fig. 7).

A good example of such a curve would be one showing compound interest. Although the amount of the interest is greater each year, it is always the *same percentage* of the total invested at the end of the previous period.

(iii) If the *absolute* increase is constant, the curve will become progressively less steep. For instance, if the increase is always (say) £5,000 per annum, the steep-

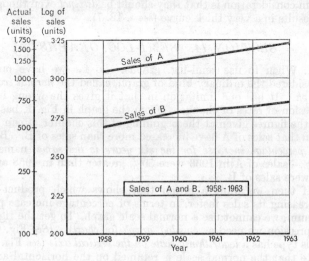

FIG. 6.—*The same figures as in Fig. 1, but plotted on a semi-log. graph*

The two curves are virtually parallel, indicating that the *rate* of increase is approximately the same for both, *i.e.* 8–10% p.a.

Sales of A

Year:	1958	1959	1960	1961	1962	1963
Sales:	1,121	1,230	1,339	1,452	1,568	1,681
Log:	3·0496	3·0899	3·1268	3·1620	3·1953	3·2256

Sales of B

Year:	1958	1959	1960	1961	1962	1963
Sales:	492	541	602	644	691	738
Log:	2·6920	2·7332	2·7796	2·8089	2·8395	2·8681

ness must lessen, since £5,000 becomes a *continually smaller percentage of the increasing total figure* (*see* curve *A* in Fig. 7).

(*b*) If *two* curves are plotted on a semi-log. graph:

   (i) The curve with the greatest slope is the one with the greatest rate of increase (*see* curves *B* and *C* in Fig. 7).

  (ii) If they are parallel the rates of increase are identical (*see* Fig. 2 and curves *C* and *D* in Fig. 7).

 (iii) If both curves over any part of the graph rise through the *same vertical distance* (say 1 in.), then both sets of figures have increased by the *same percentage*.

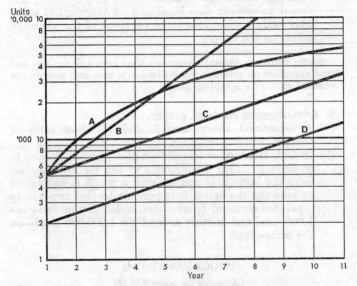

FIG. 7.—*Semi-log. graph*

Curve *A* starts at 5,000 and increases by 5,000 every year. Curve *B* starts at 5,000 and increases by 50% every year. Curve *C* starts at 5,000 and increases by 20% every year. Curve *D* starts at 2,000 and increases by 20% every year. Note that although curve *D* is parallel to curve *C* the actual size of each year's increase is considerably smaller, *e.g.* 400 as against 1,000 in year 1.

3. Construction of a semi-log. graph. Semi-log. graphs can be constructed in three ways:

(a) *By using semi-log. graph paper* (which can be bought). Points are plotted in a straightforward way, although care is needed in reading the vertical scale.

(b) *By using a slide rule to construct the vertical scale.* If the sliding section of a slide rule is removed, the printed scale can be used to mark out the vertical scale of a semi-log. graph.

(c) *By plotting the logs of the variable.* If the log. of each figure in the series is found from ordinary log. tables and these log. figures are plotted on a normal scale graph, semi-log. curves are obtained (*see* Fig. 2). Note that actual values can also be shown on the vertical scale. This enables some idea to be obtained of the values of points on the curves.

NOTE: Students should remember that zero has no log. and that therefore no attempt should be made to insert zero on the vertical scale of a semi-log. graph.

4. Advantages of semi-log. graphs.

(*a*) As explained above, semi-log. charts show rates of change.

(*b*) In addition, such charts allow a great range of values to be shown. Since the doubling of the vertical distance from the horizontal axis on such a graph is equivalent to *squaring* the value, it is possible to plot two widely separated series of figures—one series, say, around the 1,000 level and another around the 1,000,000 level—on the same graph.

PROGRESS TEST 5
(*Answers on pages* 251–2)

1. The following (fictitious) figures relate to rainfall and the profits of an umbrella shop. Show both time series on the same graph.

Year	1955	1956	1957	1958	1959	1960	1961	1962	1963	1964
Rainfall (*in.*)	61	73	65	58	49	41	55	80	73	68
Shop profits (£)	621	740	894	773	702	591	488	661	992	863

2. Comment on the following graph:

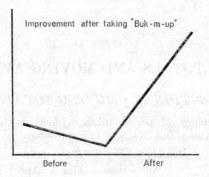

Improvement after taking "Buk-m-up"

Before   After

3. Graph the following data and then comment on the graph:*

Average temperatures at Little Fielding, 1919–64 (°c)

	Jan	Feb	Mar	Apr	May	June	July	Aug	Sept	Oct	Nov	Dec
Maximum	8	9	11	13	16	18	18	17	15	12	10	9
Minimum	−2	0	3	6	10	12	13	12	9	5	7	0

Source: *Little Fielding weather station records*

4. Plot the following time series on (*a*) a normal scale graph and (*b*) a semi-log. graph (using, however, normal scale graph paper) and comment on the graphs:*

Year	Group sales	Company A's sales
	(£000)	(£000)
1960	1,620	135
1961	1,780	154
1962	1,950	176
1963	2,140	195
1964	2,350	208

MOVING TOTALS AND MOVING AVERAGES

SECTION 15. MOVING TOTALS

1. Insufficiency of period totals. Look at the following table. Do you think business is improving?

Monthly sales of XYZ Co., 1964

Month	Jan	Feb	Mar	Apr	May	June
Sales (£)	4,000	4,100	4,200	4,300	4,400	4,500
Month	July	Aug	Sept	Oct	Nov	Dec
Sales (£)	4,600	4,700	4,800	4,900	5,000	5,100

On the face of it, business seems to be improving steadily. But, what if the sales for 1963 were as follows?

Month	Jan	Feb	Mar	Apr	May	June
Sales (£)	5,000	5,200	5,400	5,600	5,800	6,000
Month	July	Aug	Sept	Oct	Nov	Dec
Sales (£)	6,200	6,400	6,600	6,800	7,000	7,200

Clearly, business is *not* improving. Sales in January 1964 were £1,000 below those of the previous January, and each month the gap between the sales for 1964 and the same month the year before increases, until by December the difference is £2,100. So it can be seen that although each month in 1964 is better than the months before, it is worse—and progressively worse—than the same month in 1963.

2. Moving total. Obviously the figures given at first were misleading, and the question arises as to how this sort of wrong impression can be avoided. Direct comparison of the figures for one month with the same month the previous year is a possible solution, but this sort of comparison does not allow an overall trend to be easily observed. A better solution is the use of a *moving total* (or a *moving average—see s.* **16**).

Examination of the XYZ Co.'s sales figures shows that the business is seasonal—indeed, it was for this reason that the

1964 figures on their own gave a false impression. This problem of seasonal influence frequently arises in statistics and *an excellent method of eliminating such influences is to add together twelve consecutive months.*

Such a total is inevitably free of any seasonal influence since all the seasons, busy and slack, are included in the total. Moreover, if we add the twelve months immediately preceding the end of *each* month in the table we shall obtain a series of totals, one for each month. Each total will be the total for the year immediately preceding the end of that month, and the series is called a *moving total* or—more specifically in this case, since the totals are yearly totals—a *moving annual total* (M.A.T. for short).

> NOTE: Totals need not be yearly totals: they can relate to any period of time. There are, for instance, 5-year and 10-year moving totals.

3. Calculation of a moving total. Calculating a moving total is simply a matter of adding the appropriate group of periods immediately preceding the end of each individual period. However, the actual computing work can be reduced if it is appreciated that, once the first total has been found, the next total will be the same except for the difference between the new period which has been added and the old period which has been dropped. Table 2 demonstrates this method of calculating the moving annual total for the XYZ Co.'s sales.

4. Significance of a moving total. If a moving total for sales drops, it means the position is deteriorating, since such a drop indicates that the current period sales fail to equal sales for the same period the previous year. A continuing fall indicates a continuing failure of current sales to equal the previous year's sales. Conversely, a rising total indicates an improvement. Of course, if costs are being considered, then a declining total indicates improvement in the form of reduced costs.

It can be seen, therefore, that the use of moving totals helps to eliminate incorrect impressions. If such totals are graphed, the slope of the line gives a good indication of the immediate trend.

TABLE 2.   M.A.T. OF XYZ CO.'S SALES

Year	Month	Sales (£)	M.A.T. (£)	Notes on calculation
1963	January	5,000	—	
	February	5,200	—	
	March	5,400	—	
	April	5,600	—	
	May	5,800	—	There can be no M.A.T.
	June	6,000	—	until 12 months' fig-
	July	6,200	—	ures are available
	August	6,400	—	
	September	6,600	—	
	October	6,800	—	
	November	7,000	—	
	December	7,200	73,200	Total of sales Jan.–Dec. 1963
1964	January	4,000	72,200	73,200—Jan. 1963 + Jan. 1964
	February	4,100	71,100	72,200—Feb. 1963 + Feb. 1964
	March	4,200	69,900	71,100—5,400 + 4,200 etc.
	April	4,300	68,600	
	May	4,400	67,200	
	June	4,500	65,700	
	July	4,600	64,100	
	August	4,700	62,400	
	September	4,800	60,600	
	October	4,900	58,700	Add Jan.–Dec. 1964
	November	5,000	56,700	to cross-check the
	December	5,100	54,600	accuracy of this final figure.

SECTION 16.   MOVING AVERAGES

1. **Moving average.** This is simply a moving total divided by the number of periods comprising that total.

For example, look at Table 2 again. It shows the M.A.T. throughout 1964. Since each total is the sum of 12 months, the *moving average* is each moving total figure divided by 12, *i.e.*

Month	M.A.T.	Moving average
December (1963)	73,200 ÷ 12 =	6,100
January (1964)	72,200 ÷ 12 =	6,017
February	71,100 ÷ 12 =	5,925 etc.

2. **Graphing moving averages.** When graphing moving averages, care needs to be taken as to where the moving average points are plotted. Being *averages*, they must be plotted *at the mid-point of the period* of which they are the average. Thus the £6,100 just calculated above must be plotted at 30th June 1963 and the £6,017 at 31st July 1963. Note that moving totals, being *totals*, may be plotted at the *end* of the relevant period (*see s*. **13.** 2 for an explanation of this apparent inconsistency).

In order to assist the correct plotting of moving averages it is a good idea to write the average opposite the mid-point of its period when constructing the table of moving averages. For instance, the January 1964 figure of £6,017 (from 1 above) will be written opposite the half-way point between July and August 1963, thus:

Month	Actual	Moving average
July	6,200	
		6,017
August	6,400	

3. **Advantages of moving averages.**
(a) They eliminate seasonal variations.
(b) When period figures fluctuate violently, moving averages smooth out the fluctuations.
(c) They can be plotted on the same graph as the period figures without a change of scale (a M.A.T. is usually so many times bigger than period figures that it is often impossible to put both meaningfully on a graph with only one vertical scale).

PROGRESS TEST 6
(*Answer on pages 253–4*)

1. From the following annual figures calculate (a) the 3-year moving total, (b) the 3-year moving average, (c) the 10-year moving average.

Plot these, together with the individual annual figures, on the same graph. What is the difference between the 3-year moving average curve and the 10-year moving average curve?

Yearly figures 1940-64 (units)

1940	5	1945	8	1950	20	1955	9	1960	18
1941	8	1946	15	1951	16	1956	15	1961	22
1942	6	1947	10	1952	15	1957	8	1962	16
1943	12	1948	10	1953	6	1958	12	1963	14
1944	4	1949	13	1954	18	1959	14	1964	20

CHAPTER VII

Z CHARTS AND LORENZ CURVES

Although graphs are generally designed for the particular purpose for which they are required, there are two types of graph so common that their forms have become standardised. They are Z charts and Lorenz curves.

SECTION 17. Z CHARTS

1. Description of Z charts. A Z chart is simply a graph that extends over a single year and incorporates:

(a) Individual monthly figures.
(b) Monthly cumulative figures for the year.
(c) A moving annual total.

It takes its name from the fact that the three curves together tend to look like the letter Z.

2. Points in the construction of a Z chart.
(a) Very often a double scale is used on the vertical axis, one for the monthly figures and the other for the M.A.T. and cumulative figures. This is because the M.A.T. is some twelve times larger than the normal monthly figure. If the same scale were used for both curves it would mean that the curve of the monthly figures would tend to creep insignificantly along the bottom of the graph.
(b) As an example, Fig. 8 shows a Z chart for the XYZ Co.'s sales figures discussed in *s.* **15.** 1. Note where the different curves start:

    (i) *Monthly figures* at the December figure of the previous year.
    (ii) *Cumulative figures at zero.*
    (iii) *M.A.T.* at the M.A.T. figure for the December of the previous year.

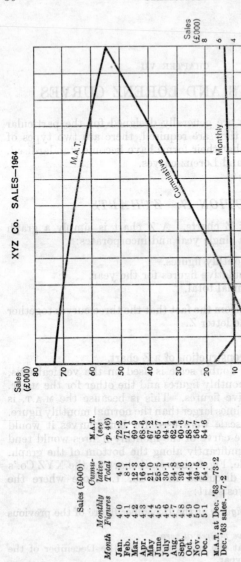

FIG. 8.—Z chart

NOTE (i) the double vertical scales, one for the M.A.T. and cumulative, the other for monthly, and (ii) that these figures are not typical; see Progress Test 7, question 1, for more typical figures

(c) Note that since a M.A.T. is the total of the twelve immediately preceding months, the M.A.T. for the final month must be the same as the cumulative total. The two curves will therefore meet at this point.

SECTION 18. LORENZ CURVES

1. Function. It is a well known fact that in practically every country a small proportion of the population owns a large proportion of the wealth. Industrialists know too that a small proportion of all the factories employs a large proportion of the factory workers. This disparity of proportions is a common economic phenomenon, and a *Lorenz curve* is a curve on a graph demonstrating this disparity.

2. Construction. To illustrate the procedure involved in the construction of a Lorenz curve, let us take the following figures:

HOLDING SIZES IN LITTLE FIELDING

Size of holding	No. of holdings	Total acreage
Under ½ acre	310	105
½ to under 1 acre	240	175
1 acre to under 5 acres	75	180
5 acres to under 15 acres	30	300
15 acres and over	25	420

The sequence of operations will then be as follows:

(a) Draw up a 6-column table as on p. 52. Insert the figures relating to the variables involved in the "No." columns, and add.

(b) Calculate each figure as a percentage of its column total and insert it in the "%" column.

(c) Insert in the "Cumulative %" column the cumulative totals of the percentages.

  NOTE: The key to constructing Lorenz curves lies in remembering that it is the *cumulative percentages* that are required.

(d) Prepare a graph with one axis for each variable, each scale running from 0 (at the origin) to 100% (*see* Fig. 9).

(e) Plot each pair of cumulative percentage figures on the graph.

(f) Starting at the origin, join these points in a smooth curve.

(g) Insert the "line of equal distribution" by joining the origin to the last point plotted.

Holdings			Total acreage		
No.	%	*Cumulative* %	*No.*	%	*Cumulative* %
310	45·5	45·5	105	9	9
240	35·5	81	175	15	24
75	11	92	180	15	39
30	4·5	96·5	300	25·5	64·5
25	3·5	100	420	35·5	100
680	100		1,180	100	

3. The line of equal distribution. If, in our example, all the holdings had been of equal acreage, then clearly the total acreage of (say) 25% of the holdings would be 25% of the total acreage of holdings in Little Fielding. Similarly, 50% of the holdings would constitute 50% of the acreage, and 75% of the holdings 75% of the acreage. If these pairs are plotted on the graph they will be found to fall on a straight line running from the origin to the last point plotted (*i.e.* the 100%; 100% point). Such a line, then, is *the curve which would be obtained if all holdings were of equal size.* It is called, therefore, the *line of equal distribution.*

4. Interpretation of Lorenz curves. The extent to which a Lorenz curve deviates from the "line of equal distribution" indicates the degree of inequality. The further the curve swings away, the greater the inequality. There is no actual measure of this inequality but its extent can be indicated by reading the curve at the point where it lies furthest from the line of equal distribution.

For example, in **Fig. 9** the curve at its furthest point from the line of equal distribution is approximately at the 87% "Holdings" and 30% "Total acreage." This means that 87% of the holdings contain 30% of the total acreage—or, put the other way round, a mere 13% of the holdings enclose 70% of the total acreage.

5. Use of Lorenz curves.

Lorenz curves can be used to show inequalities in connection with matters such as:

(a) Incomes in the population.
(b) Tax payments of individuals in the population.
(c) Industrial efficiencies.
(d) Industrial outputs.
(e) Examination marks.

In some instances, Lorenz curves can be used to compare *two series* of inequalities. For instance, if a second Lorenz curve relating to holdings in, say, Great Fielding, were super-imposed on the curve for Little Fielding in Fig. 9, then it would be possible to compare inequalities of land holding in these two communities and to see in which one holdings were nearer to being equally distributed.

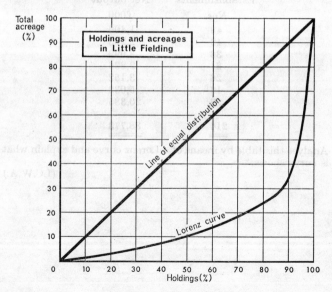

FIG. 9.—*Lorenz curve*

PROGRESS TEST 7

(*Answer on pages 254–6*)

1. From the following data construct a Z chart for 1964 and comment on the graph:*

ALPHA LTD. SALES (£)

Month	1963	1964	Month	1963	1964
Jan	15,000	17,000	July	6,000	11,000
Feb	14,000	19,000	Aug	6,000	1,000
Mar	11,000	18,000	Sept	8,000	5,000
Apr	10,000	18,000	Oct	10,000	5,000
May	8,000	18,000	Nov	10,000	8,000
June	7,000	12,000	Dec	13,000	10,000

2. The following figures come from the Report on the Census of Production for 1958:

TEXTILE MACHINERY AND ACCESSORIES

Establishments	Net output
Nos.	£000
48	1,406
42	2,263
38	3,699
21	2,836
26	3,152
16	5,032
23	20,385
214	38,773

Analyse this table by means of a Lorenz curve and explain what this curve shows.

(I.C.W.A.)

CHAPTER VIII

DIAGRAMS

Graphs are not the only way of presenting data visually. The most commonly used alternatives can be classified as follows:

(a) *Pictorial representations.*
    (i) Pictograms.
    (ii) Statistical maps.
(b) *Bar charts.*
    (i) Simple bar charts.
    (ii) Component bar charts (actuals).
    (iii) Percentage component bar charts.
    (iv) Multiple bar charts.
(c) *Pie charts.*

Each will be considered in turn and illustrative examples will be taken from the data in Table 3.

TABLE 3. DOMICILE OF STUDENTS ATTENDING LITTLE FIELDING RESIDENTIAL COLLEGE, 1960–4

| Year | Total students | Domicile in England | | |
		South	Midlands	North
1960	115	81	32	2
1961	135	85	46	4
1962	161	90	62	9
1963	150	77	59	14
1964	215	97	90	28
1964:				
Urban	160	76	62	22
Rural	55	21	28	6

Source: *L.F.R.C. records*

SECTION 19.   PICTORIAL REPRESENTATION

1. Pictograms. This form of presentation involves the use of pictures to represent data.   There are two kinds of pictogram:

(a) Those in which the same picture, always the same size, is shown repeatedly—the value of a figure represented being indicated by *the number of pictures shown* (see Fig. 10(a)).

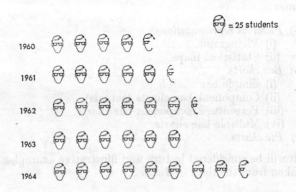

Number of students attending Little Fielding Residential College
1960-4

FIG. 10(a) *Diagrammatic representation*.   Pictogram

(b) Those in which the pictures change in size—the value of a figure represented being indicated by *the size of the picture shown* (see Fig. 10(b)).

Type (b) is definitely not recommended as it can be very misleading. If the figure being represented doubles, for example, such an increase would probably be shown by doubling the height of the picture. However, if the height is doubled the width must also be doubled to keep the picture correctly proportioned and this results in the area increasing by a factor of 4. To the eye, then, it may well appear that the figure has quadrupled!

Sometimes an attempt is made to overcome the problem by simply doubling the area, but inevitably there is always some confusion in the readers' mind as to whether heights or areas should be observed, and this type of pictogram is best avoided. (Note that three-dimensional pictures offend even more in this respect, since a doubling of height gives the impression that the volume has increased by a factor of $2 \times 2 \times 2 = 8$.)

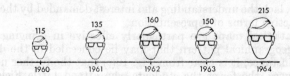

Number of students attending Little Fielding Residential College
1960–4

Fig. 10(b).—*Diagrammatic representation.* Misleading pictogram

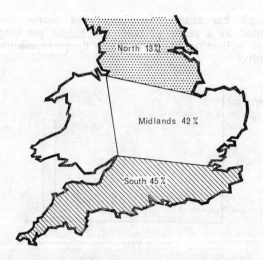

Domiciles of students attending Little Fielding
Residential College 1964

Fig. 10(c).—*Diagrammatic representation.* Statistical map

2. Statistical maps. These are simply maps shaded or marked in such a way as to convey statistical information (*see* Fig. 10(*c*)).

3. Uses of pictograms and statistical maps. These two types of diagram are very elementary forms of visual representation, but they can be more informative and more effective than other methods for presenting data to the general public, who, by and large, lack the understanding and interest demanded by the less attractive forms of representation.

Statistical maps are particularly effective in bringing out the geographical pattern that may lie concealed in the data. For instance, it is clear from Fig. 10(*c*) that the further north one goes, the fewer the students who attend Little Fielding Residential College.

SECTION 20. BAR CHARTS

1. Simple bar charts. In simple bar charts, data are represented by a series of bars: the height (or length) of each bar indicating the size of the figure represented (*see* Fig. 10(*d*)).

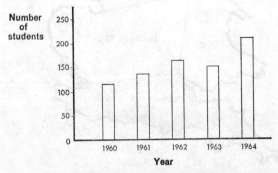

Numbers of students attending Little Fielding
Residential College 1960-4

FIG. 10(*d*).—*Diagrammatic representation.* Simple bar chart

Since bar charts are in many ways similar to graphs, virtually the same principles of construction apply (*see s.* 12)—particularly as regards showing the zero.

2. Component bar charts.

These are like ordinary bar charts except that the bars are subdivided into component parts. This sort of chart is constructed when each total figure is built up from two or more component figures. They can be of two kinds:

    (a) *Component bar chart (actuals):* when the overall height of the bar and the individual component lengths represent *actual* figures (*see* Fig. 10(*e*)).

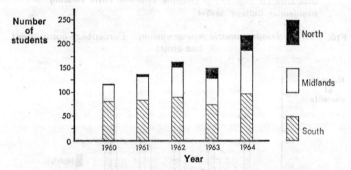

Numbers and domiciles (in England) of students attending
Little Fielding Residential College 1960 – 4

Fig. 10(*e*).—*Diagrammatic representation.* Component bar chart (actuals)

    (b) *Percentage component bar chart:* where the individual component lengths represent the *percentage* each component forms of the overall total (*see* Fig. 10(*f*)). Note that a series of such bars will all be of the same total height, *i.e.* 100%.

3. Multiple bar charts.

In this type of chart the component figures are shown as *separate bars adjoining each other.* The height of each bar represents the actual value of the component figure (*see* Fig. 10(*g*)).

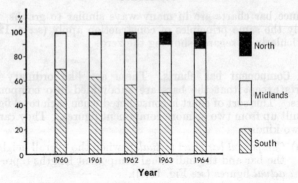

Domiciles (in England) of students attending Little Fielding Residential College 1960-4

FIG. 10(f).—*Diagrammatic representation.* Percentage component bar chart

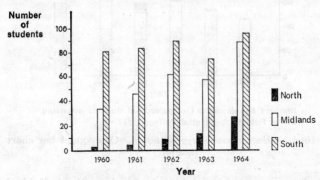

Domiciles of students attending Little Fielding Residential College 1960-4

FIG. 10(g).—*Diagrammatic representation.* Multiple bar chart

4. Uses of bar charts. They are very useful for depicting in a simple manner a *series of changes* in major figures. They are usually preferable to pictograms because:

(a) they are easier to construct,

(b) they can depict data more accurately,

(c) they can be used to indicate the sizes of component figures.

5. Which type should be used? The appropriate type of bar chart can be decided upon as follows:

(a) *Simple bar charts* where changes in totals only are required.
(b) *Component bar charts (actuals)* where changes in totals *and* an indication of the size of each component figure are required.
(c) *Percentage component bar charts* where changes in the *relative size only* of component figures are required.
(d) *Multiple bar charts* where changes in the actual values of the component figures *only* are required, and the overall total is of no importance.

Component and multiple bar charts can only be used, however, when there are not more than three or four components. More components make the charts too complex to enable worthwhile visual impressions to be gained. When a large number of components have to be shown, a pie chart is more suitable.

SECTION 21.   PIE CHARTS

1. Description. A *pie chart* is a circle divided by radial lines into sections (like slices of a cake or pie; hence the name) so that the area of each section is proportional to the size of the figure represented (*see* Fig. 10(*h*)). It is therefore a convenient way of showing the sizes of component figures in proportion to each other and to the overall total.

2. Construction. Geometrically, it can be proved that if the areas of the sections of a pie chart are in the same proportions as the basic figures, then the angles at the centre of the circle must be so too. To construct a pie chart, then, it is only necessary to draw angles at the centre of the circle in proportion to the basic figures. If the overall total was £20,000 and a component figure was £2,000, then the angle would be 2,000/20,000 × 360° = 36° (remember the total number of

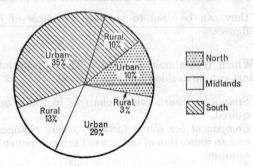

Domiciles of students attending Little Fielding Residential College 1964

Fig. 10(*h*).—*Diagrammatic representation.* Pie chart

degrees at the centre of a circle is 360). Similarly, a component figure of £5,000 would need an angle of 5,000/20,000 × 360° = 90°.

3. Uses. A pie chart is particularly useful where it is desired to show the relative proportions of the figures that go to make up a single overall total. Unlike bar charts, it is not restricted to three or four component figures only—although its effectiveness tends to dwindle above seven or eight.

Pie charts cannot be used effectively where a *series* of figures is involved, as a number of different pie charts are not easy to compare. Nor should changes in the overall totals be shown by changing the size of the "pie," for the same reason as with pictograms.

SECTION 22. OTHER DIAGRAMMATIC FORMS

Many other diagrammatic forms can be used to present data visually: the only limits are those set by human ingenuity. One interesting example is reproduced from *Which?* This publication takes a great deal of trouble to present its findings clearly and is a great user of pictorial illustration, often of no small originality. In this case a way had to be found of showing not only the average whiteness of clothes from various washing machines, but also the variability of each machine in the degree of whiteness it obtained. The diagram evolved is shown in Fig. 11. It will be seen that this diagram effectively depicts the information it was desired to convey.

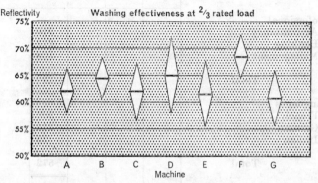

FIG. 11.—*Example of diagrammatic representation which does not employ any of the usual techniques*

The thick horizontal line at the centre of each "needle" represents the *average* whiteness of the 40 test pieces of washing. Also important is the *variation* in whiteness shown by the vertical limits of each needle. These limits indicate the range within which two-thirds of the result were likely to be found. The longer the needle, the more varied the results

Adapted from Which? *of February 1961 by courtesy of the Consumers' Association, 14 Buckingham Street, WC2*

PROGRESS TEST 8

1. Depict the data in the part table below in the form of:*

(a) A simple bar chart.
(b) A component (actuals) bar chart.
(c) A percentage component bar chart
(d) A multiple bar chart.
(e) A pie chart.

SUBJECTS STUDIED AT UPPER GUMTRY COMMERCIAL COLLEGE

Subject	Number of students				
	1960	1961	1962	1963	1964
Professional					
Accountancy				910	
Banking				212	
Management				108	
Total				1,230	
Languages					
French				302	
German				245	
Italian				25	
Total				572	
Academic					
GCE "O"				332	
GCE "A"				93	
Degree				16	
Total				441	
Total all students				2,243	

2. Represent the following (fictitious) data diagrammatically:*

HOURS OF SLEEP OF MALES OF DIFFERENT AGES

	Maximum	Minimum	Average
Baby boy	18	5	11
Young man	12	6	8
Old man	7	4	6

The data were obtained by timing the hours of sleep of the three subjects during the nights of March and April 1964.

CHAPTER IX

PUBLISHED STATISTICS

Statistical data, like other varieties of information, may be of interest to very few or to very many people. Statistics of interest to a large number of people—particularly businessmen and Government administrators—are frequently published, and some knowledge of where they can be found is an important part of the "know-how" of any statistician. Naturally, each field has its own sources and the student must discover those for his own particular field. In this chapter it is only possible to summarise details of the more general sources of published economic statistics.

SECTION 23.   REGULAR PUBLICATIONS

1. *Monthly Digest of Statistics.*

Frequency: Monthly.
Compilers: Central Statistical Office.
Contents:

  (*a*) National income and expenditure.
  (*b*) Weather.
  (*c*) Population and vital statistics.
  (*d*) Labour, analysed by sex and industry.
  (*e*) Unemployment, analysed by industry, region, sex and duration.
  (*f*) Industrial stoppages.
  (*g*) Social services.
  (*h*) Agriculture and food: production, consumption and stocks.
  (*i*) The index of industrial production.
  (*j*) Fuel and power, including coal, oil, coke, gas, electricity and petroleum.
  (*k*) Chemicals: production, sales and stocks.
  (*l*) Metals, engineering (including shipbuilding) and vehicles (including aircraft): production, sales and exports, analysed by numbers and values.
  (*m*) Textiles, hides, timber, paper, rubber, pottery and fibres (*see* Table 4): sales, production and stocks.

(n) Construction and building
(o) Retail and catering: index of sales, turnover and stocks, analysed by businesses.
(p) Transport: road (including road casualties), rail, inland waterways, shipping, airlines and passenger movements.
(q) External trade: imports and exports analysed by region and product.
(r) Overseas and home finance.
(s) Wages, analysed by industry.
(t) Indexes of prices, analysed by product.
(u) Entertainment: BBC licences, cinemas and gramophone records.

Comment: This is possibly the most important of the general publications, and students are recommended to obtain and study a current issue. In common with many other statistical publications, a guide explaining the definitions used and the methods of compilation is published periodically.

A specimen of one of the tables published is shown in Table 4. Note in this table:

(a) How monthly and weekly averages are given for earlier years to enable comparisons to be made.
(b) How production, consumption and stocks of various products are all included in the single table with no loss of clarity.
(c) That August figures are included in this issue published at the end of October.   This indicates the extent to which the statistics are up to date, a factor of great importance if the statistics are to be of any practical value.
(d) That the source of the figures is the Board of Trade.   The Central Statistical Office does not prepare statistics from raw data, but takes data from various sources.

2. *Annual Abstract of Statistics.*

Frequency: Yearly.
Compilers: Central Statistical Office.
Contents: As for the *Monthly Digest of Statistics* and in addition:

(a) Area.
(b) Education.

Comment: This is simply the annual counterpart of the *Monthly Digest of Statistics.*

TABLE 94

TABLE 4. EXTRACT FROM THE Monthly Digest of Statistics, OCTOBER 1964

Man-made fibres, hard hemps and jute

	Man-made fibres (rayon, nylon, etc.) Production			Hard hemps[1]		Jute			
	Total	Continuous filament yarn (single)	Staple fibre	Consumption	Stocks End of period	Raw jute Consumption	Jute yarn Production	Jute cloth[2] Production	Imported jute goods[2] Disposals
	Monthly averages or calendar months			Monthly averages or calendar months			Weekly averages		
	Million lb.			Thousand tons					
1960	49·33	22·38	26·95	7·37	17·78	2·67	2·73	1·58	1·18
1961	47·30	21·83	25·47	6·98	15·23	2·21	2·22	1·32	0·95
1962	52·26	24·24	28·03	7·08	15·06	2·47	2·50	1·48	0·91
1963	59·93	27·52	32·41	7·30	20·64	2·55	2·57	1·54	0·97
1963 July	60·32	28·40	31·92	6·35	17·09	1·91	2·00	1·22	0·49
August	51·83	24·96	26·88	6·17	19·26	2·05*	2·07*	1·23*	1·10
September	59·28	27·13	32·15	7·02	18·63	2·69	2·73	1·63	1·15
October	66·11	30·97	35·14	8·69	16·04	2·49	2·54	1·50	0·95
November	64·44	29·45	34·99	7·41	17·83	2·61*	2·67*	1·59*	1·01
December	67·11	30·08	37·04	6·85	20·64	2·62	2·59	1·52	1·37
1964 January	69·70	32·49	37·20	8·03	18·70	2·42*	2·47*	1·46*	1·09
February	65·22	30·29	34·93	7·34	19·96	2·76	2·76	1·63	0·50
March	68·39	30·62	37·78	6·91	17·04	2·77	2·77	1·61	1·05
April	66·92	31·11	35·81	8·61	16·84	2·66	2·62	1·53	2·01
May	69·41	32·26	37·15	7·51	16·86	2·60*	2·66*	1·56*	0·68
June	66·88	30·51	36·37	7·81	15·49	2·67	2·69	1·62	0·94
July	67·14	31·28	35·87	7·20	14·77	2·04*	2·09*	1·25*	0·78
August	60·84	27·94	32·91	5·89	19·34	1·88	1·90	1·11	0·72
September									

(1) Sisal line and manila hemp only.   (2) Estimated from consumption of yarn by jute cloth weavers.   Source: Board of Trade
(3) Weekly averages are computed from figures for calendar months. From January 1964 these figures are not comparable. The earlier figures relate to disposals by the Jute Control and imports on private account: figures from January 1964 are those published in Trade and Navigation Accounts of total imports of jute fabrics and jute sacks and bags.
* Average of five weeks.

3. *Board of Trade Journal.*

Frequency: Weekly.
Compilers: Board of Trade.
Contents:

(a) Selected indicators of the economy, including:

  (i) *Indexes of:*
  Gross domestic product,
  Industrial production,
  Consumers' income and expenditure,
  Fixed capital expenditure,
  Orders on hand,
  Prices and costs,
  Imports and exports.
  (ii) *Actuals of:*
  Changes in stocks,
  Labour,
  The balance of payments.

(b) Selected statistics, the selection varying from issue to issue.

4. *Ministry of Labour Gazette.*

Frequency: Monthly.
Compilers: Ministry of Labour.
Contents:

(a) Employed persons, analysed by industry.
(b) Overtime and short time hours, analysed by industry.
(c) Unemployment:

  (i) Numbers, analysed by region and industry.
  (ii) Duration, as at a recent date.

(d) Absenteeism due to sickness or industrial injury, on three specified days during a one-year period, analysed by region.
(e) Fatal industrial accidents and industrial diseases.
(f) Employment overseas.
(g) Weekly wage rates, analysed by industries.
(h) Index of hourly rates of pay and weekly hours.
(i) Changes in wage rates and hours of work, in full detail (including industry, district, date and class of worker).
(j) The index of retail prices.
(k) Work stoppages, showing numbers, industries, causes, principal stoppages and duration.

5. Blue Book on the *National Income and Expenditure*.

Frequency: Yearly.
Compiler: Central Statistical Office.
Contents:

(a) Gross national product.
(b) Output and expenditure.
(c) Wages and salaries, analysed by industry.
(d) Consumers' expenditure, analysed by product.
(e) Personal incomes, before and after tax.
(f) Companies' incomes and expenditures.
(g) Government (local and central) receipts and expenditure, in considerable detail.
(h) Net acquisition of financial and overseas assets.
(i) Capital formation, in considerable detail as regards type of asset, industry, sector, etc.

6. *Registrar General's returns.*

Frequency: Weekly, quarterly and annually.
Compiler: Registrar General.
Contents:

(a) *Weekly:* Summary of previous week's vital statistics.

(b) *Quarterly:*

(i) Marriages, births and deaths.
(ii) Infectious diseases, analysed by region.
(iii) Deaths, analysed by cause and sex.
(iv) Fatal accidents, analysed by cause.
(v) Industrial absence due to sickness or injury, analysed by region.
(vi) Temperatures, rainfall and sunshine.

(c) *Annually:*

Part I—Essentially same headings as above, but the data are given in greater detail.

Part II—

(i) Population estimates, analysed by region, sex, age and marital condition.
(ii) Analysis of marriages.
(iii) Analysis of divorces.
(iv) Migration.
(v) Adoption.

  (vi) Numbers of parliamentary and local government electors.
  (vii) Overseas populations.
  (viii) Fertility analysis.

  Part III—Commentary.

Comment: The Registrar General is also responsible for publishing statistics relating to the population census which is taken every ten years (*see s.* **24.** 3).

7. Other publications. There are other publications of this sort, but in the main they only re-group the statistics already detailed. Among them the most important are probably:

  (a) *Statistics on Incomes, Prices and Production*, compiled by the Ministry of Labour and published monthly. Contents as implied by the title. Tables relating to hours of work include:

   (i) Hours of work.
   (ii) Index of weekly hours.
   (iii) Average hours worked: men and women manual workers, analysed by industry.
   (iv) Overtime and short time worked.

  (b) *Financial Statistics*, compiled by the Central Statistical Office and published monthly. Contents include detailed figures relating to *financial* aspects of all economic sectors (*i.e.* Exchequer, local government, public corporations, banks, building societies, insurance, trading and hire-purchase finance companies, investment and unit trusts, *etc.*).

  (c) *Economic Trends*, compiled by the Central Statistical Office and published monthly. Contents include statistics which indicate economic trends. A feature of this publication is the number of graphs and charts given.

SECTION 24. OCCASIONAL PUBLICATIONS

1. Census of Production. At various times the Board of Trade takes a census of all production and publishes the resulting statistics. The 1958 census ran to a publication of over 130 parts, each part dealing with a single industry or a small, closely related group of industries. Each part gave tables with the following statistics:

   (i) Number of enterprises and sizes.
  (ii) Number of establishments.
 (iii) Sales.
 (iv) Purchases.
  (v) Stocks.
 (vi) Number of employees.
 (vii) Employee remuneration.
(viii) Capital expenditure on buildings, plant and machinery, and on vehicles
 (ix) Products.

2. Census of Distribution. This census is similar to the Census of Production, but is concerned with statistics relating to the distribution side of the economy. The 1961 census ran to a publication of over 13 parts. They covered the following aspects:

Part I:

(*a*) Number of establishments, turnover and persons engaged; analysed by kind of business.

(*b*) Persons engaged, analysed:

   (i) horizontally by male, female, full-time, part-time, working owners; and

  (ii) vertically by kind of business.

(*c*) Establishments, analysed by:

   (i) number of branches;

  (ii) turnover; and

 (iii) number of persons engaged.

(*d*) Retail outlets selling specified commodities; in considerable detail.

Part II: Number of establishments, turnover, and persons engaged; analysed by regions and towns; in considerable detail.

Part III: Each part carries a statistical analysis for a single region.

3. Census of Population. A census of population is taken every ten years on a specified day. The population figures are analysed in great detail in a variety of ways, including: sex, age, region, occupation, marital condition, type of dwelling and size, birthplace and nationality. Since the passing of the Census Act, 1920, the Government has had the power to hold censuses at five-yearly intervals, and it is proposed to exercise this power for the first time in 1966.

PROGRESS TEST 9

[*No model answers are given for this test. Instead, the student is referred to the section, where the answer can be found.*]

1. State where you would look for the following statistics relating to the U.K.:

   (*a*) Index of industrial production (**23. 1–3, 7 (*a*)**).
   (*b*) Index of retail prices (**23. 1–4, 7 (*a*)**).
   (*c*) Overtime worked (**23. 4, 7 (*a*)**).
   (*d*) Sales of vehicles (**23. 1; 24, 1**).
   (*e*) Exports (**23. 1, 2, 7 (*c*)**).
   (*f*) Personal incomes (**23. 5**).
   (*g*) Marriages (**23. 6**).
   (*h*) Capital expenditure (**23. 3, 5, 7 (*b*); 24. 1**).
   (*i*) Working owners in retail establishments (**24. 2**)

PART THREE

FREQUENCY DISTRIBUTIONS

CHAPTER X

FREQUENCY DISTRIBUTIONS

SECTION 25. ARRAYS AND UNGROUPED FREQUENCY DISTRIBUTIONS

Look at Table 5. What information can be gleaned from this mass of figures?

TABLE 5. RAW DATA

Mileages recorded by 120 salesmen in the course of one week

482	502	466	408	486	440
470	447	413	451	410	430
469	438	452	459	455	473
423	436	412	403	493	436
471	498	450	421	482	440
442	474	407	448	444	485
505	515	500	462	460	476
472	454	451	438	457	446
453	453	508	475	418	465
450	447	477	436	464	453
415	511	430	457	490	447
433	416	419	460	428	434
420	443	456	432	425	497
459	449	439	509	483	502
424	421	413	441	458	438
444	445	435	468	430	442
455	452	479	481	468	435
462	478	463	498	494	489
495	407	462	432	424	451
426	433	474	431	471	488

Certainly it can be seen that most of the mileages are in the 400's, though an occasional figure in the 500's is noticeable. But, once more, the limitations of the human mind make it impossible to detect whether there is any pattern in the figures. Are they spread out evenly, for example, or are there points of concentration? Here too, statistical techniques can be used to process a mass of figures relating to a single variable so that their significance can be grasped. This part of the book considers the various techniques involved.

1. Array. The mileages in Table 5 were obtained by simply listing the figures as they were given by the salesmen. Such a collection of figures recorded as it is received can be referred to as "raw data."

The first obvious step to be taken in making the raw data more meaningful is to re-list them in order of size, *i.e.* re-arrange the figures so that they run from the lowest to the highest. Such a list of figures is called an *array*. An array of the mileages in Table 5 is shown in Table 6.

TABLE 6. ARRAY OF THE RAW DATA IN TABLE 5

Mileages recorded by 120 salesmen in the course of one week

403	428	440	452	465	483
407	430	441	453	466	485
407	430	442	453	468	486
408	430	442	453	468	488
410	431	443	454	469	489
412	432	444	455	470	490
413	432	444	455	471	493
413	433	445	456	471	494
415	433	446	457	472	495
416	434	447	457	473	497
418	435	447	458	474	498
419	435	447	459	474	498
420	436	448	459	475	500
421	436	449	460	476	502
421	436	450	460	477	502
423	438	450	462	478	505
424	438	451	462	479	508
424	438	451	462	481	509
425	439	451	463	482	511
426	440	452	464	482	515

2. Ungrouped frequency distributions. An examination of the array in Table 6 suggests a further simplification. Since some figures repeat (*e.g.* 407) it would clearly simplify the list if each figure were listed once and the number of times it occurred written alongside, as in Table 7.

TABLE 7   UNGROUPED FREQUENCY DISTRIBUTION CONSTRUCTED
FROM THE ARRAY IN TABLE 6

Mileages recorded by 120 salesmen in the course of one week

Mileage	Frequency	Mileage	Frequency	Mileage	Frequency	Mileage	Frequency
403	1	434	1	456	1	479	1
407	2	435	2	457	2	481	1
408	1	436	3	458	1	482	2
410	1	438	3	459	2	483	1
412	1	439	1	460	2	485	1
413	2	440	2	462	3	486	1
415	1	441	1	463	1	488	1
416	1	442	2	464	1	489	1
418	1	443	1	465	1	490	1
419	1	444	2	466	1	493	1
420	1	445	1	468	2	494	1
421	2	446	1	469	1	495	1
423	1	447	3	470	1	497	1
424	2	448	1	471	2	498	2
425	1	449	1	472	1	500	1
426	1	450	2	473	1	502	2
428	1	451	3	474	2	505	1
430	3	452	2	475	1	508	1
431	1	453	3	476	1	509	1
432	2	454	1	477	1	511	1
433	2	455	2	478	1	515	1

Total frequency = 120

In statistics the number of occurrences is called the *frequency*, and what we have in Table 7 is called an *ungrouped frequency distribution* ("ungrouped" simply distinguishes it from the grouped distribution discussed in *s.* 26). An ungrouped frequency distribution, then, is a list of figures occurring in the raw data, together with the frequency of each figure.

Note that the sum of the frequencies must equal the total number of items making up the raw data, *i.e.* $\Sigma f = n$.

SECTION 26.   GROUPED FREQUENCY DISTRIBUTIONS

1. Description. While Table 7 (the ungrouped frequency distribution) is an improvement on the array, there are still too many figures for the mind to be able to grasp the information effectively.   Consequently it must be simplified even more. This can be done by *grouping* the figures.   For example, if all the mileages between 400 and under 420 are grouped together there are 12 occurrences in the group, that is, a frequency of 12. These groups are called *classes*.   A list of such classes together with the frequencies is called a *grouped frequency distribution*. Thus the information in Table 7 can be converted into the grouped frequency distribution shown in Table 8.

TABLE 8.   GROUPED FREQUENCY DISTRIBUTION

Mileages recorded by 120 salesmen in the course of one week

Mileages (x)	Frequency (f)
400–under 420	12
420–under 440	27
440–under 460	34
460–under 480	24
480–under 500	15
500–under 520	8
	120

2. Effect of grouping. As a result of grouping, it is possible to detect a pattern in the figures.   For instance, the mileages in Table 8 cluster around the "440–under 460" class.   However, it is important to realise that, although it brings out the pattern, *such grouping does result in loss of information*.   For example, the total frequency in the "400–under 420" class is known to be 12, but there is no longer any information as to *where in the class* these 12 occurences lie.   Increased significance has been bought at the cost of loss of information.   The exchange is well worth while, but it means that calculations made from a grouped frequency distribution cannot be exact, and consequently excessive accuracy can only be spurious accuracy.

3. Class limits. *Class limit* are the extreme boundaries of a class. Care has to be taken in defining the class limits, otherwise there may be overlapping of classes or gaps between classes. Imprecision here is a common fault. Given, say, classes of "400–420" and "420–440" miles, in which of the two would a mileage of 420 be recorded? Obviously, it could be either. Conversely, if we were told that the higher class was "421–440," a mileage of $420\frac{1}{2}$ would appear to fit into neither of them. For this reason the classes in Table 8 are stated as "400–under 420," etc. The class limits of the first class are exactly 400 miles at the lower end, and *right up to, but not including* 420 miles at the upper end (*i.e.* $419 \cdot 99$ . . .). A well-designed grouped frequency distribution will ensure that there is neither overlapping of classes nor gaps between them.

4. Discrete and continuous data. The determination of class limits can be complicated by the fact that data can be either discrete or continuous.

Discrete data are data that increase in jumps. For instance, if the number of children in families is being recorded the figures will be 0, 1, 2, 3 or 4, etc. $1\frac{1}{2}$ or $2\frac{1}{4}$ are impossible. In other words, the data increase in jumps—from 0 to 1, from 1 to 2, etc.

Continuous data, on the other hand, are data that can increase *continuously*. If (say) miles travelled are being recorded, the figures could end in any fraction of a mile imaginable, *e.g.* $425 \cdot 001$, $425 \cdot 634$, $425 \cdot 999$. . . .

When the data are discrete, classes can be stated in the form 0–4, 5–9, 10–14 . . . without any ambiguity arising, since numbers such as $4\frac{1}{2}$ are impossible. However, as future theory (*see s.* **23**, 2) demands that there be no gaps between classes, it is the convention that, in such cases, class limits are deemed to extend half a unit on either side of the stated limits, *e.g.* $0–4\frac{1}{2}$, $4\frac{1}{2}–9\frac{1}{2}$, $9\frac{1}{2}–14\frac{1}{2}$. . . .

5. Class limits and the form of raw data. In determining the true class limits attention should be paid to the form of the raw data. For instance, in the raw data of salesmen's mileages shown in Table 5 there are no fractions of a mile. Yet it is inconceivable that the mileages travelled by so many salesmen could all be exact miles. There must have been some rounding.

Now, if the figures were rounded to the nearest mile, 419·75 miles, for example, would be recorded as 420 miles. That means it would be grouped in the "420–under 440" class in Table 8. *But clearly such a mileage should be in the "400–under 420" class.* Therefore Table 8 would be incorrectly constructed. Its construction can only be correct if the raw **data** were recorded on the basis of the number of *completed* miles.

In practice such fineness would usually be unnecessary, but this example demonstrates that some care is needed in determining class limits if grouped frequency distributions are to be correctly constructed.

6. Stated and true class limits. The above discussion shows that students must be careful to distinguish between the *stated* class limits and the *true* class limits. The former are the ones *stated* in the distribution, and the latter are the *actual* limits which must be used in any work involving the figures of the distribution.

7. Class interval. This is the width of the class—in other words, the difference between the class limits. In Table 8 the class interval is 20 miles for all classes.

8. Unequal class intervals. Some sets of figures are such that, if equal class intervals were taken, a very few classes would contain nearly all the occurrences whilst the majority would be virtually empty, *e.g.* a distribution of annual salaries with class intervals of £1,000. In cases like this, it is better to use unequal class intervals. They should be chosen so that the over-full classes are subdivided and the near-empty ones grouped together, *e.g.* 0–under £500, £500–under £750, £750–under £1,000, £1,000–under £1,500, £1,500–under £3,000, etc.

9. Open-ended classes. If the first class in a distribution is stated simply as "Under . . ." (*e.g.* "Under 400 miles") or the last is stated as "Over . . ." (*e.g.* "Over 500 miles"), such classes are termed *open-ended, i.e.* one end is open and goes on indefinitely. They are used to collect together the few extreme items whose values extend way beyond the main body of the distribution.

The class interval of an open-ended class is by convention deemed to be the same as that of the class immediately adjoining it. In well-designed distributions, open-ended classes have very low frequencies and so the error that may arise from using the convention is not important.

10. Choice of classes. The construction of a grouped frequency distribution always involves making a decision as to what classes shall be used. The choice will depend on individual circumstances, but the following suggestions should be borne in mind:

(a) Classes should be between ten and twenty in number.

NOTE: For the sake of simplicity the number of classes in examples in this book will be kept very small.

(b) Class intervals should be equal wherever practicable.

(c) Class intervals of 5, 10 or multiples of 10 are more convenient than other intervals such as 7 or 11.

(d) Classes should be chosen so that occurrences within the classes tend to balance around the mid-points of the classes. It would be unwise to have a class of (say) "£2,000–under £2,100" in a salary distribution, since salaries at this level are often in round £100's, so most of the occurrences would be concentrated at £2,000, *i.e.* the extreme end of the class. This is unsatisfactory, since later theory (*see s.* **32.** 2) makes the assumption that the average of the occurrences in a class lies at the mid-point of the class.

SECTION 27. DIRECT CONSTRUCTION OF A GROUPED FREQUENCY DISTRIBUTION

Once the raw data have been recorded (as in Table 5) we may wish to construct a grouped frequency distribution directly, without going through the intermediate steps of an array and an ungrouped frequency distribution. The steps are as follows:

(a) Pick out the highest and lowest figures (Table 5: 400 and 515) and on the basis of these decide and list the classes.

(b) Take each value in the raw data and insert a check
    mark (|) against the class into which it falls (*see* Table 9).
    Note that every fifth check mark is scored diagonally
    across the previous four. This simplifies the totalling
    at the end.

(c) Total the check marks to find the frequency of each
    class.

The distribution is now complete, though the frequencies
should be added up and the total checked to see that it corres-
ponds with the total number of occurrences in the raw data.

TABLE 9. DIRECT CONSTRUCTION OF TABLE 8 FROM RAW DATA
(see Table 5)

Class	Check marks	Frequencies
400–under 420	||| ||| ||	12
420– „ 440	||| ||| ||| ||| ||| ||	27
440– „ 460	||| ||| ||| ||| ||| ||| ||||	34
460– „ 480	||| ||| ||| ||| ||||	24
480– „ 500	||| ||| |||	15
500– „ 520	||| |||	8
		———
		120

PROGRESS TEST 10
(Answer on pages 256–7)

1. Suggest classes for insertion into the "Classes" column of
grouped frequency distributions compiled from raw data relating
to:

(a) A survey of the ages of adults in a city. Questionnaires
    were sent to all people of 20 years and over, asking them
    to state their present age in years.

(b) A survey of the number of extractions made on a specific
    day by a group of dentists, the numbers ranging between
    4 and 32.

(c) Incomes per annum of all full-time employed adults in a
    town (recorded to the nearest £).

State the exact class limits of the second class chosen by you
for each of the distributions.

2. Reconstruct the grouped frequency distribution for Table 5,
using the same class interval but starting with the first class at
390 miles.*

CHAPTER XI

GRAPHING FREQUENCY DISTRIBUTIONS

SECTION 28. HISTOGRAMS

1. Description. A *histogram* is a graph of the figures in a frequency distribution. The histogram for Table 8 is given as an example in Fig. 12. This figure shows that a histogram

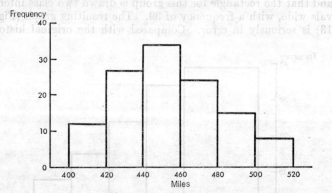

Fɪɢ. 12.—*Histogram of data from Table* 8

consists essentially of rectangles erected vertically, in which:

(*a*) the widths represent the class intervals, and

(*b*) the heights represent the respective frequencies.

Although at first sight it may appear that the heights of the rectangles are of greater importance in a histogram, the student is warned that the *areas* of the rectangles are even more important. In fact, to be absolutely correct, a histogram should be defined in such a way as to indicate that the area of each rectangle is strictly proportional to the number of observations in the class concerned.

2. Discrete distributions. If the frequency distribution is one that involves a discrete variable, it is important that the rule concerning the extension of class limits is followed (*see s. 26. 4*). This enables histograms to be constructed so that there are no gaps between the rectangles. The avoidance of gaps is vital. (A graph deliberately incorporating such gaps is a bar chart: *see s. 20.*) Histograms involving discrete variables must, therefore, show class limits adjoining each other.

3. Distributions with unequal class intervals. If, in Table 8, classes "400–under 420" and "420–under 440" were merged to give a single class, "400–under 440," the combined frequency would be 39. Now suppose we construct a histogram and that the rectangle for this group is drawn two class intervals wide, with a frequency of 39. The resulting graph (Fig. 13) is seriously in error. Compared with the original histo-

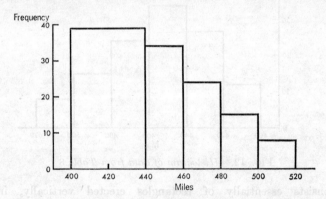

FIG. 13 —*Histogram with unequal class interval*
Incorrect construction

gram (Fig. 12), it is obvious that the area of the combined classes is much greater than the combined areas of the two separate classes.

As it is essential that the total areas should be the same, an adjustment must be made. This adjustment is quite simple, for since the "400–under 440" class has a class interval double that of the other classes, its histogram rectangle has a width double that of the other rectangles. Now, Area =

Width × Height, so a doubling of the width can be adjusted by halving the height. Thus the correct histogram is drawn with a frequency of 19½ (*i.e.* half of 39) for the "400–under 440" class (Fig. 14).

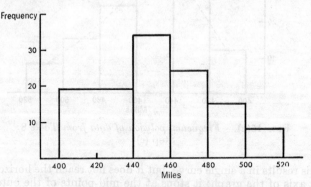

FIG. 14.—*Histogram with unequal class interval*
Correct construction

NOTE: Compared with the original histogram, this average height still does not look quite correct. This distortion arises through the loss of information as a result of further grouping.

Similarly, if a frequency distribution has a class with an interval three times the normal, the frequency of that class must be divided by three.

NOTE: Occasionally, distributions arise with no normal class interval. In such cases the smallest class interval should be assumed to be "normal."

SECTION 29. FREQUENCY POLYGONS AND FREQUENCY CURVES

1. Frequency polygon. A histogram is a graph with "steps." Instead of steps it may be desired to show a single curve rising and falling. Such a curve can be drawn in this way:

(*a*) Construct a histogram.
(*b*) Mark the mid-point of the top of each rectangle.
(*c*) Join the mid-points with straight lines (*see* Fig. 15(*a*)).

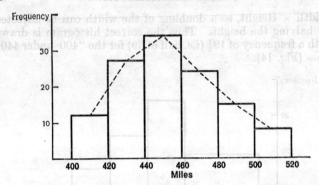

FIG. 15(a).—*Frequency polygon of data from Table* 8
Step (c)

This results in a single curve, but it does not reach the horizontal axis of the graph; it stops at the mid-points of the outermost steps. It is desirable that the curve should be "anchored" to the horizontal axis and that it should enclose an area equal to that of the histogram. The final step, then, is:

(d) Extend the curve downwards at both ends so that it cuts the axis at points which are *half a class interval beyond the outside limits of the end classes* (*see* Fig. 15(b)). This should be done even if it means that the curve crosses the vertical axis and ends in the minus part of the graph.

The resultant curve gives us a figure known as a *frequency polygon*. Fig 15(b) is in fact a frequency polygon of Table 8 superimposed on the histogram.

2. Area of a frequency polygon. It will be appreciated that in drawing a frequency polygon the corner of each rectangle cut off by the curve is equal in area to the triangle added between the point where the curve emerges from one rectangle and the mid-point of the next. Thus the area of the frequency polygon is exactly equal to the area of the histogram. This of course also explains why the curve is extended *half* a class outwards when it is brought down to meet the horizontal axis in step (d) above.

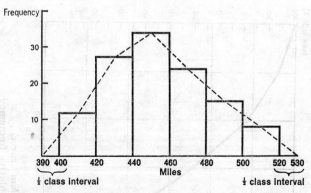

FIG. 15(*b*).—*Frequency polygon of data from Table* 8
Step (*d*)

3. Frequency curve. If the curve of a frequency polygon is smoothed so that there are no sharp points, it is known as a *frequency curve*. Normally, frequency curves should only be constructed when there are a large number of classes and very small intervals—when, in fact, the curve of the frequency polygon is virtually a smooth curve anyway. A frequency curve constructed under other circumstances tends to be inaccurate.

Again, the area under a frequency curve must be equal to the area of the histogram on which it is based.

SECTION 30.   OGIVES

1. Definition. *Ogive* is the name given to the curve obtained when the *cumulative* frequencies of a distribution are graphed. It is also called a *cumulative frequency curve*.

2. Construction.

(*a*) Compute the cumulative frequencies of the distribution, *i.e.* add up the progressive total of frequencies class by class (*see* Fig. 16, which illustrates an ogive constructed from the data in Table 8).

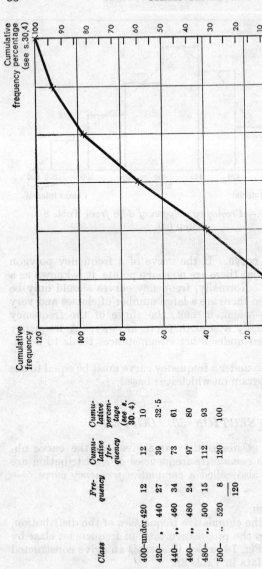

Class	Frequency	Cumulative frequency	Cumulative percentage (see s. 30, 4)
400–under 420	12	12	10
420– „ 440	27	39	32·5
440– „ 460	34	73	61
460– „ 480	24	97	80
480– „ 500	15	112	93
500– „ 520	8	120	100
	120		

FIG. 16.—*Ogive of data in Table 8* ('*less than*' *curve*)
The table alongside the graph shows the cumulative frequency distribution of the data in Table 8

(b) Prepare a graph with the cumulative frequency on the vertical axis and the classes on the horizontal axis.

(c) Plot the cumulative frequencies on the graph and join the points. Note that ogives start at:

(i) Zero on the vertical scale, and
(ii) The outside class limit of the end class.

It is very important that the cumulative frequencies are plotted at the correct place along the horizontal axis, *i.e.* at the *class limit* of the class to which they refer.

This point must be clearly understood. Consider what a cumulative frequency figure means. In Fig. 16, for example, the cumulative frequency alongside class "420–under 440" is 39. This means that there are 39 mileages which lie below 440 miles. Therefore the 39 must be plotted just below the 440 mile point (for practical graphing purposes, at 440). Similarly, the 73 relating to the "440–under 460" class means 73 mileages below 460 miles and the 73 must therefore be plotted just below the 460 mile point. In other words—to repeat—when constructing an ogive, each cumulative frequency must be plotted at the appropriate class limit of each class.

3. "Less than" and "more than" curves. Frequencies may be cumulated in two ways, by starting with the lowest or with the highest class. This means there can be two ogive curves for the same distribution (*see* Figs. 16 and 17). They are referred as "less than" and "more than" curves, the "less than" curve being the one obtained as a result of starting with the lowest class. It is by far the commoner of the two.

The term "less than" refers to the reading of the curve. For instance, in Fig. 16 it passes through the point representing a "cumulative frequency of 100" and "484 miles." This is read as "100 of the mileages are *less than* 484 miles." Similarly, at a lower point it can be seen a cumulative frequency of 60 is related to 452 miles. This means that 60 mileages are of *less than* 452 miles.

To construct a "more than" curve, the frequencies are cumulated starting at the highest class and the cumulative frequencies plotted at the *lower* class-limits.

4. Comparing ogives. It is sometimes desired to compare ogives of two different distributions. Unless the total fre-

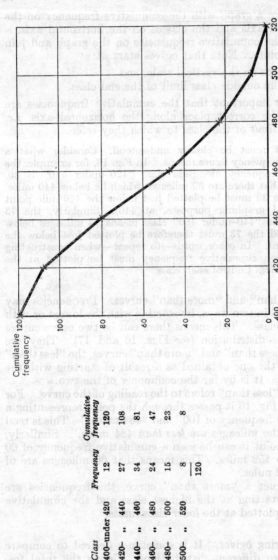

Fig. 17.—Ogive of data in Table 8 ("more than" curve)

The table alongside the graph shows the cumulative frequency
distribution of the data in Table 8

Class	Frequency	Cumulative frequency
400—under 420	12	120
420— " 440	27	108
440— " 460	34	81
460— " 480	24	47
480— " 500	15	23
500— " 520	8	8
	120	

quencies of the distributions are the same, such comparisons are virtually impossible if the ogives are constructed as out-lined above. One ogive will simply tower over the other. The difficulty is easily overcome, however, by plotting *not* the cumulative frequencies themselves but the cumulative fre-quencies *expressed as a percentage of the total of the distribution*. This results in both ogives ending at the same point, 100%, and so renders them comparable (*see* Fig. 16, noting both the percentage column in the table and the percentage scale on the right-hand side of the graph).

5. Smoothing ogives. The ogives discussed so far have consisted of a series of straight lines. Normally it is consi-dered dangerous to smooth curves relating to frequency dis-tributions, but in the case of ogives, providing the smoothed curve passes through all the plotted points, such smoothing almost always improves the graph. The reason is that occurrences are not usually spread equally throughout a class but tend to cluster in one or the other half of the class. Smoothing automatically makes some allowance for this tendency in the case of ogives and therefore improves the accuracy of the curve. Hence ogives are often smoothed.

PROGRESS TEST 11
(*Answer on pages* 257–9)

1. Construct histograms for the following data and super-impose frequency polygons on them.*

MARKS SCORED IN I.Q. TESTS BY PUPILS AT TWO DIFFERENT SCHOOLS

	Number of pupils	
I.Q. marks	School A	School B
75–under 85	15	43
85– „ 95	25	99
95– „ 105	40	54
105– „ 115	108	40
115– „ 125	92	14
Over 125	20	0
	300	250

2. Construct a histogram for the following data and super-impose a frequency polygon on it.*

NUMBER OF PAGES IN CHILDREN'S BOOKS
IN GREAT REEDING PUBLIC LIBRARY

Pages in book	Number of books
Under 50	100
50–under 100	150
100– ,, 150	80
150– ,, 200	30
200– ,, 250	20
250– ,, 300	10
300– ,, 350	6
350– ,, 400	3
400 and over	1
	400

3. Construct (a) a histogram with a frequency polygon, (b) a smooth ogive ("less than" curve), for the following data:

In a certain examination, 12 candidates obtained fewer than 10 marks; 25 obtained 10 to under 25 marks; 51 obtained 25 to under 40 marks; 48 obtained 40 to under 50 marks; 46 obtained 50 to under 60 marks; 54 obtained 60 under 80 marks, and only 8 obtained 80 marks or more.
Marks were out of 100.

4. In a subsequent examination (see question 3), a larger number of candidates sat and a grouped frequency distribution of their marks was as follows:*

Marks	Number of candidates
0–under 15	40
15– ,, 30	80
30– ,, 45	150
45– ,, 60	480
60– ,, 75	190
75– ,, 90	50
Over 90	10
	1,000

By means of ogives, compare this and the previous distribution.

5. From Fig. 16 determine:

(a) the number of mileages recorded below 470;
(b) the range of mileages that were recorded by the lowest 25% of the salesmen.

CHAPTER XII

AVERAGES

SECTION 31. DEFINITIONS

1. What is an average? In our attempt to improve the intelligibility of a mass of figures relating to a single variable we have examined frequency distributions and histograms. A quite different way of approaching the task is to try and obtain one single figure which is representative of all the figures. Such a single representative figure is called an *average*.

2. Types of average. Now, everyone knows that in politics when attempting to select a single representative for, say, Parliament there is frequently a considerable difference of opinion as to who would make the best representative. This is because different candidates represent different interests.

In a similar way there are different averages, each claiming to be representative of all the figures—though, in fact, each really is representative of only a particular *aspect* of the figures. Of these averages the most important are:

(*a*) The arithmetic mean (often referred to simply as "the mean").
(*b*) The median.
(*c*) The mode.

In addition, but much less important, are:

(*d*) The geometric mean.
(*e*) The harmonic mean.

Since each is representative of a particular aspect of the data, the selection of one of these averages will depend upon which aspect is under consideration.

3. Grouped and ungrouped data. First the student must know how to compute averages. As methods of computation differ slightly according to whether the data are grouped or not, examples relating to both grouped and ungrouped data will be given, using Tables 8 and 10 respectively. As

TABLE 10. ARRAY OF NUMBER OF CHILDREN
IN EACH HOUSE IN X STREET

Item No.	No. of children
1	0
2	0
3	0
4	0
5	0 (1st quartile)
6	0
7	1
8	1
9	1
10	1 (Median)
11	2
12	2
13	2
14	2
15	3 (3rd quartile)
16	3
17	4
18	5
19	6
	——
	33
	——

regards *grouped* data, it should be recollected that there is some loss of information when a grouped frequency distribution is compiled (*see s. 26. 2*). This loss of information means that averages cannot be computed from such distributions with complete accuracy. Any attempt to state them with absolute accuracy can only result in spurious accuracy.

SECTION 32. ARITHMETIC MEAN

1. Arithmetic mean of ungrouped data. The procedure is:

(*a*) Add up all the values.
(*b*) Divide by the number of items.

This is the average that most students will have learnt at school. Its symbol is $\bar{x}$ (called *bar x*) and the method of computation can be shown algebraically as:

$$\bar{x} = \frac{\Sigma x}{n} \quad .. \quad .. \quad .. \quad .. \quad (1)$$

(The symbols were explained in *s.* 3.)

EXAMPLE
Find the arithmetic mean of the data in Table 10

$$\Sigma x = 33; \qquad n = 19$$

$$\therefore \bar{x} = \frac{33}{19} \qquad = 1 \cdot 737 \text{ children.}$$

2. Arithmetic mean of a grouped frequency distribution.

Since there are no *actual* values in a grouped frequency distribution, it is not possible to add the values. However, it is a convention that in such distributions the occurrences within a class are assumed to be spread equally throughout the class. This means that they will be balanced equally around the mid-point of the class. It therefore simplifies the calculations relating to the mean if it is assumed that all occurrences in a particular class occur *at the mid-point of that class.* Thus the approximate sum of the values within a class is the number of occurrences (*i.e.* frequency) multiplied by the class mid-point. If this calculation is carried out for every class, an approximation of Σx can be obtained by adding all the products. After this it only remains to divide Σx by the total number of items—which is, of course, the same as the sum of the frequencies (Σf). The procedure can be shown as a formula:

$$\bar{x} = \frac{\Sigma(f \times Class\ mid\text{-}point)}{\Sigma f} \quad .. \quad .. \quad .. \quad (2)$$

EXAMPLE
Find the mean of the data in Table 8.

Class		Mid-point	f	$f \times mid\text{-}point$
400–under 420		410	12	4,920
420–	„ 440	430	27	11,610
440–	„ 460	450	34	15,300
460–	„ 480	470	24	11,280
480–	„ 500	490	15	7,350
500–	.. 520	510	8	4,080
			$\Sigma f = 120$	54,540

$$\bar{x} = \frac{54,540}{120} = 454 \cdot 5 \text{ miles}$$

NOTE: The true mean computed from the raw data of Table 5 is $454 \cdot 27$ miles. The difference arises through loss of information on grouping.

3. Short method of computing the mean.

Although the method above will always give the correct answer, the student is strongly advised to learn the following short method, which may look more complicated but in fact makes the calculations much easier:

(a) *Estimate which class contains the mean.* It does not matter how inaccurate the estimate is, although the more accurate it is, the less the work involved.

(b) *Number off the classes* on either side of the chosen class, those of lower values being minus and those of higher values being plus. The chosen class will, of course, be 0. These numbers are the *deviations* from the chosen class (symbol d).

(c) Multiply each class frequency by its deviation (fd)

(d) (i) Add these products, paying attention to the sign (Σfd), and then

    (ii) Divide by the sum of the frequencies (Σf), and finally

    (iii) Multiply by the class interval (NOTE that negative answers are very common).

(e) *Find the mid-point of the chosen class* (this figure being called the *assumed mean*) and add, or subtract as the case may be, the answer given by step (d).

The formula for this procedure is:

$$\bar{x} = Assumed\ mean + \left(\frac{\Sigma fd}{\Sigma f} \times Class\ interval \right) \quad .. \quad (3)$$

NOTE: This procedure applies to distributions with equal class intervals. For cases where the class intervals are unequal, *see* next paragraph.

EXAMPLE
Find the arithmetic mean of the data in Table 8 by the short method. The class guessed to contain the mean is "440–under 460."

Class			f	d	fd
400–under	420		12	−2	−24
420–	,,	440	27	−1	−27
440–	,,	460	34	0	0
460–	,,	480	24	+1	+24
480–	,,	500	15	+2	+30
500–	,,	520	8	+3	+24

$$\Sigma f = 120 \qquad\qquad \Sigma fd = +27$$

Assumed mean = mid-point "440–under 460" class = 450 miles.

$$\therefore \bar{x} = 450 + \left(\frac{27}{120} \times 20\right) = 450 + 4\cdot5 = 454\cdot5 \text{ miles}$$

It should be noted that the answer obtained by the short method will *always* be the same as that obtained by the long method previously discussed. There is no loss of accuracy when the short method is used.

4. Computing the mean of a distribution with unequal class intervals. If the class intervals of the distribution are unequal, the short method needs to be amended slightly, as follows:

(a) In step (b), d must be computed for each class so that d = Mid-point of class − Mid-point of "chosen" class.

(b) Step (d) (iii) is ignored.

SECTION 33.   MEDIAN

1. Median of ungrouped data. The *median* is the value of the middle item of a distribution. To find the median:

(a) Arrange the data in an array.

(b) Locate the middle item.

(c) Read off the value of the middle item.

EXAMPLE

Find the median of the data in Table 10.

(a) As Table 10 is itself an array, this step has already been taken.

(b) Since there are 19 items, the middle item must be the tenth (not $9\frac{1}{2}$). There are 9 items *below* the tenth and 9 items *above* it. Therefore the tenth is clearly the middle item. Students who are puzzled by this need only learn the following formula:

$$Middle\ item = \frac{n + 1}{2}$$

(c) The median is, therefore, the value of this item, *i.e.* one child.

It will pay students to note carefully the distinction between median (middle) item and median value. The median *item* is the middle item (in the Example, the tenth item). The median *value* is the value of this median item (1 child). It is, of course, the median value that is referred as "the median," but the median item is needed to find the median.

2. Median item of a small, even-numbered distribution.
Sometimes students are puzzled when the total number of items is an even number. In such a case there will be no single mid-item, but this is no difficulty since in any realistic set of figures the values of the middle two items will be virtually the same, and either will suffice (if they are not, then in practice it would be unwise to use the median at all).

Alternatively, the middle two items may be averaged. This would follow from the use of the formula given in (*b*) of the Example above; thus if there are 100 items, then $\frac{1}{2}(n + 1)$ = $50\frac{1}{2}$, *i.e.* the average of the 50th and 51st items.

3. Median of a grouped frequency distribution.
Again, ignorance of the actual values in a grouped frequency distribution makes it impossible to determine accurately the median value. However, it is possible to determine the median *item*. For example, in Table 8 there are 120 items. The median item is therefore the 60th.

NOTE: Since only an approximate median value can be found, it is rather pedantic to maintain that the median must be the average of the 60th and 61st items. The median item is usually considered to be the $\frac{1}{2}n$th item in a large even-numbered distribution.

Now from a cumulative frequency distribution it is possible to determine within which class the median item lies. This class is called the *median class* (note that a grouped frequency distribution is laid out as an *array of classes*). In the case of Table 8 the cumulative frequency distribution is as follows:

Miles			*Frequency*	*Cumulative frequency*
400–under	420		12	12
420–	,,	440	27	39
440–	,,	460	34	73 (median class)
460–	,,	480	24	97
480–	,,	500	15	112
500–	,,	520	8	120

The 60th item lies, therefore, in the "440–under 460" class, and so that is the median class.

The median itself is now estimated by computing the probable location of the median item within the median class. In our example, the 60th item is the 21st item from the bottom of the median class (the cumulative frequency distribution shows that the 39th item just falls in the class preceding the median class, and the 60th item is just 21 more items further on, *i.e.* 21st from the bottom of the class). Now there are 34 items in the median class and if it is assumed these items are equally spread throughout the class the median item must be 21/34ths of the way through the class. Since the class interval is 20 miles, then 21/34ths of this interval is $21/34 \times 20 \simeq 12 \cdot 4$ miles. So the median item lies $12 \cdot 4$ miles within the median class and, since this class starts at 440 miles, the value of the median item (*i.e.* the 'median') must lie at approximately $440 + 12 \cdot 4 = 452 \cdot 4$ miles.

It may seem rather complicated, but all we are doing is to determine how far the median item lies along the median class interval by means of proportions. Fig. 18, showing the position diagrammatically, may help to make things clearer. It can be seen that the median item is 21/34ths of the interval

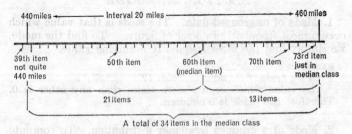

Fig. 18.—*Locating the median item within the median class*

of 20 miles, *i.e.* 12·4 miles. Therefore the value of the median item (*i.e.* the median) is $440 + 12·4 = 452·4$ miles.

Summary. To compute the median from a grouped frequency distribution:

(*a*) Compute the median item ($n/2$).

(*b*) Construct a cumulative frequency distribution and locate the median class.

(*c*) Compute how far within the median class the median item lies.

(*d*) Add the figure from step (*c*) to the bottom value of the median class to give median.

4. Median of discrete data. When the median of discrete data is calculated from a grouped frequency distribution, the answer frequently contains a fraction of a unit. Since the object of the median is to give an actual single value—that of the middle item—and since such a fraction is impossible in the case of discrete data, it is necessary to round off the answer to the nearest unit. If the data in Table 8 had related to numbers of cars, the median value of 452·4 would have been rounded to 452 cars.

When dealing with discrete data it is very important to note that the real class limits must be used in calculations, not the stated limits.

5. Determining the median from an ogive. The median can also be found by means of an ogive. This method is explained in *s.* **40. 2**.

SECTION 34. MODE

1. Mode of ungrouped data. The *mode* is that value which occurs most frequently in a set of figures. To find the mode, we simply find the most frequently occurring value.

EXAMPLE

Find the mode of the data in Table 10.

The value which occurs more times than any other is 0. Therefore the mode is 0 children.

2. Mode of a grouped frequency distribution. To compute the mode of a grouped frequency distribution correctly is, unfortunately, not so easy. Since a grouped frequency distribution has no individual values, it is obviously impossible to determine which value occurs most frequently. The best that can be done is to select the *modal class*, *i.e.* the class with the highest frequency. Yet even this can be unsatisfactory: should a different set of classes have been chosen when the original data were processed, the modal class could appear at a quite different place. Indeed, for practical purposes the student would be well advised to ignore the mode (or place it within wide limits) unless the nature of the data is such that the mode is distinct and definite, as was the case with the children in the Example above.

For examination purposes, however, the following method of finding the mode is suggested (*see* Fig. 19).

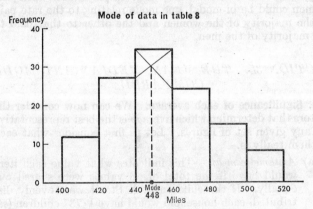

FIG. 19.—*Diagrammatic method of finding the mode*
The histogram uses the data in Table 8

(a) Construct a histogram of the grouped frequency distribution.

(b) Find the modal class (*i.e.* the class with the highest rectangle).

(c) Draw a line from the top right-hand corner of the modal class rectangle to the point where the top of the next adjacent rectangle to the left touches it. Draw a corresponding line on the opposite diagonal from the top left-hand corner to the rectangle on the right.

(d) The mode is the point where these two lines cross.

EXAMPLE

Find the mode of the data in Table 8.

See Fig. 19, which shows that the mode is 448 miles.

If the distribution has a single peak, then the following formula will give the approximate mode:

$$Mode = Mean - 3(Mean - Median) \quad .. \quad .. \quad (4)$$

3. Bi-modal distributions. When a frequency polygon (or curve) is superimposed on a histogram there is usually only one peak. Should the distribution be such that two peaks arise, the distribution is said to be *bi-modal*. Distributions normally have a single mode, but a distribution relating to (say) wage rates in a factory that employs both men and women could be bi-modal, one mode relating to the rate paid to the majority of the women and the other to that paid to the majority of the men.

SECTION 35.   THE MEAN, MEDIAN AND MODE COMPARED

1. Significance of each average. We can now consider the factors that determine which average is the best representative for any given set of figures. Let us first consider what each of them really is.

(a) *Arithmetic mean.*—This indicates what value each item would have if the total of all values were shared out equally. If the children in X Street were evenly distributed, each household would have 1·737 children (*see* Table 10).

(b) *Median.*—This is the value of the middle item. There will be *as many occurrences below this value as above it;* in other words, half the distribution lies above and half below the median. Consequently there is a 50–50 chance that any item chosen at random will lie below the median—and similarly, of course, a 50–50 chance it will lie above it.

(c) *Mode.*—As this is the value that occurs most frequently, it is the best representative of the *typical* item. It is this form of average that is implied by such expressions as "the average person" or "the average holiday." The remark that "the average holiday nowadays is two weeks" means that the *usual* holiday is two weeks, not that the mean of all holidays is two weeks. The mode is thus a familiar and commonly used average, though its name is less well known.

2. Choice of an average. The above explanations should help us to decide which average should be chosen in any particular case.

(*a*) If we wish to know the result that would follow from an equal distribution—consumption of beer per head, for instance—the *mean* is the most suitable.

(*b*) If the half-way value is required, with as many above as below, the *median* will be the choice.

(*c*) If the most typical value is required then the *mode* is the appropriate average to use.

3. Features of the mean, median and mode.

(a) *The mean:*

    (i) makes use of every value in the distribution. It can, therefore, be distorted by extreme values.

    (ii) can be used for further mathematical processing (*see s. 37*).

    (iii) may result in an "impossible" figure where the data are discrete (*e.g.* 1·737 children).

    (iv) is the best known of the averages.

(b) *The median:*

    (i) uses only one value in the distribution. It is *not*, therefore, influenced by extreme values.

    (ii) cannot be used for further mathematical processing.

    (iii) is an actual value occurring in the distribution (unless it is computed by averaging the two middle items of an even-numbered distribution).

    (iv) can be computed even if the data are incomplete. Thus in determining the median salary of a group of executives, for example, it may prove impossible to discover the salaries of the highest-paid executives. But, since these values will not affect the value of the median item, it is still possible to determine the median salary.

(c) *The mode:*

    Like the median, the mode is an actual, single value.

It can be estimated from complete data, but cannot be used for further mathematical processing.

SECTION 36.　THE GEOMETRIC AND HARMONIC MEANS

1. Geometric mean (GM).

(a) *Computation in theory:*

    (i) Multiply the values all together (*i.e.* $x_1 \times x_2 \times x_3 \ldots$) and then,

    (ii) Find the nth root of the product where n is the number of items.

(b) *Computation in practice.* The theoretical computation clearly involves a great deal of work, but this can be reduced considerably by the use of logarithms. With logs, multiplication is achieved by adding, and the nth root found by dividing by n. The formula is:

$$Logarithm\ of\ GM = \frac{\Sigma \log x}{n} \quad .. \quad .. \quad .. \quad (5)$$

To compute the GM, therefore, we must:

    (i) Add the logs of all the values;

    (ii) Divide by n.

    (iii) Look up the anti-log of the answer to (ii).

EXAMPLE

Find the geometric mean of 4, 5 and 6

$$\text{Log. GM} = \frac{\log 4 + \log 5 + \log 6}{3}$$

$$= \frac{0 \cdot 6021 + 0 \cdot 6990 + 0 \cdot 7782}{3} = \frac{2 \cdot 0793}{3} = 0 \cdot 6931.$$

$$\therefore \text{GM} = \text{anti-log } 0 \cdot 6931 = 4 \cdot 933.$$

(c) *Use of the GM.* The geometric mean is used mainly in connection with index numbers, though it can also be used for averaging ratios.

2. Harmonic mean (HM).

(a) *Computation:*

    (i) Add the reciprocals of the values; then

    (ii) Divide the sum into the number of items

The formula is:

$$Harmonic\ mean = \frac{n}{\Sigma\frac{1}{x}} \quad .. \quad .. \quad .. \quad (6)$$

EXAMPLE

Find the harmonic mean of 4, 5 and 6.

$$HM = \frac{3}{\frac{1}{4} + \frac{1}{5} + \frac{1}{6}} = \frac{3}{\frac{37}{60}} = 4\cdot86$$

(b) *Use of the HM.* The use of the harmonic mean in statistics is so restricted that discussion is best omitted in a handbook such as this.

SECTION 37. AVERAGING MEANS

1. Procedure for averaging means. If 10 students in one class have an average (arithmetic mean) of 60 marks each and 40 students in a second class have an average of 50 marks each, what is average mark of the two classes combined?

In this sort of problem there is a strong temptation to compute the mean of the averages, *i.e.* $\frac{1}{2}(60 + 50) = 55$ marks. This is quite wrong, as can be seen from the following:

(a) (i) The total mark gained by the whole of the first class must be 60×10, *i.e.* 600 marks.

> NOTE: Since $\bar{x} = \Sigma x/n$, therefore $\Sigma x = \bar{x}n$, where Σx is the total of all the values in the distribution.

(ii) Similarly, the total mark gained by the second class must be $50 \times 40 = 2,000$ marks.

(b) The combined mark of both classes, then, must be $600 + 2,000 = 2,600$ marks.

(c) These marks were obtained by a total of $10 + 40 = 50$ students, so the mean mark per student must be $2,600/50 = 52$ marks.

The *correct* procedure for computing such a combined average is as follows:

(a) Compute for each group the sum of all the values. This is done by multiplying the group mean by the number of items in the group.

(b) Add these totals to give a combined total.

(c) Divide the combined total by the combined number of items.

2. Weighted average. This combined mean is often referred to as the *weighted average* because individual group averages are "weighted" by multiplying them by the number of items in the group.

It should be noted that this particular use of a weighted average is really only a specific application of a more general idea. There are other contexts in which, when computing a mean, it is sometimes desired to give certain figures greater importance in the answer (*e.g.* index numbers). This can be done by multiplying those figures by chosen numbers called *weights*. In the example above, the weights were the number of students in each class, *i.e.* 10 and 40. The important point to remember about a mean computed from such weights is that, instead of dividing by the number of items, one divides by *the sum of the weights* (unweighted figures carry a weight of 1 in this addition). A mean so calculated is called a *weighted average*, and the appropriate formula is:

$$Weighted\ average = \frac{\Sigma xw}{\Sigma w} \quad .. \quad .. \quad .. \quad (7)$$

EXAMPLE

Find the weighted average of the following figures where Group B figures are to carry weights of 2, and Group C figures, weights of 3:

Group A: 6, 5, 3
B: 12, 14
C: 20, 22, 23

Group	No. (x)	Weight (w)	Weight × No. (xw)
A	6	1	6
A	5	1	5
A	3	1	3
B	12	2	24
B	14	2	28
C	20	3	60
C	22	3	66
C	23	3	69

$$\Sigma w = 16 \qquad \Sigma xw = 261$$

$$Weighted\ average = \frac{\Sigma xw}{\Sigma w} = \frac{261}{16} \fallingdotseq 16 \cdot 3$$

3. Accuracy and the mean. Since the mean is only a representative value of a possibly large number of very different values, it would seem pedantic to state it with extreme accuracy—even though such accuracy was not spurious. For instance, to give the mean height of a group of children as 4 ft 1 in. conveys just as much to a reader as 4 ft 1·04 in. However, in statistics the mean is frequently used in further calculations, as above, where it was used to obtain a combined mean. For this reason, it is necessary to state it with a good deal more accuracy than would otherwise be called for.

PROGRESS TEST 12

(*Answers on pages* 260–1)

1. In a series of twenty "spot checks" the following number of passengers were counted at a certain depot:*

137	136	135	136
135	135	137	138
136	137	136	136
138	137	136	137
136	136	138	135

(*a*) From these figures determine: (i) the mean, (ii) the mode, and (ii) the median.

(*b*) It is later discovered that the last observation was incorrectly recorded when the data were being collected. It should have been 35 instead of 135. Re-compute the three averages. What features of the three averages do your revised figures bring out?

2. Using the data in question 1 (p. 91):

(*a*) Compute the mean and median I.Q. of the pupils in each school.

(*b*) If 450 pupils in a third school had a mean I.Q. of 106, what would be the mean I.Q. of all the pupils in the three schools combined? [*Answer:* 104·6.

3. Find the mean and median of the data in question 2 on page 92. [*Answer:* 98·9; 83.

4. A company which makes and sells a standard article has four machines on which this article can be made. Owing to differences in age and design the machines run at different speeds, as follows:

Machine	Number of minutes required to produce one article
A	2
B	3
C	5
D	6

(a) When all machines are running, what is the total number of articles produced per hour?

(b) Over a period of three hours, only machines B, C and D were run for the first two hours, and only machines A, B and D for the last hour. What was the average number of articles produced *per hour* over this three-hour period? (I.C.W.A.)

5. A distribution of the wages paid to foremen would show that, although a few reach very high levels, most foremen are at the lower levels of the distribution. The same applies, of course, to most wage distributions.

(a) If you were an employer resisting a foreman's wage claim, which average would suit your case best?

(b) If you were the foreman's union representative, which average would you then select?

(c) If you were contemplating a career as a foreman, which average would you examine?

Give reasons for your answers.

6. Show by means of a formula the *combined mean* of three groups, the first group having n_1 items and a mean of $\bar{x}_1$; the second group, n_2 items and a mean of $\bar{x}_2$; and the third group, n_3 items and a mean of $\bar{x}_3$.

CHAPTER XIII

ALL THE -ILES

In discussing ways of clarifying a mass of data in Chapter XII, we said the median was the value of the middle item in an array. The idea of arranging figures in an array, selecting items which stand in certain positions, and then noting their values, can be developed further.

SECTION 38. QUARTILES

1. Determining quartiles of an ungrouped distribution. It will be remembered that the median item divided an array into two equal parts. It requires little imagination to see that, in the same way, each part could again be divided into halves, that is, the whole array divided into four equal parts. Now clearly the *items* which so divide the array must be items which lie a quarter, half, and three quarters of the way down the array. Thus, to take the array in Table 10, the 5th, 10th and 15th items respectively divide the whole array into four equal parts. These three items are called *quartile items*. Since the second quartile item is, of course, the median item, only the first and third quartile items are generally referred to in discussing quartiles.

Once the first and third quartile items have been found, all that remains is to read off their values from the array. In Table 10 the first quartile value (Q_1) is 0 children, and the third quartile value (Q_3) is 3 children.

2. Formulae for quartile items. Strictly speaking, the formulae for finding the first and third quartile items are:

$$First\ quartile\ item = \frac{n+1}{4} \quad .. \quad .. \quad .. \quad (8)$$

$$Third\ quartile\ item = \frac{n+1}{4} \times 3 \quad .. \quad .. \quad (9)$$

However, for a grouped frequency distribution (*see* next para.)

$$\frac{n}{4} \text{ and } \frac{3n}{4}$$

are normally quite satisfactory formulae for the quartile items.

3. Determining quartiles of a grouped frequency distribution.
To determine the quartiles of a grouped frequency distribution,
it is necessary to use the same method as was used to determine
the median. For instance, in Table 8 there are 120 items. The
quartile items are, therefore, the 30th and 90th items. By
constructing a cumulative frequency distribution, the classes
containing the quartiles can be found:

Miles			Frequency	Cumulative frequency
400–under	420		12	12
420–	,,	440	27	39 (Q₁ in this class)
440–	,,	460	34	73
460–	,,	480	24	97 (Q₃ in this class)
480–	,,	500	15	112
500–	,,	520	8	120

This distribution reveals the classes within which the
quartile items lie. The *values* of these items are found in
exactly the same way as the value of the median was found,
i.e. by assuming the items to be equally spread throughout
each class and then computing the value of the required item
by means of proportions. For example, the first quartile item
is the 30th. Since the first 12 items lie in an earlier class, it is
the $30 - 12 = 18$th item in its class of 27 items, *i.e.* it lies
18/27ths of the way into the class. As this class has an
interval of 20 miles this is equivalent to $18/27 \times 20 = 13\frac{1}{3}$
miles. Now the quartile class starts at 420 miles, so the first
quartile $= 420 + 13\frac{1}{3} = 433\frac{1}{3}$ miles.

Similarly $Q_3 = (90 - 73)/24 \times 20 + 460 = 474 \cdot 1$ miles.

NOTE: No summary of this procedure is given, as it is so
similar to the procedure for determining the median. Students
who want a summary can construct their own simply by
reading "quartile" for "median" at the end of *s*. 33. 3.

4. Use of quartiles. The median is a valuable statistical measure but, because it is the value of only one item out of a set of possibly hundreds, it often needs supplementing by other measures. One of its shortcomings, for instance, is that it gives no indication as to how far on either side of it the other values extend.

To know that the median wage in a factory is £16 per week gives us no idea of the actual level of pay received by most of the lower-paid operatives, except that it is not above £16. If, however, it is also known that the first quartile is £15 and the third £24, then it is clear that many operatives earn a wage close to the median, while some earn much more (a quarter of the operatives must earn £24 or more by the very definition of a quartile). Indeed, it is possible to go further. Since a quarter of the distribution lies below the first quartile and a quarter lies above the third, then *half the distribution must lie between the two quartiles*. It can be concluded, then, that half the operatives earn between £15 and £24 per week, whilst a quarter earn £15 or less and a quarter earn £24 or more.

From this it can be seen that a considerable amount of information will be contained in a statement that gives only three figures, if they are the median and the two quartiles. For this reason, if it is wished to summarise a large set of figures very briefly, the median and the two quartiles may be chosen as the representative figures that carry the most information.

SECTION 39. DECILES AND PERCENTILES

1. Deciles. Quartiles, we have seen, are the values attached to the items which appeared one quarter and three quarters of the way along an array. *Deciles* are the values attached to the items which appear 1/10, 2/10, 3/10, *etc.*, of the way along an array. Thus the first decile is the value of the item 1/10 of the way from the beginning of the array (in the case of Table 8, the 120/10 = 12th item). The second decile is the value of the item 2/10 of the way (in Table 8, the 120 × 2/10 = 24th item) and the, say, ninth decile the value of the item 9/10 of the way (in Table 8, the 108th item). The values of these items are found in exactly the same way as the values of medians and quartiles are found.

EXAMPLE
Find the third decile of the data in Table 8.

The third decile in the item is $\dfrac{3}{10}$ of the way along the array,

i.e. $\qquad\qquad \dfrac{3}{10} \times 120 = $ the 36th item.

From the cumulative frequency distribution shown in *s.* **38. 3** it can be seen that this item is in the "420–under 440" class and is the $36 - 12 = $ 24th item in a class of 27 items.

∴ The value of this item is $\left(\dfrac{24}{27} \times 20\right) + 420 = 437 \cdot 8$ miles.

2. Percentiles. These are *the values attached to items* 1/100, 2/100, 3/100, *etc., of the way along an array.*

EXAMPLE
Find the 85th percentile of the data in Table 8.

The 85th percentile is the $\dfrac{85}{100} \times 120 = $ 102nd item in the array.

This item lies in the "480–under 500" class and its value is $\left(\dfrac{102 - 97}{15} \times 20\right) + 480 = 486\frac{2}{3}$ miles.

3. Use of percentiles. Percentiles are particularly useful as "cut-off" values.

For example, assume that only 22% of the children in a group of primary schools can be awarded places in the local grammar school, and that selection is based on I.Q. If the children's I.Q.'s are tested and tabulated, the 22nd percentile will indicate the I.Q. level that will separate the grammar-school entrants from the others.

SECTION 40. MEDIAN AND -ILES FROM AN OGIVE

1. Relationship between ogives, medians and -iles. The ogive (*s.* **30**) can be very effectively used to determine the median or any of the -iles. The student may perhaps have realised this already, since all the above measures have been based on a cumulative frequency distribution, and the ogive is the graph of that distribution.

2. Finding medians and -iles from an ogive. To use an ogive to find the median or an -ile, it is necessary only:

(a) to compute which item in the array is required; and then
(b) to read off from the ogive the value associated with that item (using a "less than" curve).

EXAMPLE
Find the median, first quartile, third quartile, third decile and 85th percentile of the data in Table 8.

First an ogive of the data in Table 8 is constructed (Fig. 16); then:

Median.—Median item $120/2 = 60$th.   Value 452 miles.
First quartile.—Quartile item $120/4 = 30$th.   Value 433 miles.
Third quartile.—Quartile item $120/4 \times 3 = 90$th.   Value 474 miles.
Third decile.—Decile item $120/10 \times 3 = 36$th.   Value 438 miles.
85th percentile.—Percentile item $120/100 \times 85 = 102$nd.   Value 487 miles.

3. Usefulness of ogives. The use of the ogive for determining various measures like these is additional to its other use in finding "less than" or "more than" figures.   It is thus a valuable form of graph and one with which the student should be fully conversant.

PROGRESS TEST 13
(*Answers on pages 262–5*)

1. The following marks were obtained by candidates in an examination (no fractions of a mark were awarded):

Marks	No. of Candidates	Marks	No. of Candidates	Marks	No. of Candidates
0–5	2	36–40	150	71–75	120
6–10	8	41–45	200	76–80	100
11–15	20	46–50	220	81–85	60
16–20	30	51–55	280	86–90	40
21–25	50	56–60	320	91–95	17
26–30	80	61–65	260	96–100	3
31–35	120	66–70	160		
					2,240

E

(a) Find: (i) the median, (ii) the first quartile, (iii) the third quartile, (iv) the sixth decile, (v) the 42nd percentile. (*Warning:* Think carefully about class limits.)

(b) If the examining body wished to pass only one-third of the candidates, what should the pass mark be?

2. Customers' waiting times in a check-out queue at a Little Fielding self-service store were found to be as follows:

Length of wait (*mins.*)	No. of customers
No waiting	50
Waiting under $\frac{1}{2}$	210
$\frac{1}{2}$–under 1	340
1– ,, 2	200
2– ,, 3	110
3– ,, 5	170
5– ,, 10	140
10 and over	80
	1,300

(a) A few lucky customers have no waiting and a few unlucky ones have to wait over 10 minutes. How long do the middle 50% of the customers have to wait?

(b) (i) If you use the store every day, what will your mean waiting time be? [*Answer:* 2·8 minutes

(ii) You wish to reach the check-out point by 11.15 a.m It is now 11.13 as you pick up your last purchase Are the odds in your favour?

3. From the ogive in Fig. 16, find the 40th percentile. At what percentiles do (a) 500 miles; and (b) 450 miles lie?

CHAPTER XIV

DISPERSION

In Chapter XIII we tried to make a mass of data easier to grasp by describing distributions in terms of representative numbers. With this aim, we calculated an average so as to provide a single figure which was a central point in a group of figures. Unfortunately, averages can give no indication of the spread or *dispersion* of the figures.

For example, there could be two groups, each of four men. In the first group, all the men could be 5 ft 6 in. high, and in the second group they could have heights of 4 ft 6 in., 5 ft, 6 ft and 6 ft 6 in. respectively. Both groups have a *mean* height of 5 ft 6 in., but the variation in height is much greater in one than the other.

It is clearly important to find some way of measuring this dispersion and expressing it as a single figure. Such measures are called *measures of dispersion* (or *variation*) and the most important of them are:

(*a*) the range,
(*b*) the quartile deviation (semi-interquartile range), and
(*c*) the standard deviation.

SECTION 41. RANGE AND QUARTILE DEVIATION

1. Range. This is simply the difference between the highest and the lowest values. Therefore:

$$Range = Highest\ value - Lowest\ value \qquad .. \qquad .. \qquad (10)$$

EXAMPLE
Find the range of the data in Table 8 (as Table 8 is a grouped frequency distribution, reference must be made to the original array, Table 6).
Range = 515 − 403 = 112 miles.

Unfortunately the range has a grave disadvantage: it is too much influenced by extreme values. If, for example, one single salesman in the Table 8 data had travelled 627 miles, the range would have been doubled although the dispersion of the other 119 salesmen would have remained unaltered.

2. Quartile deviation. This disadvantage can be overcome by ignoring the extreme values. One way of doing this is to cut off the top and bottom quartiles, and then see what range is left. This range is called the *interquartile range*. If the interquartile range is divided by 2, the figure obtained is called the *quartile deviation* (*semi-interquartile range*), *i.e.*:

$$Quartile\ deviation = \frac{Third\ quartile\ -\ First\ quartile}{2} \quad .. \quad (11)$$

EXAMPLE

Find the quartile deviation of the figures in Table 8.

The first and third quartiles of Table 8 were calculated in *s.* **38. 3** as $433 \cdot 3$ and $474 \cdot 1$ miles respectively.

$$\therefore\ Quartile\ deviation\ =\ \frac{474 \cdot 1 - 433 \cdot 3}{2}\ =\ 20 \cdot 4\ miles.$$

SECTION 42. STANDARD DEVIATION

1. Standard deviation. This is the most important of the measures. It is computed by finding the square root of the mean of the deviations-from-the-mean squared. It is symbolised as σ (sigma). The formula for the standard deviation is:

$$Standard\ deviation\ (\sigma) = \sqrt{\frac{\Sigma(x - \bar{x})^2}{n}} \quad .. \quad .. \quad (12)$$

or, where the figures form a frequency distribution:

$$\sigma = \sqrt{\frac{\Sigma f\ (x - \bar{x})^2}{\Sigma f}} \quad .. \quad .. \quad .. \quad (13)$$

Although the basic formula for σ remains unchanged, the fact that figures can be presented in different ways and in differing complexities has resulted in four distinct methods of calculation being used. It should be noted, however, that the answer will be the same whichever method is used. The actual method applied will depend on the choice of the student, who will select a method on the basis of the figures in front of him.

2. Method 1: direct method. This is the direct application of the first formula given above.

Find the standard deviation of the following figures: 8, 6, 3, 7, 2, 8, 1, 4, 6 *and* 5.

x	$(x-\bar{x})$	$(x-\bar{x})^2$
8	$+3$	$+9$
6	$+1$	$+1$
3	-2	$+4$
7	$+2$	$+4$
2	-3	$+9$
8	$+3$	$+9$
1	-4	$+16$
4	-1	$+1$
6	$+1$	$+1$
5	0	0

$$\Sigma x = 50 \qquad\qquad \Sigma(x-\bar{x})^2 = 54$$

Applying formula (12):

$$\sigma = \sqrt{\frac{54}{10}} = \sqrt{5\cdot4} = 2\cdot32$$

NOTE: (i) $\bar{x} = 50/10 = 5$.

(ii) That, in squaring, all the minus signs disappear.

Note that the table above could be shortened by converting it into a frequency distribution. This means that the square of the deviation of any value would need to be multiplied by the frequency of that value. The Example would then be re-written as follows:

x	f	$(x-\bar{x})$	$(x-\bar{x})^2$	$f(x-\bar{x})^2$
1	1	-4	16	16
2	1	-3	9	9
3	1	-2	4	4
4	1	-1	1	1
5	1	0	0	0
6	2	$+1$	1	2
7	1	$+2$	4	4
8	2	$+3$	9	18

$$\therefore \Sigma f(x-\bar{x})^2 = 54 \text{ (as}$$
$$\text{— before)}$$

3. Method 2: using an assumed mean. The direct method can be cumbersome if $\bar{x}$ works out at an inconvenient figure. We can avoid the difficulty by taking whatever figure we wish and calling it the *assumed mean*. The formula, for frequency distributions, now becomes:

$$\sigma = \sqrt{\frac{\Sigma fd^2}{\Sigma f} - \left(\frac{\Sigma fd}{\Sigma f}\right)^2} \qquad .. \qquad .. \quad (14)$$

where $d =$ the deviation of each value from the assumed mean, *i.e.* $d = (x - Assumed\ mean)$.

EXAMPLE

Find the standard deviation of the figures in the previous example when they are arranged as a frequency distribution, and using an assumed mean.

Since any figure can be used as assumed mean, let us take 3.

x	f	$d\,(from\ 3)$	fd	fd^2
1	1	-2	-2	4
2	1	-1	-1	1
3	1	0	0	0
4	1	$+1$	$+1$	1
5	1	$+2$	$+2$	4
6	2	$+3$	$+6$	18
7	1	$+4$	$+4$	16
8	2	$+5$	$+10$	50
	$\Sigma f = 10$		$\Sigma fd = +20$	$\Sigma fd^2 = 94$

Applying formula (14):

$$\sigma = \sqrt{\frac{94}{10} - \left(\frac{20}{10}\right)^2} = \sqrt{9 \cdot 4 - 4} = 2 \cdot 32 \text{ (as before).}$$

NOTE: Since the formula calls for fd, it saves an extra calculation if fd is calculated first and fd^2 then obtained by multiplying the fd figure by d, *i.e.* $fd \times d = fd^2$.

4. Method 3: grouped frequency distribution with unequal class intervals. If the standard deviation of a grouped frequency distribution with *unequal* class intervals is required, the above method can be used—with the slight modification that d must be measured as the deviation of the mid-point of the class in question from the assumed mean.

5. Method 4: grouped frequency distribution with equal class intervals. This method is suitable where the figures are in the form of a grouped frequency distribution with *equal* class intervals.

An assumed mean is chosen that is equal to the mid-point of any desired class. Then the deviations d are measured in *whole classes*. To allow for this, the previous formula must be multiplied by the class interval. The full formula becomes:

$$\sigma = \sqrt{\frac{\Sigma fd^2}{\Sigma f} - \left(\frac{\Sigma fd}{\Sigma f}\right)^2} \times \textit{Class interval} \qquad .. \quad (15)$$

where d = deviation from the assumed mean, measured in classes.

The steps in calculating σ by this method are therefore as follows:

(a) Set out five columns headed x, f, d, fd and fd^2.
(b) Enter columns x and f from the data.
(c) Choose any class and enter in column d the deviations from it of other classes, counted in whole classes.
(d) Calculate the fd and fd^2 columns and add these columns.
(e) Apply the formula.

NOTE that since the assumed mean does not appear in the formula we do not need to specify its value. Its function is akin to that of a chemical catalyst: it helps process the end product without becoming part of it.

EXAMPLE
Find the standard deviation of the figures in Table 8.

Choose any class for the purpose of obtaining an assumed mean, say class "440–under 460 miles."

x	f	d (*in whole classes*)	fd	fd^2
400–under 420	12	-2	-24	48
420– ,, 440	27	-1	-27	27
440– ,, 460	34	0	0	0
460– ,, 480	24	$+1$	$+24$	24
480– ,, 500	15	$+2$	$+30$	60
500– ,, 520	8	$+3$	$+24$	72
	$\Sigma f = 120$		$\Sigma fd = +27$	$\Sigma fd^2 = 231$

Applying the formula:

$$= \sqrt{\frac{231}{120} - \left(\frac{+27}{120}\right)^2} \times 20 = \sqrt{\frac{231}{120} - \frac{0.81}{16}} \times 20 \simeq 27 \text{ miles.}$$

6. Variance. This is the name given to the square of the standard deviation, *i.e.* Variance $= \sigma^2$. It is important because variances can be added: for instance, if two distributions had variances of σ_1^2 and σ_2^2 respectively, the variance of the two distributions combined would be $\sigma_1^2 + \sigma_2^2$.

SECTION 43. FEATURES OF THE MEASURES OF DISPERSION

1. Units of the measures of dispersion. It should not be forgotten that the measures of dispersion are in the same units as the variable measured. For example, in Table 8 the units are miles. The range, quartile deviation and standard deviation are therefore all in miles. Had the problem involved a frequency distribution relating to ages of people (measured in years) the measures would all have been in years.

2. Advantages and disadvantages.

(a) *Range*

    (i) Very simple to calculate.

    (ii) Very simple to understand.

    (iii) Used in practice as a measure of disperson in connection with statistical quality control (a technique that employs statistical sampling theory (*see* Part Five) to determine from small samples whether or not the whole output from a process is complying with the required quality standards).

    BUT:

    (iv) Liable to mislead if unrepresentative extreme values occur.

    (v) Fails to indicate the degree of clustering. (For instance, 3, 5, 5, 5, 5, 7 has the same range as 3, 3, 3, 7, 7, 7, but the former group clusters much more closely round the mean.)

(b) *Quartile deviation*

    (i) Simple to understand.

    BUT:

    (ii) Fails to take any account of extreme values.

    (iii) Fails to indicate the degree of clustering.

(c) *Standard deviation*

    (i) Is of greatest value in later statistical work (*see* Part Five).

    (ii) Uses every value in the distribution.

       BUT:

    (iii) Difficult to comprehend.

    (iv) Gives more than proportional weight to extreme values because it squares the deviations (*e.g.* a value twice as far from the mean as another is multiplied by a factor of four—2^2—relative to the latter value).

Of the three measures, the standard deviation is the most important. Although it is virtually impossible to comprehend the significance of the standard deviation at this stage, it is of considerable use in statistics on account of its mathematical relationship to areas under the normal curve (*s.* **54.** 3).

SECTION 44. COEFFICIENT OF VARIATION

It sometimes happens that we need to compare the variability of two or more sets of figures. For example, are the figures in Table 8 more variable than those given in *s.* **42.** 2? The standard deviations are respectively 27 miles and 2·32 units. But these figures are clearly not comparable since, first, they are in different units and, second, they relate to sets of figures of quite different orders of size.

1. Coefficient of variation. We should have some idea of the degree of variability if we could find the size of a variation as compared with the average of the figures it derived from, *i.e.* calculate the standard deviation as a percentage of the mean. This measure is called the *coefficient of variation*. It is expressed by the formula:

$$\text{Coefficient of variation} = \sigma/\bar{x} \times 100 \qquad .. \qquad .. \qquad (16)$$

To compare the variability of two sets of figures would therefore involve comparing their respective coefficients of variation.

EXAMPLE
Compare the variability of the figures in Table 8 with those given in s. **42.** 2.

Table 8   *From* s. **42.** 2

σ	27 miles (*s.* **42.** 5)	2·32
$\bar{\bar{x}}$	454·5 miles (*s.* **32.** 2)	5

Coefficient of variation:

$$\left(\frac{\sigma}{\bar{\bar{x}}} \times 100\right) \qquad 6 \qquad\qquad 46$$

Conclusion: The figures used in *s.* **42.** 2 are very much more variable than those in Table 8.

PROGRESS TEST 14

(*Answers on pages* 265–6)

1. Find the standard deviations of the two distributions in question 1 on p. 91. Which has the greatest relative variability?

2. Find the standard deviation and coefficient of variation of the data in question 2 on p. 92.   [*Answer:* 72·8; 74.

3. Compute the quartile deviation of the following travelling costs:

DAILY TRAVELLING COSTS OF OFFICE STAFF

Pence per day		*Number of staff*
5–under 10		41
10– ,, 15		95
15– ,, 20		202
20– ,, 25		147
Over 25		15

4. Compute the standard deviation of the following data using

(*a*) the "direct method."

(*b*) an assumed mean:

2,450	2,461
2,460	2,449
2,455	2,452
2,441	2,451
2,448	2,455
2,440	2,443
2,452	2,458
2,444	2,463
2,446	2,453
2,459	2,440

[*Answer:* 6·96.

5 What are the main features of:*

    (a) The range.

    (b) The quartile deviation.

    (c) The standard deviation?

CHAPTER XV

SKEWNESS

INCLUDING A SUMMARY OF DISTRIBUTIONS

So far we have looked at two basic types of measure used to summarise a set of figures. Averages are used to give some idea of the *size* of the figures in the set; measures of dispersion are used to indicate the *variability* of the figures. Now we come to a third type of measure, this time concerned with the *symmetry* of the set of figures.

SECTION 45.   SKEWNESS

1. Symmetry and skewness. If the histogram of a grouped frequency distribution is drawn, it usually displays quite low frequencies on the left, builds steadily up to a peak and then drops steadily down to low frequencies again on the right. If the peak is in the centre of the histogram and the slopes on either side are virtually equal to each other, the distribution is said to be *symmetrical* (*see* Fig. 20).

On the other hand, if the peak lies to one or other side of the centre of the histogram, the distribution is said to be *skewed* (*see* Figs. 21 and 22). The further the peak lies from the centre

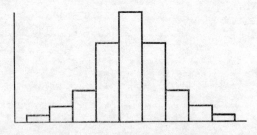

Fig. 20.—*Symmetrical distribution*

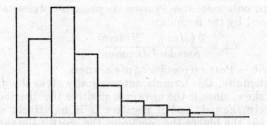

FIG. 21.—*Positive skew*

of the histogram, the more the distribution is said to be skewed.

The skewness of a distribution can be measured as regards:

(a) the *direction* of the skew; and
(b) the *degree* of skew.

2. Direction of the skew. The direction of the skew depends upon the relationship of the peak to the centre of the histogram, and is indicated by the terms *positive* skew and *negative* skew. The skew is *positive* when the peak lies to the left of the centre (*see* Fig. 21) and *negative* when the peak lies to the right of the centre (*see* Fig. 22).

3. Degree of skew. There is more than one way of measuring the degree of skewness, but at this stage the student is advised

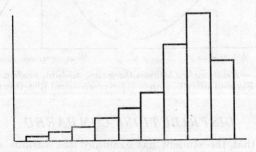

FIG. 22.—*Negative skew*

to learn only one: the *Pearson coefficient of skewness*. It is computed by the formula:

$$Sk = \frac{3\,(Mean - Median)}{Standard\ deviation} \qquad .. \qquad .. \qquad (17)$$

where Sk = Pearson coefficient of skewness.

Incidentally, this formula automatically gives the *direction* of the skew, since if the answer is positive the distribution is positively skewed, and if negative it is negatively skewed. Note that the higher the coefficient the greater the skew. If the distribution is not skewed at all, but symmetrical, the application of the formula will give an answer of zero.

4. Averages of a skewed distribution.

It is worth noting the relationship between the mean, median and mode of a skewed distribution (*see* Fig. 23(*a*)). The mode is always at the peak of the distribution and separated from the mean, which lies on the side of the longer tail, by a distance dependent on the degree of skewness. The median usually lies between the mode and the mean, though it can lie on the mode.

In the case of a symmetrical distribution the student should note that the mean, median and mode all lie at the same point: at the centre of the distribution (*see* Fig. 23(*b*)).

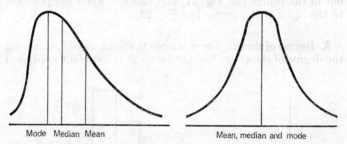

Mode   Median Mean   Mean, median and mode

FIG. 23.—*Relationship between the mean, median, mode and skew*
(*a*) Skewed distribution. (*b*) Symmetrical distribution

DISTRIBUTIONS COMPARED

Now that the student has examined the various ways in which a distribution can be described, it would pay him to select a few distributions and compare the results which follow from using each of the different ways. To this end, the information derived from working with the four distributions that have occurred in the course of Part Three are summarised below.

TABLE 11. COMPARISON OF DISTRIBUTIONS

TABLE:	8 (p. 78)	Question 1 (p. 91)		Question 2 (p. 92)
		School A	School B	
UNITS:	Miles	I.Q. marks	I.Q. marks	Pages
Mean	454·5	109·9	95·3	98·9
Median	452·4	111·5	93·3	83
Mode	448	113*	90·5*	70*
First quartile	433·3	104*	87*	50*
Third quartile	474·1	119*	103·5*	131*
Quartile deviation	20·4	7·5*	8·25*	40·5*
Standard deviation	27	12·2	11·2	72·8
Coefficient of variation	6	11·1	11·75	74
Coefficient of skewness	+0·233	−0·393*	+0·536	+0·657

*Computed for the purpose of this table

PROGRESS TEST 15

(*Answers on page* 266)

1. In earlier chapters we found that Table 8 had a mean of 454·5 miles, a median of 452·4 miles and a standard deviation of 27 miles. What is the direction and degree of skew of this distribution?

2. Compute the coefficient of skewness of the data in question 2 on p. 92, given that the mean is 98·9 pages, the median 83 pages and the standard deviation 72·8 pages.

3. Find the coefficient of skewness for the following branch sales for March 1964:

Sales (£000)	Branches
Under 10	25
10–under 20	18
20– ,, 30	8
30– ,, 40	3
Over 40	1
	—
	55

[*Answer:* +0·577

4. What is the coefficient of skewness of a distribution having a mean of 20, a median of 22 and a standard deviation of 10?

PART FOUR

CORRELATION

CHAPTER XVI

SCATTERGRAPHS

Part Three of this book was devoted to finding measures which described a *single* collection of figures. The fundamental idea now in Part Four is the examination of *two* variables—*i.e.* two collections of figures—and seeing to what extent they are related. Three techniques will be discussed, the scattergraph, regression lines and the coefficient of correlation. In order that the student may compare these techniques the two sets of figures shown in Table 12 will be used throughout for demonstration.

TABLE 12. SALES AND ADVERTISING EXPENDITURE OF THE PQP CO. LTD, 1960–4

Year	Advertising (£000)	Sales (£000)
	x	y
1960	2	60
1961	5	100
1962	4	70
1963	6	90
1964	3	80

SECTION 46. RELATIONSHIP BETWEEN TWO VARIABLES

1. **Degrees of relationship.** If a car owner were to record daily the petrol he used and the miles he covered, he would find a very close relationship between the two sets of figures. As one increased, so would the other. On the other hand, if he compared his daily mileage with, say, the daily number of marriages in New York, he would find there was no relationship at all.

The relationship between miles driven and petrol used is an obvious one, but the relationship between other sets of figures is not usually so obvious. Businessmen have found by experience that there is a definite relationship between advertising and sales, but it is often difficult to say how close the relationship is. A study of the figures in Table 12 will reveal some connection, though an uncertain one, between advertising and sales in the PQP Company. Clearly, some technique is called for to clarify this relationship.

2. Purpose of finding a relationship. Before considering such techniques the student may rightly ask himself, why bother? The answer is that knowledge of the relationship enables us to both *predict* and *control* events.

If we know there is a very close relationship between miles travelled and petrol used, it is possible to predict how much petrol will be required for a given journey—or, conversely, how far it is possible to travel using a given quantity of petrol.

Alternatively, knowledge of the relationship can be used to control car performance, since if the mileage obtained from a particular petrol consumption subsequently drops below what is expected it indicates that the engine is not functioning as it should. An overhaul will probably rectify things and so enable the previous performance figures to be attained once more.

3. Prediction involving time lag. In business the ability to predict one figure from another is particuarly useful if there is a *time lag* between the two sets of figures.

For instance, there is a close relationship between the number of plans passed by a local authority in one year relating to houses to be built, and the number of baths bought the following year. It is possible for suppliers of baths, therefore, to predict their next year's potential sales from this year's local government statistics (*see* also "Suggested answers," Answer 1 to Progress Test 5, for a further example of time lag).

A similar search goes on in the field of national and international economics for relationships involving time lag, since a knowledge of such relationships enables economists to predict the probable future economic position.

4. Independent and dependent variables. When dealing with two variables it is important to know which is the independent variable and which the dependent.

The *independent* variable is the variable which is *not* affected by changes in the other variable.

The *dependent* variable is the variable which *is* affected by changes in the other.

In the case of Table 12, changes in advertising for the year can be expected to affect sales. But a change in the sales will not directly affect advertising expenditure. Thus advertising is the independent variable and sales the dependent.

Sometimes it is not easy to decide which is which. In the case of the car-owner in para. 1, is the independent variable petrol used or miles travelled? In practice, the answer to this sort of question often depends upon the way the data are collected. If predetermined quantities of petrol are put in the tank and the distance travelled is measured, then "petrol used" is the independent variable. If, on the other hand, predetermined distances are driven and the petrol consumption subsequently measured, then the independent variable is "miles travelled."

SECTION 47.   SCATTERGRAPHS

The first technique we shall use to study the relationship between advertising and sales in Table 12 is the scattergraph. A *scattergraph* is a graph with a scale for each variable and upon which variable values are plotted in pairs.

1. Construction.
(a) Construct a graph so that the scale for the independent variable lies along the horizontal axis and the scale of the dependent variable lies on the vertical axis (*see* Fig. 24).
(b) Plot each pair of figures as a single point on the graph. Thus, in Table 12, in 1960 the £2,000 advertising and £60,000 sales form such a pair and therefore a point is plotted on the graph where the £2,000 line from the horizontal scale meets the £60,000 line from the vertical scale.

That is really all there is to a scattergraph. Its basic purpose is to enable us to see whether there is *any pattern among the points*. In the case of the Table 12 data, it is clear there is some pattern, as the points tend to rise from left to

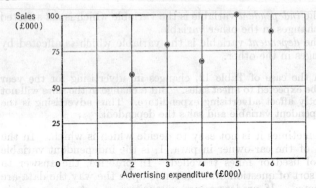

FIG. 24.—*Scattergraph of the data in Table* 12

right (Fig. 24). The more distinct a pattern is, the more closely the two variables will be related in some way.

2. The irrelevance of time. There is one point in connection with scattergraph construction it is vital to appreciate, and that is: *time does not enter into the graph at all*. In the case of the data in Table 12 we are concerned with the relationship between advertising and sales, not *when* these amounts occurred. Thus the points on the scattergraph have no time significance whatsoever.

3. The line of best fit. The value of a scattergraph can be increased by adding the *line of best fit*. This is the line judged to fit best the pattern of the points; it is drawn so as to pass centrally through the group of points (*see* Fig. 25). Since all the points cannot lie on the line, the object is to minimise the total divergence of the points from the line.

4. Estimates from a scattergraph. Once the line of best fit has been inserted, our scattergraph can be used for estimating simply by reading off from the line the sales value corresponding to any level of expenditure on advertising. Supposing £4,500 were to be spent on advertising, it can be seen from the line of best fit that this value is associated with sales of

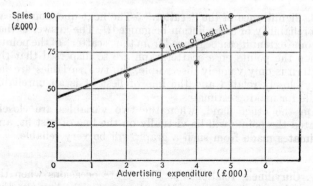

FIG. 25.—*Scattergraph of the data in Table* 12, *with line of best fit added*

£85,000. Therefore £85,000 is the estimated sales to be obtained from an advertising expenditure of £4,500.

NOTE: The value of prediction has been discussed earlier. A prediction is, of course an estimate relating to future events. However, since the techniques we shall be discussing involve estimates relating to past, present and future events, the word "prediction" will give way in the text to the more general word "estimate."

5. **The reliability of estimates.** The student may not be too happy with this estimate. He may well have noticed from the scattergraph that sales nearly as large were once associated with advertising of only £3,000; whereas on another occasion, advertising expenditure of as much as £6,000 brought is only £90,000 worth of sales. How reliable, he may ask, is the estimate of £85,000?

The answer is "Not very." The relationship here between advertising and sales is just not close enough for estimates to be made with great accuracy (as, for example, the estimates discussed earlier relating to petrol and miles would be). Yet it is still true that the *best* estimate we can make about sales, given £4,500 of advertising, is that they will be £85,000, *i.e.* any other figure estimated for sales would be even more subject to error than the £85,000.

6. Significance of the "scatter." The next question is, can the reliability of a prediction be gauged? The answer is that to some extent it can be gauged from the "scatter" of the points. When the points on a scattergraph are so dispersed that the pattern is only vaguely discernible, the two variables are *not* very closely related and the line of best fit is an unreliable guide for making estimates.

On the other hand, when the two variables are closely related the points will lie virtually on the line of best fit, and estimates made from such a graph will be very reliable.

7. Curvilinear relationship. There are occasions when the line of best fit is a curve rather than a straight line (*see* Fig. 26). When the points on a scattergraph lie close to such a

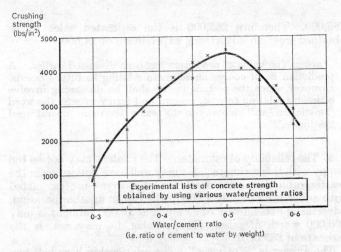

Crushing strength (lbs/in²)

Experimental lists of concrete strength obtained by using various water/cement ratios

Water/cement ratio
(i.e. ratio of cement to water by weight)

Fig. 26.—*Curvilinear relationship*

curve, estimates can be quite reliable. However, this type of relationship (termed *curvilinear*) lies beyond the scope of this book and so will not be discussed further. All the relationships we shall consider will be straight-line, or *linear*, relationships.

8. Limitations of scattergraphs. A thoughtful student may by now have realised that scattergraphs have two serious limitations, namely:

(a) *Uncertainty as to the correct position of the line of best fit.* If the best estimates are to be made from the line of best fit, it must obviously first be drawn in the correct place. So far this has depended on the judgment of the person constructing the graph. It would be much better if a mathematical method of drawing the line could be devised instead of leaving it to the artistic whim of the individual.

(b) *Lack of a measure of the closeness of the relationship.* Since the reliability of an estimate depends heavily on the closeness of the relationship between variables, the lack of any measure of the closeness limits the value of scattergraphs considerably.

The next two chapters are concerned with ways of overcoming each of these limitations.

PROGRESS TEST 16
(*Answers on pages* 267–8)

1. The I.Q.'s of a group of six people were measured, and they then sat a certain examination. Their I.Q.'s and examination marks were as follows:

Person	I.Q.	Exam. marks
A	110	70
B	100	60
C	140	80
D	120	60
E	80	10
F	90	20

Construct a scattergraph of these data, and draw the line of best fit.

(a) What marks do you estimate a candidate with an I.Q. of 130 would obtain?

(b) Estimate the I.Q. of a candidate who obtained a mark of 77.

2. Two dice were thrown and the sum of their pips doubled to give "dice value." At the same time a card was drawn at random out of a normal pack from which all court cards had been removed. The value of this card was called the "card value."

Throw	Dice value	Card value
1st	8	8
2nd	8	9
3rd	14	10
4th	22	5
5th	22	8
6th	16	3
7th	12	3
8th	6	2
9th	10	7
10th	10	5

Construct a scattergraph of these data. Is it possible to draw a line of best fit? What conclusions can you draw about the two variables?

CHAPTER XVII

REGRESSION LINES

NOTE: It is not necessary to study this chapter to understand the rest of the book. Students who are not required to study regression lines may turn at once to the next chapter.

At the end of the last chapter it was pointed out that a line of best fit drawn by eye is dependent upon the subjective judgment of the person who draws it. Consequently the position of the line will differ slightly from person to person. A line of best fit independent of individual judgment will have to be drawn mathematically. Such a line is called a *regression line*.

SECTION 48. COMPUTING REGRESSION LINES

1. Equation of the line. The general equation for any straight line on a graph is

$$y = a + bx \qquad .. \qquad .. \qquad .. \qquad (18)$$

where *a* and *b* are constants. Describing the line of best fit means, therefore, finding the appropriate values of *a* and *b*.

NOTE: It is assumed that students know this equation. To revise briefly, the *a* and the *b* are similar to the components of a two-part electrical tariff where there is a fixed charge per quarter of £*a* and a further charge of £*b* per unit of electricity used. If *x* is the number of units used in a quarter, then *y* (the total charge) = £*a* + £*b* × *x*, or *y* = *a* + *bx*. All straight lines on graphs can be expressed in this way, using appropriate values for *a* and *b*. So, to describe any line, it is only necessary to find the *a* and *b* associated with that line.

2. The method of least squares. When drawing a line of best fit, an attempt is made to minimise the total divergence of the points from the line (*see s.* **47.** 3). In computing the line mathematically, the same idea is pursued, only it has been found that the best line is one that minimises the total of the *squared* deviations. This approach is logically known as the *method of least squares*.

3. Measuring the deviations. When it comes to measuring the deviations of the points from the line, it is important to understand that statisticians do *not* measure the shortest distance between a point and the line of best fit. What they measure is either

    (*a*) the *vertical* distance between point and line, or
    (*b*) the *horizontal* distance (*see* Fig. 27).

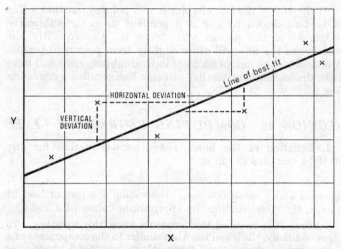

FIG. 27.—*Measuring horizontal and vertical deviations from the line of best fit*

These two different ways of measuring the deviations will produce *two different regression lines*—one minimising the total of the squared deviations measured vertically; the other minimising the total of the squared deviations measured horizontally.

This can be rather confusing, so for the moment only the calculations needed to determine regression lines will be considered. The distinction between them will be dealt with in *s.* **49.**

First, let us take the regression line in which deviations are measured vertically.   This is by far the commoner of the two.

4. The regression of *y* on *x*.

In order to find *a* and *b* in equation (18) it is necessary to solve two simultaneous equations.   They are:

$$\Sigma y = an + b\Sigma x \qquad .. \qquad .. \qquad .. \qquad (19)$$

$$\Sigma xy = a\Sigma x + b\Sigma x^2 \qquad .. \qquad .. \qquad .. \qquad (20)$$

where *n* = the number of *pairs* of figures.

Although these may appear formidable both to remember and use, they look worse than they really are (*see* NOTE, p. 142).

To help remember them, notice that the first equation is very similar to equation (18) while the second is similar to the first except there is an extra *x* somehow introduced into each term (while the *n* vanishes).   To demonstrate their use, the data of Table 12 will be employed (it will be noticed that the advertising column is already headed *x* and the sales column *y*).

EXAMPLE

Examination of the two equations shows that the only figures required are Σy, Σx, Σxy, Σx^2 and *n*; *n* in this case being 5, as there are five pairs of figures.   The other four figures can be quickly obtained by laying out the data in tabular form:

From Table 12		Computed	
x	*y*	*yx*	x^2
2	60	120	4
5	100	500	25
4	70	280	16
6	90	540	36
3	80	240	9
$\Sigma x = 20$	$\Sigma y = 400$	$\Sigma xy = 1,680$	$\Sigma x^2 = 90$

It only remains now to insert these values into the two equations and solve for *a* and *b*:

(19) $400 = a \times 5 + b \times 20$
(20) $1,680 = a \times 20 + b \times 90$

To solve:

Multiply equation (19) by 4, *i.e.* $1,600 = 20a + 80b$

Multiply equation (20) by 1, *i.e.* $1,680 = 20a + 90b$

Subtracting upper from lower: $80 = 10b$

$$\therefore \ b = 8$$

Now substitute 8 for b in equation (19), *i.e.*

$$400 = 5a + 8 \times 20$$
$$\therefore \ 5a = 400 - 160 = 240$$
$$\therefore \ a = 48$$

The regression line, therefore, is $y = a + bx = 48 + 8x$.

This line is known as the *regression line of y on x* and is the line of best fit when the deviations are measured vertically.

NOTE: Students who doubt their ability to solve simultaneous equations can derive a and b from these two formulae:

$$a = \frac{\Sigma y - b \times \Sigma x}{n}$$

$$b = \frac{n \times \Sigma xy - \Sigma x \times \Sigma y}{n \times \Sigma x^2 - (\Sigma x)^2}$$

5. The regression of x on y. If it is desired to compute the second regression line, known as the *regression line of x on y*, it is only necessary to alter the two simultaneous equations so that the x's and y's are interchanged. The equations therefore become:

$$\Sigma x = an + b\Sigma y \quad .. \quad .. \quad .. \quad (21)$$

$$\Sigma xy = a\Sigma y + b\Sigma y^2 \quad .. \quad .. \quad .. \quad (22)$$

EXAMPLE

Taking the data in Table 12 again, the only new figure required is Σy^2. This comes to 33,000, as the student can easily check. Therefore the equations are:

(21) $20 = a \times 5 + b \times 400$

(22) $1,680 = a \times 400 + b \times 33,000$

To solve:

Multiply equation (21) by 80, *i.e.* $1,600 = 400a + 32,000b$

Multiply equation (22) by 1, *i.e.* $\ \ 1,680 = 400a + 33,000b$

Subtracting upper from lower: $80 = 1,000b$

$$\therefore \ b = 0 \cdot 08$$

Substituting $0 \cdot 08$ for b in equation (21):

$$20 = 5a + 0 \cdot 08 \times 400$$
$$\therefore 20 = 5a + 32$$
$$\therefore \ a = -2 \cdot 4$$

Therefore the equation of the line is $x = -2 \cdot 4 + 0 \cdot 08y$.

This equation is *not* merely the previous one turned round. It is quite different, as the student can prove for himself if he wishes.

6. Graphing regression lines. It is quite easy to graph the regression lines once they have been computed. All one has to do is:

(a) choose any two values (preferably well apart) for the unknown variable on the right-hand side of the equation,

(b) compute the other variable,

(c) plot the two pairs of values, and

(d) draw a straight line through the plotted points.

EXAMPLE

Graph of regression lines for Table 12 as computed above:

(a) *Regression line of y on x*
  (i) Let $x = £6,000$
    ∴ $y = 48 + 8 \times 6$ (remember, x was in '000s)
      $= £96,000$ (y too was in '000s)
  (ii) Let $x = £0$
    ∴ $y = 48 + 0$
      $= £48,000$

These points, and the regression line through them, are shown in Fig. 28.

(b) *Regression line of x on y*
  (i) Let $y = £100,000$
    ∴ $x = -2 \cdot 4 + 0 \cdot 08 \times 100$
      $= \underline{\underline{£5,600}}$
  (ii) Let $y = £50,000$
    ∴ $x = -2 \cdot 4 + 0 \cdot 08 \times 50$
      $= \underline{\underline{£1,600}}$

Again, these points, and the regression line through them, are shown in Fig. 28.

SECTION 49. THE USE OF REGRESSION LINES

1. Use of the regression line of *y* on *x*. Use of the regression line first calculated in *s*. 48 is quite simple. To revert to our advertising figures (Table 12), it is only necessary to replace x in the equation by a value for advertising to obtain an estimate of the sales, y. If we again take an advertising figure of £4,500, the estimated sales will be:

$$y = 48 + 8 \times 4\frac{1}{2}$$
$$= 48 + 36 = 84, \text{ } i.e. \text{ sales of £84,000.}$$

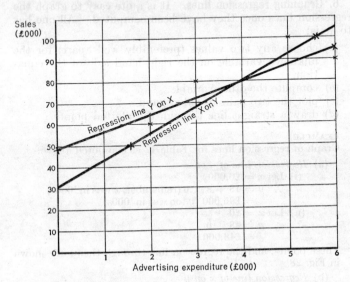

FIG. 28.—*Regression lines of the data in Table 12*

NOTE as a point of interest that the regression lines intersect at the *means of the series*—here, £4,000 and £80,000

2. Use of the regression line of x on y. In a similar way the regression line of x on y is used to estimate the value of x that follows from any given value of y. In the example so far discussed, it means estimating the advertising that would be associated with any given sales value. If, for example, sales had been £84,000, the advertising estimated to have been incurred would be:

$$x = -2 \cdot 4 + 0 \cdot 08 \times 84$$
$$= 4 \cdot 32, \text{ } i.e. \text{ £4,320.}$$

It will be seen that this is a different figure from the £4,500 advertising that gave an estimated £84,000 sales. This paradox is one of the reasons why regression lines seem so confusing to students.

3. The regression line paradox. In para. 2 an advertising expenditure of £4,320 was estimated to have been incurred, given a sales value of £84,000. Yet in para. 1, £84,000 was the estimated sales value of £4,500 of advertising. Why isn't a sales value of £84,000 associated with a single advertising figure? The reason is not easy to grasp, but some insight into the underlying reason may be gathered from the following explanation.

If the *highest* advertising value was incurred, would it be wise to predict a sales value equal to the highest recorded? Obviously not, since the highest advertising (£6,000) was associated with a sales value of only £90,000, *i.e.* £10,000 below the maximum. A better off-hand estimate would probably be around the amount actually attained—£90,000. Now if sales were £90,000, and we were unaware of the actual level of advertising expenditure, would it be wise to estimate that the highest advertising had been incurred? Since, on one occasion, sales of £100,000 followed an advertising expenditure of only £5,000, this too would be foolish. An estimate of advertising below the maximum would be more sensible.

All this means is that *given* the maximum advertising, an *estimate* of below-maximum sales is made; but *given* this specific sales figure, an *estimate* of *below* maximum advertising must be made. The "given" figure and the "estimate" *cannot be interchanged.* In other words, if an advertising figure of £s leads to an estimate of £t sales, you cannot, on learning that in a certain year sales of £t were made, estimate advertising to have been £s.

Regression lines are like one-way streets: you can only move in the authorised direction. If you want to reverse direction you must move across to the other regression line.

4. Choice of regression line. We have seen that there are two regression lines and that it is important to choose the right one. The next problem is *how* to choose the right one. Luckily the answer is quite simple: always use the line that has *the variable to be estimated on the left-hand side of the equation*. If the y variable is to be estimated, use the $y = a + bx$ ("y on x") line; if x is to be estimated, use the $x = a + by$ ("x on y") line.

5. Reliability of estimates. Although we have just been through a quite lengthy procedure for obtaining estimated values, it is important to realise that such estimates are no more reliable than those derived from a well constructed scattergraph. It simply ensures that the scattergraph *is* well constructed. The reliability of estimates depends far more on the closeness of the relationship of the figures between the variables than on the most elaborate mathematical calculations. The only reason for computing a regression line is to obtain a line of best fit free of subjective judgment (it must be admitted, though, that the regression line does improve the estimate to the extent that it obviates the possibility of a badly judged line of best fit).

A more important reason, though it does not concern us here, is that in advanced statistics the reliability of estimates made from such a line can be measured mathematically.

6. Regression coefficient. This term occasionally arises in statistical discussion. This is simply the value of b in the equations just discussed. For example, in the case of the regression of sales on advertising, the regression coefficient was 8 and in the case of the regression of advertising on sales it was $0 \cdot 08$.

PROGRESS TEST 17
(Answers on pages 268–71)

1. Determine the regression lines relating to the data in question 1 on p. 137 and estimate (*a*) the marks that would be obtained by a candidate with an I.Q. of 130, (*b*) the I.Q. of a candidate who obtained 77 marks.
Superimpose these lines on the scattergraph constructed for question 1 on p. 137.

2. Using the data in question 2 on p. 138:

(a) Compute the regression line of card value on dice value and use this line to determine the best estimate of the card value that would be associated with a dice value of (i) 4, (ii) 24.

(b) Compute the regression line of dice value on card value and use the line to determine the best estimate of the dice value that would be associated with a card value of (i) 1; (ii) 10.

(Can you now appreciate why it is necessary to compute two regression lines—one for estimating a y value from an x value, and the other an x value from a y value?)

Superimpose these regression lines on the scattergraph constructed for question 2 on p. 138.

CHAPTER XVIII

CORRELATION

We now consider the second limitation of scattergraphs mentioned at the end of Chapter XVI. There it was pointed out that the reliability of an estimate depended on the closeness of the relationship between two variables and that a measure of this closeness was essential for assessing reliability. The *coefficient of correlation* is such a measure. There are different measures of correlation, but the most generally used is one called the *Pearson product-moment coefficient of correlation*, commonly symbolised as *r*.

SECTION 50. COMPUTATION OF r

1. Formula. The formula for calculating *r* can be expressed in a number of ways. The most practical is:

$$r = \frac{\Sigma xy - n\bar{x}\bar{y}}{n\,\sigma_x\,\sigma_y} \qquad .. \quad .. \quad .. \quad (23)$$

where $n =$ the number of pairs.

2. Procedure. Examination of formula (23) indicates that to find *r* the following steps should be taken:

(a) Calculate the means of each series of figures ($\bar{x}$ and $\bar{y}$).
(b) Calculate the standard deviations of each series (σ_x and σ_y).
(c) Calculate Σxy, in other words multiply each number in the first series with its counterpart in the other (*i.e.* multiply pairs together) and then add the products.
(d) Apply the formula.

EXAMPLE
Find r *of the data in Table* 12.
  (a) Find the means.

x (advertising)	y (sales)
2	60
5	100
4	70
6	90
3	80

$$\Sigma x = 20 \qquad\qquad \Sigma y = 400$$

$$\therefore \bar{x} = \frac{20}{5} = 4 \qquad\qquad \therefore \bar{y} = \frac{400}{5} = 80$$

(b) Find the standard deviations. Since the means here are round numbers, the easiest method of calculating the standard deviations is by the "direct method" (see s. **42. 2**):

x	$x-\bar{x}$	$(x-\bar{x})^2$	y	$y-\bar{y}$	$(y-\bar{y})^2$
2	−2	4	60	−20	400
5	+1	1	100	+20	400
4	0	0	70	−10	100
6	+2	4	90	+10	100
3	−1	1	80	0	0

$$\Sigma(x-\bar{x})^2 = 10 \qquad\qquad \Sigma(y-\bar{y})^2 = 1{,}000$$

$$\therefore \sigma_x = \sqrt{\frac{10}{5}} = \sqrt{2} \qquad\qquad \therefore \sigma_y = \sqrt{\frac{1{,}000}{5}} = \sqrt{200}$$

(c) Find Σxy.

x	y	xy
2	60	120
5	100	500
4	70	280
6	90	540
3	80	240

$$\Sigma xy = 1{,}680$$

(d) Apply formula (23):

$$\frac{1{,}680 - 5 \times 4 \times 80}{5 \times \sqrt{2} \times \sqrt{200}} = \frac{1{,}680 - 1{,}600}{5 \times \sqrt{400}} = 0\cdot8$$

NOTE: r is not expressed in any units.

The computation of r is rather a lengthy business, but provided the formula is known it is not particularly involved. It is simply a matter of computing three distinct sets of figures and then using them in the formula.

SECTION 51. INTERPRETATION OF r

1. Need for experience. It has been repeatedly emphasised
that the reliability of estimates depends upon the closeness of
the relationship between two sets of figures; now that we have
a measurement of this closeness, the student is probably keen
to learn how to interpret this figure—particularly in assessing
the reliability of estimates.

Unfortunately, its interpretation depends very much on
experience. The full significance of r will only be grasped
after working on a number of correlation problems and seeing
the kinds of data which give rise to various values of r. Until
this experience has been gained the student would be wise to
interpret r very cautiously and to restrict such interpretation
to the most general terms. However, to give him a little
insight into the significance of r, its interpretation will now be
discussed in just such general terms.

2. Phrases to describe correlation. Before we examine the
numerical significance of r it would be advisable to define
certain phrases that are commonly used to describe correlation. Even better than verbal description are actual examples
shown on a scattergraph, and the degrees of correlation listed
below are illustrated in Fig. 29.

(a) *Positive correlation.*—Normally, when an increase in one
variable is associated with an increase in the other (*e.g.*
advertising and sales).

(b) *Negative correlation.*—Normally, when an increase in one
variable is associated with a decrease in the other (*e.g.*
TV registrations and cinema attendance).

(c) *Perfect correlation.*—When a change in one variable is
matched by a change of equal degree in the other
variable. If both increase or decrease together, it is
perfect positive correlation; if one decreases as the other
increases, it is *perfect negative correlation*. Perfect
correlation only exists when all the points of a scattergraph lie on the line of best fit.

(d) *High correlation.*—When a change in one variable is usually
associated with a change of a similar, but not equal,
degree in the other (*e.g.* petrol used and miles travelled).

(e) *Low correlation.*—When a change in one variable is

rarely associated with a change of similar degree in the other (*e.g.* holiday makers and marriage ceremonies).

(f) *Zero correlation.*—Here the variables are not correlated at all, and there is no relationship between changes in one variable and changes in the other (*e.g.* London bus fares and New York rainfall).

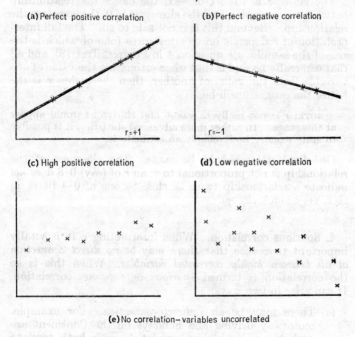

(a) Perfect positive correlation

r = +1

(b) Perfect negative correlation

r = -1

(c) High positive correlation

(d) Low negative correlation

(e) No correlation—variables uncorrelated

r = 0

FIG. 29 —*Types of correlation*

3. Numerical values of *r*. The formula for *r* is such that its value always lies between −1 and +1.

+1 means there is *perfect positive* correlation.

−1 means there is *perfect negative* correlation.

0 means that the variables are *uncorrelated*.

The closer *r* is to +1 or −1, the closer the relationship between the variables; and the closer *r* is to 0, the less close the relationship. Beyond this it is not safe to go. The full interpretation of *r* depends on circumstances (one of which is the size of the sample: *see* question 4 in Progress Test 18), and all that can really be said is that when estimating the value of one variable from the value of another, then the higher *r* is the better the estimate will be.

NOTE: *r* is not really as vague and elusive as would appear at this stage. In rather more advanced statistics, it is possible to state exactly how reliable an estimate is.

One final point should be made. The closeness of the relationship is not proportional to *r*: an *r* of (say) 0·8 does *not* indicate a relationship twice as close as one of 0·4 (it is, in fact, very much closer).

4. Spurious correlation. When interpreting *r* it is vitally important to realise that there *may be no direct connection at all between highly correlated variables*. When this is so the correlation is termed *spurious* or *nonsense* correlation. It can arise in two ways:

(a) There may be an *indirect connection*. For example, motorway driving and holidays on the Continent are probably quite highly correlated, since both tend to increase with a rising standard of living. To draw the conclusion that motorway driving *causes* Continental holidays or vice versa would be quite wrong, and a decision (say) by the Chancellor of the Exchequer to close Britain's motorways as a part of a campaign to reduce British expenditure abroad would be ridiculous.

(b) There may be a *series of coincidences*. Normally, spurious correlation cannot arise in the course of properly conducted statistical work. Laymen, however, sometimes fall into this trap. They examine the series relating to the variable they wish to predict—say the weather in June—and then hunt about amidst all sorts of data looking for a series that correlates highly with this variable. Needless to say, it is quite likely that one set of data out of the hundreds at hand will fit, even if it is something as unlikely as the number of divorces in January. Then they draw everyone's attention to the high correlation and proceed to predict June weather on the basis of it. Such predictions are, of course, quite unreliable.

5. Correlation and regression lines. Those who read Chapter XVII will probably be interested to know that the higher the correlation, the smaller the angle between the two regression lines. In the case of perfect correlation (positive or negative) the two lines will coincide and there will be only one line.

Conversely, the lower the correlation, the greater the angle between the two lines—until, when r is zero, the lines lie at right angles to each other. The "y on x" line will be quite horizontal and the "x on y" line vertical.

SECTION 52. RANK CORRELATION (r')

1. Ranking. In some sets of data the actual values are not given, only the order in which the items are ranked.

EXAMPLE

The examination results in Physics and French of a class of seven boys could be given as places, *e.g.*:

Boy	Physics	French
Allen	3	1
Birch	2	4
Clark	1	2
Davis	4	3
Evans	6	5
Ford	5	7
Gregory	7	6

2. Computation of rank correlation. Although r could be computed by using formula (23) and treating such rankings as the usual x and y series of figures, a quicker way is to use the following formula:

$$r' = 1 - \frac{6 \ \Sigma d^2}{n(n^2 - 1)} \quad .. \quad .. \quad .. \quad (24)$$

where $r' = $ the coefficient of rank correlation and

$\qquad d = $ the difference between the rankings of the same item in each series.

The computation of r' in the above Example is, therefore:

Physics rank	French rank	d	d²
3	1	2	4
2	4	2	4
1	2	1	1
4	3	1	1
6	5	1	1
5	7	2	4
7	6	1	1

$$\Sigma d^2 = 16$$

Applying formula (24):

$$r' = 1 - \frac{6 \times 16}{7(7^2 - 1)} = \frac{5}{7} = 0 \cdot 714$$

r' is, of course, interpreted in just the same way as r.

3. Notes on r'.

(a) Since there is some loss of information when rankings only are given, r' is not as accurate as the figure that would be obtained by calculating r from the full sets of marks in both examinations.

(b) Taking the rankings just given, the student should compute the coefficient of correlation between them, using the usual formula (23), and prove to his own satisfaction that the answer is the same as above.

PROGRESS TEST 18
(*Answers on pages* 271–5)

1. Compute the coefficient of correlation for the data in question 1 on p. 137.

2. Compute the coefficient of correlation for the data in question 2 on p. 138 and state what type of correlation exists between the two sets of figures.

3. Lay out the data in question 1 on p. 137 in the form of rankings and compute the rank correlation. Why does the correlation figure obtained not equal the figure obtained in the answer to question 1?

4. Determine the coefficient of correlation for the data in the following table:

Year	x	y
1962	5	17
1963	75	19

[*Answer* +1.

(Can you explain why your answer comes to this rather unexpected figure. What conclusion can you draw from this exercise regarding the interpretation of *r* in small samples?)

5. In the course of a survey relating to examination success, you have discovered a high *negative* correlation between students' hours of study and their examination marks. This is so at variance with common sense that it has been suggested an error has been made. Do you agree?*

SAMPLING THEORY

PART FIVE

SAMPLING THEORY

CHAPTER XIX

THE NORMAL CURVE OF DISTRIBUTION

SECTION 53.   THE ROLE OF SAMPLES

1. From sample to population. So far, our statistical studies have concentrated on maximising our comprehension of the groups of figures we have collected. Now we go a step further: to maximise our comprehension, not just of the figures we collect, but of *the populations we collect them from.* Indeed, this is more a leap than a step, for consider what it implies. What we have been doing so far has been to take, say, a collection of cars in a garage and find ways of describing the cars we see. Now we shall be looking at the cars in a garage and, on the basis of that sample, describing *all* cars: including the millions we cannot see.

2. Basic points. On the face of it, an attempt to formulate an all-embracing description from a tiny fraction of the total population can be no more than rash guesswork. But this is not so. There are a number of statistical laws which govern the kind of distribution usual in such work and which will ensure that our descriptions have a scientific basis. The most important of these laws—those relating to the normal curve of distribution—are examined in this chapter.

Two things, however, do need emphasising:

(*a*) Our samples *must* be random samples, otherwise we run the risk of serious error.

(*b*) We can never be absolutely certain our descriptions are correct. This means that every time we offer a description *we must indicate the probability of our description being in error.*

3. Warning and advice.

(a) *Warning:* the theory explained in this Part is subject to certain adjustments when sample sizes are small (say below 50). Therefore in this Part *large sample sizes are implied throughout.*

(b) *Advice:* revise *ss.* **28, 29** and **42** before reading any further.

SECTION 54. THE NORMAL CURVE OF DISTRIBUTION

1. Mathematical curves. Students may recall from their school algebra that curves drawn on a graph could be described by purely mathematical expressions such as $y = 10x^2 + 6x + 3$ and, because these curves were mathematical, facts about the graph could be *calculated*.

One important group of facts that can be calculated in this way concerns the area contained by the curve, and other given parts of the graph.

The task of handling statistical data can often be simplified if a mathematical curve can be found approximating to that which would be produced by plotting the actual data on a graph. By substituting the mathematical curve for the real one, we can make calculations to reveal facts about the distribution of the raw data, facts that would otherwise have been difficult to determine.

2. The normal curve of distribution. Students who have drawn a number of histograms may have been struck by the frequent recurrence of a pattern in which there is a high column in the centre of the histogram, with decreasing columns spread symmetrically on either side. If the class intervals were small enough, the frequency curve probably looked rather like a cross-section of a bell. Now it so happens that this pattern does in fact occur frequently in statistical work. There also happens to be a mathematical curve very similar to it, called the *normal curve of distribution*. It has the following features (*see* Fig. 30):

(a) It is symmetrical.
(b) It is bell-shaped.
(c) Its mean lies at the peak of the curve.
(d) The two tails never actually touch the horizontal axis, although they continuously approach it.
(e) The formula for the curve is:

$$y = \frac{1}{\sigma\sqrt{2\pi}} \; e^{-\frac{1}{2}\left(\frac{x-\bar{x}}{\sigma}\right)^2} \qquad .. \qquad .. \qquad (25)$$

but students may ignore it completely at this stage, as any mathematical data relating to the curve can easily be found in mathematical tables. What *is* important is that the mathematical properties of the curve apply equally to the actual curve of the "raw" data. In particular, areas of the graph that lie below the normal curve will correspond to areas below the actual curve.

But NOTE the inclusion of σ. It is because σ forms part of the normal curve of distribution formula that the standard deviation is so important in statistics.

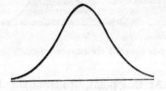

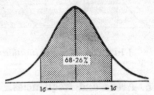

Fig. 30.—*Normal curve of distribution*

Fig. 31.—*Area enclosed between the 1 σ points*

3. Areas below the normal curve of distribution. There is a distinct relationship between σ and the areas under a normal curve. This relationship is such that if we:

(*a*) erect a line at the centre of the curve (*i.e.* at the mean),
(*b*) measure off 1σ lengths either side of this central line,
(*c*) erect perpendicular lines at these points,

then the area enclosed between the curve, the 1σ vertical lines and the axis is $68 \cdot 26\%$ of the total area enclosed by the whole curve (*see* Fig. 31). Of course, since the curve is symmetrical, the area between the central line and each 1σ line is half this value, *i.e.* $34 \cdot 13\%$.

Mathematicians can, in fact, compute the area that lies between *any* two lines, the curve and the axis—always measuring along the axis in units of σ. Obviously a table of such areas is of considerable value, and one is given in Appendix II. In this table the area between the central line, the curve, the axis and a line measured from the mean in units of σ is given as a decimal of the total area enclosed by the curve. For instance, if the line lies $1\frac{1}{2}\sigma$ from the mean, the table shows that the area enclosed is $0\cdot4332$ (*i.e.* $43\cdot32\%$) of the total area.

4. Normal curve values to be learnt. The student is advised to learn three normal curve values: those relating to the approximate areas between each pair of 1σ, 2σ and 3σ lines as shown in Fig. 32. Note that almost the entire area lies within 3σ of the mean.

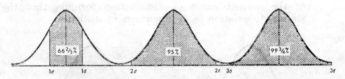

FIG. 32.—*Approximate areas beneath the normal curve*

5. Areas and frequencies. At this point, students should cast their mind back to *ss.* 28 and 29, where we discussed histograms and frequency curves. There, it was emphasised that, on graphs of distributions, areas were proportional to frequencies. This means that an area of $66\frac{2}{3}\%$ of the total area is equivalent to a frequency figure which is $66\frac{2}{3}\%$ of the total frequency. It is, therefore, quite in order to use the area values as a basis for determining frequency figures.

6. Application of the normal curve of distribution to an actual distribution. If an actual distribution has a curve similar to a normal curve, we say that the data are *normally distributed*. When we have such a distribution the area values relating to a normal curve will apply to the distribution. Thus we only have to compute the mean and standard deviation of the distribution in order to equip ourselves for determining how much of the distribution lies between any given points.

Let us now see what this means in terms of actual figures. In Part Three we found that Table 8 had a mean of $454\frac{1}{2}$ miles and a standard deviation of 27 miles. Applying the area figures of the normal curve of distribution, this means that 66⅔% of the mileages will lie between 454½ + 27 miles and 454½ − 27 miles, *i.e.* 427½ and 481½ miles. (These estimates can be checked from the ungrouped frequency distribution in Table 7, which reveals that 78 mileages lay between these limits, *i.e.* 78/120 × 100 = 65%. This is not the 66⅔% expected, but the difference arises because the Table 8 distribution doesn't quite follow a normal curve—it is slightly skewed.) Similarly, 95% will theoretically lie between the 2σ lines, *i.e.* between 454½ + 2 × 27 and 454½ − 2 × 27 = 400½ and 508½ miles (although 120 mileages really constitute too small a distribution for testing the theoretical figures).

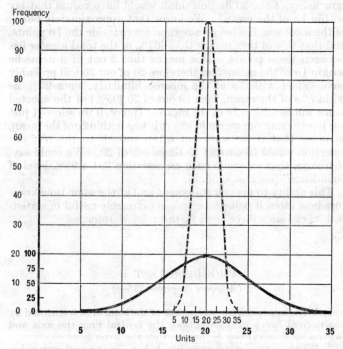

FIG. 33.—*Normal curve of distribution for a distribution having a mean of 20 units and a standard deviation of 5 units plotted twice on different scales*

Compare with Fig. 30, where the normal **curve can be** seen looking the usual shape

7. Recognising a normal curve. Students are warned that normal curves of distribution are not always immediately recognisable. Basically, they are always bell-shaped, but the "bell" may be very flat and broad or tall and thin, as shown in Fig. 33. Study of *s.* **12.** 1 will indicate the reason for these extremes: they are due simply to the stretching or compressing of the scales.

8. Probability and the normal curve. Suppose that 30 items were selected *at random* from a large normal distribution: how many of the 30 do you think would have values that lay within 1σ of the mean? We know that approximately $66\frac{2}{3}\%$ of the total area lies below a normal curve inside the 1σ points, and that this in turn means that $66\frac{2}{3}\%$ of the total *number* lies between these points. This means that 2 out of 3 items lie within 1σ of the mean, and therefore 20 of our 30 will probably have values with 1σ of the mean. Similarly, since 95% lie within 2σ of the mean, then 19 out of 20 (95%) of the selected items will be within 2σ of the mean. Hence, if we selected just *one* item at random we could assert it was within 2σ of the mean, knowing that if we were put often enough to the test our assertion would be correct 19 times out of 20. We could say, therefore, that we made such an assertion "at a 95% level of confidence" (*see* also *s.* **56.** 3).

This ability to make a statement and at the same time know just how often it will prove true is extremely useful in statistical work—as will be seen in the next chapter.

PROGRESS TEST 19
(*Answers on pages 275–6*)

1. What approximate percentage of the total area is enclosed by the normal curve of distribution, the central line, the axis and (*a*) the 2σ line, (*b*) the 3σ line and (*c*) the $2\cdot6\sigma$ line?

2. What approximate area lies below the normal curve between:

    (*a*) the lower 1σ and lower 2σ lines,
    (*b*) the lower 1σ and upper 2σ lines,
    (*c*) the lower 2σ and upper 3σ lines,
    (*d*) the lower $2\cdot6\sigma$ and upper $2\cdot6\sigma$ lines?

3. What approximate area lies below the normal curve of distribution and *outside* (a) 1σ lines, (b) 2σ lines and (c) 3σ lines?

4. Assuming that 10,000 items are normally distributed and that the distribution has a mean of 115 lbs and a standard deviation of 3 lbs:

(a) How many items have weights between: (i) 115 and 118 lbs, (ii) 112 and 115 lbs, (iii) 109 and 121 lbs, (iv) 106 and 124 lbs?

(b) If you had to pick one item at random from the whole 10,000 items, how confident would you be in predicting that its value would lie between 109 and 121 lbs?

CHAPTER XX

ESTIMATION

So far all we have found is that many distributions are what is termed normal and that, knowing the mean and standard deviation, it is possible to say how many items lie between various limits. Our next step is to see how we can apply this knowledge to samples and populations.

SECTION 55. THE STANDARD ERROR OF THE MEAN

1. The distribution of a sample. Let us assume there is a population about which we know nothing except that it exists. Unknown to us, it is normally distributed, with a mean of 20 units and a standard deviation of 5 units. In order to learn something about this population we take a random sample and graph the distribution. How will it look?

We know that in any normal distribution 1 in every 3 items will lie between the lower 1σ and the mean, *i.e.* 15 and 20 in this case. Clearly, then, in any random sample approximately 1 out of every 3 items will also lie between 15 and 20, *i.e.* $33\frac{1}{3}\%$ of the distribution of the sample. Similarly, approximately $33\frac{1}{3}\%$ of the sample items will lie between 20 and 25, 14% between 10 and 15, 14% between 25 and 30, *etc.* (*see* Fig. 34). Now let us argue backwards and say that if a normal distribution has a particular pattern as regards areas, then any distribution having such a pattern must be normally distributed (remember, a normal distribution is simply one in which the frequency curve approximates to a particular mathematical curve). This means that *the distribution of our sample is also normally distributed* (occasionally, one-sided samples will be taken, but this will be rare). Moreover, since this distribution is such that $33\frac{1}{3}\%$ of the sample items lie between 15 and 20, *etc.* it is clear that our sample standard deviation will be 5 and our sample mean will be 20.

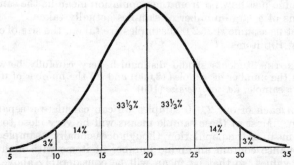

Fig. 34.—*Distribution of a sample taken at random from a population with a mean of 20 and σ of 5 units. Approximate percentages only*

However, there is just one qualification to this. We ended the argument by assuming that the proportions of sample items between various limits matched those of the population exactly. In practice our sample will *not* be an exact miniature replica of the population—no sample ever is. Chance plays a big part in the selection of items in a sample; inevitably the sample mean and standard deviation will differ a little from the population mean and deviation (though the bigger the sample the less chance there is of selecting a sample which is unrepresentative of the population).

Our final conclusion, therefore, is that the mean and standard deviation of our sample will approximate to the mean and standard deviation of the population, *i.e.*

(*a*) The best estimate of the population mean is the sample mean, and

(*b*) The best estimate of the population standard deviation is the sample standard deviation.

2. Sampling distribution of the means. If we are ever required to estimate a population mean, we can take a sample and use the sample mean as the estimate. But although we know it will be close to the population mean, we do not know how great our error may be. What we need is some measure that will tell us the extent to which sample means will deviate from the population mean. One approach to the problem is to examine just how far from the population mean lie the sample means of a large number of samples actually taken.

Let us assume that 2,000 samples are taken, the size of each being 100 items.

NOTE: Students should distinguish very carefully between (a) the number of samples (2,000) and (b) the number of items in a sample, *i.e. sample size* (100).

For each of our 2,000 samples we can calculate a separate mean. Most of these sample means will be very close to the true mean of the population, though occasionally a sample will by chance contain an undue number of items with high (or low) values, so that its mean will be considerably above (or below) the population mean.

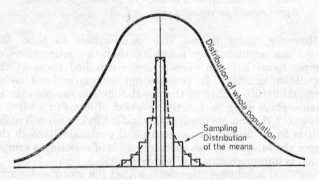

FIG. 35.—*Sampling distribution of the mean*

Next, draw a histogram of the sample means (Fig. 35). On examination, the curve of this histogram looks suspiciously like a normal curve—a very "thin" one, but a normal curve for all that. Students will thus not be surprised to learn that this distribution of means *is* normally distributed. Moreover, it can be seen that the mean of such a distribution (*i.e.* the arithmetic mean of all the sample means) will be equal to the true population mean.

To summarise: if we graph the distribution of the means of a number of samples we find that it results in a normal curve with a mean equal to the population mean. Such a distribution is called a *sampling distribution of the mean*.

3. The standard error of the mean. The next question is, what will be the standard deviation of such a distribution? Theoretically it *could* be found in the usual way, *i.e.* by taking the sample means as the variable and using the ordinary formulae for finding the standard deviation. But if this were done in practice the work involved would be so extensive that the result would hardly justify it. Fortunately, no such work is necessary, for it so happens that there is a connection between the standard deviation of the means, the standard deviation of the population, and the sample size. The connection is such that:

$$\sigma_{\bar{x}} = \frac{Standard\ deviation\ of\ the\ population}{\sqrt{Sample\ size}}$$

where $\sigma_{\bar{x}}$ is the standard deviation of the means, or the *standard error of the mean,* as it is called.

At first glance this does not seem to improve matters, as we still need to know the standard deviation of the population. However, we saw earlier that the standard deviation of the population was approximately equal to the standard deviation of a sample taken from that population. The formula can therefore be re-written as:

$$\sigma_{\bar{x}} = \frac{Standard\ deviation\ of\ the\ sample}{\sqrt{Sample\ size}} \quad .. \quad (26)$$

This means that we need to take only *one sample* in order to find the standard deviation of a distribution of the means of a whole host of samples.

SECTION 56. ESTIMATING POPULATION MEANS

1. The importance of the standard error. When we have found the standard error, what use is it? Simply this. Since 95% of the items in a normal distribution lie within 2σ of the mean of the distribution, and since the distribution of the means is normal, with a mean equal to the population mean; then 95% of the means of all samples must lie within two standard errors of the true mean of the population.

This means that if we take a single sample, then 19 times out of 20 the sample mean will lie within two standard errors of the true mean of the population. In other words, 19 *times out of 20 the true mean of the population cannot be more than two standard errors from the mean of the sample.*

2. Estimating the true mean.

Look again from the beginning. We take a sample from a large population. We find the mean of the sample and know it must be close to the true mean of the population—so close in fact that we can say it is approximately the true mean.

Unfortunately, we do not know how great our error will be in taking the sample mean as the true mean. However, if we compute the standard error from the standard deviation of our sample, we shall be able to say that 19 times in 20 the true mean will be within two standard errors of the sample mean, *i.e.* the population mean lies within the "sample mean $\pm 2\sigma$" range.

EXAMPLE

Assume that our mileages in Table 8 were but a random sample taken from a much larger population of mileages, and that we wish to estimate the true mean mileage of that population.

The mean mileage of our sample (Table 8) was $454\frac{1}{2}$ miles and its standard deviation was 27 miles.

∴ the best estimate of the mean and standard deviation of the population is also $454\frac{1}{2}$ and 27 miles.

∴ according to formula (26):

$$\text{the standard error } (\sigma_{\bar{x}}) = \frac{27}{\sqrt{120}} = 2\cdot 46 \text{ miles}$$

Now, 19 times out of 20 the true population mean is within two standard errors of the sample mean.

∴ 19 times out of 20 we can say the true population mean is between $454\frac{1}{2} \pm 2 \times 2\cdot 46 \doteq 449\cdot 6$ and $459\cdot 4$ miles.

3. Confidence levels.

It has been frequently emphasised that our conclusion will be correct 19 times out of 20. This of course is because 95% (nineteen-twentieths) of all the means fall within two standard errors of the population mean. If the chance of being wrong 1 time out of 20 is too great a risk to take, we can be safer still by widening the range. If we extend it to three standard errors, then since $99\frac{3}{4}\%$ of all means fall within three standard errors of the population mean we can be sure of being correct 399 times in 400 ($99\frac{3}{4}\%$).

These different levels of certainty are known as *confidence levels*. Any estimate of a population mean must always indicate what level of confidence has been adopted.

4. Confidence interval. In para. 3 we saw how changes of confidence level led to changes in the distance between the limits of the mean. This distance between the limits can be called an "interval," and the interval associated with any given level of confidence is called the *confidence interval*. In the example above, the 95% confidence interval is $459 \cdot 4 - 449 \cdot 6 = 9 \cdot 8$ miles.

Note that the higher the confidence level, the greater the confidence interval.

5. Summary: estimating a population mean.
(a) Take a random sample of n items.
(b) Compute the mean ($\bar{x}$) and standard deviation (σ_x) of the sample.
(c) Compute the standard error of the mean ($\sigma_{\bar{x}}$) from the formula (26).
(d) Choose a confidence level (*e.g.* 95%).
(e) Estimate the population mean as $\bar{x} \pm$ the appropriate number of $\sigma_{\bar{x}}$'s (*e.g.* $\bar{x} \pm 2\sigma_{\bar{x}}$).

6. Effect of population size. It should be noted that nothing has been said above about the size of the population. This means that *the accuracy of our estimate is quite independent of population size.*

In other words, contrary to what seems "common sense," a population of 1,000,000 calls for no bigger sample than a population of 10,000. Our accuracy depends solely on sample size and the variability of the characteristic measured.

NOTE: Strictly speaking, this is only true if the sample size is an insignificant proportion of the population size. If it is not so, the accuracy is actually *greater* than that claimed.

SECTION 57.   ESTIMATING POPULATION PROPORTIONS

1. Use of proportions. There are occasions in statistics when information cannot be given as a measure (*e.g.* miles, tons, minutes, shillings, examination marks) but only as a *proportion*, such as males in a group of people, left-wing voters in an electorate, or defective production in total production.   In these cases we are faced with estimating the population proportion from a single sample.

2. Sampling distribution of a proportion. If we took a large number of samples of (say) 100 people from a particular population we should not always find that we had the same number of males in every sample.   If the population contained slightly more females than males, we might find that our samples contained anything from 30 to 60 males, *i.e.* proportions ranging between 0·3 and 0·6.   A histogram of these proportions would result in another thin but definite normal curve of distribution having a mean equal to the true population proportion (*see* Fig. 36).

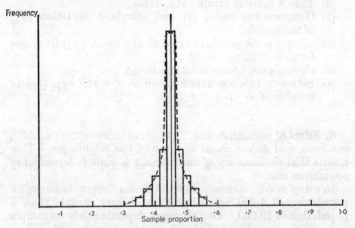

FIG. 36.—*Sampling distribution of a proportion*
This graph assumes the population proportion to be 0·45.
It shows the frequency curve derived from the histogram of
the various proportions found in a large number of samples

3. Standard error of a proportion. We could estimate the population proportion from our sample by using the sample proportion, but unless the standard deviation of this distribution—the *standard error of a proportion*—can be found, there is no way of determining the reliability of our estimate. Our other standard error formula (26) is of no value here, since it is not possible to determine the standard deviation of a proportion from a single sample. How, for instance, could you calculate the standard deviation of a sample where 43 out of 100 people were male? Fortunately, there is yet another formula available which states that:

$$Standard\ error\ of\ a\ proportion\ (\sigma_{prop}) = \sqrt{\frac{pq}{n}} \quad .. \quad .. \quad (27)$$

where p = population proportion; $q = 1 - p$, and n = sample size.

Unfortunately this formula calls for the population proportion—the very thing we do not know. Substitution of the *sample* proportion for the population proportion is, however, usually allowed if the sample size is above 50.

4. Estimating a proportion. The procedure for estimating a proportion is similar to that for estimating a mean. If we know the standard error of a proportion, all we need do is compute:

$$Sample\ proportion\ \pm\ 2\ \sigma_{prop}$$

which will, of course, give us an estimate of the population proportion at the 95% confidence level.

EXAMPLE

In a sample of 400 people, 172 were males. Estimate the population proportion at the 95% confidence level.

Sample proportion $= \dfrac{172}{400} = 0 \cdot 43$

∴ Applying formula (27):

$$\sigma_{prop} = \sqrt{\frac{0 \cdot 43 \times (1 - 0 \cdot 43)}{400}} = \sqrt{\frac{0 \cdot 43 \times 0 \cdot 57}{400}}$$

$$= \underline{\underline{0 \cdot 0248}}$$

∴ Estimate of population proportion at the 95% confidence
level = sample proportion $\pm 2\sigma_{prop}$.
    = $0 \cdot 43 \pm 2 \times 0 \cdot 0248$
    = $0 \cdot 3804$ and $0 \cdot 4796$
    $\backsimeq$ between 38% and 48%.

5. Summary: estimating a population proportion.

(a) Take a random sample of n items.

(b) Compute the sample proportion.

(c) Compute the standard error of a proportion from
    formula (27), using the sample proportion for p.

(d) Choose a confidence level (e.g. 95%).

(e) Estimate the population proportion as *Sample proportion*
    $\pm$ *Appropriate number of* σ_{prop}'s (e.g. Sample proportion
    $\pm 2\sigma_{prop}$).

PROGRESS TEST 20

(Answers on pages 276–7)

1. Estimate the population mean (a) at the 95% and (b) at the
$99\frac{3}{4}\%$ confidence levels, where the sample data are:

   (i) Mean, 950 lbs; σ, 15 lbs; sample size, 25.

   (ii) Mean, $1 \cdot 82$ ins; σ, $0 \cdot 8$ ins; sample size, 100.

   (iii) Mean, $1 \cdot 82$ ins; σ, $0 \cdot 8$ ins; sample size, 10,000.

2. Estimate, at the 95% level of confidence, the population
proportion where sample data are:

   (i) 61 males out of 100 people.

   (ii) 26 out of 49 parts were defective.

   (iii) 6,100 males out of 10,000 people.

[*Warning: care is needed with the next two questions.*]

3. The result of a sample survey of 100 flowers of a particular
type showed that the estimated mean flower height was 15 ins $\pm$
2 ins at the 95% level of confidence. The investigator decides
that he needs an estimate which is within $\frac{1}{2}$ in. of the true population mean at this level of confidence. What must his sample
size be?

4. If you wished to have a confidence level of 99% in any
survey, what would $\sigma_{\bar{x}}$ need to be multiplied by?

CHAPTER XXI

TESTS OF SIGNIFICANCE

It frequently happens in statistical work that some fact is believed to be true, yet when a random sample is taken it turns out that the sample data do not wholly support the fact. The difference could be due to (*a*) the original belief being wrong, or to (*b*) the sample being slightly one-sided—as virtually all samples are to some degree.

Clearly, tests are needed to distinguish which is the more likely possibility. Such tests will reveal whether or not the difference could reasonably be ascribed to ordinary chance factors operating at the time the sample was selected. If the difference cannot be explained as being probably due solely to chance, the difference is said to be *significant*. Tests devised to check whether it is so are called *significance tests*.

SECTION 58. TESTING A HYPOTHESIS

The first of these tests aims to find out whether or not a belief about the mean of a population can continue to be held in the face of a sample that has a mean different from the believed population mean.

1. The null hypothesis. The approach here is to make the hypothesis, or assumption, that *there is no contradiction between the believed mean and the sample mean*, and that the difference can therefore be ascribed solely to chance. This hypothesis is called the *null hypothesis*, and the object of the test is to see whether the null hypothesis should be rejected or not.

2. Testing the null hypothesis. To do this, we make use of the sampling distributions of the means (*i.e.* the thin normal curve we obtained as a result of graphing the means of a large number of samples, in *s.* **55. 2**). If the population mean is in fact the figure we believe it to be, then 95% of the means of all samples will fall within two standard errors of this figure. All that is necessary, then, is to find out whether or not the sample mean does lie this close to the believed figure. If it doesn't, the true population mean cannot be the figure it is claimed to be—unless one takes the view that the sample mean just happens to be the one mean in twenty that lies outside the "two standard errors" limits.

3. Rejection of the null hypothesis.

In other words if the sample mean lies more than two standard errors from the believed mean, one can reject the null hypothesis at the 95% level of confidence and assert that since there *is* a contradiction between the believed population mean and the sample mean which cannot be explained by chance, then the population mean cannot be the figure it was believed to be.

EXAMPLE

Assume that Table 8 relates to the mileage of 120 salesmen taken at random from a very much larger field force. Someone now asserts that the mean mileage of all the salesmen in the field force is 460 miles. Our sample mean, however, is $454\frac{1}{2}$ miles. Can the assertion be maintained at the 95% level of confidence?

NOTE—Table 8: $\sigma = 27$ miles; $n = 120$.

(a) State the null hypothesis: "there is no contradiction between the asserted mean of 460 and the sample mean of $454\frac{1}{2}$."

(b) Find the standard error of the mean. According to formula (26):

$$\therefore \sigma_{\bar{x}} = \sqrt{\frac{27}{120}} = 2 \cdot 46 \text{ miles.}$$

(c) Compute limits within which the sample mean will fall 95% of the time, *i.e.* asserted mean $\pm 2 \times \sigma_{\bar{x}}$
= $460 \pm 2 \times 2 \cdot 46 = 455 \cdot 08$ and $464 \cdot 92$ miles.

(d) Check to see whether the sample mean does lie within those limits or not. In this case our sample mean of $454\frac{1}{2}$ does *not* lie within them. Therefore the difference between the asserted mean (460) and the sample mean ($454\frac{1}{2}$) is *significant*, so the null hypothesis is rejected. Consequently, the assertion that the true mean is 460 miles cannot be held at the 95% level of confidence.

4. Non-rejection of the null hypothesis. If the null hypothesis is rejected, we conclude that the population mean is not the figure originally asserted. But if the null hypothesis is *not* rejected it is important to appreciate that we do *not* conclude that the population mean *is* the figure asserted.

Non-rejection of the null hypothesis only signifies that there is no evidence that the true mean is not as asserted; it does not mean there is evidence that it is correct.

Thus if, in the above Example, our sample mean had been 456, we would not have rejected the null hypothesis, although obviously the true population mean could as well be (say) 455 or 458—or virtually any figure in the 450's—as the asserted figure of 460. Testing a hypothesis cannot result in proof that the believed figure is true. It may only show that such a figure is probably false.

5. Confidence level and the risk of rejecting a true hypothesis. In para. 4 we came to the conclusion that the population mean could not be 460 miles, unless our sample was the exceptional one in twenty. But what if the sample *was* the odd one in twenty? In that case we would have rejected the null hypothesis when it might be true and when 460 miles could in fact have been the true population mean.

The confidence level indicates the risk one takes of rejecting a null hypothesis that might well be correct. To dismiss the assertion that 460 miles was the population mean might lead to action being taken that could result in serious difficulties should the true mean turn out to be 460 after all. Under such circumstances it may be considered that the risk of being wrong one in twenty times is too great and that only a risk of one in four hundred, at most, is justifiable. In that case a confidence level of $99\frac{3}{4}\%$ would be selected, *i.e.* the standard error would be multiplied by 3 when computing the limits.

6. Confidence level and the risk of not rejecting an incorrect hypothesis. However, raising the confidence level can result in the opposite error, since it means that one risks clinging to a believed mean of 460 when in fact it is incorrect. In the Example above, use of the $99\frac{3}{4}\%$ confidence level brings the lower limit of tolerance down to $460 - 3 \times 2\cdot46 = 452\cdot62$. Since our sample mean is above this $(454\frac{1}{2})$ we would not reject the null hypothesis.

G

In short, the selection of the confidence level depends on which error is considered the graver: to reject a hypothesis which may be true, or to fail to reject one that is wrong.

Finally, note that it is essential to select the confidence level *before* testing the hypothesis. Errors of interpretation could arise if one measured the deviation of the sample mean from the asserted population mean first, and then computed the chance of such a difference arising.

7. Summary: testing a hypothesis. The object is to test whether the difference between an asserted mean and a sample mean is significant or not.

(a) State the null hypothesis.

(b) Select the confidence level required.

(c) Compute the standard error of the mean from the standard deviation of the sample (formula (26)).

(d) Compute *Asserted mean* $\pm y \sigma_{\bar{x}}$, where y is the appropriate factor in view of the confidence level selected.

(e) Check where the sample mean falls.

  (i) If *outside* these limits, reject the null hypothesis, *i.e.* the population mean is not as asserted.

  (ii) If *inside* these limits, do not reject the null hypothesis, *i.e.* the population mean could be as asserted.

NOTE.—To test *proportion* hypothesis, simply substitute $\sigma_{proportion}$.

SECTION 59. TESTING A DIFFERENCE BETWEEN MEANS

1. Difference between means. It is quite common in statistical work to be confronted with two distinct populations which seem likely to have virtually identical means. For example, cats in the north of England are probably the same height as those in the south, that is, the mean heights of cats in the two populations are the same. Nevertheless, if a sample were taken from each population it would be unlikely that the two sample means would be identical. How could we tell whether the difference between the sample means was due solely to chance factors, or to a real difference between the two population means? In other words, how can we tell whether the difference between the means is significant?

2. Distribution of the difference between means. Assume that the two population means were the same. In that case, if a great many pairs of samples were taken and the difference found between the means of each pair (always deducting the mean heights of the northern cats from the mean heights of the southern cats), the differences would be found to be small— indeed, there would be occasions when there was no difference. When there were differences, about half of them would be plus and half minus. On only a very few occasions would there be large differences, plus or minus.

If these differences were graphed it would be found that once again the distribution would follow a normal curve, this time one with a mean of zero and extending over plus and minus values (*see* Fig. 37). And, again, 95% of the differences would lie within two standard errors of the mean of zero; in other words, *95% of the differences would not exceed two standard errors.*

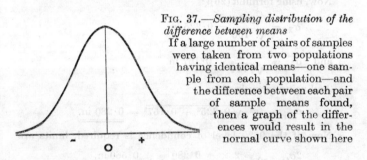

FIG. 37.—*Sampling distribution of the difference between means*
If a large number of pairs of samples were taken from two populations having identical means—one sample from each population—and the difference between each pair of sample means found, then a graph of the differences would result in the normal curve shown here

3. Testing a difference between means. The original problem now becomes one of testing to see whether or not an actual difference found exceeds two standard errors in a distribution of differences between means. If it does not exceed two standard errors, the difference can be set down to chance and one can conclude there is no evidence to prove that the two populations do not have the same mean.

First, however, it is necessary to find the standard error in a distribution of differences between means. This figure is given by the formula:

$$\sigma_{(\bar{x}_1 - \bar{x}_2)} = \sqrt{\sigma^2_{\bar{x}_1} + \sigma^2_{\bar{x}_2}} \quad .. \qquad .. \qquad .. \qquad (28)$$

where $\sigma_{(\bar{x}_1 - \bar{x}_2)}$ = the standard error of the difference between means.

We check, therefore, to see whether or not the actual difference exceeds $2\sigma_{(\bar{x}_1 - \bar{x}_2)}$. If it does, the population means are most unlikely to be the same. In statistical jargon we should say that "the difference between the means is significant at the 95% level of confidence, and therefore the populations do not have the same mean." Of course, other confidence levels could be selected, in which case $\sigma_{(\bar{x}_1 - \bar{x}_2)}$ would need to be multiplied by the appropriate factor.

EXAMPLE

Assume that:

North of England cats (x_1): sample mean 9 in.; standard deviation of sample $2\frac{1}{4}$ in.; sample size 100.

South of England cats (x_2): sample mean $8\frac{1}{2}$ in.; standard deviation of sample 2 in.; sample size 144.

Now, using formula (26):

$$\sigma_{\bar{x}_1} = \sqrt{\frac{2 \cdot 25}{100}} = 0 \cdot 225 \text{ in.}$$

and $\sigma_{\bar{x}_2} = \sqrt{\frac{2}{144}} = 0 \cdot 167 \text{ in.}$

And using formula (28):

$$\sigma_{(\bar{x}_1 - \bar{x}_2)} = \sqrt{0 \cdot 225^2 + 0 \cdot 167^2} = \underline{\underline{0 \cdot 280 \text{ in.}}}$$

Now, if the 95% level of confidence is required, limits are

$$2\sigma_{(x_1 - x_2)} = 2 \times \pm 0 \cdot 280 = \pm \underline{0 \cdot 560 \text{ in.}}$$

And the actual difference between means $= 8\frac{1}{2} - 9 = \underline{\underline{-\frac{1}{2} \text{ in.}}}$

Since this $\frac{1}{2}$ in. is just within the $0 \cdot 56$ in. limit, the difference could have arisen through chance factors and is not significant at the 95% level of confidence.

4. Summary: testing a difference between means. The object is to test whether or not the difference between two sample means is significant.

(a) Select the level of confidence required.

(b) Find the standard error of the mean $(\sigma_{\bar{x}})$ for both samples.

(c) Compute the standard error of the difference between means by formula (28).

NOTE: Since $\sigma_{\bar{x}} = \dfrac{\sigma_x}{\sqrt{n}}$, this standard error can be calculated

in one step by using the formula:

$$\sigma_{(\bar{x}_1 - \bar{x}_2)} = \sqrt{\dfrac{\sigma^2_{x_1}}{n_1} + \dfrac{\sigma^2_{x_2}}{n_2}}$$

(d) Multiply $\sigma_{(\bar{x}_1 - \bar{x}_2)}$ by the appropriate factor for the level of confidence selected.

(e) Find the actual difference between the two sample means. If the difference is below the limit found in step (d), it is not significant. If it is above that limit, the difference is significant and the conclusion can be drawn (at the chosen level of confidence) that the two populations have different means.

SECTION 60.   TESTING A DIFFERENCE BETWEEN PROPORTIONS

Problems sometimes involve *proportions* in samples instead of means. This gives little trouble, since the procedure outlined above can still be applied except that the word "proportion" should be substituted for the word "mean." Even the formula for the standard error of the difference between proportions is the same, although of course the symbols change slightly, *i.e.*:

$$\sigma_{difference\ between\ proportions} = \sqrt{\sigma^2_{prop1} + \sigma^2_{prop2}} \quad .. \quad (29)$$

NOTE: Since $\sigma^2_{proportion} = \left(\sqrt{\dfrac{pq}{n}}\right)^2 = \dfrac{pq}{n}$

then the formula can be written as:

$$\sigma_{difference\ between\ proportions} = \sqrt{\dfrac{p_1 q_1}{n_1} + \dfrac{p_2 q_2}{n_2}}$$

PROGRESS TEST 21

(Answers on pages 277–9)

1. A child welfare officer asserts that the mean sleep of young babies is 14 hours a day. A random sample of 64 babies shows that their mean sleep was only 13 hours 20 minutes, with a standard deviation of 3 hours. Test the officer's assertion at the 95% level of confidence.

2. An election candidate claims that 60% of the voters support him. A random sample of 2,500 voters show that 1,410 support him. Test his claim at the 99¾% level of confidence.

3. A sample of 200 fish of a particular species taken at random from one end of a lake had a mean weight of 20 lb. and a standard deviation of 2 lb. At the other end of the lake, a sample of 80 fish showed a mean weight of 20½ lb. and a standard deviation of 2 lb. also. An expert on fish claimed that these fish swam all over the lake and the two samples were therefore taken, in effect, from the same population. Test this assertion at the 95% level of confidence.

4. A health official claims that the citizens of city A are fitter than those of city B, and in evidence shows that 96 out of 200 citizens of city A passed a standard fitness test as against only 84 out of 200 citizens of B. Do you think he has proved his claim?

INDEX NUMBERS AND TIME SERIES

PART SIX

INDEX NUMBERS AND TIME SERIES

CHAPTER XXII

INDEX NUMBERS

In Part Three we emphasised the valuable function of statistics in reducing a mass of data, with the aid of measures, to a form easier to grasp. We now return to this aspect of statistics.

SECTION 61. THE THEORY OF INDEX NUMBERS

1. The concept of an index number. If we wish to compare several series of figures it is more than likely that their complexity will render direct comparison meaningless. If, for instance, we had information on every form of production during this year and last year (*e.g.* tons of steel produced, gallons of paint blended, TV sets manufactured, cars assembled and so on), the sheer mass of data would make it impossible to "see" in which year production was higher. Instead of such an embarrassing excess of figures, what we need is a *single* figure which in itself shows how much one year differs from another. A convenient way of doing it is to take a fairly typical year's figures as a base, and express the figures for other years as a percentage of this. Hence if the figure for 1965 were 100 and that for 1966 105, we should know that production (or whatever) was 5% greater.

Such a single figure summarising a comparison between two sets of figures is called an *index number*.

2. Complications. In the first part of Chapter XII it was pointed out that arriving at a single figure to stand for a host of others results in both:

(a) many candidates for the job of representative, and
(b) considerable loss of information when the representative figure is used in lieu of the full data.

With index numbers these two features are again present.

185

The effect of the first is to give rise to a confusing variety of types of index number and methods of calculation; the second results in doubt as to the worth of the index number when it has been obtained. In this chapter only the minimum number of types will be examined and their worth left unquestioned.

3. Index number symbols. All the different methods by which index numbers can be calculated can be expressed concisely and unambiguously as formulae, and the student is therefore advised to refer to that part of *s.* **3.** 3 where index number symbols are explained. They should all be quite clear, except possibly the phrase *base year*, which can be defined as *the year against which all other years are compared.*

4. Base 100. In many ordinary day-to-day comparisons 100 is used as a base, percentages being the most obvious example. In consequence, people have become used to such comparisons and statisticians take advantage of this fact by basing index numbers on 100.

For example, if the production of TV sets was 38,261 last year and 43,911 this year we should call last year's production 100 and this year's (by simple proportion) 115. In this way the comparison between the two years' production is made much clearer.

A few indexes use other bases, such as 10 or 1,000, but they are exceptional and there are usually good reasons for such a departure from normal practice (see *Index Numbers* by W. R. Crowe, Macdonald & Evans, 1965).

5. One-item index numbers. Where only one item is involved in comparisons between different periods, the calculation of index numbers is very simple. One year is chosen as base, and the values for other years are stated in proportion to the value of the base year, *i.e.*:

$$\text{Quantity index} = \frac{q_1}{q_0} \times 100; \text{ or}$$

$$\text{Price index} \quad = \frac{p_1}{p_0} \times 100.$$

EXAMPLE

With 1957 as base year, compute quantity and price indexes for the years 1955 to 1961:

Year	Price (£)	TV sets sold	Price index		Quantity index	
1955	45	12,912	$\frac{45}{50} \times 100 =$	90	$\frac{12,912}{21,200} =$	61
1956	48	18,671	$\frac{48}{50} \times 100 =$	96	$\frac{18,671}{21,200} =$	88
1957	**50**	**21,200**	etc.	**100**	etc.	**100**
1958	53	28,633		106		135
1959	53	35,028		106		165
1960	55	40,650		110		192
1961	60	44,531		120		210

NOTE: A one-item price index is also called a *price relative*; see *s.* **64.** 1.

SECTION 62.   WEIGHTED AGGREGATIVE INDEXES

1. Need for multi-item indexes. Unfortunately, index numbers are often wanted in circumstances where there is more than just one item. To take a common instance, we often need an index number that compares the cost of living in one year with that in another. Clearly, more than one item is involved in the cost of living!

For demonstration purposes, let us assume that only three items enter a cost-of-living index—bread, cheese and ale—and that the prices in the two years to be considered were:

TABLE 13.   THREE-ITEM COST OF LIVING INDEX

Item	1958	1964
Bread	$4\frac{1}{2}p.$ loaf	5p. loaf
Cheese	20p. lb	40p. lb
Ale	90p. keg	75p. keg

2. Difficulties involved in multi-item indexes. Our aim now is to determine a single figure which will compare the cost of living in 1958 with that of 1964. Examination of the figures above reveals at least three difficulties:

(a) Two prices have gone up and one down. As there can only be a single index number *it must be a compromise* between these two opposing price movements.

(b) The prices are given *in different units*. It is not feasible, therefore, to add together all the prices for a single year.

(c) There is no indication as to *how important* each item is in the cost of living. Obviously, bread should be considered more important than ale.

Difficulty (a) is a feature of index numbers that must always be borne in mind. Index numbers *are* compromises.

3. Weighting. Difficulties (b) and (c), on the other hand, can be overcome by *weighting*, *i.e.* multiplying the price by a number (the *weight*) that will adjust the item's size in proportion to its importance. For example, if cheese is given a weight of 10, its original price of 20p. becomes a weighted price of 200p. (£2·00).

When such a weight is selected, both the importance of the item and the unit in which the price is expressed are taken into consideration. Consequently, weighted figures are directly comparable.

Assume that weights of 120, 10 and 1 are given respectively to bread, cheese and ale. The weighted figures will therefore be:

TABLE 14.   WEIGHTED COST OF LIVING INDEX

		1958		1964	
Item	Weight	Price	Price × weight	Price	Price × weight
Bread	100	4½p.	450	5p.	500
Cheese	10	20p.	200	40p.	400
Ale	1	90p.	90	75p.	75
Total			740		975

It is now possible to compute a single index number simply by calling the total of the 1958 weighted price column 100, and finding the total of the 1964 column as a proportion, *i.e.*:

Index number for 1964 (1958 = 100) = $\dfrac{975}{740} \times 100 = \underline{\underline{132}}$.

4. Summary of procedure.

(*a*) List the items and prices.

(*b*) Select weights.

(*c*) Multiply the prices by selected weights (*weighting*).

(*d*) Add the products (*aggregating*).

(*e*) Compare the total for the base year with the total for the other year by using proportions (*indexing*).

NOTE: "Indexing" is not a word usually found in statistical books. As used here, it means expressing a comparison of two figures as an index number.

From this summary it will be clear why an index computed by this method is called a *weighted aggregative index*.

5. Formula for a weighted aggregative index. The formula for calculating such an index is:

$$Index = \frac{\Sigma\,(p_1 \times w)}{\Sigma\,(p_0 \times w)} \times 100 \qquad .. \qquad .. \qquad (30)$$

SECTION 63.   LASPEYRE AND PAASCHE

1. Quantity weighted indexes. In the previous section the actual selection of weights for a weighted aggregative index was not discussed. In practice it can be a difficult problem. One solution is to use the *actual quantities consumed* as weights. Obviously, the more bread that is consumed the more important bread is as a cost of living item. Similarly, the low consumption of, say, caviare would reflect the insignificance of such an item. An index number so computed is known as a *quantity weighted index*. Such an index differs from the one discussed above only in the use of actual quantities for weights.

2. Base year or current year quantities? Using actual quantities is all very well, but the question immediately arises as to *which* quantities? Those consumed in the base year, or those consumed in the year for which the index is required?

The answer is that either can be used—although, of course, different index numbers are obtained as a result. It so happens that each method is named after its original inventor. The one which uses base year quantities is called a *Laspeyre* price index, and the one that uses the current year quantities a *Paasche* price index.

3. Definitions and formulae.

(a) *Laspeyre price index:* a base year quantity weighted index. The formula is:

$$Index = \frac{\Sigma p_1 q_0}{\Sigma p_0 q_0} \times 100 \quad .. \quad .. \quad .. \quad (31)$$

A Laspeyre price index indicates how much the cost of buying base year quantities at current year prices is, compared with base year costs.

(b) *Paasche price index:* a current year quantity weighted index. The formula is:

$$Index = \frac{\Sigma p_1 q_1}{\Sigma p_0 q_1} \times 100 \quad .. \quad .. \quad .. \quad (32)$$

A Paasche price index indicates how much current year costs are related to the cost of buying current year quantities at base year prices.

EXAMPLE

Compute (1) *Laspeyre and* (2) *Paasche price indexes of the following data* (1958 = *base year*):

| Item | 1958 | | 1964 | |
	Price (p_0)	Quantity (q_0)	Price (p_1)	Quantity (q_1)
Bread	$4\frac{1}{2}p$. loaf	80,000 loaves	5p. loaf	100,000 loaves
Cheese	20p. lb	10,000 lbs	40p. lb	15,000 lbs
Ale	90p. keg	1,000 kegs	75p. keg	3,000 kegs

(1) *Laspeyre price index:*

Item	p_0	p_1	q_0	$p_0 \times q_0$ (£)	$p_1 \times q_0$ (£)
Bread	$4\frac{1}{2}p$.	$5p$.	80,000	3,600	4,000
Cheese	$20p$.	$40p$.	10,000	2,000	4,000
Ale	$90p$.	$75p$.	1,000	900	750
				6,500	8,750
				$\Sigma p_0 q_0$	$\Sigma p_1 q_0$

Using formula (31), Index $= \dfrac{8,750}{6,500} \times 100 = \underline{\underline{135}}$

(2) *Paasche price index*

Item	p_0	p_1	q_1	$p_0 \times q_1$ (£)	$p_1 \times q_1$ (£)
Bread	$4\frac{1}{2}p$.	$5p$.	100,000	4,500	5,000
Cheese	$20p$.	$40p$.	15,000	3,000	6,000
Ale	$90p$.	$75p$.	3,000	2,700	2,250
				10,200	13,250
				$\Sigma p_0 q_1$	$\Sigma p_1 q_1$

Using formula (32), Index $= \dfrac{13,250}{10,200} \times 100 = \underline{\underline{130}}$

4. Laspeyre and Paasche indexes contrasted. The next query a student may raise is, what difference does it make which index is chosen? As regards the final figure, there will probably be very little difference unless there has been a substantial change in the purchasing pattern. There are, however, two important practical points involving the computation and use of these indexes:

(a) Paasche numbers require actual quantities to be ascertained for *each* year of the series. This can be a big requirement. In contrast, a Laspeyre index requires quantities for the base year only.

(b) With Paasche numbers, the denominator of the formula, $(\Sigma \, p_0 \, q_1)$, needs recomputing *every year*, as q_1 changes yearly. In the case of Laspeyre numbers, however, the denominator, $(\Sigma \, p_0 \, q_0)$, always remains the same. Moreover, a consequence of this is that different years in a Laspeyre index can be directly compared with each other, whereas in a Paasche series the changing denominator means that different years can be compared *only* with the base year and not with each other.

For these reasons Laspeyre indexes are much more common than Paasche indexes.

SECTION 64. OTHER INDEX NUMBERS

1. Weighted average of price relatives index. A *price relative* is simply the price of an item in one year relative to another year—again expressed with 100 as base. Symbolically, it is

$$\frac{p_1}{p_0} \times 100.$$

Thus, bread in our earlier example being $4\frac{1}{2}p.$ in 1958 and $5p.$ in 1964, has a price relative of

$$\frac{5p.}{4\frac{1}{2}p.} \times 100 = \underline{\underline{111}}.$$

Since each price relative is, in effect, a little one-item index number (*see s.* **61**, 5), a composite index number can be obtained by *averaging* all the price relatives of items in a series. Again, weighting is necessary to allow for item importance.

EXAMPLE
Find the weighted average of price relatives index figures in Table 13 with weights of 10, 7 and 3 respectively:

Item	1958 price	1964 price	Price relative	Weight	Price relative × weight
Bread	$4\frac{1}{2}p$.	$5p$.	111	10	**1,110**
Cheese	$20p$.	$40p$.	200	7	1,400
Ale	$90p$.	$75p$.	83	3	249
				20	2,759

$$\therefore \text{Index} = \frac{2,759}{20} = 138$$

NOTE: Remember that in a weighted average you divide by the sum of the weights (see s. **37**. 2).

The formula is:

$$Weighted\ average\ of\ price\ relatives\ index = \frac{\Sigma \left(\frac{p_1}{p_0} \times w\right)}{\Sigma w} \qquad (33)$$

It should be noted, incidentally that the spread of weights in this index is much smaller than that of the weighted aggregative index. On the face of it this suggests that the drop in price of ale would have a greater influence. Yet the index is higher than before! The reason is that a price relative is quite different from a price: small prices, for instance, can have large relatives if they are unstable. For this reason, indexes using price relatives must not be quantity-weighted (though they can be value-weighted).

2. Chain index numbers. A *chain index* is simply an ordinary index in which each period in the series uses the *previous period* as base. For instance, a simple example of a one-item chain index, using some of the data given in *s.* **61**, 5, is given in Table 15.

Such an index shows whether the *rate* of change is rising (rising numbers), falling (falling numbers) or constant (constant numbers) as well as the *extent* of the change from year to year. In the example above it can be seen that although there is a steady increase in the sales of television sets the increase each year, in relation to the total sales of the previous year, is falling.

In a multi-item index such as one measuring the cost of living, a chain index is useful inasmuch as new items can be

TABLE 15. ONE-ITEM CHAIN INDEX
Sales of television sets

Year	TV sets sold	Chain index
1955	12,912	
1956	18,671	$\dfrac{18,671}{12,912} \times 100 = 144$
1957	21,200	$\dfrac{21,200}{18,671} \times 100 = 114$
1958	28,633	$\dfrac{28,633}{21,200} \times 100 = 135$
1959	35,028	$\dfrac{35,028}{28,633} \times 100 = 122$
1960	40,650	$\dfrac{40,650}{35,028} \times 100 = 116$
1961	44,531	$\dfrac{44,531}{40,650} \times 100 = 110$

introduced. For instance, if it is wished to introduce Continental holidays into such an index this year, then data for this year and last year only are required. Had a normal, non-chain index been used based on (say) 1948, there would probably have been no appropriate data available for that year and so it would be impossible to introduce Continental holidays into the index.

3. Quantity indexes. Apart from the indexes of television set sales in Table 15, every index examined in this chapter has been a *price index*, *i.e.* a measure of price changes. There are other kinds of index. An obvious one is an index of quantity.

A *quantity index* is one that measures changes in quantities. There are virtually as many different methods of computing a quantity index as there are a price index—in fact, formulae for quantity indexes can be derived from those for price indexes by simply interchanging the p and q symbols. Thus, a Laspeyre price index with a formula of

$$\frac{\sum p_1 q_0}{\sum p_0 q_0}$$

would become a Laspeyre *quantity* index with a formula of

$$\frac{\Sigma \, q_1 \, p_0}{\Sigma \, q_0 \, p_0} .$$

Weighting is particularly necessary when constructing a multi-item quantity index as it is otherwise impossible to add together tons, gallons, pairs, *etc.*

4. Value indexes. Another group of indexes relate to *value*, value being, of course, $p \times q$. Thus

$$\frac{\Sigma \, p_1 \, q_1}{\Sigma \, p_0 \, q_0}$$

is a *value index* since it compares values in the base year with values in a subsequent year.

SECTION 65. CHANGING THE BASE

1. When necessary. It sometimes happens that the user of an index wishes to change the base year. This often happens when two different series are to be compared, since it is unlikely that both will have the same base year, and so direct comparison between them would be difficult.

EXAMPLE

Assume that an index of television licences for the years 1955–61, with 1949 as base year, ran as follows:

Year:	1955	1956	1957	1958	1959	1960	1961
Index:	210	230	250	300	360	410	500

Direct comparison with the index of television-set sales computed in *s.* 61. 5 is hardly possible. To obtain such a direct comparison it is necessary to change the base year of one of the series so that both have the same base.

2. Procedure for changing the base. The procedure is as follows:

(a) Look up the index number relating to the new base year, then

(b) Divide this number into each index number in the series and multiply by 100.

This will give a new series of index numbers with the new year as its base.

> NOTE: Changing the base of a weighted index gives a series slightly different from that which would be obtained if the index had been computed entirely afresh with the new year as base. But for practical purposes the difference is rarely significant.

In the above Example, it means that to change the index of television licences from a base year of 1949 to a base of 1957, all the figures will have to be divided by 250 (the 1957 index number). To illustrate this, all the data relating to this Example may be tabulated:

Year	TV sets sold (1957 = 100) (see s. **61**. 5)	TV licences (1949 = 100)	TV licences (1957 = 100)
1955	61	210	$\frac{210}{250} \times 100 = 84$
1956	88	230	$\frac{230}{250} \times 100 = 92$
1957	**100**	250	$\frac{250}{250} \times 100 = $ **100**
1958	135	300	$\frac{300}{250} \times 100 = 120$
1959	165	360	$\frac{360}{250} \times 100 = 144$
1960	192	410	$\frac{410}{250} \times 100 = 164$
1961	210	500	$\frac{500}{250} \times 100 = 200$

Comparison of the two series is now possible and it indicates that while the rate of increase in the sales of television sets was initially greater than the rate of increase in licences, the trend was reversed in the later part of the series. If the sales index relates to one company's sales, the figures indicate that it has begun to lose its share of the market.

SECTION 66.   INDEX CONSTRUCTION

1. Factors involved.   When constructing an index number, four factors need to be considered:

(a) The purpose of the index.
(b) The selection of the items.
(c) The choice of weights.
(d) The choice of a base year.

2. Purpose of the index.   The purpose of an index must be very carefully decided, for decisions relating to the other three factors will depend on the purpose.   Moreover, the *interpretation* of the index will also depend on the purpose.

For example, an index constructed to measure change in building costs must not be used for revaluing machinery—nor even the commercial value of a building, since such an index would not take into account changes in the values of land on which such buildings are situated.

3. Selecting the items.   This can be the most difficult problem of all.   Take the construction of a cost of living index.   Obviously, bread should be included, but what about table wines?   Coal ought to be included, but how about central heating costs?   If home rentals are selected, should holiday rentals be selected too?

In the case of an index measuring employment, are part-time workers to be included?   What about self-employed workers?   In an export index, what should we do about imports which are immediately re-exported? or imports returned for some reason to the overseas supplier?   Whose share prices do we use for a share price index?

Moreover, the problem may arise as to *which* figures to take. Is a cost of living index to be based on prices in London or Manchester?   Or in Little-Comely-on-the-Ouse?

The retail price index is in fact calculated by ascertaining retail prices, in various towns throughout the country, and incorporating these prices in the national index.

The answers to such problems lie in defining the purpose of the index carefully and then selecting the items that will best achieve that purpose—although it must be realised there will always be differences of opinion.

Other problems in this category are the selection of items:

(a) *which are unambiguous:* an index of mortality from a given disease would be seriously distorted if improved diagnosis is attributing more and more deaths to the disease that would previously have been attributed to other causes; and

(b) *whose values are ascertainable:* the construction of an index relating to undetected murders would run into obvious difficulties.

4. Choice of weights. The problem here is to find weights which will result in each item being given its appropriate importance. Actual quantities may often be good weights but they are not invariably appropriate. If it were decided to take the quantities used by a "typical household" as weights, there would be some difficulty in determining a "typical household." After all, spinsters on the old age pension are very much concerned with cost of living figures and they would hardly be impressed with a heavy weighting for, say, private car travel.

But there is one factor which makes the problem of choosing weights easier. This is that a difference of opinion as regards weights does not, oddly enough, affect the index as much as one would suppose. For instance, a completely revised weight of 200 for bread in Table 14 (*i.e.* a doubling of the original weight—which was already over *nine* times as big as the other weights combined) results in an index of 124 as against a previous number of 132. Smaller revisions would result in smaller differences and this indicates that hair-splitting as regards weights is rarely worthwhile.

5. Choice of a base year. Generally speaking, the year chosen as base should be (*a*) a reasonably normal year, and (*b*) not too distant.

Sometimes a year which is significant within the series may be chosen; for example, the year Mr Khrushchev came to power might be an appropriate base year for an index of Soviet production, or the year of nationalisation might make a logical base year for U.K. coal output.

Choosing a freak year is a favourite trick of those who use statistics to mislead. A dishonest capitalist could choose a record year for profits as base and so "prove" subsequent profits to be pitifully low. A dishonest trade unionist could similarly choose a year of exceptionally full employment to "prove" that current unemployment is intolerably high.

SECTION 67. CHOOSING AN INDEX

1. Which index should be used? To this question there can only be one answer: *it depends on the circumstances.* The Laspeyre index is a good all-round one but it cannot be used if weighting figures (normally quantity) are unobtainable. In that case, the weighted average of price relatives, with weights determined on some other basis, may be appropriate. The purpose of the index is highly relevant. A chain index is obviously called for when the purpose is to indicate to what extent figures have changed in relation to the previous year. A chain index is valuable, too, where new items may need to be added and old items removed.

Finally, it must be emphasised once more that an index number is only an attempt to summarise a whole mass of data in one figure. Such a figure must inevitably be subject to many limitations and it is the responsibility of the user to balance all factors and judge:

(a) which type of index is appropriate, and
(b) the *real* significance of any single index number in a series.

PROGRESS TEST 22

(*Answers on pages* 280–3)

1. From the data below, and using 1960 as base where appropriate,

(a) Draw up:
   (i) A Laspeyre price index.
   (ii) A Paasche price index.
   (iii) A weighted average of price relatives, using the weighting:

A, 5; B, 3; C, 2.

(b) Compute:*
    (i) A quantity index for A alone.
    (ii) A price index for B alone.
    (iii) A quantity chain index for C alone.
    (iv) A Laspeyre quantity index.
    (v) (1) An index having the formula:

$$Index = \frac{\sum p_1 q_1}{\sum p_0 q_0}$$

(2) What type of index is this?

Item	1960 Price £	1960 Quantity	1961 Price £	1961 Quantity	1962 Price £	1962 Quantity	1963 Price £	1963 Quantity
A	0·20	20	0·25	24	0·35	20	0·50	18
B	0·25	12	0·25	16	0·10	20	0·12½	16
C	1·00	3	2·00	2	2·00	3	2·00	4

2. The table below relates to the weekly pay (before tax and other deductions) of the manual wage earners on a company's pay-roll:

	April 1950 Numbers	April 1950 Total pay (£)	April 1959 Numbers	April 1959 Total pay (£)
Men aged 21 and over	350	2,500	300	4,200
Women aged 18 and over	400	1,600	1,200	8,000
Youths and boys	150	450	100	560
Girls	100	250	400	1,540
	1,000	£4,800	2,000	£14,300

You are required to construct an index of weekly earnings based on 1950 showing the rise of earnings for all employees as one figure.   I.C.W.A.

3. The following three columns have been abstracted from the *Monthly Digest of Statistics*:

| | FOOD MANUFACTURING INDUSTRIES | | FOOD |
| | | | |

	Price indexes of:		Index of:
	Materials and		Retail prices
	fuel used	Output	(17/1/1956
1960	(1954 = 100)	(1954 = 100)	= 100)
January	99·4	107·5	107·8
February	98·2	107·0	107·4
March	96·4	106·2	106·8
April	96·0	106·1	106·6
May	96·3	106·4	107·3
June	95·8	106·6	108·9
July	95·7	107·2	108·8
August	95·6	107·4	106·4
September	95·2	107·0	106·1
October	94·6	106·8	107·4
November	94·9	107·2	107·6
December	95·7	107·5	108·1

Reduce these figures to a comparable basis.*

I.C.W.A.

CHAPTER XXIII

TIME SERIES

SECTION 68. INTRODUCTION

1. What is a time series? Many variables have values that change with time, *e.g.* population, exports, car registrations, company sales, employment and electricity demand. Figures relating to the changing values of a variable over a period of time are called a *time series*. For example, Table 16 is a time series showing company sales changing over time.

TABLE 16. TIME SERIES

Sales of PQP Co. Ltd, 1961–4 (tons)

Year	Quarter 1	Quarter 2	Quarter 3	Quarter 4	Total
1961	672	636	680	704	2,692
1962	744	700	756	784	2,984
1963	828	800	840	880	3,348
1964	936	860	944	972	3,712

2. Factors influencing a time series. If a graph is drawn of a time series (*e.g.* Fig. 38 relating to Table 16), the following features can often be seen:

(a) *Seasonal variation.*—A regular up-and-down pattern that repeats anually and is due to the effect of seasons on the variable.

(b) *The trend.*—An overall tendency for the curve to rise (or fall).

(c) *Random (or residual) variation.*—Odd movements of the curve which fit into no pattern at all.

Each of these three factors affects the curve and, because they all do so simultaneously, it is difficult to distinguish clearly the influence of any single one. For instance, in Table 16 it appears that seasonal influences make the fourth quarter the busiest in the year. In actual fact, the first quarter is the busiest (as will be shown later), but the combined effect of

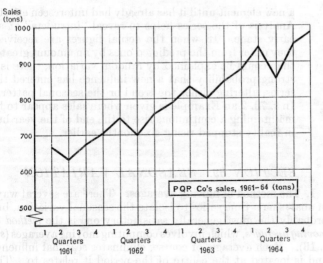

FIG. 38.—*Time series: Table* 16

seasonal influence and trend disguise this. In order to determine the influence of each factor, it is necessary to isolate each of the three factors.

NOTE: There are sometimes other factors involved, but discussion here will be restricted to these three.

3. Object of the exercise. There are two very good reasons why it is worth while isolating each factor. If its influence is known we are able to:

(a) *Predict future values of the variable.* Such knowledge is of great value. For example, if the total demand for electricity ten years from now can be estimated, the facilities that will be needed in ten years and which have a ten-year constructional period can be started at once, not in (say) six years' time, when it will be too late.

(b) *Control events.* In exercising control it is often very important to know at the earliest possible moment should a new element enter the situation. The interaction of existing factors tends to hide the appearance of a new element until it has already had unforeseen effects. Analysis of the series helps to reveal "intruders" at an early stage. If, when the actual figures are received, they differ from the predicted ones by an amount greater than could be explained by random variation, there is a strong probability that a new influence has entered the series, altering either the trend or the seasonal pattern. In *s.* **70.** 2 an Example is given where sales appear to be maintaining a continuous rise to the end of the year but in reality stopped rising six months earlier.

SECTION 69. SEASONAL VARIATION

1. The method of moving averages. There are several ways of analysing a time series to isolate the seasonal variation, but probably the most generally satisfactory one is the *method of moving averages*, which involves computing moving averages (*see s.* **16**). Each average, of course, eliminates seasonal influence and is located at the centre of the period it relates to. The figure for the season it is located against is then found as a percentage of the moving average, and this measures the variation caused by seasonal factors.

Unfortunately, if there is an even number of seasons, a moving average will inevitably be centred between two seasons. To overcome this difficulty the moving averages on either side of a particular season are averaged to give a *centred average* centred on that season. This will probably be better understood by studying Table 17.

Examination of the seasonal variation shows that there is a slight inconsistency. Quarter 1, for example, has figures of 104, 103 and 105 respectively. This is on account of random variations. To eliminate such variations, the seasonal variations are averaged:

Year	*Quarter* 1	*Quarter* 2	*Quarter* 3	*Quarter* 4	
1961	—	—	100	101	
1962	104	95	100	101	
1963	103	94	99	101	
1964	105	94	—	—	
Total	312	283	299	303	*Total*
Average	104	$94\frac{1}{3}$	$99\frac{2}{3}$	101	$= 399$

TABLE 17. ANALYSIS OF SEASONAL VARIATION

using data from Table 16 (tons)

	Quarter	Actual sales	M.A.T.	Moving average	Centred average	Seasonal variation
1961	1	672				[4]
	2	636				[4]
			2,692[1]	673		
	3	680			682[2]	100[3]
			2,764	691		
	4	704			699	101
			2,828	707		
1962	1	744			$716\frac{1}{2}$	104
			2,904	726		
	2	700			736	95
			2,984	746		
	3	756			$756\frac{1}{2}$	100
			3,068	767		
	4	784			$779\frac{1}{2}$	101
			3,168	792		
1963	1	828			$802\frac{1}{2}$	103
			3,252	813		
	2	800			825	94
			3,348	837		
	3	840			$850\frac{1}{2}$	99
			3,456	864		
	4	880			$871\frac{1}{2}$	101
			3,516	879		
1964	1	936			892	105
			3,620	905		
	2	860			$916\frac{1}{2}$	94
			3,712	928		
	3	944				[4]
	4	972				[4]

[1] This M.A.T. figure was found by adding the sales of the four quarters of 1961. Since this is only a step on the way to finding a moving average it is located at the mid-point of this period, *i.e.* between quarters 2 and 3.

[2] Centred average: mean of two moving averages on either side of it.

[3] Seasonal variation:

$$\frac{Actual\ figures}{Centred\ average} \times 100 \quad .. \quad .. \quad .. \quad .. \quad (34)$$

(Be careful not to work with this formula upside down.)

[4] No figures possible for these quarters.

It will be noted that the four quarters do not add up to 400. Averaging the seasonal variations of the quarters frequently leads to this result, but since the total of the four quarterly variations must equal 400 (*see* para. 3) an adjustment is needed to bring this about. This adjustment is often made by adding to each seasonal variation a fraction equal to:

$$\frac{Required\ total\ -\ Actual\ total}{Number\ of\ seasons}$$

i.e., in this case,

$$\frac{400\ -\ 399}{4} = \tfrac{1}{4}$$

If this formula results in a minus, subtract from the variations.

NOTE: Strictly speaking, the larger variations should carry a proportionately larger share of the adjustment, though usually the amount involved is too small to warrant such a refinement.

When a fraction as small as this is obtained, an arbitrary adjustment is more reasonable. In this example it is probably best to round the two seasonal variations with fractions to the next complete number. This would result in the final seasonal variations being:

Quarter 1	Quarter 2	Quarter 3	Quarter 4	Total
104	95	100	101	= 400

2. Summary of procedure: method of moving averages.

(*a*) List the series vertically.

(*b*) Compute the moving totals and insert them at the mid-points of each period.

(*c*) Compute the moving averages.

(*d*) If there is an even number of seasons, average the adjacent moving averages to give centred averages centred on each season.

(*e*) Compute formula (34). This gives the individual seasonal variations.

(*f*) Find the mean of the individual seasonal variations for each season.

(*g*) Adjust these means so that the sum of *all* seasonal variations is $100 \times$ *Number of seasons*. The figures arrived at after this adjustment are the final seasonal variations.

It should be noted that this procedure can be applied to any kind of season. If months are used, the only effects are that the calculations are larger and that the adjustment in step (*g*) would entail making the sum of the seasonal variations 1,200. Note too, that seasons need not be seasons of a year. Morning, afternoon and night are "seasons" in relation to electricity demands, for instance; so are certain times of day for passenger transport services.

3. Theory underlying the method of moving averages. From the computations above, quarter 1 emerges as the busiest season, with a seasonal variation of 104. Examination of the original figures in Table 16 suggests that quarter 4 should be the busiest. The contradiction arises because in this series there is a strong upward trend: if there were no seasonal variations at all, the last quarter would be distinctly higher than the first because, coming later in time, it benefits from the trend.

In the series we have examined, the trend is so steep that although quarter 4 was not as busy seasonally as quarter 1, sales in the last quarter were always higher than in the first quarter of the same year.

It is in order to eliminate the distortion of the seasonal figures by the trend that the method of moving averages is used. The approach is to find out what the figure for each season would be if there were no seasonal variation, and then relate the actual figure to it as a percentage. In *s.* **16. 3** we saw that moving averages eliminated seasonal variations and therefore such averages are used.

The adjustment in step (*g*) is needed because if some seasons are above average (where the average is 100) some must be below and, of course,

$$\frac{\Sigma \ (Seasonal \ variations)}{Number \ of \ seasons}$$

must equal 100. It follows that the sum of the seasonal variations must be 100 × *Number of seasons*.

SECTION 70.   DESEASONALISING THE DATA

1. Why deseasonalise? When examining figures subject to seasonal variation, one of the problems is to know whether (say) a relatively high figure in a busy season is due wholly to seasonal factors, or whether some other factors are involved.   If the seasonal variations are known, they can be used to remove the seasonal influences from the figures.   The resulting figures are then said to be *deseasonalised* (or *seasonally adjusted*).   The influence of factors other than seasonal variations can then be seen.

2. Computation of deseasonalised figures.   The formula is:

$$Deseasonalised\ figure = \frac{Actual\ figure}{Seasonal\ variation} \times 100 \quad .. \quad (35)$$

EXAMPLE

Assume that when the 1965 sales figures relating to Table 16 were received they were:

Quarter 1: 1,020 tons.   Quarter 3: 1,010 tons.
Quarter 2:   960 tons.   Quarter 4: 1,020 tons.

What are the deseasonalised figures and what conclusions can be drawn from them?

The deseasonalised figures are found as follows:

Quarter	Actual figure	Seasonal variation	Deseasonalised figure
1	1,020	104	$\frac{1,020}{104} \times 100 =$ 980
2	960	95	$\frac{960}{95} \times 100 = 1,010$
3	1,010	100	$\frac{1,010}{100} \times 100 = 1,010$
4	1,020′	101	$\frac{1,020}{101} \times 100 = 1,010$

The conclusion we can draw is that the upward trend has levelled out.   From the original 1965 data it seemed as though sales were on a downward trend in quarter 2 and returned to an upward trend in quarters 3 and 4.   The deseasonalised figures show that in actual fact the upward trend was maintained during quarter 2; it was in quarters 3 and 4 that the trend flattened out.

SECTION 71.   THE TREND AND THE METHOD OF SEMI-AVERAGES

1. Finding the trend.   Now that we have seen how to isolate the seasonal variation, we can examine the next factor, the *trend*.

Since moving averages indicate trend, it might be thought that the trend of any series would be given by the fourth column of Table 17.   Unfortunately, moving averages also include random variations along with the trend, so they do not result in the straight trend lines needed for prediction and control.

There are two principal ways of finding the trend.   They are:

(*a*) The method of semi-averages.
(*b*) The method of least squares.

Note, incidentally, that when graphing any trend figures it is necessary always to plot totals at the *mid-point* of the period to which they refer.

2. Features of the method of semi-averages.   This is by far the easier of the two methods of finding the trend, but it is rather crude and is apt to be inaccurate if there are any extreme values in the series.   However, providing these limitations are borne in mind, it can be usefully employed in appropriate circumstances.

3. Procedure with the method of semi-averages.
(*a*) Compute the annual totals (or totals of complete cycles, should the seasons be other than of the normal yearly kind).
(*b*) Divide the series into two halves, each containing a complete number of years.   If the overall series contains an odd number of years, omit the middle year.
(*c*) Compute the mean value of each half.

H

(*d*) Plot these two mean values on a graph at the mid-points of their respective periods and join the points. This gives the *trend line*.

EXAMPLE

In Fig. 39 an example is given of the working of this method for the series in Table 16.

SALES TREND OF DATA IN TABLE 16

Year	Total sales for year (tons)	Semi-average	Mid-point of period
1961	2,692		
1962	2,984	2,838	End 1961
1963	3,348		
1964	3,712	3,530	End 1963

Dividing line

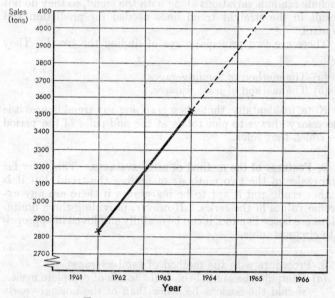

FIG. 39.—*Method of semi-averages*

4. Using the trend line for prediction. If the trend line is projected to the right, an estimate of future yearly totals can be read from it. It must be borne in mind, though, that on this particular type of graph, annual totals must be read at the mid-point of the year concerned. Thus, in Fig. 39, for example, the estimate for sales in 1965 is 4,040 tons.

SECTION 72. THE TREND AND THE METHOD OF LEAST SQUARES

Students who studied Chapter XVII will remember the method of least squares. A moment's reflection will show that a trend line is, in fact, an ordinary regression line of the variable concerned on time (since we wish to predict variable value from time and not vice versa). This means that the student who wishes to use the method of least squares to find a trend line may compute the regression line in the ordinary way if he wishes and completely ignore the procedure outlined in this section. However, it may pay him to read what follows, for a simpler method of computing the regression line is possible in a time series, owing to the fact that time values increase in equal increments.

1. Formula for the method of least squares. It is possible to state a trend line as an equation,

$$y = a + bd \qquad .. \qquad .. \qquad .. \qquad (36)$$

where y is the value of the variable concerned, a and b are constants, and d is the deviation of the required instant in time from the mid-point of the series.

NOTE: Students who skipped Chapter XVII may find the note to *s*. **48.** 1 useful here, if they read d for x.

This means that the problem becomes one of finding values for a and b. They can be determined as follows:

$a =$ arithmetic mean of the series.
$b = \Sigma yd / \Sigma d^2 \qquad .. \qquad .. \qquad (37)$

Computing a is simple enough. The procedure for b is given below, although the experienced student will be able to deduce the process from the formula.

2. Procedure for computing b.
(a) Set down the annual figures in a vertical column.
(b) Find the mid-point of the series.

(c) Against each year, insert the deviation of the mid-point of that year from the mid-point of the series. (With an odd number of years in the series these deviations will be whole years, but with an even number they will include half years.)

(d) Multiply the variable value for each year by its deviation and add the products to give Σyd.

(e) Square the deviations and add the products to give Σd^2.

(f) Apply formula (37).

EXAMPLE

Find the trend line of the data in Table 16.

Year	y (sales)	d	yd	d^2
1961	2,692	$-1 \cdot 5$	$-4,038$	$2 \cdot 25$
1962	2,984	$-0 \cdot 5$	$-1,492$	$0 \cdot 25$
Mid-point				
1963	3,348	$+0 \cdot 5$	$+1,674$	$0 \cdot 25$
1964	3,712	$+1 \cdot 5$	$+5,568$	$2 \cdot 25$
	$\Sigma y = 12,736$		$\Sigma yd = +1,712$	$\Sigma d^2 = 5 \cdot 00$

Now a = mean of the series = $\dfrac{\Sigma y}{n} = \dfrac{12,736}{4} = \underline{\underline{3,184}}$

and $b = \Sigma yd / \Sigma d^2 = \dfrac{+1,712}{5} = \underline{\underline{342 \cdot 4}}$

Applying formula (36), $y = \underline{\underline{3,184 + 342 \cdot 4d}}$.

NOTE: The mid-point of the series is the *end* of 1962. On the other hand each year's figures are, of course, *centred on the middle of the year*.

3. Use of the computed trend line. Having calculated the trend line, prediction is possible in one of two ways:

(a) The trend line can be graphed by taking any two years and:

  (i) Computing their deviations d_1 and d_2;

  (ii) Inserting these values of d_1 and d_2 in formula (36) and finding y_1 and y_2;

  (iii) Plotting these two values of y on the graph:

(iv) Joining the two points to obtain a trend line. The trend line can then be extended and the estimated values in future years read off directly.

(b) Much more simply, take the year for which a prediction is required and:

(i) Find its deviation d from the mid-point of the original series;

(ii) Insert this value in formula (36) and compute y.

EXAMPLE

Estimate the sales for 1965 from the data in Table 16.

(a) 1965 has a deviation d of $2 \cdot 5$ years from the mid-point of the series in Table 16.

(b) $\therefore y = a + bd = 3{,}184 + 342 \cdot 4 \times 2 \cdot 5 = 4{,}040$ tons.

NOTE: Here the method of least squares gives exactly the same answer as the method of semi-averages, because the series of figures is a simple series and the added sophistication of the least squares method is not really needed.

SECTION 73. RANDOM VARIATION

1. Isolating random variation. Having isolated the seasonal variation and the trend in a time series, we are left only with *random variation*. Theoretically, isolating this variation is quite simple, since all that needs to be done is to compare the actual figures with theoretical figures based on the trend and seasonal variations. Any difference must be due to random variation (or an additional factor that has not been taken into consideration).

2. Subdividing the trend. Whilst the theoretical approach is very simple, its practical execution is complicated slightly by the need to subdivide the annual trend figure into figures for each seasonal period. If we call the figure for the *seasonal* period y', then formula (36) becomes:

$$y' = \frac{a}{n} + \frac{b}{n^2} \times d' \qquad .. \qquad .. \qquad .. \qquad (38)$$

where n = number of seasons per annum, and d' = deviations measured in these periods.

The trend figure for each seasonal period may be computed by this formula.

Special care has to be taken in using the formula to count d' correctly. Remember that figures are centred at the mid-points of their periods, *i.e.* seasonal figures are centred at the mid-point of the seasons. Thus, if the deviation of quarter 3, 1964, was required in our Table 16 example, it would be determined as follows:

Number of full quarters from mid-point of the series
(end of quarter 4, 1962) to end of quarter 2, 1964   = 6
+ half a quarter for quarter 3, 1964   = $\frac{1}{2}$

$$\therefore \ d' = 6\tfrac{1}{2}$$

3. Applying the seasonal variation. The next step after computing the trend figures for each individual period is to apply the seasonal variation. This simply entails multiplying the trend figure by the seasonal variation. This gives the required theoretical figures.

4. Random variations. It only remains now to compare these theoretical figures with the actual ones. The difference will be the *random variation*. It is usually expressed as a percentage, *i.e.* the actual figure as a percentage of the theoretical figure.

There will, of course, be no pattern in this variation—as the word "random" itself implies. Hence the random variations cannot be used in predicting future figures, except in so far as they will indicate the reliability of such predictions. Thus, if the random variations are very small it is likely that the actual figures will be close to the predicted ones. Conversely, if the random variations are large, the predicted figures will be very unreliable.

5. A worked example.

Find and comment on the random variation in the data in Table 16.

The annual trend was found to be:

$$y = 3{,}184 + 342 \cdot 4 \, d \text{ (where } d = \text{deviation in years)}$$

Therefore the *quarterly* trend will be:

$$y' = \frac{3,184}{4} + \frac{342 \cdot 4}{4^2} \times d' = 796 + 21 \cdot 4d'$$

where $d' = $ deviation in quarters.

The computation of the random variation is, therefore, as follows:

Quarter		d'	Trend (from formula above)	Seasonal variation (s. 69. 1)	Theoretical figures (Trend × Seasonal variation)	Actual figures	Random variation Actual / Theoretical × 100
1961	1	$-7\frac{1}{2}$	636	104	660	672	102
	2	$-6\frac{1}{2}$	657	95	624	636	102
	3	$-5\frac{1}{2}$	678	100	678	680	100
	4	$-4\frac{1}{2}$	700	101	707	704	100
1962	1	$-3\frac{1}{2}$	721	104	749	744	99
	2	$-2\frac{1}{2}$	742	95	706	700	99
	3	$-1\frac{1}{2}$	764	100	764	756	99
	4	$-\frac{1}{2}$	785	101	793	784	99
Mid-point t							
1963	1	$+\frac{1}{2}$	807	104	839	828	99
	2	$+1\frac{1}{2}$	828	95	787	800	102
	3	$+2\frac{1}{2}$	850	100	850	840	99
	4	$+3\frac{1}{2}$	871	101	880	880	100
1964	1	$+4\frac{1}{2}$	892	104	928	936	101
	2	$+5\frac{1}{2}$	914	95	868	860	99
	3	$+6\frac{1}{2}$	935	100	935	944	101
	4	$+7\frac{1}{2}$	956	101	966	972	101

These figures indicate that the random variation is very small, and the actual figures will probably be within 1% or 2% of the predicted figures—assuming that no new factor enters the series.

6. Computing predictions from a time series.

It should be possible to see from the worked example above that *future* quarterly figures can be predicted by adding future quarters to the ones listed. Quarter 1, 1965, for example, will have a deviation d' of $8\frac{1}{2}$ and so will give a trend figure of 978. Allowing for the seasonal variation of 104, the predicted figure for the quarter will be 1,017 tons. If random variations keep within previous limits, this should be correct to within ±2%, *i.e.* the actual figure should prove to lie between approximately 1,000 and 1,040 tons.

SECTION 74. INTERPOLATION AND EXTRAPOLATION

A common technique in statistics is to plot a series of points on a graph and then draw a line of best fit across the graph. It was used in connection with scattergraphs, regression lines and can now be applied to time series trends. The line of best fit is used to predict values, and it is in this context that interpolation and extrapolation arise.

(a) *Interpolation* consists in reading a value on that part of the line which lies *between* the two extreme points plotted (*i.e.* a value on the continuous line in Fig. 40).

(b) *Extrapolation* means reading a value on the part of the line that lies *outside* the two extreme points plotted (*i.e.* a value on the dotted line in Fig. 40).

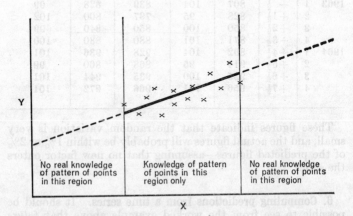

FIG. 40.—*Interpolation and extrapolation*

The distinction between the two is necessary, for although interpolation is permissible, it is considered dangerous to extrapolate. In the case of interpolation, the actual points on the graph give a sound indication of the possible error that could arise in reading a value from the line. But, where the line lies *outside* the plotted points, there is no guide at all to the degree of error. Although the plotted points may suggest the line has a steady slope, it may well be that some new, unsuspected factor comes into play at the higher or lower levels which, unknown to us, alters the slope in those regions.

For example, a scattergraph of heights and ages where ages are below 16 years would indicate continuous growth. If the height of an 80 year old man was estimated from the line of best fit of such a scattergraph, the estimate would be something like 25 ft!

In this example, we know from experience that growth stops at about 16 years of age and that extrapolation would result in serious error. But in many cases we have no experience of the events lying beyond the two extremes and so therefore do not know if extrapolations is allowable or not. It is true that the estimate may be reasonably accurate if it is read from a part of the line lying beyond, *but still close to*, one of the extreme points; but the further one moves away from the extreme point the more one must treat the estimate with caution.

PROGRESS TEST 23
(*Answer on pages* 284–6)

1. The data below relate to the populations, in thousands, of two towns A and B, between 1950 and 1958.

(*a*) Compute the population trend line for each town.

(*b*) Estimate when the populations of the two towns will be equal, and state the estimated size of the populations at that time.   [*Answer:* 1972; 144,000

Year	A	B
1950	25	200
1951	31	196
1952	36	194
1953	44	190
1954	48	189
1955	53	185
1956	60	184
1957	62	181
1958	67	180

2. (a) From the figures below compute (i) the seasonal variations, and (ii) the trend.

(b) Estimate (i) the total demand for 1965 and (ii) the demand in the last quarter of 1965.

DEMAND FIGURES (TONS) 1961–3

Year	Quarter 1	Quarter 2	Quarter 3	Quarter 4
1961	218	325	273	248
1962	444	585	445	385
1963	660	852	623	525

3. The following figures relate to units of service demanded of a service enterprise working 24 hours a day.*

(a) Find (i) the seasonal variation, (ii) the trend, and (iii) the random variation.

(b) Graph the actual figures and superimpose the trend line.

Day	Morning	Afternoon	Night
1	820	310	600
2	800	330	600
3	860	340	700
4	900	380	680

4. (For students who have studied regression lines (Chapter XVII).)

Prove that a trend line found by the method of least squares is the regression line of y on x, where x is time.* (Hint: If deviations are measured from the mid-point of a series and such deviations are in equal steps, note that the sum of these deviations must be zero.)

ESSENTIAL FORMULAE AND USEFUL FORMULAE

ESSENTIAL FORMULAE

Frequency distributions

Arithmetic mean $(\bar{x})$

Basic formula: $\bar{x} = \dfrac{\Sigma x}{n}$ .. .. .. (1)

"Short method" formula:

$$\bar{x} = \text{Assumed mean} + \left(\frac{\Sigma fd}{\Sigma f} \times \text{Class interval}\right) \quad .. \quad (3)$$

This formula is for use with frequency distributions that have equal class intervals where d = deviation in whole classes from the "assumed mean" class. If the distribution has unequal class intervals, or is an ungrouped distribution, then $d = (x -$ Assumed mean) and "$\times$ Class interval" is dropped from the formula; *see ss.* **32.** 3 and 4.

Range

Range = Highest value — Lowest value .. .. (10)

Quartile deviation

$$\text{Quartile deviation} = \frac{Q_3 - Q_1}{2} \quad .. \quad (11)$$

Standard deviation (σ)

Basic formula: $\sigma = \sqrt{\dfrac{\Sigma(x - \bar{x})^2}{n}}$ .. .. (12)

"Short method" formula:

$$\sigma = \sqrt{\frac{\Sigma fd^2}{\Sigma f} - \left(\frac{\Sigma fd}{\Sigma f}\right)^2} \times \text{Class interval} \quad .. \quad (15)$$

See note to short method formula for arithmetic mean, above.

$$Variance = \sigma^2$$

Coefficient of variation

$$\text{Coefficient of variation} = \frac{\sigma}{\bar{x}} \times 100 \quad .. \quad (16)$$

Pearson coefficient of skewness (Sk)

$$Sk = \frac{3\,(\bar{x} - \text{Median})}{\sigma} \quad .. \quad .. \quad (17)$$

Correlation

Correlation (r)

$$r = \frac{\sum xy - n\,\bar{x}\,\bar{y}}{n\,\sigma_x\,\sigma_y} \quad .. \quad .. \quad (23)$$

where n = the number of pairs.

Rank correlation (r′)

$$r' = 1 - \frac{6\,\sum d^2}{n(n^2 - 1)} \quad .. \quad .. \quad (24)$$

where n = the number of pairs, and
d = the difference between rankings of the same item in each series.

Standard errors

Standard error of the mean ($\sigma_{\bar{x}}$)

$$\sigma_{\bar{x}} = \frac{\sigma_{sample}}{\sqrt{n}} \quad .. \quad .. \quad (26)$$

Standard error of a proportion (σ_{prop})

$$\sigma_{prop} = \sqrt{\frac{pq}{n}} \quad .. \quad .. \quad (27)$$

where p = sample proportion (large samples only), and
$q = 1 - p$.

Standard error of the difference between means ($\sigma_{(\bar{x}_1 - \bar{x}_2)}$)

$$\sigma_{(\bar{x}_1 - \bar{x}_2)} = \sqrt{\sigma^2_{\bar{x}_1} + \sigma^2_{\bar{x}_2}} \quad .. \quad .. \quad (28)$$

Standard error of the differences between proportions
$$(\sigma_{diff.\ between\ proportions})$$

$$\sigma_{diff.\ between\ proportions} = \sqrt{\sigma^2_{prop_1} + \sigma^2_{prop_2}} \quad .. \quad (29)$$

Index numbers

Weighted aggregative price index

$$\text{Index} = \frac{\sum (p_1 \times w)}{\sum (p_0 \times w)} \times 100 \quad \ldots \quad (30)$$

Laspeyre price index

$$\text{Index} = \frac{\sum (p_1 \times q_0)}{\sum (p_0 \times q_0)} \times 100 \quad \ldots \quad (31)$$

Paasche price index

$$\text{Index} = \frac{\sum (p_1 \times q_1)}{\sum (p_0 \times q_1)} \times 100 \quad \ldots \quad (32)$$

USEFUL FORMULAE

Geometric mean

$$\text{GM} = \sqrt[n]{x_1 \times x_2 \times x_3 \times \ldots \ldots x_n}$$

(alternative: $\text{Log. GM} = \dfrac{\sum \log. x}{n}$) $\quad \ldots \quad \ldots \quad (5)$

Harmonic mean

$$\text{HM} = \frac{n}{\sum \frac{1}{x}} \quad \ldots \quad \ldots \quad \ldots \quad (6)$$

Weighted average

$$\text{Weighted average} = \frac{\sum xw}{\sum w} \quad \ldots \quad \ldots \quad (7)$$

Regression lines

Line equation: $y = a + bx$ $\quad \ldots \quad \ldots \quad \ldots \quad \ldots \quad (18)$

Regression line of y on x:

$$\left. \begin{array}{l} \sum y = an + b\sum x \\ \sum xy = a\sum x + b\sum x^2 \end{array} \right\} \text{Solve for } a \text{ and } b \quad \ldots \quad \begin{array}{l} (19) \\ (20) \end{array}$$

where n = the number of pairs.

Regression line of x on y:

Interchange x and y in the above simultaneous equations.

(21) and (22)

Regression coefficient

The value of b in the $y = a + bx$ regression line equation.

Price relative

$$\text{Price relative} = \frac{p_1}{p_0} \times 100$$

Weighted average of price relatives index

$$\text{Index} = \frac{\Sigma \left(\dfrac{p_1}{p_0} \times 100 \times w \right)}{\Sigma w} \qquad \cdots \qquad \cdots \quad (33)$$

Base changing

$$\text{New index number} = \frac{\text{Old index no.}}{\text{Old index no. of new base period}} \times 100$$

Deseasonalised figures

$$\text{Deseasonalised figure} = \frac{\text{Actual figure}}{\text{Seasonal variation}} \times 100 \quad \cdots \quad (35)$$

Trend line

$$y = a + bd \qquad \cdots \qquad \cdots \quad (36)$$

where y = the variable,
$\quad d$ = the deviation in time from the mid-point of the time series, $a = \bar{y}$, and
$$b = \frac{\Sigma yd}{\Sigma d^2}$$

Subdivision of the trend line

Sub-period value $y' = \dfrac{a}{n} + \dfrac{b}{n^2} d'$

where n = the number of sub-periods per cycle, and

$\quad d$ = the deviation from the mid-point of the series measured in sub-periods.

NORMAL CURVE AREAS

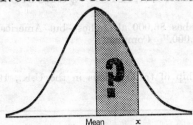

Mean   x

x is the distance the point lies from the mean measured in σ, *i.e.*

$$\frac{Value - Mean}{\sigma}$$

(if x is minus, ignore sign).

x	$Area$	x	$Area$
0·0	0·0000	1·6	0·4452
0·1	0·0398	1·7	0·4554
0·2	0·0793	1·8	0·4641
0·3	0·1179	1·9	0·4713
0·4	0·1554	2·0	0·4772
0·5	0·1915	2·1	0·4821
0·6	0·2257	2·2	0·4861
0·7	0·2580	2·3	0·4893
0·8	0·2881	2·4	0·4918
0·9	0·3159	2·5	0·4938
1·0	0·3413	2·6	0·4953
1·1	0·3643	2·7	0·4965
1·2	0·3849	2·8	0·4974
1·3	0·4032	2·9	0·4981
1·4	0·4192	3·0	0·4987
1·5	0·4332		

EXAMPLE

If a distribution has a mean of 30 and a σ of 5, what area lies under the curve between the mean and 38?

Now $n = \dfrac{38-30}{5} = 1 \cdot 6.$

The table shows that when $x = 1 \cdot 6$ the area is $0 \cdot 4452.$

∴ Area lying under the curve = $44 \cdot 52\%.$

EXAMINATION QUESTIONS

1. "Britain has 86,000 alcoholics—but America's hair-raising figure is 4,589,000." Comment.

B.S.I.

2. Membership of trade unions in the U.K., 1938, 1951 and 1960.

Membership	Number of trade unions		
	1938	1951	1960
Under 100	309	145	132
100–	286	191	176
500–	99	78	51
1,000–	116	101	97
2,500–	74	77	67
5,000–	59	43	34
10,000–	21	26	18
15,000–	21	19	26
25,000 and over ..	39	50	49
Total ..	1,024	730	650

Write a report on the changes in the sizes of trade unions over the period, using the statistics given in the above table and any derived statistics you find useful for the purpose.

U.L.C.I.

3. Write a short statistical commentary on industrial stoppages in the transport and communications industry in the period 1952 to 1961, using the figures in the following table, and compute such derived statistics as you require. What further statistical information would you require in assessing whether the transport and communications industry lost more days than other industries through stoppages in this period?

INDUSTRIAL STOPPAGES IN THE UNITED KINGDOM

	Transport and communications			All industries and services		
	Number of stoppages	*Workers involved* (000s)	*Working days lost* (000s)	*Number of stoppages*	*Workers involved* (000s)	*Working days lost* (000s)
1952	55	11	32	1,714	415	1,792
1953	73	38	69	1,746	1,370	2,184
1954	125	113	919	1,989	418	2,457
1955	118	153	1,687	2,419	659	3,781
1956	102	20	35	2,648	507	2,083
1957	121	165	998	2,859	1,356	8,412
1958	83	100	2,116	2,629	523	3,462
1959	88	30	95	2,093	645	5,270
1960	179	153	636	2,832	817	3,024
1961	138	54	230	2,686	771	3,046

I.O.T.

4. Analyse the data given below by means of secondary statistics, calculating any percentages that you think necessary.   Summarise your results in a brief report on the fire and accident insurance business.

THE "L" GENERAL ASSURANCE SOCIETY, LTD.
Fire and accident business
1962

	Fire	Accident
Premium income, 1962	£3,964,120	£4,043,551
Increase on 1961	8%	5%
Fund at end of 1962	£2,050,798	£2,971,547
Claims as percentage of premium	47%	56%
Expenses as percentage of premium	48%	35%
Underwriting surplus	£64,255	£249,318

L.C.C.

5. Explain the following statistical terms:
(a) Absolute error.
(b) Relative error.
(c) Biased error.
(d) What is the absolute error in the following amounts, which are quoted to the nearest £10,000:
       £50,000 + £280,000 + £1,560,000 − £710,000?

(e) What is the relative error in the following amounts which are quoted to the nearest 10: 500×200 A.C.C.A.

6. Distinguish between "primary data" and "secondary data," giving *two* examples of each.

Explain why secondary data must be used with great care.
                                                                    I.M.S.M.

7. What is "quota sampling"? Explain its advantages and disadvantages compared with other sampling methods for survey work.   I.H.A.

8. Discuss the advantages and disadvantages of the postal questionnaire as a method of collecting data.   L.G.E.B.

9. Examine the importance of non-response in social surveys.
                                       University of London B.Sc.

10. Draft a brief questionnaire (no more than 10 questions), to be completed by a sample of out-patients, which will provide information regarding the views of these patients on the organisation of the out-patient department.

NOTE: No questions regarding medical treatment as such are required.   I.H.A.

11. Tabulate the following information which has been taken from the *Financial Times*, 1963.

There has been a substantial increase in exports of New Zealand meat to new and developing markets in the period 1st October 1962 to 31st May 1963.   Shipments outside the U.K. totalled 86,255 tons or 27·7% of the total shipments compared with 67,500 tons or 23·4% shipped outside the U.K. in the corresponding period in 1962.   Increased shipments were sent to almost all major markets including the U.K.   Shipments to the U.K. totalled 225,000 tons (221,000).   U.S. east coast 34,700 tons (20,900), west coast, 14,500 tons (10,000), Canada east coast 6,700 tons (2,800), Japan 13,000 tons (5,700).   Meat export receipts through the banking system in the first five months of 1963 were almost £45 m., compared with nearly £37 m. at the same time the previous year.

Calculate the relevant ratios necessary to bring out the relation ships present.   R.S.A.

12. Arrange the following data in concise tabular form:

"At 10th June 1963, 479,713 persons were registered as unemployed in Great Britain.   Of these 340,570 were men, 106,272 were women, 19,322 were boys under 18 years, and the rest were girls under 18 years. The numbers temporarily stopped were 13,794 men, 432 boys, 4,117 women and 668 girls, the remainder being classed as wholly unemployed. Of this group of wholly unemployed, 47,355 men had been unemployed for not more than 2 weeks, 38,231 for more than 2 but not more than 5 weeks, 27,370 for more than 5 but not more than 8 weeks, and 213,820 for more than 8 weeks. The corresponding figures for boys were 5,234, 3,849, 2,728, 7,079; for women 14,097, 15,690, 12,202, 60,166; and for girls 3,543, 2,746, 1,951, 4,641." (Source: *Ministry of Labour Gazette*.)

Briefly describe the main features of the figures displayed in your table.   U.L.C.I.

13. On 15th August 1960, the unemployment rate in Great Britain for males was 49,700 who had been without work for less than two weeks, 121,300 over eight weeks and 53,200 over two weeks and less than eight weeks. The respective figures for females were 23,500; 38,300 and 27,500. Comparable figures for the 11th July were for males 44,900; 122,700 and 37,900 and for females 17,300; 40,£00 and 18,400. These figures include persons under 18 registered as unemployed who have had no insured employment: these numbered 205,000 and 202,300 for males in August and July respectively and for females 76,300 and 74,200 respectively.

Tabulate this information in a presentable form under a suitable title.   A.C.C.A.

14. Graph the following data in suitable form for a management committee. Draft a short statement drawing attention to the main features of the data.

	Average daily occupation of beds	Whole time nursing staff	Cost of services £ millions	Prescriptions dispensed millions	Payments to pharmacists £ millions
1951	52·2	18,521	32·1	20·8	5·3
1952	53·7	18,972	32·8	20·4	5·7
1953	54·2	19,625	33·9	20·5	5·2
1954	55·4	20,279	36·6	20·9	5·7
1955	55·4	20,783	40·1	21·2	5·8
1956	54·3	21,036	43·6	21·5	6·2
1957	54·6	21,586	45·6	20·9	7·1
1958	54·3	21,968	48·1	20·4	7·6

I.H.A.

15. Describe the differences between a natural scale graph and a semi-logarithmic graph. Indicate the type of information which is better shown on a semi-logarithmic graph.

A.C.C.A.

16. Describe how a Lorenz curve is compiled.
Construct a suitable table of personal incomes and personal tax from which a Lorenz curve can be compiled.

NOTE: The figures shown in the table need not be accurate, but must clearly indicate the type of information found in such tables.

A.C.C.A.

17. Draw any diagrams you consider helpful in depicting the information contained in the following table:

GENERAL AND SPECIALIST HOSPITALS IN HOLLAND, 1957

Ownership	No. of hospitals	No. of beds	Per cent. of all beds
Roman Catholic	111	21,300	42·1
Protestant	48	8,611	17
Non-sectarian	56	5,542	11
Municipal and Central Government	54	15,169	29·9
	269	50,622	100

Explain your choice of diagrams.

I.H.A.

18. Describe the type of chart most suitable for illustrating the following:
   (a) Sales in four areas of two products over the last four years;
   (b) Prices of three materials over the last five years;
   (c) The proportion of the total expenditure, during the previous year, of a bus company according to wages, fuel, maintenance, tyres, depreciation and other operating expenses
   (d) The traffic receipts of the British Transport Commission showing totals for British Railways, London Transport and Inland Waterways.

N.C.T.E.C.

19. Describe the information obtained in the Census of Distribution and to what practical use this information can be put.

R.S.A.

20. The managing director of your firm requires a report on the movement of prices and wages in Great Britain as a preliminary investigation pending a wage claim. State the data which would be required and give the source and the meaning of the information submitted.

L.C.C.

21. The six items of information listed below can be found in the official series of statistics. State for each:

(a) the series and Government department responsible;
(b) the frequency with which the figures appear (if irregular, the dates of the last two sets published).
(No other information is required.)

(i) A general measure of changes in the level of industrial activity;
(ii) Average changes in rates of pay of manual workers;
(iii) Numbers of skilled workers in different areas;
(iv) Gross margins in retail shops;
(v) Detailed figures of exports by quantity and value;
(vi) Changes in turnover of different types of shop.

I.C.W.A.

22. In the week following the one described in question 38, the record of deliveries of sand from the quarry is as follows:

Wt of load (cwt)	Under 10	10 and under 20	20 and under 30	30 and under 40	40 and under 60	60 and under 80	Total
No. of loads	50	61	121	78	18	2	330

Using the same axes and scales, draw two ogives to illustrate the deliveries of sand in these two weeks, distinguishing clearly between them.

Use your graph to find the median weight and the semi-interquartile range for each of the two weeks.

Compare the answer for the two weeks.

U.L.C.I.

23. In a group of 1,459 university undergraduates, 1,269 graduated and the rest failed to graduate. Using the data below, compare the arithmetic mean age on admission of those who graduated and of those who failed.

Age on admission (years/months)	Graduated	Failed to graduate
17/4	15	0
17/8	34	5
18/0	113	5
18/4	332	40
18/8	362	55
19/0	289	15
19/4	83	45
19/8	20	20
20/0	21	5

You should assume an upper age limit of 21 years.

L.G.E.B.

24. Using the data of question 23 construct the appropriate cumulative frequency curves to estimate the median age of all undergraduates, and the median age of those who graduated. Estimate also the 20th and the 80th percentiles for each distribution. Comment on your results.

L.G.E.B.

25. From the following figures taken from a price index, state what is:

(a) the median,
(b) the arithmetic mean,
(c) the lower quartile,
(d) the upper quartile,
(e) the quartile deviation,
(f) the mean deviation.

Explain the difference between the mean and quartile deviation.

53	116	70	54	36
70	98	176	139	38
67	102	161	77	137
93	133	56	93	81
81	131	185	88	54
86	92	83	60	109
95	24	117	35	57
106	19	171	81	79
105	59	55	110	186

A.C.C.A.

26. Membership of trade unions in the U.K., 1938, 1948 and 1960.

Membership	*No. of trade unions*		
	1938	1948	1960
Under 100	309	134	132
100–	286	217	176
500–	99	74	51
1,000–	116	102	97
2,500–	74	76	67
5,000–	80	60	52
15,000–	21	19	26
25,000 and over	39	51	49
Total	1,024	733	650

Source: *Annual Abstract of Statistics.*

Compare these distributions by estimating the median, the upper quartile and the highest decile (tenth) for each.

University of London B.Sc.

27. The following figures show the number of passengers carried on each of 70 journeys by an aircraft with a seating capacity of 100. Compile a grouped frequency distribution from which you can estimate the following:

(a) The average percentage capacity used;
(b) If 63 passengers is the smallest profitable load, the proportion of flights which were unprofitable.

11	12	27	57	90	72	51	76	81	71
78	76	61	25	48	67	80	78	66	32
52	26	70	53	27	67	88	67	23	96
59	74	87	61	57	24	60	63	51	52
18	43	76	99	76	64	87	12	89	38
28	87	79	90	58	29	51	45	29	84
37	82	30	76	58	33	81	55	68	91

I.O.T.

28. What are the principles underlying the construction of a histogram? Explain the relations between the histogram, the frequency polygon, and the frequency curve. Do you consider that the frequency polygon has any particular advantages over the other two forms of representation? Illustrate with a histogram the distribution of males which is given below, and use a frequency polygon to illustrate the distribution of females.

STUDENTS ADMITTED TO COURSES FOR A FIRST DEGREE

Age on admission (years)	Males	Females
17½–	15	27
18–	67	73
18½–	67	56
19–	41	49
19½–	22	20
20–	11	8
21–	5	5
22–	12	2

L.G.E.B.

29. Using the data of question 28 find the arithmetic mean age of admission for males and females separately. State precisely any assumptions that you make. Show how the two means may be combined to give the overall mean age for all students admitted.

L.G.E.B.

30. The following table concerns rates of pay and earnings by British Railways staff.

(a) Calculate the combined average rates of pay and average earnings of men and women at March 1958 and at April 1962.
(b) Find the percentage increases between the two years revealed by your results.
(c) Discuss the meaning of the difference between the increase in pay and the increase in earnings.

	Number of staff (000s)	Average rates of pay		Average weekly earnings	
Male adults:					
March 1958	502·9	£9	2s.	£12	0s.
April 1962	435·7	11	1	15	4
Female adults					
March 1958	32·8	6	18	7	7
April 1962	29·6	9	0	9	15

I.O.T.

31. The following table gives the years of construction of United Kingdom merchant vessels of 500 gross tons and over:

Year of construction			No. of vessels
January 1927 to December 1931			389
,,	1932 to	,, 1936	150
,,	1937 to	,, 1941	343
,,	1942 to	,, 1946	907
,,	1947 to	,, 1951	618
,,	1952 to	,, 1956	634

(a) Tabulate the age distribution at December 1956 of the merchant vessels, commencing with the last group, 1952 to 1956.

(b) Calculate the mean age and the standard deviation of the age distribution.

N.C.T.E.C.

32. WEEKLY INCOME OF HOUSEHOLDS IN THE U.K., 1960

Income	Number of households:	
	renting accommodation	in owned dwellings
Under £3	33	16
£3–	276	95
£6–	228	122
£10–	378	178
£14–	594	299
£20–	445	369
£30–	138	153
£50 and over	15	52
Total	2,107	1,284

From: "The Family Expenditure Survey," *Ministry of Labour Gazette,* December 1961.

Compare the two income distributions by computing means and standard deviations.

University of London B.Sc.

33. Calculate the mean and standard deviation (using short methods) for the following distribution of lengths of a component produced in a certain factory

Size (mm)		Frequency
mm	mm	
3·45 and less than 3·46		1
3·46 „ 3·47		3
3·47 „ 3·48		8
3·48 „ 3·49		12
3·49 „ 3·50		15
3·50 „ 3·51		15
3·51 „ 3·52		3
3·52 „ 3·53		2
3·53 „ 3·54		1

B.I.M.

34. (a) Define (i) median, (ii) percentile.
(b) Construct a cumulative frequency curve for the data in question 33 and from it read off the median and upper quartile.

B.I.M.

35. Calculate for the following distribution the arithmetic mean and standard deviation:

INDUSTRIAL STATUS IN GREAT BRITAIN 1951. ANALYSIS BY AGE OF MALE EMPLOYEES

Age	15–19	20–24	25–29	30–34	35–44	45–54	55–64	65 and over
Number in 000s	1	5	18	33	122	127	85	50

I.H.A.

36. For the distribution in question 35, estimate the median and quartile deviation. Explain what advantage, if any, these measures have compared with the mean and standard deviation

I.H.A

37. (a) Define the following statistical measures

(i) Mean and median.
(ii) Standard deviation and range

(b) The following figures give the radii of plastic stoppers. Calculate the mean and standard deviation of the radii.

Radii inches (thousandths)	No. of stoppers
415–	12
416–	25
417–	45
418–	53
419–	67
420–	50
421–	35
422–	26
423–	12
424–425	5
	330

L.C.C.

38. The manager of a sand quarry has kept a record of the deliveries of sand from the quarry during one week. The record is as follows:

Wt. of load (cwt)	Under 10	10 and under 20	20 and under 30	30 and under 40	40 and under 60	60 and under 80	Total
No. of loads	78	85	116	82	13	6	380

Calculate:

   (i) the arithmetic mean of the weights,

   (ii) the standard deviation of the weights.

Find the greatest possible percentage error in your answer for the arithmetic mean.

U.L.C.I.

39. The following table gives the gross weekly income of a sample of households:

			1957	1959
	Under	£3	133	87
£3 but	,,	£6	268	354
£6 ,,	,,	£8	159	152
£8 ,,	,,	£10	232	206
£10 ,,	,,	£14	619	549
£14 ,,	,,	£20	760	808
£20 ,,	,,	£30	479	628
	Over	£30	186	308

Calculate the arithmetic mean and the standard deviation *for 1957 only.* Calculate the standard error of the mean and explain its significance on the assumption that the above data are a random sample from the population of all households.

I.H.A.

40. The following table gives the length of life of 400 radio tubes.

Length of life (hours)	Number of radio tubes
300– 399	12
400– 499	32
500– 599	64
600– 699	76
700– 799	88
800– 899	60
900– 999	32
1,000–1,099	26
1,100–1,199	10
	400

Calculate:

(a) The average length of life of a radio tube:
(b) The standard deviation of the lengths;
(c) The percentage number of tubes whose length of life falls within the range mean $\pm$ 2 times the standard deviation.

N.C.T.E.C

41. (a) Explain the meaning of absolute and relative measures of dispersion, and compare their use.
(b) Estimate a measure of variation in the monthly production over the first half year, for each of the following two factories.

Output of Component Parts (thousands)

	Jan.	Feb.	Mar.	Apr.	May	June
Factory A	36	28	24	27	32	33
Factory B	73	52	51	58	63	59

L.C.C.

42. State briefly what you understand by "skewness." For the distribution on p. 237, calculate the mean, the standard deviation and the median:

Steel rings sold

Diameter (cms.)	Number (gross)
14·00–14·49	90
14·50–14·99	180
15·00–15·49	200
15·50–15·99	250
16·00–16·49	120
16·50–16·99	80
17·00–17·49	60
17·50–17·99	20

Use the figures you have calculated to obtain a measure of the skewness of the distribution.

I.C.W.A.

43.

INCOMES OF SINGLE-HANDED DENTISTS, 1955–6

Age	25–29	30–34	35–39	40–44	45–49
Average income (£)	2,380	2,410	2,420	2,570	2,260

Age	50–54	55–59	60–64	65–
Average income (£)	2,150	1,620	1,330	940

From: *Report*, Royal Commission on Doctors' and Dentists Remuneration (Cmnd. 939, 1960).

Estimate linear regression of income on age for dentists aged 40 and over from these data. How would you proceed if you take dentists of all ages and attempt a regression estimate of the age of peak earnings?

University of London B.Sc.

44. Plot the values in the following table on squared paper, and join them with a smooth curve:

x	y
1	10
2	19
3	27
5	40
6	45
7	49
8	52
9	54
11	55

(a) From your graph estimate:

    (i) the value of y when $x = 4$;

    (ii) the value of y when $x = 10$;

    (iii) the maximum value of y, and the value of x which corresponds to this value of y.

(b) Calculate the values of a and b and draw on your graph the line of best fit, $y = a + bx$. Using this line, what values of y do you get for $x = 4$ and $x = 10$?

I.C.W.A.

45. Explain what you understand by "regression" and how it may be illustrated graphically. Show that there are always two regression lines between any pair of variables, and explain the relations between them. Use the data below to illustrate the regression of:

    y = annual income at age 40

on x = age at termination of full-time education.

What would be the meaning, in this case, of the other line of regression?

x	y	x	y	x	y
14	500	15	600	18	2,000
14	525	16	1,250	19	710
14	750	16	850	20	1,900
15	630	16	1,500	22	3,000
15	810	17	1 380	23	1,860

L.G.E.B.

46. Explain in your own words the meaning of the following terms:

(a) correlation;

(b) regression;

(c) standard error of the mean.

For what purposes are such statistical methods and measures used?

I.H.A.

47. (a) Define correlation.

    (b) Calculate a coefficient of correlation between the following series A and B.

A	10	12	17	20	16
B	3	3	5	8	6

B.I.M

48. The following figures give the average weekly output of coal in the United Kingdom and the number of civil servants for twelve successive quarters in 1950–3:

Output of coal (100,000 tons)	Civil servants (000s)
40	689
41	685
36	679
44	676
46	675
39	680
45	686
43	688
42	684
38	678
47	673
48	668

(a) Calculate the coefficient of correlation between the two sets of figures.

(b) Would you agree that these figures demonstrate that a decrease in the number of civil servants results in an increase in coal production? Give reasons for your answer.

B.S.I.

49. The intelligence quotient of 12 salesmen was measured using two different methods, x and y. The results were as follows:

Salesmen	1	2	3	4	5	6
Method x	99	91	87	106	125	120
Method y	104	112	85	102	131	142

Salesmen	7	8	9	10	11	12
Method x	75	86	112	125	102	130
Method y	70	84	104	108	99	146

(a) Calculate the correlation coefficient between the two methods x and y.

(b) Draw the scatter diagram and compare the two results.

R.S.A.

50. Ten types of paint have been subjected to artificial "weathering" tests in the laboratory. The results are listed in the table below, together with those obtained under natural conditions over a longer period of time.

| Type of paint | Ranking obtained: | |
	In the laboratory	Under natural conditions
A	2	1
B	4	2
C	1	3
D	6	4
E	3	5
F	5	6
G	8	7
H	10	8
I	7	9
J	9	10

Is the laboratory test a reliable guide as to how a given paint will behave under natural conditions? I.C.W.A.

51. "The ultimate object of sampling is to generalise about the total population." Explain this statement. I.H.A.

52. A firm buys a component part from two manufacturers. Tests show that those supplied by manufacturer A have a mean life of 70 hours use with standard deviation 5 hours. Those from manufacturer B have a life of 80 hours with a standard deviation of $7\frac{1}{2}$ hours.

(a) You are asked to write a brief report for someone unacquainted with technical terms, explaining the meaning of these results and the use that can be made of them.
(b) Estimate the greatest and smallest life of the respective makes, assuming that the lives of the components are normally distributed. B.I.M.

53. A manufacturer aims to make electricity bulbs with a mean working life of 1,000 hours. He draws a sample of 20 from a batch and tests it. The mean life of the sample bulbs is 990 with a standard deviation of 22 hours. Is the batch up to standard? B.S.I.

54. A given type of aircraft develops minor trouble in 4% of flights. Another type of aircraft on the same journey develops trouble in 19 out of 150 flights. Investigate the performance of the two types of machine and comment on any significant difference. L.C.C.

55. In a sample of 540 wives of professional and salaried workers, 42% had visited their doctor at least once during the preceding three months. During the same period of a sample of 270 wives of labourers and unskilled workers, 36% had visited a doctor. By the use of an appropriate statistical test, consider the validity of the assertion that middle class wives are more likely to visit their doctors than the wives of working class husbands.

I.H.A.

56. One group of 60 patients is treated with drug A, while another group of 80 patients is given drug B. After 14 days, 12 members of the A group were free of infection; 20 members of the B group were likewise free. The doctor in charge is convinced that treatment with drug B is superior. Comment on this view, explaining the basis of any statistical test you may employ.

I.H.A.

57. In a sample of 569 wives of professional and salaried workers 45% attended weekly the local welfare centre with their infants. For a sample of 245 wives of agricultural workers, the corresponding proportion was 35%. Test the hypothesis that there is no difference between the two groups in respect of their attendance at such centres. Explain how you interpret your result.

I.H.A.

58. The following data relate to measurements of components produced by two different machines. Is there any significant difference between the output of the two machines?

Machine	Number measured	Average size	Standard deviation
A	1,200	31 in.	5 in.
B	1,000	30 in.	4 in.

I.C.W.A.

59. (a) An engineering works engaged in producing car components can make them to dimension specifications, *but* with a standard deviation of 0·004 in. Out of a total produced batch of 5,000 items, how many are likely to be within ±0·002 in. of a specified dimension? The distribution of the measurements may be taken as normal.

(b) A given computer contains 18,000 thermionic valves. The manufacturer of the valves gives the average life as 3,000 hours with a standard deviation of 50 hours. How many of the valves are likely to have to be replaced after 2,900 hours

I

usage?   The life statistics of a valve given above may be taken to refer to a Normal distribution of life.   B.I.M

60. (a) Explain concisely what is meant by sampling.

(b) What information would you require before deciding what size of sample you would employ to provide information in the nature of a statistical population?   B.I.M.

61. What do you understand by the term "statistically significant"?   Where needed illustrate your answer by hypothetical data.   I.H.A.

62. The prices and quantities sold of two commodities in two different years are shown below:

	Price (in shillings)		Quantity sold (in 000s)	
	Base year	Current year	Base year	Current year
Commodity A	10	15	120	60
Commodity B	50	60	80	100

Calculate, using quantities sold as weights:

(a) a base-weighted price index;

(b) a current-weighted price index;

and, using prices as weights:

(c) a base-weighted quantity index;

(d) a current-weighted quantity index.

Write a brief comment on the results of using the Laspeyres type in (a) and (c) and the Paasche type in (b) and (d).   B.I.M.

63.   INDEX OF INDUSTRIAL PRODUCTION

	Weight	Index 1961 (Average 1958 = 100)
Total manufacturing ..	748	114·7
Mining and quarrying ..	72	93
Construction..	126	118
Gas, electricity and water ..	54	116

(a) Explain the meaning of "Average 1958 = 100."
(b) What is the purpose of weights?
(c) Calculate the index of industrial production for 1961.
(d) If the index for gas, electricity and water subsequently rises to 138 and the other data remain the same, find the change in the total index of industrial production.

U.L.C.I.

64. The total advertising outlay by means of (1) the Press, and (2) television, are as follows:

	Press £ millions	*Television* £ millions
1958	158·4	48·0
1959	170·5	57·4
1960	197·2	71·8
1961	197·5	83·0
1962	202·0	82·5

(a) Take 1958 as base year and calculate indexes of the amounts spent on advertising in each of the given categories.
(b) Compare the two sets of indexes by means of a compound bar chart.

R.S.A.

65. The second column of the following table lists the average quantities of three metals used by a certain factory in the period 1950–2. Calculate the weighted aggregate price index for these metals for 1951 and 1952 using 1950 as the base year:

1	2	3	4	5	6	7	8
	Typical quantities used	Price per pound			Price of quantities used		
		1950	1951	1952	1950	1951	1952
Metal	(w)	P_0	P_1	P_2	P_0w	P_1w	P_2w
Copper	20,000 lb.	$0·242	$0·242	$0·242	$4,840	$4,840	$4,840
Lead	12,000 lb.	0·170	0·190	0·148	2,040	2,280	1,776
Zinc	14,000 lb.	0·175	0·195	0·125	2,450	2,730	1,750

B.S.I.

66. Describe concisely the steps involved in calculating, by the method of moving averages, a seasonally-adjusted series. Of what use is such a series in a transport undertaking? By analysing his receipts in recent years, a transport operator estimates that on average his takings each January are 20% below trend, those in February are 10% below, and those in March 5% below. In January, February and March 1963, his actual takings were £1,000, £1,100 and £1,150 respectively. After allowing for seasonal influences, would you conclude that his receipts were rising or falling during this period?

I.O.T.

67. The following table gives the quarterly sales of a product for four years.

	Quarters			
Year	1	2	3	4
1	8	22	10	9
2	22	31	21	21
3	25	28	22	28
4	34	42	41	43

Calculate a centred four-quarter moving average and derive a seasonally adjusted series.

B.I.M.

68.   HOUSING IN ENGLAND AND WALES

Number of permanent houses completed for:

		Local housing authorities	Private owners
1960	4	26,534	43,745
1961	1	22,153	38,443
	2	23,253	43,599
	3	21,459	43,673
	4	26,015	44,651
1962	1	24,416	36,201
	2	24,951	42,638
	3	25,875	43,534
	4	30,040	44,643
1963	1	13,737	27,363
	2	26,253	42,971

Source: *Ministry of Housing.*

(a) Rewrite the number of houses completed, to the nearest thousand.

(b) Calculate the trend from the approximated figures, by means of a four-quarterly moving average.

(c) Plot both series with their respective trends, on the same diagram.

R.S.A.

69. MANUFACTURERS' SALES OF GRAMOPHONE RECORDS

Quarters	£'00,000				
	1959	1960	1961	1962	1963
Jan.–Mar.	30	38	39	43	46
Apr.–June	28	27	30	33	38
July–Sept.	30	33	36	37	47
Oct.–Dec.	48	53	55	62	

Calculate values for:
(a) the trend of the sale of records, and
(b) the regular seasonal movement of the sales,
using the method of moving averages.

I.M.S.M.

70. EARNINGS IN INDUSTRY (VALUES TO THE NEAREST SHILLING)

		Men	Women			Men	Women
1956	April	235	120	1960	April	282	145
	October	238	123		October	291	148
1957	April	242	126	1961	April	301	153
	October	252	130		October	307	155
1958	April	253	131	1962	April	313	157
	October	257	134		October	317	161
1959	April	263	137	1963	April	323	164
	October	271	141		October	335	168

(a) Plot the two series of earnings given above, using an arithmetic scale graph.
(b) Calculate the trend of earnings for men, using a moving average in two's and plot the trend on the same diagram as the original series.

N.C.T.E.C.

71. Analyse the quarterly figures provided below (using annual moving averages) to show the seasonal pattern, and comment on its development since 1956.

		(in £000)		
Quarters	1956	1957	1958	1959
1	236	245	248	252
2	277	290	288	
3	263	269	262	
4	334	339	344	

I.C.W.A.

72. Define in your own words what is meant by any *three* of the following statistical terms and discuss their uses. In each case, give an example of their use in the field of transport.

(*a*) Frequency distribution;
(*b*) Random sample;
(*c*) Index numbers,
(*d*) Moving average;
(*e*) Scatter chart.

I.O.T.

73. Answer three of the following:

(*a*) The geometric mean of three numbers is A and the geometric mean of two other numbers is B. What is the geometric mean of all five numbers?
(*b*) An employee gets three successive annual rises in salary of 20%, 25% and 30% respectively, each calculated on his salary at the end of the previous year. How much better or worse off would he be if he had three annual rises of 25% each reckoned in the same way as before?
(*c*) In a factory employing 20,000 people a random sample of 200 employees showed 120 with defective eyesight. Within what limits will the number of employees in the whole factory having some eyesight defect lie?
(*d*) Selling price per unit is 10*s*. to the nearest 6*d*. Amount sold is 5,300 units to the nearest 50. Find the total value of sales and the possible error involved.

B.I.M.

74. Answer *three* of the following:

(*a*) Demonstrate that the geometric mean of two numbers cannot exceed the arithmetic average.
(*b*) Calculate, indicating the limits of the result, the product of 2,500 and 17 numbers being correct within 10% and 5% respectively.
(*c*) Write down a formula for calculating the correlation coefficient, indicating the meaning of the symbols you use.
(*d*) Explain what is meant by "confidence limits."

B.I.M.

EXAMINATION TECHNIQUE

To pass any examination you must:

1. Have the knowledge.
2. Convince the examiner you have the knowledge.
3. Convince him within the time allowed.

In the book so far we have considered the first of these only. Success in the other two respects will be much more assured if you apply the examination hints given below.

1. Answer the question. Apart from ignorance, *failure to answer the question is undoubtedly the greatest bar to success.* No matter how often students are told, they always seem to be guilty of this fault. If you are asked for a frequency polygon, *don't* give a frequency curve; if asked to give the features of the mean, *don't* detail the steps for computing it. You can write a hundred pages of brilliant exposition, but if it's not in answer to the set question you will be given no more marks than if it had been a paragraph of utter drivel. To ensure you answer the question:

(a) *Read the question carefully.*
(b) *Decide what the examiner wants.*
(c) *Underline the nub of the question.*
(d) *Do just what the examiner asks.*
(e) *Keep returning to the question.*

2. Put your ideas in logical order. It's quicker, more accurate and gives a greater impression of competence if you follow a pre-determined logical path instead of jumping about from place to place as ideas come to you.

3. Maximise the points you make. Examiners are more impressed by a solid mass of points than an unending development of one solitary idea—no matter how sophisticated and exhaustive. Don't allow yourself to become bogged down with your favourite hobby-horse.

4. Allocate your time. Question marks often bear a close relationship to the time needed for an appropriate answer. Consequently the time spent on a question should be in proportion to the marks. Divide the total exam marks into the total exam time (less planning time) to obtain a "minutes per mark" figure, and allow that many minutes per mark of each individual question.

247

5. Attempt all questions asked for. Always remember that the first 50% of the marks for any question is the easier to earn. Unless you are working in complete ignorance, you will always earn more marks per minute while answering a new question than while continuing to answer one that is more than half done. So you can earn many more marks by half-completing two answers than by completing either one individually.

6. Don't show your ignorance. Concentrate on displaying your knowledge—not your ignorance. There is almost always one question you need to attempt and are not happy about. In answer to such a question put down all you *do* know—and then devote the unused time to improving some other answer. Certainly you won't get full marks by doing this, but nor will you if you fill your page with nonsense. By spending the saved time on another answer you will at least be gaining the odd mark or so.

7. If time runs out. What should you do if you find time is running out? The following are the recommended tactics:

(a) If it is a mathematical answer, don't bother to work out the figures. Show the examiner by means of your layout that you know what steps need to be taken and which pieces of data are applicable. He is very much more concerned with this than with your ability to calculate.

(b) If it is an essay answer, put down your answer in the form of notes. It is surprising what a large percentage of the question marks can be obtained by a dozen terse, relevant notes.

(c) Make sure that every question and question part has some answer—no matter how short—that summarises the key elements.

(d) Don't worry. Shortage of time is more often a sign of knowing too much than too little.

8. Avoid panic, but welcome "nerves." "Nerves" are a great aid in examinations. Being nervous enables one to work at a much more concentrated pitch for a longer time without fatigue. Panic, on the other hand, destroys one's judgment. To avoid panic:

(a) Know your subject (this is your best "panic-killer").

(b) Give yourself a generous time allowance to read the paper. Quick starters are usually poor performers.

(c) Take two or three deep breaths.

(d) Concentrate simply on maximising your marks. Leave considerations of passing or failing until after.

(e) Answer the easiest questions first—it helps to build confidence.

(f) Don't let first impressions of the paper upset you. Given a few minutes, it is amazing what one's subconscious will throw up. Moreover it is often only the unfamiliar presentation of data that makes a statistical question look difficult: once you have looked carefully at it, it often shows itself to be quite simple.

SUGGESTED ANSWERS

Answers to most of the questions in the Progress Tests are
given either at the end of the question concerned or here. Where
for reasons of space it has not been practical to supply any answer
at all, the question has been marked with an asterisk (*)

Progress Test 2

1.   280
    500
    641
    800
    900
  —————
  3,121

Ans. = **3,100 tons**

NOTE: Since three figures are exact hundreds, this implies
that some figures are being rounded to the nearest 100. It is
assumed, therefore, that 500, 800 and 900 are approximations,
so the answer is approximated to the nearest 100 tons.

2. $1,200 \times 112 \times 4 = 537,600$.

Since the lowest number of significant figures in the rounded
figures used is two (*i.e.* 1,200 people) the answer can only contain
two significant figures.

∴ Total approximate weight of potatoes bought in a year
= 540,000 lbs.

NOTE: The 4, being an exact number, is not a rounded
number and therefore is excluded from the inspection for the
number with the lowest number of significant figures.

3. (a) $21\cdot388 \pm 0\cdot056$.   (b) $21\cdot332 \pm 0\cdot056$.

Progress Test 4

1

*Changes in passenger journeys and receipts
on British Railways, 1958–61*

(a) Passenger journeys

Type of fare	1958		1961		Change[1]	
	No. of journeys (millions)	%	No. of journeys (millions)	%	No. of journeys (millions)	%
Full fare	351	32·2	273	26·6	−78	−5·6
Reduced fare	426	39·1	435	42·5	+9	+3·4
Season ticket	313	28·7	317	30·9	+4	+2·2
Total	1,090	100	1,025	100	−65	—[2]

(b) Receipts

Type of fare	£ millions	%	£ millions	%	£ millions	%
Full fare	74	53·8	79·7	50·7	+5·7	−3·1
Reduced fare	46·1	33·5	54·1	34·4	+8	+0·9
Season ticket	17·5[3]	12·7	23·4	14·9	+5·9	+2·2
Total	137·6	100	157·2	100	+19·6	—

NOTES: The main decision in this question is whether to have the years as separate tables with passenger journeys and receipts side by side, or vice versa as shown in the answer. As the question asked for *changes* to be brought out, the layout adopted seemed preferable, the alternative layout being more appropriate to a table illustrating the *relationship between journeys and receipts* within the three-fare structure.

It was also tempting to consider using as alternative derived statistics the receipts per passenger journey (by dividing each receipt figure by its corresponding number of passenger journeys). However, valuable as these figures might be, they do not highlight *changes in the original data*, which is what the question seems to aim at.

[1] Since the table is to bring out changes between the years, a section actually detailing the changes is a logical inclusion.

[2] Note that this total must come to zero, since the fares which increase as a *percentage of the total* must exactly balance the fares that decrease.

[3] It is a favourite examiner's technique to leave "holes" in the data for a table. The student must, of course, fill in the "holes" by logical deduction.

3. *Criticisms of table:*

(a) No title.
(b) No source stated.
(c) No units given in "Weight of metal" column.
(d) (i) What are "foundry hours"?
   (ii) Since all weights of castings are covered by the first three lines of the table, what can "Others" (line 4) refer to?
   (iii) Does "Up to 10 cwts" include or exclude a casting weighing 10 cwts?
   (All these are instances of ambiguity.)
(e) Since "Up to 10 cwts" includes "Up to 4 cwts" it would seem that double-counting is occurring.

(*f*) The "foundry hours" don't add up to 2,000. What is this latter figure, then? If this total is relevant to the table, what is missing from the main body of it?

Summary. A confused table which, at best, tells little or nothing and, at worst, could mislead.

Progress Test 5

1. *See* Fig. 41.

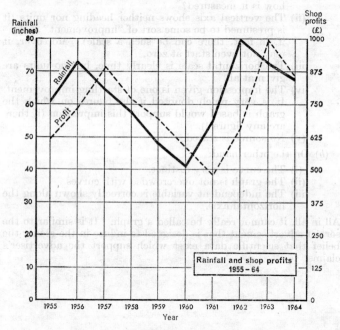

Fig. 41.—*Rainfall and shop profits*

NOTE: To answer the question it was necessary to use a double scale, and in order to bring out the relationship in the most effective manner the two scales were chosen so that the two curves occupied the same part of the graph.

As a result of such a choice of scales it becomes obvious from the graph that the two curves are almost identical, the main difference being that the rainfall curve *precedes* the profit curve by a year. This suggests that profits are closely related to the *previous* year's rainfall. (In statistics, when one curve follows another, the time difference is termed *lag*. Finding cases of lag are often useful since it means that the future value of one variable can be closely estimated from the current value of another.)

2. (*a*) This graph has the following *serious* faults:

    (i) The title is not clear. What is "improvement" and how is it measured?

   (ii) The vertical axis shows neither heading nor units (it is presumed to be some sort of "improvement" scale— if, in fact, there can be such a scale). Moreover, it may not even start at zero.

  (iii) The horizontal scale is clearly time, but no units are given at all.

  (iv) The impression given is one of startling improvement. It is very much doubted if the figures on which the graph is based would support this impression (if there are any figures!).

   (v) No source is stated.

(*b*) On the other hand:

    (i) The curve is very distinct.

   (ii) The graph is not overcrowded with curves.

  (iii) The independent variable is correctly shown along the horizontal axis.

All in all, it cannot really be called a graph. It is similar to the sort of advertisement that is designed to induce in the reader the belief that scientific data exist which support the advertiser's claims.

Progress Test 6

1. First prepare a table:

Year	Amount	3-year moving–		10-year moving–	
		Total	Average	Total[(1)]	Average
1940	5				
1941	8		6·$\dot{3}$[(2)]		
1942	6	19	8·$\dot{6}$[(3)]		
1943	12	26	7·$\dot{3}$		
1944	4	22	8·0		9·1[(4)]
1945	8	24	9·0		10·6
1946	15	27	11·0		11·4
1947	10	33	11·$\dot{6}$		12·3
1948	10	35	11·0		11·7
1949	13	33	14·$\dot{3}$	91	13·1
1950	20	43	16·$\dot{3}$	106	13·2
1951	16	49	17·0	114	13·2
1952	15	51	12·$\dot{3}$	123	13·0
1953	6	37	13·0	117	13·2
1954	18	39	11·0	131	13·3
1955	9	33	14·0	132	13·1
1956	15	42	10·$\dot{6}$	132	13·7
1957	8	32	11·$\dot{6}$	130	13·8
1958	12	35	11·$\dot{3}$	132	14·6
1959	14	34	14·$\dot{6}$	133	14·8
1960	18	44	18·0	131	
1961	22	54	18·$\dot{6}$	137	
1962	16	56	17·$\dot{3}$	138	
1963	14	52	16·$\dot{6}$	146	
1964	20	50		148	

Now *see* Fig. 42.

Difference between 10-year and 3-year moving averages: The 10-year moving average smooths out the fluctuations far more than the 3-year average—in fact, the 10-year average is nearly a straight line. However, the 3-year average is more sensitive to changes and signals a new trend sooner than the 10-year which tends to lag behind.[(7)]

NOTES: [(1)]To calculate a 10-year moving average it is first necessary to calculate a 10-year moving total.

254   STATISTICS

(2)This average is located at the mid-point of its 3-year period.

(3)A dot over a decimal digit means that the decimal is recurring.

(4)This average is located at the mid-point of its 10-year period.

(5)Totals on this graph are plotted at the *end* of the period to which they apply, and averages at the *mid-point* (*see s.* **13.** 2).

(6)A moving total of 3-years is really too short a period to give a curve of any significance. It has been included simply in order to give the student practice.

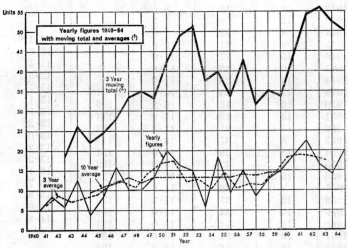

FIG. 42.—*Yearly figures* 1960–64 *with moving total and averages*

(7)Indeed, moving averages may be compared to shock-absorbers which can be built to give any kind of ride between one where every bump is felt and one that is almost perfectly smooth. However, while the latter may be ideal for riding, in economics and business some knowledge of the most recent bumps is necessary if new trends are to be noticed quickly, and therefore some compromise is needed in choosing the average.

Progress Test 7

2. *See* Fig. 43. This curve shows the extent to which the sharing of net output between establishments diverges from equality. Thus 82% of the establishments have between them only 34½%

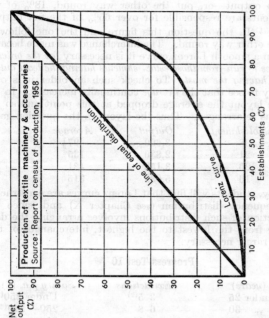

Establishments			Net output		
No.	%	Cum. %	£000's	%	Cum. %
48	22½	22½	1,406	3½	3½
42	19½	42	2,263	6	9½
38	18	60	3,699	9½	19
26 [1]	12	72	3,152 [1]	8	27
21	10	82	2,886	7½	34½
16	7	89	5,032	13	47½
23	11	100	20,385	52½	100
214			38,773		

FIG. 43.—*Lorenz curve of production of textile machinery and accessories*

of the net output—or, put the other way round, 18% of the establishments are responsible for over 65% of the net output.

NOTE: [1]In the question this figure and the one following were the other way round. The interchange was made because to obtain a smooth Lorenz curve it is necessary for *the order of the figures to run from those establishments having the least output to those having the most*. To check such an order it is only necessary to see that the *average* continually increases. In the question layout the average dropped at this point and so the order was re-arranged. Thus the layout in the question gave:

Establishments	Output	Average
38	3,699	$97\frac{1}{2}$
21	2,836	135
26	3,152	121
16	5,032	315

Normally, students will find that Lorenz curves are constructed from frequency distribution (*see* Chapter X) and, since the construction of such distributions involves arranging the data in order from the lowest to the highest, interchanges of this sort are rarely necessary.

Progress Test 10

1.

Age (years)	Extractions	Salary p.a. (£)
20–under 25	3–5[2]	Under 250[4]
25– ,, 30	6–8	250– 349[5]
30– ,, 35	9–11	350– 449
35– ,, 40	12–14	450– 549
40– ,, 45	15–17	550– 649
45– ,, 50	18–20	650– 749
50– ,, 55	21–23	750– 849
55– ,, 60	24–26	850– 949
60– ,, 65	27–29	950–1,049
65– ,, 70	30–32	1,050–1,249[6]
70– ,, 75	33–34	1,250–1,749
75– ,, 80		1,750–2,499
80– ,, 85	Class limits "6–8":	2,500–3,499
85– ,, 90	$5\frac{1}{2}$ to $8\frac{1}{2}$[3]	3,500–5,499
90– ,, 95	extractions	5,500–7,499
95– ,, 100		7,500–12,499
over 100		12,500–17,499
		17,500–22,499

Class limits of "25–under 30": 30 years exactly to up to, but not including, 35 years[1]

Over 22,500[4]

Class "250–349": £249½ to £349½[7]

NOTES: [1]It should always be remembered that ages are usually given as at the last birthday, *i.e.* rounded down. Any distribution using ages should be constructed with this in mind. In fact, students are warned that official figures often reflect this by showing *stated* limits as 20–24; 25–29, etc., and so on.

[2]A class interval of 3 is not usually recommended, but it was chosen here as a compromise. An interval of 2 would be so small that one might as well construct the distribution without any grouping at all—and so avoid the loss of information that inevitably accompanies grouping. On the other hand, an interval of 4 would result in only 7 or 8 classes.

With 3 as an interval, the distribution "looks" better if the stated lower class limits are multiples of 3.

[3]The data are discrete—you cannot have half an extraction —but the exact limits are deemed to extend half a unit on each side of the stated limits.

[4]These classes are open-ended. It is assumed that very few full-time employed adults have incomes below £250 p.a. or over £22,500 p.a.

[5]This first group of classes has been chosen so that the round hundreds fall at the class mid-points, as it is assumed that there will be a tendency for incomes to be set at the round hundred level. This arrangement is in compliance with suggestion (*d*), *s.* **26.** 10 (note, however, that incomes set at the round £50 level will unfortunately result in some undesirable clustering at the beginning of classes).

[6]Classes are unequal because the frequencies at these higher levels will reduce considerably and therefore wider classes will be required to give worthwhile frequency figures.

[7]Although salaries are usually considered a continuous variable (the discrete steps of $\frac{1}{2}p$. are really too small to render salaries a normal discrete variable), in this case the fact that the data were collected to the nearest pound changes the series to a *discrete* one, and it should be treated as such.

Progress Test 11

3. Set out the distribution:

Class			f	Cumulative f
0–under	10		12	12
10–	,,	25	25	37
25–	,,	40	51	88
40–	,,	50	48	136
50–	,,	60	46	183
60–	,,	80	54	236
Over 80			8	244

After laying out this distribution the first thing to decide, in view of the unequal class intervals is what interval should be chosen as "normal." Since three of the classes have intervals of 10, this interval has been chosen. This means that the other classes need adjustments to their frequencies in accordance with *s.* **28. 3.** These adjustments are:

Class	Divide f by:	Adjusted
10–under 25	1·5	16⅔
25– ,, 40	1·5	34
60– ,, 80	2	27
80– ,, 100	2	4

We can now construct the required graphs: *see* Fig. **44.**

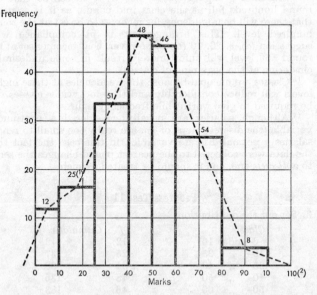

Fig. 44.—(a) *Histogram with frequency polygon of marks (first examination)*

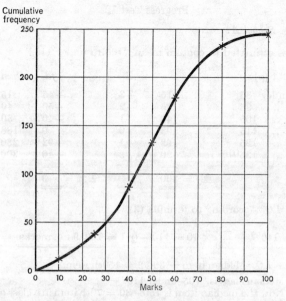

Cumulative frequency

Marks

(b) *Ogive of marks (first examination)*

NOTES:

[1]In plotting these adjusted frequencies the original frequencies do not show on the graph. Under these circumstances it is normal to write the original frequencies over the rectangles.

[2]Frequency polygons are, of course, constructed so that they extend half a class interval beyond the last class. Where the distribution has unequal classes, this extension must be made equal to *half the interval of the end class*. In this case, as the end class (80–100) has an interval of 20, the polygon must finish at half this interval beyond the top of the class, *i.e.* at 110.

[3]Note that in the construction of ogives unequal class intervals do not lead to the sort of special adjustments needed when constructing histograms.

5. (*a*) 85 mileages.
   (*b*) 400 to 432 miles.

Progress Test 12

2(a). *School A:*

Class estimated to contain mean "105 to under 115."

I.Q. (x)			d	fd	Cum.
75–under	85	15	−3	−45	15
85–	,, 95	25	−2	−50	40
95–	,, 105	40	−1	−40	80
105–	,, 115	108	0	0	188
115–	,, 125	92	+1	+92	280
125–	,, 135[1]	20	+2	+40	300

$$\Sigma f = 300 \qquad\qquad \Sigma fd = -3$$

Mean I.Q. According to formula (3),

$$\bar{x} = 110^{(2)} + \frac{-3}{300} \times 10 = 110 - 0 \cdot 1 = \underline{\underline{109 \cdot 9}} \text{ I.Q. marks.}$$

Median I.Q.: Median item $= 300/2 = 150$th item.

∴ Median class is "105–under 115."

Now the median item is $150 - 80 = 70$th item in a class of 108 items

∴ The median item lies 70/108ths into the class "105–under 115."

And since the class interval is 10 units, then 70/108ths of

the interval $= \frac{70}{108} \times 10 = 6 \cdot 5$ units.

∴ Median lies $6 \cdot 5$ units above the bottom of the "105–under 115" class *i.e.* $105 + 6 \cdot 5 = \underline{\underline{111 \cdot 5}}$ I.Q. marks.

School B:

Similarly, mean $= \underline{\underline{95 \cdot 3}}$ I.Q. marks

median $= \underline{\underline{93 \cdot 3}}$ I.Q. marks.

NOTES: [1]For the purpose of computing the mean an open-ended class is assumed to be the same size as the adjoining class (*s.* **26. 9**).

[2]"Assumed mean" is the mid-point of the chosen class, in this case "105–under 115."

4. (a)

Machine	No. of minutes per article	No. of articles per hour
A	2	60/2 = 30
B	3	60/3 = 20
C	5	60/5 = 12
D	6	60/6 = 10

Total articles per hour = 72

(b)

Machine	Production In 1st and 2nd hour	In 3rd hour	Total
A	0	30	30
B	40	20	60
C	24	0	24
D	20	10	30

144

∴ 144 articles were produced in the 3 hours.
∴ Average number of articles per hour
  $= 144/3 = 48$ articles.

5. (a) *The arithmetic mean.* The few high wages will result in this mean being the highest of the averages. Although such extreme wage payments would be unlikely to "distort" the mean seriously, their effect would result in the average looking larger than the figures in the whole of the distribution would warrant.

(b) *The mode.* In this sort of distribution the most frequently occurring wage is inevitably near the bottom, and choice of this average would result in a figure which made no allowance for the few high wages that some members of the foremen's union would be earning.

(c) *The median.* The median wage indicates the wage of the foreman who is "half way up the ladder." Half the foremen do better and half do worse. If you assume you will make a normal sort of foreman, then you may reasonably expect to be near the middle, *i.e.* earning the median wage.

6. A combined mean is found by multiplying the number of items in each group by the respective means of each group; adding the products; and finally dividing by total number of items. As a formula this can be written so:

$$\text{Combined mean} = \frac{n_1 \bar{x}_1 + n_2 \bar{x}_2 + n_3 \bar{x}_3}{n_1 + n_2 + n_3}$$

Progress Test 13

1. Cumulative frequency distribution:

Marks	f	Cum. f	Marks		Cum.
0– 5	2	2	51– 55	280	1,160
6–10	8	10	56– 60	320	1,480
11–15	20	30	61– 65	260	1,740
16–20	30	60	66– 70	160	1,900
21–25	50	110	71– 75	120	2,020
26–30	80	190	76– 80	100	2,120
31–35	120	310	81– 85	60	2,180
36–40	150	460	86– 90	40	2,220
41–45	200	660	91– 95	17	2,237
46–50	220	880	96–100	3	2,240

(a) (i) *Median:* Median item = 2,240/2 = 1,120.

∴ Median class = "51–55."

Now there are 880 items in the preceding classes. Therefore the median item is the $1,120 - 880 = 240$th item beyond the beginning of the median class, which contains 280 items.

∴ Median item lies 240/280ths of the way through the class.

Now the class has an interval of 5 marks.[1]

∴ Median value is $\dfrac{240}{280} \times 5 = 4\frac{2}{7}$ marks above the bottom of the median class.

∴ Median $= 4\frac{2}{7} + 50\frac{1}{2}^{[1]} = 54\frac{11}{14}$

But as no fractions of a mark are allowed the median must be a round number.

∴ Median = 55 marks.

(ii) *First quartile:* First quartile item $= \dfrac{2,240}{4} = 560$th

∴ Quartile class = "41–45."

∴ First Quartile $= 40\frac{1}{2} + \dfrac{560 - 460}{200} \times 5 = \underline{\underline{43 \text{ marks.}}}$

(iii) *Third quartile:* Third quartile item

$$= \frac{2,240}{4} \times 3 = 1,680\text{th.}$$

∴ Quartile class = "61–65."

∴ Third quartile $= 60\frac{1}{2} + \dfrac{1,680 - 1,480}{260} \times 5$

$= 64 \cdot 35$

Rounded to the nearest unit = <u>64 marks.</u>

(iv) *Sixth decile:* Sixth decile item

$$= \frac{2,240}{10} \times 6 = 1,344\text{th.}$$

∴ Sixth decile class = "56–60."

∴ Sixth decile $= 55\frac{1}{2} + \dfrac{1,344 - 1,160}{320} \times 5 = 58 \cdot 37$

i.e. to the nearest unit = <u>58 marks.</u>

(v) *Forty-second percentile:* Forty-second percentile item

$$= \frac{2,240}{100} \times 42 = 940 \cdot 8$$

i.e. since there can be no fraction of an item, 941st item.

∴ 42nd percentile class = "51–55."

∴ 42nd percentile $= 50\frac{1}{2} + \dfrac{941 - 880}{280} \times 5 = 51 \cdot 59$

i.e. to nearest unit = <u>52 marks.</u>

(b) If the examining body wished to pass only one-third of the candidates, the cut-off mark would need to be the mark obtained by the candidate one-third from the top, *i.e.* the $2,240 - \frac{1}{3} \times 2,240 = 1,493$rd candidate.

This candidate's marks fall in the "61–65" class and can be estimated as $60\frac{1}{2} + \dfrac{1,493 - 1,480}{260} \times 5 = 60\frac{3}{4}$

This means that the pass mark must be set at <u>61 marks.</u>

NOTE: [1]Although no fractions of a mark are given, the class limits are deemed to extend $\frac{1}{2}$ mark either side of the stated limits, *e.g.* class "51–55" is considered to have limits of "$50\frac{1}{2}$–$55\frac{1}{2}$." This means that (i) the class interval is 5, and (ii) the class begins at $50\frac{1}{2}$.

2. (a) Cumulative frequency distribution:

Length of wait (mins.)	f	Cumulative f
0	50	50
Under ½	210	260
½—under 1	340	600 (First quartile class)
1— ,, 2	200	800 (Median class)
2— ,, 3	110	910
3— ,, 5	170	1,080 (Third quartile class)
5— ,, 10	140	1,220
over 10	80	1,300

The middle 50% of the customers are those who lie between the first and the third quartiles (*see s.* **38. 4**).

First quartile item $= \dfrac{1,300}{4} = 325$th item

$\therefore$ First quartile $= \frac{1}{2} + \dfrac{325 - 260}{340} \times \frac{1}{2} = \frac{1}{2} + 0 \cdot 096 = \underline{\underline{0 \cdot 596}}.$

Third quartile item $= \dfrac{1,300}{4} \times 3 = 975$th item

$\therefore$ Third quartile $= 3 + \dfrac{975 - 910}{170} \times 2 = 3 + 0 \cdot 765 = 3 \cdot 765$

$\therefore$ The middle 50% of the customers wait between $0 \cdot 596$ and $3 \cdot 765$ minutes, *i.e.* between 36 seconds and 3 minutes 46 seconds.

(b) (ii) From the cumulative frequency distribution drawn up in (a) it is possible to determine the median.
Median item $= 1,300/2 = 650$th.

$\therefore$ Median $= 1 + \dfrac{650 - 600}{200} \times 1 = 1 + \frac{1}{4} =$

$\underline{\underline{1\frac{1}{4} \text{ minutes.}}}$

This means that half the customers wait $1\frac{1}{4}$ minutes or less and the other half $1\frac{1}{4}$ minutes or more. Now the chances are equal as to which half you will be in,[1] and therefore you will have a 50/50 chance of being at the check point in $1\frac{1}{4}$ minutes or less. Since you wish to be there in 2 minutes, the odds are definitely in your favour.[2]

NOTES: [1]Look at it this way: *all* customers must fall into one half or the other. You are one of the customers. Since there is nothing to make you fall in one half more than another, the chance of being in the first half is the same as the chance of being in the second half.

[2] Students are sometimes puzzled as to why, if your mean wait is $2 \cdot 8$ minutes, you will have a good chance of reaching the check-out point in under 2 minutes. The reason is this:

The $2 \cdot 8$ minutes is the mean waiting time over a large number of visits. Now on some of these visits the waiting time was over 10 minutes. As was pointed out in the last chapter, extreme values tend to distort the mean, and consequently these excessive waits make the mean waiting time longer than it otherwise would be. Even with the mean at $2 \cdot 8$ minutes, one wait of 10 minutes would need to be balanced by virtually three visits with no waiting time at all if the mean were to stay unchanged.

3. 40th percentile = <u>445 miles</u>.

   (a) 500 miles lies at the <u>93rd percentile</u>.

   (b) 450 miles lies at the <u>45th percentile</u>.

Progress Test 14

1. *School A.*

   Selected class: "105–under 115"

I.Q. (x)	f	d	fd	fd^2
75–under 85	15	-3	-45	135
85– ,, 95	25	-2	-50	100
95– ,, 105	40	-1	-40	40
105– ,, 115	108	0	0	0
115– ,, 125	92	$+1$	$+92$	92
over 125	20	$+2$	$+40$	80
	300		-3	447

$\therefore$ According to formula (15),

$$\sigma = \sqrt{\frac{447}{300} - \left(\frac{-3}{300}\right)^2} \times 10$$

$$= \sqrt{\frac{447}{300} - \frac{1}{10,000}} \times 10$$

$$= \sqrt{1 \cdot 49 - 0 \cdot 0001} \times 10 = \underline{12 \cdot 2 \text{ I.Q. units.}}$$

K

Coefficient of variation $= \dfrac{\sigma}{\bar{x}} \times 100$

Now by formula (3),

$$\bar{x} = 110^{(1)} + \left(\dfrac{-3}{300} \times 10 \right) = 110 - 0 \cdot 1 = 109 \cdot 9 \simeq \underline{110}.$$

$\therefore$ Coefficient of variation $= \dfrac{12 \cdot 2}{110} \times 100 = \underline{11 \cdot 1}.$

School B.

Similarly, $\sigma = \underline{11 \cdot 2 \text{ I.Q. marks}}$ and

Coefficient of variation $= \underline{11.75}.$

Therefore the variability of the I.Q.s in School B is greater than that of School A.

NOTE: [1] Mid-point class "105–under 115."

3. $Q_1 = 14 \cdot 42$ pence and $Q_3 = 21 \cdot 26$ pence.

Therefore quartile deviation $= \dfrac{21 \cdot 26 - 14 \cdot 42}{2}$

$$= \underline{3 \cdot 42 \text{ pence.}}$$

Progress Test 15

1. By formula (17),

$$\text{Sk} = \dfrac{3(454 \cdot 5 - 452 \cdot 4)}{27} = \dfrac{3 \times 2 \cdot 1}{27} = \underline{+0 \cdot 233}$$

This indicates that the direction of skew is *positive*, and that the degree of skew is $0 \cdot 233$.

2. $\text{Sk} = \dfrac{3(98 \cdot 9 - 83)}{72 \cdot 8} = \dfrac{3 \times 15 \cdot 9}{72 \cdot 8} = 0.657$

$\therefore$ Coefficient of skewness $= \underline{+0 \cdot 657}.$

4.

$\text{Sk} = \dfrac{3(20 - 22)}{10} = \dfrac{3 \times -2}{10} = -0 \cdot 6.$

$\therefore$ Coefficient of skewness $= \underline{-0 \cdot 6}$ (*i.e.* it is *negatively* skewed)

Progress Test 16

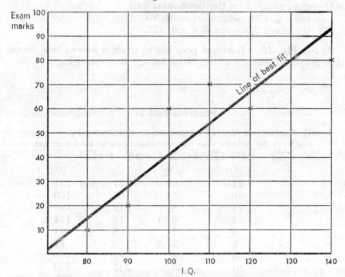

FIG. 45.—*Scattergraph of data in question* 1

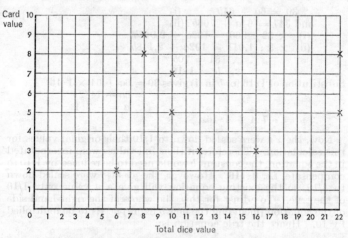

FIG. 46.—*Scattergraph of data in question* 2

1. *See* Fig. 45. Note that I.Q. is the independent variable and is therefore plotted on the horizontal axis.

    (*a*) I.Q. 130: estimated mark 80.

    (*b*) Mark 77: estimated I.Q. 127.

2. *See* Fig. 46. It is not possible to draw a line of best fit on this graph. Therefore the variables are not related.

Progress Test 17

1. (*a*) *Regression line of examination marks on IQ.*

$y = a + bx$, where $y =$ examination marks and $x =$ I.Q.

Now $\Sigma y = an + b\Sigma x$ and $\Sigma xy = a\Sigma x + b\Sigma x^2$.

$x^{(1)}$	$y^{(1)}$	xy	x^2
11	7	77	121
10	6	60	100
14	8	112	196
12	6	72	144
8	1	8	64
9	2	18	81
Σ's: 64	30	347	706

and $n = 6$

$\therefore 30 = 6a + 64b$ (i)

and $347 = 64a + 706b$ (ii)

(i) $\times 32 : 960 = 192a + 2{,}048b$

(ii) $\times 3 : 1{,}041 = 192a + 2{,}118b$

$\therefore \quad 81 = 70b$

$\therefore \quad b = 1 \cdot 16$

Substitution of $1 \cdot 16$ for b in (i) gives $30 = 6a + 64 \times 1 \cdot 16$

$= 6a + 74 \cdot 2$

$\therefore a = -7 \cdot 4$

$\therefore y = -7 \cdot 4 + 1 \cdot 16x$

Now, the x's were scaled down to 1/10 their original values for this calculation. Therefore, if their full values were incorporated in the equation, the constant b would need to be reduced by 1/10 to compensate, *i.e.* $0 \cdot 116$. However, the y's also were scaled down to 1/10, so the existing equation will give a y value only 1/10 of the true. To adjust for this, the whole of the right-hand side of the equation (including the new b figure) needs to be multiplied by 10. Hence the true equation is:

$$y = -74 + 1 \cdot 16x$$

If a candidate had in I.Q. of 130, the best estimate of his mark would be:

$$y = -74 + 1 \cdot 16 \times 130 = \underline{\underline{77 \text{ marks.}}}$$

(b) *Regression line of I.Q. on marks*

$x = a + by^{(2)}$

Now $\Sigma x = an + b\Sigma y$

and $\Sigma xy = a\Sigma y + b\Sigma y^2$

$\Sigma y^2 = 7^2 + 6^2 + 8^2 + 6^2 + 1^2 + 2^2 = 190$

$\therefore 64 = 6a + 30b$ (i)

and $347 = 30a + 190b$ (ii)

Solving ultimately gives $n = 73 + 0 \cdot 675y$

Best estimate of the I.Q. of a candidate who obtained 77 marks:

$$x(\text{I.Q.}) = 73 + 0.675 \times 77 = \underline{\underline{125}}$$

See Fig. 47 for the superimposition of these lines on the scatter-graph in Fig. 45.

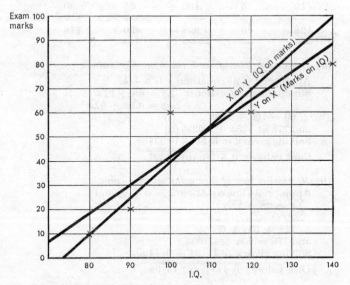

FIG. 47.—*Regression lines of data in question* 1, p. 137 *superimposed on Fig.* 45

NOTES [1]To simplify calculations the original figures have been scaled down to 1/10. Such scaling can be carried out on each series quite independently, but at the end the final equation must be adjusted to bring a and b into line with the full values.

[2]The a and b in this equation are, of course, quite different from the a and b of the equation in part (a) of the answer.

2. Let x = dice value, and y = card value, where $n = 10$.

x	y	x^2	y^2	xy
8	8	64	64	64
8	9	64	81	72
14	10	196	100	140
22	5	484	25	110
22	8	484	64	176
16	3	256	9	48
12	3	144	9	36
6	2	36	4	12
10	7	100	49	70
10	5	100	25	50
Σ's: 128	60	1,928	430	778

(a) *Regression line of card value on dice value*

Appropriate line equation: $y = a + bx$.
Simultaneous equations: $\Sigma y = an + b\Sigma x$
$\Sigma xy = a\Sigma x + b\Sigma x^2$

$\therefore 60 = 10a + 128b$ (i)
and $778 = 128a + 1,928b$ (ii)
Solving gives $y = 5 \cdot 56 + 0 \cdot 0345x$

Card values: (i) $5 \cdot 70$; (ii) $6 \cdot 391$.

(b) *Regression line of dice value on card value*
Appropriate line equation: $x = a + by$ and
$\Sigma x = an + b\Sigma y$
$\Sigma xy = a\Sigma y + b\Sigma y^2$
$\therefore 128 = 10a + 60b$
and $778 = 60a + 430b$
Solving gives $x = 11 \cdot 94 + 0 \cdot 14y$.

Dice values: (i) $12 \cdot 1$; (ii) $13 \cdot 36$.

See Fig. 48 for the superimposition of the regression lines on the scattergraph in Fig. 46.

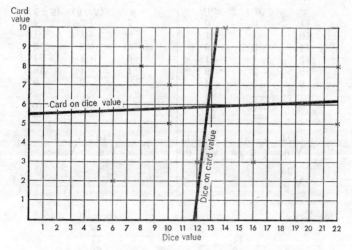

FIG. 48.—*Regression lines of data in question 2, superimposed on Fig. 46*

Progress Test 18

1. Formula (23) is the one to use.

(a) *Means*

$x^{(1)}$	$y^{(1)}$
11	7
10	6
14	8
12	6
8	1
9	2
——	——
64	30

$$\therefore \bar{x} = \frac{64}{6} = \underline{10\tfrac{2}{3}} \qquad \therefore \bar{y} = \frac{30}{6} = \underline{5}$$

(b) *Standard deviations*

Note that σ_x will be calculated using an assumed mean of 11. σ_y will be calculated using the direct method.[2]

x	d	$d^{2(3)}$		y	$(y-\bar{y})$	$(y-\bar{y})^2$
11	0	0		7	$+2$	4
10	-1	1		6	$+1$	1
14	$+3$	9		8	$+3$	9
12	$+1$	1		6	$+1$	1
8	-3	9		1	-4	16
9	-2	4		2	-3	9
	-2	24				40

$$\therefore \sigma_x = \sqrt{\frac{24}{6} - \left(\frac{-2}{6}\right)^2} = \sqrt{4 - \frac{1}{9}} \qquad \therefore \sigma_y = \sqrt{\frac{40}{6}} = \sqrt{\frac{20}{3}}$$

$$= \sqrt{\frac{35}{9}}$$

(c) Σxy

x	y	xy
11	7	77
10	6	60
14	8	112
12	6	72
8	1	8
9	2	18

$$\Sigma xy = 347$$

(d) *Applying formula* (23),

$$r = \frac{347 - 6 \times 10\frac{2}{3} \times 5}{6 \times \sqrt{\frac{35}{9}} \times \sqrt{\frac{20}{3}}} = \frac{347 - 320}{6 \times \sqrt{\frac{35}{9} \times \frac{20}{3}}}$$

$$= \frac{27}{6 \times \sqrt{\frac{700}{27}}} = +0 \cdot 885^{(4)}$$

NOTES: [1]It is quite permissible to scale down or up either or both series of figures in order to simplify calculations. Note that (i) the scaling of one series is completely independent of any scaling of the other series; (ii) since correlation is not concerned with absolute values—only degrees of change—no adjustments for such scaling need to be made later in the calculations.

(2)Both the methods used here are explained in *s*. **41**.

(3)Note that it simplifies calculation to use an assumed mean even though the true mean is already known.

(4)Note that r is not expressed in any units.

2. Formula (23) is again the one to use.

x	d_x(1)	d_x^2	y	d_y(2)	d_y^2	xy
8	-4	16	8	$+2$	4	64
8	-4	16	9	$+3$	9	72
14	$+2$	4	10	$+4$	16	140
22	$+10$	100	5	-1	1	110
22	$+10$	100	8	$+2$	4	176
16	$+4$	16	3	-3	9	48
12	0	0	3	-3	9	36
6	-6	36	2	-4	16	12
10	-2	4	7	$+1$	1	70
10	-2	4	5	-1	1	50
128	$+8$	296	60	0	70	778
Σx	Σd_x	Σd	Σy	Σd_y	Σd_y^2	Σxy

x series | *y series*

$$\bar{x} = \frac{128}{10} = 12 \cdot 8 \qquad\qquad \bar{y} = \frac{60}{10} = 6$$

$$\sigma_x = \sqrt{\frac{\Sigma d_x^2}{n} - \left(\frac{\Sigma d_x}{n}\right)^2}\ {}^{(3)} \qquad \sigma_y = \sqrt{\frac{\Sigma d_y^2}{n} - \left(\frac{\Sigma d_y}{n}\right)^{2\,(3)}}$$

$$= \sqrt{\frac{296}{10} - \left(\frac{8}{10}\right)^2} \qquad\qquad = \sqrt{\frac{70}{10} - \left(\frac{0}{10}\right)^2}$$

$$= \sqrt{\frac{724}{25}} \qquad\qquad\qquad = \sqrt{7}$$

$$= \frac{1}{5}\sqrt{724}$$

$$\therefore\ r = \frac{778 - 10 \times 12 \cdot 8 \times 6}{10 \times \frac{1}{5}\sqrt{724} \times \sqrt{7}} = \frac{778 - 768}{2 \times \sqrt{724 \times 7}}$$

$$= +0 \cdot 07.$$

The type of correlation is *very low positive*, so low as to indicate that it is virtually uncorrelated.[4]

Since there is no true correlation between the value of a thrown dice and the value of a drawn card, such slight correlation that there is must obviously be *spurious*.[5]

NOTES: Note that by careful layout all the Σ's can be computed from a single table.

[1]Assumed mean $= 12$.

[2]Assumed mean $= 6$.

[3]*See s.* **42. 3.**   Formula (14) becomes the one used here when $f = 1$ throughout.

[4]*See s.* **51.** 2.

[5]*See s.* **51.** 4.

3. | Person | I.Q. ranking | Exam. ranking |
|--------|--------------|---------------|
| A | 3 | 2 |
| B | 4 | 3 equal (*i.e.* 3.5[1]) |
| C | 1 | 1 |
| D | 2 | 3 equal (*i.e.* 3.5[1]) |
| E | 6 | 5 |
| F | 5 | 6 |

$$r' = 1 - \frac{6 \, \Sigma d^2}{n(n^2 - 1)}$$

Computation of Σd^2

I.Q.	Mark	d	d^2
3	2	1	1
4	3.5	0.5	0.25
1	1	0	0
2	3.5	1.5	2.25
6	5	0	0
5	6	0	0

$$\Sigma d^2 = \underline{\underline{3 \cdot 5}}$$

$$\therefore r' = 1 - \frac{6 \times 3.5}{6 \times (6^2 - 1)} = \underline{\underline{+0 \cdot 9}}$$

In question 1, r was $0 \cdot 885$. The difference arises through the fact that when ranking is used instead of the full set of figures there is some loss of information. This loss is reflected in the correlation values.[2]

NOTES: [1]Where there is a tie, the ranking given is the average of the ranks shared. In this case, persons B and D share the 3rd and 4th ranks. They are therefore both given the average of 3 and 4, *i.e.* 3.5.

[2]The more accurate correlation value is, of course, the one computed from the full set of figures—in this case 0·885.

Progress Test 19

[*Spurious accuracy is allowed here to assist students' checking.*]

1. (a) $\frac{1}{2} \times 95\% = 47\frac{1}{2}\%$.

   (b) $\frac{1}{2} \times 99\frac{3}{4}\% = \underline{\underline{49\frac{7}{8}\%}}$.

   (c) From Appendix II, $\underline{\underline{49·53\%}}$.

2. (a) Mean to lower $2\sigma = 47\frac{1}{2}\%$.
      Mean to lower $1\sigma = 33\frac{1}{3}\%$.
      $\therefore$ Lower 1σ to lower $2\sigma = 47\frac{1}{2} - 33\frac{1}{3} = \underline{\underline{14\frac{1}{6}\%}}$
      (*Note:* actual is $13·6\%$ [1]).

   (b) Lower 1σ to upper $2\sigma = 33\frac{1}{3} + 47\frac{1}{2} = \underline{\underline{80\frac{5}{6}\%}}$.

   (c) Lower 2σ to upper $3\sigma = 47\frac{1}{2} + 49\frac{7}{8} = \underline{\underline{97\frac{3}{8}\%}}$.

   (d) Lower $2·6\sigma$ to upper $2·6\sigma = 2 \times 49·53 \risingdotseq \underline{\underline{99\%}}$.

3. (a) $100\% - 66\frac{2}{3}\% = \underline{\underline{33\frac{1}{3}\%}}$. [Note: *Both tails required here*]

   (b) $100 - 95 = \underline{\underline{5\%}}$.

   (c) $100 - 99\frac{3}{4} = \underline{\underline{\frac{1}{4}\%}}$.

4. (a) (i) These points are at mean and upper 1σ.
      $\therefore$ Area between $= 33\frac{1}{3}\%$.
      $\therefore$ Number of items with weights between 115 and 118 lbs $= 33\frac{1}{3}\%$ of 10,000 $= \underline{\underline{3,333}}$ ($3,413$[1]).

   (ii) These points are at lower 1σ and mean.
      $\therefore$ Number of items $= 33\frac{1}{3}\%$ of 10,000 $= \underline{\underline{3,333}}$ ($3,413$[1]).

   (iii) These points are at upper and lower 2σ points (*i.e.* $115 \pm 2 \times 3$).
      $\therefore$ Number of items $= 95\%$ of 10,000 $= \underline{\underline{9,500}}$ ($9,544$[1]).

   (iv) These points are at upper and lower 3σ (*i.e.* $115 \pm 3 \times 3$).
      $\therefore$ Number of items $= 99\frac{3}{4}\%$ of 10,000 $= \underline{\underline{9,975}}$ ($9,974$[1]).

   (b) 109 to 121 lbs is $115 \pm 2 \times 3$, *i.e.* these weights lie at the 2σ points. Now, 95% of all the distribution falls between these points. Therefore 19 out of 20 items will be between 109 and 121 lbs, so any prediction that the weight of an item selected at random will lie between 109 and 121 lbs can be made at a 95% level of confidence.

NOTE: [1]This is the figure obtained if the table in Appendix II is used.

Progress Test 20

1. (i) $\sigma_{\bar{x}} = \dfrac{15}{\sqrt{25}} = 3$ lbs.

    (a) Mean estimate at 95% level = $950 \pm 2 \times 3$ = <u>944 to 956 lbs.</u>

    (b) <u>Mean estimate at $99\frac{3}{4}$% level = $950 \pm 3 \times 3$ = 941 to 959 lbs.</u>

  (ii) $\sigma_{\bar{x}} = \dfrac{0 \cdot 8}{\sqrt{100}} = 0 \cdot 08$ in.

    (a) Mean estimate at 95% level = $1 \cdot 82 \pm 2 \times 0 \cdot 08$ = <u>1·66 in. to 1·98 in.</u>

    (b) <u>Mean estimate at $99\frac{3}{4}$% level = $1 \cdot 82 \pm 3 \times 0 \cdot 08$ = 1·58 in. to 2·06 in.</u>

 (iii) $\sigma_{\bar{x}} = \dfrac{0 \cdot 8}{\sqrt{10,000}} = 0 \cdot 008$.

    (a) Mean estimate at 95% level = $1 \cdot 82 \pm 2 \times 0 \cdot 008$ = <u>1·804 in. to 1·836 in.</u>

    (b) <u>Mean estimate at $99\frac{3}{4}$% level = $1 \cdot 82 \pm 3 \times 0 \cdot 008$ = 1·796 in. to 1·844 in.</u>

NOTE the narrower limits that follow the use of a larger sample size.

2. (i) $\sigma_{prop} = \sqrt{\dfrac{0 \cdot 61 \times 0 \cdot 39}{100}} = 0 \cdot 0488$

Proportion estimate 95% level =
$0 \cdot 61 \pm 2 \times 0 \cdot 0488 = 0 \cdot 512$ to $0 \cdot 708$
$\simeq$ <u>51·2% to 70·8%.</u>

  (ii) $\sigma_{prop} = \sqrt{\dfrac{\dfrac{26}{49} \times \dfrac{23}{49}}{49}} = 0 \cdot 071$

Proportion estimate 95% level = $26/49 \pm 2 \times 0 \cdot 071$
$\simeq$ <u>38·8% to 67·2%.</u>

(iii) $\sigma_{prop} = \sqrt{\dfrac{0 \cdot 61 \times 0 \cdot 39}{10,000}} = 0 \cdot 00488$

Proportion estimate 95% level $= 0 \cdot 61 \pm 2 \times 0 \cdot 00488$
$\doteq 60 \cdot 0\%$ to $62 \cdot 0\%$

NOTE that when estimating proportions a very much larger sample size is required than is needed when estimating means in order to give estimate limits which are close enough to be worthwhile.

3. If the estimate reads ± 2 in. at the 95% level of confidence, then 2 in. $= 2 \times \sigma_{\bar{x}}$.
$\therefore \sigma_{\bar{x}} = \underline{1 \text{ in.}}$ (*i.e.* σ of sample is 10 ins.)

By formula (26), $1 = \dfrac{\sigma_x}{\sqrt{100}} = \dfrac{\sigma_x}{10}$

$\therefore \sigma_x = \underline{\underline{10 \text{ in.}}}$

The investigator wants an estimate within $\frac{1}{2}$ in. at the 95% level of confidence.
$\therefore \frac{1}{2}$ in. $= 2 \times \sigma_{\bar{x}}$ (*i.e.* the improved $\sigma_{\bar{x}}$)
$\therefore \sigma_{\bar{x}} = \frac{1}{4}$ in.

Since $\sigma_x = 10$ in., using formula (26), $\frac{1}{4} = 10/\sqrt{n}$.
$\therefore \sqrt{n} = 40$
$\therefore n = 1,600$.
$\therefore$ The sample size will need to be $\underline{\underline{1,600}}$.

4. If a 99% confidence level is required, it entails finding how far either side the mean one has to measure in order to include 99% of the total area beneath the normal curve. This in turn entails finding how far *one side* of the mean one has to measure to include $99/2 = 49 \cdot 5\%$ of the total area. Looking up the table in Appendix II, it can be seen that an area of $0 \cdot 4953$ is embraced by using $2 \cdot 6\sigma$. Therefore $\sigma_{\bar{x}}$ needs to be multiplied by $2 \cdot 6$ to give a confidence level of 99%.

Progress Test 21

1. Null hypothesis: there is no contradiction between a population mean of 14 hours and a sample mean of 13 hours 20 minutes.

Now by formula (26) $\sigma_{\bar{x}} = \dfrac{3}{\sqrt{64}} = \frac{3}{8}$ hour

If 14 hours is the population mean, then 95% sample means will fall between $14 \pm 2 \times \frac{3}{8} = 13\frac{1}{4}$ and $14\frac{3}{4}$ hours.

The actual mean is $13\frac{1}{3}$ hours and therefore lies between these limits.

Therefore the null hypothesis cannot be rejected at the 95% level of confidence, and the welfare officer's assertion is not disproved.

2. Null hypothesis: there is no contradiction between a population proportion of $0 \cdot 6$ and a sample proportion of $1,410/2,500 = 0 \cdot 564$.

Using formula (27), $p = 0 \cdot 6^{(1)}$, $q = 1 - 0 \cdot 6 = 0 \cdot 4$, and $n = 2,500$.

$$\therefore \sigma_{prop} = \sqrt{\frac{0 \cdot 6 \times 0 \cdot 4}{2,500}} = 0 \cdot 0098$$

If $0 \cdot 6$ is the population proportion, then $99\frac{3}{4}\%$ sample proportions will fall between $0 \cdot 6 \pm 3 \pm 0 \cdot 0098 = 0 \cdot 5706$ and $0 \cdot 6294$.

The sample proportion is $0 \cdot 564$, which is *outside* these limits, hence the null hypothesis must be rejected at the $99\frac{3}{4}\%$ level of confidence, *i.e.* there *is* a contradiction between the asserted population proportion and the sample proportion.

This means that the difference is significant and the population proportion is not 60%.[2]

NOTES: [1]Remember: use the true proportion for p where possible (*see s.* 57. 3). Although the true proportion is not known here, using the asserted proportion enables us to test whether or not it could be a true proportion.

[2]Note how the size of the sample improves our discrimination. The candidate claimed in effect that 1,500 out of every 2,500 people supported him. The sample gave 1,410: a mere 90 short, on a sample of perhaps only 3% or 4% of the total voters. Nevertheless, with a sample of 2,500 we were able to say that his assertion was wrong—and say this, moreover, knowing we would only make an error of wrongly dismissing such a claim once in 400 times. (We are, of course, assuming the people sampled told the truth!)

3. If the two samples were taken from the same population, it would be equivalent to two samples taken from two populations having the same mean. Therefore, to test the expert's assertion, we need to find out whether the difference between the means is significant.

Now $\sigma_{\bar{x}1} = \sqrt{\dfrac{2}{200}}$ and $\sigma_{\bar{x}2} = \sqrt{\dfrac{2}{80}}$.

By formula (28),

$$\sigma_{(\bar{x}_1 - \bar{x}_2)} = \sqrt{\left(\sqrt{\frac{2}{200}}\right)^2 + \left(\sqrt{\frac{2}{80}}\right)^2} = \sqrt{\frac{4}{200} + \frac{4}{80}}$$
$$= \underline{\underline{0 \cdot 264 \text{ lbs.}}}$$

Therefore 95% of the differences between means can extend to $2 \times \sigma_{(\bar{x}_1 - \bar{x}_2)} = 2 \times 0 \cdot 264 = 0 \cdot 528$ lbs.

The actual difference is $20\frac{1}{2} - 20 = 0 \cdot 5$ lbs. This is within the allowed limits and there is, therefore, no evidence to disprove the expert's assertion that the two samples were taken from a single population.

4. The question here is: is there a significant difference between the two proportions?

The proportion of citizens passing in A is $96/200 = 0 \cdot 48$ and the proportion of citizens passing in B is $84/200 = 0 \cdot 42$.

$$\therefore \sigma_{prop} A = \sqrt{\frac{pq}{n}} = \sqrt{\frac{0 \cdot 48 \times 0 \cdot 52}{200}} \;^{(1)}$$

and $\sigma_{prop} B = \sqrt{\dfrac{0 \cdot 42 \times 0 \cdot 58}{200}} \;^{(1)}$

By formula (29),

$$\sigma_{diff. \, prop.} = \sqrt{\sqrt{\frac{0 \cdot 48 \times 0 \cdot 52}{200}}^2 + \sqrt{\frac{0 \cdot 42 \times 0 \cdot 58}{200}}^2}$$

$$= \sqrt{\frac{0 \cdot 48 \times 0 \cdot 52}{200} + \frac{0 \cdot 42 \times 0 \cdot 58}{200}}$$

$$= \sqrt{\frac{0 \cdot 493}{200}} = \underline{0 \cdot 0496}$$

Therefore 95% of the differences between proportions do not exceed $2 \times 0 \cdot 0496 = 0 \cdot 0992$.

The actual difference between the sample proportions is $0 \cdot 48 - 0 \cdot 42 = \underline{0 \cdot 06}$.

This difference is within the allowed limit, and so is not significant at the 95% level of confidence.[2]

This means that the difference between 96 fit citizens of city A and 84 fit citizens of city B could arise through chance factors alone and the assertion that there is a difference between the proportions of fit people in the two cities is not proven.

NOTES: [1]It pays not to simplify this expression, since at the next stage it is squared, and this means that one has only to remove the square root sign.

[2]Note how a small sample in a proportion problem can mean that quite large differences can occur without the differences being significant (e.g. $96 - 84 =$ a difference of 12 in a sample size of $200 = \underline{\underline{6\%}}$).

Progress Test 22

1. (a) (i) Laspeyre price index:

Item	1960 q_0	1960 p_0 £	1960 p_0q_0 (£)	1961 p_1 £	1961 p_1q_0 (£)	1962 p_2 £	1962 p_2q_0 (£)	1963 p_3 £	1963 p_3q_0 (£)
A	20	0·20	4·00	0·25	5·00	0·35	7·00	0·50	10·00
B	12	0·25	3·00	0·25	3·00	0·10	1·20	0·12½	1·50
C	3	1·00	3·00	2·00	6·00	2·00	6·00	2·00	6·00
Σ			£10·00		£14·00		£14·20		£17·50

Using formula (31):

Laspeyre price index (1960 = 100)

Year	
1960	100
1961	$\dfrac{14\cdot00}{10\cdot00} \times 100 = 140$
1962	$\dfrac{14\cdot20}{10\cdot00} \times 100 = 142$
1963	$\dfrac{17\cdot50}{10\cdot00} \times 100 = 175$

1 (a) (ii) *Paasche price index:*

	1960	1961				1962				1963			
Item	p_0 (£)	p_1 (£)	q_1	p_1q_1 (£)	p_0q_1 (£)	p_2 (£)	q_2	p_2q_2 (£)	p_0q_2 (£)	p_3 (£)	q_3	p_3q_3 (£)	p_0q_3 (£)
A	0·20	0·25	24	6·00	4·80	0·35	20	7·00	4·00	0·50	18	9·00	3·60
B	0·25	0·25	16	4·00	4·00	0·10	20	2·00	5·00	0·12½	16	2·00	4·00
C	1·00	2·00	2	4·00	2·00	2·00	3	6·00	3·00	2·00	4	8·00	4·00
Σ				£14·00	£10·80			£15·00	£12·00			£19·00	£11·60

Using formula (32):

Year	Paasche price index 100
1960	
1961	$\dfrac{14\cdot00}{10\cdot80} \times 100 = 130$
1962	$\dfrac{15\cdot00}{12\cdot00} \times 100 = 125$
1963	$\dfrac{19\cdot00}{11\cdot60} \times 100 = 164$

1 (a) (iii) Weighted average of price relatives:

	Basic data			1961			1962			1963		
Item	1960 p_0 £	Weight		p_1 £	$\frac{p_1}{p_0} \times 100$	Price relative × Weight	p_2 £	$\frac{p_2}{p_0} \times 100$	Price relative × Weight	p_3 £	$\frac{p_3}{p_0} \times 100$	Price relative × Weight
A	0·20	5		0·25	125	625	0·35	175	875	0·50	250	1,250
B	0·25	3		0·25	100	300	0·10	40	120	0·12½	50	150
C	1·00	2		2·00	200	400	2·00	200	400	2·00	200	400
Σ		10				1,325			1,395			1,800

Weighted average of price relatives

Year	Weighted average of price relatives
1960	100
1961	$\dfrac{1,325}{10} = 132·5$
1962	$\dfrac{1,395}{10} = 139·5$
1963	$\dfrac{1,800}{10} = 180$

2. Index of weekly earnings[1]
(April 1950 = 100)

Group	April 1950[2]		April 1959			
	q_0	p_0q_0[3]	q_1[2]	p_1q_1[2]	$\therefore p_1$[4]	p_1q_0
Men aged 21 and over	350	2,500	300	4,200	14	4,900
Women aged 18 and over	400	1,600	1,200	8,000	6·67	2,668
Youths and boys	150	450	100	560	5·6	840
Girls	100	250	400	1,540	3·85	385
Totals		4,800				8,793

By formula (31),

$$\text{Index} = \frac{8,793}{4,800} \times 100 = 183$$

NOTES: Examiners are apt to ask index number questions in this form. Instead of giving price and quantity separately, they give one or the other, together with the value figure. Since $Value = p \times q$, it is necessary to divide the value figure by either the given p or the given q to obtain the missing figure.

In this question, it is the price figure that is missing, quantities and values being given. The price, i.e. wage rate, is therefore found by dividing the value by the quantity.

[1] Since a "rise of earnings" figure is required, a price index is called for (earnings here being the price paid for the labour of each worker), and it is to be based on April 1950. The best index is, then, a Laspeyre price index (formula (31)).

[2] These figures are given in the question.

[3] Note that $p_0 q_0 = Total\ earnings,\ April\ 1950$, and that this is given. There is no need, there, to compute p_0.

$$[4]\ p_1 = \frac{p_1 q_1}{q_1}$$

Progress Test 23

2. (a) (i) *Seasonal variations*

	Quarter	Demand (tons)	M.A.T.	Moving average	Centred average[1]	Seasonal variation
1961	1	218				
	2	325				
			1,064	266		
	3	273			294	93
			1,290	$322\frac{1}{2}$		
	4	248			355	70
			1,550	$387\frac{1}{2}$		
1962	1	444			409	$108\frac{1}{2}$
			1,722	$430\frac{1}{2}$		
	2	585			448	131
			1,859	$464\frac{3}{4}$		
	3	445			492	$90\frac{1}{2}$
			2,075	$518\frac{3}{4}$		
	4	385			552	70
			2,342	$585\frac{1}{2}$		
1963	1	660			608	109
			2,520	630		
	2	852			648	$131\frac{1}{2}$
			2,660	665		
	3	623				
	4	525				

Quarter	1	2	3	4	Total
1961	—	—	93	70	
1962	$108\frac{1}{2}$	131	$90\frac{1}{2}$	70	
1963	109	$131\frac{1}{2}$	—	—	
Total	$217\frac{1}{2}$	$262\frac{1}{2}$	$183\frac{1}{2}$	140	
Average	$108\frac{3}{4}$	$131\frac{1}{4}$	$91\frac{3}{4}$	70	$401\frac{3}{4}$[2]
Adjusted	108	131	91	70	400

The seasonal variations are, therefore:

    Quarter 1: 108   Quarter 3: 91

           2: 131   4: 70

(ii) *The trend*[3]

$$y = a + bd$$

Year	Demand — y[4]	d	yd	d²
1961	1,064	—1	—1,064	1
1962	1,859	0	0	0
1963	2,660	+1	+2,660	1
	$\Sigma y = 5,583$		$\Sigma yd = 1,596$	$\Sigma d^2 = 2$

$a = \bar{y} = 5,583/3 = \underline{1,861}$

and $b = \Sigma yd / \Sigma d^2 = 1,596/2 = 798$
$\therefore y = \underline{\underline{1,861 + 798d}}.$

(b) (i) *Total demand for 1965:*
1965 is three years' deviation from 1962
$\therefore$ demand $y = 1,861 + 798 \times 3$
$= 4,255,$ (say) $\underline{\underline{4,250 \text{ tons}}}$[5]

(ii) *Demand for last quarter (4) of 1965:*
First adjust the trend formula for quarters, *i.e.*:
$y' = 1,861/4 + 798/4^2 \times d'$ (where $d' =$ Deviation in quarters)
$\therefore y' = 465 + 50d'$ (rounded)
Mid-point of series = Mid-point of 1962, *i.e.* end of Quarter 2, 1962.
$\therefore$ Deviation of Quarter 4, 1965, from the mid-point of the series:

Quarters

From end of Quarter 2, 1962, to the end of 1962	2
Quarters for the years 1963 and 1964 ..	8
From beginning of 1965 to end of Quarter 3	3
End of Quarter 3 to mid-point of Quarter 4	½
	$+13\frac{1}{2}$

$\therefore$ The trend for Quarter 4, 1965:
$$y' = 465 + 50 \times 13\frac{1}{2} = \underline{\underline{1,140}}$$

$\therefore$ Demand for last quarter of 1965:
$=$ Trend $\times$ Seasonal variation
$= 1,140 \times 70 = 798,$ (say) $\underline{\underline{800 \text{ tons.}}}$

NOTES: [1]These figures are rounded.

[2]A total adjustment of $-1\frac{1}{4}$ is needed. If this is made as per formula s. **69**. 1 and the variations rounded, the figures on the next line are obtained.

[3]In practice, three years is too short a duration to obtain a reliable trend equation.

[4]These figures are the sum of the four quarters for each year.

[5]Since the estimated figures cannot be accurate to a ton, it is better to round to a reasonable number.

INDEX

A

ACCURACY, 10 ff.
  and the mean, 106
  Slide-rule, 11
  Spurious, 10–11
"ANNUAL ABSTRACT OF STATISTICS," 66
APPROXIMATION, 10 ff.
  (*see also* Rounded numbers)
  Rounding, 11
ARITHMETIC MEAN, *see* Mean
ARRAY, 76
ASSUMED MEAN:
  Application, 118, 119
  Ref., 96
AVERAGE, 93 ff.
  (*see also* Mean)
  Centred, *see* Centred average
  Choice of, 103
  Moving, *see* Moving average
  Ref., 93
  Types, 93
  Weighted, 106, 221

B

BAND CHART, 38
BAR CHART, 58 ff.
  Choice of, 61
  Component, 59
  Multiple, 59
  Single, 58
BASE CHANGING, 195
  Formula, 222
BASE YEAR:
  Choice of, 198
  Ref., 186
BIAS
  Postal questionnaire, 20
  Random selection, 22
  Systematic, 12
BI-MODAL, 102
"BLUE BOOK," 69
"BOARD OF TRADE JOURNAL," 68

C

CENSUS OF DISTRIBUTION, 71
CENSUS OF POPULATION, 71
CENSUS OF PRODUCTION, 70
CENTRED AVERAGE, 204, 205
CHAIN INDEX, 193, 199
CHART:
  Band, 38
  Bar, *see* Bar Chart
  Scatter, *see* Scattergraph
  Z, 49–51
CLASSES, 78–81
  Choice of, 81
  Interval, 80
  Limits, 79, 80
  Open-ended, 80
  Ref., 78
  Unequal, 80
CLASS INTERVAL:
  Ref., 80
  Unequal, 80, 84–5
CLASS LIMITS
  in histograms, 84
  Ref., 79
  Stated, 80
  True, 80
COEFFICIENT OF CORRELATION (r):
  (*see also* Correlation)
  Formula, 148, 220
  Interpretation, 150–52
  Numerical values, 152
COEFFICIENT OF RANK CORRELATION (r)
  see Rank Correlation
COEFFICIENT OF SKEWNESS, 126, 127
  Formula, 222
COEFFICIENT OF VARIATION, 121, 127
  Formula, 222
COMPONENT BAR CHART, 59, 61
CONFIDENCE INTERVAL, 171
CONFIDENCE LEVEL, 164, 170
  Ref., 171
  With null hypotheses, 177